Pity in Fin-de-Siècle French Culture

"Liberté, Egalité, Pitié"

Gonzalo J. Sánchez Jr.

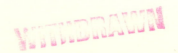

PRAEGER

Westport, Connecticut
London

Library of Congress Cataloging-in-Publication Data

Sánchez, Gonzalo J., 1961–
Pity in fin-de-siècle French culture : "liberté, égalité, pitié" / Gonzalo J. Sánchez Jr.
    p. cm.
    Includes bibliographical references and index.
    ISBN 0–275–98000–6 (alk. paper)
      1. Sympathy—France—History—19th century.   2. France—Intellectual life—19th century.
3. Sympathy—France—History—20th century.   4. France—Intellectual life—20th century.   I.
Title.
BJ703.S96S26   2004
177′.7—dc21   2003042066

British Library Cataloguing in Publication Data is available.

Library of Congress Catalog Card Number: 2003042066
ISBN: 0–275–98000–6

First published in 2004

Praeger Publishers, 88 Post Road West, Westport, CT 06881
An imprint of Greenwood Publishing Group, Inc.
www.praeger.com

Printed in the United States of America

The paper used in this book complies with the
Permanent Paper Standard issued by the National
Information Standards Organization (Z39.48–1984).

10   9   8   7   6   5   4   3   2   1

For Lucas, Aidan, Chloë, Marc, and Arlen

Contents

Acknowledgments

This book began as a research project generously funded by the American Philosophical Society. Thanks to this august body's confidence in the subject matter's promise and my potential for doing it justice, I was able to undertake rewarding investigations in 1996 at the Bibliothèque de l'Institut de France. I am grateful to the attentive and cooperative staff of this small and priceless collection, which afforded me the added enjoyment of making a daily routine out of passing under the dome of Mazarin's famous edifice. I owe a similar debt to the staff of the Bibliothèque Nationale de France's (BNF) Salle des Manuscrits, as well as to the librarians and administrators of the newer BNF's Mitterrand Library at Tolbiac. The staffs at the Bibliothèque Historique de la Ville de Paris, Harvard University's Widener Library, Columbia University's Butler Library, Boston University's Mugar Memorial Library, and the Boston Athenaeum also provided congenial and supportive environments for valuable reading and writing. I am especially obliged for their policies accommodating the importunities of a visiting scholar.

Priscilla Ferguson, Robert Paxton, Martha Nussbaum, David Cartwright, and Michael Roth commented on earlier drafts of the work-in-progress or communicated their own ideas so as to help me steer clear of errors of appreciation and approach in the subsequent composition. I owe them immeasurably more than mere thanks. Readers for the National Endowment for the Humanities, audiences at the New School for Social Research, Clark University, the City University of New York, Boston University, the École des Hautes Études en Sciences Sociales in Paris, and the Juilliard School similarly offered constructive critiques that I have incorporated. I am thankful particularly to the Centre National de la Recherche Scientifique for inviting me as a visiting fellow to participate in the history seminar led by Professor Alain Boureau.

The following individuals ensured that the challenges in bringing this work to fruition would never lead me to self-pity: William, Clare, and Margaret Sheridan; Quentin, Emma, and Lucien Bajac; Françoise Mark and Yehiel Rabinowitz; David Tedeschi; Chad Steele; William Kuhn; Santi, Evelyn, and Inès Moix; Daisy Edelson; the Abers in New Hampshire and the Buckley/Boyles in New York; and those transatlantic beacons and bournes of *francité* and fellowship: Philip Walsh and especially Lisa Jane Graham and David Sedley. I have let this work take too much time from family vacations not to publicly acknowledge what I can never privately recuse, the steadfast love for Silvia and Paul Kaminsky, Vivian and Arlene Garcia, Miriam and Peter Frometa, and Gonzalo and Silvia Sanchez. I thank also those students–Chris Mason and David Silldorf, especially–whose interdisciplinary interests and curiosities are refracted in this book and whose learning experiences have marked my own scholarship. This work belongs as much to Richard Buckley as to the credited author.

Introduction: Pity, Past and Present

We have no history of pity, or of cruelty.

Lucien Fèbvre[1]

When we believe we are merely recreating the grief and pain of a beloved person, our pity exaggerates them; but perhaps it is our pity that speaks true, more than the sufferers' own consciousness of their pain, they being blind to that tragedy of their existence which pity sees and deplores.

Marcel Proust
Sodome et Gomorrhe[2]

Pity is a term of enormous utility for the cultural historian and interpreter of the humanities. It is an analytical guide to the process by which cultures attach value to nonrational components of social life, accord moral status to sentiments, and make assumptions about how to judge others—for pity is almost invariably yoked to justice as mutually exclusive alternatives. Moreover, the variegated and changing lexicon of pity makes it a fruitful subject for historical linguistics and discourse analysis.

French academic philosophers, educators, and novelists in the *fin-de-siècle*, broadly demarcated as the years between 1880 and 1914, engaged in a historically significant scrutiny of pity and its relation to ethics, politics, literature, gender, and education. The present book is devoted to documenting and exploring this significant scrutiny. France had an especially strong tradition of thinking on pity that derived not only from Christian-*pieta* associations—this it shared with many other cultures—but from the canon of more secular ideas dating back to at least the seventeenth century. From that century through the nineteenth, the educated and arguing elites of France focused sustained attention on pity and its value as social sentiment and moral guide. A classic pedigree legitimated preoccupations with pity, from the early ascetic distrust of the philosophers Pascal and Descartes and the moralists the duc de la Rochefoucauld and the marquis de Vauvenargues, through its rehabilitation by the Enlightenment *philosophes*, especially Diderot, Montesquieu, Rousseau, and Voltaire. Throughout the nineteenth century, the cultivation of pity was at the heart of romantic humanitarianism and the "religion of suffering humanity," as seen in the works of Hugo, Lamartine, and Michelet. The lengthy, but essential, "Prologue" highlights some of the authoritative foundations of this lineage.

I privilege the end of the nineteenth century because there was a heightened concern with pity in these years, as the term was thrust simultaneously into the center of two related debates: is pity an appropriate adjunct to virtue, and is its cultivation a quintessentially French quality? Moreover, all those who wished to take the pulse of a rapidly changing France had to wrestle with pity precisely because its ancestry—consecration in literary tradition, association with the Revolution, attachment to Rousseau's ambiguous legacy, and heterodox relation to both Christian and Republican welters of ideas—was made a basis of this examination. For the French, the very word "pity" and its pacifying contexts evoked images of social and intellectual constancy: a metaphysics of national comfort inhered in the word. Indeed, one of the figures we will be encountering could write in 1895 (appropriately, in a study of la Rochefoucauld): "The evolution of the idea of pity would suffice as a gauge of changes in our social state."[3] The analysis of this chiastic relationship—between changes in the idea of pity and in *fin-de-siècle* society—is the red thread running through this book.

Fin-de-siècle France was a particularly sensitive cultural landscape for pity, in part because these were the foundation years of the Republican political system, which was very much a moral order, and in part because these years witnessed a revival of the philosophy of sentimentalism and the renewal of interest in the old-school problem of the rift between reason and sentiment. Pity was pivotal to assorted logics of alternation in these years: individual-social; feminine-masculine; secular-Christian; public sphere-private space; classical-modern; philosophy-psychology and philosophy-literature; sentiment-reason; and universal-national. Determining how these oppositions were adjudicated within various disciplinary settings and given rhetorical formulations is a vast and vital historical undertaking; the more modest goal of this book is to elucidate the place of pity in these mediations.

The chapters in Part I disclose the contexts that made pity a synecdoche for various disciplinary transformations, particularly the challenges of sentimentalism and "affective philosophy" to the eclectic legacy of French philosophy and education. The fusion of promotion and examination—prescription and description—characterized the attention given to pity. My analysis of the interest in pity within *fin-de-siècle* philosophy relies heavily on the debates and problematics engaged in by academic thinkers, especially members of the *Académie des sciences morales et politiques*. A historical reconstruction of these deliberations can disclose the broader culture's assumptions. If, along the way and in paraphrasing the participants,[4] we rediscover neglected philosophers and moralists and revisit the milieu of French philosophy in its pre-Bergson years, then we will also have added some useful material to the history of French thought. Whereas the first chapter documents how pity was described and analyzed, the second chapter shows how it was prescribed, especially in Françisque Bouillier's essay, "De l'influence sur la pitié de la distance, du temps, et du lieu" ["On the Influence of Distance, Time, and Place on Pity"]. Overt appeals to the traditional connotations of pity validated reformers' tutelary roles in an updated social context. The prescriptive dimension of pity was extended to its logical site: the school. The question for educators was simply posed: is pity educable? Chapter 3 reports their unsurprisingly confirmatory responses.

Part II introduces concerns for, confrontations around, and contradictions within uncomplicated beliefs about pity. The consensual tenets on pity were complexified by the bursting onto the French philosophical scene of Arthur Schopenhauer and Friedrich Nietzsche, the former proposing pity as the quasi-mystical source of morality, the latter its great naysayer. The critic Alexandre Baillot wrote: "In preaching a universal pity to those who are capable of it, Schopenhauer addressed himself specifically to the French."[5] Chapter 4 makes sense of this and similar claims about Schopenhauer and Nietzsche. The confrontation with Nietzsche's legacy, in *fin-de-siècle* France as well as today, decidedly looms over this study. Chapter 5 explores a specific debate and a signal affair that pitted pity against justice. Social developments in the Third Republic, especially secularism, socialism, and the Solidarity movement, posed new challenges to traditional thought on social concord. Debate on the movement known as Solidarity and on the dyad charity-fraternity was revelatory of what was at stake when pity was prescribed or proscribed as a pro-social virtue. The Dreyfus affair was one catalyzing event that set in opposition the exclusive promotion of pity or justice in a vituperative public debate with mortal human risks. These two words were often rhetorically twined in both sides' emotive appeals.

The accession of females to French secondary and higher education after 1880, together with the amalgam of a Republican pedagogy for girls with received ideas on femininity and gender relationships, marked a singularly propitious time for reworking sentimentalism and pity into official curricula. In Chapter 6, I survey the study programs offered in the *Revue universitaire*, especially the questions that rhetorically transcribe the wish to inculcate pity in young women. The curricula for the *École normale des jeunes filles*, for example, raised questions such as: Why is pity essential for women? In doing so, they exposed the contradiction between the universalist claim made on behalf of an ethically meliorist pity and its gendered form.

Literary debates in the *fin-de-siècle* were always about more than literature: philosophers adverted to literary works, and literary types ranged themselves around metaphysical and social stances. Literature and philosophy were overlapping cultural "fields" (in Pierre Bourdieu's sense) of rhetoric and discourse; philosophy, for instance, was "literary" in both form and vocation. Pity was a key marker in this drawing of promiscuous boundaries. Part III of the book first notes the sensational reception accorded by French critics and public to European writers like Tolstoy, Dickens, and Ibsen, who evangelized a tender emotionality keyed to pity. That these sources were non-French rendered the value of pity more unstable and fraught with repercussions for supposedly national traditions. But French writers were also engrossed by pity during these years. Émile Zola, the Goncourt brothers, Paul Bourget, Octave Mirbeau, Léon Bloy, Pierre Loti, Anatole France, and Marcel Proust, among others, put pity to narrative use in mediating self and society and as an intermediary between the real and ideal. These authors championed incompatible philosophical and political doctrines, yet the nettled relationship between the communicability of emotions and the paradoxes of authorship suggested a focus on "pity" as both subject and strategy of their fictions. This part avails itself of the interests and methodology of the sort of work done by Sarah Maza in *Private Lives and Public Affairs: The "Causes Célèbres" of Prerevolutionary France*: "These questions have to do with the interrelation of public and private issues in the genesis of political ideologies; with the relationship between narrative and ideology; and, more broadly, with the status of fiction in historical analysis."[6]

All of the authors studied here, literary or philosophic, help us detect a covert dimension of the preoccupation with pity: its coupling to social and moral contagion, to the propinquity and promiscuity that the hurly-burly living together of *fin-de-siècle* society threatened. For them pity, like hygiene and domestic architecture, was a response to the very modern problem of how to live together, a response to the fundamental predicament of nineteenth-century thought, that of the relationship between the individual and society. This study highlights the existence of a prevailing belief that there was a civilizing process intrinsic to, and furthered by, pity. Relevant to a cluster of hypotheses of Norbert Elias, Georg Simmel, and Max Weber, such a view championed pity as a *technic* of civilization that did not entail the "disenchantment of the world"; pity was a necessary part of the democratization and expansion of inner life, counteracting alienating modernity.

Can writings—especially literary confections, elaborate philosophical conceptions, and sociological postulates—ever render sentiments intelligible or reflective of the wider society's lived experience? Some dubiety is built into our project: skepticism about what individuals or their writings really mean—beyond the etymological assumptions with which they work—when they invoke pity as a shibboleth, wield it as a reforming tool, or vaunt it as worthy of truly human flourishing. A methodological vade mecum is thus apposite before commencing our narrative. Much of this book is essentially a study of rhetoric, of philosophical-literary discourse interpreted as operating as a logic of appeal. Pity in *fin-de-siècle* France was, in this sense, highly rhetorical, brandished as a prescriptive machination in order to scrub away social and epistemological asperities. The appeal to pity was a pacifying, traditionalist, and, in many ways, conservative rhetoric of emotional entreaty for a changing social milieu. As Kenneth Burke writes: "For rhetoric as such...is rooted in an essential function of language itself, a function that is wholly realistic, and is continually born anew; the use of language as a symbolic means of inducing cooperation in beings that by nature respond to symbols."[7] This book describes how an appeal to readers' sense of traditional "pity" in the writings of French philosophers, pedagogues, and novelists interacted, in the sociopolitical sphere of the *fin-de-siècle*, with the interest in studying and promoting this very virtue.

The categorization of this sentiment is also an important methodological stake. As we shall see, pity was portrayed by its French acolytes as a virtuous sentiment. Moreover, I argue that it was sheathed by them within the trappings of a full-blown cognitive theory *avant la lettre*. In one of the many diachronic similarities disclosed by this book, this cognitive approach to pity as belonging to the genus of sentiment tallies with recent useful definitions of sentiment as "socially articulated symbols and behavioral expectations, as opposed to private feelings."[8] William Reddy has handily coined a neologism for this dimension of sentiment: "emotives."[9] By examining pity as a socially articulated sentiment, as a rhetorical "emotive," we avoid the snare of having to excavate experiential subjectivities.

The fact remains—it is our point of departure—that pity was a centripetal force in French intellectual and social life in the *fin-de-siècle*. Indeed, if there were an equivalent in French moral and social thought for Raymond Williams' *Key Words*, pity would figure prominently, far more so than its alphabetical position.[10]

Is pity a more or less democratic sentiment? If it is considered a sentiment, how to construe it as a moral attribute? Could its cultivation ameliorate social discord? Is it a gendered quality, adjudicated exclusively to the feminine? Another diachronic resemblance with which my research originated is that these questions were asked not only by *fin-de-siècle* thinkers and writers but also by our contemporary philosophers, psychologists, and moralists. Just as the pity tradition that was taken over in the *fin-de-siècle* had antecedents, so it has had descendants. Indeed, over the past twenty or so years, there has been a veritable explosion of philosophical and historical works on the emotions, passions, and sentiments.[11] (See the "Bibliography" for works indicating the substance and range of ideas informing my approach.) Some of these efforts have been inspired by the neo-Aristotelian vogue in contemporary philosophy; others by trends in philosophical historiography, especially the renewed study of pity in Greek tragedy and philosophy, or pity's Anglophone pedigree: Hobbes, Hume, and Adam Smith. These efforts have generally embraced what they see as the positive role of pity in moral and social life. With the emergence of the controversial biological postulate of innate altruism, various branches of psychology, philosophy, and the social sciences have engaged in conceptual and empirical investigations into the connections between emotions and benevolence, especially in the helping professions—medicine, social work, and psychotherapy. The preponderance of discussions on pity in recent years has probably been linked to Nietzsche's philosophy, specifically to his vehemently anti-pity stance. One of the leading figures in the philosophical reevaluation of pity has been Martha Nussbaum, who in works on classical philosophy, literature, the emotions, and Nietzsche, has both analyzed and championed (a combination similar to that of French philosophers of a century ago) a compassionate pity: "Rousseau seems right that, followed through rigorously enough, pity supports something like democratic equality: democracy because pity sees the value to each person of having a choice in his or her way of life and in the political conception that governs it; equality because it concerns itself at least with the provision to all of a basic minimum welfare. We can now observe that pity constructs an emotional analogue of the original position in John Rawl's *A Theory of Justice*."[12]

But very little historical treatment has been allocated to sentiment and pity in *fin-de-siècle* France, either their social manifestations or inquiries into them. Moreover, the philosophical and psychological disciplines have largely ignored or minimized the trails left by French predecessors. This study therefore hopes to restore historical perspective to contemporary discussions on pity and ethics, politics and literature. Through its twofold dedication to the French history of ideas on pity as sentiment, this book too participates in the spirit of rehabilitation of contemporary works while hoping to fill a lacuna.

So pity is with us today, as it very much was in *fin-de-siècle* France: what of an instructive nature do the two periods share, and where do they differ? For starters, a terminological trap: pity's definitional multivalence distorts the affective experience the discourse hopes to signify. Pity, compassion, sympathy, empathy, and mercy are near synonyms, conceptually related but distinct words that are often used together and often opposed, with supposedly differing social and moral consequences. The semantic instability has only grown throughout this century—pity's denotative and connotative capacities have shown incredible powers of expansion. The confusions beg all sorts of questions in the diachronic study of linguistics that are far beyond the scope—and competence—of this study. But it is useful to remember that the French of the *fin-de-siècle* almost uniformly used the term "pitié" to connote the meanings and contexts that are today shaded over a wider range of terms in the English language. Moreover, the term for them denoted an unvaryingly positive sense of sentimental communion with others' "weal and woe." If pity is back with us today, it often does not speak its—or this—name: it is often a subset or synonym of compassion and sympathy and liable to be a pejorative complement to these.[13] Indeed, much of the writing on pity today in Anglo-American philosophy centers on parsing the particularities of other-directed emotions. For French writers on pity in the *fin-de-siècle*, the situation was reversed: "pitié," the equivalent of the Greek *eleos* and the Latin *pieta*, always comprised compassion and sympathy as the dominant case.

Another difference concerns the issue of *francité*—"Frenchness." Most recent thinking on sentiment and ethics has presumed the universality of pity. Writers in the *fin-de-siècle* did so too—up to a point. Not only did they complicate their ideas with reference to gender and to "civilization," but also they were self-conscious of national and linguistic traditions coalescing around the term "pitié." If I often refer to "the" or "a" "French" tradition, philosophy, or problematic, it is not within an essentialist frame of reference, nor with the belief in the existence of national characteristics in philosophy or in philosophical or moral characteristics of nations. However, the rhetorical panoply exploited in the last century included a certainty as to the salience and pertinence to a national-linguistic community of specific theoretical problems and tropes. Most of the figures I cite believed in a "Frenchness" typifying their thought, and in fact this suppositional quality was made into the source of invidious anxiety. If geographical, historical, linguistic, and ideological commonalities authorize the use of the adjective "French," it is only with these caveats in mind.[14]

The study of pity cannot be conceded to any single discipline or national-linguistic tradition; there are too many moral and epistemological stakes. The following study is therefore unapologetically interdisciplinary and discursive—in truth, cross-disciplinary.[15] This book does not hesitate to make the history of ideas relevant to present discussion—or, conversely, to import the present into the past. Indeed, one of my goals is to point scholars from different disciplines—philosophy, sociology, social psychology, history, and comparative literature—to where lines of inquiry similar to theirs have been opened in the past and with what results.[16] Our subject is therefore of more than historical interest—in at least two senses of the term, chronological and disciplinary. "Pities" past and present, French- and English-language, can play off each other to reveal basic assumptions about our societies and our humanity. That is the premise and hope of this book.

NOTES

1. Lucien Fèbvre, "Sensibility and History: How to Reconstitute the Emotional Life of the Past," *A New Kind of History: From the Writings of Fèbvre*, Peter Burke, ed., K. Folca, trans. (London: Routledge & Kegan Paul, 1973), 18. For an analysis and critique of Fèbvre's influential pronouncement, especially on its methodological assumptions, see Barbara H. Rosenwein, "Worrying about Emotions in History," *American Historical Review* 107:3 (June 2002): 821–45, where the author takes apart the "grand narrative" of emotions reflected in the history of *mentalités* earlier in the twentieth century: "There is a clear theoretical underpinning for the grand narrative. It is a particular model of the emotions, one that prevailed when Huizinga, Fèbvre, Bloch, and Elias were writing and that prevails today in our very language and in popular conceptions of the emotions. This is the 'hydraulic model'" (834–35).

2. Marcel Proust, *Sodom and Gomorrha*, K. Scott Moncrieff, trans. (London: Chatto and Windus, 1951), 201–02 . ["...quand nous croyons seulement recréer les douleurs d'un être cher, notre pitié les exagère; mais peut-être est-elle qui est dans le vrai, plus que la conscience qu'ont de ces douleurs ceux qui les souffrent, et auxquels est cachée cette tristesse de leur vie, que la pitié, elle, voit, dont elle se désespère."] *Sodome et Gomorrhe* (Paris: Gallimard, 1988).

3. Jean Bourdeau, *La Rochefoucauld* (Paris: Hachette, 1895), 192. ["Le progrès de l'idée de pitié suffirait à marquer le changement de l'état social."] Translations from French into English are mine throughout this book unless otherwise noted.

4. Although I am largely indebted to Dominick LaCapra's notion of "dialogic reading," I also profess myself a practitioner of what he qualifies more circumspectly as "synoptic": "paraphrastic approach (that) remains geared to reporting the 'findings' of reading for summarizing the meaning of large runs of texts or documents in a concise, lucid manner." See Dominick LaCapra, *History and Reading: Tocqueville, Foucault, French Studies* (Toronto: University of Toronto Press, 2000), 34. See also Martin Jay, "Two Cheers for Paraphrase: The Confessions of a Synoptic Intellectual Historian," in *Fin-de-Siècle Socialism and Other Essays* (New York: Routledge, 1988), 52–63.

5. Alexandre Baillot, *L'influence de la philosophie de Schopenhauer en France (1860–1910)*. (Paris: Librairie Philosophique J. Vrin, 1927), 14.

6. Sarah Maza, *Private Lives and Public Affairs: The "Causes Célèbres" of Prerevolutionary France* (Berkeley: U of California Press, 1993), 10.

7. Kenneth Burke, *A Rhetoric of Motives* (Berkeley: U of California Press, 1969), 43.

8. Rosenwein, "Worrying about Emotions in History," 824 n. 12. See also Janet Todd, *Sensibility: An Introduction*: "But a 'sentiment' is also a thought, often an elevated one,

influenced by emotion, a combining of heart and head or an emotional impulse leading to an opinion or principle" (London: Methuen, 1986), 7.

9. William Reddy, *The Navigation of Feeling: A Framework for the History of Emotion* (Cambridge: Cambridge UP, 2001).

10. There does exist a French-language equivalent of Williams' concept, defined by Georges Matoré: "Le *mot-clé* désignera donc non une abstraction, non une moyenne, non un objet, mais un être, un sentiment, une idée, vivants dans la mesure même où la société reconnaît en eux son idéal. Nous proposons ici, remarquons-le, non une typologie abstraite mais une coördination hiérarchique fondée sur des termes auxquels les contemporains reconnaisaient eux-mêmes un caractère fondamental." ["*Key-word* thus designates not an abstraction, an average, nor an object, but rather a being, a sentiment, an idea, given life to the degree that society recognizes in them its ideal. Note that what is proposed here is not an abstract typology, but a hierarchical coordinate based on terms in which contemporaries themselves recognize a fundamental characteristic."] (*La Méthode en léxicologie* [Paris: M. Didier, 1953], 68).

11. A perfectly frank note is hit by Michael Stocker, who writes: "At the same time I was struck by philosophers' strangeness about emotions, I was also struck and heartened by the explosion of philosophical works on emotions and moral psychology. Many of these works also argued against those strange philosophical treatments or lack of treatment of emotions." In Michael Stocker and Elizabeth Hegeman, *Valuing Emotions* (Cambridge: Cambridge UP, 1996), 3. See especially Martha Nussbaum's *Upheavals of Thought: The Intelligence of the Emotions* (Cambridge: Cambridge UP, 2001).

12. Martha Nussbaum, "Compassion: The Basic Social Emotion," *Social Philosophy and Policy* 13:1 (1996), 40. For a similar discussion of Rawls in *Upheavals of Thought*, see pages 340–42. In this latter work, Nussbaum has shied away from the term "pity" in favor of "compassion," which subsumes it: "'Pity' has recently come to have nuances of condescension and superiority to the sufferer that it did not have when Rousseau invoked *pitié*, and still does not have when 'pity' is used to translate the Greek tragic terms *eleos* and *oiktos*. I shall avoid it here because of those associations....I shall use the term 'compassion,' but my analysis shall focus on the standard cases where compassion is linked to undeserved misfortune, and is thus coextensive with pity, in its older use" (301 n. 6).

13. Although Joel Davitz, in *The Language of Emotion* (New York and London: Academic Press, 1969), shows how traditional usage still attaches itself to pity. For example, he cites the Lorge-Thorndike Frequency, in which "Pity" merits an "A" ("greater than 50 per 1,000,000 words used") (11).

14. See Frédéric Worms, "Au-delà de l'histoire et du caractère: l'idée de philosophie française, la Première Guerre mondiale et le 'moment 1900,'" *Revue de Métaphysique et de Morale* (July-September 2001): 63–81: "Thus the 'moment 1900' is characterized in its philosophy by shared problems, such as the foundation and numerical nature of mathematics, time and psychological experience, being and the critique of consciousness....To recount such moments around these problems cannot entirely avoid the issue of their more general geographical and historical dimensions, those which, as we have seen, join together philosophical characteristics with national characteristics in such a way as to allow a reciprocal correlation, and to seek the philosophical disposition of a nation in its political activity" (78–79). ["Ainsi le 'moment' 1900 est-il caractérisé en philosophie par des problèmes communs tels que celui du nombre et de la fondation des mathématiques, du temps et de l'expérience psychologique, de la vie et de la critique de la connaissance....Décrire de tels moments autour de tels problèmes ne peut permettre en effet d'éviter entièrement la question de leur épaisseur géographique et historique plus générale, celle qui, comme on l'a vu plus haut,

reliait les caractères philosophiques aux caractères nationaux au point de permettre l'identification inverse et la caractérisation philosophique des nations dans leur action politique."]

15. I rely on—and hope to fulfill—LaCapra's definition of the term: "Cross-disciplinarity is different from additive interdisciplinarity in that it explores problems that cut across existing disciplines, and it may lead to an unsettling and rearticulation of disciplinary lines, possibly even giving rise to newer objects of study and disciplinary formations, or at least to newer emphases, concentrations, and specializations." In *History and Reading*, 192.

16. See Richard Harvey Brown: "Seen in this way, the writing of history is a moral activity of retrospection. By retrospectively viewing the past the historian creates space for perspectively viewing the present." In *Social Science as Civic Discourse: Essays on the Invention, Legitimation, and Uses of Social Theory* (Chicago: U of Chicago P, 1989), 107.

Prologue: Composing the French Pro-Pity Tradition

Each sentiment has its history, and this history is curious, because it is, if we may so speak, an abridged history of humanity. Although the feelings of the human heart do not undergo any permanent change, yet they feel the effect of the religious and political revolutions which are going on in the world. They retain their nature, but change their expression; and it is in studying these changes of expression that the literary critic writes, without classifying it, the history of the world.[1]

In this approach, emotions have a history, and it is not enough to examine economic, social, and cultural structures either in isolation or in combination. One cannot begin to appreciate the sweep and significance of historical change unless one examines emotional management and its strengths and failures, its vital role in relationships and meanings, its links to authority and rebellion, and its destabilization by war, famine, or technological progress.[2]

Pity was a key word, a "mot-clé," comprising salient ideas in varied French discursive contexts. So we first need to retrace the historical trajectory of influential views on the meanings, objects, and moral worth of pity. Our goal is to provide both the *loci classicus* and the chronological and thematic markers that gave genealogical grounding to *fin-de-siècle* thinking on pity. The chronological presentation of this "Prologue" does not imply that I take a teleological view of French engagements with pity, even if the protagonists of a century ago often understood their engagement in cumulative, progressivist terms—remember Jean Bourdeau's claim that "the evolution of the idea of pity would suffice as a gauge of changes in our social state."

The terms "pity tradition" and "doctrinaire pity" figure prominently in this study and indeed were invoked explicitly or implicitly by some of our thinkers, so it is important to provide here their general conceptual bearings. The two phrases condense the consensus in *fin-de-siècle* philosophy and criticism around pity as a natural, benevolent sentiment central to social virtue as well as to French identity.

Etymological dictionaries help us detect both changes and constancy in the meaning of "pity" over centuries. What they reveal is that *pitié* is more distinctive, polysemous, and less bifurcated in French than in English. For centuries it conventionally denoted a sentiment of misericord, consecrated by Christianity and carrying the full weight of an emotional response to human suffering:

At first, *piétet* (1050) and *pitet* (1080), are descended from the Latin *pietas*, a word derived from *pius* (*pie, pieux*), with both sacred and profane meanings and which, with its meaning of a "sentiment of devotion toward the gods, family, and country," furnished *piété*. During the imperial period, *pietas* began to signify clemency, the sentiment of misericordious kindness shown by the Emperor; then, in the language of Christians, the sentiment of compassion, kindness, and charity. The word entered French with its Christian value of "compassion," but also as the inheritor of values both profane and religious. It made its way into the locution, "that inspires a sentiment of pity." In Old French it also comprised the related ideas of concern, distress, and suffering.[3]

Georges Gougenheim recently insisted on the singularity of the French etymological borrowing from the Latin, which "profoundly penetrated the soul of the French:"

Under the Roman Empire, the word *pietas*, enlarging its meaning, was used to express sentiments of benevolence and compassion regarding others. The word provided two words in French: *pieta*; the second, *pitié*, is the result of an evolution that is, if not wholly popular, nonetheless attests to a borrowing that quickly entered the expressions of common speech. *Pitié* extends the sense that the Latin had already taken; one that must have profoundly penetrated the soul of the French. French is the sole language that was led to adopt this dual evolution of a Latin word.[4]

"French is the sole language that was led to adopt this dual evolution of a Latin word"—a learned "piety" and a widespread, demotic "pity" that denotes sentimental communion.

Frédéric Godefroy, in his masterfully compendious *Dictionnaire de l'ancienne langue française et de tous ses dialectes, du IXème au XVème siècles*, of 1889, declined the manifold vocabulary of premodern *pitié*: "*pitable*: 'tender, pious, pitying;' *pitace* (pitasse, pitache): 'doux, pieux, pitoyable,' 'augmentation of pity;' *pittance*: 'pity' (also linked to religious service of same name); *pite*: 'adj., one who shows pity, pitying;' *pitéablement*: 'from pity, by pity;' *piteer, pitier, pitoyer*: 'v. in., to have pity, take pity on, to be moved;' *piteor (piteour)*: 'someone who pities;' *pitos* (-tous, teus, teux, teulz, toulz, toux, tieux, tells, dos, doux, piet): 'adj., compassionate, pious, who takes pity on;' *pitosement*: 'adv., pitiable, with pity'".[5]

Most of these terms are adjectives, adverbs, or intensifiers. In erudite, literary discourse up through the sixteenth century, the noun form of *pitié* was less frequently employed than the adjective *pitoyable*, and it was deployed in declamatory locutions rather than as a noun signifier for a sentiment with an ideational component.[6] Indeed, almost all of the examples that Littré supplied in the 1860s for his definition of *pitié* as a noun denoting "a sentiment that takes hold at the sight of sufferings and which moves us to ease them," dated from no earlier than the seventeenth century.[7]

The seventeenth century was a time of revival of interest in, and rehabilitation of, the sentiments and "passions."[8] The theater, poetry, and the visual arts participated equally in this reappraisal. Racine, Boileau, and LeBrun were representative figures.[9] Racine's illustration of the Aristotelian dynamics of pity was especially remarked by his contemporaries and was to be a privileged object of study in the eighteenth and nineteenth centuries. The abbés Guyot and d'Olivet, for example, engaged in published grammatical disputations on Racinean pity in the early eighteenth century:

> "'If from so much misfortune some pity moves you.'" "I dare not," says the Author, "condemn this sentence, but I dare less approve it." (Why? Note the reason). "I believe," he says, "that pity is said only of persons, whereas compassion is used as much for people as for things. 'Have pity on me. Have compassion on my woes.'" Heavens! What scrupulousness! Where on earth does M. d'Olivet get this distinction? It's certainly not from the usage current in spoken language, even less so from that of written language.[10]

The prioritization of pity over compassion, as in this example, would continue to characterize French distinctions between the two concepts and link seventeenth- and eighteenth-century usages.

Boileau, too, poetically declaimed praise of Aristotelian tragic pity: "In all you write, observe with care and art/ to move the Passions, and incline the Heart. / If, in a laboured act, the pleasing Rage/ Cannot our hopes and fears by turn engage,/ nor in our mind a feeling of Pity raise;/ in vain with learned scenes you fill your plays".[11] La Fontaine's exasperated quip (*boutade*) about children, "Cet âge est sans pitié" ["that age is without pity"] from "Les deux pigeons" in *Les Fables*, also became a canonical reference in discussions on pity.

Sheila Page Bayne has scrutinized French ideas on emotions and the absorption with pity in a study of "weeping, emotion, tears, and literature" during the seventeenth century. Distinguishing between "sentimental" and 'intellectual' tears, Bayne cites the seventeenth-century alignment of pity with the latter as a quintessential example of the dissimilarity: "A similar pattern reveals itself when we turn to another source of intellectual tears: pity. We have referred to intellectual tears as those responding to causes that transcend the individual, and we have seen that one such cause is the abstract concept with an emotional connotation strong enough to cause weeping. Not only abstract virtues and ideas come under the heading of intellectual tears; pity is also an emotion transcending the individual."[12] Bayne's reading of La Fontaine's *Amours de Psyche et de Cupidon* teases out the intimate relations between pity and "intellectual" tears:

> An examination of the arguments presented by Ariste and Acante gives us an idea of how pity was considered to be pleasurable and in what ways tears of pity were enjoyable tears....That is to say, weeping is one of the commonest things in the world, but weeping for pity, "pour le malheur d'autrui," is a particular, rare and privileged form of weeping....Ariste evokes the connection of pity to virtue and reminds his listeners of "la satisfaction intérieure des gens de bien." The idea of the elevation of human beings through pity is most strikingly presented by Ariste.[13]

Bayne concludes by demonstrating the relevance of pity and "intellectual" tears to most of seventeenth-century drama: "It is clear that pity was regarded as a pleasure, and that much of the success of 17th-century tragedy depended on it. This is notable also in contemporary remarks on tears and pity in the theater. These passages suggest that pity, for the theater-goer of the 17th century, was associated with transcendent spiritual values."[14]

This self-transcending dimension was evident in most seventeenth-century definitions of pity, whether pleasurable or painful, as a moral good. From the beginning to the close of that century, this approbatory ethical dimension appeared in dictionary definitions of pity. Jean Nicot's *Thrésor de la langue français* of 1606 is an example:

Pity and "compassion that one feels for the misery of another," *Miseratio, Commiseratio*; "Pity one feels for a poor person, and the misericord one shows him in offering him one's goods," *Eleemosyna*; "Who has pity for someone," *Misericors, Clemens*; "I have pity and compassion for human frailty," *Fragilitatis humanae miseratio subit*; "If God does not pity us," *Nisi Deus nos respexerit*; "Lose all pity and affection that one should feel for another," *Exuere humanitatem.*[15]

Omitting the corresponding Latin but maintaining the same dolorous sense, the *Dictionnaire de l'Académie française* of 1694 defined pity similarly: "Pity: 'Compassion. Sentiment for the woes, for the miseries of another.'"[16]

The French term during the age of the Sun King thus incorporated dysthemic, but potentially pleasurable, connotations—"souci, détresse, douleur, misère, souffrance" [worry, distress, sorrow, misery, suffering]—with socially beneficial and theologically significant consequences—"bonté miséricordieuse, compassion, bonté, charité" [misericordious benevolence, compassion, goodness, charity]. This affective unity— an other-regarding emotion prompting socially useful, religiously syntonic, and aesthetically satisfying responses—was the distinctive version of pity inherited by the *fin-de-siècle* and bounds the concept I analyze in this book. Even today, a cursory look at the contemporary *Thesaurus Larousse* shows the constancy of this definition: "Pity: 'compassion; sympathy; moved; goodness; charity; humanity; clemency; leniency; goodness of heart; misericord; grace; mercy; heartbreaking; poor; unfortunate; *pieta*; Jeremiad; lamentation; wailing; grief; weeping.'"[17] How different this is from the English-language evolution of the term!—the *Thesaurus Larousse* lists "condescension; disdain; scorn; affliction; distress; misery" as *antonyms* of pity, whereas the equivalent terms in English have lodged themselves at the very center of "pity's" more pejorative meaning.[18]

If pity was a key word in French language, not all claims made on its behalf were condoned. We also encounter misprisions and contestation, which were sanctioned, especially by those who accepted the term's referents but were uneasy with its purported effects. Because pity came to have a morally and socially uniform sense in the seventeenth century, it became an easy target for those who wished either to complexify or to minimize it. This included especially those moralists of the seventeenth and eighteenth centuries who were stylistically partial to maxims, aphorisms, and apophthegms. Why the nondiscursive moralists should be more hostile to pity than other writers—the later example of Nietzsche is a striking confirmation—is an interesting question that has yet to receive sustained attention. La Rochefoucauld, Vauvenargues, Chamfort, and Pascal were ambivalent at best to the broadest claims made for pity.

François, duc de La Rochefoucauld (1613–1680), was unequivocally hostile to pity: "Pity is often a way of feeling our own misfortunes in those of other people; it is a clever foretaste of the unhappiness we may some day encounter. We help others to make sure they will help us under similar circumstances, and the services we render them are, properly speaking, benefits we store up for ourselves in advance."[19] Other maxims were equally jaundiced: "There is often more pride than kindness in our pitying the misfortunes of our enemies; we give them proofs of our compassionateness to bring home to them our superiority." [20] In his *Portrait*, La Rochefoucauld painted a more nuanced picture of his rejection of a manipulative pity: "I am little susceptible to pity, and would like to be not at all. However, there is nothing I would not do to relieve a suffering person, and truly I believe that one should do everything in one's power, including even demonstrating much compassion for their troubles, for the unfortunate are so stupid that this does them a world of good; but I also hold that it is enough to be satisfied with the display, and to carefully guard against possessing it."[21]

Luc de Clapiers, the Marquis de Vauvenargues (1715–1747), wrote that "pity is less tender than love."[22] But he also claimed that "it is a sign of ferocity and baseness to insult a disgraced person, especially if they are wretched; there is no villainy which misery does not turn into an object of pity for sensitive souls."[23] Sébastien-Roch-Nicholas Chamfort (1740–1794) penned the following maxims: "Generosity is but the pity of noble souls"; "pity is only a secret falling back on ourselves at the sight of another's woes, the which we could also be victims."[24]

Similarly, Pascal, in his *Pensées*, wrily counseled that "we should pity this one and that; but we should have for the former a pity born of tenderness and for the latter a pity rising from scorn."[25] What these figures spanning nearly two centuries shared in common was an insurgence against the univalent equation of pity with virtue; they wished to balance compassion and commiseration with a healthy dose of individualism and a mistrust of others' needs and claims.

Descartes is the most important representative of the nonaphoristic, rationalist distrust of pity as motor sentiment and moral quality. His analyses epitomize challenges to the early-modern pro-pity tradition. In *Passions of the Soul*, he made pity a small subset of one of the six major passions, sadness: "But when it [good and evil] is represented to us as pertaining to other men, we may esteem them either as worthy or unworthy of it; and when we esteem them worthy, that does not excite in us any other passion but joy….But if we esteem them unworthy of it, the good excites envy and the evil pity, which are species of sadness."[26] By splicing pity to envy and condescension and subsuming them all under sadness, Descartes in essence minimized pity: "For the rest, since hatred and sadness should be rejected by the soul, even when they proceed from true knowledge, this should with greater reason be the case when they proceed from some false opinion."[27] Pity, as a form of sadness that is passive and non-instrumental, is the self-love of the weak: "Those who feel themselves very feeble and subject to the adversities of fortune appear to be more disposed to this passion than others, because they represent the evil of others as possibly occurring to themselves; and then they are moved to pity more by the love that they bear to themselves than by that which they bear to others."[28]

Still, Descartes held that the "noble-minded" can also be accessible to pity, in a way that combines the past, in the person of Aristotle, and anticipates the near future in the figure of la Rochefoucauld—he fused representational capacities to a sense of superiority to create a distancing but satisfying sociability:

And there is this difference here that while the ordinary man has compassion on those who lament their lot because he thinks that the evils from which they suffer are very vexatious, the principal object of the pity of the greatest men is the weakness of those whom they see bemoaning their fate, because they do not consider that any accident which might possibly happen would be so great an ill as is the cowardice of those who cannot endure it with constancy; and although they hate vices, they do not for all that hate those whom they see subject to them, but only pity them.[29]

Descartes' position was a nuanced version of Stoicism. He did argue that pity could be a sort of criterion of moral worth, in that it is absent only among the evil: "But it is only the evilly disposed and envious, who naturally hate all men, or those who are so brutal and blinded by good fortune, or rendered so desperate by evil fortune that they do not consider that any evil can happen to them, who are insensible to pity."[30]

The emotive and semantical gap between Descartes and La Rochefoucauld, on the one hand, and the later eighteenth century, on the other, is enormous. The Enlightement conspicuously embraced pity, sensibility, passions, tears, weeping, and benevolence—rhetorical and representational. The abbé Féraud's *Dictionnaire critique de la langue française* of 1787 defined pity using positive misericordious synonyms and illustrated usages with the literary examples that had accrued through canonicity: "Pity: s.f. 'Compassion, sentiment of sorrow provoked in us by the woes, the misfortunes of others.' 'To have pity' (without an article), 'to be moved by pity.' 'Tragedy should provoke terror and pity.' 'Pitiless heart,' etc. 'Take pity on' governs the usages: 'Take pity on the state to which you see me reduced' (*Crébillon*)."[31] Linguistic usage, literary representation, the concern with sociability conjoined to make of the eighteenth century an "age of pity," in Anne Vincent-Buffault's phrase.[32]

The Enlightenment *philosophes* especially rehabilitated an unequivocally "good"—that is, socially virtuous—pity against the stringent rationalism and distrustful individualism of the earlier century. Diderot, the baron d'Holbach, Montesquieu, Rousseau, and Voltaire were the figures most crucial to this revaluation. Voltaire declared in a letter written late in his life: "Yes, pity is the antidote to all the scourges of this world; that's why Jean Racine took as the motto for the collected edition of his Tragedies, 'fear and pity.'"[33]

Diderot and his *Encyclopédie* were an instant *locus classicus*.[34] In the *Encyclopédie*, pity was classified as a moral concept whose existence attested to the innate goodness of humanity:

Pity (ethics), is a natural sentiment of the soul, which we experience at the sight of those who suffer or are in distress. It is not true that pity originates from self-consciousness....Thus we owe more of the noble and merciful actions of this world to the goodness of hearts than to philosophical speculation. Nothing so honors humanity than this generous sentiment; it is, of all the movements of the soul, the softest and most delectable in its effects.[35]

This construal of pity as a universal, natural, and humane passion facilitating intrasocial goodness was rendered canonical by the *Encyclopédie*, trumping the earlier moralists' maxim-driven denigration and supplanting literary renditions of pro-social sentimentalism. Indeed, the Encyclopedists, in taking pity away from elite moralists' pen and placing it on the side of the heart against philosophy and apostrophizing it as that which bestows upon Humanity its greatest honor, composed a veritable paean to pity:

"The hand of springtime covers the earth in flowers," says the inspired Brahmin. Such is sensitive and benevolent pity with respect to the sons of misfortune. She wipes their tears, she softens their afflictions. This pauper drags his poverty from place to place; he has neither clothing nor shelter—place him under the protective wings of pity. He is chilled to the bone— warm him up; he is overcome with fatigue, revive his forces, lengthen his days, so that your soul may live.[36]

The dithyrambic penchant of this period for beatitudes has been called a "deism of sensibility" by Paul Bénichou: "There resulted, as a heroic complement to humanist optimism, a sort of lay version of the Christian cult of suffering: the minister of humanity, whether philosopher or poet, like a secular Christ, established his titles through his tribulations."[37]

Montesquieu's *Lettres Persanes* is another key *locus* depicting pity as a social virtue, an adjunct to both justice and charity. The character Usbek writes to Mizra recounting the mythic story of the Troglodytes. After relating in "Letter XII" the destruction of the Troglodytes through their own cupidity and ferocity, Usbek narrates how they found temporary surcease through the intervention of two wise and piteous leaders: "These two men were very singular. They had some knowledge of Humanity and Justice. They loved Virtue, and were united as much by the Rectitude of their own Minds, as by the Corruption of their countrymen. They were witnesses of the common Desolation, and no farther concerned in it than they were led to by Pity. The Destruction of their Neighbors was a Motive of farther Union."[38] For Montesquieu, wisdom, pity, and justice are the mutually sustaining curatives for an ailing social order (and thus for his own monarchy, in this cautionary tale).

The baron d'Holbach, in his *Morale universelle, ou les devoirs de l'homme fondés sur sa nature*, promoted pity while noting its relatively weak hold on most humans— hence the need for a pedagogy of sentiment, a stance that would be recuperated in the *fin-de-siècle*. Against La Rochefoucauld and other detractors of the supposed self-regarding egotism of pity, d'Holbach argues that the sentiment brings real benefit to both beneficiary and benefactor:

From the relief given to he who suffers there also results a real relief to the person providing it; a very soft and sweet pleasure that reflection further increases through the idea of having done somebody some good, of having gained some rights to their affection and merited their thanks, of acting in such a way as to prove that we possess a sensitive and tender Heart; a disposition that all men wish to find in their brethren, and whose absence would lead one to believe that one is poorly made.[39]

D'Holbach claims, however, that this "disposition" is, unfortunately, relatively rare: "But pity, as everything shows us, is quite rare on earth; the world is full of an enormous crowd of insensitive beings, whose hearts are barely moved if at all by the misfortunes of their fellow beings."[40] So an education onto pity is all the more essential, especially in a society shot through with inequality: "Education must ceaselessly work upon the sensitivity of princes, the powerful, and all those who are destined to benefit from luxury…this is how the sentiment of pity may be developped in hearts that nature has endowed with sensibility."[41]

Jean-Jacques Rousseau gave the central impetus to pity's renewed cachet. Rousseau's *Second Discourse* is the cynosure of the valorization of pity and became the core of subsequent debates (as it still is today). In this work on "the origins of inequality," he argued that there are two principles prior to reason: self-preservation and pity. He posited this schema in order to confute Hobbes (like Hume and Smith in their related arguments): "I do not believe I need fear any contradiction in granting to men the only Natural virtue which the most extreme Detractor [Hobbes] of human virtues was forced to acknowledge. I speak of Pity, a disposition suited to beings as weak and as subject to so many ills as we are; a virtue all the more universal and useful to man as it precedes the exercise of all reflection in him, and so Natural that even the Beasts sometimes show evident signs of it."[42] Like Aristotle, Rousseau evidenced pity's power in spectators' passions: "Such is the pure movement of Nature prior to all reflection: such is the force of natural pity, which the most depraved morals still have difficulty destroying, since in our theaters one daily sees being moved and weeping at the miseries of some unfortunate person people who, if they were in the Tyrant's place, would only increase their enemy's torments."[43]

Rousseau seconded the Anglo-Scottish moral-sentiment theorists yet went further in his attribution of pro-social worth to pity:

Mandeville clearly sensed that, for all their morality, men would never have been anything but monsters if Nature had not given them pity in support of reason; but he did not see that from this single attribute flow all the social virtues he wants to deny men. Indeed, what are Generosity, Clemency, Humanity, if not Pity applied to the weak, the guilty, or the species in general? Even Benevolence and friendship, properly understood, are the products of a steady pity focused on a particular object; for what else is it to wish that someone not suffer, than to wish that he be happy?[44]

Rousseauian pity is not the multivalent sentiment that had been taxonomized by many predecessors; it is rather a unitary sentiment with a social intentionality that inheres in human nature. Rousseau reinforced this claim by conceiving pity not only as a moral virtue but also as a nomological standard undergirding justice and all other mechanisms inclining to sociability:

It is therefore quite certain that pity is a natural sentiment which, by moderating in every individual the activity of self-love, contributes to the mutual preservation of the entire species. It is pity that carries us without reflection to the assistance of those we see suffer; pity that, in the state of Nature, takes the place of Laws, morals, and virtue, with the advantage that no one is tempted to disobey its gentle voice; pity that will keep any sturdy Savage from robbing a weak child or an infirm old man of his hard-won subsistence if he can hope to find his own elsewhere; pity that, in place of that sublime maxim of reasoned justice, *Do unto others as you would have them do unto you*, inspires in all men this other maxim of natural goodness, much less perfect but perhaps more useful than the first: *Do your good with the least possible harm to others*. It is, in a word, in this Natural sentiment rather than in subtle arguments that one has to seek the cause of the repugnance to evil-doing which every human being would feel even independently of the maxims of education.[45]

Rousseau's pity is vast and consequential: with it he sought to replace the "golden rule" ethics of the Judeo-Christian heritage and other deontological arguments. That so expansive a role is incumbent upon it is due to the fact that pity is nature's guarantee that a species can vouchsafe its existence against potential "evil-doing" from individual members.[46]

It was Rousseau's matchless contribution to thinking on pity to have made of it the keystone of a sentiment-based moral, social, linguistic, and literary theory, and this in a more thoroughgoing, metaphysical and prescriptive manner than the Anglo-Scottish moral-sentiment theorists had made of sympathy. Much of nineteenth-century thought on pity would encounter Rousseau as an unavoidable landmark.

Within a decade of Rousseau's death, there already were attempts to come to grips with the spur he provided to formulations on pity. For example, J.-N. Étienne de Bock, in a book titled *Recherches philosophiques sur l'origine de la pitié et divers autres sujets de morale*, tried to counter Rousseau's attack on political culture by arguing that pity is not found in nature but rather cultivated by civil society: "After establishing that man in the state of nature is cruel, it remains for us to see how civilization, in fostering his imagination and other faculties, brings forth pity."[47]

Another Rousseauian figure promoting a pro-pity sentimentalism was Bernardin de Saint-Pierre, whose *Études de la Nature*, first published in 1784, and *Paul et Virginie*, in 1787, were popular phenomena with their sentimental, pastoral, and sublime raptures. The cult of sensibility he promoted was indissolubly paired with pity:

The feeling of innocence is the first spring of pity; which is why we are more moved by the unhappiness of a child than that of the elderly. This is not, as some philosophers have claimed, because the child has fewer means and wants, because indeed it has more while the aged is often ill and moves ineluctable towards death, just as the child is entering life—it's because the child has never caused offense, is innocent....When an aged person is virtuous, an ethical feeling about his troubles increases in us; which obviously proves that human pity is not an animal sentiment. Similarly, the sight of Belisarius is very moving. If you add to it that of a child holding out its hand to gather some coins for this renowned blind man, the notion of pity is even greater.[48]

Notice the budding commonplaces in Bernardin de Saint-Pierre's argument: adjudication of innocence and guilt and a diagnostic for proximate mechanisms of social sentiments. The title of the work—*Études de la nature*—assumes the innateness of pity. His works were a major source for nineteenth-century Romanticism, more widely read at this later time than during the earlier revolutionary decades.

There is a crucially causal nexus in the emergent French pity tradition between the stimulus of Rousseauian pity on the French Revolution and, in turn, of the French Revolution on pity. This is in part the subject of William Reddy's immensely useful work, which also informs the signification of "sentimentalism" that is used throughout this book: "Sentimentalism taught that pity, benevolence, love, and gratitude were expressions of the same natural sensitivity, the root of morality, and the foundation of all social bonds, and that stimulating these feelings was the best protection against unruly passions and a necessary training for virtue."[49] And:

But here I wish to insist on the special emotional character of some (but not all) of these new practices, as the novel view of emotions as a force for good in human affairs, and on the enthusiasm for emotional expression and intimacy—for emotional refuge from a prevailing code of honor—expressed by many actors central to events leading up to and following the outbreak of the Revolution. I propose to call these linked features of the age collectively "sentimentalism."[50]

Reddy argues that the Enlightenment was a spur to, and avatar of, this sentimentalism: "Recent work suggests that 'sentimentalism' grew out of a central concern of the Enlightenment period—the question of human nature—and that virtually all major figures accepted, in part, the sentimentalist answer to this question....Feelings of benevolence, pity, love, and gratitude gave shape to moral judgments and rendered moral action pleasurable."[51] The *philosophes* also drew political conclusions from their intellectual commitment to sentimentalism, basing the incentive for political reforms on the need to express and nurture altruistic passions: "Not the least of these implications was the idea that natural benevolence, love, gratitude, and pity ought to serve as a basis for political reform as well as personal choice."[52]

But, Reddy argues, the example of Robespierre's Terror showed that sentimentalism failed as an "emotional regime."[53] Moreover, the backlash against the Terror occluded a sentimentalist pity-politics: "After the fall of Robespierre, however, the role of emotions in politics was brought into question. Within a few years, reigning ideas about emotions were radically altered; even their role in prior decades was covered over and denied."[54] I part company with Reddy's argument that sentimentalism was erased, except for "traces," from 1794 until recent study of it: "Sentimentalism, although its doctrines had been discredited and were no longer admissible as public justification for actions or norms of judgement, lived on as a private code of behavior, available to shape affective ties within the family, between lovers."[55] This book demonstrates that many of the same public philosophical valorizations and political associations perdured over a century later, in the nineteenth century's *fin-de-siècle*. At this latter date, the pro-pity consensus was strikingly similar to that of the Enlightenment; yet, as Reddy rightly argues, many of its precursors and *loci classicus* were reintroduced for debates as if they had been simply forgotten.

The Revolution did not totally discredit sentimental pity, even if it did devalue its

Rousseauian version. In fact, the years 1789–1794 gave social and political substance, as well as polemical rigor, to the abstractions of pity. The Revolution was a crucible for the claims on behalf of pity's cohering capacities; for fellowship and suffering were among the Revolution's affective modes. Sympathetic fraternity was the Revolution's ordeal, exaltation, and downfall. Both pro-and anti-revolutionary writers battled for the right to pity's mantle. The question for post-Rousseauian pity was not its reality but its prescriptive political role and its historical lessons—an ideological pity.

Like Reddy, David Denby has written recently on the fate of sentimentalism in the post-Revolutionary transition up to the 1820s. He summarizes and analyzes Rousseau's *Émile*:

What of Rousseau's treatment of pity, *bienfaisance*, alms-giving? A large part of Book IV of *Émile,* up to the "Profession de foi du vicaire savoyard," is devoted to Émile's education in pity and *bienfaisance*, evidently conceived as key elements in the development of the adolescent's "reason and passions," and as crucial in the building of a bridge between the individual and the society in which he must live....Pity, then, plays an important role in Émile's moral development: the relation between the growing social subject and the surrounding society is envisaged to a considerable extent through the cognition, internalisation and transformation of the spectacle of human suffering.[56]

Denby also further maintains that Rousseuaian pity is the epitome of sentimentalism:

The first maxim which Rousseau offers to guide this process is a revealing one: "Il n'est pas dans le cœur humain de se mettre à la place des gens qui sont plus heureux que nous, mais seulement de ceux qui sont plus à plaindre." This is of course perfectly consonant with sentimentalism's predilection for the victim, and for the downward social displacement of the sentimentalising process: it is the spectacle of misfortune which is crucial for the formation of the moral sense.[57]

Denby likewise invokes Diderot as a pre-Revolutionary model for a piteous sentimentalism: "And they are together the condition for the communicative aesthetic which Diderot evokes in a famous passage: 'Hommes, venez apprendre de lui à vous réconcilier avec les maux de la vie; venez, nous pleurerons ensemble sur les personnages malheureux de ses fictions, et nous dirons: "Si le sort nous acable, du moins les honnêtes gens pleureront aussi sur nous."'"[58] In a chapter titled "Sentimentalism in the Rhetoric of the Revolution," Denby persuasively claims that "the language of sentiment, and crucially the notion of pity, becomes a central symbolic enjeu of Revolutionary debate at this point in the Revolution."[59] Just as Reddy situates Robespierre implacably at the rhetorical crossroads of pity, Denby stresses the Incorruptible's arbitrating influence: "But it is Robespierre who develops the theme in all its complexity, putting sensibility at the heart of the debate. The first objective of Robespierre's intervention is to adjudicate between the competing claims of pity and rigour:...'who is the true victim?'"[60] With the Terror, "Republican heroism is thus a transcendence of pity and sympathy, and is a particularly laudable virtue in a woman."[61] Reddy, too, notes how the Montagnards arrogated to themselves the right of legitimating pity: "Saint-Just, Robespierre, and others even warned their fellow revolutionaries against 'false pity.' To have pity and spare the life of a convicted aristocrat, of a nonjuring priest, of a counter-Revolutionary peasant, endangered the larger acts of benevolence by which the Revolution had dismantled the Old Regime and restored to the people what they had lost. False pity became itself suspect and grounds for the death penalty."[62]

Denby analyzes a noncanonical and nontheoretical source to show how the Revolution's discursive struggles over pity had practical consequences for ordinary individuals:

The difference between the experience of the sentimental traveler in the first book [François Vernes' *Voyageur sentimental*] and now is that in the Revolutionary situation, the narrator cannot go about his business of charitable activity in the same open way as before: he would lay himself open to the charge of assisting the enemies of the Revolution, "la pitié allait me criminaliser aux yeux de ceux que le courage de la férocité rendait tout-puissants." Such accusations of counter-revolutionary motivation were of course directed at the language of pity in the years 1793–94.[63]

Sentimentalist pity did not emerge intact from these rhetorical collisions, but a pro-pity philosophy was still tenable. Both Reddy and Denby establish this point in the fiction and ideas of Mme. de Staël. Denby deems her the highest avatar of post-Revolutionary pro-pity thinking:

Finally, Madame de Staël goes on to insist, as she will on numerous occasions throughout her career, on the relationship of pity to the Revolution. She takes issue with the Robespierrist notion that "la pitié est un sentiment puérile qui s'oppose à toute action nécessaire à l'intérêt général," and describes the Terror as "un système continuel, et par conséquent à froid, de méconnaître toute pitié." In her view, revolutionary situations, characterized by their suspension of the "état social" and the introduction of passion into public reasoning, need the voice of pity more than any other circumstance.[64]

Denby concludes his discussion of de Staël's writings with her fiction, specifically *Delphine*: "*Delphine*...returns to the truth which was amply demonstrated in the opening phase of the novel: love and pity are inseparable emotions, which can never 'triompher l'un de l'autre.'"[65]

Reddy similarly argues (somewhat against the grain of his own thesis): "The sentimentalist interlude could not be simply expunged, however.... [Staël]'s liberalism, crystallized in her remarkable essay of 1800, *De la littérature dans ses rapports avec les institutions sociales*, retained essential elements of the sentimentalist credo."[66]

Other representative, if not canonical, polemicists reflect the schema traced by Denby and Reddy. The royalist Joseph-François Michaud (1767–1839), for example, carried on a correspondence concerning the politics of pity with the abbé Jacques Delille, author of a celebrated poem titled *La Pitié*.[67] In the first letter, dated March 2, 1802, Michaud substantiated the Rousseauian idea of pity: "What sentiment is better able to preserve stability in the social order than that which helps us to mend the inequities of fate, and which, in societies where the unfortunate are abandoned, renders citizens more generous than the polity, and love more fruitful than laws?"[68] But to this line of reasoning he attached decidedly non-Rousseauian elements: "The word *pietas* articulated at once the concern one shows for the wretched, respect for the gods, love for family, and loyalty to one's country...thus pity lent its tears to brilliance; she presided over the birth of the arts, and watched over the preservation of morals."[69]

A pity that maintained most of its Rousseauian associations had emerged unscathed from the Revolution, Michaud and Delille agreed. In fact, this pity had attenuated the upheaval's horrors: "The Revolution looked after the sacred flame of Pity amidst all the horrors of tyranny, and perhaps it is to her that we owe the good fortune of having preserved something of our humanity during the recent past."[70] Michaud concluded his letters by appealing to the socially restorative features of pity, harking back to Enlightenment pity: "Nothing is more capable of reassuring us as to the end of our troubles than to see the newfound interest in images of pity...the ancients were penetrated by this idea, depicting the goddess of pity wearing an olive wreath."[71]

That the pro-pity consensus existed and continued to develop after the Revolution is also reflected in linguistic usage. The *Gradus français ou dictionnaire de la langue poétique*, by L. J. M. Carpentier (1822), retained the same definition as the earlier *Encyclopédie*, Nicot's *Thrésor*, and *Académie*:

"Pity:" sentiment of sorrow provoked in our souls by the troubles and woes of others. Syn.: Compassion, commiseration, the length of the latter seemingly excluding it from poetic language; sensitivity. *Epit.*—charitable, benevolent, helpful, sensitive, gentle, tender, protective, painful, peaceful, leisurely, noble, generous, active, tranquil, false, feigned, unworthy, criminal, mortal, cruel, imploring, excited, haughty, prideful, offensive, insulting. *Périph.*—care, compassionate.[72]

Carpentier's *Gradus* also cites the following *loci classicus*, some of which had accrued to the pro-pity tradition since the Encyclopedists' days: "But soon the haughty Islander confessed/ Pity's soft influence o'er his harden'd breast/ For Pity's voice still prompts us to bestow/ Some lenient Balm to lighten human woes."[73] Racine remained an obligatory reference: "That despite the pity that clutches me I should bathe in a child's blood—No, Sire."[74]

Benjamin Constant, like his friend Mme. De Staël, preserved a valorization of pity through the Revolution: "Suffering rouses in us both that which is most noble in our nature, courage, and that which is most tender, sympathy and pity. It teaches us to fight on our behalf and feel for others."[75] Victor Kocay, in *L'Expression du sentiment dans l'oeuvre de Benjamin Constant*, also argues for Constant's commitment to sentimentalism: "According to Constant...morality is not always a desire for self-protection nor a forfeiture of personal happiness. It is also a sentiment for the other, a sentiment of sympathy, even of pity or of justice."[76] Constant's *Adolphe* is the epitome of a sentimental novel.

François Guizot was less partial to pity but acknowledged its significance in human affairs, especially in its relation to justice. In 1822, before his "moment,"[77]

Guizot wrote a reasoned tract against the death penalty for political "crimes." He pleaded on behalf of justice-claims, not pity, in arguing for punishments that fit the crime:

It is true that if the punishment appears excessive, if it outrages moral sentiments rather than pacifies them, if it turns the reaction of horror at a crime that it set out to arouse into pity for the guilty instead, then it loses its intended effect and goes against its own nature.... However, even amidst the softest temperaments, pity never lays such exclusive possession to the heart of men that in seeing a great punishment inflicted on a great crime it immediately forgets the crime and focuses solely on the sufferings of the chastisement. Pity too has its sense of justice, and when this justice is not rendered indignant, the severity of the sentence exercises its powers over consciences as much or more so than fear.[78]

But, Guizot signally continued, pity is a legitimate and cautionary sentiment against punishments that do not fit the crime, especially political ones:

These are the effects of the politically prosecuted person's heading to the death penalty...all the statements of the political prisoner that one is to hoist up on the scaffold become the subject of a lively interest, of sustained commentaries; the most minor details of his fate provoke vivacious and obstinate sentiments, even among those who would not have dared do what he has done, who would normally take only a tepid interest in him, had not the terrible fate that weighs upon him not stirred up from the bottom of hearts all the elements of pity and of sympathy.[79]

Guizot's paralleling of pity and justice, with its retrospective echoes of the Revolution—he constantly referred to the events of the early 1790s in *De la peine*—would be a capital theme for nineteenth-century thought.

In the early part of the century, the cultivation of pity—and the Revolution's cautions on it—was at the heart of romantic humanitarianism and the "religion of suffering humanity." This was the "time of the prophets," in Bénichou's phrase; the nineteenth century was shot through with doctrines of secular theology, of quasi-religious humanitarian utopias and of writers and thinkers as "new spiritual powers," a new sacerdocy.[80]

Lamartine, Michelet, and Hugo made of pity the determining criteria in history's march toward humane progress.[81] Michelet's pity was most typical and pertinacious: "If I acknowledge any miracle, if I think that man is an exception in nature, it's not because of his intelligence but because of pity."[82] For him, the Revolution and all history confirmed the necessary role of this presocial, essential pity: "May this impulse of pity sustain me for the two volumes that will conclude my *History*! 'The enormous pity that existed in the kingdom of France,' according to the Maid's words, that's the real historical inspiration."[83] Michelet was also instrumental in forging a specifically gendered pity, an attribute of femininity, which would be ripe with consequences for the *fin-de-siècle* and its female pedagogy: "The first appearance of women in the history of heroism (beyond the family sphere) took place, as one would expect, through an élan of pity."[84]

Like Michelet, Lamartine saw the conjunction of pity and the Revolution as disclosing a fundamental lesson about social morality: "Pity is not a vain word among humans....It is a generous justice of the human heart, more perceptive and infallible in the end than the inflexible justice of the mind....If the absence of all pity is a crime among despots, why would it be a virtue in a republic?"[85] This was a lesson to be drawn not only from the Revolution but from all of human history: "History, setting aside for a moment its partiality for popular causes, has no other motive, other glory, other duty than pity."[86]

Victor Hugo also exploited the lessons of the Revolution to insert pity as the philosophical kernel of a poetics of sentimental sociability. In novels and poems, he both advocated pity and delineated its perils and promises, as in "La Pitié Suprême,"[87] which is a poetic snapshot of what in the *fin-de-siècle*—when we next encounter similarly totalizing literary enterprises—was to become what I call a demotic pity: a plain-language, unequivocal connotation of pity as a misericordious feeling that calls forth humans' better angel.

In all its different domains, politics, ethics, and literature, the romantic-humanitarian evaluation of pity was uniformly positive. The literary critic Saint-Marc Girardin, for example, continued the Aristotelian-Rousseauian promotion of a piteous aesthetic: "It is this which constitutes the crowning glory of the Greek art; it excites pity without exhausting it; it mingles sorrow and resignation in the plaints of its victims, in order that they may inspire at the same time pity and respect, and that the two sentiments may temper each other in the bosom of the spectator."[88] We should also advert here to a summary of nineteenth-century linguistic practice and prescriptive codification, for this etymological history makes clear that pity was construed as a natural sentiment of sociability, a cognitive spur to benevolent action. The *Trésor de la langue française: Dictionnaire de la langue du XIXème et du XXème siècle (1789–1960)* crystallizes this definition of *pitié* from the nineteenth century: "A. Sentiment of affliction that one feels at the woes and sufferings of another, and which leads to seeing them relieved; disposition to feel this sentiment. Syn.: 'to feel sorry, commiseration, compassion, misericord.'"[89] In nineteenth-century usage, pity comprised compassion and was prior to it: "Locution and expression: 'Have pity on someone.' 'Be seized with compassion for someone.'...'Look upon someone with pity.' 'Feel the sentiments of compassion for someone.'—'To feel taken by pity for someone.' 'Feel compassion for somebody.'—(to be) 'without pity,' (to be) 'without human feeling.' 'Burn, massacre, hunt someone down without pity.'"[90]

In definitions and examples, the *Trésor* systematically linked pity to literary models and to early-Christian *pieta*, two associations that were to play an important part in *fin-de-siècle* sentimentalism: "2. a. Pity taken as a quality or virtue of the soul. 'Tragedy should excite terror and pity.' B. Religion. Synon. of misericord. 'Divine pity; God of pity; Lord, take pity; (May) God have pity on my, their soul'....'Pity and mercy'—'Christ of pity.' Christ represented iconographically with the five wounds of the Passion with a resigned attitude.' 'Virgin, Madonna, Notre-Dame of pity.' Synom. of *pieta*.'"[91] A further characteristic of pity that is revealed by etymological history is its inextricable connections to justice: "Total or partial grace accorded someone guilty of a crime or who was conquered."[92] The *Trésor* also takes note of condescending and pejorative connotations: "D. Scornful sorrow. 'Disdainful, haughty pity'; 'what a pity!' Balzac, *Peau de chagrin*, 1831, 287: 'The sentiment which man bears with the greatest difficulty is pity, especially if he merits it. Hate is a tonic, it makes one live, it inspires vengeance; whereas pity kills it, weakens even more our flaws.'"[93] We should note here in passing—as we shall take it up more fully in later chapters—that pity was neither semiasologically nor ethically pure: contestation over its meaning and virtues was a continuing part of the debate over sentimentalism. If pity was not a single idea or term, this manifold context was also not rotely digested. Nonetheless, the *Trésor* indicates the seeming ubiquity of pity in nineteenth-century writings: "Literary frequency: 6,518. Frequency in religious literature: 19th century: a. 10,749; b. 7,628."[94]

Most recent scholars of the subject—Bénichou, Denby, Dunn, and Reddy, for example—are correct in focusing on the earlier nineteenth century as a bridge across the potential *aporia* represented by the Revolution. Midcentury official philosophy and "realist" literature seemed to mark a pause in the recuperation of a pro-pity sentimentalism.[95] Victor Cousin's constricting rationalism and middle-of-the-road "eclecticism" were especially a gridlock for pity—his watchword for both ethics and epistemology was "désintéressement." Reddy can rightly claim that Cousin makes his case for the "erasure" of sentimentalism:

Then, in a section entitled "Other Defective Principles," he takes a few pages to refute the core doctrine of sentimentalism...It is certainly true, Cousin concedes, that we derive pleasure from accomplishing an admirable action, an act of benevolence or generosity. It is also true that, when we see others suffer, we may feel "pity" or "sympathy," a form of suffering of our own that urges to act to help them. But if we do good solely because it brings pleasure, or if we help others solely to avoid the pain of pity, then we are actually only pursuing our own interest, maximizing our own pleasure. However, Cousin has already argued at length that morally good action must be based on disinterested motives.[96]

But just as the Revolution served as both reflection and deflection of Enlightenment ideas on pity, the change around 1870—the Commune, Republicanism, the challenge of German models of philosophy and education, democratized education—provided a renewed context that prevented pity's erasure from the palimpset of traditionally received ideas.

The best and most appropriate site for detecting this post-1870 relevance of pity and for registering its renewed impact in philosophical and political discourse is the *Grande Encyclopédie*, a compendium of official, progressivist, tradition-honoring attempts in the *fin-de-siècle* to classify and disseminate positivist material in the spirit of the Enlightenment *philosophes*.[97] If we take apart at length and then dialogically reconstruct its extensive entry on "Pity," we will be in a better position to understand the discursive background to *fin-de-siècle* debates and arguments that occupy this book.

The author, Camille Mélinand, a philosopher and Republican pedagogue whom we shall encounter again in a few chapters, begins with a definition that relates pity to sympathy and links it to the philosophy of Schopenhauer: "Pity is one type of sympathy, it is sympathy for suffering, that is to say the fact of sharing it, of feeling the suffering of another. Pity expresses itself physically through tears; that's what was shown by Schopenhauer, who among philosophers was the one who spoke of pity with the greatest profundity."[98] Literature and theater confirm this dimension: "In a novel or a play, there are almost foolproof ways to provoke tears…since our pity is infallibly stimulated."[99]

Mélinand taxonomizes pity in accordance with sentimentalist philosophy and its categories of will, feeling, liberty, imagination, and experience, as well as its criterion of tears:

At first sight it appears that pity is an instinctive, impulsive sentiment…or a sort of vibration in common with others. But that's only a very superficial view. Doubtlessly, pity *begins* with such a mechanical repurcussion, but real pity, pity in the fullest sense of the term, is an entirely different thing. It comprises intellectual and intentional elements; it is not a state, but rather an *act*. In truth, pity only deserves that name if we do not remain within this first moment of automatic vibration: if, rather, I fix my attention on the suffering of another; if, by an effort, I tear myself from egotistical thoughts and individual sensations; if I bend my imagination so as to enter into the soul of another. Real pity is thus an *act of will*….Real pity involves an *effort* to surpass ourselves, to beat with the heart of another, to become one with our "fellow creature." Real *pity* is even an act of *liberty*: there is reason to believe that a being without freedom would be incapable of it.[100]

Mélinand's evocation of a "real" pity is an obsessive leitmotif that sought to inoculate the sentiment against falsely and weakly egotistical versions of it; in this enterprise, he had recourse to the psychological and emotive terminology of the pro-pity tradition that buttressed his philosophical claims:

Thus pity, even though it is instinctive at its start, requires an act of freedom, and relies even more on two factors: the strength of the imagination and the richness of experience…in a word, real and deep pity is a sort of foresight; it is the throbbing and intense vision of that which happens in a heart. Moreover, in order to be capable of pity, "experience" is necessary; in truth, in order to "enter into" the sentiments of another, there is no other means but to have experienced them oneself….As a result, one could say that a certain depth of pity requires a singular tenacity and vitality of the *memory*; because "experience" is nothing else but a treasure, more or less rich, of *memories*.[101]

This defense of a "real" pity calls for a critique of la Rochefoucauld—one font of the false version of it as weakly egotistical: "Even la Rochefoucauld's formula is quite superficial: for, I might have an interest in *faking* pity in expectation of my own sorrows, but *not to feel it in itself*. That which la Rochefoucauld may be able to explain are pity's external demonstrations, not pity itself."[102]

"Real pity" is thus truly other-directed and possesses ethical worth. Schopenhauer's presence is again capital for Mélinand's account:

Real pity is thus to rudimentary pity…what reason is to instinct….That's why pity has incomparable moral worth. First of all, pity's moral distinction is apparent….If then it is disinterestedness which is the essence of morality, there is every reason to believe that pity is the moral sentiment par excellence: because it is through pity that we free ourselves from egoism; it is through pity that we negate, if we can put it thus, egoism, since we suppress the barriers that separate individuals, since we "identify" with others. And this is why Schopenhauer sought in pity the very principle of the sole "criterium" of ethics.[103]

Mélinand takes a sidewise swipe at the Cousinian nonsentimental reading of "désintéressement."

Other debates central to *fin-de-siècle* pity, especially concerning justice and charity, are also touched upon in Mélinand's version of Schopenhauer in the *Encyclopédie*: "Not only is pity essentially good, but it is also fruitful in practice and the source of a multitude of virtues. One could even argue with Schopenhauer that justice and charity are born out of pity....Even the idea of the equality of all humans, which is one of the essential ideas in ethics, may be considered to have its origin as much in pity as in rationality."[104]

Pity is not only a valuable ethical fundament but also improves upon Kantian morality:

Finally, a "morality of pity" offers another advantage over traditional morality: it protects animals....It is a weakness of the "morality of duty" (that is, in sum, Kantian morality), to not really be able to prove this immorality—on the other hand, if we take as our starting point pity, there is nothing more self-evident: a human who is cruel to animals, thus betraying a real absence of pity, deserves condemnation and indignation. Moreover, we should note with Schopenhauer that pity, even if we take it to be the source of morality, does not bar abstract formulas, rules of conduct, fixed principles.[105]

Mélinand's conclusion is also Schopenhauerian: "So why then is pity good? According to Schopenhauer, it is because pity is the profound *truth*. Egoism is foremost an *error*....If we cannot follow Schopenhauer that far, it suffices to change the wording slightly: instead of saying: *identity* of all humans, we would say: solidarity, kinship, identity of nature and of fate. Thereby the doctrine becomes almost incontrovertible."[106]

Mélinand's entry in the *Encyclopédie* thus confirms the impulsion Schopenhauer provided to the French pro-pity tradition and also deploys all the terms that were to become a hallmark of pro-pity thinking in the *fin-de-siècle*: "almost incontrovertible."

The components of the pro-pity discursive community represented by Mélinand were varied: philosophical and literary signposts; the Enlightenment; the Revolution; changed social conditions during the nineteenth century that encouraged greater propinquity while provoking stridently adversarial political doctrines; and a romantic expressiveness that unshackled sentiments from the classical carapace that had molded the seventeenth century's tepid reaction to pity—all of these created a philosophical and literary culture wherein demotic pity thrived as a presumptive social virtue and communicative strategy. When writers debated pity or appealed to it in their prescriptive tracts or in their fictions, it was with the accretions given it by the *moralistes*, by Enlightenment *philosophes*, especially Rousseau, and by romantic humanitarianism that they made sense of the word as a vector of multiple meanings: ethical, social, and patrimonial, among them.

This is a study of a period in French thought and letters when this tradition and its exemplars had contemporaneous accents and stakes—and from which we can still learn today. For my claim is that the pro-pity intellectual community, from the nineteenth century until just after the *fin-de-siècle*, presented an important and instructive example of cognitive theory about sentiments and emotions, *avant la lettre*.[107] At the risk of presentism,[108] I wish to argue that the thinkers, ideas, and problems examined in this book offer both a genealogy of, and parallel to, contemporary debate and positions on sentiments, emotions, and their relationship to ethics. This "Prologue" thus reconstitutes the historiographical landmarks of a recent history that is also the historiography of contemporary intellectual history.

NOTES

1. Saint-Marc Girardin, *Lectures on Dramatic Literature, or, The Employment of the Passions in the Drama*, Robert Gibbes Barnwell, trans. (New York: Appleton & Co., 1849), 21.

2. William Reddy, "Sentimentalism and Its Erasure: The Role of Emotions in the Era of the French Revolution," *The Journal of Modern History* 72:1 (March 2000): 119.

3. *Le Robert, Dictionnaire historique de la langue française*, vol. 2 (Paris: Dictionnaires Le Robert, 1992), 1532. ["d'abord *piétet* (1050) et *pitet* (1080), est issu du latin *pietàs*, mot dérivé de *pius* (pie, pieux), de sens sacré et profane, et, qui, avec son sens propre de 'sentiment de dévotion envers les dieux, les parents, la patrie,' a donné *piété*. À l'époque impériale, *pietàs* a commencé à désigner la clémence, le sentiment de bonté miséricordieuse dont fait preuve l'empereur, puis, dans la langue des chrétiens, le sentiment de compassion, la bonté, la charité. Le mot est passé en français avec la valeur chrétienne de 'compassion,' mais il est héritier des valeurs à la fois profanes et réligieuses. Il est entré dans la locution *c'est pitié, c'est une pitié de* (1306), 'cela inspire un sentiment de pitié.' Il recrouvrait également en ancien français l'idée voisine de souci, le fait de la détresse, ou de la souffrance."]

4. Georges Gougenheim, *Les Mots français dans l'histoire et dans la vie*, vol. 1, 2nd ed. (Paris: A. & J. Picard, 1966), 119. ["sous l'Empire romain le mot *pietas*, élargissant son sens, sert à exprimer des sentiments de bienveillance et de compassion à l'égard des autres hommes. Ce mot a fourni au français deux mots: ...l'autre, *pitié*, résulte d'une évolution qui n'est peut-être pas entièrement populaire; mais qui du moins atteste un emprunt qui a pénétré de bonne heure dans la langue populaire....*Pitié* continue le sens élargie qu'avait pris le mot en latin. Ce sens avait dû pénétrer profondement dans l'âme du peuple. Le français est la seule des langues ramenés à offrir cette double évolution du mot latin."]

5. Frédéric Godefroy, *Dictionnaire de l'ancienne langue française et de tous ses dialectes, du IXème au XVème siècles* (1889. Repr. New York: Kraus Reprint Corp, 1961), 178–80. ["*pitace* (pitasse, pitache): 'doux, pieux, pitoyable;' *pitable*: 'augmentatif de pitié;' *pittance*: 'pitié;' *pite*: 'adj., qui a de la pitié, pitoyable;' *piteablement*: 'par pitié, pieusement;' *piteer, pitier, pitoyer*: 'v. in., avoir pitié, s'apitoyer, s'attendrir;' *piteor* (*piteour*): 'celui qui a pitié;' *pitos*: (-tous, teus, teux, teulz, toulz, toux, tieux, tells, dos, doux, piet): 'adj., compatissant, pieux, qui a pitié de;' *pitosement*: 'adv., pitoyablement, avec pitié.'"] See also Frédéric Godefroy, *Léxique de l'ancien français*, J. Bonnard and Am. Salmon, eds. (Paris: Librairie Honoré Champion, 1964), where the Latin "pitable-piu" leads to "pitié" (395).

6. See also Edmond Huguet, *Dictionnaire de la langue française du seizième siècle*, vol. 6 (Paris: Didier, 1965), who cites many more example of *pitoyable* than *pitié*.

7. Paul-Emile Littré, *Dictionnaire de la langue française*, vol. 5 (Chicago: Encyclopaedia Britannica, 1994), 4730–31 [originally published 1863–1869]: "[un] sentiment qui saisit à la vue des souffrances et qui porte à les soulager." Littré cites among many others Racine, Bishop Louis Bourdaloue, Corneille, La Fontaine, Maleherbe, Voltaire, Buffon, and Rousseau. Racine's verses are especially prominent among Littré's examples.

8. Raymond Baustert argues, in a discussion of Castiglione's *Courtier* and its impact in France, titled, "L'honnêteté en France et à l'étranger: étude comparative de quelques aspects" (*Horizons Européens de la littérature française au XVIIè siècle*, Wolfgang Leiner, ed. [Tubingen: 1988]): "C'est que malgré le renouveau stoïcien au seizième siècle, la tradition favorable à la passion était resté vivante en France" (259). ["Despite the Stoic revival of the sixteenth century, the pro-passion tradition in France had retained its vitality."]

9. See Charles Le Brun's *A Method to Learn to Design the Passions*, John Williams, trans., Alan T. McKenzie, intro. (Los Angeles: U of California P, 1980). Jennifer Montagu, in *The Expression of the Passions: The Origins and Influence of Charles Le Brun's "Conférence sur l'expression générale et particulière"* (New Haven, CT: Yale UP, 1994), linked Le Brun and Racine through the painter's representations of pity for an edition of the latter's plays of 1676.

10. ["'Si de tant de malheurs quelque pitié te touché.' 'Je n'ose, dit l'Auteur, condamner cette phrase, et j'oserais encore moins l'approuver' (Pourquoi? Ecoutez la raison) 'Il me semble,' dit-il, 'que *pitié* ne se dit que des personnes; au lieu que *compassion* se dit tant des personnes que des choses. "Ayez pitié de moi." "Ayez compassion de mes maux."' Ciel! Quelle délicatesse! Mais où M. d'Olivet prend-il cette distinction? Ce n'est pas assurément dans l'usage de la *langue parlée*, encore moins dans celle de la *langue écrite*"]. Abbé Pierre François Guyot, *Racine vengé, ou Examen des remarques grammaticales de M. l'abbé d'Olivet sur les oeuvres de Racine* (Avignon: 1739), 68.

11. ["Que dans tous vos discours la passion émue/ Aille chercher le coeur,/ l'échauffe et le remue./Si d'un beau mouvement l'agréable fureur/ Souvent ne nous remplit d'une douce *terreur,*/ Ou n'excite en notre âme une *pitié* charmante,/ En vain vous étalez une scène savante".] Boileau, *Art poétique*, "Chant III" (Paris: Gallimard, 1985), 240, lines 15–25. (*The Art of Poetry*, John Dryden, trans. [London: R. Bently and S. Magnes, 1673], 30–31.)

12. Sheila Page Bayne, *Tears and Weeping: An Aspect of Emotional Climate Reflected in Seventeenth-Century French Literature*. Etudes littéraires françaises: 16 (Tübingen: Gunter Narr Verlag, 1981), 72. For a similar point, see C. Badiou-Monferran, Anne Coudreuse, and Bruno Delignon, "La promotion esthétique du pathétique dans la seconde moitié du XVIIè siècle: Passions, emotions, pathos," *La Licorne* 43 (1997): 75–94.

13. Bayne, 72–73.

14. Bayne, 74. Bayne's point here is supported by one of the subjects of her study, Jean-François Senault, who in *The Natural History of the Passions*, wrote: "If we judge [others] unworthy of the good that is happend to them; that raiseth Envy in us; if we think them not to deserve the Evil that is befallen them, then we are affected with *Pity or Commiseration*" (*Natural History of the Passions* [London: Printed by T. N. for James Magnes, 1674], 128–29). In *The Use of the Passions*, Senault's similar argument against Stoicism was even more adulatory of pity: "For Self-love hath put us so much out of order, that Divine Providence hath been fain to make us miserable by Pity, so to interest us in the miseries of others; did she not touch us, we should not seek out a remedy for them" (*The Use of the Passions*, Henry, earl of Monmouth , trans. [London: John Sims, 1671], 508).

15. ["Pitié et 'compassion qu'on a de la misère d'aucun,' *Miseratio, Commiseratio*; 'Pitié qu'on a d'un povre, et la miséricorde qu'on luy fait en luy aidant de ses biens,' *Eleemosyna*; 'Qui a pitié d'aucun,' *Misericors, Clemens*; 'J'ay pitié et compassion de la fragilité humaine,' *Fragilitatis humanae miseratio subit*; 'Si Dieu n'a pitié de nous,' *Nisi Deus nos respexerit*; 'Perdre toute pitié et affection qu'un homme doit porter à l'autre,' *Exuere humanitatem*."] Jean Nicot, *Thrésor de la langue française* (Paris: A. et Je. Picard, 1606), 483.

16. ["Compassion. Sentiment de douleur pour les maux, pour les misères d'autruy."'] *Dictionnaire de l'Académie française* (Paris: 1694), 2:243.

17. ["Pitié:" 'compassion; sympathie; attendrissement; bonté; charité; humanité; clémence; indulgence; mansuétude; miséricorde; grâce; merci; crève-coeur; pauvre;

malheureux; pietà; Jérémiade; lamentation; plainte; déplorer; pleurer.'"] *Thesaurus Larousse: des mots aux idées, des idées aux mots*, Daniel Pechoin, ed. (Paris: Larousse, 1991), 609 ("Pitié").

18. ["condescendance; dédain; mépris; affliction; détresse; misère."] Henri Bertaud du Chazaud's *Le Robert, Dictionnaire des synonymes* (Paris: Dictionnaires Le Robert, 1983), confirms the *Thesaurus Larousse's* usage, providing the following entry for "Pitié:" "I. favorable ou neutre: apitoiement, attendrissement, bonté, charité, coeur, commisération, compassion, compréhension, humanité, indulgence, mansuétude, miséricorde, sensibilité, sympathie; II. Par extension: grâce, merci; III. non-favorable: dédain, mépris" (355). ["I. Favorable or neutral: caringly, tenderness, goodness, charity, heart, commiseration, compassion, understanding, humanity, indulgence, goodness of heart, mercy, sensitivity, sympathy; II. By extension: grace, mercy; III. Unfavorable: disdain, scorn."]

19. *The Maxims of La Rochefoucauld*, Louis Kronenberger, trans. (New York: Vintage Books, 1959), 83, #264.

20. ["il y a souvent plus d'orgueil que de bonté à plaindre les malheurs de nos ennemis; c'est pour leur faire sentir que nous sommes au-dessus d'eux que nous leur donnons des marques de compassion."] François VI de la Rochefoucauld, *Maximes, suivies des réflexions diverses, du Portrait de la Rochefoucauld par lui-même* (Paris: Editions Garnier Frères, 1967), 105, #463.

21. ["Cependant il n'est rien que je ne fisse pour le soulagement d'une personne affligée, et je crois effectivement que l'on doit tout faire, jusques à lui témoigner même beaucoup de compassion de son mal, car les misérables sont si sots que cela leur fait le plus grand bien du monde; mais je tiens aussi qu'il faut se contenter d'en témoigner, et se garder soigneusement d'en avoir."] Rochefoucauld, *Maximes*, 356–67. We have occasion later to consider further la Rochefoucauld's views on pity in a discussion of Nietzsche, whose better master he was in the matter.

22. ["la pitié est moins tendre que l'amour."] Vauvenargues, *Réflexions et maximes* (Paris: Gallimard, 1971), 210, #827.

23. ["c'est une marque de férocité et de bassesse d'insulter un homme dans l'ignominie, s'il est, d'ailleurs, misérable; il n'y a point d'infamie dont la misère ne fasse un objet de pitié pour les âmes tendres."] Vauvenargues, 129, #387.

24. ["La générosité n'est que la pitié des âmes nobles;" and "la pitié n'est qu'un secret repli sur nous-mêmes, à la vue des maux d'autrui dont nous pouvons être également les victimes."] Chamfort, *Maximes et anecdotes* (Monaco: Incidences, 1944), 122, #318.

25. ["on doit avoir pitié des uns et des autres; mais on doit avoir pour les uns une pitié qui naît de tendresse et pour les autres une pitié qui naît de mépris."] In *Encyclopédie philosophique universelle: II. Les notions philosophiques, dictionnaire*, vol. 2: *Philosophie occidentale, M-Z*, Sylvain Auroux, ed. (Paris: Presses universitaires françaises, 1990), 1961.

26. Descartes, *Passions of the Soul*, in *The Philosophical Works of Descartes*, vol. 1, Elizabeth S. Haldane and G.R.T. Ross, eds. and trans. (Cambridge: Cambridge UP, 1973), 360 ("Article 62, Mockery, Envy, Pity"). Anthony Levi, in his discussion of Descartes' *Traité des passions*, touches upon the seventeenth-century pro-pity context that informs Descartes' work: "[after 1650]... the moralists give increasing attention to the social order....Classical literature turns to the fundamental questions with an earnestness unknown to the Baroque. Racine, Pascal, Mme. de La Fayette are keenly disturbed by the tragic dilemmas of the human condition which had left Montaigne serene and unperturbed." In *French Moralists: The Theory of the Passions, 1585–1649* (Oxford: Clarendon Press, 1964), 336.

27. Descartes, *Passions of the Soul*, 394.

28. Descartes, 415: "Article 186: Those Who Are the Most Given to Pity."

29. Descartes, 416: "Article 187: How the Most Noble-Minded Are Touched by This

Passion."

30. Descartes, 416: "Article 188: Who Are Those Who Are Not Touched by It."

31. ["*Pitié*. s.f. Compassion, sentiment de douleur qu'excitent dans nous les maux, les misères d'autrui. 'Avoir pitié de' (sans article) 'être touché de pitié.' 'La tragédie doit exciter la terreur et la pitié.' Coeur *sans pitié*, etc. 'Prendre pitié' régit de: 'Prends pitié de l'état où tu me vois réduit' (Crebillon)."] Féraud, *Dictionnaire critique de la langue française*, vol. 3 (Marseille: J. Mossy Père et fils, 1787), 169.

32. Anne Vincent-Buffault writes of "collective emotion" linking experience and society, especially concerning pity: "Dans les deux cas la pitié est le ressort essentiel de l'émotion collective." ["In both cases, pity is the indispensable spring of collective emotion."] *Histoire des larmes, XVIIIème–XIXème siècles* (Paris: Rivages, 1986), 39. Like Bayne, Buffault argues that pity and weeping are effective means of identification with the Other. Buffault locates the peak of this sensibility in the eighteenth century, the "age of pity": "Cette participation par les pleurs aux souffrances d'autrui qui se transforment en larmes délicieuses quand on y porte remède, cet attendrissement plus général sur le malheur de l'humanité signalent un nouveau rapport à l'autre régi par l'identification sensible. L'optimisme philanthropique n'est pas encore réglé par la pudeur: il produit des signes démonstratifs. Modèle de sociabilité naturelle, c'est un âge de la pitié où la visibilité de l'émotion reste centrale." ["This involvement in the suffering of others through tears, which are transformed into delicious tears when solutions are at hand, this more general sensitivity to the suffering of humanity signals a new relationship to the Other, governed by responsive identification. Philosophical optimism is still not regulated by a sense of shame: it causes demonstrative signs. A model of innate sociability, this is an age of pity where the visibility of emotion retains a central place."] (43–44)

33. ["Oui, la pitié est le contre-poison de tous les fléaux de ce monde; voilà pourquoi Jean Racine prit pour devise, dans l'édition de ses tragédies, 'crainte et pitié.'"] Cited by Littré, *Dictionnaire de la langue française*, 4730. See also R. S. Ridgeway, *Voltaire and Sensibility* (Montreal: McGill's-Queen's UP 1973).

34. See John Spink, "Diderot et la réhabilitation de la pitié," in *Colloque international Diderot (1713–84)*, Anne-Marie Chouillet, ed. (Paris: Aux amateurs de livres, 1985), 51–60. Spink argues, in effect, that "la Nouvelle Philosophie et, surtout, la Philosophie des Lumières, ont réhabilité la passion de la pitié, jusqu'alors méprisée et même condamnée." ["The new philosophy and, especially, the Enlightenment, rehabilitated the passion of pity, theretofore disdained and even reproved."] (51)

35. ["*Pitié* (Morale), c'est un sentiment naturel de l'âme, qu'on éprouve à la vue des personnes qui souffrent ou qui sont dans la misère. Il n'est pas vrai que la pitié doive son origine à la réflexion....Aussi devons-nous beaucoup moins les actions nobles et miséricordieuses à la philosophie qu'à la bonté du coeur. Rien ne fait tant d'honneur à l'Humanité que ce généreux sentiment; c'est de tous les mouvements de l'âme le plus doux et le plus délicieux dans ses effets. Tout ce que l'éloquence a de plus tendre et de plus touchant, doit être employé pour l'émouvoir."] *Encyclopédie, ou Dictionnaire raisonnée des sciences, des arts et des métiers*, Diderot and d'Alembert, eds. (Paris: Briasson [etc.], 1757): vol. 12, 662–63.

36. ["'La main du printemps couvre la terre de fleurs, dit le bramine inspiré.' Telle est à l'égard des fils de l'infortune la pitié sensible et bienfaisante. Elle essuie leurs larmes, elle adoucit leurs peines....Ce pauvre traîn sa misère de lieu en lieu; il n'a ni vêtement, ni demeure, mets-le à l'abri sous les ailes de la pitié; il transit de froid, réchauffe-le; il est accablé de langueur, ranime ses forces, prolonge ses jours, afin que ton âme vive."] Diderot, 663.

37. Bénichou, *The Consecration of the Writer, 1750–1830* (*Le sacre de l'écrivain*), Mark J. Jensen, trans. (Lincoln: U of Nebraska P, 1999), 16–17, 277.

38. ["Il y avait dans ce pays deux hommes bien singuliers: ils avaient de l'humanité; ils connaissaient la justice; ils aimaient la vertu. Autant liés par la droiture de leur cœur que par la corruption de celui des autres, ils voyaient la désolation générale et ne la ressentaient que par la pitié; c'était le motif d'une union nouvelle."] Montesquieu, *Lettres Persanes* (Paris: Bookking International, 1994), 43–44.

39. baron d'Holbach, *Morale universelle, ou les devoirs de l'homme fondés sur sa nature* (Amsterdam: Marc-Michel Rey, 1776), 154. In Chapter viii, titled "De la compassion ou de la pitié" ["Du soulagement donné à celui qui souffre, il en résulte un soulagement réel pour la personne qui lui donne du secours; plaisir très-doux, que la réflexion augmente encore par l'idée d'avoir fait du bien à quelqu'un, d'avoir acquis des droits sur son affection, d'avoir mérité sa reconnaissance, d'avoir agi d'une façon qui prouve que l'on possède un Coeur tendre et sensible; disposition que tous les hommes désirent trouver dans leurs semblables, et dont l'absence ferait croire que l'on est mal conformé."]

40. d'Holbach, 156. ["Mais la pitié, comme tout le prouve, est très rare sur la terre; le monde est rempli d'une foule d'êtres insensibles, dont les coeurs ne sont que peu ou point rémués par les infortunes de leurs semblables."]

41. d'Holbach, 158–59. ["L'éducation devrait sans cesse exercer la sensibilité des princes, de grands et de ceux qui sont destinés à jouir de l'opulence....C'est ainsi que le sentiment de la pitié pourrait être développé dans les coeurs que la nature a doués de sensibilité."]

42. Jean-Jacques Rousseau, *The "Discourses" and Other Early Political Writings*, Victor Gourevitch, ed. and trans., Cambridge Texts in the History of Political Thought (Cambridge: Cambridge UP, 1997), 152.

43. Rousseau, 152. But in the *Lettre à d'Alembert sur les spectacles*, Rousseau polemicized against this Aristotelian attitude: "I hear it said that tragedy leads to pity through fear. So it does; but what is this pity? A fleeting and vain emotion that lasts no longer than the illusion which produced it; a vestige of natural sentiment soon stilled by the passions; a sterile pity which feeds us a few tears and which has never produced the slightest act of humanity. Thus the sanguinary Sulla cried at the account of evils he had not himself committed" (*Politics and the Arts: Letter to M. d'Alembert On the Theatre*, Allan Bloom, trans. and ed. [Glencoe, IL: Free Press, 1960], 24). Rousseau here does not inveigh against the sentiment of pity but against the simulation of it by the decadent arts more marked by their luxury than by the sincerity of their passions. His polemic is significant for our discussion in Part III, as he writes elsewhere in this *Letter*: "In giving our tears to these fictions we have satisfied all the rights of humanity without having to give anything more of ourselves; whereas unfortunate people in person would require attention from us" (25).

44. Rousseau, *The Second Discourse*, 153. For good accounts of Anglo-Scottish promotion of sympathy as an ethical principle, see John Mullan, *Sentiment and Sociability: The Language of Feeling in the Eighteenth Century* (Oxford: Clarendon Press, 1988), which focuses especially on sentimentalism in the works of David Hume, Samuel Richardson, and Laurence Sterne; and G.R. Morrow, "The Significance of the Doctrine of Sympathy in Hume and Adam Smith," *The Philosophical Review* 32 (1923): 60–78.

45. Rousseau, *The Second Discourse*, 154.

46. Rousseau revised this bedrock principle somewhat in his *Essay on the Origin of Languages*: "The social affections develop in us only with our knowledge. Pity, although natural to man's heart, would remain eternally inactive without imagination to set it in motion. How do we let ourselves be moved to pity? By transporting ourselves outside ourselves; by identifying with the suffering being. We suffer only to the extent that we judge it to suffer; we suffer not in ourselves but in it. Think how much acquired knowledge this transport presupposes!" In *The "Discourses" and Other Early Political Writings*, 267–68. The differences between a pre-social and social pity, the first based on instinct and the latter

premised on imagination, are probably only an apparent contradiction—Rousseau was getting at the same problem from both sides of the nature-culture divide. But this contrast is relevant to later debate on pity and to evaluations of Rousseau's contributions to theories on pity. See, for example, Derrida's views in our Conclusion.

47. ["Après avoir établi que l'homme dans l'état de nature étoit cruel, il nous reste à faire voir comment la civilization, en développant son imagination et ses autres facultés, produit la pitié."] J.-N. Etienne de Bock, *Recherches philosophiques sur l'origine de la pitié et divers autres sujets de morale* (London: 1787), 68.

48. ["C'est le sentiment de l'innocence qui est le premier mobile de la pitié; voilà pourquoi nous sommes plus touchés des malheurs d'un enfant que de ceux d'un vieillard. Ce n'est pas, comme l'ont dit quelques philosophes, parce que l'enfant a moins de ressources et d'espérances, car il en a plus que le vieillard, qui est souvent infirme et qui s'avance vers la mort, tandis que l'enfant entre dans la vie: mais l'enfant n'a jamais offensé; il est innocent....Lorsqu'un vieillard est vertueux, le sentiment moral de ses malheurs redouble en nous; ce qui prouve évidemment que la pitié de l'homme n'est pas une affection animale. Ainsi, la vue d'un Bélisaire est très attendrissante. Si on y réunit celle d'un enfant qui tend sa petite main afin de recevoir quelques secours pour cet illustre aveugle, l'impression de la pitié est encore plus forte."] Bernardin de Saint-Pierre, *Etudes de la nature* (Paris: Firmin Didot Frères, 1853), 397. Jacques-Henri Bernardin de Saint-Pierre (1737–1814) was Professeur de Morale at the École Normale Supérieur and a member of the Académie after 1803. The mention of Belisarius in his comments may indicate that Bernardin de Saint-Pierre had in mind Jean-François Marmontel's five-act tragedy of 1769, *Bélisaire*, which was also the basis for Jacques-Louis David's painting for the Salon of 1781, "Bélisaire demandant l'aumône," which today hangs at the Musée des beaux-arts, Lille.

49. William Reddy, "Sentimentalism and Its Erasure," 127.

50. Reddy, *The Navigation of Feeling: A Framework for the History of Emotion* (Cambridge: Cambridge UP, 2001), 146. Janet Todd also furnishes a definition of "sentimentalism" relevant to our concerns: "It is possible, however, to extricate 'sentimentalism.' Once employed only pejoratively to suggest affectation and excessive emotional display, it was used by Sir Leslie Stephen in *English Thought in the Eighteenth Century* as 'the name of the mood in which we make a luxury of grief.' More recently the word has come to denote the movement discerned in philosophy, politics, and art, based on the belief in or hope of the natural goodness of humanity and manifested in a humanitarian concern for the unfortunate and helpless" (*Sensibility: An Introduction*, 6).

51. Reddy, "Sentimentalism and Its Erasure," 111, 120.

52. Reddy, 122.

53. The phrase is Reddy's invention : "Central to the life of individuals, open to deep social influence, emotions are of the highest political significance. Any enduring political regime must establish as an essential element a normative order for emotions, an 'emotional regime.'" (*The Navigation of Feeling*, 124). A similar and equally useful concept is Barbara H. Rosenwein's notion of "emotional communities:" "People lived—and live—in what I propose to call 'emotional communities.' But the researcher looking at them seeks above all to uncover systems of feeling: what these communities (and the individuals within them) define and assess as valuable or harmful to them; the evaluations that they make about others' emotions; the nature of the affective bonds between people that they recognize; and the modes of emotional expression that they expect, encourage, tolerate, and deplore" ("Worrying about Emotions in History," 842).

54. Reddy, "Sentimentalism and Its Erasure," 111.

55. Reddy, *The Navigation of Feeling*, 147; see also 304–10. Martha Nussbaum has similarly written: "In thinking about who Nietzsche's opponents are, we need to be aware that *pitié* is not common as a central ethical term in nineteenth-century texts: in Comte,

Renan, etc., one tends to find, instead, phrases such as *sentiments fraternels* and *fraternité*. Rousseau's usage, with its strong links to the Greco-Roman tradition, seems not to have survived the Revolution" (*Upheavals of Thought*, 303).

56. David Denby, *Sentimental Narrative and the Social Order in France, 1760–1820* (Cambridge: Cambridge UP, 1994), 129, 132.

57. Denby, 130.

58. Denby, 80. Denby glosses Diderot's lines as follows: "If the formulation is not revolutionary in the social or political action which it implies, it clearly articulates the notion that the text, read and wept over, is to be the site of a community of like minds drawn together by their common reaction to a common scene. Lessing's formulation of the notion of the democratisation of subject-matter similarly links it to the possibility of identification. Pity and fear are not felt for the person to whom they occur; they arise from 'our similarity to the suffering person,' and are 'for ourselves.'" (80)

59. Denby, 151.

60. Denby, 152–53.

61. Denby, 156. Denby further explains: "The discursive constitution of deserving victims, and of the speaker as their most fierce defender, becomes a statement of Revolutionary legitimacy, just as the correct and incorrect use of pity become an indicator of political position. These conflicts confirm, in my view, the interlocking of sentimentalism and the Revolution: they intensify and in some cases transform a symbolic and discursive association which was culturally available because of the place of sentimental narrative in the Revolution's beginnings" (161). Susan Dunn analyzes the ways in which this same discursive battle was updated by Hugo and Lamartine (see later).

62. Reddy, *The Navigation of Feeling*, 195.

63. Denby, *Sentimental Narrative and the Social Order in France*, 52.

64. Denby, 197–98.

65. Denby, 224.

66. Reddy, *The Navigation of Feeling*, 205.

67. M. Michaud, *Le printemps d'un proscrit, suivi de plusieurs lettres à M. Delille sur la pitié* (Paris: Chez Giguet et Michaud, 1804). The abbé Delille translated Virgil (the *Georgics*, in 1769, and the *Aeneid*, in 1804) as well as Milton (*Paradise Lost*, 1805). He also wrote rhetorical verse based on fashionable ideas and was given the chair in poetry at the Collège de France by the Consulate. The subject of Virgil and pity would still be relevant to the debate on pity a century later, when another clerical figure, the abbé Moulard, engaged it.

68. ["Quel sentiment est plus propre à maintenir l'équilibre dans l'état social, que celui qui nous aide à réparer les injustices du sort, et qui, dans les sociétés où les malheureux sont abandonnés, rend les citoyens plus généreux que la cité, et l'amour meilleur que les lois?"] Michaud, 173. On Michaud, see Alfred Michiels, *Histoire des idées littéraires en France au XIXè siècle* (Paris: 1863. Génève: Slatkin Reprints, 1969-1970), 502–5.

69. ["le mot *pietàs* exprimait à la fois l'intérêt qu'on porte au malheur, le respect pour les dieux, l'amour pour les parents, le dévouement à la patrie....Ainsi la pitié prêtoit ses larmes au génie; elle présidait à la naissance des arts, et veillait à la conservation des moeurs."] Michaud, 173, 176.

70. ["Elle [the Revolution] entretenait ainsi le feu sacré de la Pitié au milieu des horreurs de la tyrannie, et c'est à elle peut-être que nous devons dans les derniers temps, d'avoir conservé quelque chose de la nature humaine."]Michaud, 197.

71. ["Rien n'est plus propre au contraire à nous rassurer sur la cessation des troubles, que de voir qu'on prend enfin quelque intérêt aux images de la pitié...les anciens étaient pénétrés de cette idée, aussi réprésentaient-ils la déese de la pitié avec une guirlande d'olivier."] Michaud, 239–40. Denby concluded his work with an analysis of Delille and Michaud: "There is much work to be done on this realignment. Just one direction is suggested by the

use of the notion of *pity* by Delille and Michaud: developing and making explicit the conservative potential of Rousseau's model of Clarens, these writers offer the reassuring and nostalgic picture of an organic society in which pity neutralises and renders acceptable a rigid hierarchy….At the same time, as in the later Vernès but I think with different ideological implications, the figure of the chain of being and the conceptual framework of theodicy reemerge, with pity representing part of that mysterious alchemy which produces Good out of Evil, happiness out of perceived suffering, Order out of the perceived inequality of social existence" (*Sentimental Narrative and the Social Order in France*, 246).

72. ["'Pitié:' Sentiment de douleur qu'excitent dans notre âme les maux, les misères d'autrui. Syn.: Compassion, commisération, la longueur de ce dernier semble l'exclure de la langue poétique, sensibilité. *Epit.*—Charitable, bienfaisante, secourable, sensible, douce, tendre, tutélaire, douleureuse, paisible, oisive, noble, généreuse, active, tranquille, fausse, feinte, indigne, criminelle, fatale, cruelle, suppliante, excitée, superbe, orgueilleuse, offensante, insultante. *Périph.*—soins, compatissants."] L.J.M. Carpentier, *Le gradus français ou dictionnaire de la langue poétique* (Paris: 1822), 922.

73. Carpentier, 922. ["'Mais la *pitié* que l'aimable nature/ Mit de sa main dans le fond de nos coeurs,/ Pour adoucir les humaines fureurs,/ Se fit sentir à cette âme si dure.' (Voltaire, *La Pucelle*, ch. 19".] (*La Pucelle, or the Maid of Orleans: A Poem in 21 Cantos from the French of M. de Voltaire* (London: 1796).

74. Carpentier, 922. ["'Que, malgré la pitié dont je me sens saisir, / Dans le sang d'un enfant je me baigne à loisir!/ Non, seigneur' (Racine, *Andromaque*, Act. 1, sc. 2)."]

75. ["la douleur reveille en nous, tantôt ce qu'il y a de plus noble dans notre nature, le courage, tantôt ce qu'il y a de plus tendre, la sympathie et la pitié. Elle nous apprend à lutter pour nous, à sentir pour les autres."] Benjamin Constant, *De la Religion considérée dans sa source* (Paris: Bossange père, 1824–1831): vol. 4. On Benjamin Constant and the connection between romantic sentimentalism and politics, in addition to the work of Kocay, see K. Steven Vincent, "Benjamin Constant, the French Revolution, and the Origins of French Romantic Liberalism," *French Historical Studies* 23:4 (Fall 2000): 607–37, especially 625–35.

76. ["selon Constant…la morale n'est pas toujours un désir de protection ni un sacrifice du bonheur personnel. Il est également un sentiment à l'égard de l'autre, un sentiment de sympathie, de pitié même, ou de justice".] Victor Kocay, *L'Expression du sentiment dans l'oeuvre de Benjamin Constant*. Studies in French Literature 48 (Lewiston, NY: Edwin Mellen Press, 2001), 32.

77. See Pierre Rosanvallon, *Le Moment Guizot* (Paris: Gallimard, 1985).

78. ["Il est vrai que si la peine paraît excessive, si elle révolte plus de sentiments moraux qu'elle ne s'en concilie, si elle change en pitié pour le coupable l'horreur du crime qu'elle voulait inspirer, elle perd son effet et va contre son dessein….Cependant, et au sein même des moeurs les plus douces, la pitié ne possède jamais si exclusivement le coeur de l'homme, qu'en voyant un grand châtiment mérité par un grand crime, il oublie soudain le crime pour ne songer qu'aux souffrances du châtiment. La pitié a aussi sa justice, et quand cette justice n'est point offensée, la gravité de la peine exerce son pouvoir sur la conscience comme sur la peur."] Guizot, *De la peine de mort*, 2nd ed. (Bruxelles: Hauman, 1838), 30.

79. ["Voilà l'effet des poursuites politiques qui marchent vers la peine de mort…toutes les paroles de l'accusé politique qu'on pousse à l'échaffaud deviennent le sujet des entretiens les plus animés, des plus entraînants commentaires, que les moindre détails de son sort excitent les sentiments les plus vifs, les plus obstinés, même chez des hommes qui n'auraient point fait ce qu'on lui impute, qui prendraient à lui un assez médiocre intérêt, si la terrible destinée qui pèse sur lui ne mettait en jeu toutes les puissances morales, n'aillait remuer au fond des coeurs tous les éléments de la pitié et de la sympathie."] Guizot, 134–35.

80. Paul Bénichou, *Le Temps des prophètes: Doctrines de l'âge romantique* (Paris:

Gallimard, 1977). A perfect demonstration of Bénichou's thesis is Henry Bérenger's *La conscience nationale* (Paris: Armand Colin, 1898), in which the author lays out a genealogy of the contemporary possibility of merging religion and a scientific psychology in a "religion of the inner life": "La religion de la vie intérieure deviendra-t-elle la religion de la France? Mettra-t-elle fin aux vieux fanatismes comme aux nouvelles intolérances? Nous pouvons d'autant mieux l'espérer que depuis cent ans la religion de la vie intérieure a été préparée et professée par quelques-unes des plus grandes âmes françaises. Jean-Jacques Rousseau, Lamartine, Lamennais, Michelet, Quinet, ont été les magnifiques annonciateurs de cette religion nouvelle. Plus près de nous, Ernest Renan, Jean-Marie Guyau, Edouard Schuré, Auguste Sabatier, lui ont donné une nouvelle force et une plus grande profondeur" ["Will the religion of inner life become the religion of France? Will it put paid to both old fanaticisms and new intolerance? We can hope all the more so in that for one hundred years the religion of interiority has been primed and preached by some of the greatest French souls. Jean-Jacques Rousseau, Lamartine, Lamennais, Michelet, Quinet, have been the splendid heralds of this new religion. Closer to our own day, Ernest Renan, Jean-Marie Guyau, Edouard Schuré, and Auguste Sabatier, have given it a new power and a greater depth."] (144–45)

81. On pity and the romantic humanitarian imagination, see Susan Dunn, "Michelet and Lamartine: Regicide, Passion, and Compassion," *History and Theory* 28:3 (November 1989): 275–95, and *The Deaths of Louis XVI: Regicide and the French Political Imagination* (Princeton: Princeton UP, 1996). Dunn argues in both these works that pity was a virtue embraced by both writers as well as an operative concept in their work: "But not only was pity central to Michelet's and Lamartine's visions of 19th-century history and concepts of revolutionary and political morality, it also extended to their attitudes towards historiography. They envisaged pity, to which revolutionaries, kings, and politicians were so ambivalent, as the basis for historiography and as the fundamental moral mission for the historian" ("Michelet and Lamartine," 276).

82. ["Si je me reconnais un miracle, si je sens que l'homme est une exception dans la nature, ce n'est pas à l'intelligence, c'est à la pitié."] Dunn, "Michelet and Lamartine," 278. Dunn glosses on this dictum: "His compassion for the sufferings of others, heightened by his feelings of sorrow and loss at the time of his first wife's death in 1839, convinced him that mourning and tears were the source of his ability to fathom and resurrect the past, that his craft and power as an historian derived, not from his intellect, but from this wealth of emotion and empathy....Pity was the emotional medium of a spiritual merging with the past" (285). In his account of the end of Jacobinism in the *History of France*, Michelet titled two sections: "La sortie des prisons—l'explosion de la pitié," and "Aveugle réaction de la pitié" (In *Oeuvres completes*, vol. 21 [1872–1874], Paul Viallaneix, ed. [Paris: Flammarion, 1982]).

83. ["Puisse ce mouvement de pitié me soutenir dans les deux volumes qui vont achever mon *Histoire*! 'La grande pitié qu'il y (avait) au royaume de France,' selon le mot de la Pucelle, c'est la véritable inspiration historique."] Dunn, "Michelet and Lamartine," 285. Michelet's position on pity and the Revolution is opposed to that of Hannah Arendt in *On Revolution*: "And yet, he reached the conclusion that the Revolution failed because of the absence of pity and grace, not justice" (Dunn, 284).

84. ["La première apparition des femmes dans la carrière de l'héroisme (hors de la sphère de la famille) eut lieu, on devait s'y attendre, par un élan de pitié."] Michelet, *Les Femmes de la révolution* (Paris: A. Delahays, 1854), 13. In this chapter on the "Héroisme de Pitié," Michelet vaunts the actions of Mme. Legros, who fought against arbitrary detention at the Bastille in 1783.

85. ["la pitié n'est pas un vain mot parmi les hommes....Elle est une justice généreuse du coeur humain, plus clairvoyante au fond et plus infaillible que la justice inflexible de l'esprit...Si l'absence de toute pitié est un crime dans le despotisme, pourquoi donc serait-ce une vertu dans les républiques?"] Dunn, *The Deaths of Louis XVI*, 190. Dunn also comments

in "Michelet and Lamartine:" "Like Michelet, Hugo, and other believers in Romantic humanitarianism, Lamartine regarded pity as the highest form of human justice, the foundation of politics and morality" (290–91). And: "In the wake of Jacobin pitilessness and the regicide, Michelet and Lamartine pursued compassion and amnesty as essential elements in their humanitarian ideology and as guideposts in the writing of history. The intuition that pity and compassion were the supreme form of justice, central to politics, nationhood, as well as to historiography, was born from encounters between historians and the executed king" (295).

86. ["L'histoire, oubliant un moment sa partialité pour les causes des peuples, n'a plus d'autre cause, d'autre gloire et d'autre devoir que la pitié."] Dunn, "Michelet and Lamartine," 292.

87. ["Car les pleurs sont sacrés; ils sortent, pur dictame,/ les pleurs humains du coeur, les pleurs divins, de l'âme;/ Dis que, s'éxaminant soi-même, on se résout/ A chercher le côté pardonnable de tout,/ Dis qu'on a rejeté l'amertume chagrine,/ Le réel se dévoile, on sent dans sa poitrine/ Un coeur nouveau qui s'ouvre et qui s'épanouit./ Un ange vit un jour les hommes dans la nuit;/ Il leur cria du haut de la sereine sphère:/ -Attendez; je vous vais chercher de la lumière. /Il revint apportant dans sa main la pitié./ L'homme, humble ou grand, large esprit, âme,/ Tatant le sort ainsi qu'on suit dans l'ombre un mur,/ A peur de la pitié comme d'un puits obscur,/ Et préfère la haine, et s'attache à la corde/ Du mal pour ne pas choir dans la miséricorde."] Victor Hugo, "La Pitié Suprème," in *Oeuvres Complètes*, vol. 10, Jean Massin, ed. (Paris: Club français du livre, 1967), 1250–54, stanzas 737–47.

88. Saint-Marc Girardin, *Lectures on Dramatic Literature*, 23.

89. ["A. Sentiment d'affliction que l'on éprouve pour les maux et les souffrances d'autrui, et qui porte à les (voir) soulager; disposition à éprouver ce sentiment. Syn.: 'apitoiement, commisération, compassion, miséricorde.'"] *Trésor de la langue française: Dictionnaire de la langue du XIXème et du XXème siècles (1789–1960)*, vol. 13 (Paris: Editions du Centre national de recherche scientifique [Gallimard], 1988), 437 ("Pitié").

90. ["Loc. et expr.- 'Prendre qqn. en pitié.' 'Etre pris de compassion pour quelqu'un'...– 'Regarder qqn en pitié.' Éprouver pour quelqu'un des sentiments de compassion...– 'Se sentir pris de pitié pour quelqu'un.' 'Éprouver de la compassion pour quelqu'un'...– '(Être) sans pitié.' (Être) sans sensibilité humaine. 'Immoler, massacrer, poursuivre qqn. sans pitié.'"] *Trésor de la langue française*, 437.

91. ["2. a. La pitié considérée en tant que qualité, vertu de l'âme. 'La tragédie doit exciter la terreur et la pitié.' b. Religion. Synon. de miséricorde. 'Pitié divine; Dieu de pitié; Seigneur, prends pitié; (Que) Dieu ait pitié de mon, son âme'...'Pitié et merci'...'Christ de pitié'. 'Christ représenté iconographiquement avec les cinq plaies de la Passion dans une attitude d'acceptation'- 'Vièrge, Madone, Notre-Dame de pitié.' Synom. de *piétà*."] *Trésor de la langue française*, 437.

92. ["C. Grâce totale ou partielle accordée à une personne coupable d'une faute ou qui a été vaincue."] *Trésor de la langue française*, 437.

93. ["D. Mépris apitoyé. Pitié dédaigneuse, hautaine; 'quelle pitié!' Balzac, *Peau chagrin*, 1831, 287: 'Le sentiment que l'homme supporte le plus difficilement est la pitié, surtout quand il la mérite. La haine est tonique, elle fait vivre, elle inspire la vengeance; mais la pitié tue, elle affaiblit encore notre faiblesse.'"] *Trésor de la langue française*, 437.

94. ["Freq. abs. littér.: 6,518. Freq. rel. littérature: XIXème siècle: a. 10,749; b. 7,628."] *Trésor de la langue française*, 437.

95. Although Naomi Schorr, in *George Sand and Idealism* (New York: Columbia UP, 1993), persuasively argues that the seeming "realism" of Sand's fiction has been both misunderstood and at the source of her devaluation from canonical status.

96. Reddy, *The Navigation of Feeling*, 221–22.

97. "La *Grande Encyclopédie* paraît de 1885 à 1902, sous l'impulsion et la direction

d'André Berthélot, en trente et un volumes in-4. C'est un inventaire alphabétique, conçu dans un esprit fortement historique, des lettres, sciences et arts, en même temps qu'une mise au point de leur évolution dans le temps jusqu'à leurs manifestations de l'heure." ["The *Grande Encyclopédie* appeared between 1885 and 1902, under the impetus and direction of André Berthélot, in 31 volumes in quarto format. It was an alphabetical inventory, conceived in a strongly historical spirit, of letters, sciences and arts, and at the same time an update on their progress in time up to their present-day manifestations."] Pierre Nora, ed., *Les Lieux de mémoire*. I: *La République* (Paris: Gallimard, 1984). André Berthélot was the son of the famous chemist. Born in 1862, he entered Parisian politics as a Radical in 1894 and was elected to the Chamber in 1898 as a Dreyfusard deputy. He became secretary-general of the *Encyclopédie* in 1885. See C.-E. Curinier, ed., *Dictionnaire national des contemporains*, vol. 2 (Paris: B. Brunel, s.d.), 277.

98. ["La pitié est une forme de la sympathie, c'est la sympathie pour la souffrance, c'est-à-dire le fait de partager, de ressentir la souffrance d'autrui. La pitié s'exprime physiquement par les larmes; c'est ce qu'a montré Schopenhauer, un des philosophes qui ont parlé de la pitié avec le plus de profondeur."] *La Grande Encyclopédie: Inventaire raisonné des sciences, des lettres, et des arts*, vol. 26, André Berthélot, ed. (Paris: Société Anonyme de la Grande Encyclopédie: 1885–1902), 992.

99. ["Dans un roman ou dans un drame, il y a des moyens presque infaillibles de provoquer les pleurs…car notre pitié est infailliblement excitée."] *La Grande Encyclopédie*, 992.

100. ["Il semble, au premier abord, que la pitié soit un sentiment irrefléchi, instinctif…ou une sorte de vibration à l'unisson des autres. Or ce n'est là qu'une vue très superficielle; la pitié *commence* sans doute par cette espèce de contrecoup mécanique, mais la pitié vraie, la pitié au sens plein du mot, est tout autre chose. Il y entre des éléments intellectuels et volontaires; ce n'est pas un état, c'est réellement un *acte*. En effet, la pitié ne mérite ce nom que si je n'en reste pas à ce premier moment d'ébranlement automatique: si je fixe mon attention sur la souffrance d'autrui; si, par un effort, je m'arrache à mes pensées égoïstes, à mes sensations individuelles; si je tends mon imagination pour passer dans l'âme d'un autre. La pitié réelle est donc un acte de *volonté*….La pitié réelle est un *effort* pour sortir de nous-mêmes, pour palpiter avec le cœur d'un autre, pour ne faire qu'un avec nos 'semblables.' La *pitié* réelle est même un acte de *liberté*: il y a lieu de croire qu'un être sans liberté en serait incapable."] *La Grande Encyclopédie*, 992–93.

101. ["Ainsi la pitié, quoique instinctive en son principe, exige un acte de liberté, elle dépend encore de deux conditions: la force de l'imagination et la richesse de l'expérience…la pitié réelle et profonde en un mot est une sorte de divination; elle est la vision intense et palpitante de ce qui se passe dans un cœur. D'autre part, pour être capable de pitié, il faut de 'l'expérience;' en effet, 'pour entrer' dans les sentiments d'autrui, il n'y a guère d'autre moyen que de les avoir soi-même éprouvés….On pourrait dire par conséquent qu'une certaine profondeur de pitié exige une ténacité et une vivacité singulières de la *mémoire*; car 'l'expérience' n'est rien autre chose qu'un trésor plus ou moins riche de *souvenirs*."] *La Grande Encyclopédie*, 993.

102. ["La formule même de la Rochefoucauld reste bien superficielle: car, en prévision de mes propres chagrins je puis avoir intérêt à *feindre* la pitié, mais *non pas à l'éprouver*. Ce que la Rochefoucauld expliquerait peut-être, ce sont les actes extérieurs de la pitié, ce n'est pas la pitié elle-même."] *La Grande Encyclopédie*, 993.

103. ["La vraie pitié est donc à la pitié rudimentaire…ce que la raison est à l'instinct….C'est pourquoi la pitié a une valeur morale incomparable. Tout d'abord, l'excellence morale de la pitié est évidente….Si donc c'est le désintéressement qui est l'essence de la moralité, il y a bien des chances pour que la pitié soit le sentiment moral par excellence: car c'est par la pitié que nous nous affranchissons de l'égoïsme; c'est par la pitié

que nous nions même, pourrait-on dire, l'égoisme, puisque nous supprimons les barrières qui séparent les individus, puisque nous nous 'identifions' avec un autre. Et c'est pourquoi Schopenhauer a cherché dans la pitié le principe même de le 'critérium' unique de la moralité."] *La Grande Encyclopédie*, 993.

104. ["Non seulement la pitié est essentiellement bonne, mais elle est féconde dans la pratique, elle est la source d'une foule de vertus. On pourrait même soutenir avec Schopenhauer que la justice et la charité naissent de la pitié....L'idée même de l'égalité de toutes les personnes humaines, qui est une des idées essentielles de la morale, peut avoir son principe dans la pitié tout aussi bien que dans la raison."] *La Grande Encyclopédie*, 993–94.

105. ["Enfin, une 'morale de la pitié' présente, sur la morale traditionelle, un autre avantage: elle protège les animaux....C'est donc une faiblesse, pour la 'morale du devoir' (c'est-à-dire en somme la morale de Kant), de ne pas pouvoir vraiment démontrer cette immoralité—au contraire, si nous prenons comme principe la pitié, rien de plus évident: l'homme cruel envers un animal, trahissant par là même une réelle absence de pitié, mérite le blâme et l'indignation. Il faut remarquer d'ailleurs, avec Schopenhauer, que la pitié, même si on la reconnât comme source de la moralité, n'exclut pas les formules abstraites, les règles de conduite, les principes fixes."] *La Grande Encyclopédie*, 994.

106. ["Pourquoi maintenant la pitié est elle bonne? D'après [Schopenhauer] c'est parce qu'elle est la *vérité* profonde. L'égoisme est avant tout un *erreur*....Si l'on ne veut pas suivre Schopenhauer jusque-là, il suffira de modifier un peu les termes: au lieu de dire: *identité* de tous les hommes, on dira: solidarité, parenté, communauté de nature, de destinée. Dès lors la doctrine deviendra presque indiscutable."] *La Grande Encyclopédie*, 994.

107. "In the cognitive view, emotions are part of a process of perception and appraisal, not forces striving for release. Denying that emotions are irrational, cognitive psychologists see them as resulting from judgements about 'weal or woe'—that is, about whether something is likely to be good or harmful, pleasurable or painful, as perceived by each individual". Barbara H. Rosenwein, "Worrying about the Emotions in History," 836. See especially Nussbaum, *Upheavals of Thought*.

108. I share LaCapra's view: "It should be noted, however, that the critique of presentism need not lead to a defence of a study of the past in and for itself. It should be related to a combination of objective reconstruction and dialogical exchange that provides the genealogy of present discourses and practices, thereby placing one in a more informed position to critically appraise and, if warranted, attempt to change them" (*History and Reading*, 194 n. 27).

Part I: Pity at the Center of a Renascent Sentimentalism

But it seems that never have those great ideas, pity, charity, pardon, penetrated hearts so profoundly since the time of Christ as they do today.

Émile Boutroux[1]

The terms gradually die when the functions and experiences in the actual life of society cease to be bound up with them. At times, too, they only sleep, or sleep in certain respects, and acquire a new existential value from a new social situation. They are recalled then because something in the present state of society finds expression in the crystallization of the past embodied in the words.

Norbert Elias[2]

A serious difficulty encountered when trying to define a word that conveys a state or wave of feeling is the individual character of all emotion...our individual sentiments are not isolated, they model themselves on those of the group in which we live, for at bottom individuals live through and by others.

Pierre Dumonceaux[3]

We explore in this section the ubiquity of pity and sentiment that Boutroux perceived in the rhetoric around him and try to understand its place within the philosophical milieu of his colleagues. *Fin-de-siècle* France was a ground propitious to pity, in part because this was the founding period of the Republican political and educational system; philosophy, ethics, and the human sciences then took a marked turn toward the applied and prescriptive, a turn that focused pity in its sights. Developments in the Third Republic, especially secularism, socialism, and the rise of new disciplines, posed challenges to traditional social and moral thought and philosophical beliefs. Pity was invoked as one way to embody an imagined community when the contours of the social and intellectual order were ominously tenuous; its *loci classicus* gave pity immediate access to the communal *imaginaire* of thinkers, reformers, and pedagogues. This presence amounted to an ironic development: midcentury ethics had disavowed sentimentalism, yet when it returned, it was hailed for its orthodoxy and its *francité*. Its innovatory status had the look of something déjà-vu.

The philosophical engagement with pity thus heralded a return of the repressed: the overarching philosophy of sentimentalism comprising pity, which we encountered in the "Prologue," had been relegated to a rhetorical romantic humanitarianism with a purchase on popular discursive fields, while philosophy and the social sciences mostly allied themselves with stringent rationalism and/or eclecticism. Pity as a key word for philosophical theories on human nature and sociability returned with a vengeance, showing how historical changes in thinking on sentiments and emotion-categories are never irrevocably forward-thrusting, but rather circumstantial and historicist—as many of these *fin-de-siècle* French figures themselves understood.

Pity is not one idea covering one object, nor was it susceptible of being canalized into one disciplinary approach, especially when philosophical and scientific disciplines in *fin-de-siècle* France were in a contestatorial mode. But this is precisely what made pity a capital trope for the *fin-de-siècle* in efforts to engage encompassing issues of human nature within a complexifying society. Moral philosophers, psychologists, and *littérateurs* with a concern for ethics laid a proprietary claim to issues relevant to pity, because the notion was both familiar and fungible. The problem of the relationship between the individual and society was the key question for thinkers of the late nineteenth century.[4] This problem usually generated practical philosophic and psychological propositions of a socially propaedeutic nature. Pity received renewed consideration because of its relevance to, and possibility for renewal within, this thought. It was seized upon as a talisman that the general philosophic and literary fields deployed both for protection against, and in order to coopt, the intrusions of newer and more empirical disciplines— experimental psychology, neocritical philosophy, and, especially, sociology. Metaphysics and philosophically oriented psychology were in a crisis mode, and moral obligation was its crisis-theme *par excellence*.

The contours and causes of this "crisis" are generally well analyzed. John I. Brooks's *The Eclectic Legacy: Academic Philosophy and the Human Sciences in Nineteenth Century France* and Jean-Louis Fabiani's *Les philosophes de la république* showed how the Cousinian legacy of hybrid Cartesian and Kantian rationalism, on the one hand, and a pick-and-choose scientism, on the other, commanded a respectful paternity for decades,[5] often stymieing—when not indirectly influencing—both more adventurous approaches to philosophy's traditional concerns and fresh departures in psychology and sociology.[6] The tenor of Academic philosophy in the midnineteenth century had been anti-materialistic, anti-positivist, synthetic, Cousinian, exigently rationalist (with an admixture of Cartesian religious faith), and disinclined to grant ethical status to nonrational faculties. Plato, Aristotle, Descartes, and, to a lesser extent, Kant were the quartet with which most philosophical problems, especially moral and metaphysical, were played; the perennial preoccupations with free will, causality, teleology, deism, dualism, and epistemology were the fixed points of their conceptual universe, and despite the inroads of romanticism and the pro-pity tradition or of associationist and evolutionary psychology, they helped to denigrate the status of sentiments. In 1881 the list of philosophic works taught as "Classics" ("Livres Classiques") in secondary education were: Descartes, *Discours sur la méthode et premier méditation*; Leibniz, *La Monadologie*; Cicero, *de Legibus* (first book); Seneca, *De vita beata*; Plato, *la République*; and Aristotle, *Morale à Nicomaque*. Academic philosophy was, in short, conservative.

Others have noted the imperviousness of French philosophy to foreign developments, so that critical challenges and newer orientations were never attended to; still others have noted that this crisis was, above all, rhetorical—that it concerned philosophy's own standing in society and its role in imposing moral requirements.[7] William Logue, in *From Philosophy to Sociology: The Evolution of French Liberalism, 1870-1914*, argues that the goal of "Eclecticism" was to protect philosophy from charges of having caused the Revolution—and hence, by implication, that with a new dispensation after 1870, philosophy lacked both a mission and guidelines. Jean-Louis Fabiani, as well as Christophe Charle, in *Paris, fin de siècle: culture et politique*, and Terry N. Clark, in *Prophets and Patrons: The French University and the Emergence of the Social Sciences*, have argued that philosophy was mainly fixated on pedagogy in these years, as Republicans created another quasi-official, *juste-milieu* system of thought geared to perpetuating democratic civism, in the way that Cousin had created "Eclecticism" as a school of middle-road ideas between religion and materialism, constitutionalism and monarchy. Contemporaries were themselves cognizant of crisis, manipulating a diagnosis on behalf of their preferred remedies. Many of the works that we shall come upon in this Part make use of the term "crisis"—usually in a rhetorical manner.

These means of helping us make sense of nineteenth-century French philosophy, both contemporary and reconstructive, are good ones. I merely wish to add to the intellectual history of the nineteenth century, especially the *fin-de-siècle*, by stressing the innovations surrounding sentimentalism, on the one hand, and by focusing on the omnipresent discourse concerning the split between reason and sentiment, on the other—subjects that have been minimized. If there is an increasing historiographical consensus on the significance of Cousinian philosophy in the midcentury and the role of figures such as Théodule Ribot, Pierre Janet, and Émile Durkheim in challenging it as they tried to fashion new "human sciences" by the *fin-de-siècle* (here the work of Brooks is especially useful), there is less scrutiny of, much less any accord on, the renewed interest in late-eighteenth-century theories on human nature. What I wish to argue is that a large group of philosophers, from the most pedantic pedagogues of the Republic's educational system and professional academies to Henri Bergson and other philosophic innovators of the early twentieth century, took a look at their academic, patrimonial legacy and plunged into the tenebrous waters of sentiment and pity in order to ascertain whether the latter could serve as moral foundation and social glue. Many concluded that they could; most that they could not; all the same, the return of sentimentalism made it an inevitable touchstone of social thought. Sentimentalist rhetoric was not merely raked up again in its earlier form—a novel convergence of defensive metaphysics and burgeoning psychologism united around new studies of the will (which had been essential to eclectic philosophy),[8] collective psychology,[9] the sentiments, and their association with cognition; and linked these to an abiding preoccupation with ethics. Dominick LaCapra was right on the mark in remarking, "Moral philosophy increasingly became the religion of mass democracy and its conception of the essence of all religion."[10]

This inquiry does go against the grain of intellectual history by focusing on the lesser lights of that history, not because they "fit" my argument but because in the years between the respective dominance of Cousin and Bergson, much of the work done in French ethics and philosophy was carried out within the camaraderie of institutions such as the *Académie des sciences morales et politiques* (ASMP), lycées and universities, reviews and bureaucracies, by figures known today mostly as "teachers of"— Émile Boutroux as teacher of both Durkheim and Bergson, Alphonse Darlu as Proust's teacher, and so on. By virtue of their institutional affiliation and pedagogic reach, these men (all members of the ASMP were indeed of the same gender) had an incomparable authority and impact in their own day, as well as representativity. André Canivez wrote: "Let us try now to understand the renewal of academic philosophy after 1870…never had they exercised a more profound influence on youth than in the period under study. Until the end of the century, the prestige of a Professor, and especially of the Philosophy Professor, did not cease to grow, not only in the provinces, but also in Paris, where the finest minds always ended up gathering."[11] Like Canivez and Brooks, who believe that thinkers such as Jules Lachelier, Charles Renouvier, and Jules Lagneau helped revamp a philosophy made stale by the ghostly hold of Cousin, I believe that many of these lesser figures have been unjustly ignored or depreciated.

My argument amends the historiography of *fin-de-siècle* philosophy by giving much more place in it to the reason-sentiment divide in ethics, a rift that has traditionally been relegated to its more obvious home in the late eighteenth century, especially in Great Britain. For it is possible to make a strong reading of this presumed dichotomy as an unjustly neglected trope of *fin-de-siècle* French philosophy. Rather than considering this reinvestment in deeply-rooted issues as a paltry symptom of blockage or a rhetorical reheating of old chestnuts, the renewed attention can also be seen as a preliminary to new departures. Just as the dominant position of Enlightenment sentimentalism was united to the late eighteenth-century discourse on moral obligation, so, too, was the return of sentimentalism fundamental for the pondering of ethical duty in the *fin-de-siècle*. If to philosophize is mostly to recapitulate the history of philosophy (as Alasdair MacIntyre and Charles Taylor would have us believe[12]), and if the history of philosophy is consonant with its own historiography, then a major philosophical realization of *fin-de-siècle* French philosophy was its rendezvous with the Hume-Kant perplex of the late eighteenth century.

Pity is not the philosophers' stone upon which every strand of *fin-de-siècle* thought can be bolted together. Pity was not *the* problematic for *fin-de-siècle* philosophy, but it was an important red thread running through that problematic— the shared problems of knowledge and ethics, of living together and knowing together. The questions that were asked about pity—and that indeed have come to be asked about it now—had special resonance and legibility within that problematic: is pity natural or a social artifice? Is it more closely linked to a pessimistic or optimistic view of humanity? Is it physical or mental? Can it serve as the basis for political association? What type of study is more appropriate to it? Is it a distinctively French notion? Most meaningfully, perhaps, is pity educable?

Our first task is to inspect the context of sentimentalism and especially that in which pity was judged as a moral sentiment. In the late nineteenth century, a few observers coined this reappearance of sentimentalism "affective philosophy."[13] After first documenting the multitude of ways in which various thinkers deployed "pity" as they ventured around the contemporary philosophical environment updating sentimentalist philosophy, we then examine a related context: discussions about the intersubjectivity of consciousness and the prospects of individuals knowing of, and feeling about, each other in a changing society. The emphasis on sentiment and pity can be seen here as reinforcing notions of subjectivity that were in trouble.[14] It can also be seen, *pace* Sarah Maza, as validating a counterintuitive aspect of Habermas's notion of the "public sphere:" "A central feature of this 'public sphere' was then, paradoxically, a preoccupation with matters common to the scattered 'subjectivities' of its inhabitants and which we would call 'private.'"[15]

We next consider the theme of civilizing progress and its relation to the pedagogical possibilities of pity, especially as formulated by Françisque Bouillier, Gabriel Tarde and, to a lesser degree, Ludovic Carrau, Gustave LeBon, and Pierre-Félix Thomas. This chapter makes the case that a self-conscious appeal to traditional pity validated reformers' self-assumed prescriptive role (often with conservative political implications) in a changing society and was instrumental in giving legitimacy to the nascent field of collective (mass) psychology. In the subsequent chapter, we look at how Théodule Ribot and other pioneering philosopher-psychologists took their cues from Schopenhauer and tried to shift disciplinary balances toward the empirical in creating a properly observable psychological philosophy of pity, especially as this coincided with the emerging prominence of will as subject matter.

NOTES

1. *Morale sociale: leçons professées au Collège libre des sciences sociales*, Émile Boutroux, préf. (Paris: Félix Alcan, 1899), 33. ["Cependant, il semble que ces grandes idées de pitié, de charité, de pardon, n'avaient jamais pénétré aussi profondément les coeurs depuis les jours du Christ, qu'aujourd'hui."]

2. Norbert Elias, *The Civilizing Process: The History of Manners and State Formation and Civilization*, Edmund Jephcot, trans. (Oxford: Blackwell, 1994), 6-7.

3. ["Une sérieuse difficulté quand on enterprend de définir un mot qui exprime un état ou un mouvement de la sensibilité est le caractère individuel de toute sensibilité...notre sensibilité personnelle n'est pas isolée, elle se modèle sur celle du groupe où nous vivons, car l'individu existe au fond par les autres et pour les autres."] Pierre Dumonceaux, *Langue et sensibilité au XVIIème siècle: l'évolution du vocabulaire affectif* (Génève: Librairie Droz: Publications Romanes et Françaises, 131: 1975), 9.

4. See William Logue, *From Philosophy to Sociology: The Evolution of French Liberalism, 1870-1914* (De Kalb: Northern Illinois UP, 1983), 56.

5. For the opinion that Victor Cousin and his brand of eclecticism were responsible for an increasingly stale status quo, see Fabiani, *Les philosophes de la République* (Paris: Editions de Minuit, 1988), 82; W.M. Smith, "The 'Two Cultures' in Nineteenth Century France: Victor Cousin and Auguste Comte," *Journal of the History of Ideas* (1965), 45-58. For a contemporary analysis by someone immersed in these currents, see Boutroux, "La Philosophie en France depuis 1867," *Revue de métaphysique et morale* (1908); republished in *Nouvelles études d'histoire de la philosophie* (Paris: F. Alcan, 1927), 139-93.

6. Fabiani cogently analyzes the links between the "crisis" mode in ethics and the anti-sociology defensiveness of professional philosophers: "Mais c'est surtout une prise de position en faveur d'une restauration métaphysique qui diminue la part des sciences sociales....L'augmentation de la part relative de la morale s'explique par l'apparition de nouvelles questions de morale civique et de morale sociale...les recherches sociologiques ne sont jamais intégrées en tant que telles: elles sont toujours traitées comme des questions morales" (*Les philosophes de la République*, 37, 52). ["But it's especially the position in favor of a restoration of metaphysics that dimishes the role of the social sciences....The relative increase in the role of ethics can be explained by the appearance of new questions of civic and social morality...sociological investigations are never treated as such: they are always treated as ethical issues."] This reading conflicts with William Logue's thesis in *From Philosophy to Sociology*, to wit, that the emergence of a "new liberalism" "was nothing less than the replacement of a liberalism based on a metaphysical philosophy by a liberalism based on sociology" (2).

7. Ernest Renan's *La réforme intellectuelle et morale de la France* (Paris: Lévy Frères, 1871) is the classic, ideological account of the shock to philosophical and pedagogical comforts provoked by loss in the Franco-Prussian War. See also Claude Digeon's excellent narrative, *La crise allemande de la pensée française, 1870-1914* (Paris: Presses universitaires de France, 1959). See also the arguments of André Canivez, *Jules Lagneau: Essai sur la condition du professeur de philosophie jusqu'à la fin du XIXème siècle* (Strasbourg: Association des publications de la Faculté des lettres de Strasbourg, 1965).

8. See Brooks, *The Eclectic Legacy: Academic Philosophy and the Human Sciences in Nineteenth Century France* (Newark: U of Delaware P, 1998), 47.

9. See the by-now classic accounts: Susanna Barrows, *Distorting Mirrors: Visions of the Crowd in Late Nineteenth-Century France* (New Haven, CT: Yale UP, 1981); Robert A. Nye, *The Origins of Crowd Psychology: Gustave LeBon and the Crisis of Mass Democracy in the Third Republic* (Beverly Hills, CA: Sage, 1975).

10. LaCapra, *Emile Durkheim: Sociologist and Philosopher* (Ithaca, NY: Cornell UP, 1972), 50.

11. ["Essayons maintenant de comprendre le regain de la philosophie universitaire après 1870....jamais ils n'exercèrent une influence plus profonde sur la jeunesse qu'à la période que nous étudions. Jusqu'à la fin du siècle, le prestige du professeur, et notamment du professeur de philosophie, ne fera que croître non seulement en province, mais à Paris où finissent par se rassembler les meilleurs esprits du pays."] André Canivez, *Jules Lagneau*, 113.

12. See MacIntyre's essay, "The Relationship of Philosophy to its Past," which criticizes philosophy's presentist bias by utilizing the valorization of affective experience as one example, and Taylor's "Philosophy and its History," both in *Philosophy in History: Essays on the Historiography of Philosophy*, J. B. Schneewind and Quentin Skinner, eds. (Cambridge: Cambridge UP, 1984), 31-48. Taylor pleads forthrightly for the historicity of philosophy: "Philosophy and its history are one" (17).

13. Such was the term used by a few writers of the time, as we shall now see. More recent equivalents are imperfectly useful—equally technical and neologistic. See, for example, Jean Maisonneuve, *Les Sentiments (Que Sais-je?)*, 10th ed. (Paris: Presses universitaires de France, 1973), who coined the terms *psychosociologie affective* and *affinité psychosociologique* ("psychosociological affectivity" and "psychosociological affinity").

14. See Rei Tarada's argument about more recent works in *Feeling in Theory: Emotion after the "Death of the Subject"* (Cambridge, MA: Harvard UP, 2001): "The texts discussed below suggest that historically, the idea of emotion has been activated to reinforce notions of subjectivity that could use help" (14).

15. Sarah Maza, *Private Lives and Public Affairs*, 13. Maza's point concerns the late eighteenth century.

Chapter 1: "Affective Philosophy": Pity as Cognitive Sentiment

Sentiment has never been vanquished in its external conflict with reason.

Gustave LeBon[1]

The citation that opens this part was articulated by Émile Boutroux (1845–1921) as part of a series of lectures on ethics offered to the educated general public on the eve of the twentieth century. The full paragraph—"But it seems that never have those great ideas, pity, charity, pardon, penetrated hearts so profoundly since the time of Christ as they do today. They have marked our sensibility with an almost painful quivering. We hear them in the words of the legislator; they appear even on the stage"—reveals a culture of sentimental rhetoric receptive to pity that typified the "emotional community" in which philosophers toiled, against which they often combated, and to which they contributed in any case.

Boutroux, who held the Chair in the History of Philosophy at the Sorbonne from 1888 until 1907 and, as president of the jury of the *agrégation* in philosophy, was an influential educator, could not escape the fascination with ethical obligation.[2] A leading figure of "metaphysical positivism,"[3] underrated in his time and largely forgotten today—except as Durkheim's colleague and mentor[4]— Boutroux was the author of works that reveal the intermingling of ethics and epistemology characteristic of this milieu. In his preface to the lectures published as a collected volume, Boutroux gave a dramatic adumbration of his colleagues' challenge in defining and defending a contemporary ethic: "Morality of course has broad principles. But today these do not suffice. We need to know what exactly are our duties to civilization and for the precise conditions in which we find ourselves."[5] Boutroux's remarks on the ambient sensibility are like a leitmotif of *fin-de-siècle* philosophy: crisis and obligation, ethics, social complexity, and the problematic of pity were embraced in bewildering proximity.

At first sight this rhetoric may look like self-important imprecations emanating from the *esprit de corps* of undervalued intellectuals offering their services as social prophets. Indeed, from the times when Cousinian eclecticism held sway in the midcentury to the early years of the Third Republic, the "broad principles of morality" comprised an agreed-upon triad of approaches: the ethics of self-interest and pleasure (usually folded into the rubric of "Utilitarianism"); that of sympathy (associated with Adam Smith); and duty (an admixture of Judeo-Christian tradition, deontology, and Kantianism).[6] The latter was the doctrinal preference. There appeared to be a ready-made template for teachings on ethics, one that had sufficed for generations of students. But now, or so Boutroux claimed, "duties to civilization and for the precise conditions in which we find ourselves" made of these three options something less than conclusive choices. Rhetoric and reality—philosophical disquisitions and social transformations—called upon other contenders for moral leadership.

Ethical obligation was the Rosetta stone of *fin-de-siècle* French philosophy. The question of moral foundations was *the* social and moral question of moment for philosophers and reformers, one that both privileged moral philosophers' status and reopened a panoply of problems. My argument is that the "crisis" of moral foundations was also the backdrop for the return of sentimentalism and that contemporary problems that raised questions about the nature of moral action reintroduced a more formal philosophical engagement with pity. In attempting to solve the "crisis" of moral obligation, late-century French moralists (in this they revealed direct filiations to their seventeenth- and eighteenth-century precursors) gave a searching look at nonrational sources of ethics and returned to the question of the moral status of sentiments. Pity was a key word and analytical commonplace in this enterprise. The thinkers we study elaborated theories of pity as a social virtue, even when they tried to minimize the consequences.

We concentrate on the professional philosophers associated with the *Académie des sciences morales et politiques* (ASMP), who were representative of Third Republic philosophy and were concerned with its practical dimensions. The youngest affiliate of the *Institut*, chartered in 1793, the Académie—abbreviated here henceforth as the ASMP—was in its first years composed of political thinkers and "politilogues," such as the Prince Charles-Maurice de Talleyrand, Pierre-Claude-François Daunou, Jean-Jacques Régis de Cambacerès, the abbé Sieyès, Joseph Lakanal, and the abbé Grégoire. Suppressed by Napoleon in 1803 as a "nest of intellectual oppositionists," it was reorganized by Guizot in 1832.[7] Presided by Tocqueville in 1852 and by Bergson during World War I, its institutional life and internal politics were of a very elite variety. It was one of the few true sites of cross-disciplinarity in public intellectual life, mixing members from fields as diverse as Egyptology, linguistics, archaeology, history, philosophy, and political science—as evidenced in the contents of its publication, the *Journal des savants*. But it was also a conservative bunch, in the sense that its membership was self-selecting, hence chary of young turks, and mostly consecrating late-career reputations, and also in the sense that in order to preserve its field of autonomy, it could never get too politically far ahead of whatever regime was in power. Many of its sessions, as made public in the published *Séances*, were consecrated to ethical questions.[8] Most of its members betrayed a preoccupation with pity only in the context of their pursuit of what they took to be the philosophic Holy Grail: the foundations of moral obligation.

I want to emphasize two characteristics revealed by this pursuit. The first was the struggle to fit an orthodox Kantianism ("neocriticism") into the dominant ethical discourse. Kantian ethics became the "quasi-official morality of the Third Republic,"[9] and both the philosophers who wished to validate this orthodoxy and those wanting to challenge it adverted to moral phenomenon, like sentiments, not previously within their ken. This view of sentiment was different from the Smithian idea of sympathy—as opposed to Smith's emphasis, this sentimentalism was more concerned with the "weal and woe" of Others. Second, the novel fusion between critical rationalism and sentiments fashioned a sort of cognitive theory of sentiments *avant la lettre*, one whose terms were often left unanalyzed by its proponents and that is strikingly similar to positions held today. For them, sentiments were distinct from emotions—the former were cognitive and volitional; the latter, visceral and reactive. This distinction was not without a difference—the former, exemplified by pity, were allowed into the inner sanctum of moral virtues. The thinkers discussed here typify variants of both characteristics.

Alfred Fouillée (1838–1912) was a member, as of 1893, of the ASMP who taught at the École Normale Supérieur and who was a pragmatic, pro-Republican democrat, prolific in his writings and interests and similar to Boutroux in influence and consequent neglect.[10] He wrote, in *La réforme de l'enseignement philosophique et moral en France*: "philosophy is the civic religion of democracies and we must confess that we could not grant much confidence to any future reform without philosophy. If priest and King go together, one has also always united these two titles: philosopher and citizen."[11] He addressed the "moral crisis" while evoking Schopenhauer and pity in a review of the varied thinking on moral obligation: "'It is easy to preach morals,' said Schopenhauer, 'hard to establish its foundations.' The current crisis of morals proves this. Everything is open to question; nothing appears firmly established anymore, or at least self-evident—not universal evolution, not the 'altruism' of positivists, not the pessimists' pity and their new nirvana, not the Kantians' duty, nor the transcendent good-in-itself of the spiritualists."[12] Fouillée's is a model synopsis, with its historical self-consciousness of "crisis," anxiety about moral certainty, and despair over ethical pluralism, at the same time taking care to summarize competing theories, and its acknowledgment of pity as a moral principle—while placing it on the side of pessimism. Through Fouillée we see the larger discursive context within which pity resurfaced and through which Schopenhauer made his entry.

Fouillée had to confront directly the ontological and moral status of sentiment, a task to which he turned in his theory of *idées-forces*—an epistemological concept wherein ideas have volitional potential. In his *L'Évolutionnisme des idées-forces* of 1890, Fouillée summarized his problematic with this question: "do we quash the intellectual and moral dimensions of sentiments, desires, loves of all sort, in order to reduce them entirely to nervous sensations, visceral, muscular, passively received from the exterior by an impotent conscience?"[13] Fouillée's answer to his rhetorical question was, not surprisingly, a negation—sentiments are cognitive and volitional.

Fouillée elaborated this answer in a follow-up work of 1893, *La psychologie des idées-forces*. He defined sentiment as cognitively anterior to emotion.[14] As such, sentiments have myriad psychological and social consequences: "Every manifestation of the sentiments has, by definition, a psychological facet and, moreover, a social one: in reality, there is only actual *expression* if there is a feasible *interpretation* of the gestures of other beings who form, together with him, a society...For us, it is really this psychological law of solidarity or sympathy that governs and explains all the details of expression."[15] The monistic series leading from sentiment to emotion, idea, and volition takes on apperceptive reality only in an intersubjective realm. *Idées-forces* are sympathetic by definition: sentiment is both innate and socially constitutive. Fouillée performs a twofold division of sentiment into self-directing and other-directed, dolorous and joyous—as others, such as Françisque Bouillier and Gabriel Tarde, would also do. For him, *sympathie* is the quintessential other-directed sentiment: "And thus it is with sympathy: nature does not know of the isolation of the egoistic ideal; she connects, she combines, unites. Like heat and light, she cannot give life and sensibility to a certain spot without having it shine on others; far from sealing 'morals,' she opens them up to others...a sad idea has in its train innumerable painful *feelings*."[16]

Here is the ground favorable to pity—not that sympathy serves as its synonym in Fouillée's use (we must always keep in mind that *pitié* was an almost univalent expression of "pity"), but rather that the doleful recognition of the Other generates the moral cognition and engagement that are the hallmarks of the pro-pity tradition and of its basis in cognitive theory.

The possibility of a moral sentimentalism became an obsessive focus of philosophers associated with the ASMP. The revenant fault lines of moral philosophy in late-nineteenth-century France were those of the Kant-Hume debate of the late eighteenth century: autonomous reason versus innate inclinations, deontological duty versus altruistic sentiment. The institutional position-taking around Kantian hegemony facilitated this rerun. Fouillée's is an exemplary case. In the third of his book-length explorations of *idées-forces*, titled *Morale des idées-forces*, he grappled with Kant in order to free up discursive space for sentimentalism; in doing so, he both indulged a *tu quoique* argument against Kant[17] and granted full epistemological standing to pity: "Even the sentiment of *pity* and *tender sympathy*, if it preceded the contemplation of that which should constitute duty and becomes a determining principle.... We can only propound duty by loving it and because we love it as a condition of goodness. The morality of love and goodness, by the mediation of *idées-forces*, is one and the same with morality based on reason."[18] Lastly, Fouillée argued, pity is the sentiment that is on a par with universal reason—it too has cosmic implications: "Do we know, at any rate, whether the aid given to someone who suffers is not worth more, in itself, than the sky above our heads? Let us give that assistance and there will have been somewhere in this vast universe a tiny corner where one creature had pity on another creature."[19] For Fouillée, pity could often be taken as a more effective guide to benevolence than disinterested reason.

The reason-sentiment debate pitted contemporaries against each other and the present against the past—the role of sentiment served as a diachronic link. Jean Bourdeau (1848–1928), a popularizing philosopher and *littérateur* whose studies of Nietzsche and Tolstoy we come across in later chapters and who was also a member of the ASMP, confided to a correspondent: "Kant's morality poses a psychological question of the highest importance from a purely scientific viewpoint, as from an educational one—to wit, how can a human act without an emotional motive? I am persuaded of the contrary. Kant exalts reason because he is passionate about it."[20] Frédéric Rauh (1861–1909), another member of the ASMP, ingeniously tried to claim Kantianism as a form of sentimentalism: "Whatever the case may be, the theory of the categorical imperative ties Kant to the morality of sentiment, because it measures the moral value of an act according to the intensity of a certain subjective state."[21] In the most aptly titled work of this period, *La philosophie affective*, Bourdeau volunteered this estimation of the supposed reason-sentiment split in a comment on Fouillée: "Mr. Fouillée believes that the verve behind a sentiment's impulse can arise from ideas, whereas we are inclined to the contrary viewpoint.... Sentiments are the masters and ideas their humble servants. Sentiments push us where they want."[22] This line of reasoning vouchsafed the encroachment of sentimentalism into academic philosophy.

Charles Renouvier (1815–1903), one of Émile Durkheim's teachers and formative influences, contributed to the revalorization of sentiment despite himself, in an article on "Kant et Schopenhauer: le principe de l'obligation morale" ("the principle of moral obligation": if Kant was the touchstone of moral philosophy, Schopenhauer was its stumbling block and, later, part of its new cornerstone), explaining the French obsession with rationalist ethics through an odd combination of psychologism and ethical imperativism: "Realizing that their personal sentiments were capable of deceiving them, they concluded that they had no other means to obviate error than to seek in things the impersonal truths that they *should* make the rule for their sentiments and their wills."[23] Renouvier faults this rationalist outlook for its intellectual vacuity yet concedes that only Kantianism can convincingly counter untrustworthy sentiments.

The various ways and reasons for reverting to the sentiment-reason rift were reflected in the work of generalists not associated with the ASMP—the many public philosophers, *littérateurs*, and *journalistes philosophes* who wrote for an educated public. They, too, tended to promote pity; they, too, attempted to buttress that endorsement with support from landmark figures in the reason-sentiment debate, revisiting la Rochefoucauld, Spinoza, the Enlightenment *philosophes*, and Spencer, among others, in the hopes of recuperating piteous sentiment for their different social and ideological positions.

Ferdinand Brunetière, for example, used some of the ink he spilled on the pages of the *Revue des deux mondes* to sketch the outlines of an altruism he hoped to detach from the "new" (Spencerian) conception of morality. He usually polemicized against contemporary literature—typically finding in his mental crosshairs Zola and "naturalism"—but he also penned articles or books intended as general and popularizing contributions to ethics. He wanted to protect pro-social sensibility and pity against the infringements of secular and modernizing culture. Betraying a rhetorical traditionalism, Brunetière's assault on an alienating modernity required circling back to the anti-pity protagonists of a simpler, earlier era. In an article on "Question de morale," he wrote: "It has always appeared and still appears evident to me that to teach, for example, along with the 'divine' Spinoza, that 'pity is unworthy of the wise,' is to proffer a dangerous utterance."[24] In this typical animadversion, Brunetière seized upon Spinoza's denigration of pity not solely as a straw man; part of the vigor attached to the debate on pity involved precisely the awareness of a tradition of thinking about pity that restored relevance to figures as varied as Spinoza, la Rochefoucauld, Rousseau, and Michelet.

Like Spinoza, la Rochefoucauld was the moralist to whom a proper discernment of pity required reference, among both academic philosophers and *littérateurs*. Jean Bourdeau made both figures central to his outline of the progress of moral sentiments in his monograph on *La Rochefoucauld*, which begins with a thumbnail sketch of the evolution of pity: "The inexpressive Spinoza, in his *Ethics*, considers pity in almost the same terms as la Rochefoucauld, 'a bad and sterile sentiment.' Nothing is worthy of pity, nor of hate. We must alleviate misery and do good through reason, and leave compassion to the masses. Spinoza turns aside pity so that it not trouble the metaphysical freedom of his mind, la Rochefoucauld because it is not a noble or a disinterested sentiment."[25] Bourdeau intends this summary as criticism of la Rochefoucauld and Spinoza and as a teleological account of the triumph of sentimentalism in the historical battle between reason and sentiment. He situated the rehabilitation of pity in the eighteenth century, part of a new faith in secular progress that did away with rational astringency in favor of sentimental harmony. Bourdeau's was a perfect example of the triumphalist discourse on the pity tradition that restored the accents of the reason-sentiment debate.

In Bourdeau's narrative, Voltaire and Rousseau are sentimentalism's trailblazers, whereas la Rochefoucauld and, with him, the entire seventeenth century are the superseded paths:

In the eighteenth century the idea of progress spreads. The moralists of the seventeenth century hardly think of it. Pascal observes that human inventions are ever advancing, but that goodness and wickedness in the world remain the same. Voltaire replies: "I dare side with the party of humanity against that sublime misanthrope; I dare declare that we are neither as wicked or unhappy as he claims; humans are not like other animals, we feel for our species a natural benevolence. Nature has given us a disposition to pity."[26]

Bourdeau's reconstituting argument deployed the crucial motifs of pity: the belief in moral improvement and its concomitant, the softening of mores. He did so by using an intellectual Baedeker that revisited the key sites of the reason-sentiment confrontation, a cursus not dissimilar to that of our "Prologue:" Pascal, la Rochefoucauld, Voltaire, and Revolutionary sentimentalism.

A competition for philosophy students sponsored by the ASMP in 1890, on the subject of the "role of sentiment or moral instinct in contemporary theories," is one indicator of the shifting tide on sentimentalism. The first competitor's *mémoire* proceeded under sentimentalism's universal assumption that "sentiment" always connotes altruism, never egoism, "that sentiment is divided into moral sense and sympathy, leaving in silence the egoistical sentiments."[27] The contemporary sentimentalist paradigm held that "sentiment" was always other-directed and hence capable of being harnessed to socially beneficent ends; the possibility of self-regarding sentiments never entered this calculus—indeed, much effort was directed at repudiating la Rochefoucauld and other authoritative sources for this view and later, as we shall see, Nietzsche, la Rochefoucauld's inheritor.

It was to the fourth *mémoire* that the reporter, the politician Charles Waddington (1819–1914), devoted greatest attention and approval and to which he applied the classificatory periodization of this era, with Kant, Rousseau, and the Scottish philosophers as central figures:

With the eighteenth century, a new era opens up in ideas on morality; sensibility, until then disparaged, assumes precedence over reason. From theory sentimentalism passes into practice. Essay 4 is in agreement with number 2 in attributing to Jean-Jacques Rousseau, if not the paternity of the sentimental system, at least the decisive influence in this direction. Instinct is declared good, and under the name of conscience, becomes the infallible guide to conduct. Thanks to it, preternaturally egotistical humans become capable of pity, of benevolence; justice and society are founded.[28]

Given that questions for *concours* were faithful indicators of the wider intellectual and pedagogical community's concerns, so that the prized entries reflected a broader discourse, these analyses mirrored the persistent encounter with the sentiment-reason divide in ethics.

Between the claims of egoistic and altruistic sentiments, the ethical grounds were not neutral; all our moralists agreed peremptorily that "sentiment" was corrival with solicitude and fair-mindedness. For example, despite his mordant rationalism, Renouvier, in *La science de la morale*, a work that William Logue reckons "the unrecognized masterpiece of nineteenth-century philosophy,"[29] still sketched a theory of "interpersonal passions" that struggled to define sentiments as cognitive spurs: "It will suffice to place an agent in the presence of a good or evil presently felt by another person, and to infer that he/she conceives this good or evil as capable of affecting himself. Benevolence or malevolence will at that point become *sympathy* or *antipathy*…this natural disposition to partake of and emulate other agents' internal and also external alterations, appears to be the root of the passion in question."[30] Renouvier did not claim that moral judgment arises from the affective mechanisms of sympathy, compassion, and pity, nor did he hope to base a deontological ethics on them, but he did assimilate sentiments to moral considerations, viewing them as evaluative bridges between the self and the "weal and woe" of others. He thus grappled with ethical duty in such a way as to admit sentiments, even if he did not give them pride of place. Indeed, toward the end of his life Renouvier "regretted" that he had not included a more affirmative discussion of pity in *La science de la morale*—"if I had to do a second edition of it, I would have added a few pages on goodness, on pity" [31]—and the addition that he wished to be part of the corpus of his ethical legacy was later used to inculcate pity in female pedagogy, as we shall soon see. That Renouvier wanted to rethink pity out of a feeling of neglect is itself emblematic of a shift in the tenor of the times— from the Cousinian rationalism and Kantian criticism that had inspired *La science de la morale* to the sentimentalism of the *fin-de-siècle*, which made coming to terms with pity in 1902–1903, when Renouvier confided his avowals, part of any moralist's obligatory thematic.

Paul Janet (1827–1898), professor of philosophy at the Sorbonne, a disciple of Cousin—as determined as the latter in his desire to reconcile Aristotle and Kant—and member of the ASMP from 1864, gave sustained attention to sentiment in a prolific career of commentary and analysis, a career that was of paramount and conservative influence pedagogically in the *fin-de-siècle*.[32] In an early work, he offered a glossary of the affective inclinations: "More important are the inclinations toward other humans...if it is a matter of torments, *compassion* or *pity*."[33] For Janet, pity is the pathetic component of sympathy, together comprising the only other-regarding sentiments worth an ethical presumption: "Sympathy is a sentiment so close to the moral sentiments that an ingenious Scottish philosopher, Adam Smith, based an entire moral system on this principle."[34] Sympathy is so close, so related to "moral sentiment," that Janet grasps Smith's position but cannot make it his own. Janet desperately beckons back Kant: "Kant is surely right when he speaks of that false sentimentality or mawkishness...we must take care not to fall into effeminate softness or into a silly philanthropy which sacrifices justice to insipid sentiment."[35] Here we can detect an early form of the gendered turn in sentimentalism—and also, as Janet Todd has remarked, how an excessively rhetorical investment in sentimentalism led to the coining of the neologism, "sensiblérie."[36] Yet Paul Janet would not completely denigrate pity out of Kantian allegiance—if a piteous sentimentalism there must be, he would prefer to rid pity of its fatalistic and dysthemic associations, of its pessimistic connotations:

Men being necessarily unhappy, the only moral law is to pity, and if possible, to relieve, their woes: the true principle of action is pity, *das Mitleid*. Even if we should grant this, it would still be true that philosophy, having for its object the relief of human woes, would by that means give them all the happiness which they can have; while at the same time one who should act in accordance with it would also secure for himself the best and purest enjoyment. The principle of pity does not, then, exclude the principle of happiness.[37]

Such was sentimentalism's ascendancy that Janet would prefer to place it under the sign of hedonism. Indeed, part of the attraction of Aristotle as a complement to Kant was his acceptance of the tender sentiments, including pity: "When one reads, and becomes profoundly imbued with, Kant's philosophy, one finds one's self in a strange moral condition: one repents of one's good sentiments, and suffers remorse for them. 'What!' says one to himself. 'I love my friends, I love my children, I love mankind! I am endowed with pity and tenderness! All this has no moral value. Why did not nature make me an egoist?'"[38] Pity, tenderness, and love, Janet concedes, do have moral value, and so he chides Kant for disparaging them. All of these qualities, which Janet opposed to Kant's astringent rationalism, are the very premises of sentimentalism and its sensitivity to others' "weal and woe." This is the contradiction between a rising sentimentalism—Janet wrote in 1873—on the one hand, and Kantianism, on the other. As the precepts of sentimentalism were embraced, Kant's grip as unquestioned master over academic philosophy was to some extent loosened.

In a later sweeping introduction to philosophy that he coauthored with Gabriel Séailles (1852–1922),[39] Janet adverted to philosophy's history in order to explain ethics and reviewed the pro-pity tradition as part of this sequential cursus. The authors whose thought he reviewed valorized Christianity over Stoicism and Helvétius over Hobbes because the former of each pairing used misericord as moral criterion: "But the charity of the Stoics was a rational sentiment, the result of reflection, and of the consciousness of human dignity. Christian charity is deeper, more ardent.... Charity consists in desiring the moral good, the perfection of our neighbor, and in the alleviation of his woes. Towards the guilty it is shown in forgiveness and pity."[40] Conversely and seemingly at cross-purposes, the authors favored Helvétius's Stoic rendering of Hobbes's pity over the original: "Pity for others in their misfortunes is the fear we have that the like calamity may befall ourselves. The doctrines of Helvétius were at once a continuation and a contradiction of Hobbes...while to Hobbes all the cause of division and hatred was the interest of the individual, Helvétius discovered, in the working of the laws of this interest, the principles of tolerance and sympathy."[41] The authors cited Helvétius after first paraphrasing Hobbes in order to promote the former's version of pity as socially normative. They preferred the altruistic and sentimental dimensions authorized by Helvétius and not Hobbes—sentimentalism with a French twist.

The rendezvous with sentiments facilitated a valorization of pity, which was conceived as preeminently altruistic and other-directed. What exactly were the denominational contours of this *pitié*—what did they want it to mean, and what role did they want it to fulfill? Most of our thinkers were not curious as to its social or physiological mechanisms. For them, pity was a traditional quality whose specificity was left unexamined in deference to its practical moral consequences. It trailed in the wake of the sentimentalism that they gladly received from the past.

Other thinkers attempted to articulate a position on sentiment that would place it as a discernible entity at the heart of revived philosophy—especially Théodule Ribot, as we will see. The common denominator of their efforts was to efface the caesura between reason and sentiment, to replace this split by a notion of the latter whose enlarged sphere of pertinence assimilated the former—a full-blown cognitive theory of feeling, in short. For example, in an article titled "Les sentiments et les idées," Joseph Milsand (1817–1896) of the ASMP argued that "the distinctive feature of sentiment is to be broader than ideas, to comprise as part of themselves the objective discernment that then become ideas."[42] Another commonality was the almost monomaniacal insistence on classifying and categorizing the sentiments.

Frédéric Paulhan (1856–1931) made a series of attempts in the 1880s to establish firmer contours for sentimentalism's "affective philosophy." In 1887, Paulhan wrote: "The different general categories of the affective phenomena that I wish to acknowledge are: 1. *passions, sentiments, affective impulses* and *affective gestures*; 2. *affective feelings*; 3. *emotions*."[43] Among these categories, it is sentiment, naturally, that is essential for a cognitive[44] form of sentimentalism, hence for ethics:

Since sentiments and passions have much power to shape our acts, and since our acts are important to society, we can differentiate sentiments not by the organs from which they originate, but by the nature of their object. This also has the benefit of affording a transition between psychology and sociology through ethics, whose fundaments are psychological and its effects social. Sentiments are then divided into: 1. *anti-altruistic* sentiments....2. *egoistic* sentiments.... 3. *altruistic* sentiments, including the sentiments of love and sympathy, which have for their objects beings who are more or less similar to us (humans, animals), pity, etc.[45]

For Paulhan, then, sentiments are distinguished from other mental or physiological data and from other virtues by their bipartite sequence: a psychological cause (interiority) with a social (interpersonal) effect. Their psychology is a clearly cognitive one. We will return to Paulhan's explanations of pity in a later context.

Sentimentalism and, with it, pity thus attempted to fuse the imperative sentiment-reason dualism. It was also invoked in the perennial context of another, Cartesian dualism: the objectivity/subjectivity of consciousness. For morality as much as epistemology was keyed to this debate: essentially it is—like knowledge— a matter of Otherness. Thus, from Durkheim's *conscience collective* to Bergson's intuitionism to the neospiritualist revival of Cousin's notion of "désintéressement," the problem of alterity was another leitmotif of *fin-de-siècle* philosophy, subsequently overlooked. The problem of other minds was the way ethics was treated by Fouillée: "There thus exists in the very makeup of the intellect a sort of 'altruism,' which is the intellectual requirement of altruistic conduct; there is a disinterestedness required of thought, which makes it so that we cannot conceive of others but by 'putting ourselves in their place,' put ourselves inside them through thought. Consciousness is thus linked by its very foundations to other beings."[46] For Fouillée, "altruism"—a still-fresh Comtean neologism that he carried by the scruff of its neck—captured the dual dimensions of an intersubjective, anoetic consciousness moving beyond itself. Altruism is thus perfectly situated between psychology and metaphysics, and morality is the intersubjective arena in which other-aware consciousnesses participate reciprocally. It is truly synoptic: "Let us assume, on the contrary, that I put myself entirely 'in your place,' that I have an absolute and tangible consciousness of my effect on you as on me; then you cease to be a specter, a phenomenon, simply a thing: you become a consciousness, a living person, equal to me; I have an awareness of you as if you were me, and your consciousness is now one with mine."[47]

Morality excavates an objective space that facilitates epistemological operations, and conscience is like an inchoate substance around which knowledge and feeling coalesce: "To have full knowledge of beings, it would be necessary to know them from the inside, enter inside them and feel like they feel. But inner knowledge, once again, is consciousness. Complete intellectual satisfaction would then come from a universal consciousness that unites at one and the same time you, me, and all."[48] Fouillée apostrophized an epistemological altruism that shared a pan-psychic quality with Schopenhauer's philosophy.

The ethical status of a cognitively sentimental pity gained a foothold with the increasing interest in intersubjectivity—it was the "moral instinct" that could interlace dualism. Through Fouillée's position we perceive how the concern of French philosophy with sentiment was given epistemological stature and how sentiment was conceived within dualisms that authenticated its practical moral instrumentality. For Fouillée, sentiment like knowledge is moral because it is other-directed; egoistic impulses are excluded from moral and deliberative consideration since they are a form of solipsistic ignorance. So Fouillée's epistemological transcendence comprised pity: "Contemporary philosophy, far from ridiculing moral instinct, is more and more inclined to validate it, for it discovers in it an almost infallible intuition of the profoundest laws of life. Instead of seeing in pity an 'illusion,' for example, it sees in it on the contrary the primary and surest way of stripping away the illusion of a solitary and autonomous self."[49] Fouillée promoted pity as a tool for unmasking the "illusion" of subjectivity. His approach here may be usefully labeled an "idealism of sentiment," for he conceived of sentiment as inextricably bound up with mental representations, with pure ideas, rather than with tangible cognitive processes: "*Sentiments* comprise ideas by their very definition, in a people as in an individual; there can be no moral, aesthetic, social sentiments, etc., without moral, aesthetic, social ideas, etc."[50] With Fouillée, the return of sentimentalism, an extreme version of the cognitive theory of sentiments, and intersubjectivity all went hand in hand.

This intellectual development—intersubjectivity premised on a cognitive theory of sentiments—may have sounded an abstruse tone, yet its proponents closely aligned intersubjectivity with an observable social complexity. Camille Hémon, for example, based sentiment on socialization: "the not less fundamental law of suggestion and sympathetic contagion demonstrates how, subjected to the continual influences of his brethren, that same individual associates his sentiments to theirs, and thus becomes socialized and civilized."[51] The civilizing and socializing process, according to Hémon, is triggered by the intersubjectivity actuated by sentiments—specifically, by sentimental contagion and suggestion.[52] Indeed, it is the intersubjective dimension of sentiment that acts as its social safeguard: "On the other hand, if an individual eludes for one instant these artificial conditions of existence, during a great danger, for example, or under the influence of a pressing need, every social sentiment, generosity, pity, human respect, etc., will quickly disappear in the awakening of basic instincts, theretofore masked or repressed by sincere social considerations and conventional sentiments."[53] The rhetoric of an intersubjective and piteous sentimentalism was partly, then, a stratagem for evoking the prerogatives of "civilization" and "society" over egoism and its putatively primitive arrangements.

In a book-length work predating Hémon's by seven years, Julien Pioger also laid out a sentimentalist scheme keyed to social complexity. Its very title—*La Vie sociale, la morale et le progrès*—demonstrated the triad of overlapping issues that impart explanatory resonance to intersubjective pity. Pioger's quasi-Durkheimian thesis is that sensibility is keyed to social differentiation: "It is only through the widening of social differentiation that we witness the solidarising role of the convergence of modes of feeling."[54] For Pioger, pro-social sentiments such as pity are made possible by the intersubjectivity inherent in sociability: "It is the same with sociability. It is the reciprocal reactions among members or constituent parts of an identical social body that produce these tendencies, these attractions that we render by various expressions, instinct, sympathy, love, pity, etc., and to which we implicitly attach a more or less vague idea of mentalism."[55] This line of reasoning, grounding as it does pro-social sentiments in a complex cultural milieu, helps mark a watershed in the Rousseauian moment in sentimentalism.

There were ideological reasons, of course, for devaluating Rousseau's version of pity, especially among those who blamed Rousseauian romanticism for various political and social problems.[56] We must note, as we shall do with greater elaboration, that the pro-pity discourse of the *fin-de-siècle* disfranchised Rousseauian naïveté and primitivism. In accounts such as Pioger's, fellow-feeling is a product of, not a counterweight to, social—and perforce political—complexity. In fact, integral to renewed sentimentalism was the distinction drawn between emotion and sentiment by reference to the latter's political dimensions. Jean Izoulet (1854–1929) phrased it this way: "*Sentiment* like desires is related to the political body. Therefore we must not explain the difference between sensation and sentiment as the difference between the body and some supposed 'soul,' but as the difference between the animal body and the social body."[57] Pioger thus links sentimental complexity to social complexity in a way that implicitly advocates both: "It is simple now to grasp the fact that social sensations necessarily must multiply proportionately to the frequency and the intensity of social relations.... We perfectly understand that we acquire, develop, and abstract our common idea of affection, sympathy, pity, goodness, beauty, according to the extent of our perceptions and comparisons."[58]

All these thinkers, whatever their position on the philosophical field—Izoulet and Pioger were more receptive to sociology and the human sciences than most colleagues—accentuated social intersubjectivity and shunned Rousseauian misology. For them intelligence is required for an apperceptive grasp of the Other. So, for example, Elie Rabier (1846–1932), whose thought is summarized by Brooks as "intelligent empiricism"[59] and who became the state's director of l'*Enseignement secondaire* between 1889 and 1906 and, as such, was instrumental in determining some of the programs of study (syllabi) that we encounter in the *Revue Universitaire*, argued for an other-directed morality that is both intersubjective and fostered by acumen:

The truly sympathetic human, the good, charitable human, is one whose own self, instead of completely monopolizing consciousness, is always ready, on the contrary, to relinquish this prized place to the idea of an unfamiliar self.... This entails the importance of *intelligence* as the prerequisite of sympathy. It is necessary for the sorting out and interpreting of signals, for imagining what they mean internally or externally to living beings. That's why the lack of sympathy often results from lack of intelligence.[60]

The sensible conscience in society calls for deciphering sentiments in order to socialize. Much debate about pro-social pity centered on whether these signs were the more effective if they were more dolorous and dysthemic. Rabier contradicted la Rochefoucauld by arguing for the inherently virtuous nature of distress: "La Rochefoucauld's theory is false...suffering moves the soul, suffuses it with softness, sympathy, pity. Human sadness is perhaps the strongest bond in human society."[61] For Rabier as for other pro-pity thinkers, sentiments are the safeguard of social cohesion and the least capricious manifestation of cognition.

Another figure helping to decouple the objectivity-subjectivity dualism that had so dominated French philosophical paradigms and did so with the help of sentiment was Henri Bergson, for he retraced the ground of pity covered by currently less hallowed philosophers in order to arrive at the philosophical promised land of intuitionism. In his *Essai sur les données immédiates de la conscience*, Bergson situated pity at the interstices of "psychological states" and "moral sentiments."[62] He dismissed la Rochefoucauld's condescension toward pity, seeing in the duc's target only "lesser forms of pity."[63] "Real pity," Bergson echoed sentimentalists, "consists less in fearing suffering than in craving it. A slight desire, which one would hardly wish to see fulfilled, but which one elaborates despite oneself, as if nature had committed a great injustice and it were necessary to avoid any suspicion of complicity with her. The essence of pity is thus a need to humiliate oneself, a longing for abasement."[64] Like Schopenhauer, Bergson saw an inimical relationship between pity and nature, which gave the former its abundantly moral character. Pity is fecund because contrary to mere facticity. It is also, Bergson held, not devoid of ego-satisfactions: "This painful wish, moreover, has its charms, because it hoists us up in our own esteem, and makes us feel superior to those worldly goods from which our thought momentarily separates itself."[65] The motions of the Bergsonian consciousness never seep outward toward others in self-forgetfulness; consciousness is both intelligent and intuitive, circling back to its source after its apperceptive engagement with the world.[66] Like the sentimentalists before him and like Ribot, as we shall see, all of whom situated pity within the overlapping boundaries of a philosophical psychology and ethics, Bergson treated pity as processual and developmental: "The increasing intensity of pity consists then in a qualitative sequence, in the progression from disgust to fear, from fear to sympathy, and from sympathy itself to humility,"[67] a process requiring the Other so that the Self may be enriched.

I have been delineating the philosophic deployment of *pitié* as an ethical sentiment, one that dated from Enlightenment sentimentalism but that was suddenly opportune in the *fin-de-siècle*'s attempt to master and work through the impasse between sentimentalism and reason. Not every philosopher of late-nineteenth-century France elucidated these issues with pity as his intellectual implement; but those who did were almost uniformly in agreement about the rhetorical and epistemological operations it could perform. The analysis and prescription of its self-evident social and political virtues were left for others, whom we shall now take into our account.

NOTES

1. Gustave LeBon, *Aphorismes du temps présent*, in *Gustave LeBon: The Man and His Works*, Alice Widener, trans. and ed. (Indianapolis: Liberty Press, 1979), 270.

2. Boutroux was elected to the Académie des sciences morales et politiques (Philosophy Section) on May 21, 1898 and named director of the Fondation Thiers in 1902. He was elected to the Académie Française in 1914. From 1915 until his death six years later, Boutroux's thought and prolific writings were fixated on anti-German chauvinism. See Archives Nationales (AN), Series AJ16/985 and F17/22028; and also Christophe Prochasson and Anne Rasmussen, *Au nom de la Patrie: les intellectuels et la première guerre mondiale*

(1910–1919) (Paris: Editions de la Découverte, 1996), 189, 192–93. He was also a good friend of Prime Minister Raymond Poincaré and a leading member of the pro-Dreyfus intellectual group that issued the "Appel à l'Union" during the affair. (See Bibliothèque nationale française, Salle des Manuscrits, N.A.Fr. 25170, Papiers Lavisse, vol. 5, especially the letter dated 3 December 1898 drafted by Boutroux. See also BNF, Ms. N.A.Fr. 15995 [Papiers Poincaré, vol. 4].

3. Isaac Benrubi classified Boutroux as a leading exemplar of the third main line of French philosophy, "metaphysico-spiritual positivism" (see *Contemporary Thought of France*, Ernest B. Dicker, trans. [New York: Alfred A. Knopf, 1926]). See also Mary Jo Nye, "The Boutroux Circle and Poincaré's Conventionalism," *Journal of the History of Ideas* 40 (1979): 107–20.

4. Fabiani places Boutroux at the highest echelon of the philosophical hierarchy: "Au sommet, les philosophes—Boutroux, Fouillée, Ravaisson—qui sont aussi des professeurs" ["At the summit, those philosophers—Boutroux, Fouillée, Ravaisson—who are also professors."] (*Les philosophes de la République*, 87.) Maurice Barrès thought highly of him: "Pourquoi M. Boutroux n'est-il pas célèbre? Mais la célébrité, c'est un amusement, une petite satisfaction de vaniteux. Le véritable intérêt, c'est d'agir sur des cerveaux, de modifier des êtres. Tel penseur, de qui le nom ne passe pas le cercle de ses disciples, envoie son idée retentir très avant dans le monde." ["Why is Mr. Boutroux not famous? But fame is a little game, a contentment for the vain. The real importance is to have an effect on minds, to change people. A given thinker whose name is not known beyond the circle of his followers makes his ideas splash into the world."] Barrès, *Journal de ma vie extérieure*, François Broche and Eric Roussel, eds. (Paris: Editions Julliard, 1994), 446.

5. ["La morale, sans doute, a des principes généraux. Mais, aujourd'hui, ils ne suffisent pas. Nous voulons savoir quels sont précisément nos devoirs, au point de civilisation et dans les conditions particulières où nous nous trouvons."] Boutroux, *Bulletin de la société française de philosophie,* ii.

6. See Brooks, *The Eclectic Legacy*, 52.

7. Rose de Laval, "La plus jeune Académie de l'Institut de France," *Historia* 579 (March 1995), 94–96. See also Georges Picot, *L'Institut de France* (Paris: Librairie Renouard, 1907). For information on the ASMP's history, bylaws, members, and so on, see AN, F17/3612. See also Terry N. Clark, *Prophets and Patrons: The French University and the Emergence of the Social Sciences* (Cambridge, MA: Harvard UP, 1973), 57–60.

8. See Brooks, *The Eclectic Legacy*: "The term *science morale* or *science des phénomènes moraux* was commonly used throughout the nineteenth century to refer to either the study of mind or the study of morals....Moreover, the moral sciences connoted an introspective, traditional approach best represented by the Académie des Sciences Morales et Politiques, which was largely hostile to Positivism" (22). "This body [ASMP] had a larger contingent of philosophers, nearly all eclectic spiritualists" (94).

9. Brooks, 155.

10. Like Boutroux, Fouillée was also one of the philosophers characterized by Benrubi as a "metaphysico-spiritual positivist," and sited on the "summit" of professional philosophy by Fabiani (*Les philosophes de la République*, 87). Logue credits him with bringing a social-science dimension to philosophy (*From Philosophy to Sociology*, 13–14), characterizing his thought as "libéralisme réformiste" (111). On Fouillée's views on Darwinian evolution, see Robert A. Nye, *Masculinity and Male Codes of Honor in Modern France* (Berkeley: U of California P, 1998), 88–89. Brooks notes both Fouillée's eclecticism and differences from Boutroux: "Fouillée left the university in 1875, after only three years at the École Normale, and his thought, which centered around what he called the *idée-force*, became more eclectic than neospiritualist. By contrast, Boutroux remained within the

university throughout his career and developed the essential themes of neospiritualism" (*The Eclectic Legacy*, 280–81).

11. ["la philosophie est la religion publique des démocraties et nous avouons que nous n'aurions pas grande confiance dans l'avenir d'une réforme sans philosophie. Si prêtre et roi vont bien ensemble, toujours on a rapproché ces deux titres: philosophe et citoyen."] Cited in Canivez, *Jules Lagneau*, 285.

12. ["'Il est facile de prêcher la morale, a dit Schopenhauer, difficile d'en établir les fondements.' La crise actuelle de la morale en est la preuve. Tout est remis en question; aucun principe ne paraît encore solidement établi ou du moins à lui seul suffisant, ni celui de l'évolution universelle, ni 'l'altruisme' des positivistes, ni la pitié et le nouveau nirvana des pessimistes, ni le devoir des Kantiens, ni le bien en soi et transcendant des spiritualistes."] Alfred Fouillée, *Critique des systèmes de morale contemporain* (Paris: G. Baillière, 1883), v.

13. ["faut-il supprimer le côté intellectuel et moral des sentiments, désirs, amours de toutes sortes, pour les réduire en entier à des sensations nerveuses viscérales, musculaires, passivement reçues du dehors par une conscience impuissante à réagir?"] Fouillée, *L'Evolutionnisme des idées-forces* (Paris: Félix Alcan, 1890), 170.

14. ["L'émotion est donc, en définitive, le changement soudain apporté par le sentiment ou développement antérieur des états de conscience, à leur direction, à leur vitesse, à leur extension; elle est comme l'effet mécanique, et non statique, du plaisir et de la douleur dans le domaine mentale."] ["Emotion is certainly then a sudden change brought forth by the sentiment, or a prior change in states of consciousness, in their direction, speed, and scope; emotion is like the mechanical and not static effect of pleasure and pain in the mental sphere."] Fouillée, *La psychologie des idées-forces* (Paris: Félix Alcan, 1893), 136.

15. ["Toute expression des sentiments a, par définition même, un côté psychologique et, qui plus est, social: il n'y a, en effet, *expression* véritable que s'il y a *interprétation* possible des mouvements par d'autres êtres formant avec le premier une société....Selon nous, c'est en effet cette loi psychologique de solidarité ou de sympathie qui régit et explique tous les faits d'expression."] Fouillée, *La psychologie des idées-forces*, 143.

16. ["Et il en est de même de la sympathie: la nature ne connaît pas l'isolement de l'idéal égoisme; elle rapproche, elle confond, elle unit. Comme la chaleur et la lumière, elle ne peut donner la vie et la sensibilité sur un point sans les faire rayonner sur les autres; loin de fermer les 'morales,' elles les ouvre toutes sur autrui...une idée triste a bientôt pour cortège des myriades de *sensations* pénibles."] Fouillée, *La Psychologie des idées-forces*, 166.

17. ["La morale de Kant est trop huguenot et, qui plus est, trop prussienne; il semble, au premier aspect, que ce soit le militarisme transporté dans l'ordre morale. Ce n'est là, pourtant, que l'apparence intérieure. Au fond, Kant, lui aussi, n'accepte la forme universelle du devoir que parce qu'il a l'amour intime de la bonté."] ["Kant's ethics is too Huguenot and, what's more, too Prussian; it appears at first blush a form of militarism carried over into the moral domain. That's only, however, a matter of appearances. At bottom, Kant himself accepts the categorical form of duty because he has a thorough love of goodness."] Fouillée, *La Psychologie des idées-forces*, 253.

18. ["Même le sentiment de *pitié* et de *tendre sympathie*, s'il précède la considération de ce que doit être le devoir et devient un principe determinant....Nous ne pouvons poser le devoir qu'en l'aimant et parce que nous l'aimons comme condition de la bonté. La morale de l'amour et de la bonté, par l'intermédiaire des idées-forces, ne fait donc qu'un avec la morale de la raison."] Fouillée, *La Psychologie des idées-forces*, 267.

19. ["Sait-on, d'ailleurs, si le secours donné à celui qui souffre ne vaut pas plus, à lui seul, que tout le firmament sur nos têtes? Donnons ce secours, et que, dans l'immense

univers, il y ait un petit coin, où un être, en face d'un autre être, aura eu pitié."] Fouillée, *La Psychologie des idées-forces*, 267.

20. ["La morale de Kant pose une question psychologique de la plus haute importance au point de vue de la science pure, comme au point de vue de l'éducation—à savoir si l'homme peut agir sans motif affectif. Je suis persuadé du contraire. Kant éxalte la raison, parce qu'il en a la passion."] Bibliothèque Nationale, Salle des Manuscrits, N.A.Fr. 18340. Letter to Arvède Barine, dated March 2, 1904.

21. ["Quoiqu'il en soit, la théorie de l'impératif catégorique rattache Kant à la morale du sentiment, puisqu'elle mesure à l'intensité d'un certain état subjectif la valeur morale de l'acte."] Frédéric Rauh, *Études morales* (Paris: Félix Alcan, 1911), 118. This was part of a chapter whose problematic was "les sentiments moraux." Rauh taught at Lycées in Vendôme and Valenciennes until 1886, then in Paris, at the Ecole normale supérieur in 1900, and finally at the Sorbonne from 1908 until his death the following year. For further information on Rauh, see AN, F17/21577.

22. ["M. Fouillée estime que la vigueur de l'impulsion des sentiments peut leur venir des idées, tandis que nous nous inclinerons vers l'opinion contraire...les sentiments sont les maîtres et les idées leurs humbles servantes. Les sentiments nous poussent où ils veulent aller."] Bourdeau, *La Philosophie affective: nouveaux courants et nouveaux problèmes dans la philosophie contemporaine* (Paris: Félix Alcan, 1912), 117–21.

23. ["En voyant que leurs sentiments personnels étaient sujets à les tromper, ils ont conclu que pour éviter l'erreur ils n'avaient pas d'autre moyen que de chercher dans les choses les vérités impersonelles dont ils *devaient* faire la règle de leurs sentiments et leurs volontés."] Charles Renouvier, in *La critique philosophique* (9:1), 139. In a study of Renouvier's thought, William Logue noted Renouvier's anti-sentiment philosophy of moral obligation: "It is gravely important, however, that the passions remain in a supporting role, for altruism or Christian love for one's fellow man can offer no stable rules for moral conduct. Renouvier showed that a morale of love was a morale that easily adopted the maxim that the ends justify the means....To his Christian critics, Renouvier responded that the age of [morals based on] charity in theory was, in practice, an age of blood." In *Charles Renouvier, Philosopher of Liberty* (Baton Rouge: Louisiana State UP, 1993), 78–79.

24. ["Il me paraîssait, il me paraît toujours évident, que d'enseigner par exemple, avec le 'divin' Spinosa, que 'la pitié est indigne du sage,' c'est proférer une parole dangereuse."] Ferdinand Brunetière, "Question de morale," *Revue des deux mondes* (September 1, 1890), 215.

25. ["L'impassible Spinoza, dans *L'Ethique*, juge la pitié presque dans les mêmes termes que la Rochefoucauld, 'un sentiment mauvais et stérile.' Rien n'est digne de pitié, ni de haine. Il faut soulager la misère et faire le bien par raison, et laisser la compassion au peuple. Spinoza écarte la pitié pour ne pas laisser troubler la liberté métaphysique de son esprit, la Rochefoucauld parce qu'elle n'est pas un sentiment noble, ni un sentiment désintéressé."] Bourdeau, *La Rochefoucauld*, 84. Bourdeau similarly brandished a *tu quoique* argument against la Rochefoucauld in the next paragraph: "Cette pitié toutefois que la Rochefoucauld désapprouve dans son *Portrait*, et qu'il va rabaisser dans ses *Maximes*, il s'en prévaut dans ses lettres et dans ses *Mémoires*. Parlant de la révolte des paysans écrasés d'impôts qu'il a réprimée dans son gouvernement de Poitou, il écrit en 1643: 'Je ne désavoue point que leur misère ne me fit regarder avec pitié leur rébellion.' Il demande à Mazarin de lui accorder le droit de grâce, il en use si largement qu'il n'en couta la vie ni l'honneur à aucun des sujets du roi" (Ibid.). ["The same pity of which la Rochefoucauld disapproved in his *Portrait*, and which he will deprecate in his *Maximes*, he boasts of in his *Mémoires*. Speaking of the peasants' revolt against crushing taxes, which he subdued in his government of Poitou, he writes in 1643: 'I do not deny that their misery made me look

upon their revolt with pity.' He asked Mazarin to give him the power of clemency, and he made so great a use of it that he did not take the life or honor of any of the King's subjects."]

26. ["Mais au XVIIIème siècle commence à se répandre l'idée de progrès. Les moralistes du XVIIème n'y songent guère. Pascal constate que les inventions des hommes vont en avançant, mais que la bonté et la malice du monde en général restent les mêmes. Voltaire lui répond: 'J'ose prendre le parti de l'humanité contre ce misanthrope sublime; j'ose assurer que nous ne sommes ni si méchants, ni si malheureux qu'il le dit; l'homme n'est pas comme les autres animaux, il a pour son espèce une bienveillance naturelle. La nature lui a donné la disposition à la pitié.'"] Bourdeau, *La Rochefoucauld*, 178, 180.

27. ["que le sentiment se subdivise en sens moral et en sympathie, passant sous silence les sentiments égoists."] "Rapport sur le concours ayant pour sujet le rôle du sentiment ou de l'instinct moral dans les théories contemporaines, par Charles Waddington, le 19 juillet 1890," *Séances de l'Académie des sciences morales et politiques*, 628.

28. ["Avec le 18ème siècle, s'ouvre une ère nouvelle pour les idées morales: la sensibilité, jusque-là dédaignée, prend le pas sur la raison. De la théorie, le sentimentalisme passe dans la pratique....Le mémoire 4 est d'accord avec le numéro 2 pour attribuer à Jean-Jacques Rousseau, sinon la paternité du système sentimental, du moins une influence décisive en ce sens. L'instinct est proclamé bon, et, sous le nom de conscience, il est le guide infaillible de la conduite. Grâce à lui, l'homme d'abord égoiste devient accessible à la pitié, à la bienveillance; la justice et la société sont fondées."] "Rapport sur le concours," 633–34. Waddington was elected to the ASMP on February 14, 1888; for more biographical information, see AN, F17/21879.

29. Logue labels Renouvier's thought as *personalisme* and comments on the relevance of his ethics in relation to pity: "But he believed that the idea of a right of defense at least provided the basis for rational judgement and discussion, whereas the principles of love or altruism were more easily corrupted and furnished no basis of measure unless regulated from without by rational considerations....Renouvier did not deny the importance of the emotions in determining behavior, nor did he deny that they could make a positive contribution to moral action, they were simply inadequate as a foundation for moral action." *Charles Renouvier: Philosopher of Liberty*, 59–60. Canivez, too, reminds us that "Si, de cette fin-de-siècle, H. Bergson reste le maître incontestable de la philosophie, Renouvier et Lachelier ont plus d'importance" (*Jules Lagneau*, 268).

30. ["Il suffira de placer l'agent en présence d'un bien ou d'un mal actuellement obtenus par une autre personne, et de supposer qu'il se représente ce bien ou ce mal comme pouvant toucher lui-même. La bienveillance et la malveillance deviendront alors *sympathie* et *antipathie*...cette disposition naturelle que nous avons à participer aux modifications tant internes qu'externes des autres agents et à les imiter, et qui paraît être la racine de la passion dont il est question ici."] Renouvier, *Science de la morale* (Paris: Librairie philosophique de Ladrange, 1869), 403.

31. ["si j'avais eu à en faire une seconde édition, j'aurais ajouté quelques pages sur la bonté, sur la pitié."] Cited in *Renouvier: derniers entrétiens*, Louis Prat, ed. (Paris: A. Colin: 1904), 95.

32. Janet first attracted attention in 1848, when he won the ASMP's essay competition asking to "comparer la philosophie morale et politique de Platon et Aristote avec les doctrines des plus grands philosophes modernes sur les mêmes sujets" ["compare the moral and political philosophy of Plato and Aristotle to those of the greatest modern philosophers"]. See AN, F17/3612, as well as F17/20993. For biographical information, see AN, AJ/16/1153. See also Brooks: "Janet was an eclectic spiritualist who held the chair of the history of philosophy at the Faculty of Letters. He was also a member of the Conseil supérieur de

l'instruction publique—the highest body in the French educational system—and of the Académie des Sciences Morales et Politiques. These positions made him influential in academic matters. ("Philosophy and Psychology at the Sorbonne, 1885–1913," 130). See also Logue, who stresses the fact that Janet was the most historical of eclectics and whose lecture course in 1867 on Kant marked the most serious study of Kant in France (*From Philosophy to Sociology*, 37). But on his conservative (retarding) influence, see Brooks, *The Eclectic Legacy*; and LaCapra, who recounts how Janet warned Alfred Espinas, concerning the latter's thesis, that sociology lead to madness (*Émile Durkheim*, 81).

33. ["Plus importantes sont les inclinations relatives aux autres hommes...s'il s'agit particulièrement de souffrances, la *compassion* ou la *pitié*."] Janet, *Eléments de morale* (Paris: Charles Delagrave, 1870), 21–22.

34. ["La sympathie est un sentiment si voisin du sentiment moral, qu'un ingénieux philosophe écossais, Adam Smith, a fondé sur ce principe un système moral."] Janet, 104.

35. ["Kant a sans doute raison, s'il veut parler de cette fausse sentimentalité ou sensiblérie...il faut prendre garde à ne pas tomber dans des tendresses efféminées ou dans une philanthropie niaise qui sacrifie la justice à une fade sensibilité."] Janet, 276.

36. "In France where 'sensibilité' translated the English 'sensibility,' a new term 'sensiblérie' developed to distinguish sensibility from the debased and self-indulgent kind." Todd, *Sensibility: An Introduction*, 8.

37. Janet, *The Theory of Morals*, 85.

38. Janet, 354.

39. Séailles wrote tomes of appreciation on his contemporaries, including Renan, Renouvier, and Lachelier. Maurice Paléologue, the diplomat who published his widely cited *Journal de l'affaire Dreyfus*, recounted his evenings at the salon of the Dreyfusard Mme. Euphrasie Aubéron de Nerville (one of the prototypes for Proust's fictional Mme. Verdurin) with Séailles, who was favorable to Dreyfus's cause, in attendance (*My Secret Diary of the Dreyfus Case, 1894–99*, Eric Mosbacher, trans. [London: Secker and Warburg, 1957], 83–84). For more biographical information on Séailles, see AN, F17/22331.

40. *History of the Problems of Philosophy*, Ada Monahan, trans., Henry Jones, ed. (London: Macmillan, 1902), 48.

41. Janet and Séailles, 72–73.

42. ["le propre des sentiments est d'être plus large que les idées, d'inclure comme une partie d'eux mêmes les perceptions objectives qui deviennent des idées."] Joseph Milsand, *La critique philosophique* (9:1), 109.

43. ["Les différentes classes générales des phénomènes affectifs que je propose de reconnaître sont: 1. les *passions*, les *sentiments*, les *impulsions affectives* et les *signes affectifs*; 2. les *sensations affectives*; 3. les *emotions*."] Frédéric Paulhan, *Les Phénomènes affectifs et les lois de leur apparition* (Paris: Félix Alcan, 1887), 170.

44. ["Comme les *besoins*, en effet, le sentiment et la passion sont des tendances organiques senties. Mais les sentiments sont surtout des besoins cérébraux; le mot de passion s'applique aux besoins intenses accompagnés de désirs excessivement violents."] ["Like *needs*, in fact, sentiment and passion are truly felt organic tendencies. But sentiments are above all else cerebral needs; the term passion is applied to intense needs accompanied by excessively violent desires."] Paulhan, *La Physiologie de l'esprit* (Paris: Germer Baillière, s.d.), 87.

45. ["Comme les sentiments et les passions ont beaucoup de pouvoir pour déterminer nos actes, comme nos actes importent à la société, on peut distinguer les sentiments non plus par la nature des organes qui leur donnent naissance, mais par la nature de leur objet. On a ainsi l'avantage de fournir une transition entre la psychologie et la sociologie en passant par la morale, dont les bases sont psychologiques, dont les effets sont sociaux. Les sentiments se

divisent alors en: 1. sentiments *anti-altruistes*... 2. sentiments *égoistes*... 3. sentiments *altruistes*, comprenant les sentiments d'amour, de sympathie, qui ont pour objet des êtres plus ou moins semblables à nous (hommes, animaux), la pitié, etc."] Paulhan, 88.

46. ["Il existe ainsi dans la constitution même de l'intelligence une sorte 'd'altruisme,' qui est la condition intellectuelle de l'altruisme dans la conduite; il y a un désintéressement nécessaire à la pensée, qui fait que nous ne pouvons pas ne pas concevoir les autres, nous 'mettre à leur place,' nous mettre en eux par la pensée. La conscience se trouve ainsi, par son fond même, reliée à tous les autres êtres."] Fouillée, "Les transformations futures de l'idée morale," *Revue des deux mondes* (September 15, 1890), 306.

47. ["Supposons, au contraire, que je me mette pleinement 'à votre place,' que j'aie la conscience entière et concrète de mon action en vous comme en moi, vous cessez d'être un spectre, un phénomène, une simple chose: vous devenez une conscience, une personne vivante, égale à moi; j'ai conscience de vous comme si vous étiez moi, et votre conscience ne fait plus qu'une avec la mienne."] Fouillée, "Les transformations futures de l'idée morale," 308.

48. ["Pour avoir la pleine intelligence des êtres, il faudrait les connaître par le dedans, se mettre en eux et les sentir comme ils se sentent. Or la connaissance par le dedans, encore une fois, c'est la conscience. La pleine satisfaction intellectuelle, ce serait donc la conscience universelle, unissant à la fois moi, vous, tous et tout."] Fouillée, 310.

49. ["La philosophie contemporaine, loin de ridiculiser l'instinct moral, tend de plus en plus à le justifier, car elle y découvre une intuition presque infaillible des lois les plus profondes de la vie. Au lieu de voir dans la pitié une 'illusion,' elle y voit au contraire le premier et le plus sûr moyen de dépouiller l'illusion du moi isolé et se suffisant à lui-même."] Fouillée, "Les transformations futures de l'idée morale," 319. Fouillée borrowed the logic and terms of this argument from Schopenhauer.

50. ["Un *sentiment* enveloppe l'idée même dans sa définition, pour un peuple comme pour un individu; il n'y a pas de sentiments moraux, esthétiques, sociaux, etc., sans des pensées morales, esthétiques, sociales, etc."] Fouillée, *La France au point de vue morale* (Paris: Hachette, 1911), 367.

51. ["la loi non moins fondamentale de suggestion et de contagion sympathique nous a montré ensuite comment, soumis aux incessantes influences de ses semblables, ce même individu identifie ses sentiments aux leurs, et, par là, se civilise et se socialize."] Camille Hémon, "Conflits des sentiments égoists et des sentiments sociaux," *Revue des cours et conférences* 9:2 (June 20, 1901), 709.

52. For more recent accounts of a similar yet more analytical nature, see Elaine Hatfield, John Cacioppo, and Richard Rapson, eds., *Emotional Contagion* (Cambridge: Cambridge UP, 1994).

53. ["par contre, l'individu échappe un instant à ces conditions artificielles d'existence, dans un grand danger, par exemple, ou sous l'empire d'un besoin impérieux, tous les sentiments sociaux, générosité, pitié, respect humain, etc. auront tôt fait de s'évanouir devant le réveil des instincts élémentaires, naguère masqués ou refoulés par les sincères réflexions sociales et les sentiments de convention."] Hémon, "Conflits des sentiments égoistes et sentiments sociaux," 710.

54. ["Ce n'est qu'au fur et à mesure de la différenciation sociale que nous voyons le rôle solidarisant de la convergence des modes se sentir."] Julien Pioger, *La Vie sociale, la morale, et le progrès* (Paris: Félix Alcan, 1894), 101.

55. ["il en est de même de la sociabilité. Ce sont les actions et réactions réciproques entre les membres ou parties composantes d'un même corps social qui engendrent ces tendances, ces attractions que nous traduisons par des expressions diverses, instinct, sympathie, amour, pitié, etc., et auxquels nous attribuons implicitement une idée plus ou moins vague de

psychisme."] Pioger, 103.

56. This was the case, for example, with Pierre Laserre's *Le Romantisme français: Essai sur la révolution dans les sentiments et dans les idées au XIXème siècle*, 4th ed. (Paris: Mercure de France, 1907): "L'individu n'éprouvait aucune tendance à sortir de l'isolement, soit pour s'unir aux autres, soit pour les asservir. Il est absurde, mais plein de sens, qu'avec cette nullité psychique, Rousseau attribue à ses primitives la 'pitié.' Le spectacle de cet animal qui reçoit les coups paisiblement et qui pleure, quand il voit frapper, est d'une tristesse où il y a de l'ignoble." ["The individual felt no need to escape his solitude, either to unite himself with or to subjugate others. It is absurd yet meaningful that with such a psychological non-entity, Rousseau ascribes 'pity' to these primitives. The spectacle of this creature who passively accepts blows and cries at the striking of them is so sad as to be ignoble."] (58)

57. ["Le *sentiment*, comme l'aspiration, a trait au corps politique. Il ne faut donc pas expliquer la différence de la sensation et du sentiment par la différence du corps et d'on ne sait quelle 'âme,' mais par la différence du corps animal et du corps social."] Jean Izoulet, *La Sainte Cité ou l'anti-Marxisme* (Paris: Albin Michel, 1895), 313. A professor of philosophy first at the Lycée Bourg-en-Bresse and then at Douai, in Paris at Henri IV and Condorcet, he became "Professeur de philosophie sociale" at the Collège de France. As secretary to Paul Bert in 1881, Jules Ferry asked him to offer 60 lectures on the "psychology of ethics" to all Parisian educators.

58. ["Il est facile maintenant de comprendre que les sensations sociales doivent nécessairement se multiplier proportionellement à la fréquence et à l'intensité des rapports sociaux....Nous comprenons parfaitement que nous acquérons, développons et abstrayons notre idée générale d'affection, de sympathie, de pitié, de bonté, de beauté, au fur et à mesure de l'extension de nos perceptions et comparaisons."] Izoulet, 154–55.

59. See Brooks, *The Eclectic Legacy*, 146.

60. ["L'homme vraiment sympathique, l'homme bon, l'homme charitable, c'est celui dont le moi propre, au lieu de s'accaparer à lui seul toute la conscience, est toujours prêt, au contraire, à céder cette place si chère à l'idée d'un moi étranger....De là résulte l'importance de *l'intelligence* comme condition de la sympathie. Elle est nécessaire pour démêler, interpreter les signes, se représenter ce qu'ils impliquent à l'intérieur ou à l'extérieur des êtres vivants. C'est pourquoi le défaut de sympathie provient souvent du défaut d'intelligence."] Ellie Rabier, *Leçons de philosophie*, 5th ed. (Paris: Hachette, 1896), 495–96.

61. ["La thèse de la Rochefoucauld est fausse....la douleur attendrit l'âme, la pénètre de douceur, de sympathie, de pitié. Les tristesses humaines sont peut-être le lien le plus fort de la société humaine."] Rabier, 517, 520.

62. Henri Bergson, *Essai sur les données immédiates de la conscience*, in *Oeuvres complètes*, André Robinet, ed.., Henri Gouhier, intro. (Paris: Presses universitaires de France, 1970), 16. Bergson was elected to the ASMP's Philosophy Section on December 14, 1901.

63. ["les formes inférieures de la pitié."] Bergson, 16.

64. ["consiste moins à craindre la souffrance qu'à la désirer. Désir léger, qu'on souhéterait à peine voir réalisé, et qu'on forme pourtant malgré soi, comme si la nature commétait quelque grande injustice, et qu'il fallut écarter tout soupçon de complicité avec elle. L'essence de la pitié est donc un besoin de s'humilier, une aspiration à descendre."] Bergson, 16.

65. ["Cette aspiration douloureuse a d'ailleurs son charme, parce qu'elle nous grandit dans notre propre estime, et fait que nous nous sentons supérieurs à ces biens sensibles dont notre pensée se détache momentanément."] Bergson, 16–17.

66. See Armand Laquièze, who considered Bergson one of the three great metaphysicians of pity, alongside Schopenhauer and Nicoli Hartmann (1862–1950). In

Étude analytique sur la pitié (Lyon: E. Vitte, 1943), 88.

67. ["L'intensité croissante de la pitié consiste donc dans un progrès qualitatif, dans un passage du dégoût à la crainte, de la crainte à la sympathie, et de la sympathie elle-même à l'humilité."] Bergson, *Essai sur les données immédiates de la conscience*, 17.

Chapter 2: The "Altar" of Civilization

The meliorative promise of pity was ultimately more important than its value as a philosophical wedge against dualism. Many of those who wished pity would help shape the contours of an imagined community viewed this as a matter of how rather than why. Françisque Bouillier (1813–1899) of the ASMP authored an essay on pity in 1882 that laid out nothing less than a civilizing mission for this virtue: "De l'influence sur la Pitié de la distance, du temps et du lieu" ["On the Influence of Distance, Time, and Place on Pity"].[1] His reflections on pity were as much those of a philosopher as of an official pedagogue—he had been inspector-general of secondary education since 1864. The essay's problematization and approach were guided by concerns with the place of pity in social progress and solidarity.

More specifically, Bouillier wished to consider—as do students of pity today—whether and why pity diminishes in intensity and efficacy across historical time and social and geographic space.[2] Bouillier believed that all individuals have a limited horizon of moral concern yet argued for the desirability of furthering pity's reach. Indeed, he claimed that evidence of the cultivation of pity is a hallmark of civilized progress and compensation for diminishing religious faith; his ideas thus essayed a formulation of guiding emotives.[3]

Bouillier clearly did not wish to indulge the pathetic fallacy, since he began by arguing that, in the best of all possible worlds, pity would play a lesser role in human affairs than joy: "According to Rousseau and Schopenhaeur, the human heart only sympathizes with misfortunes, and not the successes, of others.... In our opinion, human nature is better than that...it is true that this sympathetic sentiment is weaker than the corresponding sentiment of pity, or even that it is often stifled by the jealousy that often gets in the way; but it is not any less natural to the human heart."[4] But if pity is more contagious than happiness, this is a reflection, albeit regrettable, of the intractability of worldly woes—the pathetic is more human than the euphoric. Bouillier reckons that if suffering there must be, then the more pity, the better for society.

Bouillier claimed peremptorily that pity is a causally irreducible and metaphysically *a priori* sentiment, focusing instead on its reach and efficacy. He first posited a classic law of inverse proportion: "We must insist on the law of diminution to which sympathy and pity are subjected as their objects recede from us…. how much of our hearts and our pity are left on the side of the road, so to speak, when the tragic or poignant detail happens beyond our borders!"[5] Central to both pity and sympathy is the imagination, which, he held, can counteract the attenuation that distance effects on pity:

The intervention of the mind should play a much greater part when pity has to take in woes that are out of sight, and the unfortunate who are far from us. Here in effect it is necessary that we should have read or heard more or less dramatic accounts, that more or less vivid pictures should form in our minds…. Rousseau said the same: "one becomes sensitive only when their imagination moves and leads them out of themselves."[6]

Bouillier made pity dependent on representational capacities, acknowledging the role of literature and the arts as educators of sentiment (a cherished contemporary theme). Bouillier's anodyne paraphrase of Rousseau was thus not without deeper significance. Like Fouillée, Bouillier aimed to base a pro-pity sentimentalism in the mind—he, too, was a cognitivist. Pity, he wished to persuade, is about intelligence and imagination more than "heart" or "nature"—against the easy association of it with natural man or inherent innocence, Bouillier advanced a civilizing mission, an imperialism of pity, as it were: "With each new means of communication discovered in the world, pity penetrates further afield; new horizons are uncovered for international benevolence…. Let us not forget a not inconsiderable influence, for example, that of the press, which augments the others, which diffuses and proliferates them, which is throughout the entire world the greatest vehicle for the sentiment of pity."[7]

Bouillier's pity was resolutely anti-Rousseauian in its acceptance of mass culture and social complexity. Unafraid of the propaganda of feelings, with its pitfalls of potential inauthentic manipulation and dissemination of the pathetic fallacy, Bouillier embraced the modern possibilities of print media: "Just as it widens its reach ever farther, pity becomes ever more inventive and ingenious in enlarging its capacities and makes even the most lukewarm and least generous converge with its aims. It takes advantage of all means of publicity, advertisements, large posters in every color, the hundred voices of the press, the eloquent appeals daily repeated on behalf of victims."[8] Whereas others might distrust the heteronymous motives in furtherance of pity, Bouillier waxes indulgent: "Even if lacking charity and virtue, there is still in all these various forms of benevolence a laudable part attributable to the noble and touching sentiment of pity, whose augmentation is of great importance for the good of society. Moreover, when we consider the goal to be attained, too much severity would be out of place."[9] Bouillier hews to a consequentialist view of pity, whereby he commends this virtue more for its effect on social welfare than as integral to individualistic ethics. Indeed, in forging an imagined community of the morally concerned, the former comprises the multitudinous benefits of the latter.

Bouillier contributed to the sentimentalist correction of the Rousseauian bias against the alliance of sentiment with civilization. Like the other figures and tropes from the past that were revived as references by *fin-de-siècle* sentimentalism, Rousseau's seminal views on pity were reiterated for the sake of a generous modification. Bouillier's sweepingly comprehensive commitment to a progressing pity led him to rectify Rousseau and then to conclude with a call for inculcating pity. His steadfastness in defending the possibilities of moral progress was another offshoot of the rendezvous with the reason-sentiment divide: the question of moral advancement had been key to the Enlightenment; it was a pole around which the thought of Kant and Condorcet was oriented.[10]

Bouillier risked confusing his issues, emptying out the precise contents of pity while seeming to detect it everywhere at work behind headlines and appeals, and mistaking his own tolerance of all displays of solicitude for a diagnosis of its spread. But what Bouillier's account lacked in psychological and terminological precision (unlike most of our other figures, e.g., he elided the difference between pity and sympathy, despite his title) was made up for by more careful consideration of the social dimensions of pity's cultivation—by an eye for form if not substance. Bouillier ecumenically accepted all methods for disseminating pity: "Pity, increasingly enlarged in our hearts by education, practices, and examples, and also faced with less distress soliciting it in every direction and dividing its attention, will direct itself of its own accord, at the first entreaty and without any other incentive or allure, to relieve every suffering. But as long as this progress has yet to occur, at least to the degree we have indicated, we cannot condemn the recourse to other, less pure and disinterested, motives."[11] Even when habilitated by other motives, pity was still praiseworthy.

Bouillier's intention in positing this contrast was to call for a pedagogical pity that would work by reflection rather than contagion. The question of emotional contagion had vexed the burgeoning sentimentalism of the *fin-de-siècle*—behold the archly aphoristic formulation of LeBon: "All manifestations of psychic life can be contagious but it is the emotions in particular which propagate themselves in this manner. Contagious ideas are the syntheses of affective elements."[12] Bouillier wanted to promote a version of pity not freighted with the overtones of "contagion." Nor did he fear that "interestedness"—a depreciatory term left over from the Cousinian lexicon—would vitiate pity; pity is of a piece and will be spread further afield and across time, with increasing efficacy. Suffering is its constant; education and modernization are its variables. Bouillier's emphasis on a sentimental education reflected the pedagomania of the late nineteenth century and targeted implicitly the dualisms we encountered earlier—the sentiment-reason rift and the Cartesian divide between the rational and thus educable, and the irrational. By bringing pity across these gulfs, Bouillier made it as universal and as inculcable as the rational faculties:

Increase the sentiment of pity for all that suffers around us, in combating that double law of decrease that we have pointed out, extend it progressively to all of humanity, keep from that very delicate flower anything that could harm or dry it out—therein lies one of the great duties of teachers, families, and even rulers. We cannot exaggerate the place we should give to the cultivation of this exquisite sentiment and to the mental faculties necessary to its development. La Fontaine said about children: "That age is without pity." That is true only of poorly educated youth. In effect, as soon as children can conceive of suffering through experience and learning, they become naturally sympathetic and pitying.[13]

Bouillier here played on all the keys used to compose the full scale of pro-pity themes: sentiment as moral, linked to duty; family, government, and, especially, schools, indissociably participating in the effective germination of pity; an imagined communal solidarity flowing from pity; lastly and repetitively, the centrality of pedagogy in conquering those imaginative distances and lapses of times that are nemeses of pity.

Bouillier's conclusion is a plea both disabused and passionate:

Pity once had an altar consecrated to it in Athens, in the heart of the city. It is necessary that it have one in all of our hearts. That in lieu of superior sentiments, such as those of duty, religion, and charity, more or less weakened, pity at least soften further the hearts and comportment of all. That all may have pity, even of the stranger or foreigner in our midst, that each of us, even in the midst of revolutions and public catastrophes, retain pity for each other. Finally, may pity preserve us from the worst excesses; that, lacking all else, it be a safeguard, a supreme resource of humanity and of civilization during the crises that may confront us![14]

This is a prayer for pity perched between hope and despair, a peroration that limns as many dangers and discloses as many values to which pity is central as Freud's *Civilization and Its Discontents* with its equivalent summoning of Eros. Like Freud, Bouillier was looking for a safeguard against nihilism; was on the side of civilization against anarchy, order against revolution (the Revolution); believed in the meliorist power of education. Like Freud, he was imbued with a metacultural perspective that looked to historical development, to evolution and decline, to crisis and renewal, as thematic guides. His Pity differed from Freud's Eros in that it was not exclusively secular—even though the example he offered was Athens's altar to pity (a not negligible touch in a classicist educational milieu that enjoyed the accents of Greco-Roman antiquity).[15]

Bouillier's article was an emotive exercise in metanarrative appeal, beseeching the reading and teaching elites to instill a pity that would guarantee civilizing progress, vouch for the social order in a complexifying society, and be a token of community imagined and thus actualized—and, not least, a post-Commune echo of the Revolutionary-era debate on the character of pity as a unifying virtue for the body politic: "that each of us, even in the midst of revolutions and public catastrophes, retain pity for each other."[16]

In a work published a few years later, Bouillier returned to a similar theme in discussing the legitimacy of practicing history as a form of measurement of, and judgment on, moral progress. A historian is above all a moralist, he claimed, and like all moralists must assess epochs and cultures on a scale of indulgence and severity, with pity and censure as the contrasting criteria. The basis for a historian's judgment must be an intuition of the subjects' capacity for reasoned self-control: "If he imagines the hard and terrible living conditions of savages and barbarians, perhaps he will be more prone to pity than to another sentiment regarding these distant and wretched ancestors, despite all their savagery."[17] Bouillier then argues that progress obtains when societies *en masse* opt for pity over cruelty: "But from the sixteenth to the seventeenth centuries a change occurred in hearts and minds; there was less belief in evil spells and more pity for the witches which some parliaments still burned at the stake."[18] This is a line of reasoning that Bouillier wields to whack the Revolution's apologists over the head: "It has often been remarked that, on the contrary, never was that word sensibility more lavished, almost like a deceptive lure, than on the eve of the most bloody and pitiless executions of the Revolution."[19] For Bouillier, pity has historical and evaluative salience.

Bouillier condescends when he recommended the same pity-centered judgment for arbitrating contemporary social problems, in what amounts to a covert equation of the marginalized in his society with earlier "barbarians." Suicides especially deserve pity: "I have pointed out elsewhere—without wishing to completely absolve them—that of all those whom morality condemns, the wretches who kill themselves are deserving above all others of pity. If you imagine the interior of such a distressed soul, your pity will be so great that it will win out over the rigorous judgments of religion and morality."[20] Since Bouillier here invoked a pity that assumes a difference in kind between judge and judged, we are perhaps authorized in criticizing him for not consistently upholding his vision of an imagined community sentimentally constituted—not to mention the psychological naïveté about the cause of suicide, later rectified by Durkheim. His logic also renders impossible a social and moral ideal whereby universal pity obviates the very problems that here confirm the superiority of a few in their opportunity to display sentimental virtue. Indeed, if for Bouillier moral progress is possible, if pity is both an evaluative mode and metaphor for such progress, the basic social and metaphysical data of morality are intractable: "you will never eradicate from this supposed earthly paradise the greatest woe, the toughest hardship—death."[21] Here is Bouillier's Freudian Thanatos matching the correspondingly piteous Eros; here is his Schopenhauerian quietism in search of tender surcease—a deathly fiction bordering on social passivity. Yet Bouillier renders great intellectual service in placing pity next to questions of justice, and he adumbrates something like the "democratization of inner life" that presupposes, and results from, pity.

Bouillier confronted directly the Rousseauian legacy that had to be superannuated in order to reverse the correlation between civilization and "natural" humanity, for if pity was a sign of complexification and civilization, then indeed Rousseau had to have gotten things backward; and so a look at "primitive" societies, facilitated by a disciplinary dovetailing with the nascent anthropological investigations, formed part of the required rendezvous with pity.

Julien Pioger also placed pity squarely on the side of civilization, as a way of classifying "developed" or "primitive" societies. In a discussion of the social basis of morality, he, too, assumed social complexity as prior to sentiment: "Whether the example is *pity* (Schopenhauer), sympathy (Adam Smith), or self-interest, we would say that our poor 'fuegano' seems very little capable of conjuring up the general idea of *pity*, sympathy, or self-interest."[22] Doubtlessly, Pioger had learned about the natives of Tierra del Fuego from the anthropological literature; equally doubtless is Pioger's inversion of Rousseau, wherein he posits the idea of pity as capable of revelation only to a society whose complexity precedes its discernment and expression. There is no "natural" pity apart from civilization.

Another contributor to the pro-pity case on civilization was Ludovic Carrau (1842–1889), a moral philosopher influenced both by Kantian idealism and sentimentalism.[23] Carrau tackled the Rousseauian question by arguing that pity did exist in "primitive" societies, but only in a potential state:

We believe we have more than sufficiently demonstrated that in primitives, the seeds of all the main virtues are to be found in a position of instinctive predisposition. It is doubtful, of course, whether that constitutes true morality. However, there is something here that is more than merely sensatory. When a savage reacts to an impulse of pity, of charity, do you think that he is not aware of thereby behaving better than if he gave in to egoistic or vengeful impulses?[24]

"Savages" favor pity over egoism; they, too, are potential sentimentalists. They must be, because even if they do not display "proprement la moralité," the civilizing process could never come about if it were not based on a piteous *telos* leading the less socialized toward complexity and morality: "Doubtlessly it cannot be repeated enough that primitive humans, savages, have only a very vague awareness of this ideal and this duty; but they are not wholly lacking in them. Otherwise, the subsequent progress of human morality, which entails the ever-growing action of intellect and reason, would remain unintelligible."[25] For Carrau, as for the contemporaneous proponents of pity, intelligence and reason fertilize the germs of a sentimental morality that, given the right concatenation of conditions, leads to social progress—cognition is intellectual; sentiments are cognitive; ergo, society is both a mental and sentimental phenomenon.

Carrau unambiguously claimed that what drives an other-directed, pro-pity morality forward is this civilizing imperative. Moreover, he addressed the nominalist debate about the relationship between sentiments and their designation so as to rebuff any challenge to his ascription of feelings to people who may lack the capacity to name them: "Generosity, pity, charity are not any the more absent from the human heart.... And it is relevant here to point out the weakness of the argument that is made of the absence of certain words in primitive idiom.... Just because a language is still too simple to set down abstractions such as moral precepts for conduct does not mean that the sentiments manifested by this or that action are any the more unknown to the hearts of the humans who speak it." [26] The lack of a vocabulary corresponding to imputed sentiments becomes yet another argument on behalf of the role of intelligence in conveying ethical sentiments ever upward, toward civilization.

Gabriel Tarde (1843–1904), a member of the ASMP and a social philosopher known subsequently as Durkheim's lesser foil,[27] elaborated for complex societies the links that these imperial observers of the progress of pity wished to forge upon "primitive" peoples. Tarde's philosophical social-science was predicated on an equation between social complexity, synonymous with progress and order, and sentimental refinement: "the clearest and plainest moral progress consists of the magnification of the heart as it matches the numerical increase in society."[28] The "social logic of sentiments" as conceived by Tarde is such that it is foremost a sentimental logic of society.

This logic is premised on a developmental scheme whereby the hardness of simple societies evolves through contact and complexity into the tenderness of civilized nations. In another reversal of the Rousseauian paradigm, Tarde envisions contact guiding socialization, which leads to affective contagion and imitation, which leads to pity and sympathy, leading ultimately to progress and civilized unity: "Let us see here the *dialectic* of social logic.... In incessantly increasing the ratio of sympathetic sentiments at the expense of the antipathic ones that are related to it, the result is the *continual enlargement of the social group, in extent and depth.*"[29] If compensation and contagion are key terms for Tarde as for Bouillier, Tarde sees social density as leading to sentimental intricacy through the richness and quantity of pro-social feelings: "All the older affective sentiments...remain despite their changes in outward appearance...while others have emerged—links of professional camaraderie; feudal or monarchical loyalty; democratic 'fraternity;' humanitarian pity. An *addition* of affective sentiments has arisen in the course of the heart's evolution."[30]

Is pity truly like Freud's Eros, supposedly holding society together, and can it explain diachronic changes in the social order? There was a certain philosophical milieu, that of Bouillier, Tarde, Carrau, and Pioger, that clearly shared an approach inclining them to think so: pity released people, permitting them to escape the crushing gravity of cultural and solipsistic claustralness. This milieu shared a fear and a hope: a fear that industrializing societies, with their estrangement from smaller, more intimate, and highly integrated social groupings to broader, more distant, more complex networks of relationships would lead humans to become cold, calculating, and dehumanized; a hope that sentiments could be canalized into the civilizing process. For them, moral progress and duty would be threatened by modernization unless sustained by pro-social sentiments.

These authors promoted pity as a humanizing virtue—both for civilized and "primitive" societies. But in prescribing pity, they did not delve deeply into its constituent regions, whether psychological or physiological. They deemed it both as a self-evidently cognitive and a contagious sentiment. Not so with the pioneers of synthetic psychology and empirical sociology, for whom pity had first to be taken apart, understood, and described before it could be prescribed.

NOTES

1. Elected to the ASMP on December 11, 1872, François-Cyrille ("Françisque") Bouillier began his pedagogical career as professor in Lyon, where he became president of the *Académie impériale* in 1856. Subsequently he became rector of the University of Clermont in 1864. Nominated to the *Conseil d'instruction publique* in 1864, he became director of the *École Normale* in 1867.

2. The subject unites ancient and recent reflections on pity: "Aristotle held that danger evokes fear if you or someone very close to you is endangered and that it evokes pity if the person at risk is not so close but still close enough. We would extend this to hold that we

typically feel only sadness, not fear or pity, for those who are very far from us" (Michael Stocker and Elizabeth Hegeman, *Valuing Emotions*, Cambridge Studies in Philosophy [Cambridge: Cambridge UP, 1996], 121).

3. The work of Max Weber, Norbert Elias—and even Gustave LeBon—could be usefully juxtaposed to Bouillier's argument on this latter point. I use the term "emotives" in the sense suggested by Reddy in *The Navigation of Feeling*.

4. ["Selon Rousseau et Schopenhauer, il n'y aurait de sympathie dans le coeur humain que pour les malheurs, et non pour les prosperités d'autrui....À notre avis, la nature humaine vaut mieux que cela...il est vrai que ce sentiment sympathique est plus faible que le sentiment correspondant de la pitié, ou qu'il est même étouffé par l'envie qui trop souvent vient à la traverse; mais il n'en est pas moins tout aussi naturel au coeur de l'homme."] Françisque Bouillier, "De l'influence sur la Pitié de la distance, du temps et du lieu," *Académie des sciences morales et politiques: séances et travaux* 118 (1882), 58.

5. ["Insistons sur cette loi de décroissance à laquelle sont soumises la sympathie et la pitié, à mesure que leurs objets reculent loin de nous....Combien plus de notre coeur et de notre pitié ne restera-t-il pas en route, pour ainsi dire, si le fait tragique ou émouvant a eu lieu hors de la frontière."] Bouillier, 63, 66.

6. ["Bien plus grande encore doit être cette part de l'intervention de l'esprit, quand la pitié s'étend à des maux qui sont hors de nos yeux, et à des malheureux qui sont loin de nous. Ici en effet il est nécessaire que nous en ayons lu ou entendu des récits plus ou moins dramatiques, que de peintures plus ou moins vives s'en forment dans notre esprit....Rousseau a dit de même: 'nul ne devient sensible que quand son imagination l'anime et le transporte hors de lui.'"] Bouillier, 60–62. We should note the similarities between Bouillier's views here and those of Jacques Derrida, who also comments on Rousseau's linking of pity and imagination. (*Of Grammatologie*, Gayatri Chakravorty-Spivak, trans. [Baltimore and London: Johns Hopkins UP, 1976.] See my Conclusion.

7. ["A chaque voie nouvelle de communication ouverte dans le monde, la sympathie pénètre plus avant; des horizons nouveaux s'ouvrent à la bienfaisance internationale....N'oublions pas une influence non moins considérable, celle de la presse, qui s'ajoute à toutes les autres, qui les propage et les multiplie, qui est dans le monde entière le grand véhicule des sentiments de sympathie et de pitié."] Bouillier, "De l'influence sur la Pitié," 50.

8. ["De même qu'elle s'étend de plus en plus au loin, la pitié devient aussi de plus en plus inventive et ingénieuse pour augmenter ses ressources et faire concourir à son oeuvre, par divers attraits, même les tièdes et les moins généreux. Elle met en oeuvre tous les moyens de publicité, les annonces, les grandes affiches de toutes les couleurs, les cent voix de la presse, les appels éloquents et chaque jour répétés en faveur des victimes à secourir."] Bouillier, 73. In their investigation of "Fear-Arousing and Empathy-Arousing Appeals to Help: The Pathos of Persuasion," Shelton and Rogers would side with Bouillier on mass communication's potential for cultivating social sentiments: "If our theories of attitude change are to apply to mass media as well as face-to-face communication, then our messages must frequently appeal for help for the unseen and unknown others in the same plight" (*Journal of Applied Social Psychology* 11:4 [1981], 376).

9. ["Cependant, à défaut de charité et de vertu, il y a, dans toutes les formes variées de la bienfaisance, une part louable à faire à ce sentiment si noble et si touchant de la sympathie et de la pitié dont les développements sont de si grande importance pour le bien de la société. Quand d'ailleurs on considère la fin à atteindre, trop de sévérité ne serait pas à sa place."] Bouillier, "De l'influence sur la Pitié," 75.

10. Kant had asked: "is the human race in constant progress?" Bouillier devoted his first book to outlining an answer: "Our goal is to determine whether virtue increases in the world,

like the arts and sciences, like civilization itself; or whether it decreases, as is the opinion of certain disgruntled souls; or, finally, whether it remains at a standstill, neither advancing nor receding, despite differences in time and mores." ["Notre but est de rechercher si la vertu va en croissant dans le monde, comme les sciences et les arts, comme la civilisation elle-même; ou si elle va en diminuant, selon le sentiment de quelques esprits chagrins, ou enfin si elle demeure immobile, sans avancer ni reculer, malgré toute la différence des temps et des moeurs."] In Bouillier, *De la querelle des anciens et des modernes en morale* (Paris: Académie des sciences morales et politiques, 1869), 6. His subsequent writings on pity and history constituted his programmatic answers. For more on this broad question and more specifically on its relation to sentimentalism at the turn of the eighteenth century, see Joan Dejean, *Ancients against Moderns: Culture Wars and the Making of a Fin-de-Siècle* (Chicago: U of Chicago P, 1997).

11. ["La pitié, de plus en plus développée dans les coeurs, par l'éducation, par les moeurs, par les exemples, et aussi en face de moins de misères qui la sollicitent dans tous les sens et l'obligent à se partager, se portera d'elle-même et toute seule, au premier appel, sans nulle autre mobile ou attrait, au-devant de toutes les souffrances à soulager. Mais tant que ce progrès n'aura pas eu lieu, on ne saurait condamner, au moins dans la mesure que nous avons dite, le recours à des mobiles auxiliaires, moins pur et moins désintéressés."] Bouillier, "De l'influence sur la Pitié," 77.

12. Gustave LeBon, *Opinions and Beliefs*, in *The Man and His Works*, 207.

13. ["Accroître le sentiment de la pitié pour tout ce qui souffre autour de nous, en réagissant contre cette double loi de décroissance que nous avons signalée, l'étendre progressivement jusqu'à l'humanité tout entière, écarter de cette fleur si délicate ce qui peut la blesser et la dessécher, voilà un des grands devoirs des maîtres, de la famille et même des gouvernants. On ne saurait faire dans l'éducation une part trop grande à la culture de ce sentiment exquis et aux facultés de l'esprit nécessaires à son développement. La Fontaine a dit en parlant des enfants: 'Cet âge est sans pitié.' Cela n'est vrai que de l'enfance mal élevée. Sitôt en effet, qu'il a pu se faire une idée de la souffrance par sa propre expérience, l'enfant est naturellement sympathique et pitoyable."] Bouillier, "De l'influence sur la Pitié," 78.

14. ["La pitié avait autrefois à Athènes un autel au milieu de la ville; il faudrait qu'elle en eût un dans tout les coeurs. Qu'à défaut des sentiments supérieurs de devoir, de religion, de charité, plus ou moins affaiblis, la pitié du moins adoucisse encore davantage les moeurs et le coeurs de tous! Que tous aient pitié, même de l'étranger, que tous, même au milieu des révolutions et des commotions publiques gardent la pitié les uns pour les autres! Que la pitié enfin nous préserve des derniers excès, et qu'à défaut de tout le reste, elle soit une sauvegarde, une ressource suprême de l'humanité et de la civilisation dans les crises que nous pouvons avoir à traverser."] Bouillier, 79.

15. Bouillier was right—"Pity" had an altar at Athens late in the fifth century B.C.E. See John Travlos, *Pictorial Dictionary of Athens* (New York: Praeger, 1971): "The Altar of the Twelve Gods was considered the central point from which road distances were measured....This altar also served as a place of asylum and probably because the protection of suppliants was such an essential part of the cult in this shrine from the 5th century B.C.E. onward, the goddess Pity came to be worshipped there; she joined the Twelve Gods as the Thirteenth and a special altar to her was set up in the enclosure. In time the name Altar of Pity came to apply to the whole shrine" (458). In "The Altar of Pity in the Athenian Agora," Homer A. Thompson writes: "by the time of Statius and of Pausanias the Altar of the Twelve Gods had been moved elsewhere leaving the sanctuary to Pity alone" (*Hesperia* 21 [1952], 49, 51). As to the decoration and iconography of the Altar, Thompson ventures that four extant panels depicting Orpheus and Eurydice, Medea and her daughters, Theseus and

Perithoos, and Heracles in the garden of the Hesperides were part of the original décor: "It is time now to consider whether the themes of the four reliefs can be brought into relation with what we know of the Athenian conception of Pity. That conception was comparatively simple and close to our own: compassion inspired by the misfortunes common to human life, and especially toward strangers in distress. One aspect of the general conception is stressed repeatedly by the literary sources, viz. the pity inspired by a grievous situation that has come about through a reversal of fortune" (65, 69). [Thompson dates the Altar to 420–410 B.C.E]. There are classical Greek and Roman sources on the Altar of Pity with which the French of Bouillier's time would have been acquainted. Pausanias wrote of it in his *Description of Greece* (Book I: 17, 1), Wilt S. Jones, trans. (Cambridge, MA: Harvard UP, 1959), 81. The diffusion of Pausanias in France, where his works were first translated in 1731 and then again in 1814, is the subject of the essay by Olivier Gengler, "Les traductions françaises de Pausanias," *Les Études classiques* 67:1 (1999), 63–70. Bouillier would have been familiar not only with Pausanias but with Statius's *Thebaïs*. Other sources that would have been known to Bouillier and that inflected accounts of classical antecedents of the pro-pity tradition, were Philostratus, *Letter 39* (70), "To a Woman:" "Furthermore, the Athenians welcomed Demeter when she was in exile, and Dionysius when he was shifting his abode, and the sons of Heracles when they were wandering about; it was at that time that the Athenians also set up the Altar of Compassion (*eleos*), as a thirteenth god, to whom they poured libations, not of wine and milk, but of tears and of respect for suppliants. Do you also erect this altar, and show pity on a man who is in distress, so that I may not be twice exiled, both deprived of my country and foiled of my love for you; for, if you take pity, I am forthwith restored" (*The Letters of Alciphron, Aelian, and Philostratus*, Allen Rogers Benner and Francis H. Fobes, trans. [Cambridge, MA: Harvard UP, 1949], 497–99); Diodorus of Sicily (mentioned by Thompson, "The Altar of Pity in the Athenian Agora"), in *Complete Works*, vol. 5, Book 13: 22, C. H. Oldfather, trans. (Cambridge, MA: Harvard UP, 1950), 185; Apollodorus, *The Library*, Book 2: 8, 1, Michael Simpson, trans. (Amherst: U of Massachusetts P, 1971).

16. It is here that we can call Bouillier's association of pity and civilization truly "conservative" in the political sense. David Denby, in *Sentimental Narrative and the Social Order in France, 1760–1820*, writes of the "reassuring and nostalgic picture of an organic society in which pity neutralizes and renders acceptable a rigid hierarchy."

17. ["S'il se représente les dures, les terribles conditions d'existence des sauvages et des barbares, peut-être sera-t-il plus porté à la pitié qu'à tout autre sentiment envers ces lointains et misérables ancêtres, malgré tout leur barbarie."] Bouillier, *Nouvelles études familières de psychologie et de morale* (Paris: Hachette, 1887), 24.

18. ["Mais, du seizième au dix-septième siècles, un changement s'est fait dans les esprits et dans les moeurs; on a moins foi aux maléfices et l'on prend en pitié les sorciers que quelques parlements font encore brûler."] Bouillier, *Nouvelles études*, 33.

19. ["Jamais, au contraire, on l'a souvent remarqué, ce mot de sensibilité, comme un appât trompeur, n'avait été plus prodiguée qu'à la veille des plus sanglantes, des plus impitoyables exécutions de la Révolution."] Bouillier, *Nouvelles études*, 34. This issue, of course, harks back to Brissot, Robespierre, and De Staël and forward to Hannah Arendt. See the works of Reddy and Denby.

20. ["Entre tous ceux que la morale condamne, et sans vouloir les absoudre, j'ai déjà fait voir ailleurs combien les malheureux qui se tuent sont dignes entre tous de pitié. Représentez-vous l'intérieur de cette âme désolée, et votre pitié sera si grande qu'elle l'emportera peut-être sur les jugements les plus rigoreux de la religion et de la morale."] Bouillier, *Nouvelles études*, 327–28.

21. ["vous ne pourrez jamais bannir de ce prétendue paradis sur terre la plus grande des

misères, la plus dure des épreuves, celle de la mort."] Bouillier, *De la Conscience en psychologie et en morale* (Paris: Germer-Baillière, 1872), 154.

22. ["Que si on veut nous donner comme explication la *pitié* (Schopenhauer), la sympathie (Adam Smith), ou l'intérêt, nous répondrons que le cerveau de nôtre pauvre Fuégien nous semble bien peu susceptible de conçevoir l'idée générale de *pitié*, sympathie ou d'intérêt"]. Julien Pioger, "Origines et conditions sociales de la moralité," *Revue philosophique de la France et de l'étranger* 37 (January–June 1894): 634–56.

23. For biographical and career information on Victor-Marie-Joseph-Ludovic Carrau, who taught at the University of Besançon from 1870 to 1881 and at the Sorbonne from 1881 to 1888, see AN, AJ16/1000 and F17/20343. His thesis was an *Exposition critique des théories des passions chez Descartes, Malebranche, et Spinoza.*

24. ["Nous croyons avoir surabondamment établi qu'en eux [primitives] se trouvent, à l'état de disposition instinctives, les germes des principales vertus. On peut douter, il est vrai, si c'est là proprement la moralité....Cependant il y a là autre chose que de la pure sensibilité. Quand le sauvage obéit à un mouvement de pitié, de charité, pense-t-on qu'il n'ait pas quelque conscience de mieux faire que s'il cédait à l'impulsion de l'égoisme ou de la vengeance?"] Ludovic Carrau, *La Conscience psychologique et morale dans l'individu et dans l'histoire* (Paris: Perrin, 1887), 288–89.

25. ["Sans doute, et l'on ne peut trop le répéter, l'homme primitive, le sauvage n'ont qu'une conscience très vague de cet idéal et de cette obligation; mais elle ne saurait leur faire entièrement défaut; autrement, les progrès futures de la moralité humaine, qui implique l'action toujours croissante de l'intelligence et de la raison, resteraient éternellement incompréhensibles."] Carrau, "La Moralité chez les sauvages," *La Revue politique et littéraire* 2:1 (July 3, 1880), 33.

26. ["La générosité, la pitié, la charité ne sont pas davantage absentes du coeur des hommes....Et à ce propos il ne sera pas inutile de signaler la faiblesse de l'argument que l'on tire de l'absence de certains mots dans les idiomes sauvages....De ce qu'une langue est trop rudimentaire encore pour traduire des abstractions, comme les qualités morales de la conduite, ne s'ensuit-il que les sentiments qui se manifestent par telles ou telles actions soient nécessairement étrangers au coeur des hommes qui la parlent."] Carrau, "La Moralité chez les sauvages," 32.

27. On the Durkheim-Tarde debates concerning the relationship of sociology and philosophy, see LaCapra, *Émile Durkheim*, 54–55; Brooks, *The Eclectic Legacy*, who remarks: "But Durkheim's most formidable rival was Tarde. As we have seen, many of Durkheim's positions were either formulated or articulated in opposition to Tarde. Durkheim's insistence on purely sociological explanations opposed Tarde's methodological individualism and psychologism" (229). On Tarde's views on sexuality and the duel, see Nye, *Masculinity and Male Codes of Honor in Modern France*, 113, 172, 184–85.

28. ["le plus clair et le plus net du progrès moral a consisté dans l'élargissement du coeur, parallèle à l'accroissement numérique des sociétaires."] Tarde, "La Logique sociale des sentiments," *Revue philosophique de la France et de l'étranger* 36 (July–December 1893), 563.

29. ["Voyons quelle est ici la *dialectique* de la logique sociale....En faisant grandir sans cesse la proportion des sentiments sympathiques aux dépens des sentiments antipathiques qui leur sont liés, [résulte] *l'agrandissement continuel du groupe social en étendue et en profondeur.*"] Tarde, 567. Tarde's emphasis on imitation was as much a key word for him as contagion. See especially "Extra-Logical Laws of Imitation," in *On Communication and Social Influence: Selected Papers*, Terry N. Clark, ed. and intro. (Chicago: U of Chicago P, 1969).

30. ["Tous les anciens sentiments affectueux...subsistent en somme malgré des

changements de forme...et d'autres ont apparu, liens de camaradérie professionnelle, fidélité féodale ou monarchique, 'fraternité' démocratique, pitié humanitaire. Il y a eu *addition* de sentiments affectueux, au cours de l'évolution du Coeur."] Tarde, "La logique sociale des sentiments," 571. On Tarde's idea of "moral atavism," see Nye, *Masculinity and Codes of Honor*, 218.

Chapter 3: Between Social Psychology and Pedagogy

AFFECTIVE PSYCHOLOGY

Affective logic: Until now, psychologists recognized only rational logic. They have begun to add affective logic, or that of feelings, which is absolutely distinct from rational logic.... Affective logic directs most of our actions...The force of certain sentiments can become such that not only intelligence but also the most evident self-interests of the individual remain without influence.[1]

Jean Bourdeau coined the revived sentimentalism "affective philosophy." Given the disciplinary contestation in *fin-de-siècle* France, especially between philosophy and the emergent social (or human) sciences, newer methodologies were bound to claim the "affective" in philosophy. The burgeoning field of psychology especially disputed the hegemonic entitlement of academic philosophy to promote or define pity; sentimentalism could be seen as inviting an approach that was exactly what the "new" moral psychology offered in contradistinction to official philosophy. Moral psychology in the *fin-de-siècle* was at the crossroads of long-standing obsessions with ethics and the newfangled promise of experimentalism. Théodule Ribot (1839–1916) saw himself as a pioneering psychologist of morality, one who could help tether a cognitive theory of sentiment to a new discipline.

Ribot first taught at Laval from 1872 until 1882 and then at the Sorbonne from 1885 to 1888 and at the Collège de France from 1888 until his retirement in 1901.[2] Elected in 1899 to the ASMP's philosophy section, he was as well placed as anyone to navigate the rough waters between the perennial metaphysics and the newer psychology. His intellectual attitude broke free from the mold of much *juste-milieu* philosophy—he was receptive to ideas from abroad, to the sciences, and to undercurrents in French thought. He was a devoté of Schopenhauer, Nietzsche, and Tolstoy and generated articles on all three during his tenure as director of the *Revue philosophique* from 1888 to 1895; he was among the first in France to consecrate a book-length critical study to Schopenhauer, in 1874, thereby inaugurating the confrontation with the German that was to be a touchstone for reflections on pity.[3] Indeed, Ribot heeded intellectual developments in Germany, especially those in psychology, to which he devoted a book in 1879, *La Psychologie allemande contemporaine* (*Contemporary German Psychology*).[4] Ribot also opened the pages of the *Revue philosophique* to nontraditional interests by publishing work from psychologists, neurologists, and medical physiologists.[5]

In his courses at the Collège de France,[6] of which his original lecture notes are conserved as manuscripts at both the Bibliothèque Nationale de France and the Bibliothèque de l'Institut de France, Ribot revealed to his students that his ambition in studying sentiments was to poach the territory of traditional ethics: "sentiments have for a long time been treated under a purely philosophical method; some have carried on as *moralists*, others as *metaphysicians*...for me the study of sentiments is the *most material* part of psychology."[7] This was a heretical pronouncement: sentiments, as distinct from passions or emotions, were always approached as an abstract, never as a material phenomenon. Moreover, Ribot alighted on a way to revivify approaches to moral sentiments by latching them to an overarching paradigm of willpower and proposing a datum of study that would be seen as objective: pain. All those who had accorded the validity and intersubjectivity of socializing sentiments had begged fundamental epistemological questions: *how* does pity arise within the subject, and what binds it to consciousness? Ribot hoped to counter the old-fashioned moralists by proposing preliminary semantical and methodological clarifications: pro-social sentiments are first individual rather than *apriori*, supraindividual. Pain is primordial among the individual sensations; it is the quintessential if heretofore ignored datum of the moral realm:

The similarity between physical and moral pain will be our theme. On this question, the bibliography is completely useless: everything remains to be done. This is not because little has been written on it; but rather that the authors were moralists or theologians, optimists or pessimists, all concerned with proving and justifying the value of pain, to adjudicate between pleasure and pain on this earth, etc.—all of which are questions beyond our competence. Nobody, on the other hand, has concerned himself with the *nature* of moral pain—it is this psychological study which we will attempt.[8]

For Ribot pain is divisible into two representative components: "purely representational pains can be classified into two large groups: 1. egoistic pain; 2. sympathetic or altruistic pains."[9] That is, some pains draw us back inside ourselves; others lead us outward, to the world of persons and of things. Like the moralists he overtly criticized, Ribot gave precedence, both in interest and in value, to "sympathetic" or "altruistic" pain:

With sympathetic or altruistic pains, the difficulties are greater, and reductionism thornier. All these pains can be reduced to sympathy (a collective term comprising the totality of nonegoistic pains). The question would then be whether sympathy, in its basic form, can be reduced to purely physical states. I would remark to you here that the problem of sympathy is a very big question.[10]

It is precisely those social dimensions Ribot had averted in order to plumb individual subjectivity that render sympathy knottier. Ribot's argument here partly contradicts his earlier hedonistic epistemology and is in direct Humean filiation: "when animals live together, there is sympathy among them. And certainly, in addition to their individual conscience, there is a social conscience.... The power of the intellect is at every instant dependent on sentiment; a great intelligence is in general propped up by a great passion. It is not reason that uses passion, but passion which makes use of reason to reach its ends."[11] Not only did Ribot revisit the Kant-Hume reason-sentiment divide, but he also helped prop up embryonic efforts to substantiate collective (mass) psychology. With his emphasis on an intersubjective "social conscience," Ribot's language and conclusion resembled Durkheim's *conscience collective*.[12] In Ribot's version, sociability is "sympathy"'s space, and contagion is the precursor of a moral conscience. Intelligence is implicated in the amplification of sentiment. Reason is the capstone to the process of sentimental expression; indeed, the affective self is parent to the rational self. It was this logic in Ribot's thought that LeBon settled on to legitimate his own outlook on mass psychology, in a favorable commentary on his colleague's work: "The affective self constitutes the most fundamental element of a personality."[13]

Ribot approved of pity as sympathy's highest and morally most complex facet: "The immediate, unthinking impulses of pity for the unfortunate, be they foreigners, enemies, or criminals, even animals...even egoism in the best sense cannot explain the behavior of the good Samaritan."[14] Ribot reprised the terms of his more traditional philosophical contemporaries, despite his earlier distancing: the "strangers, enemies, and criminals" of Bouillier, Pioger and Carrau; the animals dear to Paulhan; the Tardian overtones of "good Samaritan;" indeed, the entire pro-pity language that belittles egoism.

It seems that the valorization of pro-social sentiments had the better of Ribot's attempt at pioneering a new methodology. Where he had first anchored his approach in physiology, collapsing sentiments into the more basic category of physical sensations, specifically pain, he ultimately veered toward mass psychology. Perhaps the problem was one of judgment, and Ribot did not want his enterprise to founder on the shoals of Fact and Value. Perhaps he realized that he could not fit pro-social sentiments unto the procrustean bed of aversive responses. Sympathy—perforce pity—is at the nodal point of contact among biology, sociology, and morality. Like the philosophers and sociologists that Ribot wished to circumvent, he believed in a "law of association" and the indissolubly social character of tender sentiments ("douleurs morales").

Ribot also resembled his colleagues of the ASMP in his belief that moral pain was developmentally twined to the cultivation of intelligence. In his lecture course of 1893–1894 on the subject of the "Psychology of Sentiments," he postulated during his very first lesson that "the reason for the advance of sentiments...the essential, fundamental, perhaps only cause, is the development of the intelligence, intellectual states, imagination, and reason."[15] Ribot's uncertain probing through the sentiment-reason relationship led him to tergiversate between the language of physiological sensation and that of cognitive sentimentalism.

In the published version of these lectures, Ribot claimed that intelligence was responsible for furnishing the third and decisive element to the physiopsychological kernel of socializing sentiments so that they grow to conscious, social dimensions. The sequence is as follows: biological trigger ("sensation"); "tender emotion" (synonymous with "bienveillance," "compassion," "pitié") that becomes self-representational; then intellectual harnessing, making of the composite whole a "sentiment." Other-directed emotions would be too weak were they to rest on the foundations of the first two elements alone: "Could a society depend on this state alone? Stability requires more stable bonds, moral links."[16] The requirements of society, the cognitive template for sentiments, implicate the primacy of intelligence.

As with Bouillier's and Fouillée's words, we see in those of Ribot an emphasis on the civilizing reciprocity of social sentiments as they become interlocked with the higher mental faculties. Ribot stressed the civilizing imperative of sentiments no less than did his nonempirical associates of the ASMP. The contradiction formerly espied between sensations and intelligence is only apparent, for these belong to two different stages in the elaboration of sentiments:

the first thing that must be done is to rid ourselves of a preconception inculcated by our language that would undermine our theme: to wit, the belief that sympathy, sympathetic tendencies or sentiments are synonyms of benevolence, tenderness, pity, altruism.... In a psychological sense, the word "sympathy" has nothing to do with benevolence; it's the existence of identical dispositions in two or more members of the same species, or of two different species...notice that no moral element is involved.[17]

"The existence of identical dispositions in two or more members": this omnibus disposition of sympathy is putatively amoral, or premoral, but of course it is this precise interstitial quality that was made the basis of morality by the return of sentimentalism, pro-pity sociability, and the emerging mass psychology. Ribot wished to indicate a break between this "disposition" and the "truly moral" qualities of pity, goodness, tenderness, and altruism so that he could ally the latter terms with social and cognitive processes.

In his clearest working out of the nettled relationship between an organic and contagious sympathy, on the one hand, and a cognitively developed sentiment of altruism, on the other hand, Ribot deployed spatial metaphors: "Affective sympathy becomes sympathy in the common sense of the word solely through the addition of a second affective state which is different from it: tender emotions, altruism, compassion, pity. But this must be added to basic sympathy for sympathy to be established in its full form."[18] Sentimentalism is thus placed in two different orbits—the first, foundational, consisting of a "sympathetic instinct;" the second, revolving around the first, comprises those "tender emotions" that pro-pity thinkers had always lumped together with the first.

His most consistent version on the sentiment of which pity was a subspecies could be sketched as follows: the social phenomena of pity comprises binary elements, a "mechanical unity" with biological roots and wide plasticity, and an affective additive, the "tender emotion" itself, which adds the sympathetic solidarity permitting us first to feel and then to express pity. Intelligence then corroborates, validates, and cultivates this expression.[19] Civilized density of feeling is the result.

What remains of the sentimental commonplaces on pity in Ribot's thinking? Pity has been moralized and psychologized at once: like its fellow amalgams, altruism and compassion, it is a "tender emotion" that supplements the purely psychophysiological datum, sympathy (or altruism, according to successive versions), together with which it orients an individual toward a disposition to goodness, "bienveillance." Pity holds a larger place in Ribot's thinking on sympathy than the other "tender emotions" leading to social virtue. In the published *Psychology of Sentiments*, Ribot hazarded that pity may be a uniquely structured emotion, drawing its composition from ancestral or unconscious roots.[20] In all this, Ribot attested to the appeal that sentimentalism still retained over the scientific imagination and its nascent disciplinary configurations.

Jean Bourdeau, in *La Philosophie affective*, titled his analysis of Ribot's thought "La psychologie anti-intellectualiste de M. Ribot" ["The Anti-Intellectualist Psychology of Mr. Ribot"]. Ribot's importance was attested by Bourdeau's critical superlative: "We do not believe we exaggerate when we point to his last book on *The Psychology of Sentiments* as the most important essay to have appeared since the work of Taine on *Intelligence*."[21] But Bourdeau did not endorse what he took to be the pathetic basis of Ribot's epistemology: "Pain being indissociable from the human condition, what better side to take than to softly caress its incurable sadness?...Melancholy pity (the 'luxury of pity') lacks nobility when it has no other object than our own cherished self."[22] Bourdeau paraphrased Ribot in order to point out and criticize (mistakenly) the solipsistic and asocial nature of a pity based on internal sensation rather than external affectivity. Bourdeau believed pathos became ethos only when it stopped "luxuriating" in the ego and was directed toward others. So he saluted (contradictorily) Ribot's approach to social sentiments and his sequencing of psychological processes:

At the lowest level, before being moral, sympathy is biological. It expresses itself by the imitation of motor inclinations; this is the case with Panurge's sheep, with the contagion of yawning, laughter, with the simultaneous impulses of crowds. At a higher level are added compassion, pity. One sees even ants pick up their wounded from the field of battle.... The existence of social instincts in animals allows us to verify their innateness. The irresistible impulse to help others also exists among humans. The example of the good Samaritan defies all the analyses of la Rochefoucauld.[23]

For Bourdeau, Ribot's signal contribution was the distinction he proposed between "sentiments," on the one hand, and "emotions" and "passions," on the other, so that "sentiment" would be coupled only with pro-social feeling—and pity is an exemplar of this latter category. Bourdeau reprised Ribot's image of the Good Samaritan and carried on the pro-pity tradition's argument with la Rochefoucauld. In his contemporaries' eyes, what Ribot had done was to deepen and expand a pro-pity sentimentalism by furnishing a multifarious nomenclature that would pave the way for greater epistemological suppleness.

Frédéric Paulhan's is an important example. In *The Laws of Feeling*, he began with the same observation about the state of research that Ribot voiced in his fourth lecture: "The laws of feeling, on the other hand, are very little known; certain particular forms of sensibility...have been studied with some care, especially in their outward manifestations and their social effects; we also have many theories relating to pleasure and pain, and there are interesting books on the emotions and passions; but the results cannot be compared with those obtained in other psychological fields."[24] In contradistinction to the "outward manifestations" and "social effects" that preoccupied the moralists of sentiment, Paulhan, like Ribot, wished to confect an explanation rooted in internal states. For him, the means to penetrate the coppice of semantic confusion was to acknowledge that all sentiments were "compound impressions," a "synthesis of feelings," or what he also termed "the harmony and synthesis of affective phenomena."[25]

In order to explain these phenomena, Paulhan turned for help to Herbert Spencer and to two of his models, "the luxury of pity" and "the luxury of grief" (the latter term borrowed by Spencer from Sir Leslie Stephen). Paulhan hoped thereby to import and rectify Spencerian phenomenology:

My criticism of Spencer's explanation is that it does not account for all the phenomena. Indeed, there are some forms of the luxury of pity that it fails to explain—the egoistic pleasure of pity, for example. For it would be a mistake to believe that pity is at all times wholly generous; in fact, it may be attended by very varied egoistic pleasures. To begin with, there may be a feeling of pride, due to an almost unconscious examination of one's own conduct, or a simple feeling of well-being attributable to the vague awakening of the idea of freedom from the misfortunes one is commiserating upon—to the simple effect of contrast.[26]

At first view, Paulhan's account favors the egoistic, self-regarding interpretation of pity that recalls la Rochefoucauld and Spinoza—the anti-pity tradition. Paulhan concludes, however, by completely shifting gears and reinforcing his adherence to a pro-social logic: "Lastly, in my opinion, the pleasure of compassion arises in its purest and most complete form from the tendency to help those we pity, when that tendency is in harmony with most of our ideas or feelings.... We find further verification of this in the fact that if the tendency to relieve the suffering person is too strongly checked pity becomes as a rule wholly painful."[27] Paulhan finds, then, that the desire to help others, the "tendency to relieve the suffering person," characterizes the "purest and most complete form" of other-directed sentiment. With this conclusion, Paulhan ended up, not unexpectedly and like Ribot, with a pro-social, pro-pity affirmation.

Alexander Shand, observing from Britain, also judged Ribot in terms similar to Bourdeau's and Paulhan's, alternately praising and condemning him for his classifications. Shand applauded Ribot for his "study [of] the Passions—the most important and comprehensive systems of the human mind itself."[28] Like Ribot, Shand allied emotions to disinterested sentiments, of which pity was the loftiest illustration:

Now pity seems to be an essentially disinterested emotion. For pity is the name of a sorrow that we feel on behalf of another person: Every emotion has a potential disinterestedness, so far as among the stimuli which excite it are some which excite it on behalf of another individual instead of on behalf of oneself.... These higher systems we shall call "sentiments" to distinguish them from the lesser system of the emotions.[29]

Shand called upon the like-minded Ribot because he, too, reiterated a hierarchy of emotions in which "sentiments" were superior to "emotions." He, too, remarked the divorce between the Cousinian notion of "disinterestedness" and its disparagement of sentiment: for those whose thought partnered Ribot's, the very dynamism of sentiments was invested in disinterestedness. Pity was the perfect exemplum.

The presence of Shand in this exchange should demonstrate what does not need proving: that there was an important cross-cultural and interdisciplinary dialogue even then; even then, the belief in a specifically French pedigree to pity did not prevent receptiveness to other approaches. This was the significance of an important discussion of pity that took the shape of a review in 1901 of an article that had appeared in the *American Journal of Psychology*, an experimental survey and essay titled "Pity."[30] The article corroborated most of the themes cherished by French promoters of pity, for example, the authors' definition of pity as a pro-social virtue: "The legitimate *expression* of pity is some act directed toward the relief of suffering and the subjective easement following objective betterment.... We may conceive of pity as primordially a sentiment undetermined in any special direction, but as predisposing man to sympathize with suffering wherever met."[31] Or their sense of it as a civilizing quality: "Thus we see how pity, which like charity begins at home, tends to irradiate toward cosmic dimensions.... Thus pity irradiates and contributes elements to benevolence, patience, toleration, chivalry, humanity and all the social traits."[32] Or again, the importance they attribute to the imagination, especially to fiction, in inculcating pity: "Fiction, therefore, performs now the function of an Aristotelian catharsis in discharging harmlessly the virus of psychic rudimentary organs: *Imagination* is another covariant of pity and a momentous agent of altruism generally...All that quickens the humanistic exercise of this faculty makes for pitifulness."[33] Perhaps most relevant to its reception by the French reviewer was the authors' stress on educability and pedagogy: "The *pedagogy of pity* opens a problem as large and difficult as its psychology...to *pity aright* is a very important part of the education of the heart.... Everything indicates thus that pity is plastic, pliable, and therefore educable."[34]

This was the sort of article destined to find an echo in France, and it did. The reviewer for the *Revue philosophique de la France et de l'étranger* was Dr. Jean Philippe, colleague and collaborator of Alfred Binet and, as "chef de travaux du laboratoire de psychologie physiologique à la Sorbonne," a representative of the vanguard psychology that was least invested in commonplace notions of an abstract pity.[35] He summarized the article's methodology, findings, and definitions in a lengthy article of his own; but he consecrated the greatest fraction of his intervention to questions of educability and to the relationship of pity and justice:

It remains to be determined whether the educator should cultivate it: on this point, two theories are clearly opposed. One views pity as a sign of weakness in the individual and in society and which has nothing to do with the sentiment of justice; they note its expansion during periods of decadence and disturbances, for example, during the decline of Rome with its train of paid consolers and weepers. Others show its necessity. In truth, everything depends on the direction given pity by its origins, because it hinges on, at the same time, affectivity, sympathy, imagination, etc., which orient it in the most diverse directions (witness animal shelters).[36]

For Philippe, the rich promises of educability prevailed over further study of psychology and justice.

On the whole, the rush to a sentimental education in pity was given priority over firmer disciplinary investigations into the psychological dynamics and social nature of the sentiment. Pity could have been—should have been, I would argue, if enough care had been taken to think through the possibilities—grafted to a social psychology that gained only a tenuous disciplinary footing in France. Given that meta-social approaches like those focusing on contagion or *conscience collective* touched tangentially on the terrain of pity, a way of thinking about the latter that was no longer tied down by customary tropes could have been fruitful, both to sentimentalism and to social psychology. (I have purposely avoided closer scrutiny of the thought of that towering figure of disciplinary rearrangements, Durkheim, as well as that of the only somewhat lesser figure of Lucien Lévy-Bruhl, both of whom were supreme *moralistes* and philosophers obsessed with the relationship of reason and sentiment, and of individual and society. But much work has already been consecrated to their ethical thought; and it would take an entire tome, much less a chapter, to address their lateral contribution to pity.[37] A figure such as Hippolyte Taine, who was a partisan of English Associationist psychology and not in the least receptive to sentimentalism, was marginal to Academic philosophy and pedagogy.[38]) Instead, thinking about it was displaced onto innovations in programs of study, especially as Republican pedagogy and, later, female instruction necessitated distinctive features.

THE PEDAGOGY OF PITY

Here emerges the possibility of an *education of sentiments* and, reciprocally, an *education through sentiments*.

Camille Hémon[39]

The promoters of pity took its prescriptive dimensions to a logical conclusion: the school. If pity was valorized as a social good, then a fitting corollary was to prescribe it as an educational goal. Thinking on pity held that intelligence was developmentally twined to sentiment; that pity had to be instilled in individuals if a complex society was to hold together; that the tradition on pity was itself a subject worth studying. Given the Third Republic's pedagomania, the advent of universal primary schooling, the accession of females to state-sponsored schooling, and the establishment of a program of required study in moral philosophy beginning in 1882,[40] the promoters of pity eagerly propounded an affirmative answer to the question: is pity educable?

This was the governing assumption of those ranging from Françisque Bouillier, who had called for a pedagogical pity that works by reflection and cultivation, to Jean Philippe, the reviewer of Saunders and Hall's English-language article in the *American Journal of Psychology*. In this section we examine three interrelated issues: the reevaluation of traditional ideas on the possibility of educating sentiments, a likelihood that had to be confirmed if programs of study were to follow; then these programs themselves, first in the manuals and textbooks of moral philosophers and psychologists such as Pierre-Félix Thomas's *The Education of the Sentiments*, Émile Boirac's *Elementary Course in Philosophy*, Paul Janet's *Traité élémentaire de philosophie* and Pierre Janet's *Manuel du Baccalauréat de l'enseignement secondaire: philosophie*, or Camille Mélinand's *Course of Moral Philosophy*; and third, the official, uniform curriculum of secondary education, as encoded in the *Revue Universitaire*, which formulated standardized curricula for courses and questions for the baccalaureate examination. We will see that issues surrounding pity and the effort to promote it as a civic virtue were a prominent feature of the curricula and questions listed in the *Revue*. In a later Chapter we deal exclusively with the inculcation of pity in a specifically feminine pedagogy.

Pity prospered in the imagination, was strengthened by intelligence, and had to be channeled along the proper social course—or such was the budding consensus among educators. But how and when was this sequence to be introduced? An earlier tradition held the belief about childhood best expressed by La Fontaine: "that age is without pity." This literary and rhetorical tradition had to be infirmed before a new pedagogy could be put in place.

There is an exemplary account of the educability of pity that rhetorically invests the full range of assumptions, themes, and recommendations of this discourse. In a study of *L'éducation des sentiments*, Pierre-Félix Thomas devoted one chapter to "De la pitié," offering at first a perspective thoroughly grounded in historical cataloging but then insisting on the moral conditions that have updated this virtue.[41] Thomas acknowledged pro-pity precedents as if they were perennial and uncontested: "this sentiment plays such a considerable role in life, and moralists have left us many penetrating insights on it."[42] But then he shifted to an etiological analysis: "it is useful to examine here more closely its causes and effects, in order to see its true nature."[43] Thomas defines the nature of pity by tweaking the classic language of the pro-pity tradition, which in turn helps model the contemporaneous consensus: "In genuine pity we thus find two different if inseparable elements: a painful emotion similar to the other's emotion, which is to say, a suffering caused by the sight of that other's suffering, and a tendency more or less dynamic to come to their aid. Thanks to the latter, pity is so benevolent and fruitful; thanks to it, too, pity contrasts with the hypocritical kindness that is rarely active."[44] Pity is dynamically altruistic: "Pity is thus the altruistic sentiment par excellence."[45]

Thomas next proposed a précis of what was the major rhetorical contribution to the pro-pity tradition in the *fin-de-siècle*: situating pity at the junction of reason and imagination, making it historical by rendering it an attribute of civilization and therefore susceptible of change in space and time and through education, as well as by cleaving to suppositions about femininity:

But pity is far from being found in equal activity and liveliness in everyone: first of all because it has its causes, as we have shown, in sensitivity and imagination, faculties that are different according to individual and era. If women know better than men do how to sympathize with all hurts, if they know how to find the consoling words for all the unfortunate, it is because, in general, they have a livelier imagination and sensitivity than do we.[46]

This is, after all, a treatise on the educability of emotions, so Thomas insists on the possibility of inculcating pity: "Let us add, however, that reason and the will are often precious auxiliaries for pity; thanks to these supports, pity becomes considered, enlightened, perseverant, and thus more practical."[47] Yet pity could not mold a social solidarity were it to depend on reason and will alone. Emotional contagion is the privileged vector of social solidarity: "Finally, perhaps more than any other sentiment, pity is characterized by contagion: if before a pauper who stretches his hands out to an indifferent crowd, a passerby suddenly stops and speaks to this wretch with warmth and cares about his distress; soon you shall see a circle forming around him, and when his alms fall into the bowl, it is rare indeed that others will not soon do so as well."[48] Thomas does not claim that this contagious emotion is unmitigatedly healthy, but it is the sort of social reality that makes an ideal subject for pedagogy: "but it is necessary to acknowledge its existence if we wish to teach our students how to use it wisely when we develop their pity."[49]

In writing of "developing" pity as a socializing virtue, Thomas clearly disclosed a pro-pity agenda: "Let us see then what services pity can provide us when she is utter and sincere. The first is to mitigate our egoism: 'Humans, writes Rousseau, would never have been anything but monsters had not nature given them pity to back up reason; it is that which moderates in each of us our self-love.'…Second, pity brings humans closer together…. Does not history prove that pity has always bred miracles among us?"[50] As a socializing virtue, practice and not theory should most occupy thinking on pity—attention to its education: "We have just examined pity in itself and pointed out the general consequences it entails; it remains for us to demonstrate what can and should be its role in education."[51]

In the section devoted exclusively to education, Thomas began with the obligatory reference to La Fontaine, to which he added another from La Bruyère: "First of all, are children really capable of this sentiment? —We know La Fontaine's opinion on this topic. It is summed up in the verse with which one has often reproached him: 'that age is without pity.' That opinion is equally La Bruyère's: 'children,' says he, 'do not like to suffer hurts but gladly inflict them.'"[52] Thomas revisits tradition only to contradict it: "but what is absolutely certain is that pity emerges at an early age, and reveals itself in acts whose meaning is not in the least dubious."[53] If children lack a socially aware sense of pity, this is because they are still untrained: "We must admit, however, that in many cases our children evince a surprising insensitivity; but what are its causes? The first among them is their lack of experience."[54] And so education of the sentiments must be timely and comprehensive:

To accomplish this new task, it is to the child's sensibility and imagination that we should first have recourse. If we lead him or her gradually to reflect on the sufferings of others, to compare those sufferings to those he or she already knows; if we know how to choose the readings he or she must master, and draw their attention to unfortunate events that occur within their circle, their primary indifference will soon disappear. They will not only learn to recognize the woes that may one day strike them, but also to share them and pity them in others. Moreover, since pity is contagious, let us show ourselves pitying to the unfortunate, and may our pity be directed in priority to those whom nature has cruelly disinherited, because more than any other they have a right to our aid.[55]

To the fatalistic poetic dismissals of La Fontaine and La Bruyère, Thomas responds with a programmatic prescription centered on education.

This prescription was specified in the manuals of the Republican schooling system; texts that marked a change in appraisals of the cognitive and ethical status of sentiments. If we compare three official philosophy textbooks diachronically, from 1843 to 1879, we can detect the gradual encroachment of a rhetorical pedagogy of sentimentalism: Adolphe Franck's *Dictionnaire des sciences philosophiques* (1843), Charles Jourdain's *Notions de philosophie* (1852), and Paul Janet's *Traité élémentaire de philosophie* (1879).

These leading primers were geared to the standardized syllabus of lycée and university philosophy, [56] and furnished a gloss on the four basic categories of that curriculum: ethics, logic, religion, and epistemology. The first of these manuals, Franck's, pays no attention to sentiments in psychology or philosophy. The second edition, dating from 1875, does incorporate a lengthy section on Schopenhauer, who is treated adversely and whose notion of pity is completely ignored.[57] Jourdain's *Notions* stressed *sensibilité* rather than sentiments and in its focus on the state as the locus of moral obligations included "pity" only as a *"penchant."*[58] Janet's *Traité*, in contrast, consecrates much greater attention to sentiment, epistemologically and narratively. Janet defined sentiment as a cognitive quality: "or else emotions do not have a corporal seat, and have instead as their cause an idea, a thought; they are then called sentiments."[59] Furthermore, sentiment is a hybrid moral and intellectual attribute: "Sentiments are thus inclinations that lead us toward intellectual and moral elements."[60]

In direct filiation with the pro-pity cognitive theory of sentiment, Janet defends pity against la Rochefoucauld's denigration, in a lengthy and vituperative critique: "All of [la Rochefoucauld's] contentions are false, superficial, and gross.... Pity is all that is most natural and most spontaneous in the human heart; the presence of suffering makes each of us suffer, without a closing-in upon ourselves. This is a simple and immediate factor, which is just as innate a part of us as self-love."[61] Unlike Franck and Jourdain, Janet's text expanded on a social ethics of pity under the rubric of "philanthropic inclinations," assembling Hobbes, Rousseau, Schopenhauer, and Descartes in the process:

The very need that humans feel for society appears to prove that it is altogether natural and not artificial...beyond this first seed, there is another to which Rousseau drew attention, pity, which, even in a state of nature, unites humans. Schopenhauer, despite his misanthropy, believed in the natural pity of humans for each other and makes of it the foundation of his ethics.... Pity, as a disposition to suffer the same woes as those who are miserable, is but a form of sympathy; but in so far as it is a sadness caused by that suffering and a desire to ease those who have woes, it is a form of benevolence and philanthropy.[62]

Like the other philosophers who viewed sentiments as developmentally linked to social complexity, Janet, too, argued that "if sentiments give rise to society, it is also reciprocally true that these sentiments only arise and flourish in and through society.... We should not conclude from this that sentiments are thus artificial: for since humans are essentially social, what is more natural than the emergence of social sentiments?"[63] Janet's *Treatise* thus evinces a thorough investment with the rhetorical and pedagogical weight of a sentimental ethics, reflecting a trend of *fin-de-siècle* thought.

The instruction manuals and textbooks conceived expressly for the Republican school system would accentuate this trend. In the *Dictionnaire de pédagogie et d'instruction primaire*, that "cathedral of primary schooling,"[64] first composed in 1887 as a primer for the burgeoning Republican catechism, Gabriel Compayre (1843–1913) penned a lengthy entry on "Sensibilité" that justified the educability of sentiments:

The careful study of the slow and continual progress of sensibility, as it raises itself little by little from the cruder pleasures of the senses to the finest emotions of the Heart, is the best refutation one can bring to bear on the error of educators who, like Rousseau, wish to wait until the fifteenth year before beginning to bring out the moral sentiments. One cannot start cultivating too soon the moral sensitivity of a child.[65]

The existence of sentiments in need of guidance validated the pedagogical enterprise, and education was a guarantor of civilizing sentiments—an obligatory encounter with Rousseau helped make this reciprocal point.

Émile Boirac (1851–1917), a quintessential Republican pedagogue, began a discussion of sentimentalism in his preparatory guide for philosophy, *La Dissertation philosophique* (1890), by focusing students' attention on distinctions and classifications: "Distinguish sentiment from sensation. Enumerate, classify, and define the primary sentiments."[66] Boirac then led the students to an advocatory discussion of "Sentimental Doctrines," in which they had to obviate Spinoza's anti-pity stance—"'pity is the sadness born from someone else's misfortune'"[67]—by commenting on and criticizing it.

In a longer textbook published four years later, Boirac came back to his charges with more explicit instructions. Boirac wanted to indoctrinate his young readers to sentimentalism: "All the more reason why one cannot, as the Stoics wanted to, remove sensibility from human nature. Such a mutilation is neither *possible* nor *desirable*. It is necessary that an *idea* become *sentiment* in order to *move* the will."[68] And so students had to learn to argue the merits of sentimentalism: "Show the reciprocal influence of thought on sentiment and sentiment on thought."[69] In doing so, they also had to engage la Rochefoucauld: "La Rochefoucauld said: 'The mind is often the dupe of the heart.' While acknowledging the truth of this maxim, can it not be reversed to say that often the heart is the dupe of the mind?"[70]

Paul Janet's manual proposed a fuller historical and classificatory approach to sentimentalism. In his perspective, "social inclinations" supply the key to moral phenomena and confound the naysayers of earlier tradition: "*Social* or sympathetic *tendencies* that have as their object fellow-humans have been the subject of much philosophical discussion. Certain authors, such as la Rochefoucauld in his *Maxims*, and later Helvétius in his book on *L'Esprit*, have denied their existence."[71] Janet, unlike his illustrious predecessors, will affirm their existence in a complete catalog: "These social sentiments comprise, in different aspects, *philanthropy, sociability, benevolence, sympathy, compassion, pity, friendship, gratitude*."[72] Janet validates social sentiments by providing a thesaurus that students could make synonymous with moral inclinations.

Camille Mélinand, author of the entry on "Pity" in the *Encyclopédie* from our Prologue, was more explicit in his pedagogical advocacy of pity. In his manual, *Cours de philosophie morale*, he urged his students to consider other-directed feelings as the highest expression of moral obligation: "The active form (and no longer only negative) of the same duty is the urge towards relieving sufferings we have not ourselves caused. Soothe the most pain that is possible—that's already an admirable project. And this project can be indefinitely expanded: because one must look for *misfortune* in all its forms, since it is the cause of innumerable woes."[73] The hierarchy of other-directed feelings begins with pity: "For all these duties toward suffering, the bountiful *sentiment* is *pity*, which consists in feeling, as if it were ours, the pain of another; and in so doing thereby almost quashes individual boundaries in becoming 'one with the other.'"[74] Prescription, advocacy, and indoctrination: pity was at the center of the inculcation of ethical sentimentalism.

Perhaps the most convincing, because official and ubiquitous, example of the widespread consensus on prescribing pity in education was the use made of it in the *Revue Universitaire,* which presented a mandatory syllabi for use by all teachers through the directives of the education ministry, starting in 1892 (the *Revue Universitaire* began publication that year, a decade after the important educational reforms of the Third Republic). The examination questions for primary, secondary, and upper-level students listed in the *Revue* reveal the diligent commitment to pity in official curricula. We will turn in Chapter 6 to the indoctrination of a specifically feminine pity as rendered in the *Revue*'s curricula for the *Écoles secondaires des jeunes filles*; for now, we look at the two frameworks within which pity thrived in the *Revue*'s pages: the reexamination of the sentiment/reason divide in morality and the role of pity in literature. The first was an affirmation and pedagogical application of the problematic we have seen at work; the second was a newer interest, echoing the charged atmosphere of the competition between the literary and philosophical fields.

Sentimentalism was omnipresent in the *Revue*, as both injunction and model. In its second year, the *Revue* published an account of the subject most preoccupying the teaching of philosophy for secondary-school boys: "The role of sensibility in moral life." This was to be the subject of the "Essay" for the *baccalaureate*: "Those philosophers who do not at all want virtue to rely on sentiment should take a look at the world; they should consider all the ugliness of reality, social injustice, the innumerable hurts of history.... They will understand then that above all else it is necessary to safeguard moral law, and far from disowning sentiments, they will claim its assistance against the overwhelming force of passions."[75] Essay topics for the *baccalaureate* were never open-ended; they came with guiding assumptions, and here these comprised a notion of sentiments as sustaining moral principle, together with an opposition between sentiments (pro-social) and "passions" (synonymous with "force, pride, self-interest"). This pedagogical form of indoctrination was a way to articulate emotive desiderata for a rising generation.

The *Revue* revealed that, in 1899, the "Dissertation" (Essay) in philosophy for the *baccalaureate* still focused on legitimating sentimentalism: "Sentiment and reason. Their nature, legitimate role in the life of individuals and nations."[76] In 1901, students in courses of ethics were asked to review the matter of whether "fraternity could be based on solidarity of interests."[77] The guidelines indicated that the answer could only be no, for pity was more closely linked to fellow-feeling, to a real solidarity of weal and woe:

We can all say with the poet: "I love the majesty of human suffering." Or more simply, without concerning ourselves with the majestic character assumed by these sufferings in the eyes of the poet, we can say: "I love he/she who suffers because they suffer." Yes, we are often led to love our fellow beings by *pity*, and not only by *pity* for the great calamities that sometimes overwhelm their fragile and uncertain existence…. That sympathy for all and that distinctive pity for the unfortunate are so powerful that they arouse each day, even among the least refined natures, acts of devotion bordering on sacrifice, and they are so widespread that some moralists of the positivist school have seen in them the only forces in our nature capable of combating human egoism.[78]

The rhetoric of persuasion was here meant to indoctrinate a dolorous sense of other-directed sentiment, rather than self-interest, as the key to fraternity. So that the tendentious instructions conclude with a justification of Michelet's romantic-humanitarian pity: "The souls in which this sympathy, this appreciation for the great spectacles of the past, is most lively, like that of Michelet, for example, are they not the most capable of pity, the most tender and warm, and truly fraternal?"[79]

The sentimentalist discourse permeating these curricular directives included the same compulsory references to traditional figures and tropes as that employed by contemporary theorists. The same allusions perdured: La Fontaine, Rousseau, Aristotle, and Descartes, for example. In 1908 the essay question for the *Agrégation de Philosophie* was on "The role of passions in ethics according to Descartes."[80] In 1910, it was Aristotle's turn to serve as a vector for meditating on the very French virtues of pity. A lengthy question posed to students in classics yoked together Aristotle, Racine, and Corneille in a deliberation on the "sources of dramatic pity:"

"Aristotle, far from demanding perfect heroes, on the contrary wishes that tragic characters…be neither completely good nor totally wicked. He does not want them to be exceptionally good, because the chastisement of a good person would provoke more indignation than pity in a spectator; nor that they be excessively wicked, because one does not pity a villain." These important lines from Aristotle's *Poetics*, thus summarized and commented by J. Racine, can equally provide material for a French composition: "Study the principal characters of Corneillian and Racinian drama in relation to the famous theory of Aristotle on *terror* and *pity*, taken as the two principal forces of dramatic emotion."[81]

This exposé, coinciding with themes that have once again returned to considerations on literature today, combined the three essential ingredients of a doctrinaire pity: landmarks of French literature—Racine and Corneille—validate and exemplify Aristotelian pity so perfectly that both classic and French compositions can be oriented around the three authors; literary pity codifies a real ethical sentiment; reflections on pity must perforce themselves be both literary and philosophical and, above all, emotive.

This doctrinaire literary pity, about which we learn more in its own Chapter, was part and parcel of pedagogical instruction in the *fin-de-siècle*. The topic for the *Agrégation* in Latin in 1896 was representative:

"And looking at the typical impact of Athenian tragedy on the souls of its spectators, we can say that Plato was more justified in prohibiting its practice than Aristotle in promoting it; because, since tragedy consists of the immoderate reactions of *fear* and *pity*, it turns the theater into a school of fright and compassion, where one learns to be afraid of all dangers and to become upset at all misfortune. Such was the desire to weep that there were fewer virtues than woes set out on stage, out of fear that a soul brought up to venerate heroes would be incapable of abandoning itself to pitying the wretched." [Saint-Evrémond, *De la tragédie ancienne et moderne* (1672)][82]

The point of the exercise was for the student-postulant to challenge Saint-Evrémond, himself writing in defense of the "moderns" vs. the "ancients" in an earlier "culture war," by valorizing just what this earlier authority denigrated, thereby trumpeting the modernity of sentimentalism and of the pro-pity appraisals that can now be made of all literature.

Thus *lieux communs* and *loci classicus* were constantly recuperated or challenged in order to teach pity right. In 1901, the question for the *Dissertation française* required students to "Discuss Corneille's idea: 'Tragedy should provoke pity and fear.'"[83] The additional expository guidelines were rhetorically precise: "If it is true that this sentiment is provoked in us by portrayals of our fellow-creatures suffering, when we fear that their misfortunes may also befall us, is it not also true that it is excited more strongly by the sight of woes happening to someone in our circumstances, whom we resemble completely, than by the view of calamities that make the greatest monarchs tumble from their thrones?"[84] The intersubjective qualities ascribed to pity in this elucidation were accompanied by an emphasis on Republican equality; together with fraternity, pity was aligned with a notion of social closeness—a democratization of both inner and outer life.

Corneille was also conscripted for the *Agrégation* in grammar for 1903, when students were asked to expound on excerpts from the "Préface" to *Don Sanche d'Aragon*, "from 'I would say even more; that tragedy should excite pity' to 'You know better than I all that I am saying.'"[85] In 1905, La Bruyère's literary pity made an appearance for the *Dissertation française*: "Social satire and the sentiment of pity in La Bruyère, in reference to the article on Peasants (*De l'homme*)."[86] The same year, the *Composition française* for the *Licence ès lettres* called for a commentary on Brunetière's valorization of La Bruyère's pity: "'La Bruyère accepted the society of his day less easily than did Molière, and we see emerge in him a pity that does not exist in Boileau. It is the humanitarian ideal that begins to surface.'"[87] Brunetière's view and the corroboratory reading that is expected to accompany it were in equal measure indicative of the new doctrinaire pity that took on officious force in pedagogy—a teleological view by which pity is judged as a marker of progress, humanism, and thus recuperated for a modernity still in touch with tradition.

Students in the program for the *Enseignement secondaire des garçons* were mandated in 1906 to answer this essay question: "What reflections are aroused in you by these thoughts of a contemporary writer: 'The more I think about human life, the more I believe that we need give it as witnesses and judges Irony and Pity. Irony and Pity are two good counselors: one, by smiling, makes life loveable; the other, which cries, renders it sacred' (Anatole France, *Le Jardin d'Épicure*)."[88] We come back to Anatole France toward the end of this study. Here it is important to retain the notion that a not insignificant aspect of the educational setting of *fin-de-siècle* France was bathed in the sentimentalism of which Boutroux remarked, one in which pity was both explored and indoctrinated.

It is also important to note that this dual engagement with pity—disciplinary and educational—had become largely doctrinaire, by which I mean both univocally positive and national-cultural: vested in French traditions, authors, and language. So it was all the more necessary to confront the new theories on and challenges to pity originating from Germany in the latter part of the nineteenth century.

NOTES

1. Gustave LeBon, *Opinions and Beliefs* , 185, 188.

2. See biographical information in AN, AJ16/1025 and AJ16/1434. For Ribot's career, as well as his ambivalent relationship with Paul Janet and Alfred Espinas, see Brooks, "Philosophy and Psychology at the Sorbonne, 1885–1913," and especially the chapter in *The Eclectic Legacy*, "Eclectic Buddhist: Théodule Ribot." Ribot's training at the École Normale in Paris was in philosophy, and he began his career as a professor of philosophy in the French secondary-school system. Although Ribot was not trained as a psychologist or as a psychiatrist, he did as much as any contemporary to promote new trends in psychology. He became interested in English associationist psychology, and in 1870 he published a work that would be translated as *Contemporary English Psychology*, an exposition of the theories of the Mills, Spencer, Alexander Bain, and others. This was one of the first complete and supportive accounts of developments across the Channel, and it played a large role in introducing the empiricist and utilitarian (if not experimental) approaches that were to help change French psychology. See also Benrubi, who writes about Ribot's novel contributions: "In the first place then he stands for the emancipation of the individual philosophical sciences from metaphysics" (*Contemporary Thought of France*, 35).

3. Ribot, *La Philosophie de Schopenhauer* (Paris: Germer-Baillière, 1874). See the next chapter.

4. In 1880, Ribot penned a letter to Lachelier commissioning an article for the *Revue* that included this categorical distinction between German psychology and French philosophy: "Couldn't you send me a small study that I would print under the form of a 'Miscellany' and which could be titled 'Philosophical Pedagogy in Germany?' The study would concern itself with showing in *which* ways this teaching is conceived and taught in different universities. I remember that you once told me something quite sound on the

distinction between empirical psychology and the theory of knowledge. This is absolutely unheard of in France, at least in education" ["ne pourriez vous pas m'envoyer un petit travail que j'imprimerai sous forme de 'Variétés' et qui aurait pour titre 'l'Enseignement philosophique en Allemagne?' Il s'agirait dans cette étude de montrer de quelles manières cet enseignement est conçu et donné dans les diverses universités. Je me souviens que vous m'avez dit une chose très juste sur la distinction entre la psychologie empirique et la théorie de la connaissance. Cela est absolument inconnu en France, dans l'enseignement du moins."] Letter dated May 8, 1880, in Bibliothèque de l'Institut, MS 18742, "Lettres adressées à Jules Lachelier."

5. Michael S. Roth, "Remembering Forgetting: *Maladies de la Mémoire* in Nineteenth-Century France," *Representations* 26 (Spring 1989): 49–68, writes of Ribot's phenomenological project: "Thus the problem for Ribot, a problem that Fouillée thought insoluble in the positivist paradigm, was to understand how indivisible moments can create continuity. If memory is made up of instants, how does consciousness find a *sens* in the past?" (55). Ribot's preoccupation with memory, upon which Roth focuses, led Ribot to formulate what came to be known as "Ribot's Law." See Ian Hacking, *Rewriting the Soul: Multiple Personality and the Sciences of Memory* (Princeton, Princeton UP, 1995), as well as Brooks, *The Eclectic Legacy*, 88, 177.

6. On the circumstances of his leaving the Sorbonne for the Collège de France, see Brooks, "Philosophy and Psychology at the Sorbonne," 132.

7. ["les sentiments ont été très longtemps traités par une méthode purement philosophique; les uns ont procédé en *moralistes*; les autres, en *métaphysiciens*...pour moi, l'étude des sentiments, est la partie la *plus matérielle* de la psychologie."] Théodule Ribot, "Les Sentiments et les états affectifs, cours, 1888–89," in Bibliothèque de l'Institut de France, MS 18174: "1er leçon, Introduction."

8. ["L'identité de la douleur physique et de la douleur morale, tel sera notre thème. Sur cette question, la bibliographie est absolument nulle: tout est à faire. Ce n'est pas qu'on n'ait beaucoup écrit là-dessus; mais les auteurs étaient des moralistes ou théologiens, des optimistes, des pessimistes, tout préoccupés de prouver l'utilité de la douleur, d'en trouver la justification, de faire la part du plaisir et de la douleur sur la terre, etc.—toutes questions qui ne sont pas de notre compétence. Aucun ne s'est occupé de la *nature* de la douleur morale; c'est cette étude psychologique que nous avons à faire."] Ribot, leçon 4.

9. ["les douleurs purement représentatives peuvent se classer en deux grands groupes: 1. les douleurs égoistes; 2. les douleurs sympathiques ou altruistes."] Ribot, leçon 4. It would be interesting to trace the parallel between Ribot's grappling with this physiological-representational relationship and Freud's version of the same task. Freud would, within a decade, explore much of the same psychic territory in elaborating his theory of instincts and would make use of "ego-cathexis" in a manner equivalent to Ribot's focus.

10. ["Avec les douleurs sympathiques ou altruistes, les difficultés sont plus grandes, et la réduction plus embarassant. Toutes ces douleurs peuvent se ramener à la sympathie (mot collectif embrassant la totalité des douleurs non égoistes). La question serait donc de savoir si la sympathie, dans sa forme élémentaire ne se ramenérait pas à des états purement physiques. Je vous ferai remarquer tout d'abord que la question de la sympathie est une grosse question."] Ribot, leçon 4.

11. ["lorsque des animaux vivent ensemble, il y a entre eux sympathie. Et en définitif, autre leur conscience individuelle, ils ont une conscience sociale....La puissance de l'intelligence est à chaque instant sous la dépendance du sentiment; une grande intelligence est en général soutenu par une grande passion. Ce n'est pas la raison qui se sert de la passion, mais la passion qui se sert de la raison pour arriver à ses fins."] Ribot, leçon 4.

12. See LaCapra, *Émile Durkheim*: "In the normal state of society, the *conscience collective* would be the shared psychological ground of practical reason and solidarity in the personalities of members of society: it would be objectively real and subjectively internalized at the same time;" "in one sense, [*conscience collective*] was the socio-psychological ground of a common culture in the personalities of members of society" (17, 89).

13. Gustave LeBon, *Opinions and Beliefs*, 166–67.

14. ["Les impulsions de pitié, instantanées, irréfléchies, pour les malheureux, que ce soient des étrangers, des ennemis, des criminels, des bêtes mêmes...l'égoisme le mieux entendu ne saurait expliquer la conduite du bon samaritaine."] Ribot, *La Psychologie des sentiments* (Paris: Félix Alcan, 1896), 234.

15. ["(la) cause de l'évolution des sentiments...cause essentielle, fondamentale, peut-être unique, c'est le développement de l'intelligence, des états intellectuelles, de l'imagination, et de la raison."] Ribot, Bibliothèque Nationale de France, MS 18184.

16. ["Une société pourrait-elle reposer sur ce seul état? La stabilité exige des liens plus solides, les liens moraux."] Ribot, *La Psychologie des sentiments*, 287.

17. ["la première chose à faire est de se débarrasser d'un préjugé inculqué par le langage, et qu'est propre à vivier notre sujet: à savoir de croire que sympathie, tendance ou sentiments sympathiques soient synonymes de bienveillance, tendresse, pitié, altruisme....Du sens de la psychologie, le mot sympathie n'a rien à voir avec la bienveillance, c'est l'existence de dispositions identiques chez deux ou plusieurs individus de la même espèce, ou de deux espèces différentes...remarquez qu'il n'y entre aucun élément moral."] Ribot, IX léçon: "Tendances sympathiques."

18. ["La sympathie affective devient la sympathie au sens courant du mot, mais seulement par la jonction d'un second état affectif qui lui est étranger, qui est autre: les émotions tendres, l'altruisme, la compassion, la pitié. Mais ceci doit s'ajouter à la sympathie primitive pour qu'elle soit constituée sous sa forme complète."] Ribot, *La Psychologie des sentiments*, 235.

19. See Laquièze, *Étude analytique sur la pitié*, 27–28, 60.

20. Laquièze, 60–61.

21. ["Nous ne croyons pas exagérer en signalant son dernier livre sur la *Psychologie des sentiments*, comme l'essaie le plus important qui ait paru, depuis l'ouvrage de Taine sur l'*Intelligence*."] Jean Bourdeau, *La Philosophie affective*, 64.

22. ["La douleur étant inséparable de la condition humaine, quel meilleur parti prendre que d'en caresser mollement l'incurable tristesse?...L'apitoiement mélancolique ('luxury of pity') manque de noblesse, quand il n'a d'autre objet que notre cher moi."] Bourdeau, 69.

23. ["Au plus bas degré, avant d'être morale, la sympathie est biologique. Elle se traduit par l'imitation des tendances motrices; c'est le cas des moutons de Panurge, de la contagion des bâillements, du rire, de l'entraînement simultané des foules. A un degré supérieur s'y joignent la compassion, la pitié. On voit jusqu'aux fourmis relever leurs blessés sur le champ de bataille....L'existence de l'instinct social chez les animaux permet d'en constater l'innéité. L'impulsion irrésistible vers le bien des autres existe aussi chez les hommes. L'exemple du bon samaritaine défie toute les analyses de la Rochefoucauld."] Bourdeau, 73–74.

24. Frédéric Paulhan, *The Laws of Feeling*, C. K. Odgen, trans. (New York: Harcourt, Brace, and Co., 1930 [1884]), 1.

25. Paulhan, 98.

26. Paulhan, 99. Paulhan's language here echoes that of Mondion de Montmirel, "en plaignant les autres, nous nous félicitons secrètement de ne pas souffrir les mêmes maux," ["in pitying others, we secretly congratulate ourselves for not suffering the same woes"] and anticipates that of Bergson by a few years. (See the "Prologue.")

27. Paulhan, "The Laws of Feeling," 100–102.

28. Alexander F. Shand, "M. Ribot's Theory of the Passions," *Mind* 16 (1907): 477.

29. Alexander F. Shand, *The Foundations of Character: Being a Study of the Tendencies of the Emotions and Sentiments* (London: Macmillan and Co., 1914), 48, 49, 50.

30. The authors were F. H. Saunders and G. Stanley Hall: "Pity," *American Journal of Psychology* 11: 1–4 (October 1899–July 1900): 534–91. The article elucidated the responses to a questionnaire on eleven items. The authors favored an evolutionary understanding of pity, based on the cultural transmission of adaptive responses. Hunger was one instance of this: "*hunger* in some form was cited as that which had excited the deepest pity.…When we reflect that the great majority of animals find their grave in the maw of others and that the struggle for survival has been largely for food, we can understand that it speaks well for the race that pity in this field even for those of an alien race and at a great distance, who suffer from famine, is so effective" (535, 537).

31. Saunders and Hall, 580–81.

32. Saunders and Hall, 587.

33. Saunders and Hall, 589–90.

34. Saunders and Hall, 580–81, 590.

35. Jean Philippe was a specialist in psychometry and committed to surmounting the mind-body dualism. He was the author of an important work in his own right, *L'image mentale* (Paris: Félix Alcan, 1903), as well as a collaborator with Binet in the latter's book, *La Psychologie expérimentale*, of which he authored Chapter 7: "Psychométrie."

36. ["Reste à savoir si l'éducateur doit le développer: et sur ce point, deux théories s'opposent nettement. Les uns observent que la pitié est pour l'individu et la société un signe de faiblesse qui n'a rien à faire avec le sentiment de la justice: ils notent son développement aux époques troubles de décadence, p. ex. vers le déclin de Rome, avec les pleureuses, les consolateurs, etc. D'autres en montrent la nécessité. En réalité, tout dépend de l'orientation que lui donnent ses origines, car elle relève à la fois de l'affectivité, de la sympathie, de l'imagination, etc., qui l'orientent (témoin les hospices d'animaux), dans les directions les plus diverses."] Dr. J. Philippe, "Revue: 'La Pitié,'" *Revue philosophique de la France et de l'étranger* 52 (July-December, 1901), 703.

37. On Durkheim as a *moraliste*, see LaCapra, *Émile Durkheim*, 2, 288–89. Much of the work of Stjepan G. Meštrović has been devoted to making a case for the influence of Schopenhauer on Durkheim and, more generally, on sociology, especially as the latter two privilege sentiment and compassion: "…Simmel, Wundt, Ribot, Tönnies, Jung, Pareto, Mosca, LeBon, and Tarde. Most of them lamented the loss of heart that accompanied so-called progress, and most of them may be considered as Schopenhauer's disciples in some fashion" (*The Coming Fin-de-Siècle: An Application of Durkheim's Sociology to Modernity and Postmodernism* [London and New York: Routledge, 1991], 41). See also idem., *Durkheim and Postmodern Culture* (New York: Aldine de Gruyter, 1992); and "Moral Theory Based on the 'Heart' versus the 'Mind:' Schopenhauer's and Durkheim's Critiques of Kantian Ethics," *Sociological Review* 37:3 (August 1989): 431–57.

38. Although in his lessons on art, Taine commented favorably on Delacroix's painting using the terms of pro–pity sentimentalism: "On n'a jamais senti plus à fond, par une sympathie plus personnelle, avec une pitié plus largement étendue, le drame douleureux de la vie." "Il faisait sortir la pitié, le désespoir, la tendresse, et toujours quelque émotion déchirante ou délicieuse de ses tons violacés et étranges, de ses nuages vineux brouillés de fumés charbonneuses, de ses mers et de ses cieux livides" (*Philosophie de l'art*, 18th ed. [Paris: Hachette, 1921], 118). ["Never has one felt more deeply, with a more personal sympathy and more expansive pity, the painful drama of life." "He let transpire pity, despair,

tenderness, and always some excruciating or delicious emotion, from his strange and purplish hues, his wine-red clouds hazy with charcoal smoke, his purplish seas and skies."]

39. ["De là se tirait la possibilité d'une *éducation du sentiment* et, réciproquement, d'une *éducation par le sentiment.*"] Camille Hémon, "Conflits des sentiments égoistes et des sentiments sociaux," 706.

40. See the article "Morale," in *Dictionnaire de pédagogie et d'instruction primaire,* Ferdinand Buisson, ed.: "L'Etat peut donc et doit enseigner la morale. Mais selon que cet enseignement s'adressera à des enfants ou à des élèves-maîtres, il sera donné suivant des programmes differents." ["Thus the State can and should teach morality. But depending on whether this instruction is targeted to infants or master-pupils, its contents will use different syllabi."] (vol. 2, part 2, 1969). This article was written shortly after the 1882 program was decreed, in justification of the Republican state's arrogating to itself what had been accepted as the church's and family's prerogative. See also Guillaume Jost and André Cazès, eds., *Ministère de l'instruction publique: l'inspection de l'enseignement primaire* (Paris: Imprimérie nationale, 1900): "L'enseignement de la morale."

41. The very subheadings of the chapter are a historiographical review of the French pity tradition: "Of pity. Definitions of Descartes, Bossuet, la Rochefoucauld. Elements which it involves. Its causes. Sentiments which it rouses in those who are its object. II. Under which conditions is pity valuable? Opinions of Epictetus and Charron. Rebuttal of these opinions. Benefits conferred by pity. Of false pity. III. The role of pity in education. Are children open to this sentiment? The opinions of la Fontaine, de la Bruyère, Victor Hugo. Whence arises the insensitivity of children? IV. Ways of evoking and guiding pity." ["I. De la pitié. Définitions de Descartes, de Bossuet, et de la Rochefoucauld. Eléments qu'elle implique. Ses causes. Sentiments qu'elle inspire à ceux qui en sont l'objet. II. À quelles conditions la pitié est-elle utile? Opinion d'Epictète et de Charron. Réfutation de cette opinion. Services rendus par la pitié. De la fausse pitié. III. Rôle de la pitié dans l'éducation. Les enfants sont-ils accessibles à ce sentiment? Opinion de la Fontaine, de la Bruyère, de Victor Hugo. D'où vient l'insensibilité des enfants? IV. Moyen d'éveiller et de diriger la pitié."] P.-F. Thomas, *L'éducation des sentiments* (Paris: Félix Alcan, 1899), 192.

42. ["ce sentiment joue un rôle si considérable dans la vie, et les moralistes nous en ont laissé tant d'analyses pénétrantes."] Thomas, 192.

43. ["qu'il est utile de l'examiner ici de plus près, afin d'en bien voir la nature, les causes et les effets."] Thomas, 192.

44. ["Dans la pitié véritable nous trouvons donc deux éléments distincts, bien qu'inséparables: une émotion pénible semblable à l'émotion d'autrui, c'est-à-dire une souffrance causée par la vue de sa souffrance, et une tendance plus ou moins vive à la secourir. C'est grâce à ce dernier élément que la pitié est si bienfaisante et si féconde; c'est par lui, également, qu'elle s'oppose à la bonté hypocrite qui est rarement agissante."] Thomas, 192–93.

45. ["La pitié est donc bien le sentiment altruiste par excellence."] Thomas, 193.

46. ["Mais…il est loin de se trouver chez tous également vif et agissant; c'est qu'il a d'abord ses causes, comme nous l'avons montré, et dans la sensibilité et dans l'imagination, et que ces deux facultés diffèrent suivant les individus et les temps. Si la femme sait mieux que l'homme compatir à toutes les douleurs, si elle sait trouver des paroles consolatrices pour toutes les infortunes, c'est que, en général, elle a une sensibilité et une imagination plus vives que les nôtres."] Thomas, 193–94. The rhetorical opposition between "women" and "we"— the omniscient community of male readers and actors—is capital to theories on the inculcation of pity.

47. ["Ajoutons, cependant, que la raison et la volonté sont souvent, pour la pitié, de précieux auxiliaires; c'est grâce à ces auxiliaires qu'elle devient réfléchie, éclairée,

persévérante, partant d'autant plus utile."] Thomas, 194.

48. ["Enfin, la pitié, plus encore peut-être que nos autres sentiments, a pour caractère d'être contagieuse: qu'auprès d'un pauvre qui tend la main à la foule indifférente, un passant tout à coup s'arrète; qu'il interroge ce malheureux, lui parle avec affection, et s'intéresse à sa misère; aussitôt on fait cercle autour de lui, et, quand son aumône tombe dans la sébile, il est rare que beaucoup d'autres immédiatement ne l'y rejoignent."] Thomas, 194.

49. ["mais il est nécessaire d'en constater l'existence, si nous voulons pouvoir, en développant la pitié chez nos enfants, leur apprendre à l'utiliser sagement."] Thomas, 195.

50. ["Voyons donc, lorsqu'elle est sincère et complète, quels services elle nous rend. Le premier est d'atténuer en nous l'égoisme: 'Les hommes, dit Rousseau, n'eussent jamais été que des monstres, si la nature ne leur eût donné la pitié à l'appui de la raison; c'est elle qui modère, en chacun de nous, l'activité de l'amour de soi'....En second lieu, la pitié rapproche les hommes....L'histoire ne nous prouve-t-elle pas, d'ailleurs, que la pitié a toujours parmi nous enfanté des miracles?"] Thomas, 197.

51. ["Nous venons d'étudier la pitié en elle-même et de signaler quelles conséquences généralement elle entraîne; il nous reste à montrer quel peut et quel doit être son rôle dans l'éducation."] Thomas, 198.

52. ["Et, d'abord, les enfants sont-ils bien accessibles à ce sentiment?—On connaît sur ce point l'opinion de La Fontaine. Elle se résume dans ce vers qu'on lui a souvent reproché: 'Cet âge est sans pitié.' Cette opinion est également celle de La Bruyère: 'les enfants, dit-il, ne veulent point souffrir le mal et ils aiment à en faire.'"] Thomas, 198.

53. ["mais ce qui est absolument certain, c'est que la pitié, de très bonne heure, fait en eux son apparition, et se manifeste par des actes dont le sens n'est point douteux."] Thomas, 199.

54. ["Il faut cependant reconnaître que, dans bien des cas, nos enfants font preuve d'une insensibilité surprenante; mais quelles en sont les causes? Ces causes se trouvent d'abord dans leur inexpérience."] Thomas, 199.

55. ["Pour remplir cette nouvelle tâche, c'est à la sensibilité et à l'imagination de l'enfant que nous devons, en premier lieu, recourir. Si nous l'amenons graduellement à réfléchir aux souffrances des autres, à comparer ces souffrances à celles qu'il connaît déjà; si nous savons choisir les lectures qu'il doit faire, et appeler son attention sur les événements fâcheux qui se produisent dans son entourage, son indifférence primitive bientôt disparaîtra. Il apprendra non seulement à connaître les maux qui le peuvent frapper, mais encore à s'y associer et à les plaindre. En outré, puisque la pitié est contagieuse, montrons-nous nous-mêmes pitoyables aux malheureux, et que notre pitié aille de préférence à ceux que la nature a cruellement déshérités, car plus que tous les autres ils ont droit à nos secours."] Thomas, 201.

56. Brooks writes in *The Eclectic Legacy*: "I would like to bring to light the pervasiveness of the philosophy of the syllabus in the discourse of the early human sciences, because I think it continued to inform much of the thought and practice of these disciplines long after they claimed their independence" (18).

57. The entry on Schopenhauer was written by Émile Charles, in Franck, ed., *Dictionnaire des sciences philosophiques*, 3rd ed. (Paris: Hachette, 1885), 1558–63.

58. Jourdain, *Notions de philosophie*, 8th ed. (Paris: Hachette, 1863), 13–14.

59. ["ou bien elles (émotions) n'ont pas de siège corporel, et elles ont pour cause une idée, une pensée; elles s'appellent alors *sentiments*."] Janet, *Traité de philosophie*, 6th ed. (Paris: Librairie Ch. Delagrave, 1889), 243.

60. ["sentiments sont les impulsions et inclinations qui nous portent vers des choses intellectuelles et morales."] Janet, 244.

61. ["Tout cela est faux, superficiel et grossier....La pitié est tout ce qu'il a de plus

naturel et de plus spontané dans le coeur humain; la présence de la souffrance nous fait souffrir, sans aucun retour sur nous-mêmes. C'est là un fait simple et immédiate, qui fait aussi bien partie de notre constitution que l'amour de soi."] Janet, 255.

62. ["Le besoin même que les hommes ont de la société paraît bien prouver qu'elle est naturelle et non factice….outre ce premier germe, il y en a un autre que Rousseau a signalé, la *pitié*, qui, même dans l'état de nature, réunit et rapproche les hommes. Schopenhauer, malgré sa misanthropie, croit à la pitié naturelle des hommes les uns pour les autres et en fait le principe de sa morale….La pitié, en tant qu'elle est une disposition à souffrir le même mal que ceux qui souffrent, n'est qu'un mode de la sympathie: mais en tant qu'elle est une tristesse causée par cette douleur et un désir de soulager ceux qui souffrent, cela est un mode de la bienveillance et de la philanthropie."] Janet, 323.

63. ["si ces sentiments donnent naissance à la société, il est aussi vrai réciproquement que ces sentiments ne se développent et ne se perfectionnent que *par* et *dans* la société….Il n'en faut pas conclure que ces sentiments soient artificiels pour cela: car puisque l'homme est essentiellement social, quoi de plus naturel que l'apparition de sentiments sociaux?"] Janet, 325.

64. The phrase is Pierre Nora's, in his essay "Le *Dictionnaire de pédagogie* de Ferdinand Buisson: Cathédrale de l'école primaire," in *Les lieux de mémoire*, I: *La République* (Paris: Gallimard, 1984), 353–78.

65. ["L'étude attentive de ces progrès lents et continues de la sensibilité, s'élevant peu à peu des plaisirs les plus grossiers des sens jusqu'aux émotions les plus délicats du Coeur, c'est la meilleure réfutation qu'on puisse opposer à l'erreur des pédagogues qui, comme Rousseau, veulent attendre la quinzaine année pour développer les sentiments moraux. On ne saurait trop tôt cultiver la sensibilité morale de l'enfant."] Gabriel Compayre, "Sensibilité," in *Dictionnaire de pédagogie et d'instruction primaire*, vol. 2:2, Buisson and Guillaume, eds. (Paris: Hachette, 1887), 2021.

66. ["Distinguer le sentiment de la sensation. Enumérer, classer et définir les principaux sentiments."] Émile Boirac, *La Dissertation philosophique* (Paris: Félix Alcan, 1890), 53.

67. ["'la pitié, c'est la tristesse née de la misère d'autrui.'"] Boirac, 53.

68. ["À plus forte raison ne peut-on, comme le voulait le stoïcisme, retrancher la sensibilité de la nature humaine. Cette mutilation n'est ni *possible* ni *désirable*. Il faut que *l'idée* se fasse *sentiment* pour *mouvoir* la volonté."] Boirac, *Cours élémentaire de philosophie*, 7th ed. (Paris: Félix Alcan, 1894), 32.

69. ["Montrer l'influence réciproque de la pensée sur le sentiment et du sentiment sur la pensée."] Boirac, 32.

70. ["La Rochefoucauld a dit: 'L'esprit est souvent la dupe du coeur.' Tout en reconnaissant la vérité de cette maxime ne peut-on la retourner et dire que souvent aussi le coeur est la dupe de l'esprit?"] Boirac, 37.

71. ["Les *inclinations sociales* ou sympathiques qui ont pour object les autres hommes, ont étes le sujet de beaucoup de discussions philosophiques. Certains auteurs, comme la Rochefoucauld dans ses *Maximes*, et plus tard Helvétius dans son livre sur *L'Esprit*, ont nié leur existence."] Janet, *Manuel du baccalauréat de l'enseignement secondaire: philosophie*, 3rd ed. (Paris: Vuibert et Nony, 1905), 161.

72. ["Ces sentiments sociaux présentent sous divers aspects, la *philanthropie*, la *sociabilité*, la *bienveillance*, la *sympathie*, la *compassion*, la *pitié*, *l'amitié*, la *reconnaissance*."] Janet, 100.

73. ["La forme active (et non plus seulement négative) du même devoir, c'est l'élan vers le soulagement de souffrances que nous n'avons pas causées. Soulager le plus de douleurs qu'on pourra, c'est déjà un admirable programme. Ce programme s'étend indéfiniment: car il faut aller *vers la misère* sous toutes ses formes, puisqu'elle est la source de souffrances sans

nombre."] Camille Mélinand, *Cours de philosophie morale* (Paris: Universelle par correspondance de Paris, s.d.), 84–85.

74. ["Pour tous ces devoirs envers la douleur, le *sentiment* fécond est la *pitié*, qui est le fait de ressentir, comme si elle était notre, la peine d'autrui, et par là de supprimer presque les barrières individuelles, en ne faisant plus qu'un avec 'l'autre.'"] Mélinand, 86.

75. ["Que ces philosophes qui ne veulent point que la vertu s'aide du sentiment, jettent les yeux sur le monde; qu'ils considèrent toutes les laideurs de la réalité, les injustices de la société, les douleurs sans nombre de l'histoire....Alors ils comprendront qu'il faut sauver avant tout la loi morale, et, loin de répudier les sentiments, ils en invoqueront le secours contre la force accablante des passions."] *Revue Universitaire* 2 (1893:1) (Paris: A. Colin, 1893), 254.

76. ["Le sentiment et la raison. Leur nature, leur rôle légitime dans la vie des individus et des nations."] *Revue Universitaire* 8 (1899:2), 285.

77. *Revue Universitaire* 1902:1 ("Peut-on fonder la fraternité humaine sur la solidarité des intérêts?")

78. ["Tous nous pouvons dire avec le poète: 'J'aime la majesté des souffrances humaines.' Ou, plus simplement, sans aucun souci du caractère auguste que revêtent ces souffrances aux yeux du poète et de l'âge, nous pouvons dire: 'j'aime celui qui souffre parce qu'il souffre.' Oui, nous sommes souvent conduits à l'amour pour nos frères humaines par la *pitié*, et non pas seulement la *pitié* pour les grandes catastrophes qui viennent de temps en temps bouleverser leur existence frêle et incertaine....Cette sympathie pour tous et cette pitié spéciale pour les malheureux sont si puissantes qu'elles suscitent chaque jour, chez les natures les moins raffinées, des actes de dévouement qui vont jusqu'aux sacrifices, et elles sont si universelles que certains moralistes de l'école positive ont vu en elles les seules forces de notre nature capables de lutter contre l'égoisme humain."] *Revue Universitaire* (1902:1), 314.

79. ["Les âmes où cette sympathie, cette admiration pour les grands spectacles du passé est le plus vive, comme celle de Michelet, par exemple, ne sont-elles pas aussi les plus accessibles à la pitié, les plus tendres et les plus chaudes, les plus vraiment fraternelles?"] *Revue Universitaire* (1902:1), 315.

80. ["L'usage des passions en morale selon Descartes."] *Revue Universitaire* (1908:1), 80.

81. ["'Aristote, bien éloigné de nous demander des héros parfaits, veut au contraire que les personnages tragiques...ne soient ni tout à fait bons, ni tout à fait méchants. Il ne veut pas qu'ils soient extrêmement bons, parce que la punition d'un homme de bien excitéroit plus l'indignation que la pitié d'un spectateur; ni qu'ils soient méchants avec excès, parce qu'on n'a point pitié d'un scélérat'....Ce texte important de la *Poétique* d'Aristote, ainsi résumé et commenté par J. Racine, peut également fournir une matière de composition française: 'Etudier les principaux personnages du théâtre cornélien et du drame racinien par rapport à la célèbre théorie aristotélicienne de la *terreur* et de la *pitié*, considérées comme les deux principaux ressorts de l'émotion dramatique.'"] *Revue Universitaire* (1910:1), 282.

82. ["'Et à considérer les impressions ordinaires que faisait la tragédie dans Athènes, sur l'âme des spectateurs, on peut dire que Platon était mieux fondé pour en défendre l'usage, que ne fut Aristote pour le conseiller; car la tragédie consistant, comme elle faisait, aux mouvements excessifs de la *crainte* et de la *pitié*, n'était-ce pas faire du théâtre une école de frayeur et de compassion, où l'on apprenait à s'épouvanter de tous les périls, et à se désoler de tous les malheurs?...Telle était l'envie de lamenter, qu'on exposait bien moins de vertus que de malheurs, de peur qu'une âme élevée à l'admiration des héros ne fût moins propre à s'abandonner à la pitié pour un miserable.' (Saint-Evrémond, *De la Tragédie ancienne et*

moderne [1672])."] *Revue Universitaire* (1896:2), 89.

83. ["discuter cette idée de Corneille: 'La tragédie doit exciter de la pitié et de la crainte.'"] *Revue Universitaire* (1907:1), 93.

84. ["Or, s'il est vrai que ce dernier sentiment ne s'excite en nous par la représentation que quand nous voyons souffrir nos semblables et que leurs infortunes nous en font appréhender de pareilles, n'est-il pas vrai aussi qu'il y pourrait être excité plus fortement par la vue des malheurs arrivés aux personnes de notre condition, à qui nous ressemblons tout à fait, que par l'image de ceux qui font trébucher de leurs trônes les plus grands monarques?"] *Revue Universitaire* (1907:1), 93.

85. ["depuis 'Je dirai plus; la tragédie doit exciter de la pitié'...jusqu'à: 'Vous savez mieux que moi tout ce que je vous dis.'"] *Revue Universitaire* (1903:1), 204.

86. ["La satire sociale et le sentiment de pitié chez La Bruyère, à propos de l'article sur les Paysans (*De l'homme*, 128)."] *Revue Universitaire* (1905:1), 259.

87. ["'La Bruyère s'est moins aisément arrangé que Molière de la société de son temps, et l'on voit percer chez lui une pitié qui n'est pas dans Boileau. C'est l'idée d'humanité qui commence à se faire jour.'"] *Revue Universitaire* (1905:2), 80.

88. ["Quelles réflexions vous inspire cette pensée d'un auteur contemporain: 'Plus je songe à la vie humaine, plus je crois qu'il faut lui donner pour témoins et pour juges l'Ironie et la Pitié. L'Ironie et la Pitié sont deux bonnes conseillères: l'une, en souriant, nous rend la vie aimable; l'autre, qui pleure, nous la rend sacrée.' (Anatole France, *Le Jardin d'Épicure*)."] *Revue Universitaire* (1906:1), 179.

Part II: Patrimonial, Social, and Pedagogical Anxieties around Pity

In preaching a universal pity to those who are capable of it, Schopenhauer addressed himself specifically to the French.

Aléxandre Baillot[1]

Schopenhauer and Nietzsche combined to make a confrontation with pity more ineluctable in *fin-de-siècle* France. The next chapter makes sense of Baillot's and similar claims about the two German philosophers. When Schopenhauer and Nietzsche made their mark in France, their *francité* or "frenchness" was the contentious subject. Nietzsche himself wrote: "In this France of the spirit, which is also the France of pessimism, Schopenhauer is even more at home than he has ever been in Germany, his main work has already been translated twice, the second time excellently, so that I now prefer to read Schopenhauer in French."[2] Pity was also a prism through which to inspect Nietzsche in French thought—but an incongruous one: the pity tradition made him comprehensible at the same time as it simplified and limited his philosophical reach. Moreover, with both Schopenhauer and Nietzsche, larger tensions between description and prescription were in evidence: analysis of their thought on pity was always accompanied by assessment.

Appraisals of Schopenhauer and Nietzsche often were a function of the precedence given either justice or pity in commentators' value-system. Indeed, *fin-de-siècle* thinkers and social reformers debated whether justice or pity should be given priority as a principle of social attachment. In Chapter 5, we look at two specific contexts—one a debate and the other a signal, if dramatically drawn-out, event—that pitted justice against pity: the discussion around the movement known as Solidarity, and the Dreyfus affair. Stances on Solidarity were especially revealing of the stakes involved in prescribing or proscribing pity. In addition to the works of Léon Bourgeois, Henri Marion, and especially

Georges Fonsegrives's *Solidarité, pitié, charité: examen de la nouvelle morale*, this chapter studies the oppositional pairings elaborated by political philosophers in works where pity/justice were posited as inescapable alternatives. The Dreyfus affair offers a good case study of the antithetical uses of the terms pity and justice in a clamorous public debate with more than impersonal perils. Most often these words were rhetorically twined in the partisans' emotive appeals to both sides—Dreyfusard and anti-Dreyfus. The equation for the concomitant partisans followed a certain logic of alternation: injustice called upon pity as a corrective, but when justice successfully did its work (at the last), pity was held in abeyance.

As we saw in the last chapter, schools' syllabi granted an important part to the analysis and inculcation of pity. Chapter 6 highlights the study programs and questions conveyed by the *Revue Universitaire* that attempted to indoctrinate pity in young women. Not only were questions on pity a prominent feature of the curricula listed in the *Revue*, but so was the effort to promote pity as both a civic and gendered virtue. The accession of females to secondary education and to some university posts after 1880, with attendant anxieties about received ideas on femininity and gender relationships, was deemed a singularly propitious time for revising a sentimental education. Many of the programs for the *École secondaire des jeunes filles*, for example, included questions such as: "Why is pity essential for women?" Young ladies were expected to cultivate pity, which in turn would cultivate Frenchmen.

In all three chapters we see concerns for, confrontations around, and contradictions within the categorical doctrines of pity we examined in the previous chapters.

NOTES

1. ["En prêchant l'universelle pitié à ceux qui en sont capables, Schopenhauer s'adressait, de ce fait, particulièrement aux Français."] Alexandre Baillot, *L'influence de la philosophie de Schopenhauer en France (1860–1900)* (Paris: Librairie Philosophique J. Vrin, 1927), 14.

2. Friedrich Nietzsche, *Nietzsche Contra Wagner*, in *The Portable Nietzsche*, Walter Kaufmann, ed. (New York: Penguin, 1968), 671–72.

Chapter 4: Schopenhauer and Nietzsche

Arriving at the right time, Schopenhauer played a considerable role in France: on the one hand by offering his conception of the world for the consideration of thinkers; on the other, by putting forward pity as the supreme law to moralists, love as the basis of pain to psychologists, and to the hopeless, salvation through total renunciation and liberating consciousness.[1]

A vital impetus to debate on pity was provided by two German-language philosophers who had a belated, galvanizing impact in France: Arthur Schopenhauer and Friedrich Nietzsche. One was the melancholy promoter of a pity-based ethics (*Mitleids-moral*); the other, its great nemesis, "Zarathustra" the anti-pitier. (It is not incidental that French readers, in contradistinction to contemporary practice, consistently translated as *pitié* the word at the crux of the Germans' disagreement, *mitleid*.)[2] Together, they helped keep pity at the center stage of ethics in France and provoked a sense of nationalistic anxiety about its patrimony.

French sentimentalist thought of the *fin-de-siècle* refused to give moral standing to egoistic impulses; only altruistic, piteous sentiments were granted salience as moral motives. The crux of the Schopenhauer-Nietzsche disputation centered on this very question; their respective philosophies found receptive soil in France. Schopenhauer, who died in 1860, entered French philosophic awareness belatedly. The diffusion and acceptance of his works and ideas really began after 1870,[3] coinciding with the post–Prussian War nationalist and moral crises: "Schopenhauer, the foreign philosopher most widely read in France in the last quarter of the century."[4] Perhaps not so coincidentally, Schopenhauer's thinking had undergone a pronounced apolitical transformation after the failed European revolutions of 1848,[5] and he now posthumously navigated another political revolution, across the shores of the Rhine, to renewed relevance.[6]

The purpose here is not to reexamine Schopenhauer's critical reception in France[7], but rather to ascertain the vital importance of Schopenhauerian pity for French thought. Indeed, the imputed "Frenchness" (*francité*) of Schopenhauer's ideas became part of the compulsion to classify his philosophy and update pro-pity thinking. I maintain that it is not fortuitous that Schopenhauer's impact in France was at a maximum when pro-pity sentimentalism was also ascendant. Schopenhauer's was the antithesis of eclectic philosophy.[8] The first stab at attracting a French readership for Schopenhauer, in 1856, had been inconsequential. It was only with the article consecrated to him by Paul-Armand Challemel-Lacour (1827–1896)[9] in 1870 that Schopenhauer got posthumous traction. In 1874, Ribot dedicated a book-length study to him, and in 1876 Ernest Renan was avidly trying to publicize him.[10] By 1880, Schopenhauer's work, with the paramount exception of *The World as Will and Representation* and the *Aphorisms*, had been translated into French; by then, he was thoroughly à la mode.

That vogue had everything to do with the reciprocal relationship between his "Frenchness" and pro-pity ethics, for there was an attempt to naturalize Schopenhauer, to assimilate him to French philosophical and ethical traditions, after 1870. Bourdeau could claim, in support of a subscription drive to commemorate the centennial of the German's birth, scheduled for February 22, 1888: "We could recall for our part how much Schopenhauer was inspired by French genius, by our eighteenth-century authors and our physiologists of the nineteenth."[11] Janet also asserted Schopenhauer's *francité*: "This semi-French education had a rather large influence on the mind of our philosopher, and it is not reckless to assume that it contributed to giving him the taste for clarity and precision, the horror of metaphysical jargon, that distinguishes him in a particular manner from the philosophers of his time and country."[12] In a seminal comparative essay of 1880, Janet teased out the affinities between Schopenhauer's will-centered philosophy and the earlier physiology of Pierre-Jean-Georges Cabanis (1757–1808) and Marie-François-Xavier Bichat (1771–1802). He argued that Schopenhauer's conception of the will was "French": "Whatever the origins of his ideas may be, it is from us that they came; it is to our own philosophers that we should render homage. This is something that is often forgotten by the zealous admirers of all things German. We exalt Schopenhauer while forgetting Cabanis and Bichat.... the only point that we have wished to highlight is the French origins of Schopenhauer's philosophy."[13]

Janet was consistent in his Francocentric linkages: in a *laudatio* to Marie-François-Pierre Maine de Biran (1766–1824), he equated the founder of an eclectic will-centered French philosophy with the increasingly renowned German: "The activity of the self has no influence over the sentiments of the heart or over love. We can only lend ourselves to the receptivity of the spirit...one can relate him equally here to another German philosopher who has become famous, Schopenhauer."[14]

Challemel-Lacour, although sympathetic to Schopenhauer's goals, nonetheless characterized his philosophical system as a mere "work of literature;" yet he too wrote along lines similar to Janet: "If we had to characterize the brilliant aspect of Schopenhauer's talent, I would say that above all he is a painter of the life and temperament of humans, a moralist in the *French* sense of the word; he was educated at the school of Montaigne, la Rochefoucauld, la Bruyère, Vauvenargues, Chamfort,

Helvétius, whom he cites at every step."[15]

Schopenhauer's "Frenchness" was partly a product of the tradition-honoring and classificatory impulses operative in academic philosophy. But it was also a result of the attempt to factor new ideas through sentimentalism and the moralists' tradition. These elements account for the immense critical interest in two basic aspects of Schopenhauer's thought: his "pessimism" and pity-ethics.

Schopenhauer's (in)famous pessimism—the claim, in *The World as Will and Representation*, that the nonexistence of the world would have been preferable to its existence, since the will, the ground of all existence, leads inexorably to suffering so that the only true remedy is the ablation of desire and thus the eradication of the basis of being—was at first a source of horrified attraction.[16] Consider the case of Elmé Caro (1825–1887), a dinosaur of the ASMP, who was elected to that body on February 6, 1869 and to the Académie Française in 1874 and who taught at the Sorbonne until 1887. He was the author of such alarmist works as *Étude de morale sur les temps présents* (1875), and *Problèmes de morale sociale* (1887), as well as tendentious commentaries on contemporary philosophers, gathered as *Philosophie et philosophes* (1888). He upbraided Schopenhauer's bleak vision, which he reproved as un-French and nihilistically revolutionary. Indeed, Caro, Bourdeau's father-in-law, laid down his claims with ridiculous brusqueness, charging, among other things, that Schopenhauer belonged to a race of beer-drinkers and "there is no danger that pessimism will ever adapt itself to the land of the vine and especially in France; Bordeaux clarifies and brightens ideas and Burgundy chases away nightmares."[17] Trivial caricature aside,[18] Caro refused to abide Schopenhauer for political reasons, since he saw pessimism as an auxiliary to revolution: "And one should not think that this evil is simply intellectual or literary: it affects souls and public morality, and sooner or later translates into political and social catastrophes."[19] The specter of the national disaster of 1870–1871 and its residual Germanophobia hung over Caro's screed; but so did the earlier Franco-French debate on the political standing of sentiment. In a reversal, conservative anti-Republicans would recuperate Schopenhauerian pessimism in the late 1880s and 1890s.[20]

Schopenhauer's pity-based morality truly drew him onto the French philosophical stage. The pessimist, the metaphysician, the psychologist of the will—all facets of his thought were subordinated to that of the pro-pity moralist—an exercise later reinforced by the pairing with Nietzsche. Before we analyze reactions to, and appropriations of, Schopenhauerian pity, it is indispensable that we outline his cogent views as located in his writings.

It is fitting that Schopenhauer's pity-based theory of morality was given its first, pithy exposition in answer to a competition sponsored by the Royal Danish Society of Scientific Studies on the appropriately Kantian-Humean question, "What are the grounds of morality?"[21] Schopenhauer's answer is the basis of the essay published as *On the Basis of Morality (Über die Grundlage der Moral)* of 1839, where, after subjecting Kant's ethics to a harsh critique, he proposed, especially in section 16, an ethics of pity meant to be both ontological and descriptive. He claimed that his system was so consonant with common sense that "my solution to the problem will remind many of the egg of Columbus"[22]—a system intended as the elucidation of the principle whose maxim is, "Injure no one; on the contrary, help everyone as much as you can."[23]

The philosophical quandary arises from the fact that this maxim describes behavior that is universally approved, yet why it is so has gone unsolved. Furthermore, this maxim encounters an immediate hurdle: humanity's "boundless egoism," which is the enemy of justice and indeed of all other-directed virtues.[24] By definition, Schopenhauer argues—with nine "proofs" at hand—"the absence of all egoistic motivation is, therefore, *the criterion of an action of moral worth*"[25]—"*egoism* and the *moral worth* of an action absolutely exclude each other."[26]

But how is it that the self can break through to a concern with the "weal and woe" of others?

It is the everyday phenomena of pity [*mitleid*], of the immediate *participation*, independent of all ulterior considerations, primarily in the *suffering* of another, and thus in the prevention or elimination of it; for all satisfaction and all well-being and happiness consist in this. It is simply and solely this pity [*mitleid*] that is the real basis of all *voluntary* justice and *genuine* loving-kindness. Only insofar as an action has sprung from pity [*mitleid*] does it have moral value; and every action resulting from any other motive has none. As soon as this pity [*mitleid*] is aroused, the weal and woe of another are nearest to my heart in exactly the same way, although not always in the same degree, as otherwise only my own are.[27]

Thus, pity is defined by Schopenhauer as that feeling for another whereby "I suffer directly with him, I feel his woes just as I ordinarily feel my own; and likewise, I directly desire his weal in the same way I otherwise desire my own."[28] Here we see the integral relationship of pity and pessimism, for in a suffering-based cosmos pity is incessantly beckoned; the circle among pity-pitier-pitied is as perpetual as that linking birth-suffering-death.

The revelation of the ontological unity of Being that underlies all differentiated wills is the antidote to both egoism and the nihilism induced by suffering, as well as the first step to true pity: "In the last resort, it is this knowledge to which every appeal to gentleness, leniency, loving-kindness, and mercy instead of justice, is directed. For such an appeal is a reminder of that respect in which we are all one and the same."[29] A self-transcending pity, not duty or reason, is therefore the true grounds of morality. It is, Schopenhauer claims, the *urphänommen* of morality, the "great mystery of ethics."[30]

Schopenhauer's claims for pity as the basis of ethics are consistently broad. For him, it is a metaphysically irreducible principle; it is causally antecedent to justice and philanthropy, the two highest manifestations of social virtue. The former corresponds to the first half of Schopenhauer's guiding maxim: "the first degree of the effect of pity [*mitleid*] is that it opposes and impedes those sufferings which I intend to cause to others by my inherent antimoral forces;"[31] the latter is the functional equivalent of the second clause, "help everyone as much as you can." As "confirmation" of the truth of a *mitleid-morals*, Schopenhauer appeals to the commonsense psychology underlying the universal disapproval of cruelty: "nothing shocks our moral feelings so deeply as cruelty does. We can forgive every other crime, but not cruelty. The reason for this is that it is the very opposite of pity [*mitleid*]."[32] So that pity [*mitleid*], a "boundless compassion," is "the firmest and surest guarantee of pure moral conduct, and needs no casuistry."[33]

The primacy accorded pity in its binary antagonism to justice points us to understanding why Schopenhauerian pity was taken seriously in France. So does the self-conscious manner in which Schopenhauer set about situating himself against the anti-pity tradition in France: "The foundation I have given to ethics certainly leaves me without a predecessor among the school philosophers.... For many of them, the Stoics, for instance...Spinoza...Kant...positively reject and condemn pity [*mitleid*]. On the other hand, my foundation is supported by the authority of J. -J. Rousseau, who was undoubtedly the greatest moralist of modern times."[34] So Schopenhauer himself confirmed the rationale of those who wanted to highlight the *francité* of his pro-pity ethics.

Schopenhauer's case for an ethics founded on pity was reinforced by arguments in *The World as Will and Representation* and in his more accessible collection *Parerga and Paralipomena*, whose last chapter of volume 1, "Aphorisms on the Wisdom of Life," was published in a separate, popular edition in France as *Aphorismes sur la sagesse dans la vie*. Schopenhauer's brief for pity was emphatically anti-Kantian; it further eroded the rationalists' confidence in logical axioms of ethics and reinforced sentimentalism. Schopenhauer thus became the counterweight to Kant that Hume had never been for the French in the reason-sentiment divide—this was partly the source of his prominence and lisibility, I would argue. Indeed, in answer to the question prompted by Baillot's claim that "in preaching a universal pity to those who are capable of it, Schopenhauer addressed himself specifically to the French"—Why especially to the French? —I would make the case that sentimentalism in late-nineteenth-century France and its concerns with the foundations of morality and the respective roles of reason and sentiment made especially fertile soil for Schopenhauer's pity-morals. We can now turn to some of the interpretations that substantiate this claim.

Schopenhauer's *francité* and his promotion of pity made for facile comparisons. For example, Bourdeau, in his monograph on la Rochefoucauld, contrasted the two philosophers by situating them within traditional thinking on pity: "Schopenhauer borrows from la Rochefoucauld his theory of pity, 'which is only the sight of our own woes in those of another.' But he wants us to turn away from the sight of human perversity to that of the anguish of human existence. He thus makes of pity the cardinal virtue: not to know it is to place oneself beyond humanity."[35] In his last engagement with Schopenhaeur, in 1912, where he showed himself more unsympathetic to the German's philosophy, Bourdeau nonetheless coupled him to Rousseau: "Like Rousseau he exaggerates compassion, which he reconciles to his misanthropy in that despite the wickedness of humans we should pity their misfortunes. The morality of compassion is but the prelude to the morality of renunciation, which alone leads to Redemption."[36] By the time Bourdeau wrote these lines, he had become acquainted with Nietzsche's attacks on pity. This may account for the shift in vocabulary from the earlier rendering of Schopenhauerian *mitleid* as *pitié* to its translation here as both *compassion* and *pity* and thus be one way in which Bourdeau wished to save the essential French concordance of Schopenhauer's concept from the brunt of Nietzsche's opprobrium, for Bourdeau, even at this latter date, still agreed with

Schopenhauer that the problem of the foundation of moral obligation was the "biggest problem in human existence."[37] But Bourdeau had come to reprove Schopenhauerian pity because, like Nietzsche and under his influence, he linked pity to pessimism and asceticism, both of which he disdained. On the eve of the Great War, we see through Bourdeau the mutual waning of Schopenhauer's reverberations in French philosophy and the hold of a pro-pity ethics.

Schopenhauer's pity-based system of morality was inserted into the sentiment side of the debate with rationalism—often to the detriment of Schopenhauer. Fouillée, who was influenced in his philosophy of *idées-forces* by Schopenhauer, did not believe that "pity and the new nirvana of the pessimists" was a sufficient moral principle.[38] Nourrisson objected in 1891 that Schopenhauerian pity was devoid of sanctions—the essential criterion for a persuasive axiom in ethics: "Can duty be replaced by pity, which Schopenhauer wishes to make the basis among all beings, owing to the identity of their nature? Does not such an ethics, insofar as it is an ethics, remain lacking in sanctions?"[39]

Paul Janet also argued that Schopenhauerian pity could be an ethical imperative only if subjected to the *idea* of pity, which alone could set duty in motion. This cognitive reinterpretation of Schopenhauer's theory renders Janet a proponent of rational eudemonism. Moreover, pity does not replace duty, as Schopenhauer claimed; rather, it serves to trigger another ideational complex of obligation:

Let us suppose, with Schopenhauer, that pity is the essential principle of morals; suppose that, since all men have, as he maintains, only one and the same essence, the good of others is our own good: then I would say that we would feel ourselves obliged to promote the good of other men, or at least to prevent them from suffering, even when our passions were drawing us in a direction contrary to that of pity.... so long as this idea remains, however feeble may be his pity, however strong his anger, it is impossible that he should feel it permissible to yield to his strongest passion, while that which his conscience tells him is the better, remains torpid.... But from this general principle I deduce this rule: Act in such a way that you may sympathize to the greatest possible extent with other men. It is a categorical imperative.[40]

The ingeniousness with which Janet formulates a categorical imperative of pity (of all things!) demonstrates to us the need to quarantine Schopenhauerianism within compassable boundaries. Janet needed to safeguard the Kantian categorical imperative against Schopenhauer's apostasy. But this led to the inspired equation of pity with reason. Schopenhauer thus goaded an ethics accommodating of pity even in those who, like Janet, were not willing to accept all the doctrines of sentimentalism.

Renouvier, another rearguard champion of rationalism, was among the leading neo-Critical philosophers to take Schopenhauer's metaphysics seriously. In a lengthy article published in *L'Année philosophique*'s third issue, in 1892, on Schopenhauer's "metaphysics of pessimism," he studied—in order to critique—the links that the German tried to forge among individuation, noumenal appearance, and pity. Renouvier was a singular detractor in that he pointed to the apparent paradox involved in positing pity as a way to surmount the delusion of selfhood and self-sufficiency:

We must go further and note that pity or love, and not only justice, disappear in the transformation effected by Schopenhauerian metaphysics…. these sentiments, even taken at the highest degree of generalization possible, extended to yet larger and larger groups, still imply a relationship to someone other than the self and, thus, presuppose to some degree the principle of individuation. The acknowledgement of the universal unity of identities, which is the explanation of the basis of pity and charity, thus leads to this odd assertion: that it is for oneself that one has pity, that at bottom one loves only oneself.[41]

For Renouvier, it was Schopenhauer's hatred of individuation that lay beneath both his metaphysics and his ethics.

Renouvier returned to this topic in a chapter of his neo-Kantian treatise of 1897, *Philosophie analytique de l'histoire*: "La morale du pessimisme: Principe de la pitié" ["The Ethics of Pessimism: Principle of Pity"]. Here, he stressed what he judged to be Schopenhauer's debased Buddhism that obliges an ethics premised on pity: "The ethics of pessimism is a direct consequence of the doctrine that evil is connected to the will to life, and of the universal resemblance of beings. In effect, asceticism is always a battle of the will against life, and pity, which is Schopenhauer's ethical fundament, hinges, according to him, on the feeling of a community of misery."[42] Renouvier's paraphrase of Schopenhauer's dysthemic pity seems anodynely fair-minded. Like Bourdeau, Renouvier stressed the links among pity, pessimism, and asceticism; unlike Bourdeau, he judges these through a glass rationally: "Kantian and Schopenhauerian *a prioris* are in agreement in their shared opposition to utilitarian ethics; and up to that point, in fact, they provide the same criterion for moral acts, from which all consideration for the agent's happiness is severely excluded. The mystical and ascetic character of this pessimistic ethics has its source in a sentiment that Schopenhauer fuses to the intuitive consciousness of the identity of Being."[43] In contradistinction to the philosophers who disparaged Schopenhauer's pity as inferior to rational duty and in a modification of his wholesale critique of 1892, Renouvier here analyzed the difference as lying between utilitarianism and hedonism, on the one hand, and German *a prioris*—duty and dolorous sentimentalism—on the other. The antinomian project of judging and merging Kant and Schopenhaeur, the one by the other, fascinated Renouvier, even as he preferred Kant: "But it is he, Schopenhauer, who, because of his particular habit of envisaging sentiment—one could almost say a physical feeling—as the source of all moral acts, and of mistaking the idea of law for that of a commandment intimated from the outside, who found himself incapable of understanding the basics of Kantian imperatives."[44]

But by stressing the intersubjective and synesthetic quality of Schopenhauerian pity--as Mélinand was to do in the *Encyclopédie*--Renouvier praised its explanation of crying: "The theory of pity provided Schopenhauer with a remarkable psychological explanation of *crying*, which he correlates in all cases—even those in which we are moved by our own distress—to pity and not to the feeling of distress itself. This explanation seems a solid and fortunate one, even if the author was inspired to it by his theory of the correspondence between the subject and object of pity, even when they differ as phenomena."[45] Renouvier's interpretations innovated pro-pity thinking in allying pity and duty with a noneudemonistic amativeness. Love, Renouvier argued, is a circumscribed instance of pity: "the conclusion is that pure love is essentially pity, whether the suffering to be relieved be great or small...love and pity cannot be divided from the sentiment of a certain kinship of nature."[46] Renouvier's admixture here is uniquely French, indicating the extent of the reach of sentimentalism. Indeed, most other pro-pity theorists or sentimentalists never went so far as to identify pity with love, either humane or sacred.[47] If Renouvier's intercession was intended to salvage an alternative amative explanation of attachment to Schopenhauer's unrelieved ascetic pessimism, it still profited sentimentalism.

For that matter, in the article for *L'Année philosophique* he had concluded that Schopenhauer, despite or because of his faulty metaphysics, was a salutary influence on philosophy for his backing of sentiment over reason; even if Renouvier believes, *contra* Schopenhauer, that the former should serve to sustain selfhood:

The entry of Buddhism—which had been so distant—in Western philosophy can have a positive dimension: the acknowledgement of pain as essential both to organic and moral life and experience...we are already disenchanted with those purely intellectualist doctrines that led philosophers to turn aside from these great truths.... The necessary condition for a veritable optimism, in philosophy as in religion, should take as its subject not just the individual, but also, and essentially, the personality, the *salvation of the self.*[48]

Buddhism was used almost as an adjective that supposedly helped explain Schopenhauer's metaphysics—and thus it served to divorce what was eminently not assimilable into French tradition (pessimism) from what was (pity). Paul Challemel-Lacour dismissed the contents of Schopenhauer's ethics as unworthy of French thought because of what he claimed was its bastardized Buddhism:

To regard, on the contrary, that the will is a common source from which every being flows and that, varied only in appearance, is nonetheless identical in each, is to eliminate the barrier separating individuals.... it is also a way to enthrone pity over egoism—pity, which is the sympathetic repercussion in the human heart of all sufferings; pity, which moralists unanimously proclaim as the origin of all virtues, the commencement of love, and which slowly but surely leads one to absolute renunciation and puts one in a position to outsmart the tricks of fate and to escape the eternal illusions with which nature encircles one. Here we are at the height of Buddhism. These ideas are an emanation of the counsels of despair that have always flourished in India.[49]

On the other hand, Rodolphe Dareste (1824–1911), member of the ASMP, great jurist (sitting on the Cour de cassation from 1877 until his death), and historian of law (an editor of the *Revue historique du droit français et étranger* from 1855 until 1907), credited Schopenhauer with creating a vogue for Hindu legal philosophy.[50]

The French response to Schopenhauer exhibited the same classificatory impulse that dominated the reason-sentiment debate; the discussion of pity on the tails of a foreign figure imposed genealogical precision. In addition to the almost requisite references to la Rochefoucauld and Rousseau, there were also allusions to contemporary figures. Alphonse Darlu (1849–1921) of the ASMP[51] in 1899 paid tribute to Schopenhauerian pity within a threefold context: its relationship to the history of ethics; to French traditions; and to metaphysical theories of morality. In the first, Darlu classified Schopenhauerian pity as "one of the most important contributions to ethical theory in recent times," under the rubric of "spiritualism:"

One of the first to appear is Schopenhauer's morality of pity…we must surely acknowledge the powerful action that it has exercised over European thought in the last half-century…. It may be that our own Loti, whose most beautiful books have a taste of ash, is indebted to him…. In order to destroy evil, it is necessary to abjure individual existence, to mingle one's heart with that of others. Pity intuits the identity of all beings. It tears the veil of Maya. It is the great mystery of moral life.[52]

Darlu accorded Schopenhauer's ethics of pity a large impact on European thought of the previous half century and then brought it back within national boundaries by assimilating it to Pierre Loti, a writer of tales, novels, and travelogues who was gaining renown at just this time and whose narratives of pity we explore in the next part. That fiction and Schopenhauerian pity were thus consolidated was telling. Yet Darlu's description is not prescriptive: "We believe that the ideas of pity, charity, admiration, flow from the very sources of moral life, and that their deterioration would simultaneously diminish that life. However, they correspond to only one of the two movements comprising the soul's rhythm. The soul cannot completely escape itself without ceasing to be. It must seek within itself the necessary strength to love without. Real goodness consists of strength and not weakness."[53] Darlu turned the tables on Schopenhauer, situating within the self the pro-social sentiments that are summoned for the sake of others.

Georges Fonsegrive expressed similar reservations at first contact with Schopenhauer's ideas on pity, only to accept a modified rendering a few years later. His qualms had less to do with a bias for rationalist metaphysics or neospiritualism than with a dislike of pessimism, which contaminated pity for him by making it nihilistic and quietistic rather than truly caritative. Rejecting—perhaps misunderstanding—Schopenhauer's equating pity with philanthropy, Fonsegrive argued for a difference between pity and goodness:

Schopenhauer wished to reduce almost all social morality to this sentiment, all duties toward other beings. But pity is not goodness; it is only a tender sentiment at the sight of the woes of others. For it to become goodness, it is necessary to introduce an active principle, an *élan* towards the being who suffers, a respect for that being, a belief in his/her worth. To be good, to do good, is not solely to release someone from their woes, but to strengthen the weakened being, to beckon him or her to a heightened state, to an ascent and exaltation of life itself.[54]

Fonsegrive valued pity insofar as it was linked to a receptivity to others' weal and woe; but the more active disposition that would undercut the very need for further pity is *bonté*, which surpasses pity in primacy and purport, especially since Schopenhauerian pity is inextricably linked to pessimism, which undermines the metaphysical underpinnings of *bonté*: "But pity obviously presupposes that life has a value, that it is worth more than nothing. To be good one must love, and the pessimist cannot love, since nothing is loveable because nothing has any value. Thus Schopenhauer would reproach any institution and any conduct that seeks to boost individuals in the world and life itself."[55]

Fonsegrive, while criticizing Schopenhauerian pity as an insufficient spur to goodness, nonetheless employed it as a signpost in a teleological moral itinerary: "The ancient Westerners knew little of pity. Human suffering seems to have moved them little. They gladly turned away from its manifestations rather than seeking to relieve it. It is in the East that Buddhism, based on the contemplation of all the evils that assail humanity, created a religion of pity. Schopenhauer wished to reduce ethics to that sentiment."[56] Fonsegrive's attempt to draw an analogy between Schopenhauer and a supposedly "Oriental" pity was a commonplace, translating the wish to insulate French intellectual practices from too much external innovation.

Théodule Ribot, in his epochal monograph on Schopenhaeur in 1874,[57] fastened onto the importance of pity in the German's philosophy. Ribot identified pity as the very pith of Schopenhauer's theory of the will and hence as congruent with his own interests. After paraphrasing Schopenhauer's view of it as the basis of sociability— "Pity alone is the real basis of all free justice and all true charity"—Ribot saw its main feature as the "complete negation of the will to life...characteristic of saints, anchorites, vedics, Christians."[58] The ascetic aspect of pity clearly renders it a character-virtue rather than an act- or duty-based regulator: "It is in being and not in activity that freedom is found."[59] But pity's very asceticism, Ribot argues, causes it to be an inadequate ethical ground rule, since will is essential to determining moral value.

Ribot's ambivalence about the relationship between pity and the will helps explain the attraction of Schopenhauer for him and perhaps the subsequent tenor of his psychological treatises as well. The study of the "will" (*volonté*) was a major preoccupation of *fin-de-siècle* thinkers because it touched on the most important problems of self and society. Will implies dynamic individuality, difference, and divergence. The scrutiny of the self-regarding will also entailed an analysis of other-regarding pity, since oppositional pairings were the rule: Schopenhauer was pro-pity and abjured the will, whereas Nietzsche was anti-pity and pro-will (to simplify for the moment). Ribot's work can be seen, in part, as venturing to arbitrate among these positions.

Did this enthrallment with Schopenhauer not betoken an impasse in French philosophy? The simplest answer might be that Schopenhauer's nationality and pessimism acted after 1870 as anomalous incentives to reconsider the pity tradition and its assumed patrimony. Frédéric Paulhan put it this way: "Schopenhauer answered well enough to our need...moreover, the unfortunate circumstances that our country had passed through rendered us perhaps more capable of appreciating the bitter pleasure of lost illusions and also, without a doubt, of favorably welcoming theories from foreign countries, even or especially one which defeated us."[60] To look up the word "pity" in *fin-de-siècle* French reference books invariably meant to happen upon Schopenhauer. In l'abbé Élie Blanc's (1846–1927) *Dictionnaire de philosophie ancienne, moderne, et contemporaine* (1906), "Pitié" was given a cognitive definition with almost exclusive reference to Schopenhauer: "Sentiment of sympathy and commiseration that arises from the sight of others' woes. Acknowledged or even provoked and directed by reason, pity becomes a virtue. But Schopenhauer could not make of it the fundament of ethics."[61] Mélinand similarly used Schopenhauer as the distinct authority for his article on "Pitié" in *La Grande Encyclopédie*.

Schopenhauer's antipodes in this as in other regards was Nietzsche, who also saturated French thinking on pity. That the two were closely associated in this thinking is a sign of both the real-life relationship between the elder pessimist and his younger, onetime acolyte—in *Twilight of the Idols*, an epitome of his thought, Nietzsche gave Schopenhauer a rare accolade: "*Schopenhauer*. Schopenhauer, the last German worthy of consideration"[62]— and the fact that the ethics of pity was central to both.[63]

Like Schopenhauer, Nietzsche made his mark in France with his *francité* at issue.[64] Many early commentators laid him out on the procrustean bed of the French moralists' tradition,[65] and found his dimensions remarkably like la Rochefoucauld's. As was also the case for Schopenhauer, pity served as a lens through which to behold Nietzsche's ideas; it refracted some of the other complex components of his work: antiChristianism, atheism, anti-democracy, and anti-idealism. Most commentators misrepresented this concatenation, preferring to harness him both to French intellectual traditions and to Schopenhauer.

In truth, other than Schopenhauer and Wagner, Nietzsche's models, those against whom he cut his philosophical teeth, were a roll call of French classics: Montaigne, Pascal, la Rochefoucauld, Rousseau. Taine and Renan, two contemporary legatees, were also consequential. Even Nietzsche's Schopenhauerian flirtation and repudiation were added reasons to measure him by traditional yardsticks, since Schopenhauer was himself incorporated into this tradition.[66] Or as Nietzsche wrote, as cited earlier: "In this France of the spirit, which is also the France of pessimism, Schopenhauer is even now more at home than he has ever been in Germany; his main work has already been translated twice, the second time excellently, so that I now prefer to read Schopenhauer in French."[67]

Nietzsche's condemnation of pity would henceforth be twined to Schopenhauer's sponsorship.[68] "Schopenhauer was hostile to life; therefore, pity became a virtue for him,"[69] Nietzsche claimed, and this argument resounded in French writings on both men.

Nietzsche's attacks on pity are strewn all over his texts and concentrated most forcefully in two works, *Thus Spoke Zarathustra* and *On the Genealogy of Morals*, as well as central to *Human, All Too-Human*; *Daybreak*; *The Gay Science*; *The Antichrist*; and *Twilight of the Idols*. These views are often more nuanced and developmentally complex than Nietzsche himself suggested,[70] for pity is not just Nietzsche's polemic, it is also his analytic. Nietzsche's aphoristic style, seized upon by *fin-de-siècle* French commentators as a point of convergence with the moralists' tradition, helps mask the thoroughness of his grappling with pity. In *The Gay Science* he rhetorically replied to his own demand, "Where does your greatest danger lie—In pity?" and the bulk of his case against pity draws out the full range of meanings behind this question and answer. In *Nietzsche Contra Wagner*, he observed: "The more a psychologist—a born and inevitable psychologist and unriddler of souls—applies himself to the more exquisite cases and human beings, the greater becomes the danger that he might suffocate of pity."[71] In *Twilight of the Idols* he again declaimed:

Saying Yes to life even in its strangest and hardest problems, the will to life rejoicing over its own inexhaustibility even in the very sacrifice of its highest types—*that* is what I called Dionysian, *that* is what I guessed to be the bridge to the psychology of the *tragic* poet. *Not* in order to be liberated from terror and pity, not in order to purge oneself of a dangerous affect by its vehement discharge—Aristotle understood it that way—but in order to be *oneself* the eternal joy of becoming, beyond all terror and pity—that joy which included even joy in destroying.[72]

Nietzsche's most sustained argument against pity is in *Zarathustra*, where pity is apostrophized as the autobiographical Zarathustra's "last temptation" and "greatest sin"—with Schopenhauer as the blandisher. Zarathustra's *bildungsroman* is an education in overcoming pity: "But what is human distress to me? My final sin, which has been saved up for me—do you know what it is? *Pity!*" And: "consideration and pity have ever been my greatest dangers, and everything human wants consideration and pity. With concealed truths, with a fool's hands and a fond, foolish heart and a wealth of the little lies of pity: thus I always lived among men."[73] Pity is warded off as injurious not only to truly human flourishing but to love and creativity. Nietzsche put this forward with aphoristic tempestuousness:

Verily, I do not like them, the merciful who feel blessed in their pity: they are lacking too much in shame. If I must pity, at least I do not want it known; and if I do pity, it is preferably from a distance....One ought to hold to one's heart; for if one lets it go, one soon loses control of the head too. Alas, where in the world has there been more folly than among the pitying? And what in the world has caused more suffering than the folly of the pitying? Woe to all who love without having a height that is above their pity![74]

Nietzsche's argument is thus myriad: pity is indulged in by the weak for their pleasure and power: "'Pity is needed,' says the third group. 'Take from me what I have! Take from me what I am! Life will bind me that much less!' If they were full of pity through and through, they would make life insufferable for their neighbors;" "When the great man screams, the small man comes running with his tongue hanging from lasciviousness. But he calls it his 'pity.'"[75] But since these perverse pleasures and powers are instantiated by Others, they are not self-creative or -transcending; pity brings about unintended consequences ("folly"); it is inferior to a love ("great love") that respects human autonomy and dignity:

Whether it be a god's pity or man's—pity offends the sense of shame. And to be unwilling to help can be nobler than that virtue which jumps to help. But today that is called virtue itself among all the little people—pity. They have no respect for great misfortune, for great ugliness, for great failure.... thus be warned of pity: from there a heavy cloud will yet come to man. Verily, I understand weather signs. But mark this too: all great love is even above all its pity; for it still wants to create the beloved. "Myself I sacrifice to my love, *and my neighbor as myself*"—thus runs the speech of all creators. But all creators are hard. Thus spoke Zarathustra.[76]

Pity is contrary to forgetting, which is essential to all striving and creativity, in that pity holds off the "much bitter dying" that renders forgetfulness vital—"This is my pity for all that is past: I see how all of it is abandoned."[77] Pity also holds on to a supposed truth about others' situation, when in fact creative falsehood is a precondition for living.

This is not all—if "God is dead," as Nietzsche notoriously announced, "He" died from pity, the poisonous emotion: "Thus spoke the devil to me once: 'God too has his hell: that is his love of man.' And most recently I heard him say this: 'God is dead; God has died of his pity for man.'"[78] Because pity imposes an inhibiting view of suffering and dependence, its ultimate consequence is destruction, especially self-destruction. Indeed, the decisive reason for Nietzsche's joining the battle against pity is his wish to tetanize suffering against pessimism; he wishes to embrace suffering as vital and hence as erroneously interpreted by those who cannot encompass existence with an *amor fati*. Pity obtrudes from the heart of the meaning of suffering:

The most spiritual human beings, if we assume that they are the most courageous, also experience by far the most painful tragedies: but just for that reason they honor life because it pits its greatest opposition against them.... They still have pity on my accidents; but *my* word says, "Let accidents come to me, they are innocent as little children." How could they endure my happiness in accidents and winter distress and polar-bear caps and covers of snowy heavens—if I myself did not have mercy on their *pity*, which is the pity of grudge-joys and drudge-boys, if I myself did not sigh before them and chatter with cold and patiently *suffer* them to wrap me in their pity.[79]

Nietzsche's contrast between pity and a "hard" or "great" love that has nothing to do with the Pauline-Christian commands to "love thy neighbor" was intelligible to those French who, including Renouvier and Fonsegrive, had disserted on this relationship. More significantly, it reiterated some of la Rochefoucauld's contentions. The duc's ideas helped buttress *Human, All too-Human* (1878), and his view of pity especially worked its way into Nietzsche's *Daybreak* and *Zarathustra*. In *On the Genealogy of Morals*, Nietzsche acknowledged la Rochefoucauld's cardinal importance to the pity tradition, one that he mistakenly regarded as unmitigatedly reprobatory: "For this overestimation of and predilection for pity on the part of modern philosophers is something new: hitherto philosophers have been at one as to the *worthlessness* of pity. I name only Plato, Spinoza, la Rochefoucauld and Kant—four spirits as different from one another as possible, but united in one thing: in their low estimation of pity."[80] More noteworthy than Nietzsche's wrapping himself in the mantle of his illustrious anti-pity predecessors is his judgment of where sentimentalism had led modern philosophers: to the "overestimation of and predilection for pity."

The nexus on pity formed by the troika of la Rochefoucauld, Schopenhauer, and Nietzsche was the subject of Jean Bourdeau's *La Rochefoucauld*. Bourdeau, who was to illuminate the work of all three in articles and monographs,[81] placed la Rochefoucauld at the last crossroads of French anti-pity thought, from which the two Germans bifurcated. In Bourdeau's account, the eighteenth century begins an optimistic disinheriting of la Rochefoucauld's views: "Revolutionary sentimentalism is even further removed from the views of la Rochefoucauld than the rationalism of the reformist school."[82] In the nineteenth century, Bourdeau sees both Schopenhauer and Nietzsche laying claim to la Rochefoucauld; but although he offers a skillful account of Nietzsche's affinity to the Frenchman, it is the former, he insists, who has best followed and transformed la Rochefoucauld's stance. Moreover, Schopenhauer rather than Nietzsche is on the civilizing side of pro-pity progress:

Today we live in the midst of a more peaceful, egalitarian society: for us, honor is inseparable from justice. The evolution of the idea of pity would suffice as an indicator of changes in our social state. La Rochefoucauld, like the ancients, gave it little importance.... In the 17th century, one only pitied the members of one's own caste; Voltaire wanted us to pity everyone; Rousseau was moved only by the humble; Schopenhauer requires us to be pitiable even to animals, and bases all morality on pity; Tolstoy sees in it the only religion...for the best among us, these are not vain words.[83]

We return to the chiastic relationship between pity and progress that acted as an evolutionary marker for *fin-de-siècle* thinkers. The indicators affixed to the names of la Rochefoucauld, Schopenhauer, and Nietzsche best illuminated this chiastic relationship. Bourdeau's claims are paradigmatic: moral progress comes after la Rochefoucauld, through the very virtue of pity that the duc derided; it is situated in the recent past, embodied and emboldened by French enlightenment sentimentalism; it is now highlighted by German philosophers and in literature from abroad—and all this progress inheres in, and is represented by, the word pity. These, to paraphrase Bourdeau, are not vain claims. They are diametrically opposed to Nietzsche's appropriation of the pity tradition and weigh against his claim to its complete proprietorship.

Nearly a decade later, Bourdeau detected another wave of change in the vogue for pity, after having spread beyond Schopenhauer in the 1880s with the impetus of foreign literature, especially Tolstoy's: "Just yesterday, Schopenhauer, Tolstoy held the scepter. We were moved, life's sufferings were depicted in the darkest of colors, a warm pity was exalted, 'the religion of suffering humanity.'"[84] But this was "yesterday," for Nietzsche—as he had hoped—had come to weigh more and more against pity.

Bourdeau's story had now to be updated: while Tolstoy had bolstered the legacy of Voltaire, Rousseau, and Schopenhauer, Nietzsche was now a tonic counterweight. Lucien Arréat, for example, assessed the comparative strengths of Nietzschean and Tolstoian pity:

But Nietzsche soon scrambles and disfigures his clearest ideas, and pushes them to an exaggerated frenzy, either because, out of hatred for the feminine and for what he labels "slave morality" he banishes pity and sympathy, which are nonetheless natural forces.... Tolstoy arrives at the same conclusion as Nietzsche; he arrives there by exaggerating pity, a profound sentiment that is a corrective to his doctrine, but which nonetheless renders his heroes as incapable of social duty, as refractory to the exigencies of communal life, as the absence of pity renders Nietzsche's heroes.[85]

While we deal more fully in the next part with Tolstoy's impact on discussions of pity in France, we can remark here how Bourdeau, too, saw Nietzsche as counteracting the Russian writer's influence in France, much as the younger German had done vis-à-vis Schopenhauer: "Nietzsche thus proposes an opposing view to that of Tolstoy. He expounds a warrior's morality; Tolstoy, that of the nurses, the stretcher-bearers of the Genevan Red Cross, who carry off the wounded and dress their wounds, and whose compassionate souls want to see all men, instead of tearing each other apart, hug each other."[86]

Rousseau joined Tolstoy as a requisite reference point for Nietzsche: "Irreconcilable enemy of our society filled with lies, like Rousseau was the last century, like the latter he calls for a return to instinct, to nature—in the most refined of styles—but with this essential difference: that Rousseau was a plebian before whom stood an aristocratic world, whereas in the very democracy prophesized by Rousseau, which today is in the process of being completely actualized, Nietzsche is the most arrogantly patrician soul that can be conceived."[87] Bourdeau's drawing on Rousseau, who had been interred in the Panthéon in 1878, was not simply fortuitous—Rousseau incarnated one of the three "images of man" that Nietzsche had pondered in his early work (Schopenhauer and Goethe were the other two). Rousseau exercised a fitfully ambivalent fascination on Nietzsche.[88]

The juxtaposition was not perforce favorable to Rousseau the Frenchman. Pierre Laserre, an early disciple of the Action Française and initial champion of Nietzsche, contrasted Rousseau and Nietzsche to the latter's benefit: "It is in this earthly world that Rousseau's disciples—confused Christians, marked by a fake naturalism—dream of seeing realized the perfect happiness of humanity…. Against these idylls, generous in appearance but in their consequences basically ugly, Nietzsche is on the side of the Montaignes, Hobbes, la Rochefoucaulds, de Maïstres, in short, all the far-sighted."[89]

Laserre's contention clarifies the reception accorded Nietzsche's attacks on pity and their relevance to Rousseau's inheritance, for the French pity tradition was partly a social-contract one, where altruism functioned as a political guarantor of solidarity, keeping autonomy and fellow-feeling in harmony. Rousseau had made of pity the pre-social mechanism of all human moral capacity, the highest virtue of the human animal's interpersonal communicability. Both pity and justice—Rousseau did not sever the connections between them—were indispensable poles of the Rousseauian tradition, and Nietzsche undermined both by pointing to their bad faith. Henri Lichtenberger (1864–1941) noted this implicitly Rousseuaian dimension to Nietzsche's notoriety in France: "Nietzsche acknowledged that nature does not recognize such a distinction, good and evil, that it has neither justice nor pity."[90]

Lichtenberger devoted a long exposition to Nietzsche's *pitié contre pitié*. He avoided an overtly polemical or patrimonial account, admirably detailing citations and paraphrases; but he folded Nietzsche's censure of pity into a biographical paean:

it is neither out of cold-heartedness nor lack of acquaintance with pain that he showed himself so tough towards suffering humanity…life held for him rigors that were hardly ordinary; his tragic fate perhaps gave him the right to show himself less willing to pity human miseries and weaknesses; the courageous and proud thinker who never allowed himself to curse existence…and who, under perpetual threat of death or insanity maintained until the end his passionate hymn in honor of an eternally young and bountiful life.[91]

Lichtenberger melded into this stance a possibly more baleful Social-Spencerian argument whereby he interpreted Nietzsche as condemning pity because it ran counter to European hegemony: "Christianity and the religion of pity have effectively contributed to the deterioration of the European race."[92]

Another early appreciation of Nietzsche that grasped his thought in its opposition to pity and *francité* appeared in *La Revue de Paris* in 1895. Explaining Nietzsche's ideas to a general readership, the author, Léonie Bernardini, the only female allowed to intervene in this discussion (and the author of an earlier study on *Richard Wagner* [1882]), wrote:

Of all the products of this century to which Nietzsche takes an axe, as if they were the unhealthy outgrowths of decomposing bodies, none is more hateful to him than the Religion of Pity, in which we claim to have found the last nobility and only refuge for disbelieving souls. With an admirable acuity, Nietzsche pursues his diagnosis of it even into its innermost corners. He demonstrates how it hypertrophies from hidden roots in our exasperated sensibilities, our sick nerves and weakened wills…he probes the very depths of the conscience of our times in order to unmask that morbid taste for tears, that delight in our own anxiety which give to modern Pity somewhat of a sadistic underside and which find expression in an odd way in an entire current of modern art.[93]

Bernardini's overwrought analysis exposes both contemporary sensibility and Nietzsche's challenge to it. It also invokes Nietzsche's *francité*: "It would be interesting in this regard to study Nietzsche's attitude towards French thought. In these times of intellectual 'Germanization,' we might be discomfited to see that it is a German who re-establishes in us a respect for our national genius, a sentiment of our former superiority over Europe."[94] Bernardini reinforces the impression that pity and *francité* were mutually indispensable registers for the interpretation of Nietzsche in the *fin-de-siècle*.

The official academics and members of the ASMP who had grappled with Schopenhauer also uniformly contended with Nietzsche's denigration of pity. Alfred Fouillée was a notable example. He devoted considerable energy to skewering Nietzsche, peremptorily dismissing him as an unoriginal follower of his own son-in-law, Jean-Marie Guyau, whose *Esquisse d'un moral sans obligation ni sanction* Nietzsche had favorably annotated in 1885.[95] Fouillée, though influenced by Schopenhauer in his conception of *idées-forces*, had conceded that the culture of pity springing up about him was excessive and that Nietzsche was thus offered an easy target: "*Zarathustra* is partly also a legitimate reaction against the overly sentimental morality made fashionable by those who preach a 'religion of suffering humanity.'"[96] But Fouillée does not engage Nietzsche on these terms, for he trivializes his motives and impugns his sanity while reversing the pity-valuation on him in a *tu quoique* argument: "In reading Nietzsche, one is torn between two sentiments, admiration and pity (even if he would reject the latter as an insult), because there is in him, amidst much elevated thought, something unhealthy and, as he loved to say himself, 'perverse.'"[97] Moreover, he, too, needed to align Nietzsche within identifiable coordinates in French tradition so as both to grasp his originality and to attenuate the import of his stance against pity—with la Rochefoucauld as the reference de rigueur: "Nietzsche had as predecessors not only la Rochefoucauld and Helvétius, but also

Proudhon, Renan, Flaubert, and Taine."[98] Obsessed with Nietzsche's fatalism and his idea of "eternal return," Fouillée sides more closely with Schopenhauer against Nietzsche:

But, added Schopenhauer, when one has acquired a consciousness of universal woe, one cannot feel anything but an infinite pity for the world and an infinite desire to be done with it. Nietzsche, on the contrary, wishes to persuade us to feel an infinite exhilaration in the face of this woe—similar to that of the bacchants; it is this state that he describes as Dionysian. Thus, to the tragic and pessimistic sense of existence there gives way in Nietzsche an enthusiastic and optimistic sentiment, without however the fundamental conception of the will to life having changed…. But isn't Nietzsche, who believes himself to be more optimistic than Schopenhauer, engulfed in a more profound pessimism?[99]

Chopping Nietzsche down to Schopenhauer's terms—"Nietzsche's doctrine, like that of Schopenhauer, is a philosophy of the will"[100]—helped Fouillée make the limited sense of Nietzsche that tradition and a focus on *volonté* allowed.

Fouillée devoted one chapter of his opuscule on *Nietzsche et l'immoralisme* to the *condamnation de la pitié*, in which, as we have noted, he rejected the more overwrought claims of the culture of pity. But Fouillée was willing to go only so far in this dismissal—he wanted to make certain that French thought could still maintain a caritative advantage over Nietzsche's more radical thrusts: "Nietzsche unduly confuses charity with pity and with the sentimentalism made fashionable by Tolstoy and Dostoievsky, and by all the followers of the religion of suffering."[101] Fouillée did not believe that the pity attacked by Nietzsche—the antithesis of Tolstoy's positive version—is the only variant and therefore that Nietzsche's censure does not have to be taken or left on its own terms. The authority of Spinoza helped him rally around an alternative tradition:

Spinoza had already claimed, "pity is, in itself, bad and useless," but only "for a soul who is guided by reason." And by pity he meant the sensible and nervous emotion, the *passion* of *compassion*. But that great mind took care to qualify his statement: "It is expressly to be understood that I speak here of the man who lives according to reason. For if a person is never led, either by reason or by pity, to come to the aid of another, he surely deserves the name of inhuman, because he no longer resembles a human." Spinoza thus refuted Nietzsche.[102]

Fouillée was thus consistent in siding against passion or emotion *per se* in its claim to trump reason; nonetheless, he championed a cognitive notion of pity that exonerated it from Nietzsche's deleterious allegations. He also adulterated Spinoza's thought—an avowed model for Nietzsche and a bane of sentimentalism—into an apologetics of pity.

Fouillée took pity from what he understood to be Nietzsche's mordant grip by making it a prelude to charity and citing Guyau as his authority: "To salvage this idea, it suffices to remark that pity or spontaneous sympathy is neither real Christian charity nor the moral goodness of philosophers….Guyau had already answered in advance: 'Suffering is blunted when it unites hearts like a lover does and raises them all in the same beat; just like pity, pain becomes sweet.'"[103] Fouillée subordinates pity to charity and goodness, hoping to disarm Nietzsche's critique of it.

In a later work, *Le Moralisme de Kant et l'amoralisme contemporain*, Fouillée launched a covert attack on Nietzsche, the "contemporary amoralist" incarnate, and in the process abandoned his earlier reticence toward pity. By linking Nietzsche to Kant, Fouillée associated the radical German to the traditional rationalist, placing both on the opposite side of sentiment, thus perpetuating the crisis in moral theory. Fouillée's brief against Kant was a model of the slippery-slope mode of comparative analysis—for him, Kant's categorical imperative is responsible for opening the way for Nietzsche's harsh valuation of sentiment: "Kant is not exempt from all responsibility for the paradoxes of the hedonists and worshippers of might, of whom Stirner and Nietzsche are the most audacious advocates. In fact, Kant portrayed human feeling as essentially 'vitalistic' and 'animal,' thus hedonistic and egoistic. In a general way he described human nature as having an amoral or even immoral power of development."[104] Fouillée argued that all Nietzsche had to do was vaunt what Kant had devalued: "But what Kant condemned, Nietzsche put all his 'courage' into praising."[105] This had its most egregious consequence in Nietzsche's denunciation of the least hedonistic and egoistic form of sensibility, pity: "Sympathy and pity, for Hobbes and la Rochefoucauld, were an egoistic precaution; for Nietzsche, they are forms of cowardice, a weakness, a sagging of the will to power, an unnatural sentiment. Does the lion pity the prey it devours?"[106] Fouillée placed Nietzsche even further from the pro-pity tradition than Hobbes and la Rochefoucauld by interpreting his condemnation as more stridently pejorative than their prudential, "precautionary" ambivalence. German rationalism carried within itself the seeds of (im- or a-) moralism—the implication is that French thought was free of both Kantian and Nietzschean extremes.

Fouillée's case against Nietzsche was built on an imaginative amalgam of physiology and cognitive idealism: "The great law of 'stimulus-response,' which has as its corollary *imitation*, tells us that a child cries in seeing others cry.... This nervous unison does not yet represent a disinterested altruism, but neither does it represent an 'egoism,' strictly speaking.... The life of Others, even despite ourselves, penetrates us, becomes ours."[107] This assertion goes against both the heart of the James-Lange theory of emotions and Nietzsche's claim that distance—"the pathos of distance"—is the appropriate range for human sociability: if "nature" vouchsafes interpersonal closeness, as revealed by the purely physiological phenomenon of crying, then Nietzsche's hunter-prey dichotomy is invalidated. Fouillée, moreover, recognized a more idealistically active pity:

The mechanism of passive pity by which nature puts each of us in a position of acknowledging, or even, to a certain degree, feeling that which another suffers, has been described a hundred times; but as long as there is in me nothing but the mechanical play of nerves there is no active sympathy or benevolence. Real pity begins, not when I suffer passively and nervously with you, but when, conceiving in thought a social ideal whereby our sufferings should be shared, and wishing to achieve this ideal, I *wish* therefore to suffer with you. I agree then to my own suffering.[108]

Fouillée distinguished a "real" from a "passive" pity, and the distinction passed through the power of individual cognition and will to harness sentiment. The promptings of sentiment are the proximate mechanism for setting in motion a "social ideal," whose conception is philosophically anterior and superior to mere sensation—a true cognitive theory of sentiment, again *avant la lettre*. The content-less "social ideal" that Fouillée has in mind must be the polar opposite of Nietzsche's—much closer to the Schopenhauerian vision of an equality of suffering that creates an imagined community.

Fouillée's definition of "real pity" posits something very like Kant's "kingdom of ends" as the alternative to Nietzschean "amoralism:"

Would Nietzsche see in pity a cowardly sentiment of *my own woe* in the woes of another? No, what involves me in your suffering is not my woe, nor even exclusively your misery. Something rises above us both that, in controlling us both, brings us closer together: this is the idea of universal solidarity or even universal justice. In the sufferings that your rational will is forced to endure as one endures an enemy force, there is a sort of injustice, and it is the more or less conscious sense of this injustice that makes me want to help you.[109]

Fouillée's position is comparable to Janet's similar categorical-imperative revision of Schopenhauer in *The Theory of Morals*. Fouillée likewise subordinated the sentiment of pity to a transcendent philosophical idealism: "an ideal of universal solidarity" that is both cognitively prior to and socially constitutive of sentiment.

Fouillée's thinking conveys the panoply of themes updated by the confrontation with Schopenhauerian and Nietzschean pity: the relationship between will and reason; the motor role of sentiment; the self-other divide; and social responsibility. Fouillée split the differences between the two Germans; what remains he called "real pity," a sentiment that is realized in self-conscious idealism: "It is this voluntary union *in idea* that constitutes real and active pity: all the rest appears to me as only an external inducement, the mechanism generated by unintelligent nature in order to incite me to surpass myself and it."[110] The physiology of pity is subordinate to its ideational content; "real pity" (a term that recurred as a leitmotif from Janet to Bergson) is cognitively social.

Fouillée concluded this book by rhetorically subverting Nietzsche in favor of pity: "Nietzsche only accepts 'tonic' sentiments, but active pity is 'tonic' and fortifying: it is a deployment of a powerful and disinterested sentiment provoked by two *idées-forces*: an idea of justice in which we are all equal and an idea of benevolence by which we are brothers. To flee from the idea of another's pain is thus the only real cowardice, not as Nietzsche believes."[111] Fouillée opposed his notion of *idées-forces*—which combines sentience and the motive power of sentiment in precisely the way the cognitive theory of pity is now envisioned—to Nietzsche's more egoistic conception.

The changes in Théodule Ribot's thinking on sentiments in response to Nietzsche and Schopenhauer's ideas are a further example of the influence they exerted over moral psychology in France.[112] Unlike Janet, who in his essay of 1880 was interested simply in demonstrating the influence of French philosophy on Schopenhauer, Ribot wished to synthesize both of these strands into a new psychology of will and sentiment. Although he had rejected Schopenhauer's "metaphysical" account of "universal pity" in the *Psychology of Sentiments*, he had concluded that work with praise for the gist of Schopenhauer's approach to intersubjective emotions.

His encounter with Nietzsche's work led Ribot to privilege the "tonic" over tender emotions. In his later *Essai sur les passions*, the Nietzschean "will to power" was now at the center of his preoccupations: "We can however set aside certain passions that, however different they are in appearance and goal, seem to me to come from a basic tendency…that one can summarize with Nietzsche's phrase, *the will to power*."[113] This "basic tendency," which is prior to the tripartite structure dominating Ribot's earlier scheme (emotions, passions, sentiments) is further characterized by him as a propensity to "individual expansion:" "Until now we have seen one single tendency, organic or sexual, transform itself into passion. The following study is not as uncomplicated. We pointed out earlier an individual's basic tendency to self-expansion, his 'will to power,' which expresses itself both physically and psychically. It appears to us to be the original source of many diverse passions."[114] Nietzsche provided Ribot with some of the lexicon to hone his psychological theory.

Another category of thinkers was less goaded to rethink their ideas by Nietzsche's challenge than to reject him en bloc: Catholic apologists for whom pity was a synecdoche for all the values maligned by Nietzsche. This was the case with Fonsegrive, who shed his prior anti-Schopenhauerian animus and embraced pity in reaction to Nietzsche. Whereas he had proffered love and charity as virtues higher than pity in *Morale et société*, he now vindicated pity in *Solidarité, pitié, charité*, partly in reaction to Nietzsche. In doing so, Fonsegrive epitomized the view that Nietzsche's attack was a dangerous prototype of all the other un-Christian, anti-spiritual philosophies—Darwinism, socialism, or solidarism. The quality shared by all these threats is materialism: "by substituting nature for God, necessity for Goodness, we are no longer allowed to hear the voices of the spirit, only the lessons of nature; and those lessons are a hymn to inequality, a triumphal appeal to power, an insult to weakness and misery, a condemnation of pity."[115]

In a chapter devoted specifically to appealing Nietzsche's verdict against pity, Fonsegrive rehabilitated a Christian pity that he had previously equated with, and therefore abandoned to, Schopenhauerian pessimism. The "true meaning of Christian pity," Fonsegrive now maintained, is "less a slacking of the life force than a reaction against the obstacles opposed to life, less an abnegation than a fresh burst."[116] Like Fouillée's idealistic rehabilitation of a "real pity," Fonsegrive countered Nietzsche's devaluation by placing pity at the center of a creative spiritual revolt against nature and necessity: "Nietzsche reproves the Christian for not having the courage to rebel. However, the Christian lives in a perpetual state of rebellion, he rises up against evil, and he revolts against every misery."[117] This counterargument missed Nietzsche's mark, since the *mal* and *misère* that Fonsegrive took for granted are precisely the preconceptions of the pity-perspective that Nietzsche tore asunder. But Fonsegrive desired to redeem a worldly commitment for the Christian that conferred to both pity and suffering an affirmative quality, and so he contradicted both Schopenhauer and Nietzsche: "Pity that is directed against misery, every type of woe—for there are many other miseries than material poverty—does not dispirit a Christian in his love of life."[118] Fonsegrive's *bête noires*, Nietzsche, Schopenhauer, and socialism, were all foils in this outlook—morality cannot be reduced to poverty, nor is Christianity nihilistic. The link among these contentions is pity, a Christian pity of charity and *agape*.

Fonsegrive was to come to an even more vigorous defense of pity when confronted by the movement and ideas known as Solidarity. Even in this context, one that pitted juridical notions of equity against sentimental notions of pity, Schopenhauer and Nietzsche were figures of reference, as we shall now see.

NOTES

1. ["Venu à son heure, Schopenhauer a joué un rôle considérable en France: d'une part en offrant sa conception du monde à la méditation des penseurs; d'autre part, en proposant aux moralistes la pitié comme loi suprème, aux psychologues l'amour comme le principe de la douleur, et aux désespérés le salut par le renoncement totale et la connaissance libératrice."] Alexandre Baillot, *L'Influence de la philosophie de Schopenhauer en france*, 20.

2. See Walter Kaufmann's "Introduction" to his edition of *The Portable Nietzsche* (New York: Penguin, 1980): "*Mitleid* has almost invariably been rendered by 'pity,' although 'compassion' would have the advantage that it too means literally 'suffering with.' The two English terms, however, do not have entirely the same meaning, and it is no accident that Aristotle, Spinoza, and la Rochefoucauld, of whose precedent Nietzsche makes much, have all been translated in the past as criticizing '*pity*.'" (4) See, on the contrary, E.F.J. Payne's translation of Schopenhauer's *On the Basis of Morality* (Providence, RI: Berghahn Books, 1995), where *mitleid* is always translated as "compassion." In recent commentaries and translations, the two English terms have been used interchangeably to render both Schopenhauer's and Nietzsche's *mitleid*, but "compassion" seems to be gaining the upper hand—a noticeable chronological change in linguistic practice away from that of the French period under review. See, for example, Maudemarie Clark and Alan J. Swensen's recent translation of *On the Genealogy of Morals* (Cambridge, MA: Hackett, 1998), where Nietzsche's *mitleid*—and his attacks on it—is translated uniformly as "compassion."

3. The only full-length, though hardly thorough, treatments of the reception of Schopenhauer in France are René-Pierre Colin, *Schopenhauer en France: Un mythe naturaliste* (Lyon: Presses universitaires de Lyon, 1979), and Alexandre Baillot, *L'Influence de la philosophie de Schopenhauer en France*. A shorter but still invaluable study is the recent essay by Anne Henry, "La réception de Schopenhauer en France," in *Schopenhauer: Essays in Honor of His 200th Birthday*, Eric von der Luft, ed. (Lewiston, NY: Edwin Mellen Press, 1988), 188–215. See also Thomas West, "Schopenhauer, Huysmans and French Naturalism," *Journal of European Studies* 1 (1971), 313–24.

4. ["Schopenhauer, le philosophe étranger le plus lu en France dans le dernier quart du siècle."] Fabiani, *Les philosophes de la République*, 114.

5. On Schopenhauer's activities during the 1848 Revolution in Frankfurt, as well as for a general biographical account, see Rudiger Safranski, *Schopenhauer and the Wild Years of Philosophy*, Ewald Osers, trans. (Cambridge: Cambridge UP, 1989), 322–25.

6. Jean Bourdeau wrote: "Celle [la philosophie] de Schopenhauer est tout imprégnée du conservatisme réactionnaire de la Sainte-Alliance. Sa renommé, qu'il attendait avec un orgueil si sûr de lui-même, a commencé à se répandre en Allemagne après les déceptions de 1848; elle a gagné la France au lendemain de la guerre et de la Commune. Schopenhauer est le philosophe des lendemains de révolution." In *La Philosophie affective*, 27 ["Schopenhauer's philosophy is steeped in the reactionary conservatism of the Holy Alliance. His fame, which he expected with a self-assured pride, began to spread in Germany after the disap-

pointments of 1848; it spread to France right after the war and the Commune. Schopenhauer is the philosopher of revolutionary repercussions."]

7. See Paul Janet, "Un Philosophe misanthrope: Schopenhauer," *Revue des deux mondes* (May 15, 1877); Jean Bourdeau, *Philosophie affective*, 19; Anne Henry, "La réception de Schopenhauer en France."

8. Brooks, *The Eclectic Legacy*, 81.

9. In "Un Bouddhiste contemporaine en Allemagne, Arthur Schopenhauer," *Revue des deux mondes* (May 15, 1870), republished as a separate volume. Together with *Études et réflexions d'un pessimiste*—written in 1861–1862, but published only posthumously by Joseph Reinach in *La Grande revue* over four issues in the Spring of 1900 and then collected in one volume by Charpentier in 1901—these two works have been reprinted recently in the series *Corpus des oeuvres de philosophie en langue française* (Paris: Fayard, 1993). The legitimacy of Schopenhauer's appropriation of Buddhism, the main thesis of Challemel-Lacour's appreciation, has been probed recently. See the debate among Roger-Pol Droit, "Schopenhauer et le Bouddhisme: une 'admirable concordance?'" in von der Luft, ed., *Schopenhauer*, 123–28; Joan Stambaugh, "Thoughts on the Innocence of Becoming," *Nietzsche-Studien* 14 (1985), 66; Graham Parkes, "The Orientation of the Nietzschean Text," in *Nietzsche and Asian Thought*, Parkes, ed. (Chicago: U of Chicago P, 1991), 3–19; Dorothea W. Dauer, *Schopenhauer as Transmitter of Buddhist Ideas* (Berne: Herbert Land, 1969).

10. See letter to Charles Ritter, dated September 12, 1876, in Ernest Renan, *Correspondance*, vol. 2: 1872–1892 (Paris: Calmann-Lévy, 1928).

11. ["Nous pourrions rappeler à notre tour combien Schopenhauer s'est inspiré du génie français, de nos auteurs du XVIIIème siècle et de nos physiologistes du XIXème."] Jean Bourdeau, "Le Bonheur dans le pessimisme: Schopenhauer d'après sa correspondance," *Revue des deux mondes* (August 15, 1884), 917.

12. ["Cette éducation demi-française eût une assez grande influence sur l'esprit de notre philosophe, et il n'est pas téméraire de supposer qu'elle a contribué à lui donner ce goût de la clarté et de la précision, et cette horreur du jargon métaphysique qui le distingue d'une manière particulière entre les philosophes de son temps et de son pays."] Janet, "Un Philosophe misanthrope: Schopenhauer," 275, 287.

13. ["Quelle que soit l'origine de ces idées, c'est de chez nous qu'elles sont venues; c'est à nos propres philosophiques qu'il faut en faire honneur. C'est ce qu'oublient trop souvent les admirateurs intempestifs de tout ce qui vient d'Allemagne. Nous exaltons Schopenhauer; nous avons oublié Cabanis et Bichat....le seul point que nous ayons tenu a mettre en lumière, ce sont les origines françaises de la philosophie de Schopenhauer."] Paul Janet, "Schopenhauer et la physiologie française: Cabanis et Bichat," *Revue des deux mondes* (May 15, 1880), 59.

14. ["L'activité du moi n'a aucune influence directe sur les sentiments du coeur ou de l'amour. Nous ne pouvons que nous prêter à la réceptivité de l'esprit...On peut le rapprocher également d'un autre philosophe allemand, devenu célèbre, Schopenhauer."] Janet, *Les Maîtres de la pensée moderne* (Paris: Calmann Lévy, 1883), 398, 401.

15. ["S'il fallait caractériser le côté brillant du talent de Schopenhauer, je dirais que c'est avant tout un peintre de la vie et des humeurs des hommes, un moraliste dans le sens *français* du mot; il est instruit à l'école de Montaigne, de la Rochefoucauld, de la Bruyère, de Vauvenargues, de Chamfort, d'Helvétius, qu'il cite à chaque pas."] Challemel-Lacour, *Études et réflexions d'un pessimiste. Un Bouddhiste contemporaine en Allemagne: Arthur Schopenhauer*, 196.

16. See, for example: Ph. Bridel, "Pessimisme," *Encyclopédie des sciences religieuses*,

vol. 10, F. Lichtenberger, ed. (Paris: Librairie Sandoz et Fischbacher, 1881); René Doumic, "Deux moralistes 'fin-de-siècle:' Chamfort et Rivarol, *Revue des deux mondes* (February 15, 1896), 277–78. Pierre-Félix Thomas argued against Schopenhauer in a chapter of *Morale et éducation* dedicated to "pessimisme." Janet lectured on Schopenhauer's pessimism at the Sorbonne—see *Principes de métaphysique et de psychologie, leçons professés à la faculté des lettres de Paris, 1888–1894* (Paris: Charles Delagrave, 1897), 389.

17. ["il n'y a pas de danger que le pessimisme s'acclimate jamais dans le pays de la vigne ni surtout en France; le vin de Bordeaux éclaircit les idées et le vin de Bourgogne chasse les cauchemars."] Elmé Caro, *Le Pessimisme au XIXème siècle* (Paris: Hachette, 1878), 124. See Logue, *From Philosophy to Sociology*, who studied Caro as an apogee of second-generation Cousinian philosophy and regards him as the defender of metaphysics against positivism and materialism, as well as Brooks, *The Eclectic Legacy*, who narrates Caro's disagreements with Ribot (77–78, 90–91). More biographical and professional information can be found in AN, F17/20340.

18. Or perhaps not so trivial: in these years of nationalist anxiety, viticultural metaphors were deployed in literary and intellectual domains as a way of securing the support of an eminently superior domain; even more defensively so as economic and ecological conditions (phylloxera) threatened France's viticultural supremacy.

19. ["Et que l'on ne croie pas que le mal soit simplement intellectuel et littéraire: il affecte les âmes, la moralité publique, et tôt ou tard se traduit en catastrophes politiques et sociales."] Caro, 199.

20. See René-Pierre Colin, *Schopenhauer en France*, 125.

21. The exact question was: "Are the source and foundation of morals to be looked for in an idea of morality lying immediately in consciousness (or conscience) and in the analysis of other fundamental moral concepts springing from that idea, or are they to be looked for in a different ground of knowledge?" Schopenhauer's answer, the only one submitted to the judges, did not receive a prize. See David Cartwright's "Introduction" to Schopenhauer's *On the Basis of Morality*.

22. Schopenhauer, *On the Basis of Morality*, 46.

23. Schopenhauer, 69.

24. Schopenhauer, 131.

25. Schopenhauer, 140.

26. Schopenhauer, 141.

27. Schopenhauer, 144. The translator of this edition, E.F.J. Payne, uses "compassion" uniformly for *mitleid*; previously, most others translated Schopenhauer's *mitleid* as "pity." The distinction implicit in Payne's usage, as well as in that of other contemporary commentators—in so far as they are not arbitrary—seems to be that pity denotes an active feeling, compassion the moral notion constituting it ("I *feel* pity for," therefore I "*have* compassion").

28. Schopenhauer, 143.

29. Schopenhauer, 210–11.

30. Schopenhauer, 144.

31. Schopenhauer, 149.

32. Schopenhauer, 169. It might be noteworthy here that Richard Rorty makes a curiously similar point, since he considers that "the inability to notice that one is being cruel is the cardinal human sin." Eschewing the sentimental terminology of a pity-morality, Rorty's term for this principle of consideration is "solidarity"—an odd echo of the French pity-solidarity debate, the subject of our next chapter. See Rorty, *Contingency, Irony, and Solidarity* (Cambridge: Cambridge UP, 1989), 189–198.

33. Schopenhauer, 172.

34. Schopenhauer, 183.

35. ["Schopenhauer emprunte à la Rochefoucauld sa théorie de la pitié, 'qui n'est que la vue de nos propres maux dans les maux d'autrui.' Mais il veut que nous détournions nos regards de la perversité des hommes, pour les fixer sur la détresse de l'existence humaine. Il fait de la pitié la vertu cardinale: ne la point connaître, c'est se mettre hors de l'humanité."] Bourdeau, *La Rochefoucauld*, 182–83.

36. ["Avec Rousseau il magnifie la compassion qu'il concilie avec sa misanthropie, en ce sens qu'en dépit de la méchanceté des hommes nous devons nous apitoyer sur leur infortune. La morale de la compassion n'est que le prélude de la morale du renoncement, qui seule conduit à la Rédemption."] Bourdeau, *La Philosophie affective*, 25.

37. Bourdeau, 130.

38. Alfred Fouillée, *Critique des systèmes de morale contemporain* (Paris: Germer Baillière, 1883), v.

39. ["Le devoir peut-il être remplacé par la pitié [*mitleid*], que Schopenhauer prétend fonder entre tous les êtres sur l'identité même de leur nature? Une telle morale, si tant est que ce soit une morale, ne reste-t-elle pas destituée de sanction?"] Nourrisson, "Rapport sur le concours ayant pour sujet le pessimisme, 28 juillet 1886," *Mémoires de l'Académie des sciences morales et politiques* XVII (1891) (Paris: Firmin-Didot, 1891), 375.

40. Janet, *The Theory of Morals*, 138-40. But see Chapter 1, where we discussed Janet's move away from a strict Kantianism to a synthetic approach combining Aristotle and Schopenhauer.

41. ["Il faut aller plus loin et remarquer que la pitié ou l'amour périt, et non pas seulement la justice, dans la transformation que lui fait subir cette métaphysique…ces sentiments, même en leur plus grande généralisation possible, étendus à des groupes de plus en plus grands, sont toujours des rapports à quelque autre que soi, et, par conséquent, supposent à un degré ou à un autre l'individuation. La reconnaissance de l'unité et de l'identité universelle, l'explication du fait de la pitié ou charité par le fait de l'unité, reviennent donc à cette affirmation: que c'est de soi qu'on a pitié, et qu'au fond on n'aime que soi."] Charles Renouvier, "Schopenhauer et la Métaphysique du pessimisme," *L'année philosophique* 3 (1892), 45.

42. ["La morale du pessimisme est une conséquence directe de la doctrine du mal attaché au vouloir-vivre, et de l'universelle identité des vivants. En effet, l'ascétisme se montre partout comme une lutte de la volonté contre la vie, et la pitié, principe de l'éthique de Schopenhauer, dépend selon lui…du sentiment de la communauté de misère."] Renouvier, *Philosophie analytique de l'histoire: les idées, les religions, les systèmes* (Paris: Ernest Leroux, 1897), 409.

43. ["L'apriorisme de Kant et celui de Schopenhauer s'accordent dans une opposition commune à la morale utilitaire; et jusque-là elles fournissent en fait le même critère des actes moraux, d'où la considération du bonheur de l'agent est sévèrement exclue. Le caractère mystique et ascétique de cette morale du pessimisme a sa source dans un sentiment, que Schopenhauer joint à la connaissance intuitive de l'identité des êtres."] Renouvier, 411.

44. ["Mais c'est lui, Schopenhauer, qui, à raison de sa propre habitude d'envisager la source de tous les actes moraux dans le sentiment—on pourrait presque dire physique—et de confondre l'idée de loi avec celle d'un ordre intimé du dehors, s'est trouvé incapable de s'assimiler les ens des impératifs kantiens."] Renouvier, "Kant et Schopenhauer: le principe de l'obligation morale," *La Critique philosophique* 9:1, 25.

45. ["La théorie de la pitié a fourni à Schopenhauer une remarquable explication psychologique du *pleur*, qu'il rapporte dans tous les cas, y compris celui où nous sommes émus

par nos propres douleurs, à la *pitié*, et non point au sentiment de la douleur en elle-même. Cette explication paraît heureuse et bien fondée, quoiqu'elle ait été inspirée probablement à son auteur par sa théorie de l'identité du sujet et de l'objet de la pitié, même alors qu'ils sont différents dans le phénomène."] Renouvier, *Philosophie analytique de l'histoire*, 412.

46. ["il résulte de là que l'amour pur est essentiellement de la pitié, grande ou petite que soit la peine à soulager....l'amour et la pitié ne peuvent se séparer du sentiment d'une certaine communauté de nature."] Renouvier, 411–12.

47. The point of Vladimir Jankélévitch's discussion of pity in *Les Vertus et l'amour*, vol. 2: *Le Traité des vertus* (Paris: Flammarion, 1986), is to diminish its standing in relation to a metaphysically and socially preferable Love.

48. ["L'entrée en scène du bouddhisme dans la philosophie occidentale, qui en était si éloignée, peut avoir une heureuse signification: ce serait la reconnaissance de la douleur comme essentielle à la vie organique et à la vie morale du monde de l'expérience...on est déjà désenchanté des doctrines purement intellectualistes qui servaient aux philosophes à se détourner de ces grandes vérités...condition nécessaire d'un véritable optimisme qui, en philosophie de même qu'en religion, doit prendre pour sujet non seulement, mais l'individu et, essentiellement, la personne, *le salut de la personne*."] Renouvier, "Schopenhauer et la Métaphysique du pessimisme," 61.

49. ["concevoir au contraire que la volonté est le fonds commun d'où tout être jaillit, et que, diversifiée seulement par le jeu des apparences, elle est cependant identique en tous, c'est supprimer la barrière qui sépare les individus....C'est introniser la pitié à la place de l'égoisme, la pitié, qui est le retentissement sympathique de toute souffrance dans le coeur de l'homme, la pitié, que les moralistes proclament unanimement le principe de toutes les vertus, l'initiation à l'amour, qui peu à peu vous achemine au renoncement parfait et vous met en état de déjouer les tromperies du destin, d'échapper à l'éternelle illusion dont la nature vous enveloppe. Nous sommes ici en plein Bouddhisme. Ces idées sont une émanation des doctrines désespérées qui de tout temps ont fleuri dans l'Inde."] Challemel-Lacour, *Études et réflexions d'un pessimiste. Un Bouddhiste contemporaine en Allemagne*, 231-32. If it is true that Schopenhauer makes ample references to "Asia" and to Vedic scripture, especially the *Upanishads*, as well as to Hinduism, Brahmanism, and Buddhism, he does so as much in opposition to what he considers the crudely inhumane aspects of Christian dogma and European rationalism as in agreement with these beliefs.

50. ["La science du droit hindou a fait, depuis quelques années, des progrès remarquables."] Rodolphe Dareste, *Études d'histoire du droit* (Paris: L. Larose et Forcel, 1889), 60.

51. The "neospiritualist" Darlu (Brooks, *The Eclectic Legacy*, 170) also exercised an intellectual influence on Marcel Proust. See H. Bonnet, *Alphonse Darlu: le maître de philosophie de Marcel Proust* (Paris: A. G. Nizet, 1961). For more biographical information on Darlu, see AN, AJ16/1028.

52. ["L'une des premières qui se présentent est la morale de la pitié de Schopenhauer...il faut bien reconnaître l'action puissante qu'il a exercée sur la pensée européenne dans ce dernier demi-siècle...Je ne sais pas si nôtre Loti, dont les plus beaux livres ont un goût de cendre, ne lui doit pas quelque chose....Pour détruire le mal, il faut renoncer à la vie individuelle, il faut confondre son coeur avec celui des autres. La pitié pressent l'unité des êtres. Elle déchire le voile de Maya. Elle est le grand mystère de la vie morale."] Alphonse Darlu, "Classification des idées morales du temps présent," in *Morale sociale: Leçons professées au Collège libre des sciences sociales*, 31.

53. ["Nous pensons que les idées de pitié, de charité, d'admiration sont puisés à la source même de la vie morale, et qu'elles ne sauraient s'affaiblir, sans que cette vie di-

minuait. Cependant elles ne correspondent qu'à un des deux mouvements qui forment le rythme de l'âme. Car l'âme ne peut sortit absolument d'elle-même, sans quoi elle cesserait d'être. Elle doit chercher en elle la force nécessaire pour aimer au dehors. La vraie bonté est faite de force et non de faiblesse."] Darlu, 34–35.

54. ["Schopenhauer voulut réduire à ce sentiment à peu près toute la morale sociale, tous les devoirs envers les autres êtres. Mais la pitié n'est pas la bonté; elle n'est qu'un sentiment tendre à la vue des maux d'autrui. Pour qu'elle se tourne en bonté, il faut y introduire un principe actif, un élan vers l'être qui souffre, un estime pour cet être, une croyance à sa valeur. Être bon, faire du bien, ce n'est pas seulement délivrer des maux, c'est développer l'être amoindri, c'est l'appeler à un accroissement, à une ascension, à une exaltation de la vie."] Georges Fonsegrive, *Morale et société* (Paris: Bloud et cie., 1907), 179. Born on October 19, 1852 and passing away on February 18, 1917, Fonsegrive was a doctrinaire Catholic and anti-Republican professor of philosophy who began his pedagogical career in the Dordogne and worked his way up to various lycées in Paris, ending up at his death at the Lycée Buffon. He was a director of the conservative Catholic *La Quinzaine* and also contributed to the anti-Republican *Le Monde* and the *Gazette de France* in the 1890s and 1900s. See AN, AJ16/1076, which contains glowing inspection reviews by Darlu and Lachelier.

55. ["Mais cela (pitié) suppose évidemment que la vie a une valeur, que l'être vaut plus que rien. Pour être bon il faut aimer, et le pessimiste ne peut pas aimer, car rien n'est aimable, puisque rien ne vaut. Aussi Schopenhauer condamnerait-il toutes les institutions et toutes les mœurs qui viseraient à augmenter dans le monde l'être et la vie."] Fonsegrive, *Morale et société*, 179.

56. ["Les anciens Occidentaux ont peu connu la pitié. La souffrance humaine paraît les avoir assez peu émus. Ils se détournaient volontiers de son spectacle plutôt qu'ils n'aimaient à la soulager. C'est en Orient que le bouddhisme, fondé sur la considération des maux qui assaillent l'humanité, a créé une religion de la pitié. Schopenhauer voulut réduire (la moralité) à ce sentiment."] Fonsegrive, 179.

57. See Anne Henry, "La réception de Schopenhauer."

58. ["La pitié seule est la base réele de toute libre justice et de toute vraie charité"— "négation complète du vouloir-vivre, saints, anchorites, védics, chrétiens."] Ribot, *La Philosophie de Schopenhauer* (Paris: Germer Baillière, 1874), 118.

59. Ribot, 132.

60. ["Schopenhauer répondait assez bien à notre besoin...de plus, les circonstances malheureuses que notre pays avait traversées nous rendaient peut-être plus capables d'apprécier le plaisir amer de la perte des illusions et sans doute aussi d'accueillir favorablement des théories arrivées de pays étrangers, même ou surtout de celui qui nous avait vaincus."] Paulhan, *Le Nouveau mysticisme* (Paris: Félix Alcan, 1891), 28–30.

61. ["Sentiment de sympathie, de commisération que fait naître la vue des maux d'autrui. Acceptée ou même provoquée et dirigée par la raison, la pitié devient une vertu. Mais Schopenhauer ne pouvait en faire le principe de la morale."] L'abbé Elie Blanc, *Dictionnaire de philosophie ancienne, moderne, et contemporaine* (1906, reprinted New York: Burt Franklin, 1972), 954.

62. Nietzsche, *Twilight of the Idols*, in *The Viking Portable Nietzsche*, 527.

63. David Cartwright maintains that Nietzsche argued, in effect, at cross-purposes with Schopenhauer. In his "Kant, Schopenhauer, and Nietzsche on the Morality of Pity," (*Journal of the History of Ideas* [January 1984]), where he aligns Nietzsche closer to Kant than to Schopenhauer, Cartwright argues: "The main reason I say this is that the emotion referred to by Schopenhauer is free from the pejorative cast that is associated with pity....This pejorative cast, lacking in compassion, is in full flower in the emotions Nietzsche analyzes....If what I

say is true, any comparison between Nietzsche and Schopenhauer's conceptions of *Mitleid* should take into account that although they use the same German noun, they are referring to different emotions" (96, n. 46). In the later "Schopenhauer's Compassion and Nietzsche's Pity" (*Schopenhauer-Jahrbuch* 69 [1988], 557–69), Cartwright asserts even more explicitly that their use of *mitleid* refers to different phenomena: "it is best to understand Schopenhauer's conception of '*Mitleid*' as 'compassion' and Nietzsche's as 'pity'" (557). Joan Stambaugh similarly contends that Nietzsche lacked the idea of compassion in his writings. See "Thoughts on Pity and Revenge," *Nietzsche-Studien* 1 (1971), 27–35. See also T.L.S. Sprigge, "Is Pity the Basis of Ethics? Nietzsche versus Schopenhauer," in *The Bases of Ethics*, William Sweet, ed. (Milwaukee: Marquette UP, 2000).

64. The following is a partial list of useful works on Nietzsche's reception in France: Généviève Bianquis, *Nietzsche en France* (Paris: Félix Alcan, 1929); Eric Hollingsworth Deudon, *Nietzsche en France: L'antichristianisme et la critique, 1891–1915* (Washington, DC: UP of America, 1982); Brendan Donnellan, *Nietzsche and the French Moralists* (Bonn: Bouvier, 1982); Louis Pinto, *Les neveux de Zarathoustra: la réception de Nietzsche en France* (Paris: Editions du Seuil, 1995); W.D. Williams, *Nietzsche and the French* (Oxford: Blackwell, 1952). See also Christopher E. Forth, "Nietzsche, Decadence, and Regeneration in France, 1891–95," *Journal of the History of Ideas* 54 (1993), 97–118, where Henri Albert and the *Mercure de France*, Nietzsche's greatest champions in the 1890s, are given their due. Albert's own book-length study, *Nietzsche* (Paris: 1903) is, however, a dull-witted work.

65. Even today the comparisons continue within Nietzsche studies; see David Molner, "The Influence of Montaigne on Nietzsche: A Raison d'Être in the Sun," *Nietzsche-Studien* 22 (1993), 80–93.

66. See Molner, 82; Anne Henry, "La réception de Schopenhauer en France," 189; Charles S. Taylor, "Nietzsche's Schopenhauerianism," *Nietzsche-Studien* 17 (1988), 45–73.

67. *Nietzsche Contra Wagner*, in *The Viking Portable Nietzsche*, 671–72.

68. Nietzsche had written to a correspondent: "Pity, my dear friend, is a kind of hell, regardless of what Schopenhauer's disciples may say" and "but that Schopenhauerian 'pity' has always caused the greatest mischief in my life—so I've every reason to favor moral philosophies which ascribe a few *other* motives to moral conduct, and don't try to reduce all human excellence to 'fellow-feelings.' For this isn't just an effeminacy...but a serious practical danger. One should make one's own ideal of humankind prevail, and overpower one's fellow humans as well as oneself with it—that's acting creatively! But that requires keeping a tight rein on your pity, and treating what is contrary to your ideal as an enemy." Cited in Cartwright, "The Last Temptation of Zarathoustra," 51–52.

69. Nietzsche, *The Antichrist*, in *The Viking Portable Nietzsche*, 7.

70. For some recent, perceptively critical assessments of Nietzsche's views on pity, in addition to those of Cartwright, cited earlier, see Michael S. Green, "Nietzsche on Pity and *Ressentiment*," *International Studies in Philosophy* 24:2 (1992), 63–76; Martha Nussbaum, "Pity and Mercy: Nietzsche's Stoicism," in *Nietzsche: Morality and Genealogy*, Richard Schacht, ed. (Princeton: Princeton UP, 1994); Richard Schacht, *Nietzsche* (London: Routledge and Kegan Paul, 1983); Frank Cameron, "Beyond Pity and Cruelty: Nietzsche's Stoicism," *De Philosophia* 13:2 (1997), 191–206; Oliver Conolly, "Pity, Tragedy, and the Pathos of Distance," *European Journal of Philosophy* 6:3 (December 1998).

71. Nietzsche, *Nietzsche Contra Wagner*, in *The Viking Portable Nietzsche*, 677.

72. Nietzsche, *Twilight of the Idols*, in *The Viking Portable Nietzsche*, 562–63.

73. Nietzsche, *Thus Spoke Zarathustra*, in *The Viking Portable Nietzsche*, 354, 297. Cartwright offers a subtle argument that Nietzsche's critique was a positive incorporation

and supplementing of Schopenhauer, in "The Last Temptation of Zarathustra," 67–68. See also Roger Hollinrake, *Nietzsche, Wagner, and the Philosophy of Pessimism* (London: George Allen and Unwin, 1982), who sees *Zarathustra* as a response to Schopenhauer via Wagner's operas, the *Ring Cycle* and *Parsifal*.

74. Nietzsche, *Thus Spoke Zarathustra*, 200–02. See John Burt Foster, *Heirs to Dionysius*, 76–77.

75. Nietzsche, *Thus Spoke Zarathustra*, 158.

76. Nietzsche, 377–378.

77. Nietzsche, 314.

78. Nietzsche, 202. "But he *had* to die: he saw with eyes that saw everything; he saw man's depths and ultimate grounds, all his concealed disgrace and ugliness. His pity knew no shame: he crawled into my dirtiest nooks. This most curious, overobtrusive, overpitying one had to die" (378).

79. Nietzsche, *Twilight of the Idols*, 524; *Zarathustra*, 286–87. See Georg Simmel, *Schopenhauer and Nietzsche* (Amherst: U of Mass P, 1986 [1907]), 11.

80. Nietzsche, *On the Genealogy of Morals* (New York: Vintage), 19.

81. He was recommended to Nietzsche by Hippolyte Taine, in a letter of December 14, 1888. See Smith, *Transvaluations*, 39.

82. ["Le sentimentalisme révolutionnaire est plus éloigné encore des vues de la Rochefoucauld que le rationalisme de l'école réformiste."] Bourdeau, *La Rochefoucauld,* 180.

83. ["Nous vivons aujourd'hui au sein d'une société plus pacifique, plus égalitaire: l'honneur est pour nous inséparable de la justice. Le progrès de l'idée de pitié suffirait à marquer le changement de l'état social. La Rochefoucauld, comme les anciens, en faisait peu de cas....Au XVIIème siècle, on ne plaignait guère que les gens de sa caste; Voltaire veut qu'on plaigne tout le monde; Rousseau ne s'attendrit que sur les humbles; Schopenhauer exige qu'on soit pitoyable même envers les animaux, il fonde toute morale sur la pitié; Tolstoï y voit la seule religion....Pour les meilleurs d'entre nous ce ne sont point là de vaines paroles."] Bourdeau, 192–93. The link between honor and justice is partly the subject of Robert A. Nye's *Masculinity and Male Codes of Honor in Modern France*.

84. ["Hier encore Schopenhauer, Tolstoï tenaient les sceptres. On s'attristait, on nous peignait sous les plus noires couleurs les misères de la vie, on exaltait la pitié cordiale, 'la religion de la souffrance humaine.'"] Bourdeau, *Les Maîtres de la pensée contemporaine* (Paris: Féix Alcan, 1904), 106.

85. ["Mais il [Nietzsche] brouille et défigure bientôt ses plus claires idées, et les pousse jusqu'au grossissement du délire, soit que, par haine du féminisme et de ce qu'il nomme la 'morale d'esclaves,' il bannisse la pitié et la sympathie, qui n'en sont pas moins des forces naturelles....Tolstoï aboutit au même résultat que Nietzsche; Tolstoï y arrive par l'exagération de la pitié, sentiment profond qui est le correctif de sa doctrine mais qui n'en fait pas moins son héros aussi impropre aux devoirs sociaux, aussi rebelle aux nécessités de l'existence commune, que l'absence de pitié faisait le héros de Nietzsche."] Lucien Arréat, *Dix ans de philosophie* (Paris: Félix Alcan, 1901), 133, 138.

86. ["Nietzsche offre ainsi la contre-partie de Tolstoï. Il expose la morale des combattants; Tolstoï, celle des infirmiers, des brancardiers de la Croix de Génève, qui ramassent les vaincus et pansent leurs blessures, et dont l'âme compatissante voudrait voir tous les humains, au lieu de s'entre-déchirer, s'embrasser les uns les autres."] Bourdeau, *Les Maîtres de la pensée contemporaine*, 134.

87. ["Irréconciliable ennemi de notre société pleine de mensonge, comme l'était Rousseau au siècle dernier, comme Rousseau il exige le retour à l'instinct, à la nature,—dans le style le plus raffiné,—mais avec cette différence essentielle que Rousseau était un plébéien

devant lequel se dressait un monde aristocratique, tandis que dans cette démocratie prophé-tisée par Rousseau, aujourd'hui en voie de se réaliser entièrement, Nietzsche est l'âme la plus orgueilleusement patricienne qui se puisse concevoir."] Bourdeau, 121.

88. See Keith Ansell-Pearson, *Nietzsche Contra Rousseau: A Study of Nietzsche's Moral and Political Thought* (Cambridge: Cambridge UP, 1991).

89. ["C'est de ce monde même que les disciples de Rousseau—chrétiens déréglés, mar-qués d'un faux naturalisme,—rêvent de voir s'accomplir le parfait bonheur de l'humanité....Contre cet idyllisme, généreux d'apparence, mais, par ces conséquences, si laid au fond, Nietzsche est du côté des Montaignes, des Hobbes, des la Rochefoucauld, des de Maïstre, des clairvoyants enfin."] Pierre Laserre, *La Morale de Nietzsche* (Paris: Editions de La Mercure, 1902), 56–58. Laserre argued that Nietzsche was a proponent of classicism (against "degenerate" Romanticism) and of hierarchy and power (against debilitating democ-racy). In a later edition of 1917, Laserre tried to inoculate Nietzsche against the strains of Great War chauvinism by claiming that he was a "good German," more French than those French like Rousseau.

90. ["Nietzsche a reconnu que la nature ignore cette distinction, bien et mal, qu'elle n'a ni justice ni pitié."] Henri Lichtenberger, *La Philosophie de Nietzsche* (Paris: Félix Alcan, 1894), 275. Lichtenberger's was the first monograph devoted to Nietzsche published in France. See Pinto, *Les Neveux de Zarathoustra*, 53. For more biographical and professional information on Lichtenberger, see AN, AJ16/6066.

91. ["ce n'est ni par sécheresse de cœur ni faute de connaître les douleurs qu'il se mon-tre si dur pour l'humanité souffrante...la vie eût pour lui des rigueurs peu communs; sa tragique destinée lui confère peut-être le droit de se montrer moins prompt à s'apitoyer sur les misères et les faiblesses humaines; le penseur vaillant et fier qui...ne s'est jamais laissé aller à maudire l'existence...et qui, sous la menace perpétuelle de la mort ou de la folie a soutenu jusqu'au bout...son hymne passionné en l'honneur de la vie éternellement jeune et féconde."] Lichtenberger, 183–84.

92. ["le christianisme et la religion de la pitié ont efficacement contribué à la dégradation de la race européenne."] Lichtenberger, 123.

93. ["Parmi ces productions de notre siècle, auxquelles Nietzsche s'attaque avec la hache ainsi qu'à ces efflorescences maladives qui germent de la décomposition des grands corps, nulle qui lui soit plus odieuse que cette Religion de la Pitié, où nous croyons tous avoir trouvé la dernière noblesse et le seul refuge des cœurs qui ne croient plus. Avec une admira-ble sûreté de coup d'œil, Nietzsche en poursuit le diagnostic jusqu'en nos fibres les plus secrètes. Il montre de quelles racines cachées elle s'hypertrophie dans nos sensibilités ex-aspérées, dans nos nerfs malades et nos volontés affaiblies...il sonde jusqu'au fond de la conscience de son temps pour y mettre à nu ce goût morbide des pleurs, cette volupté de notre propre angoisse qui donnent à la Pitié moderne comme un dessous de sadisme et se caractérisent de si étrange manière dans toute une branche de l'art contemporain."] L. Ber-nardini, "Les idées de Frédérick Nietzsche," *La Revue de Paris* 2:1 (January-February 1895), 217.

94. ["Il pourrait être intéressant, à ce propos, d'étudier l'attitude de Nietzsche à l'égard de la pensée française. En ces temps de 'germanisation' intellectuelle, peut-être serions-nous confus de voir un Germain nous rappeler au respect de notre génie national, au sentiment de notre ancienne supériorité sur l'Europe."] Bernardini, 223.

95. See Fouillée, *Nietzsche et l'immoralisme* (Paris: Félix Alcan, 1902), ii. For a recent account of the affinity between the two, see Dominique Pécaud, "'Ce Brave Guyau,'" *Nietzsche-Studien* 25 (1996), 239–54.

96. ["*Zarathoustra* c'est aussi une réaction en partie légitime contre la morale trop sen-

timentale mise à la mode par ceux qui prêchent la 'religion de la souffrance humaine.'"] Fouillée, *Nietzsche et l'immoralisme*, vii.

97. ["En lisant Nietzsche, on est partagé entre deux sentiments, l'admiration et la pitié (quoiqu'il rejette cette dernière comme une injure), car il y a en lui, parmi tant de hautes pensées, quelque chose de malsain et, comme il aime à le dire, de 'pervers.'"] Fouillée, viii.

98. ["Nietzsche a eu pour prédécesseur non seulement la Rochefoucauld et Helvétius, mais encore Proudhon, Renan, Flaubert, et Taine."] Fouillée, "La Religion de Nietzsche," *Revue des deux mondes* 71:1 (January-February 1901), 567.

99. ["Mais, ajoutait Schopenhauer, quand on a acquis la conscience de la misère universelle, on ne peut plus éprouver qu'une pitié infinie pour ce monde et un désir infinie de l'anéantir. Nietzsche, au contraire, veut nous persuader d'éprouver une ivresse infinie, analogue à celle des bacchantes; et c'est cet état qu'il décrit sous le nom de dionysien. Ainsi, au sentiment tragique et pessimiste de l'existence succède, chez Nietzsche, le sentiment enthousiaste et optimiste, sans que cependant la conception fondamentale du vouloir-vivre soit changée....Nietzsche, qui se croit plus optimiste que Schopenhauer, n'est-il point englouti dans un pessimisme plus profonde?"] Fouillée, 588.

100. ["La doctrine de Nietzsche, comme celle de Schopenhauer, est une philosophie de la volonté."] Fouillée, 564.

101. ["Nietzsche confond indûment la charité avec la pitié et avec le sentimentalisme mis à la mode par Tolstoï et Dostoiewsky, par tous les adeptes de la religion de la souffrance."] Fouillée, *Nietzsche et l'immoralisme*, 146–47.

102. ["Spinoza avait déjà dit que 'la pitié est, de soi, mauvaise et inutile,' mais seulement, 'dans une âme qui vit conduite par la raison.' Et il entendait par pitié l'émotion sensitive et nerveuse, la *passion* de la *compassion*. Mais ce grand esprit avait soin d'ajouter: 'Il est expressément entendu que je parle ici de l'homme qui vit selon la raison. Car, si un homme n'est jamais conduit, ni par la raison ni par la pitié, à venir au secours d'autrui, il mérite assurément le nom d'inhumain, puisqu'il ne garde plus avec l'homme aucune ressemblance.' Spinoza réfutait ainsi Nietzsche."] Fouillée, 148.

103. ["Pour redresser cette idée, il suffit de faire observer que la pitié ou sympathie spontanée n'est ni la vraie charité des chrétiens, ni la bonté morale des philosophes....Guyau avait répondu d'avance: 'La souffrance s'émousse lorsqu'elle unit les coeurs comme fait un aimant et les soulève tous d'un même battement; ainsi que la pitié la douleur devient douce.'"] Fouillée, 149.

104. ["Kant n'est pas exempt de toute responsabilité dans les paradoxes des hédonistes et des adorateurs de la force, dont Stirner et Nietzsche se sont faits les plus audacieux défenseurs. En effet, Kant a représenté la sensibilité humaine comme de nature essentiellement 'vitale' et 'animale,' donc hédoniste et égoiste. Il a, d'une manière générale, décrit la nature humaine comme une puissance de développement amorale ou même anti-morale."] Fouillée, *Le Moralisme de Kant et l'amoralisme contemporaine* (Paris: Félix Alcan, 1905), viii. Max Stirner (1806–1856), posthumously known for his work translated as *The Ego and His Own: The Case of the Individual against Authority*, was a faddish thinker in the *fin-de-siècle*. See John Carroll, *Break-Out from the Crystal Palace: The Anarcho-Psychological Critique, Stirner, Nietzsche, and Dostoyevsky* (Boston: Routledge and Kegan Paul, 1974); Ronald Paterson, *The Nihilist Egoist: Max Stirner* (London: Oxford UP, 1971).

105. ["Mais, tandis que Kant condamne, Nietzsche mettra tout son 'courage' à approuver."] Fouillée, *Le Moralisme de Kant et l'amoralisme contemporaine*, ix. Cartwright's "Kant, Schopenhauer, and Nietzsche on the Morality of Pity," also aligns Kant and Nietzsche on one side, Schopenhauer on the other. See also Charles Renouvier's "Kant et Schopenhauer: le principe de l'obligation morale," as well as both Janet's *Eléments de mo-*

rale and *Theory of Morals*, all discussed in Chapter 1.

106. ["La sympathie et la pitié, pour Hobbes et la Rochefoucauld, étaient une prudence égoiste; pour Nietzsche, elles sont une lâcheté, une faiblesse, un affaissement de la volonté de puissance, un sentiment contre nature. Est-ce que le lion a pitié de la bête qu'il déchire?"] Fouillée, *Le Moralisme de Kant et l'amoralisme contemporaine*, 275–76.

107. ["La grande loi de 'réponse au stimulus,' qui a pour corollaire l'*imitation*, fait que l'enfant pleure en voyant pleurer....Tout cet unisson nerveux ne constitue pas encore un altruisme désintéressé, mais il ne constitue pas non plus un 'égoisme' proprement dit ou conscient....La vie d'autrui, même malgré nous, pénètre dans la nôtre, devient la nôtre."] Fouillée, 276. Fouillée's example of crying is similar to Renouvier's and Mélinand's interpretation of Schopenhauer.

108. ["On a cent fois décrit le mécanisme de la pitié passive par lequel la nature met chacun en état de comprendre et même de sentir à un certain degré ce qu'un autre souffre; mais, tant qu'il n'y a en moi que le jeu mécanique des nerfs, il n'y a encore ni sympathie active, ni bienveillance. La vraie pitié commence, non lorsque je souffre passivement et nerveusement avec vous, mais lorsque, concevant par la pensée un idéal de société au sein duquel les peines seraient partagés, et voulant réaliser cet idéal, je *veux* par cela même souffrir avec vous. Je consens alors à ma souffrance."] Fouillée, 276.

109. ["Nietzsche y [pitié] verra-t-il un lâche sentiment de *mon propre mal* dans le mal d'autrui? Non, ce qui me préoccupe en votre souffrance, ce n'est pas mon mal, ce n'est pas même exclusivement votre mal. Quelque chose s'élève au dessus de nous deux qui, en nous dominant l'un et l'autre, nous rapproche l'un de l'autre: c'est un idéal de solidarité universelle et même de justice universelle. Dans la souffrance que votre volonté raisonnable est forcée de subir comme on subit une puissance ennemie, il y a une sorte d'injustice, et c'est le sentiment plus ou moins obscur de cette injustice qui fait que je voudrais vous secourir."] Fouillée, 277.

110. ["C'est cette union volontaire *en idée* qui constitue la vraie et active pitié: tout le reste ne m'apparaît que comme l'occasion extérieure, le mécanisme produit par la nature inintelligent pour m'exciter à la dépasser et à me dépasser."] Fouillée, 278.

111. ["Nietzsche n'accepte que les sentiments 'toniques' mais la pitié active est 'tonique' et réconfortante: elle est une déploiement de sentiment désintéressé de puissance suscité par deux idées-forces: une idée de justice dans laquelle nous sommes égaux, une idée de bienveillance au sein de laquelle nous sommes frères. Fuir devant la douleur d'autrui voilà donc la seule vraie lâcheté, et non pas, comme le croît Nietzsche."] Fouillée, 278.

112. For a general discussion of the relationship between Ribot and Nietzsche, see Hans Erich Lampl, "Flair du Livre: Friedrich Nietzsche und Théodule Ribot," *Nietzsche-Studien* 18 (1989), 573–86.

113. ["On peut cependant mettre à part quelques passions qui, si différentes qu'elles soient dans leur allure et leur but, me paraissent sortir d'une tendance fondamentale...qu'on peut résumer en la formule de Nietzsche, *la volonté de puissance*."] Ribot, *Essai sur les passions*, 3rd ed. (Paris: Félix Alcan, 1910), 50–51. On the reciprocal influence of Ribot on Nietzsche, see Ignace Haaz, *Les Conceptions du corps chez Ribot et Nietzsche* (Paris: L'Harmattan, 2002).

114. ["On a signalé plus haut la tendance fondamentale de l'individu à l'expansion de son être, sa 'volonté de puissance,' qui se déploie sous une forme tantôt physique, tantôt psychique. Elle nous paraît la source originelle de passions très diverses."] Ribot, 71.

115. ["en substituant la nature à Dieu, la nécessité à la Bonté, on ne nous a plus permis d'entendre les voix de l'esprit, mais seulement les leçons de la nature et ces leçons sont une hymne à l'inégalité, un appel triomphal à la force, une insulte à la faiblesse et à la misère,

une condamnation de la pitié."] Georges Fonsegrive, *Solidarité, pitié, charité: Examen de la nouvelle morale* (Paris: 1912), 38.

116. ["moins un affaisement de la vie qu'une réaction en face des obstacles qui s'opposent à la vie, moins un abattement qu'un sursaut."] Fonsegrive, 55.

117. ["Nietzsche reproche au chrétien de ne pas avoir le courage de se révolter. Le chrétien vit cependant en état de révolte perpétuelle, il s'insurge contre le mal, et il se révolte contre toutes les misères."] Fonsegrive, 57.

118. ["la pitié qui s'adresse à la misère, à toute misère—car il y a bien d'autres misères que la pauvreté d'argent—ne saurait déprimer chez les chrétiens l'amour de la vie."] Fonsegrive, 57.

Chapter 5: The Solidarity Movement and the Dreyfus Affair

I show pity most of all when I show justice,
For then I pity those I do not know,
Which a dismissed offense would after gall;
And do him right that, answering one foul wrong,
Lives not to act another.

William Shakespeare, *Measure for Measure*

I claim that the rich man's pity for the poor is insulting and against human fraternity. Spare the poor your pity, they have enough of that. Why pity and not justice? You have an account with them. Pay up. It is not a sentimental matter, it a business proposition.

Anatole France[1]

"Liberty, equality, pity:" which of these should society and its institutions most favor, and why assume a choice has to be made among them? Towering over these questions is the figure of Justice, which is intricately related to all of these qualities. If the relationship between the individual and society was the cardinal politicophilosophical problem of the *fin-de-siècle*, and if sentimentalism was one way to address it, then its related concepts had to be matched up to the overarching theme of justice. This chapter outlines and analyzes the debates surrounding the Solidarity movement and the Dreyfus affair, a catalyzing event that pitted the exclusive promotion of pity against that of justice. We encounter figures not only from philosophy and the ASMP but also from the wider society, all of whom invoked a rhetorically charged sense of doctrinaire pity in the hope that it could mobilize emotive transformations in a bewilderingly polarized society.

Problems of justice in the *fin-de-siècle* posed the same threat to pity as had the Revolution of 1789. Implicit in the sentimentalist discourse was the assumption that the two terms, pity and justice, had social and moral dimensions that, *grosso modo*, could be differentiated—that pity *or* justice is the logic of alternation sustaining the body politic; that notions of fairness and impartiality are incompatible with those surrounding pity.[2] Today, in an emotional and intellectual climate far different from that of *fin-de-siècle* France, these assumptions still exercise many a philosopher and social scientist.[3]

Pity was thus placed within a welter of social, psychological, and disciplinary settings addressing a parallel jumble of issues, poverty, charity, social justice, and socialism among them. Poverty and charity, especially, were two essential poles of *fin-de-siècle* French thought and quotidian reality.[4] In a culture whose cupidity, avarice, and inequality were amply documented in novels, newspapers, and court cases, social injustice was a not inconvenient verity. If millions were poor or went hungry in France every day, another sizable number were able to feel better about themselves by dispensing charity, the palliative measure most commended by the church and by hierarchical privilege.[5] In addition to its Christian ancestry, charity harbored conceptually allied notions of individualism, idealism, and liberty.[6]

Both secular republicanism and socialism, though often opposed, agreed in pointing to justice—social, economic, and juridical—as the best corrective to inequities, rather than charity. The justice-charity dispute mirrored a religious-secular clash that implicated pity. We first sample a range of pronouncements prioritizing charity against justice in order to situate pity in this argument and then survey the positions taken on justice and pity in response to Solidarity.

There were those, seemingly in the minority, who believed pity would unite charity and justice. Camille Mélinand, for example, condemned egoism as a basis for linking charity and justice: "Basic justice, 'negative' justice, consists first of all simply in *not making someone suffer*. Indeed this simple duty is extremely important in daily life…. As always, egoism is the enemy. To spare all those blows to the feelings of others, it is not only necessary not to be immersed in oneself; it is necessary to think of others, turn oneself toward and love them. In short, charity is needed even where there is justice."[7] For Mélinand, justice and charity are rooted in an innate tendency of other-directed sentiment: "The real relationship between justice and charity can thus now reveal itself. They are not two different types of duties: for they are the same. They are simply two different ways of accomplishing one's duty: one can do so by pure reason, because one *understands* human solidarity; one can also do so through love. Charity is thus not a duty that differs from justice, but the élan, the flame that inspires, warms, and unites justice."[8] If justice and charity are equally other-directed, they arise from different springs: reason and love. The combination of charity and love is accorded active precedence over abstract justice: "justice therefore comprises respect and mutual aid; charity is the love that must support, enliven, give warmth to the practice of justice."[9]

Edouard Maneuvrier similarly complemented and completed justice with charity: "It is necessary to think up a perfectible and progressive justice, extending and clarifying itself at the same time as the mind…. But to what today does it fall, if not by right then in fact, these domains to be conquered? To charity. It is therefore charity that will provide justice with new, positivistic laws, morally obligatory and also effective."[10] Maneuvrier's account gives charity the same teleologically progressivist and civilizing nuances that sentimentalism granted to pity. Charity is pity's proxy, the operational manifestation of social sentiment.

In a treatise misleadingly titled *La Justice par l'état* (1899), Paul Lapie (1869–1927) also showed partiality toward charity as the socially progressive sentiment:

In every respect, charity is just another name for justice. Individual charity is but a more scrupulous justice, more enlightened and profound. Social charity is the justice that prevents humans from dying needlessly.... But charity does not say, as does justice: "to each according to his rights;" it says: "to each according to his needs."...To create nurseries, protect early childhood, and raise abandoned children—and also to take care of the sick—is not merely to do the work of sentimental philanthropy, it is to do the work of justice.[11]

Lapie gave an ordered declension whereby justice equaled "social charity" and charity a "philanthropic sentimentalism" pregnant with meliorist projects. Lapie ultimately conflated charity and justice in the hopes of preserving an other-directed sentimentalism that need not adjudicate between them.

Most commentators of the era who equated the two or who gave precedence to the eleemosynary did so by invoking Christian idealism (as shown by the example of Fonsegrive). A case in point is Charles de Ponthière, who, in a work titled *Charité, justice, propriété*, proposed a pro-charity argument founded on Christian inequality: "Charity creates, justice only preserves; charity is fecund, whereas justice contents itself with protecting that which love of neighbor has already created.... The working of the whole certainly needs organization; but what could organization do—justice—without its basis—charity? Charity, the very heart of Christianity, is as immortal as the latter."[12]

We see here that traditional Christian virtues comforted sentimentalism and protected against what was fearful in a changing *fin-de-siècle* society. Christian idealism was given pride of place in a competition sponsored by the ASMP on "the moral elements necessary to the normal development of democracy in modern societies." Benjamin-Constant Martha (1820–1895) offered a summary of the winning essay: "The Gospels were even in advance of equality in recognizing to humble people and the poor a sort of moral superiority in the eyes of Divine justice, in the name of the value of suffering; and that all it took was to shift principles and transport them from the religious to the social world in order to arrive at democracy."[13] Martha's observations are loaded with the presuppositions and values that absorbed pity into the religion-secularism clash: evangelical virtues subtend democracy; other-directedness is the premise of politics; suffering is the basis of virtue. Charity for him was not purposely corralled with pity. Indeed, charity is the preferred alternative to justice because, more so than pity, it drew legitimation exclusively from Christian tradition and thus is more decisively religious. But there was a series of rapprochements between charity and pity that began to join both terms as essential bulwarks against an exclusive justice—they were allies on the amative flank of justice.

For these thinkers, pity was a corollary to Pauline virtue, and its Christian connotation was a further backing to charity's claims against justice. For example, Émile Boutmy (1835–1906) of the ASMP offered the following argument in a pamphlet written for a broad audience: "In order to extend and propagate in future generations the fruits of his divine immolation, Christ, through his doctrines but especially by his example, raised above all others—which are nothing without it—the virtue which is the most pure and sublime expression of human solidarity: *charity*."[14]

If these members of the ASMP promoted the Augustinian version of Pauline charity over secular justice, Paul Janet based a similar preference on what he saw as the supposed metaphysical liberty inhering in charity: "Distinctions between the duties of justice and those of charity—justice is absolute, without restrictions or exceptions; charity, just as compulsory as justice, is more independent in its application. It chooses its time and place, its recipients and means—its beauty lies in its freedom."[15] For Janet, a sentimental fraternity was the counterweight to an unfeeling justice calibrated to material concerns. In a textbook for Parisian high school students, Janet devoted a chapter to the "principles of social morality—justice and charity." Justice and charity frame social morality, and Janet instructed students that all virtues and vices could be lined up behind these two headings. His classification was summary and schematic, befitting a textbook: "Vices: Denunciation, treason, calumny, falsehood, indiscretion, tyranny, etc. Virtues: misericord (pity), equity, magnanimity, faith, munificence, mercy, severity, etc."[16] Janet divided the virtues pertaining to justice and charity along the lines of two character types: "Two types of characters: strong characters and soft or tender characters: the former more inclined to justice, the other to charity."[17] Character-virtues were usually given precedence in moral reflection (Théodule Ribot wrote: "we must note moreover that all religions have never promised eternal rewards to qualities of mind but to qualities of character, by an exact sense of their just relations"); sentimental fraternity was more salient to ethical discernment than intelligence, and Janet divided justice-charity around the former.

Defenders of a Christian charity most often had another explicit agenda: to anathematize socialism. The Comte d'Haussonville (1843–1924) of the ASMP, for example, championed Christian charity against socialism. He asked: "Rich people's obligation to transmit their wealth…is this a duty of justice or one of charity?"[18] Haussonville's answer was in the form of a semantic arbitration: "Undeserved is not synonymous with unjust. A good worker reduced to destitution is the victim of an undeserved misery and not of an unjust misery." In an essay for the *Revue des deux mondes*, he insisted that charity is best reconciled to liberty: "To the despondency over freedom, which is the primary cause of socialism, can be added another, more noble in nature: many charitable people who until now were satisfied with giving alms, seek today to relieve in a more effective manner the poverty of which they are the troubled witnesses."[19] Liberty is the despair of socialism because it tends to selfishness and seems incapable of remedying suffering; allied to charity, however, liberty overcomes these pitfalls: "I would say that the true principle is this: liberty tempered by charity."[20] This charity is explicitly Christian: "But the voice that said for the first time, 'My children, love each other as you love yourself,' carried out a not less enormous moral revolution. Christianity is in effect the only religion that made of love of one's neighbor a law of conscience and an instrument of salvation."[21] Christian caritative fraternity unites subjectivity and social welfare in much the same way that sentimentalist philosophers saw pity as doing.

Fouillée, too, gave otherworldly charity ontological precedence over sublunary justice: "It is on divine charity that theologians base the very love of man for man and, as a consequence of that love, human justice and law…. The first thing to know is whether charity, thus based on theological solidarity and alone posited as a foundation, truly entails justice."[22] Fouillée answered affirmatively. For him, charity is not confined to actions relieving poverty and misery but extended to all existential connections to the Absolute as lived out among fellow mortals. Mortality was very much the point; Fouillée conceived of justice as metaphysically inadequate, for the same reason that made both pity and religion inevitable—suffering and death: "If the State must always have as its primary role the guarantee and sanction of justice, it will not, for all that, remove the need for private benevolence nor, as a result, for the moral virtues of charity or fraternity. However perfect a collectivist society, it will always have woes to relieve. 'One need not,' says a communist, 'console the suffering; one must defeat suffering itself.' Easy to say! Do away also with death!"[23] For Fouillée, sympathetic solidarity trumped material solidarity.

The Solidarity movement complicated the charity-justice debate and directly enmeshed pity. Positions on Solidarity were especially instructive of the stakes involved in promoting or denigrating pity. "Solidarity" was a genuinely novel term and movement in social and ethical thought in *fin-de-siècle* France. The word actually designates two different concepts that usually, but not always, merged: a generic secular substitute for older precepts of moral fealty and the wider political program associated with Léon Bourgeois.[24] The former sense was a technical borrowing from jurisprudence;[25] the latter came to be designated as upper-case "Solidarity."

Henri Marion (1846–1896) was a leading sponsor of solidarity in the first sense. His arguments mixed both an arrogation and a rejection of Rousseau's thought, for he argued, *pace* Rousseau, that moral solidarity arose from sentiments, especially from sympathy and pity, which were natural phenomena; yet, *contra* Rousseau, he held that no social contract was needed to explain the move from solidaristic impulses to actual sociability: "One can no longer find anybody who would claim that the social state has a contractual beginning: everyone acknowledges that humans are basically 'social animals.' So the principal link in society is, together with necessity, but even prior to and more important than need, sympathy."[26] Marion referred to "sympathy" in its association with *sensibilité* rather than the Spencerian sense of contagion: "And as for the worries and sadness caused by sympathy, they apparently have their sweetness, because at the very moment one suffers from them, one would not exchange them for egoistic indifference. Do we not willingly go to the theater to seek them out, and are we not indebted to the poet or novelist who provides us with them?"[27] Marion established a secular principle of social attachment on nonegoistic pathos, on a sentimental fraternity that the representational arts gratify.

Marion's sense of "solidarity" was congruous with sentimentalism, whose advocates welcomed it.[28] Marion disserted on solidarity in a manner reassuring to them because he was ultimately a partisan of charity and pity in the dispute with justice. For him, solidarity was an updated secular cloak for traditional charity. He apostrophized charity in *Leçons de morale*: "Charity is essentially active…. In order to be complete and have its full value, justice must be crowned by charity…. In order to always be just toward everybody, indulgence and goodness are necessary: charity, meaning love, is thus the best guarantor of justice."[29] Like other partisans of charity, Marion faulted justice as mechanistic and lacking in altruism: "Thus justice is but the first stratum of morality; it is a support for virtue properly speaking rather than virtue itself. Virtue begins there and then rises higher: virtue is essentially charity, meaning the profound and dominant sentiment of the excellence of the human person."[30]Marion's was a "soft" version of charity's dispute with justice. The obdurate clashes occurred when upper-case "Solidarity" sized up charity and, in its train, pity.

Léon Bourgeois and the enthusiasts of this movement saw their ideas as tackling the problems between justice and charity. The "preface" to Bourgeois's *Essai d'une philosophie de la solidarité*, by Alfred Croiset, affirmed this purpose: "Justice, distinguished from charity by an old convention and emptied, so to speak, of all deep feeling, has something in it that is dry and narrow. Charity, in the contemporary sense of the term (which is not the primordial and truly Christian sense), expresses a sort of sentimental and gratuitous condescension of a superior toward an inferior.... The word 'solidarity,' borrowed from biology, marvelously answers this obscure but profound need."[31] Bourgeois essayed a doctrine that, beyond terminological rehabilitation, would constitute a wholesale eclipse of charity and a secularization of sentimental ethics. For him, social solidarity is antithetical to sentimental solidarity; disparate individuals are more easily—and verifiably—united in the former than in the latter. Bourgeois put it this way: "Charity or love is the giving of oneself; paying up is not giving, when one pays what one owes.... I say to those who do good: you think you are being charitable; rid yourself of this error, since you are simply repaying a debt; do not show so much smugness."[32] Here Bourgeois reprised the post-Revolutionary argument that sentimental responses to injustice, inequality, and suffering were luxuries of *sensibilité*.

Solidarity touched a nerve in ethical thought in *fin-de-siècle* France. The question that moralists attempted to answer is how to identify what is distinctively moral in the human condition. Solidarity reformulated the question by relating it to social phenomena rather than individual liberty—it attempted a sociological recasting of ethics. In this it participated in the enthrallment with mass psychology and sociology characteristic of this epoch. The only ethical *a prioris* that the Solidarists presupposed were the very contingency of social and historical factors—one is born among others in a certain time and place. Moral liberty is thus never abstract; if it is universal, this is only because all humans are social beings. The Solidarists thus hoped to launch a revolution in moral philosophy by turning away from the individual and his or her cognitive and sentimental faculties.[33]

Alphonse Darlu recognized this threat: "It is totally natural to bring a sociological conception to morality, which leads to the doctrine of solidarity. There is where we must look for the originality of the idea of solidarity, if I am not mistaken. Until now morality, even when it preached charity, placed itself in an individual's point of view. Charity counsels us to treat all humans, no matter whom, as our neighbor, our brethren. Solidarity attaches us to a given collectivity."[34] Darlu's contrast of individualism with socialization frightened defenders of charity and pro-pity sentimentalism, provoking resistance.

The more strident opposition to Solidarity was thus truly conservative in the political sense. This was the case with that curmudgeonly calumniator of socialism, Gustave LeBon. He, too, perceived the enormously attractive power of Solidarity: "The movement in favor of solidarity, that is to say, the association of similar interests, which is so generally evident, is perhaps the most definite of the new social tendencies and is probably one of those that will have the greatest effect on our evolution."[35] Whereas "for many people the term 'social solidarity' always recalls, to some extent, the idea of charity," LeBon paraphrases Solidarity's governing precepts in order to underscore the opposition between the terms: "The term solidarity signifies merely association, and by no means charity or altruism."[36] LeBon insists that the Solidarists see charity as they do pity—as a pejorative and inadequate sentiment: "It is possible to found a durable institution on interest, which is a solid and unchanging sentiment, but not on philanthropy, which is a fluctuating and always ephemeral sentiment. Philanthropy is also too akin to pity to inspire any gratitude in its objects."[37] LeBon regrets the coming age of pro-justice solidarism and its eclipse of pro-pity, pro-charity sentimentalism: "In the future evolution of the world the mind will be ruled by interests, not by sentiments. Pity, charity, and altruism are the survivors, without prestige and without influence, of the past that is dying before our eyes. The future will no longer know them."[38] LeBon repudiates such a future. Indeed he proposes some break-speed measures pertinent to the pity-justice debate that, even or especially in an age of democratization, will avert the full brunt of justice-claims in mass politics. For example:

We should cling vigorously to the jury. It constitutes, perhaps, the only category of crowd that cannot be replaced by any individuality. It alone can temper the severity of the law, which, equal for all, ought in principle to be blind and to take no cognizance of particular cases. Inaccessible to pity, and heeding nothing but the text of the law, the judge in his professional severity would visit with the same penalty the burglar guilty of murder and the wretched girl whom poverty and her abandonment by her seducer have driven to infanticide.[39]

The jury of peers is one class of crowd that LeBon would tolerate in the coming age of mass politics, specifically because it is the one grouping in which sentiments can escape their otherwise ubiquitous death sentence and serve as counterpoise to both severity and stupidity.

Louis Joseph Proal, who contended that romantic-humanitarian literary sentimentalism had predisposed juries toward excessive indulgence and clemency, argued the contrary about the pity-jury relationship:

Pity for the authors of crimes of passion is an excellent sentiment, but only on condition that it does not degenerate into silly sentimentality; that it does not absolve the guilty of all healthy consciousness of their sin, and does not disorganize society by letting criminals off scot-free. There is a marked tendency nowadays toward a certain false sentimentality; people weep over murderers, but quite forget their victims' sufferings; lavish all their pity on lovers who turn assassins, but keep none for husbands poisoned by wives.[40]

Proal rejected the Aristotelian valorization of pity: "Aristotle held that the Stage purges our passions by making them more refined and pure. I hold an exactly contrary opinion—that by giving an extraordinary intensity to our passions, it makes these more violent and less pure.... But Dramatic Art should not consist merely in violently stirring the spectator's emotions. When Aristotle said Tragedy has for aim to excite pity and terror, he was unduly restricting its domain."[41] So Proal preferred that juries deliberate with reason and not pity in mind: "The pity a jury feels for the woman who has been forsaken and has taken revenge into her own hands springs from genuine good nature, but after all sentimentality is not the proper frame of mind for giving judgment. Pity, like every other sentiment, must be governed by reason. Besides, a jury ought not to lavish all its commiseration on the love sorrows of women, who are so open to temptation; let it keep a little for the victims."[42] Proal's words help us locate the reason and sentiment divide on the gender fissure.

Members of the ASMP were just as assiduous in battling solidarism, if less motivated than LeBon by an overtly conservative political agenda. In 1903, the *Académie* devoted its entire summer session to a very one-sided debate on Solidarity, publishing the proceedings as *La Solidarité sociale, ses nouvelles formules.*[43] Most commentators beckoned pro-charity arguments to combat Solidarity by trotting out a doctrinaire sense of pity. These were the terms employed by Charles Brunot (1860–1938): "What the Solidarists want, along with Baudrillard, is that, while 'leaving alone adults and the strong,' society 'help children and the weak to live;' they want 'society to have a heart, but no frailty;' and for a rule they give to it justice, not pity."[44] He judged this as too one-sided and claimed that Solidarity would ultimately invite a sentimentalist reaction: "It is not that, beyond the limits of stringent justice, a Solidarist must remain insensible to human misery. It is not any more prohibited for him to have a heart and love his fellow man than it is for any other person. But he acts then according to the inspiration of his own sentiments and not according to the rational rules of his own doctrine."[45] Brunot here followed the wider defection to the sentiment side of the debate: "Sentiment is in reality a more active agent than pure ideas. Of all the elements whose connections comprise social solidarity, it is, if not the strongest, then the most fecund."[46] The cognitive theory of sentiments trumps the antiquated logomachy of philosophies of impartiality:

In order to be able to conclude in contradistinction to the disciples of V. Cousin, the Solidarists find themselves in a position of having to demonstrate that the duty to benevolence is comprised within the very rational idea of justice, and they struggle mightily to do so. But the psychology that compels these tours de force is today generally abandoned. Not only are intelligence or rationality no longer considered by psychologists as independent and superior faculties, but they are subordinated to sentiment, to the will.[47]

Émile Boutroux echoed Brunot, with the added suspicion that Solidarity's rational postulates subtended statist goals: "The so-called solidarist doctrine was conceived with an eye to basing benevolent duties no longer on charity or love, as if on a subjective and gratuitous sentiment, but rather on a scientific idea and rational principle capable of justifying the intervention of public powers."[48] Boutroux also detected a tacit caritative ideal in Solidarity's precepts: "The solidarity erected as a dogma by the Solidarity movement is, at bottom, a sentiment, a belief, a hope. It is sympathy coming to the aid of the deprived, and the use of public powers in society toward that end, since those of the individual are insufficient."[49] Like Brunot, Boutroux turned the tables on Solidarity, which for him was a secular interloper in charity's domain.

The most explicit contrast between solidarity and pity that did not take the latter quality as simply a handmaiden to charity was that issued by Georges Fonsegrive. Much as he had earlier done with Schopenhaeur and Nietzsche's ideas, he drew the consequences for pity of the Solidarity movement's pro-justice claims against charity. In a work that encompassed all three concepts we have been analyzing—*Solidarité, pitié, charité: examen de la nouvelle morale*—Fonsegrive sided with the latter two against Solidarity, while granting them noticeable autonomy. The nominative weight of each term in this period is attested by the fact that they were grouped together in one title.

Fonsegrive's opening salvo against Solidarity was to accuse it of committing something very much like the naturalist fallacy—that what is natural is morally binding. He maligned two schools of thought for their alleged indulgence of this fallacy: the Spencerian "struggle of the fittest" and the Nietzschean notion of the *übermensch*: "Through our unwholesome pity, we place obstacles to the law of natural selection, we hinder human progress, we weigh down humanity's ascent toward the heights."[50] With enemies like these, pity needs friends, and with Spencer and Nietzsche allied against it, pity needs Fonsegrive's version of Christianity.

Christianity offered a better solution to the problem of social attachment than Solidarity; it was also an enrichment of pity. Fonsegrive contended that grace, the product of the theodicic covenant between God and man, is the link between haves and have-nots, among generations and societies: "And we proclaim together with Christianity, which came long before M. Bourgeois, that man is born a debtor…everything we have, we have through grace and pardon…. I owe nothing to other humans if I do not owe first of all and primarily to God."[51] Christianity alone can reconcile weak and strong, and motivate pity on behalf of justice and equality, two virtues that must be Evangelical and not secular if they are to count as "goodness," for they embrace any human effort whose goal is to replace natural inequality with divinely reflected sociability.

Like Rousseau in *Discourse on the Origins of Inequality* and *On the Social Contract*, Fonsegrive was consumed by the search for a moral and civic antidote to natural inequality; his explicitly religious solution posited goodness ("bonté") and pity as the specifically human escapes from the "natural" order. That this view did not entail any liberal or democratic political arrangements was not paradoxical, for Fonsegrive's conception of goodness—subjective and idealistic—required that it avoid contact with any secular arrangements.

Frédéric Rauh, like Fonsegrive, promised to summon the word pity in a discussion of "La Justice," in a work we earlier discussed, *Étude de morale*; specifically, in a subheading on "La misère et le sentiment de la pitié." Rauh supports the generalization that opens his discussion—"Today we mostly concur in the sentiment that deprivation should be eliminated"[52]—with an appeal to sentimentalism: "It is not true that we cease to be rational as soon as we appeal to sentiment or to faith. To be reasonable is to take responsibility for one's conscious states no matter what they may be: reason is independent of its contents. In social matters, sentiment is creative; and to acknowledge an irresistible élan of the heart is as *positivistic* as to recognize a physical fact. We need not have a phobia about sentiments."[53] But how does sentiment create and what form should it take? "But that's not the question. What we need to know is whether charity can and should take on a more juridical and legal form; and that cannot be decided *a priori*."[54] The institutional framework of justice-claims—juridical or legal—is not as important as the sentimental *a priori*, which is the need to obliterate egoism. Rauh espouses the characteristically sentimentalist position that misery—a social fact—induces pity, which then obligates a series of actions, charitable in nature, whose legal and institutional status then becomes the nub of the problem. Although Rauh's title seems to pledge a discussion "du sentiment de la pitié," not once does he actually deploy the word. What does it mean to imply and connote pity amid such an assortment of social themes? A pity that hides its label behind the concept is a virtue both diffused and defused. It is also a virtue that elides into charity, which becomes its proxy.

Eugène Ehrhardt was equally ambivalent about pity's relation to charity, invoking the term in a traditional way—by appealing to Schopenhauer's authority, connecting the German's views on pity to those on the fundaments of right and law: "Schopenhauer also took a position concerning the problem of the origins of the nature of law. His theory forms a sort of pendant to that of the basis of morality. It is, so to speak, the negative side of the morality of pity. Justice is nothing other than pity to a lesser degree."[55] Ehrhardt did not believe, however, that Schopenhauerian pity fully explained legality: "We can see that Schopenhauer's theory is original. Right is purely negative, it arises when acts of egoism and violence have offended the sense of pity that humans, or at least the members of certain groups, feel for each other, and in order to react against these acts of violence. But in the presence of such claims, we cannot but ask: according to what principles and which rules is the reaction against injustice carried out?"[56] Ehrhardt feels obligated to discuss Schopenhauerian pity in a summary of possible ways out of the "actual crisis in the philosophy of law," but can embrace only the metaphysical impetus behind the theory, not the substantive relationship between pity and justice.

The fact that these debates reveal a tentative acknowledgment of change in society and attempt to facilitate this process by formulating emotive ideals is significant as a form of psychocultural analysis of the elite *zeitgeist*. In this context, we see even more clearly than in earlier chapters that the word pity was summoned as a pacificatory agent, a mollifying incantation for society. But was this not merely an irenic bromide? For there is something unsatisfactory about these disquisitions on justice, charity, and pity—a sense of a breach between rhetoric and reality; between position-taking and action; an impotence in imposing emotives other than the illusion of power granted by participating in debates at official institutions. We would need to study how sentimentalism was translated into concrete decisions and dominating discourses within such bureaucracies connected to justice as courtrooms, administrative panels, and the military or rights-movements such as feminism and anti-vivisectionism.[57] Was there an outpouring in these venues of *argumenta ad misericordia*? To what effect?

Did sentimentalism and the language of pity help attenuate the excesses of inequality, physical violence, capital punishment, or dueling, for example?

Lacking the resources and space to address such crucial questions, I can here apply a very broad template of the debate on justice and pity through the tangible example of the Dreyfus affair. The Dreyfusards and anti-Dreyfusards made use of these terms following a logic of alternation: injustice called upon pity as a corrective; but when justice supposedly did the work it was called upon to do, pity was kept in abeyance. In this very relevant regard, the Dreyfus affair repeated many of the strategies and tropes of the pity debate during and after the Revolution, with the question of who were piteous victim and unpitiable villain once again dramatically posed.

Dreyfus himself—often emotionally withdrawn, a man of stoic dignity and heroic endurance, who never once played to the pathetic in his judges or interlocutors—was not beyond invoking pity as the emotion pertinent to his situation. In the last entry of the journal he kept on Devil's Island, Dreyfus wrote with a posthumous sense of trampled optimism: "On the day that the truth will come to light, I request that my beloved wife and children receive the pity inspired by so great a misfortune."[58] This was the closest Dreyfus ever came in his pronouncements destined for publication to an overt *argumentum ad misericordia*. On a later occasion, however, when he faced his judges at the retrial in Rennes, he dismissed pity as inadequate to his claims on justice; indeed, he turned the tables of the presumed justice-pity antagonism on his accusers: "I had but one duty: to appeal to reason and the conscience of the judges. It is I who have pity for the men who dishonored themselves by condemning an innocent man through the most criminal methods."[59]

Oddly, Dreyfus agreed in this regard with his persecutors, who also divided pity and justice. For example, in an editorial dated September 10, 1896, *L'Eclair* asked that the books be thrown at Dreyfus, using these terms:

If this doubt in favor of the traitor should continue to grow, it is believed, even within the military, that it would be appropriate to dot all the I's and to very frankly reveal on what irrefutable grounds the Court-Martial based its decision to brand as a traitor to the country the man who seems to be benefiting excessively from an inexplicable sense of pity and a feeling of doubt which seems more generous than perspicacious.[60]

Doubt entertains pity and justice hard-heartedness: both sides agreed on this, which made the Dreyfusards the pro-pity faction in the years just after 1894.

This chronological movement in the antithetical relationship is most clearly seen in the polemical writings of Georges Clemenceau, the great firebrand defender of the Dreyfusard cause—and just as importantly, the great enemy of the causes garrisoned by the anti-Dreyfusards. In his first articles for the daily *L'Aurore*, gathered together in the volume *L'Iniquité*, Clemenceau drew on pity as an indignant counterclaim to the shame of justice's wrongs. In one example, Clemenceau envisioned pity as the motive source for combating injustice: "Contradictory forces battle within man. Instead of pouring out sterile principles, let us benefit from every possibility in order to indicate our surprise at our brief existence on this earth by an act of pity that takes us beyond ourselves."[61] Clemenceau's pity is that other-regarding, intersubjective principle conceived of by contemporary sentimentalists. He qualified it as an "act" accomplishing an array of consequences, including something akin to mercy, by binding an emotional predisposition.[62] Like moralists and novelists, Clemenceau fastened pity to a recognition of mortal limits and the melancholy acceptance of time's passage.

In a later article supporting a general pardon for all those implicated in the affair—especially its second unwitting victim, Colonel Picquart—Clemenceau conflated Communard and Dreyfusard amnesty to assert the superiority of sentiment over reason and pity over justice:

Thus I propose that we not execute anybody, and even offer amnesty to those who have survived the violence of our time. In good and in evil we are all very fragile. From this equilibrium should arise progress. Less misleading than fallible reason, sentiment pushes us to carry out that painful procedure through the great charity of mankind. Give sentiment its due. Pity for the vanquished, indulgence to the vanquishers, that is the meaning of my vote for amnesty.[63]

Soon, however, in response to the granting of an appeal of Dreyfus's verdict, Clemenceau would counsel that both justice and pity should share in the same altruistic sentiment and form a *bloc* against injustice. He did so in opposition to what he saw as the sham Christian manipulation of charity by Dreyfus's opponents: "All the State's powers have pronounced themselves unanimously against justice. The Christian preachers who spout the official pity of the Church in its places of worship have not come up with one charitable word.... It's too much. The Supreme Court has stood up and to the ruling powers, deaf to pity, has hurled the saving word: 'Justice.'"[64] Justice is the goal to which pity is an adjutant, not surrogate. Indeed, Clemenceau concluded this series of articles with a call for vengeance against the Republic's adversaries, rather than with an appeal to pity.

As the Dreyfusard cause gained decisive momentum, there was a corresponding shift away from pity in Clemenceau's appeals. In fact, when "pity" was objectivized as an *enjeu* in the affair, Clemenceau handled it tentatively, even defensively:

It is a sad time when one has to defend oneself against having taken pity on the undeserved suffering of a human creature. Thus it is ordained by the sectarian mentality of Rome, sowing hatred and the banishing from humanity of all that is not subject to the Vatican. As to me, I admit that I pitied the Jew tortured in the name of the Gospels, as I would have pitied the Christian tormented in the name of the law of Moses or of Mohammed. But I have always maintained that above that sentiment that I admit, a passion of generosity higher and vaster controlled all of this battle against the worst manifestations of the human soul.[65]

The pathos of injustice beckons pity as its active analogue and moral spur; the march of justice requires the "more generous" engagements of justice, equality, and fraternity.

Beyond Clemenceau's example, pity was also exploited for any perspective that could obviate or complement justice claims. After the smarmy forgerer Colonel Henry gave up his ghost, a memorial fund was set up to erect a monument, and the fund's appeal used the commonplaces of a pity-language. One of the fund's promoters, the abbé Caperan, referred to the monument as a "memorial of pity."[66] For their part, the Dreyfusard party came to see pity, as it was increasingly equated with pardon rather than acquittal, as inadequate. Joseph Reinach, for example, argued, "within a month, a pardon will be no more than a measure enacted out of pity."[67] Conversely, General de Gallifet, the defense minister who acquiesced in pardon, gave this presidential prerogative the character of a pity-appeal, not a justice-claim: "We will also submit to the act which a deep feeling of pity has dictated to the president of the Republic."[68] Pity-pardon (*pitié-clemencia*) were again twined in opposition to the hard claims of justice, reprising their long tradition in tandem; during the Dreyfus affair, they were wielded respectively and successively according to who was winning the unequal battle in the courts of law.

In both of these examples, the Solidarity movement and the Dreyfus affair we see positions taken up around justice and pity, charity and solidarity that responded to appraisals of pro-social sentimentalism. In both cases, a doctrinaire, rhetorical, and defensive pity was wielded against tribulations of modernity.

NOTES

1. ["Je tiens la pitié du riche envers le pauvre pour injurieuse et contraire à la fraternité humaine. Epargnez au pauvre votre pitié, ils n'en ont que faire. Pourquoi la pitié et non pas la justice? Vous êtes en compte avec eux. Réglez la compte. Ce n'est pas une affaire de sentiment, c'est une affaire économique."] Anatole France, "Conte pour commencer gaiement l'année," *Opinions sociales* (Paris: G. Ballais, 1902).

2. Hannah Arendt's *On Revolution* (1977) is a particularly striking rendition of this dichotomy, with specific reference to the French Revolution and use of the term "solidarity:" "Pity may be the perversion of compassion, but its alternative is solidarity" (88). Her larger argument in this book is also relevant here, as well as to other themes we have encountered: "Pity, because it is not stricken in the flesh and keeps its sentimental distance, can succeed where compassion always will fail; it can reach out to the multitude and therefore, like solidarity, enter the market-place. But pity, in contrast to solidarity, does not look upon both fortune and misfortune, the strong and the weak, with an equal eye; without the presence of misfortune, pity could not exist, and it therefore has just as much vested interest in the existence of the unhappy as thirst for power has a vested interest in the existence of the weak....Pity, taken as a spring of virtue, has proved to possess a greater capacity for cruelty than cruelty itself. 'Par pitié, par amour pour l'humanité, soyez inhumains!—these words, taken almost at random from a petition of one of the sections of the Parisian Commune to the National Convention, are neither accidental or extreme; they are the authentic language of pity" (88–89).

3. See, among other examples, Martin Hoffman, "The Contribution of Empathy to Justice and Moral Judgment," in *Empathy and Its Development*, Nancy Eisenberg and Janet Strayer, eds. (Cambridge: Cambridge UP, 1987); Robert Solomon, *A Passion for Justice* (Reading, MA: Addison-Wesley, 1990); Vladimir Jankélévitch, *Les Vertus et l'amour*, vol. 2: *Traité des vertus*.

4. In addition to the many organizations and leagues devoted to charity, even *La Critique philosophique* sponsored a competition for Ff 10,000 on the following question: "Rechercher les meilleurs moyens d'arriver à l'extinction du pauperisme, la charité, malgré les efforts les plus généreux, étant impuissante à le faire disparaître" (9:1, 15). ["Look into the best means of achieving the extinction of poverty, since charity, despite its most generous efforts, is powerless to make it disappear."]

5. There was also a historiographical echo of the *fin-de-siècle*'s interest in charity and its ecclesiastical connotations. See, for example, Léon Cahen's "Les idées charitables à Paris au XVIIème et au XVIIIème siècles d'après des compagnies paroissales" (*Revue d'histoire moderne et contemporaine* 2 [1900–1001], 5–22), who favored the word pity in his account of the church's endorsement of charity: "le XVIIème siècle est l'âge d'or de la charité privée: il suffit de citer le nom de Saint Vincent de Paul pour évoquer le souvenir de ce grand mouvement de pitié et d'amour....C'est l'Eglise qui consacre les bonnes oeuvres; il faut être dans l'Eglise pour mériter la *pitié* des fidèles" (5, 9). ["The 17th century is the golden age of private charity: it is enough to cite the name of Saint Vincent de Paul in order to evoke the memory of this great movement of pity and love....It was the Church that devoted itself to good works; but one had to be a member of the Church to deserve the *pity* of the faithful."]

6. See William Logue: "Charity was never the bad word in France that a minority of English liberals tried—unsuccessfully even in their own counrty—to make it" (*From Philosophy to Sociology*, 26).

7. ["La justice élémentaire, la justice négative consiste d'abord à *ne pas faire souffrir*, tout simplement. Or ce simple devoir est d'une importance extrême dans la vie quotidienne....Comme toujours, c'est l'égoïsme qui est l'ennemi. Pour épargner tous ces froissements aux autres, il faut n'être pas uniquement concentré sur soi; il faut penser aux autres, être tourné vers eux, les aimer. Bref, il y faut de la charité, quoi qu'il n'y ait là que justice."] Camille Mélinand, *Cours de philosophie morale*, 85.

8. ["Le véritable rapport entre justice et charité peut donc maintenant nous apparaître. Il n'y a pas là deux espèces de devoirs: car se sont les mêmes. Il y a seulement deux façons différents de faire son devoir: on peut le faire par pure raison, parce qu'on *comprend* la solidarité humaine, on peut aussi le faire par amour. La charité n'est donc pas un devoir différent de la justice, mais l'élan, la flamme qui inspire, échauffe et unifie la justice."] Mélinand, 42.

9. ["la justice comprend donc le respect et l'entr'aide; la charité est l'amour qui doit soutenir, vivifier, échauffer la pratique de la justice."] Mélinand, 77.

10. ["Il faut concevoir une justice perfectible, progressive, s'étendant, s'éclairant en même temps que l'esprit lui-même....Mais à qui appartiennent actuellement, sinon en droit, mais au moins en fait, ces domaines à conquérir? À la charité. C'est donc la charité qui fournira à la justice des lois nouvelles, positives, non plus seulement obligatoires moralement, mais effectivement."] Edouard Maneuvrier, "Une thèse individualiste sur l'idée de l'Etat," *Revue Universitaire* (February 15, 1896), 339.

11. ["À tous égards, la charité n'est qu'un nom de la justice. La charité individuelle n'est qu'une justice plus scrupuleuse, plus éclairée et plus profonde. La charité sociale, c'est la justice qui évite aux hommes une mort imméritée....Mais la charité ne dit pas comme la justice : 'à chacun selon son mérite;' elle dit : 'à chacun selon ses besoins'....Créer des maternités, protéger la première enfance, élever les enfants abandonnés—et de même soigner les malades,—ce n'est pas seulement faire œuvre de philanthropie sentimentale, mais c'est faire œuvre de justice."] Paul Lapie, *La Justice par l'état: étude de morale sociale* (Paris: Félix Alcan, 1899), 159–60. Lapie was the author of several educational manuals and became rector of the University of Paris (the Sorbonne) in 1925. On Lapie's relationship to Durkheim and his importance in diffusing social philosophy throughout the educational system, see LaCapra, *Durkheim*, 44.

12. ["La charité édifie, la justice ne fait que sauvegarder, la charité est féconde, la justice se borne à protéger ce que l'amour du prochain a instauré....Les rouages ont besoin d'organisation sans doute; mais que ferait l'organisation—justice—sans le fonctionnement–charite? La charité, coeur même du Christianisme, est immortelle comme lui."] Charles de Ponthière, *Charité, justice, propriété* (extrait de l'*Association Catholique*) (Paris: X. Rondelet et cie., 1899), 9.

13. ["Que l'Évangile a été même au-delà de l'égalité en reconnaissant aux petits et aux

pauvres une sorte de supériorité morale devant la justice divine au nom du mérite de la souffrance, qu'il a suffi de déplacer les principes et de les transporter du monde religieux dans le monde social pour en faire sortir la démocratie."] Benjamin Martha, "Rapport," in *Mémoires de l'Académie des sciences morales et politiques de l'Institut de France* XV (Paris: Firmin-Didot, 1887), 607–8. Another member of the ASMP (elected on June 1, 1872), Martha was a classical scholar and the author of studies on *Le Parthénon et le génie grec*; *Études morales sur l'antiquité* (Paris: Hachette, 1883); *Mélanges de littérature ancienne* (Paris: Hachette, 1896); and *Moralistes sous l'empire romain* (Paris: Hachette, 1865). He was a relative of Colonel Picquart. See BNF, N. A. Fr. 25170, Papiers Lavisse, vol. 5: Affaire Dreyfus. For further personal and professional information on Martha, see AN, F17/22983.

14. ["Pour répandre et propager dans toutes les générations à venir les fruits de sa divine immolation, le Christ, par ses doctrines et surtout par son exemple, a élevé au-dessus de toutes les autres—qui ne sont rien sans elle—la vertu qu'est la plus pure et la plus sublime expression de la solidarité humaine: *la charité.*"] Boutmy, *La Solidarité humaine* (Paris: s.d.), 12–13. Boutmy wrote various works on British and continental politics and philosophy, including an analysis translated in 1904 as *The English People: A Study of Their Political Psychology*, as well as *Taine, Scherer, Laboulaye* (Paris: A. Colin, 1901), and *Philosophie de l'architecture en Grèce* (Paris: Germer Baillière, 1870). He was a Dreyfusard intellectual, associated with Boutroux, Janet, and Bourgeois. He was also the founder of the École libre des sciences politiques. See "Les Professeurs de l'Ecole libre des sciences politiques et la constitution d'une science du politique en France," in *Le Personnel de l'enseignement supérieur en France aux 19ème et 20ème siècles*, Christophe Charle et Régine Ferré, eds. (Paris: Editions du centre nationale de la recherche scientifique, 1985), 261–72; Christophe Prochasson, *Les Années éléctriques*, 212. Boutmy was elected to the ASMP on March 26, 1898.

15. ["Distinctions entre les devoirs de justice et les devoirs de charité—La justice est absolue, sans restriction, sans exception; la charité, tout aussi obligatoire que la justice, est plus indépendante dans l'application. Elle choisit son lieu et son temps, ses objets et ses moyens—sa beauté est dans sa liberté."] Paul Janet, *Cours de psychologie et de morale: 2ème année—morale théorique et morale pratique* (Charles Delagrave, 1891), 301.

16. ["Les vices: Délation, trahison, calomnie, fausseté, indiscrétion, tyrannie, etc. Les vertus: miséricorde (pitié), équité, magnanimité, confiance, libéralité, clémence, sévérité, etc."] Janet, 316.

17. ["Deux sortes de caractères: les caractères forts et les caractères doux et tendres: les uns plus portés à la justice, les autres à la charité."] Janet, 316.

18. ["L'obligation pour le riche de communiquer sa richesse...est-elle un devoir de justice ou un devoir de charité?"] Haussonville, *Socialisme et charité* (Paris: Calmann Lévy, 1895), 372. Othénon-Bernard de Cléron, le Comte d'Haussonville, was the author of, among other works, *Misères et remèdes* (Paris: Calmann-Levy, 1892), and *Socialisme et charité* (Paris: Calmann-Levy, 1895). He was elected to the ASMP on November 24, 1904.

19. ["À ce découragement de la liberté qui est la cause première du mouvement socialiste, s'en ajoute une autre, plus noble de sa nature....Beaucoup de personnes charitables auxquelles jusqu'à présent l'aumône avait suffi cherchent aujourd'hui le moyen de soulager, d'une façon plus efficace, les misères dont elles sont les témoignes affligés."] Haussonville, "Socialisme d'état et socialisme chrétien," *Revue des deux mondes* (June 15, 1890), 842.

20. ["je dirais que le principe véritable est celui-ci: la liberté temperée par la charité."] Haussonville, 861.

21. ["Mais la voix qui a dit pour la première fois, 'Mes petits enfants, aimez-vous les uns les autres,' n'en a pas moins opéré dans le monde une grande révolution morale. Le christianisme est en effet la seule religion qui ait fait de l'mour du prochain une loi de la conscience et un

instrument du salut."] Haussonville, 863–64.

22 ["C'est sur la charité divine que tous les théologiens font reposer l'amour même de l'homme pour l'homme et, comme conséquence de cet amour, la justice humaine, le droit humain....Le premier point est de savoir si la charité, ainsi fondée sur la solidarité théologique et posée seule en principe, implique véritablement la justice."] Alfred Fouillée, *Critique des systèmes de morale contemporain* (Paris: G. Baillière, 1883), 374.

23. ["Si l'État doit toujours avoir pour principal rôle d'assurer et de sanctionner la justice, il ne supprimera pas pour cela la nécessité de la bienfaisance privée, ni, par conséquent, la vertu morale de la charité ou de la fraternité. Quelque parfaite que soit la société collectiviste, elle aura toujours des maux à soulager. 'Il ne faut pas,' dit un communiste, 'consoler les souffrans; il faut supprimer la souffrance.' Vous en parlez à votre aise! Supprimez donc aussi la mort!"] Alfred Fouillée, "La question morale, est-elle une question sociale?" *Revue des deux mondes* (August 1, 1900), 497.

24. See J.E.S. Hayward's excellent and definitive article: "Solidarity: The Social History of an Idea in Nineteenth Century France," *International Review of Social History* 4 (1959): 261–84.

25. And in turn helped influence subsequent juridical notions. See *Guide to the Law and Legal Literature of France*, Edwin M. Borchard and George Wilfred, eds. (Washington, DC: Library of Congress, 1931), 41.

26. ["On ne trouverait plus personne aujourd'hui pour soutenir que l'état social est d'origine conventionelle: tout le monde avoue que l'homme est essentiellement un 'animal social.' Or le lien principal de la société, c'est, avec le besoin, mais avant et plus que le besoin même, la sympathie."] Henri Marion, *De la solidarité morale* (Paris: Germer Baillière, 1880), 158–59. For information on Marion's career, see AN, F17/21253. On Marion and the duel, see Nye, *Masculinity and Male Codes of Honor*, 181.

27. ["Et quant aux inquiétudes et aux tristesses dont la sympathie est la cause, elles ont apparement leur douceur, car, au moment même où l'on en souffre, on ne les échangerait pas pour l'insouciance égoiste. Ne va-t-on pas à plaisir les chercher au théâtre; et ne savons-nous pas gré au poète ou au romancier qui nous les procure?"] Marion, 159.

28. See Charles Renouvier's review of Marion's *De la solidarité morale*, in *La Critique philosophique* 9:1 (October 1880). See also Elmé Caro, "La Solidarité morale (Henri Marion)," Paul Janet, "Rapports verbaux: de la solidarité morale," both in *Séances de l'Académie des sciences morales et politiques* 115 (Paris: Alphonse Picard, 1881); as well as Caro's review, "La Solidarité Morale," *Revue politique et littéraire* 3:1 (January 1881).

29. ["La charité est essentiellement active....Pour être complète et avoir tout son prix, la justice doit se couronner de charité....Pour être toujours juste envers tout le monde, il faut de l'indulgence et de la bonté: la charité, c'est-à-dire l'amour, voilà donc, en un sens, la meilleure sauvegarde de la justice."] Henri Marion, *Leçons de morale*, 171.

30. ["Ainsi la justice n'est que la première assise de la moralité, c'est le support de la vertu proprement dite plutôt que ce n'est la vertu elle-même. La vertu commence là et s'élève au-dessus: la vertu, c'est essentiellement la charité, c'est-à-dire le sentiment profond et prédominant de l'excellence de la personne humaine."] Marion, 284.

31. ["La justice, distinguée de la charité par un long usage et vidée, pour ainsi dire, de toute sensibilité, a quelque chose de sec et d'étroit. La charité, au sens courant du mot (qui n'est pas le sens primitif et vraiment chrétien), exprime une sorte de condescendance sentimentale et gratuite de supérieur à inférieur....Le mot de 'solidarité,' emprunté à la biologie, répondait merveilleusement à ce besoin obscur et profound."] Léon Bourgeois, *Essai d'une philosophie de la solidarité* (Paris: Félix Alcan, 1902), ix–x.

32. ["La charité ou l'amour, c'est le don de soi; payer n'est pas donner, quand on paie ce

que l'on doit....Je dis à ceux qui font le bien: vous croyez faire la charité; détrompez vous, vous payez seulement votre dette; n'en ayez pas tant d'orgueil."] Bourgeois, 59, 61.

33. But Hayward claims, on the contrary, that Solidarity came to re-center and re-introduce individualism in the *fin-de-siècle*: "Solidarity: The Social History of an Idea in Nineteenth Century France," 269.

34. ["Il est tout naturel de porter cette conception [sociologique] dans la morale, ce qui conduit à la doctrine de la solidarité. C'est là, si je ne me trompe, qu'il faut chercher l'originalité de l'idée de solidarité. Jusqu'ici la morale, même quand elle enseignait la charité, se plaçait au point de vue de l'individu. La charité nous avertit de traiter tout homme, quel qu'il soit, comme nôtre prochain, nôtre frère. La solidarité nous attache à une collectivité déterminée."] Darlu, "Classification des idées morales du temps présent," 122–23.

35. Gustave LeBon, *The Psychology of Socialism*, from *The Man and His Works,* 137. On LeBon's influence in the *fin-de-siècle*, see Prochasson, *Les Années élèctriques*, where he characterizes LeBon not as a *universitaire* but as a vulgarizer and popularizer whose influence was owed to being a *Directeur de collection* for Flammarion's "Bibliothèque de philosophie scientifique" (66–67).

36. LeBon, 342.

37. LeBon, 351.

38. LeBon, 357.

39. LeBon, 173.

40. Louis Joseph Proal, *Passion and Criminality: A Legal and Literary Study* (Paris: C. Carrington, 1901), 583.

41. Proal, 587, 603.

42. Proal, 615.

43. Académie des sciences morales et politiques, *La Solidarité sociale, ses nouvelles formules*, *Séances de l'Académie des sciences morales et politiques* 160 (Paris: A. Picard, 1903). The Académie met weekly during June and July. A series of seminars more hospitable to Solidarity was held at the same time at the École des hautes études sociales. See Terry Clark, *Prophets and Patrons*: "The École [des hautes études sociales] shared the EPHE's [École pratique des hautes études] cooperative research emphasis and arranged several seminars with leading university figures. One of the best known was on 'solidarity,' presided over by the apostle of Solidarity, Léon Bourgeois. Outstanding *universitaires* in the seminar included the philosophers Duelaux, Alphonse Darlu, Xavier Léon, and Frédéric Rauh, the political economist Charles Gide, and Ferdinand Buisson" (159). Even here, however, not all of the participants were necessarily receptive to Solidarism. Take Charles Gide, for example, as cited by Lucien Arréat, in *Dix ans de philosophie*: "M. Gide relève plus particulièrement l'apport du sentiment logique, auquel correspond l'idée de justice prise au sens étroit, et le rôle social si important de la sympathie. Il justifie, contre Spencer, la charité, qui est aussi un produit de l'évolution; il ne veut pas qu'elle soit exclue des contrats, mais qu'elle les imprègne; la charité acceptée par tous ne serait que la Loi" (123). ["Mr. Gide emphasizes more specifically the contribution of rational sentiment, to which corresponds the idea of justice taken in the strictest sense, and the important social role of sympathy. He defends charity against Spencer, which is also a product of evolution; he does not want it to be excluded from contracts but that it permeate them: charity admitted by all would be nothing less than the Law"].

44. ["Ce que les solidaristes...veulent avec Baudrillard, tout en 'laissant faire les adultes et les forts,' la société 'aide à faire' les enfants et les faibles, ils veulent que la 'société ait du coeur, mais pas de faiblesse;' et ils lui donnent la justice comme règle, non la pitié."] ASMP, *La Solidarité sociale, ses nouvelles formules*, 76–77. Brunot taught at Lyon and then in Paris from 1891 until 1928. See AN, F17/24348.

45. ["Ce n'est pas qu'au delà de la stricte justice, le solidariste reste insensible aux misères humaines. Il ne lui est, pas plus qu'à d'autres, interdit d'avoir du coeur et d'aimer les hommes. Mais il agit alors selon l'inspiration de ses sentiments et non plus selon les règles rationelles de sa doctrine."] *La Solidarité sociale*, 75–76.

46. ["Le sentiment est en effet un agent plus actif que l'idée pure. De tous les éléments dont la connexion forme la solidarité sociale, c'est sinon le plus fort, du moins le plus fécond."] *La Solidarité sociale*, 77.

47. ["Dès lors, pour pouvoir conclure à l'inverse des disciples de V. Cousin, les solidaristes se voient obligés de démontrer que le devoir de bienfaisance rentre dans l'idée toute rationnelle de la justice, et ils s'y évertuent. Mais la psychologie qui leur impose ces tours de force est aujourd'hui généralement abandonnée. Non seulement l'intelligence ou la raison n'est plus considérée, chez les psychologues, comme une faculté indépendante et supérieure, mais elle est subordonnée au sentiment, à la volonté."] *La Solidarité sociale*, 125.

48. ["La doctrine dite solidarisme a été constituée en vue de faire reposer le devoir de bienfaisance, non plus sur la charité ou l'amour, comme sur un sentiment subjectif et libre, mais sur une idée, sur un principe scientifique et rationnel, propre à justifier l'intervention de la force publique."] *La Solidarité sociale*, 124.

49. ["La solidarité que le solidarisme érige en dogme, c'est, dans le fond, un sentiment, une croyance, une aspiration. C'est la sympathie, tendant à venir en aide aux déshérités, et à utiliser pour cet objet les forces de la société, puisque celles des individus sont insuffisants."] *La Solidarité sociale*, 124.

50. ["Par nôtre pitié malsaine, nous mettons obstacle à la loi de sélection, nous retardons le progrès humain, nous alourdissons l'élan de l'humanité vers les cimes."] Fonsegrive, *Solidarité, pitié, charité: examen de la nouvelle morale*, 36.

51. ["Et nous proclamons avec le christianisme, bien avant M. Bourgeois, que l'homme est né débiteur...tout ce que nous avons, nous l'avons par grâce et pardon....Je ne dois rien aux hommes si je ne dois d'abord et premièrement à Dieu."] Fonsegrive, 44, 46.

52. ["Nous avons presque tous aujourd'hui le sentiment que la misère doit être supprimée."] Rauh, *Études de morale*, 358.

53. ["Il n'est pas vrai qu'on cesse d'être raisonnable sitôt qu'on fait appel au sentiment ou à la foi. Être raisonnable, c'est situer ses états de conscience quels qu'ils soient: la raison est indépendante de son contenu. En matière sociale, le sentiment est créateur; et constater un élan du coeur irrésistible est aussi *positif* que constater un fait physique. Il ne faut pas avoir la phobie du sentiment."] Rauh, 360–61.

54. ["Mais là n'est pas la question. Il s'agit de savoir si la charité peut et doit prendre aujourd'hui une forme juridique et légale; or, cela ne peut se décider *a priori*."] Rauh, 362.

55. ["Schopenhauer a pris également position vis-à-vis du problème de l'origine de la nature du droit. Sa théorie forme une sorte de pendant à celle qui est à la base de la morale. C'est pour ainsi dire la morale de la pitié sous une forme négative. La justice n'est autre chose que la pitié à un degré inférieur."] Eugène Ehrhardt, *La Notion du droit et le christianisme: introduction historique. La crise actuelle de la philosophie du droit* (Paris: Fischbacher, 1908), 132–33.

56. ["La théorie de Schopenhauer, on le voit, est originale. Le droit est purement négatif, il se forme lorsque des actes d'égoisme et de violence ont offensé les sentiments de pitié que les hommes, ou du moins les membres de certains groupes, éprouvent les uns à l'égard des autres, et pour réagir contre ces actes de violence. Mais en présence de semblables affirmations, on ne peut s'empêcher de se demander: d'après quelles principes et quelles règles se fait la réaction contre l'injustice?"] Ehrhardt, 133.

57. On how Schopenhauer and the language of pity propelled the anti-vivisection

movement, see John Vyvyan, *In Pity and in Anger: A Study of the Use of Animals in Science* (Marblehead, MA: Micah, 1988); Andreas-Holger Maehle, "The Ethical Discourse on Animal Experimentation, 1650–1900," *Clio Medica* 24 (1991), 203–51.

58. Cited by Jean–Denis Bredin in *The Affair: The Case of Alfred Dreyfus* (New York: George Braziller, 1986), 133.

59. Bredin, 404.

60. Bredin, 165.

61. ["Des forces contradictoires sont en conflit dans l'homme. Au lieu de nous répandre en préceptes stériles, mettons toute chance à profit pour marquer la surprise de notre courte existence par l'acte de pitié qui nous prolonge au delà de nous–mêmes."] Clemenceau, *L'Iniquité* (Paris: P.-V. Stock, 1899), viii.

62. See Jeffrie G. Murphy and Jean Hampton, *Forgiveness and Mercy* (Cambridge: Cambridge UP, 1988), for a contemporary perspective on pity and mercy.

63. ["Donc, je propose de ne fusiller personne, et même d'amnistier ceux qui ont survécu aux violences de nos temps. Dans le bien et dans le mal nous sommes très fragiles. De cette compensation doit se dégager le progrès. Moins trompeur que la raison faillible, le sentiment nous pousse à faciliter cette opération douloureuse par la grand charité des hommes. Laissons faire le sentiment. La pitié aux vaincus, l'indulgence aux vainqueurs, voilà le sens de mon vote pour l'amnistie."] Clemenceau, *L'Iniquité*, 339.

64. ["Tous les pouvoirs de l'Etat se sont prononcés d'ensemble contre la justice. Les prédicateurs chrétiens qui débitent la pitié officielle de l'Eglise en ses temples n'ont pas trouvé une parole de charité....C'est trop. La Cour suprême s'est levée et aux maîtres du pouvoir, sourds à la pitié, elle a jeté le mot saveur: 'Justice.'"] Clemenceau, *Vers la réparation* (Paris: P.-V. Stock, 1899), 439.

65. ["Triste temps où il faudra se défendre d'avoir pu s'apitoyer sur les malheurs immérités d'une créature humaine. Ainsi le veut l'esprit sectaire de Rome semant la haine et la mise hors l'humanité de tout ce qui n'est pas sujet du Vatican. Pour moi, j'en fais l'aveu, j'ai eu pitié du juif torturé au nom de l'Évangile, comme j'aurais eu pitié du chrétien supplicié au nom de la loi de Moïse ou de Mahomet. Mais j'ai toujours dit qu'au dessus de ce sentiment dont je fais l'aveu, une passion de générosité plus vaste et plus haute dominait toute cette bataille contre les pires manifestations de l'âme humaine."] Clemenceau, *La Honte* (Paris: P.-V. Stock, 1903), 172.

67. Bredin, *The Affair*, 352.

68. Bredin, 430.

69. Bredin, 434.

Chapter 6: EnGendering Pity

Thus is woman: complete altruism, pity, and devotion, because completely maternal and loving.[1]

The *fin-de-siècle* was a time of ferment for gender relations: education and labor were among the domains subject to redefinitions and renegotiations between the sexes, one in which the male continued to hold the upper hand.[2] No terrain was more emblematic of these skirmishes than that of education. Young women were finally admitted in state-sponsored secondary schools beginning in 1880.[3] The "Sée" laws, named after the Deputy Camille Sée, were passed on December 21, 1880 and July 26, 1881, the latter date at which was decreed the organization of an *École Normale Supérieure de jeunes filles*, in order to "recruit female professors for the secondary education of young girls."[4] On 14 October 1881, this *École Normale Supérieure* was established at Sèvres. By 1886, there were 10,000 female students in 112 state-run secondary or higher schools—25 students at Sèvres,[5] with the bulk in 16 lycées, 19 collèges, and 76 *cours secondaires*.[6] By 1914, this composite total numbered 38,000.[7]

The Republic was especially keen on the school as its defining site and mission—it was seen as the crucible for changes in mores and ideals. This was particularly true of a Republican education for and of young women.[8] For André Berthélot, public education of young girls was "one of the Republic's fundamental creations."[9] For M. Burdeau, the Chamber's *rapporteur* for the Education Ministry's budget of 1887, it was "the representative work of the present régime."[10] Indeed, in the *Dictionnaire de pédagogie et d'instruction primaire*: "'Woman' is hardly worthy of mention and only under three headings that scarcely take us out of the realm of the school: 'girl,' which leads us directly there through the legislative history of her education; 'Teacher,' which appears as the normal product of this education; and 'Mother,' whose reason for being is to prepare the child for this future."[11]

Given this combination of Republican pedagomania and perennial concerns over the role of women in society, debates and discussions on how and why to educate young females proliferated during the 1880s.[12] This debate continued in much the same language until the Great War. The two constants of this discussion were, first, that it was carried out almost exclusively among men[13] and, second, that it assumed female pedagogy had to be different in kind from that offered to young males, for even among the most fervent advocates of universal schooling for girls, there was an assumption that women had a more sentimental and piteous character that destined them for a circumscribed role (maternal, house-bound) and that entailed a particular pedagogy.[14] This elemental premise has been usefully labeled "maternalism."[15] Republican maternalism, of which Rousseau was the inspiriting force and *locus classicus*, was especially significant for the combination of pedagogy and pity.[16] Michelet, as we have seen, also helped forge this sentimental-ist Republican discourse: "pity, which is inert and passive in men, who are more resigned to others' woes, is in women a very active sentiment, very violent, which sometimes becomes heroic and pushes them commandingly to the most daring acts."[17]

For example, Octave Gréard offered this typical argument, which he used in support of government funding for female schooling: "Two things, in fact, should be considered in education: the acquisition of knowledge and the development of faculties. One cannot be conceived of without the other. However, they differ from each other to a certain degree, according to whether men or women are concerned.... The first concern of an education that is well directed must thus be to guarantee to that young girl an elevated moral culture that shapes the moral person."[18] Gréard's conclusion disingenuously detaches a female "nature" different from that of the male in order to inoculate against coeducation:

Let us be careful not to appear to want to change women into men, and in order to introduce greater might into the couple, let us not remove from it grace and sweetness…whereas we make decisions through reason, she listens to her heart, and tenderness has no source more profound, devotion more given to complete abandon. Her exquisite sensibility quivers at every breath: movable, passionate, fearless, never hoping by halves, she feels and at the same time mirrors the most diverse emotions.[19]

Female pedagogy must take into account women's nature—sentimental—and destination: the home. André Berthélot put it this way: "It is important that young girls should be educated in such a way that when they become mothers one day, they be able to convey to their children a truly modern and liberal instruction."[20] Republican pedagogy was not intended to form "bas-bleus" or "garçon-manqués"—so, neither Greek nor Latin was to be taught females, nor math or applied sciences.[21]

Ferdinand Buisson (1841–1932), one of the most important pedagogues of the early Third Republic,[22] and a Republican advocate of women's suffrage and of Dreyfus's cause, argued: "Whatever the case may be, women appear to us today, more than at other times, governed by the Heart, sensibility, imagination, by all that sort of affective and intuitive qualities.... These treasures of sensibility and imagination that overflow your Heart, do you know where they must unfold? Around yourselves, in the humble and sweet circle of your family. You dream of being an angel: be an angel of the household."[23] These were the words of someone who was correctly taken in 1883 for pedagogically progressive and who, as counselor to Jules Ferry, helped frame the terms of deliberation on female education. They echoed wider postulates on women's "essence," place, and destiny.[24]

The consequences of this configuration—female pedagogy, male hegemony, Republican schooling, and long-standing assumptions on the sentimental nature of "true womanhood"—had enormous relevance for the inculcation of pity. Schools could be sites of indoctrination in pro-pity sentimentalism, as we saw in Chapter 3. Yet if the advent of state schooling for girls made the pedagogy of pity still more pertinent, the rhetorical strategies used in a gendered school system revealed a significant paradox that would vex and, ultimately, undermine a doctrinaire sentimental education of pity: since females were assumed to be more emotional and piteous, what does this suggest about the universalism attributed to sentiments and, specifically, pity? The supposedly universalist assumption held that intelligence was developmentally twined to sentiment and that pity had to be instilled in individuals if a complex society was to hold together. Was it a coincidence that Bouillier penned his paean to pity in 1881, just when female pedagogy came to the fore? Had he not insisted on the universal meliorist character of pity? Granted the Third Republic's pedagomania and the consensus on the alleged emotional disposition of females, the notion of pity necessarily took on special, but incongruous, dimensions. As a virtue that could and must be intellectually comprehended and developed through education, pity had a place of honor in the Republican school. But if this place was reserved more so for women than men, what were the implications for the putative unifying force of sentiment and the pedagogical cultivation of a socially facilitating pity?

The emotives that the young Republic tried to engender as principles of social attachment and pacification thus ran up against previous "emotional regimes" predicated on gender. The transformative anxieties provoked by changing ideas on femininity and the other results of an invented "intersexual science" primed over neutered, cosmopolitan conceptions of pity. Although pity would for some time continue to be categorized as a cosmopolitan virtue—and not only by Bouillier—and addressed by males as a communal quality, it was specifically proposed to young ladies, who were expected to cultivate pity, which in turn would nurture (male) Frenchmen.[25] In this sense, pity as a keyword was the specifically Republican contribution to maternalism. Ida-R. Sée, the wife of Camille Sée, wrote a book on *Le Devoir maternel* (*Maternal Duties*), which included the following passage on "The Education of Sentiments:"

Woman herself better complies with sentiments, she discerns them more surely; her soul corresponds with the juvenile soul by a secret affinity. It is the mother who will awaken or enlarge the child's heart; if she responds to his first hurts with tenderness and pity, if she knows how to suffer alongside him, knows how to share his affectionate feelings for things…. Pity, patience, devotion, altruism, can thus be taught by a careful integration, by a patient labor that only a mother can undertake. Such a beckoning of heart to heart will be much more salutary than lessons on ethics![26]

The maternalist emphasis on pity and correlative sentiments thus became the focus of awkward inversions: males were in the discomfiting position first of promoting sentiment, a formerly feminized quality, for an apparently universal, but actually male, public sphere; and then of having to fully assume the formerly elided and supposedly female dimensions of pity and sentiment in order to safeguard what they were now obliged to acknowledge as the maleness of social arrangements. (A similar reversal was operated by Gabrielle Reval in her fictionalized account of life at the *École Normale Supérieure* at Sèvres, where she puts these words into the mouth of the imaginary counterpart to the real-life director, Mme. Jules Favre: "Disciples of Socrates, Epictetus, or of Kant, you must firmly uphold the promise made to yourselves of living according to your beliefs, of always obeying your conscience…. Beware of a false pity for yourselves and for others; often it is nothing but disguised cowardice.")[27] This untimely contradiction had vast, if at first imperceptible, consequences: pity became fixed within canonical pedagogical and literary fields as an at once doctrinaire and increasingly "feminine" virtue.

In this chapter, we look first at pronouncements on women and gender that stressed the fundamental importance of pity to a notional feminine character. Then I analyze in greater detail the official programs that reflected the gendered edification unto pity, as listed in the *Revue Universitaire* as well as in manuals for female secondary education. The courses included in the *Revue*, especially those granting certificates for employment in the *enseignement secondaire des jeunes filles*,[28] were a sort of Republican sentimental catechism. They betray assumptions on the altruistic temperament of young women, a disposition supposedly to be fortified through the study of tradition and tropes. Pity was adjudicated as a special feminine educational obligation in order to bridge the fracture between modernity and tradition, the Republic and "true" France, civilization and progress, the "maternalist" home and civil society, the inner self and communicability—in short, all the fault-lines signaled by anxieties over gender.

Ludovic Carrau was a proponent of the cosmopolitan, civilizing pity that worked through consciousness-raising. Yet at the kernel of this progress was a maternal pity: "In the life of savages, it is the women who offer us the most touching examples of sympathy, pity, devotion. One would say that maternal love, so often thwarted in its object by the abominable practice of infanticide, pours itself out in a more tender compassion for the woes of the stranger, the unknown."[29] The evolution of pity operates teleologically from the "savage" to the civilized through the basic mechanism of maternal instinct. Women, that is, harbor the germs of pity no less than they do the seeds of life.

Carrau touched upon some of the other dimensions of the gendered pro-pity consensus—for example, the alignment of a rational justice, implicitly associated with the masculine, against an involuntary, visceral pity, coupled to the feminine: "Justice is rather a matter of intelligence, of reason; charity is the involuntary, almost unconscious overflowing of the heart. It is harder to be truly just than to be adorably charitable."[30] This was a perspective that would be parroted in a later study program: for the *Agrégation de l'enseignement secondaire des jeunes filles* in 1909, the essay question on "morale, psychologie" was: "Women have been reproached for having a sense of pity, but not that of fairness; of being moved by obvious sufferings, but indifferent to remote justice. What is true in these claims? What psychological and pedagogical conclusions can you draw from them?"[31] Women were more piteous than men, less capable of abstract justice—this was the doctrinaire feminine pity that had, *mutatis mutandis*, psychological and pedagogical consequences whose lessons must be learned (and taught).

If women were "reproached" for this purported discrepancy between the senses of pity and justice, it was only a rhetorical rebuke—it was regarded with uniform approbation by those who addressed this supposed opposition. For example, Etienne Lamy (1845–1919)—another Republican functionary— celebrated the growing role of women in society and their greater access to education by pointing to the sentimental benefits that would redound to men: "In their greater liberty and increased influence, these voices rejoice in the reparation of a long injustice, in the legitimate exercise of a force necessary to the world and the dawn of a civilization where women will perhaps initiate men in that which the latter most lack and in which women are richest: sweetness, misericord, pity, goodness, the virtues of love."[32] Lamy reverses the tropes of the justice-pity antagonism by accenting the latter's benefit to men once the "injustice" of unequal access to social goods is repaired. Intrinsic to women, pity benefits men.

So for these pedagogues the education of women unto pity was not an exercise in the difficult. It was a question of harnessing "nature," since women were viscerally predisposed to tender emotions. Joseph Donaudy, for example, opined that "today's woman obviously can be distinguished from men by the following two points: 1. She is more sentimental; 2. She is more pitying, more altruistic."[33] This means that female education is directed more toward sentiment than to rational faculties: "It is true that women are regulated too much by sentiment and not enough by intelligence; but, by a fair compensation, she is more sensitive than men to the best of all these sentiments, altruism, and less than he to the worst."[34] Donaudy is in perfect agreement with Lamy's contention that female pity compensates male obdurateness and that it compensates the male virtue of justice: "She may not be capable of imagining the need for a law or for the diminution of the number of unhappy fellow-citizens, but she will give herself over to relieve individually the unfortunate, the sick, the guilty even; always goodness, and goodness without reflection."[35] This goodness may be specifically feminine, but it is also socially necessary: "Should an occasion arise, a catastrophe, a public misfortune, and one sees the ranks of women in a society come together in the same flight of pity and fraternal charity for the unfortunate more frequently than is the case with men."[36] The sexual division of sentimental labor makes for a good division of social labor and points toward necessary pedagogical directions.

Like Carrau, Donaudy also attributes women's piteous disposition to their maternalism: "And that is because women are wholly, one could say, maternity."[37] The social and pedagogical applications of this maternal character follow inexorably: women's place is in the hearth, as keeper of the familial and religious flames without which society cannot subsist:

Religious dogma, since it deals with that which is mysterious, that is to say, that which is unknowable by the intellect, can in truth only appeal to sentiment; for its part, religious ethics, like all ethics, necessarily presuppose pity or altruism. Woman, sentimental and altruistic, is thus altogether chosen as the apostle of this dogma and the example of fraternal morality.... The prompting to pity of a judge through the mediation of women has even been instituted as a dogma by Catholicism, which made of the Virgin Mary the advocate of sinners before God.[38]

If women were ostensibly more sentimental and piteous than men, why cultivate this singularity, and why not teach against the grain? Because the pro-pity consensus was an exemplary way to unite both secular Republicans and Catholics around the belief that a woman's place is in the home, especially if this dictated a detour through the democratic state's secular school system.

Célestin Bouglé (1870–1940) endorsed such views, hoping to replace jingoistic male attitudes toward war by a justice that calls for female pity as a counterweight: "In fact, if you prepare yourselves for war, it is in order to limit as much as possible the harm it does to men. If you follow in the steps of the army, it is pity which leads you by the hand, pure pity, which carries within it future peace."[39] Through Bouglé's oration we see one chronological marker of doctrinaire feminine pity—on the eve of the Great War, pity is handed to women for safekeeping because they are its rightful guardians. As such, they influence the destinies of men: "Sociologists take pleasure in repeating that 'the entire social mechanism rests, in the last analysis, on opinions.' Opinions, in their turn, run on sentiments. Or who does not know the depths to which—by her approbations and her indignations, her smiles and her tears—woman is capable of altering the sentiments of men?"[40] By indoctrinating a feminine pity, men cannot help helping themselves. And so Bouglé concluded his lay sermon:

"It is necessary to resist evil, but first within oneself!" "One must be courageous in times of war, but first in times of peace!" If you know how to extend around you these two truths, you will have satisfied the most noble requirements of Christian morality and modern morality; you will have worked for the real progress of humanity, for you will have contributed to shaping, in your role as women, a race of beings among whom pity is allied to courage and which will be, in every sense of the word, men of heart.[41]

Pity and courage in war, secular and Christian morality—women were hallowed as the junction among these essentialist attributes.

Females needed to be educated for such an imperative role. Philosophy and teacher-training syllabi throughout nearly three decades of the "long" *fin-de-siècle* (from the early 1880s until 1914) stressed sentiment and, especially, pity as subjects to be tackled on behalf of young female charges. The relations between moral education and teacher-training were especially close; ethics were a larger component of girls' schooling than that of boys, and practical philosophy was a preferred field of study for women entering higher education. Henri Marion, for example, wrote about moral training in female pedagogy: "In the third year, the program offers a full course on practical ethics, in which the enumeration of duties is preceded by summary ideas.... What is most original in the philosophical teaching of young girls is the program for the course in applied pedagogical psychology."[42]

The *Revue Universitaire* reveals the concern demonstrated by the pedagogical establishment with a feminine sentimental education. The Republican *Ministère de l'instruction publique* established exams and "detailed syllabi and plans of study for the secondary schooling of young girls" on July 28, 1882.[43] On January 5, 1884, an *agrégation pour l'enseignement secondaire des jeunes filles* was instituted, and two days later a *certificat d'aptitude pour l'enseignement secondaire des jeunes filles*. Four themes germane to a gendered pro-pity sentimentalism were drawn in to these programs: the role of altruistic emotion in education; the relation of justice to pity and to charity; the inculcating of literary *loci* and tropes of the French pity tradition; and the promotion of pity as an ethical virtue. These themes correspond to the theoretical-emotive writings we have analyzed, thus reinforcing the sense that pro-pity sentimentalism of the *fin-de-siècle* shifted from problematic to consensus to doctrine. That these themes were supposed to be mastered by prospective teachers of young girls also confirms our sense that this had become a specifically feminine doctrinaire pity.

Both young ladies and their would-be instructors were supposed to be versed in the terms of sentimentalism. In 1897, the examination question for the *certificat d'aptitude à l'enseignement secondaire des jeunes filles* was: "Analysis of the 'morals of sympathy.'"[44] The terms of "affective philosophy" were supposed to be widely inculcated. The crossroads of the *fin-de-siècle*, the year 1900, saw the proliferation of sentimentalist questions across disciplines and programs. These questions reveal that the topics debated by philosophers, psychologists, and social scientists over the past two decades had filtered through to the larger society and were susceptible of indoctrination. For example, a question for the *licence philosophique* drew its substance from the ambient affective philosophy: "The nature of Emotion and the classification of affective reality."[45] In order to obtain the *agrégation de philosophie*, the essay required an equal familiarity with sentimentalism: "Egoism and altruism. Are these two tendencies equally fundamental and primary?"[46] Presumably, the chances of passing were significantly better if the answer was anchored by a "no" on behalf of altruism.

A significant feature of this pedagogical sentimentalism was how it was fastened to literary *loci* that reinforced and revised traditionalism. In 1905, Vauvenargues was treated with this respect in the question for the *certificat d'aptitude à l'enseignement secondaire des jeunes filles*: "'All our proofs,' said Vauvenargues, exist only to make things known to us with the same certainty as we get through sentiment.' Do you share his opinion? What role would you give to intuition and to sentiment in our intellectual and moral development?"[47] Descartes was yet another *de rigueur* dignitary. In 1911, the essay question for the *agrégation de philosophie* was: "The role of passions in morality according to Descartes."[48] That same year, la Rochefoucauld and Rousseau were drawn into the literature question proposed for the *classes de l'enseignement secondaire des jeunes filles*: "During the 17th century, one took pride in being 'reasonable;' in the 18th century, in being 'sensitive;'" in the 19th, in being 'humane.' Illustrate to what sort of logical and profound evolution these diverse conceptions of morality correspond."[49] The guidelines specified that la Rochefoucauld should be considered the prototype of seventeenth-century "reasonableness" and Rousseau that of eighteenth-century "sensitivity"— together, they were signposts of an ethical evolution toward contemporary humanitarianism.

The importance especially of Rousseau is clear: as both the consummate philosopher of sentiment and a theorist of feminine pedagogy, his was a traditional authority that had to be confronted. For example, in 1906, the examination question on the subject of *Éducation, pédagogie* for Sèvres was: "Assess this thought of Rousseau: 'To keep pity from degenerating into weakness, it must be generalized and spread to the whole human race. We must have more pity—from reason and out of love for our own—on our species than on our neighbor, and it is terribly cruel toward our fellow men to pity the wicked.'"[50] The question was not meant to be of merely historical interest or solely an "appreciation" of Rousseauian thought: it was specifically for and about pedagogy, and Rousseau's dictum was meant to serve as a teaching guide.

In 1907, the female students in this same program were asked to reflect on Rousseau's sturdy contemporaneity: "What do you think is the cause of the indifference, barely hidden by a veil of admiration, for Voltaire's works, whereas those of Rousseau are still marked by a passionate interest?"[51] In 1910, the case for Rousseau's ubiquity was put before students with even greater emphasis: "A contemporary critic has written: 'Rousseau seizes us through all of our faculties: in politics, morality, poetry, and novels, one finds him everywhere, at the entrance to all the avenues of the present.' Assess the depth and universality of Rousseau's influence."[52] Rousseuaian sentimentalism was all-pervading in *fin-*

de-siècle pedagogy. If this is unsurprising, it is remarkable by comparison to his relative absence from theoretical pronouncements of the period, which gave him lesser weight in the revival of sentimentalism.

It was for girls and their teachers that the unambiguous qualities of Rousseauian "sensitivity" as cited in the question of 1911 had to be rendered explicit. The following year's question in *Morale and psychologie* for the *classes de l'enseignement secondaire des jeunes filles* required this reflection: "What does it mean to be 'sensitive?' Give the psychological and historical meaning of this adjective. What nuance can you detect between a sensitive personality and a sensible soul? Is sensitivity always a type of generosity of the heart and mind? Are there not dangerous sensibilities?"[53] In 1914, any doubts about the correct answer to the former question—the psychological springs of sentiment—were occluded in the question on pedagogical psychology for the *classes de l'enseignement secondaire des jeunes filles*: "Of the danger of detaching sentiment from action. Good sentiments have value only insofar as they are translated into action. It is their psychological role to act as motors."[54] Among pedagogues, the motor-role of sentiment had become a commonplace.

This psychological postulate was condignly germane to female pedagogy, and so the question for the *certificat d'aptitude à l'enseignement secondaire des jeunes filles* in 1910 was: "In what manner and by which means can one educate a young girl's will? Does this education seem to you to be as important for a woman as that of the sentiments?"[55] The inferences concealed in this question are worth restating: sentiments must be carefully handled in female pedagogy; will and intelligence are not as essential as sentiment. In any case, nothing can be done with the former that does not presuppose perfecting the latter, since the social and moral repercussions of such a perfectioning are enormous: "It has been claimed that sensibility in a woman is like the languages in Aesop's fables, the best and worst of things. Show all the bad that, gone wrong, and all the good, because well-directed, this sensibility can give rise to in social and moral life."[56]

The "directions" to be taken, of course, *pace* Lamy, Buisson, et al., was maternal and traditional. Female sentiments were at their most useful, socially and ethically, when guiding young women back to their traditional habitus, so that the role of altruistic sentiment itself in education was to bring females to the self-conscious realization of their aptness for what they were in any case unconsciously primed: "Maternal love taken as the source and model for sympathetic sentiments: 1. Identify the maternal element that is to be found in the noblest human sentiments.... 2. Of the moral and social importance of the hearth as a means of guaranteeing between mother and child the relations needed to fashion sympathetic sentiments."[57] A woman's place must be in the home if sympathetic sentiments are to be cultivated for the greater benefit of the wider society. Behind the indoctrination of maternal tenderness lies a wide paradox: the catechism betrays the belief that sentiments by themselves are not as effective as sentiments that have been trained, that the doctrine of sentimental*ism* is prior to the effusion of sentimental acts otherwise taken as given. This is a prophylactic rhetoric of male anxiety.

Such a paradox was born out of a belief and a fear—a belief in the disciplining effect of education on sentiment and a fear that without this curb, male egoism could go unchecked: "'I was born to attach myself to love, not hate,' answered the ancient Antigone. Show how this beautiful phrase should be the motto of all women, not so as to turn them into bleating and somewhat burdensome sheep in times of trouble, but rather so that they maintain thereby a sense of serenity, of piteous intelligence, because our hatreds and rancors, even those which seem to be justifiable, always contain much egoism and often misunderstanding."[58] Young women had to be instructed in virtues that were *sui generis*. This tuition also had to be sized up against the justice that was deemed a male virtue and that sentimentalism ritually invoked as its antagonist.

In 1906 instructors had to come to grips with Montesquieu, one of the obligatory references in the tradition upholding the justice side of the tether: "Discuss this thought of Montesquieu: 'Almost all the virtues consist in a specific relation of one man to another; for example, friendship, love of country, and pity are particular relationships. But justice is a general relation. So all the virtues that destroy this general relation are not virtues.'"[59] Again, the purpose of the exercise must have been less to discuss this opinion than to find a way around its dilemma.

The mandatory textbook in ethics for female secondary education placed Renouvier's last reflections on the relations among pity, justice, and charity at the core of its lesson on *sentiments altruistes*. This relationship as conceived by the manual—*Leçons de morale théorique et notions historiques: Enseignement des jeunes filles: Écoles normales*—made Renouvier's pro-pity change of heart about his magnum opus, *La science de la morale* (1869), the point of departure for its lesson. In a chapter on the "rôle du sentiment dans la morale," the authors first turned to benevolence: "Let us assume sentiments are benevolent. Let us consider them as elements or factors of morality and analyze them from this point of view."[60] This provides an immediate connection to other-directed sentiment: "But our morality is neither completely *individual* nor *internal*: it has a *social basis*, it comprises elements of sympathy and altruism."[61] Pity encompasses these latter two virtues, so the "Exercises" proposed for the students include the question: "How can one reconcile the revulsion against evil and pity?"[62] The authors imply that pity should not remain passive, that it need not accept irremediable evil and can act on behalf of the ameliorable. This sense is corroborated by the reading assignment they propose under the rubric "notions historiques"—"à lire: Renouvier, 'la pitié.'"[63] Ancel and Dugas wanted to draw attention to the connection of pity to justice and charity, thereby making it more actual, social, and practicable.

The excerpt from Renouvier does not come from *La science de la morale* but from his comments in *Derniers entretiens*, where he confided in 1902 and 1903 to his interlocutor, Louis Prat, his feelings about the former work: "If I could have done a second edition, I would have added some pages on goodness, on pity."[64] And this, Renouvier reveals, because he believes pity is highly pedagogical: "I wish that we would make every effort to cultivate in our children the sentiment of pity."[65] Pity is an inescapable subject matter for education, especially since it is actuated through justice: "Pity, if it is properly interpreted, leads to justice."[66] Renouvier concludes by lamenting his inability to furnish a thorough account of pity, principally because other views have been either incomplete or partial, especially Schopenhauer's:

The analyses that have been made of this sentiment appear to me to be unsatisfactory. For pity to be awakened in us, it is not necessary—this is Schopenhauer's theory—that each person consider himself *as a unique and universal being*, it is enough to admit for all humans a commonality of origin and destiny, *an intimate solidarity in poverty and suffering.* I believe all humans are capable of feeling pity, because all men deeply feel injustice, or that which is the same thing, the pain of living.[67]

Renouvier links pity to justice because the former is the basic reaction to injustice. Renouvier believes that, given the omnipresence of evil and suffering, especially their undeserved manifestations, pity will need to be nurtured as a countervailing cultural power: "It is because pain seems to us unwarranted that pity blossoms in our souls. It is not necessary that we love those whom we see suffer: they can be strangers, indifferent to us, animals. Their fate is to suffer, ours is to suffer, so we have pity. Pity may be defined: 'the soul's revolt against the malice of evil.'"[68] The "soul's revolt against the malice of evil:" this is not the sort of definitional abstraction, with its rational purity, that one expects from a neo-Kantian. The point of the lesson, as it has been condensed for young females, is the evocation of a rationally sanctioned emotive discourse that alerts them to evil and sensibility. Pity is the principal virtue here because it accomplishes a twofold objective: encourages the nurturing of other-directed attentiveness (the sufferings of others, even of strangers and animals) and puts students on their guard against evil. The fact that the one excerpt that follows from *La science de la morale* is the section on "Solidarité morale" reveals how social solidarity is the purpose of exploiting Renouvier's regret *apropos* pity.

There was nothing specifically feminine about Renouvier's views of pity; his phrases invoke "tous les hommes" or "nous." It is rather the use that Ancel and Dugas, the authors of these *Leçons*, make of him that renders this guidance specifically feminine. Through reading and discussion exercises, young girls are tutored on the proper relationship to justice and misfortune with pity as the intermediary.

In other manuals as well as in the *Revue Universitaire*, female pedagogy enthroned the literary *loci* and tropes of the pity tradition and promoted pity as a virtue distinct from either justice or charity. In 1892, the essay required of students in philosophy in the *enseignement secondaire des jeunes filles* was: "How can one cultivate the sentiment of pity in a child's soul?"[69] The "how" of this question begged a normative "should." In 1897 the condition for an *agrégation de l'enseignement secondaire des jeunes filles* passed through an "analysis and critique of the morality of pity."[70] The best way to indoctrinate pity was to make students conversant with the pros and cons of its ethical significance, in line with traditional sources and contemporary consensus.

The *Revue* betrayed the educational establishment's partiality to pro-pity conceptions of female development. In 1900, for example, this was the question with which teachers were to drill girls on the subject of "éducation, pédagogie:" "Tell us what you think of pity, its moral and social value, from 'One must not remove the altar from the temple, nor pity from the hearts of men.'"[71] Echoes of Bouillier's essay of 1881 are as clear as is the tendentious phrasing that perforce leads to a positive estimation of the "moral and social value" of pity.

In 1902, the adjectives "sincere" and "tactful" were introduced to qualify the sort of pity to be instilled: "It has been said that 'pity is the best type of alms.' How can a sincere and tactful pity alleviate the unfortunate who are its object?"[72] This prudential and effective pity was followed by further terminological nuances in 1910, when girls were asked, in the "quatrième année" of "Morale, psychologie:" "Demonstrate, using examples, the nuances of meaning that exist among pity, indulgence, and benevolence. Also show that these are the qualities desired par excellence in women, but the most dangerous to employ for oneself and others if not constrained by reason."[73] Here we have the essence of a doctrinaire feminine pity as disclosed by official pedagogy: pity, benevolence, and indulgence are feminine qualities par excellence, in need of rational cultivation and direction. Pity is feminine by definition and by fiat; and this is knowable and directable only through that certified instrument, the Republican school.

It is also knowable through its teleological dimensions—in 1909 the candidates for the *certificat d'aptitude à l'enseignement secondaire des jeunes filles* were asked to reflect on the "historical evolution of the sentiment of pity. Show how it tends to substitute itself today to the sentiment of duty, of which it is an essential and necessary, but not sufficient, element."[74] Pity replaces duty: this is the historicist and sentimentalist turn in ethics in vulgate version.

The advocacy of pity was integrated into wider and more comparative historical contexts. In 1910, the *agrégation de l'enseignement secondaire des jeunes filles* imposed the following reflection: "'A century of pity is only fertile,' it has been said, 'if it is also a century of energy.' Do the two qualities not seem to you to be equally necessary to establish a just and decent society?"[75] Sincere, discreet, decent, and feminine—to these qualification was added that of energetic, which served to link pity to the allegedly more masculine qualities of "just" and "noble." Another "noble" context for pity was that of the righteous morality of suffering: "Pain and sadness. Show their relations and their differences; their moral worth and danger. General guidelines: pain makes us known to ourselves; it also reveals others to us: pity and solidarity are born from suffering, which is why they are most customary among the humble."[76]

In 1913, the question in pedagogical psychology for all *classes des lycées et collèges, enseignement secondaire des jeunes filles* reverted back to the query posed in exactly the same terms in 1892: "How can one cultivate the sentiments of pity in a child's soul?"[77] This repetition across two decades confirms the static and doctrinaire property of pro-pity tuition.

The connections between pity and literature became as much a commonplace in schools' syllabi as in critical discussion.[78] The commonplace figures in thinking on pity were the subject of examination questions and official syllabi—La Fontaine, Corneille, Boileau, Pascal, Nietzsche, and Anatole France and, as we have seen, Descartes, la Rochefoucauld, and Rousseau. They had become, under the impulsion of sentimentalism, the "classics" of pity, in much the same way that they were also part of the nascent movement of "classics" in the *fin-de-siècle* Republican school.[79] For example, the problem posed by La Fontaine's *bon mot*, that children are without pity, a phrase that seriously preoccupied pedagogical theorists, gained all the more weight in the context of practical instruction. In 1913, the *composition française* for the *classes de l'enseignement secondaire des jeunes filles* was: "La Fontaine said of children: 'that age is without pity.' Reflect on your own infantile cruelty, since you are at the age when one leaves behind childhood."[80] The following directives were issued to teachers in guiding the students' responses: "Search for the causes: 1. Carelessness, inexperience, and inability to put oneself in another's place; 2. egoism and vanity; 3. rebellion against authority."[81] La Fontaine had to be wrong, must be instructed as being wrong, in order to preserve the other-regarding, self-restraining enterprise proper to schooling. So, too, Nietzsche had to be gainsaid:

A contemporary German philosopher claims that the truly great man, the peerless person, the "übermensch," must be as hard as diamond, indifferent to the suffering of others and detached from all pity. You will first of all determine if it is desirable, supposing it is even possible, to forsake pity. Then you will show that the types of "übermensch" that we find in Corneille—and especially don Diego, the old Horace, Augustus—are neither unyielding nor insensitive.[82]

This was a female pedagogy of pity that took its French literary *loci* seriously and that took up the cudgels against Nietzsche with as much insistence as wielded by disparaging philosophers and critics.

Corneille's tragedy and Boileau's implicitly Aristotelian criticism of its unities also merited attention: "Boileau rebuked Corneille for having introduced a new motive in tragedy: admiration. Must we blame Corneille, and does the fact that he resorted to admiration make him really neglect the two great tragic passions: terror and pity?"[83] This question came to the defense of Corneille by using the fixed tenets of pity that, in literature no less than in ethics—both combined in pedagogy—was instilled as a doctrine.

Even the implacable Pascal could be reconciled to pity by pedagogues. In 1910, the literature component of the *certificat d'aptitude à l'enseignement secondaire des jeunes filles* required an essay on "The sense of 'pity' in Pascal's *Pensées*. Show how it permeates that book which is so severe toward human weakness."[84] Pascal, who had been a classic reference against pity, was now recruited as a member in good standing of pro-pity sentimentalism—indeed, his

Pensées were permeated by a "sense of pity"—thus demonstrating the willful reconsiderations brought about by the pedagogues of pity.

Contemporary literary figures also came to figure as pedagogical classics on the subject of pity. This was true of Anatole France—an instant contemporaneous classic in any sense—who was made the subject of the following question for the *classes de l'enseignement secondaire des jeunes filles* in 1919: "Comment on this thought of Anatole France: 'Suffering, what a divine unknown! We owe it everything that is good in us, everything that gives life value; we owe it pity, courage, we owe it all the virtues.'"[85] The commonplaces surrounding a pedagogical pity are here gathered around Anatole France's aphorism: the moral worth of suffering; the importance of pity to this value; the assimilation of a piteous cognition to virtue.

We have encountered most of these literary figures earlier: La Fontaine, la Rochefoucauld, Pascal, Corneille, Descartes, Rousseau, Nietzsche, and Anatole France. We are thus in a position to confirm that the study programs did engage the pity tradition in a way that was faithful to its *loci classicus*. What is noteworthy beyond the fidelity to a received tradition, however, is the impulse to reinvest all of it with a straightforward and lisible promotion of pity, one, moreover, whose characteristics are expedient to female pedagogy. To speak to pity and teach it were to be cognizant of the special responsibility that women had to tend its flame in the patriarchal temple.

Did women and men share a common humanity that could be understood and educated through the same rational and emotive tools? The turn to sentimental philosophy implied an affirmative answer. But when it came to pedagogy, the omnipresent moralizing instrument of Republican France, the advocates of pity as a socializing sentiment—far stronger than its detractors—managed both to complicate and simplify this answer with a gendered "yes, but..." Pity had to be inflected with feminine accents so as to maintain women's placatory role in a *fin-de-siècle* society beset by the promises and threats of change. Civilizing and modernizing imperatives were thus both served by a feminine education unto pity.

NOTES

1. ["La femme est ainsi: toute altruisme, pitié et dévouement, parce que toute maternité et toute amour."] J. Dody (pseud. of Joseph Donaudy, b. 1862), *Les questions sentimentales en sociologie* (Paris: V. Giard et E. Brière: 1905), 16.

2. The launching of an imprint titled *Bibliothèque biologique et sociologique de la femme* by the publishing house O. Doin attested to this ferment, viewed as conflictual by definition. See the statement of mission: "those problems of morality and economic activity in which men and women are in conflict and which comprise that which one may call intersexual Science." ["ces problèmes de morale et d'activité économique où les hommes et les femmes sont en conflit et qui constituent ce que l'on peut appeler la Science

intersexuelle"].

3. For a progressivist account of this development, see Octave Gréard, *L'Enseignement secondaire des filles. Mémoire présenté au conseil académique dans la séance du 27 juin 1882* (Paris: Delalain, 1882). Gréard was one of the founders of the Republic's educational system and a member of the ASMP, elected on May 15, 1875.

4. In addition to Gréard's account, see the laws, decrees, and documents compiled by Antoine Villemot, *Étude sur l'organisation, le fonctionnement et les progrès de l'enseignement secondaire des jeunes filles en France, de 1789 à 1887* (Paris: Paul Dupont, 1887). The citation is from page 10. The text of Sée's intervention before the Chamber is reproduced in Françoise Mayeur, *L'Éducation des filles en France au XIXème siècle* (Paris: Hachette, 1979), 185–86. Her verdict on Sée's labors, in *L'Enseignement secondaire des jeunes filles sous la Troisième République* (Paris: Presses de la fondation nationale des sciences politiques, 1977), is that they were Condorcetian in spirit: "In the mind of a Ferry or of a Camille Sée, initiatives on behalf of the education of women were inspired largely by Condorcet, whose style and mode of thought are easily recognizable in Camille Sée." ["Dans l'esprit d'un Ferry et d'un Camille Sée, les initiatives en faveur de l'éducation des femmes sont inspirées essentiellement par Condorcet dont le style et la forme de pensée se reconnaissent aisément chez Camille Sée"] (13). See also Sée's own relation in *Lycées et collèges de jeunes filles: documents, rapports et discours à la chambre des Députés et au Sénat; décrets, arrêtés, circulaires, etc.* (Paris: 1886).

5. See Françoise Mayeur on the specificities of the *École de Sèvres*, marked by the person of its *Directrice*, Mme. Jules Favre, in *L'Éducation des filles en France au XIXème siècle*, 151–52.

6. Mayeur, 7–8.

7. Mayeur, 167. By 1929, the number had increased to 50,157. Cited by Karen Offen, "The Second Sex and the Baccalauréat in Republican France, 1880–1924," *French Historical Studies* 13 (1983), 252–86.

8. "For the future of the Republic, it is necessary to organize an education for girls. Paul Bert and Jules Ferry consecrated themselves to this, with all the more of a free hand in that the structures of female pedagogy are almost nonexistent" ["Pour l'avenir de la République, il faut donc organiser l'éducation des filles. Paul Bert et Jules Ferry s'y consacrent, avec d'autant plus de liberté que les structures, en matière d'enseignement féminine, sont presque inéxistantes"]. Cited by Mona Ozouf, *L'école, l'église et la République* (Paris: Seuil, 1982), 95. See also Linda Clark: "Ferry and his allies reformed girls' education in order to remove women from the influence of the church and its monarchical allies and to mold future generations of mothers supportive of republican ideology" ("Bringing Feminine Qualities into the Public Sphere: The Third Republic's Appointment of Women Inspectors," *Gender and the Politics of Social Reform in France, 1870–1914*, Elinor A. Accampo, Rachel Fuchs, and Mary Lynn Stewart, eds. [Baltimore: Johns Hopkins UP, 1995], 155.

9. ["l'une des créations fondamentales de la République."] Villemot, *Étude sur l'organisation, le fonctionnement et les progrès de l'enseignement secondaire des jeunes filles en France*, 10. André Berthélot, born in 1862, was the son of the famous chemist. He entered Parisian politics as a Radical in 1894 and was elected to the Chamber in 1898, where he was among the Dreyfusard activists. He became secretary-general of the

Encyclopédie in 1885. For more biographical information, see C.-E. Curinier, ed., *Dictionnaire national des contemporains*, vol. 2 (Paris: B. Brunel, s.d.), 277.

10. ["l'oeuvre caractéristique du régime actuel."] Villemot, *Études sur l'organisation*, 10.

11. ["la 'Femme' même, ne semble digne de figurer que sous les trois espèces qui ne nous font guère sortir de l'école: 'Fille,' qui nous y mène tout droit par l'histoire législative de son instruction; 'Institutrice,' qui paraît le débouché normal de cette instruction; et 'Mère,' dont c'est la raison d'être d'y préparer l'enfant."] Pierre Nora, "Le *Dictionnaire de pédagogie* de Ferdinand Buisson: Cathédrale de l'école primaire," *Les Lieux de mémoire*, 372.

12. Some of the debates are transcribed in dossiers in AN, F17/12964. In addition to the work of Gréard, the following are essential: Paul Rousselet, *La pédagogie féminine* (Paris: Ch. Delagrave, 1881); Antoine Villemont, ed., *Enseignement secondaire: Documents* (Paris: P. Dupont, 1889), and idem., *Étude sur l'organisation, le fonctionnement et les progrès de l'enseignement secondaire des jeunes filles en France, de 1789 à 1887*; Paul Janet, "L'éducation des femmes," *Revue des deux mondes* 1883 (5), 48–83; Henri Marion, *Étude de psychologie féminine: l'éducation des jeunes filles* (Paris: Armand Colin, 1902); Étienne Lamy, "La femme et l'enseignement de l'Etat," *Revue des deux mondes* (April 1, 1901), 602–29; H. Boiraud, "Sur la création par l'état d'un enseignement secondaire féminin en France," *Paedagogica Historica* 21 (1977), 21–36; Léon Dubreuil, "Paul Bert et l'enseignement secondaire féminin," *Revue d'histoire économique et sociale* 18 (1930), 205–40; Karen Offen, "The Second Sex and the Baccalauréat in Republican France;" Mona Ozouf, *L'école, l'église et la République*, esp. Chapter 3, "L'Éducation des filles;" and Françoise Mayeur's works, cited.

13. The committee of the Conseil supérieur de l'instruction publique that approved the laws of the 1880s on female education was all-male: MM. Belot, Berné, Blutel, Berson, Clédat, Dognon, Mariot, and Rancès. But see Linda Clark's important discussions of the role of female pedagogical inspectors as relays between the administration and schools: "Bringing Feminine Qualities into the Public Sphere: The Third Republic's Appointment of Women Inspectors," and "A Battle of the Sexes in a Professional Setting: The Introduction of *Inspectrices Primaires*, 1889–1914," *French Historical Studies* 16 (Spring 1989), 96–125.

14. See Karen Offen: "Its products were to be skilled, well-read, and gracious wives and mothers—suitable companions, as we have said, for the new male replublican elite of France" ("The Second Sex and the Baccalauréat in Republican France," 257).

15. See Seth Koven and Sonya Michel, in "Womanly Duties: Maternalist Politics and the Origins of the Welfare States in France, Germany, Great Britain, and the United States, 1880–1920," *American Historical Review* 95 (October 1990), who define maternalism as "ideologies that exalted women's capacity to mother and extended to society as a whole the values of care, nurturance and morality....It extolled the private virtues of domesticity while simultaneously legitimating women's public relationships to politics and the state, to community, workplace, and marketplace....Maternalism challenged the constructed boundaries between public and private, women and men, state and civil society" (1099). See also Annelise Maugue, *L'Identité masculine en crise au tournant du siècle, 1871–1914* (Paris: Editions Rivages, 1987): "Maternité constitutes such a 'school of tenderness and forgetfulness of self' that a woman lives out her

relationships with her entire entourage, including adults, and even the whole universe, as a mode of abnegation." ["La maternité constitue une telle 'école de tendresse et de désintéressement' que la femme vit ses relations à tout son entourage, adultes compris, et à l'univers entière sur la mode de l'abnégation"] (27).

16. Clark writes of the specifically Republican version of maternalism: "The republic's renaming of nursery schools from *salles d'asile* to *écoles maternelles* in 1881 signified not only that their central function was educational rather than charitable but also that their teachers offered a kind of maternal care to children aged 2 to 6 whose mothers worked outside the home. Official curricula and textbooks for girls' schools spelled out the dimensions of republican motherhood. Republican mothers were dutiful and self-sacrificing" ("Bringing Feminine Qualities into the Public Sphere: The Third Republic's Appointment of Women Inspectors," 149).

17. ["la pitié, inerte, passive chez les hommes, plus résignés aux maux d'autrui, est chez les femmes un sentiment très actif, très violent, qui devient parfois héroïque et les pousse impérieusement aux actes les plus hardis."] Michelet, *Histoire de la révolution française*, vol. 2, viii.

18. ["Deux choses, en effet, sont à considérer dans l'éducation: l'acquisition des connaissances et le développement des facultés. L'une ne se conçoit pas sans l'autre. Cependant elles diffèrent l'une de l'autre dans une certaine mesure, selon qu'il s'agit des hommes ou des femmes....Le premier souci d'une éducation bien dirigée doit donc être d'assurer à la jeune fille cette haute culture morale qui crée la personnalité morale."] Gréard, *L'enseignement secondaire des filles*, 102.

19. ["Gardons-nous de paraître vouloir changer les femmes en hommes, et, pour faire entrer dans le ménage plus de force, n'allons pas en faire sortir la douceur et la grâce....où nous nous décidons par raison, elle écoute son Coeur, et la tendresse n'a pas de source plus profonde, le dévouement de plus complet abandon. Sa sensibilité exquise vibre à tous les souffles: mobile, passionnée, ne craignant, n'espérant jamais à demi, elle ressent tour à tour et réfléchit admirablement les émotions diverses."] Gréard, 109–10.

20. ["il importe que les jeunes filles soient élevées de façon que, quand elles seront un jour mères de famille, elles puissent communiquer à leurs enfants une instruction vraiment moderne et libérale."] Cited in Villemot, *Étude sur l'organisation, le fonctionnement et les progrès de l'enseignement secondaire des jeunes filles en France*, 81.

21. See Françoise Mayeur, *L'enseignement secondaire des jeunes filles sous la Troisième République*, 149; and Karen Offen, "The Second Sex and the Baccalauréat in Republican France," 258–59.

22. Buisson was Directeur de l'enseignement primaire in 1879, Professeur de science de l'éducation at the Sorbonne in 1896, deputy from Paris in 1902, president of the *Ligue des droits de l'homme* in 1914, President of the *Ligue de l'enseignement* in 1918, and the Nobel Peace laureat in 1927. See Christophe Charle's entry in *Les professeurs de la faculté des lettres à Paris*, vol. 1: *1809–1908* (Paris: Éditions du centre nationale de la recherche scientifique, 1985), 38–40; Pierre Nora, "Le *Dictionnaire de pédagogie* de Ferdinand Buisson;" Mona Ozouf's prosopographical entry in *L'école, l'église et la République*, 239–40.

23. ["Quoi qu'il en soit, la femme nous semble aujourd'hui, plus encore qu'autrefois, dominée par le Coeur, par la sensibilité, par l'imagination, par tout cet ordre de qualités

affectives….Ces trésors de sensibilité et d'imagination dont votre Coeur déborde, savez-vous où il faut les répandre? C'est autour de vous, dans l'humble et doux cercle de la famille. Vous rêvez d'être une ange: soyez l'ange du foyer."] "L'éducation laïque de la jeune fille (Discours à la société pour l'instruction élémentaire, 22 juillet 1883)," in *La foi laïque: extraits de discours et d'écrits (1878–1911)* (Paris: Hachette, 1912), 25, 29–31.

24. See William Reddy, *The Invisible Code*: "That 'public' has for so long meant 'male' is not in itself a new contention, but it is a contention whose implications have only begun to be teased out. In particular, the relationship between gender and emotion, between the 'female' and the 'personal,' 'sentimental,' or private,' is so intimate and elemental that it has shaped and continues to shape public action, although actors often have no awareness of it" (6).

25. See David Bell, "To the extent that French authors believed that political action and historical evolution determined national character, they also generally saw these two factors working through a particular intermediary: women. For if national character was in some senses identical to or symbiotically linked to *moeurs*, *moeurs* themselves were the province of women, both because of women's general influence on social interactions and their specific role in educating the young" ("The Unbearable Lightness of Being French: Law, Republicanism and National Identity at the End of the Old Regime," *The American Historical Review* 106:4 [October 2001], 1227).

26. ["La femme obéit elle-même mieux aux sentiments, elle les devine plus sûrement; son âme s'accord avec l'âme enfantine par une secrète affinité. C'est la mère qui éveillera ou développera le Coeur de l'enfant; si elle répond à la première douleur par la tendresse et la pitié, si elle sait souffrir avec lui, partager son sentiment d'affection pour les choses….La pitié, la patience, le dévouement, l'altruisme se peuvent ainsi enseigner par une lente assimilation, par un travail patient que la mère seule peut tenter. Bien mieux que les leçons de morale cet appel du Coeur au Coeur sera salutaire!"] Ida-R. Sée, *Le Devoir maternel* (Paris: Eugène Figuière, 1911), 70–72.

27. ["Disciples de Socrate, d'Epictète, ou de Kant, ayez en vous-mêmes le ferme propos de vivre conformément à votre loi, d'obéir toujours à votre conscience….Gardez-vous d'une fausse pitié pour vous-mêmes et pour les autres; souvent ce n'est qu'une lâcheté déguisée."] Gabrielle Reval, *Les Sèvriennes* (Paris: Ollendorff, 1900), 91. On the controversial question of whether females should be taught exclusively by women, see Charles Jacquard, "L'éducation morale à l'école," *Le Volume* 20:1 (1907–1908); "La formation morale des professeurs femmes," *Revue Universitaire* (1912:2); Mlle. F. Teutscher, "Sur Quelques insuffisances de l'enseignement féminin," *Revue Universitaire* (1911:1), 33–37.

28. See Karen Offen: "the *brevets de capacité primaire élémentaire* and *primaire supérieur*, which had previously been attainable only through the girls' primary schools. These certificates qualified their holders for the sole vocation then deemed respectable for women, that of primary schooteacher" ("The Second Sex and the Baccalauréat in Republican France," 262).

29. Ludovic Carrau, *La Conscience psychologique et morale dans l'individu et dans l'histoire*, 282. ["Ce sont les femmes qui, dans la vie sauvage, nous offrent les plus touchants exemples de sympathie, de pitié, de dévouement. On dirait que l'amour maternel, si souvent frustré de son objet par l'abominable pratique de l'infanticide, se

déverse en compassion plus tendre sur les maux de l'étranger, de l'inconnu."]

30. ["La Justice est plutôt affaire d'intelligence, de raison; la charité est le déborde-ment involontaire, presque inconscient, du Coeur. Il est plus difficile d'être vraiment juste que d'être adorablement charitable."] Carrau, 282.

31. ["On a reproché aux femmes d'avoir le sens de la pitié, non celui de l'équité; d'être touchées des souffrances visibles, indifférentes à la justice lointaine. Qu'y a-t-il de vrai dans ces allégations? Quelles conclusions psychologiques et pédagogiques en tirez-vous?"] Revue Universitaire (1909:2), 455.

32. ["Dans sa liberté grandie et dans son influence étendue, ces voix célèbrent la réparation d'une longue injustice, l'exercice légitime d'une force nécessaire au monde et l'aurore d'une civilisation où la femme introduira peut-être ce qui manque davantage aux hommes et ce dont les femmes sont les plus riches: la douceur, la miséricorde, la pitié, la bonté, les vertus de l'amour."] Etienne Lamy, La Femme de demain (Paris: Perrin, 1914), 48. Lamy, a Catholic of the Left, was elected to the Assembly in 1877; he was also editor of Le Correspondant from 1903 to 1909 and was received by the Académie Française in 1905.

33. ["La femme actuelle, bien évidemment, se distingue de l'homme par les deux points suivants: 1. Elle est plus sentimentale; 2. Elle est plus pitoyable, plus altruiste."] J. Dody, Les Questions sentimentales en sociologie, 10.

34. ["La femme se détermine trop par le sentiment et pas assez par l'intelligence, c'est vrai; mais, par une juste compensation, elle est plus sensible que l'homme au meilleur de tous les sentiments, à l'altruisme, et moins que lui au plus mauvais."] Dody, 14.

35. ["Elle ne sera pas capable d'imaginer la nécessité d'une loi ou diminuer le nombre de ses concitoyens malheureux, mais elle donnera tout son dévouement pour soulager individuellement les malheureux, les malades, les coupables même; toujours la bonté, et la bonté sans la réflexion."] Dody, 16–17.

36. ["Vienne une occasion, une catastrophe, un malheur public, et dans un même élan de pitié et de charité fraternelle pour les malheureux, on voit, bien plus que chez les hommes, se confondre tous les rangs féminins de la société."] Dody, 17.

37. ["Et cela sans doute parce que la femme tout entière est, peut-on dire, une maternité."] Dody,15.

38. ["Le dogme religieux, puisqu'il traite de ce qui est mystérieux, c'est-à-dire inconnaissable par l'intelligence, ne peut en effet faire appel qu'au sentiment, et de son côté la morale religieuse, comme toute morale, présuppose nécessairement la pitié ou l'altruisme. La femme, sentimentale et altruiste, est donc toute désignée comme apôtre du dogme et exemple de la morale fraternelle....Cette inspiration de la pitié au juge, par l'intermédiaire de la femme, a même été érigée en dogme par le catholicisme, qui a fait de la vierge Marie l'avocat des pêcheurs auprès de Dieu."] Dody, 19, 21.

39. ["En réalité, si vous vous préparez à la guerre, c'est pour limiter autant qu'il est en vous le mal qu'elle fait aux hommes. Si vous suivez l'armée à la trace, c'est la pitié qui vous conduit par la main, la blanche pitié, qui porte en son sein la paix future."] Bouglé, "La Paix et la femme (conférence prononcée à Toulouse, le 28 juin 1909, devant une assemblée de l'Union des femmes)," in Vie spirituelle et action sociale (Paris: Edouard Cornély, 1902), 95–96. A sociologist, friend, and colleague of Durkheim, Bouglé taught at Montpellier in 1898, at Toulouse in 1900; in Paris, he was Professeur de philosophie sociale at the Sorbonne beginning in 1901. He was influenced by German thought (his first work

was the *Notes d'un étudiant français en Allemagne*). See AN, AJ16/5885. For a discussion of his activities during the Great War—the context for this citation—see Prochasson and Rasmussen, *Au nom de la Patrie: les intellectuels et la première guerre mondiale (1910–1919)*, 201–02.

40. ["Les sociologues se plaisent à répéter que 'tout le mécanisme social repose, en dernière analyse, sur des opinions.' Les opinions, à leur tour, roulent sur des sentiments. Or qui ne sait jusqu'à quelle profondeur—par ses admirations et par ses indignations, par ses sourires et par ses larmes—la femme est capable de modifier les sentiments de l'homme."] Bouglé, 98.

41. ["'Il faut résister au mal, mais d'abord en soi-même!' 'Il faut être courageux en temps de guerre, mais d'abord en temps de paix!' Si vous savez répandre autour de vous ces deux vérités, vous aurez satisfait aux plus nobles exigences et de la morale chrétienne et de la morale moderne; vous aurez travaillé au progrès véritable de l'humanité, car vous aurez contribué à former, pour votre part de femmes, une race d'êtres dans le sein desquels la pitié se marie au courage et qui soient ainsi, dans tous les sens du mot, des hommes de cœur."] Bouglé, 125.

42. ["En troisième année, le programme présente un cours complet de morale pratique, où l'énumération de devoirs est précédée de notions très sommaires....Ce qu'il a de plus original dans l'enseignement philosophique des jeunes filles, c'est le programme du cours de psychologie appliquée à l'éducation."] Henri Marion, *Étude de psychologie féminine*, 355, 357.

43. ["programmes détaillés et le plan d'études de l'enseignement secondaire des jeunes filles"]. Villemot, *Étude sur l'organisation, le fonctionnement et les progrès de l'enseignement secondaire des jeunes filles en France, de 1789 à 1887*, 65.

44. ["Analyse de la 'morale de la sympathie.'"] *Revue Universitaire* (1897:1), 94.

45. ["Nature de l'émotion et classification des faits affectifs."] *Revue Universitaire* (1897:1), 421.

46. ["Égoisme et altruisme. Ces deux inclinations sont-elles également fondamentales et premières?"] *Revue Universitaire* (1897:1), 522.

47. ["'Toutes nos démonstrations, a dit Vauvenargues, ne tendent qu'à nous faire connaître les choses avec la même évidence que nous les connaissons par le sentiment.' Etes-vous de son avis? Quelle part accordez-vous à l'intuition, au sentiment dans notre développement intellectuel et moral?"] *Revue Universitaire* (1905:1), 453.

48. ["L'usage des passions en morale selon Descartes."] *Revue Universitaire* (1911:1), 72.

49. ["Au XVIIème siècle, on se piquait d'être 'raisonnable;' au XVIIIème siècle d'être 'sensible,' au XIXème, d'être 'humain.' Montrez à quelle évolution profonde et logique correspondent ces diverses conceptions de la morale."] *Revue Universitaire* (1911:1), 88.

50. ["Appréciez cette pensée de Rousseau: 'Pour empêcher la pitié de dégénérer en faiblesse, il faut la généraliser et l'étendre sur tout le genre humain. Il faut, par raison, par amour pour nous, avoir pitié de nôtre espèce encore plus que de nôtre prochain, et c'est une très grande cruauté envers les hommes que la pitié pour les méchants.' (Rousseau, *Émile*)."] *Revue Universitaire* (1906:1), 86.

51. ["D'où vous paraît provenir l'indifférence, à peine voilée d'admiration, qui s'attache aujourd'hui aux oeuvres de Voltaire, tandis qu'un intérêt passionné s'attache

toujours à celle de Rousseau?"] *Revue Universitaire* (1907:1), 377.

52. ["Un critique contemporain a dit: 'Rousseau nous prend par toutes nos facultés: en politique, en morale, dans la poésie, dans le roman, on le trouve partout, à l'entrée de toutes les avenues du temps présent.' Appréciez la profondeur et l'universalité de cette influence de Rousseau."] *Revue Universitaire* (1910:1), 492.

53. ["Qu'entendez vous par être 'sensible?' Donnez le sens psychologique et historique de cet adjectif. Quelle nuance établissez-vous entre un caractère sensitif et une âme sensible? La sensibilité est-elle toujours une forme de la générosité du cœur et de l'esprit? N'y a-t-il pas de dangereuse sensibilités?"] *Revue Universitaire* (1912:2), 273.

54. ["Du danger de dissocier le sentiment de l'action. Les bons sentiments n'ont de valeur qu'autant qu'ils se traduisent en acte. C'est leur rôle psychologique d'être des moteurs."] *Revue Universitaire* (1914:1), 90.

55. ["De quelle manière et par quels moyens peut-on faire l'éducation de la volonté chez une jeune fille? Cette éducation vous paraît-elle aussi importante pour une femme que celle des sentiments?"] *Revue Universitaire* (1910:1), 277.

56. ["On a prétendu que la sensibilité, chez la femme était, commes les langues d'Ésope, la meilleure et la pire des choses. Montrez tout le mal que déréglée et tout le bien que bien dirigée elle peut enfanter dans la vie morale et sociale."] *Revue Universitaire* (1912:1), 87.

57. ["L'amour maternel considéré comme source et modèle des sentiments sympathiques. 1. Dégager l'élément maternel qui se retrouve dans les plus nobles sentiments humains....2. De l'importance morale et sociale du foyer comme moyen d'assurer entre la mère et l'enfant les rapports nécessaires à la formation des sentiments sympathiques."] *Revue Universitaire* (1913:2), 457.

58. ["'Je suis née pour m'unir à l'amour, non à la haine,' répondait l'Antigone antique. Montrez que cette belle parole devrait être la devise de toutes les femmes, non pour les transformer en brébis bêlantes et passablement encombrantes aux heures de troubles, mais pour qu'elles y maintiennent un centre de sérénité, d'intelligence pitoyable, parce que nos haines, nos rancunes, même celles qui nous paraissent les mieux fondées, comportent toujours beaucoup d'égoisme et souvent d'incompréhension."] *Revue Universitaire* (1913:2), 181.

59. ["Discuter cette pensée de Montesquieu: 'Presque toutes les vertus sont un rapport particulier d'un certain homme à un autre; par exemple, l'amitié, l'amour de la patrie, la pitié sont des rapports particuliers. Mais la justice est un rapport générale. Or toutes les vertus qui détruisent ce rapport général ne sont pas des vertus.'"] *Revue Universitaire* (1906:1), 76.

60. ["Tenons les sentiments pour bienfaisants. Regardons-les comme des éléments ou facteurs de la moralité et analysons-les à ce point de vue."] J. Ancel and Léon Dugas, *Leçons de morale théorique et notions historiques. Enseignement des jeunes filles: Écoles normales*, 3rd ed. (Paris: Fernand Nathan, 1918), 9.

61. ["Mais notre moralité n'est pas tout *individuelle* ou *interne*: elle a une *base sociale*, elle comprend des éléments de sympathie et d'altruisme."] Ancel and Dugas, 10.

62. ["Comment peut-on concilier l'horreur du mal et la pitié?"] Ancel and Dugas, 14.

63. ["To read: Renouvier, 'on pity.'"] Ancel and Dugas, 14.

64. ["Si j'avais eu à en faire une seconde édition, j'aurais ajouté quelques pages sur la bonté, sur la pitié."] Ancel and Dugas, 274; citation of Prat is in *Charles Rénouvier:*

derniers entrétiens, 95.

65. ["Je voudrais que l'on s'ingéniait à développer chez nos enfants le sentiment de la pitié."] Renouvier, cited in Ancel and Dugas, 274.

66. ["La pitié, si elle est bien interprétée, conduit à la justice."] Renouvier, cited in Ancel and Dugas, 274.

67. ["Les analyses qui ont été faites de ce sentiment me semblent insuffisantes. Il n'est pas nécessaire, pour que la pitié s'éveille en nous—c'est la thèse de Schopenhauer—que chacun des hommes se considère *comme un être unique et universel*, il suffit d'admettre pour tous les hommes une communauté d'origine et de fin, *une étroite solidarité dans la misère et dans la souffrance*. Je crois tous les êtres humains capables d'éprouver la pitié, parce que tous les hommes sentent profondément l'injustice ou, ce qui est la même chose, la douleur de vivre."] Renouvier, cited in Ancel and Dugas, 274–75.

68. ["C'est parce que la douleur nous semble immérité que la pitié fleurit dans notre âme. Il n'est pas nécessaire que nous aimions ceux que nous voyons souffrir: ils peuvent être des étrangers, des indifférents, des animaux. Leur lot est de souffrir, notre lot est de souffrir, et nous avons pitié. La pitié pourrait être définie: 'la révolte de l'âme contre la méchanceté du mal.'"] Renouvier, cited in Ancel and Dugas, 275.

69. ["Comment peut-on développer les sentiments de la pitié dans l'âme de l'enfant?"] *Revue Universitaire* (1892:1), 21.

70. ["analyse et critique de la morale de la pitié."] *Revue Universitaire* (1897:1), 94.

71. ["Dites ce que vous pensez de la pitié, de sa valeur morale et sociale d'après 'Il ne faut pas ôter l'autel du temple, ni la pitié du coeur de l'homme.'"] *Revue Universitaire* (1900:1), 540. The source of this citation is not certain. In *Mes Cahiers: 1896–1923* (Guy Dupré, ed. [Paris: Plon, 1994]), Maurice Barrès cites this exact phrase and attributes it to Phocion. On Phocion and the apopthegms attributed to him, especially in Plutarch's *Lives* (vol. 8: *Phocion*), see Lawrence A. Tritle, *Phocion the Good* (London: Croom Helm, 1988). I have not been able to find this expression in Plutarch, Cornelius Nepos, or other accounts of Phocion, including Tritle's. Phocion was a student of Plato, and his death was linked, especially by Plutarch, to that of Socrates, as a sacrifice to the demagogic leadership of Athens. Poussin painted two versions of Phocion's "Death" (thus linked also to David's "Death of Socrates"). Racine studied Plutarch. The following writers all cited Phocion: Holbach, *La Morale universelle*; A. Chénier, *Épitres*; Chateaubriand, *Essai sur les Révolutions*; Marivaux, *Le Télémaque travesti*; Fénélon, *Dialogues des morts*; P.-A. Guys, *Voyage Littéraire de la Grèce*; J. Esprit, *Fausseté des vertus humaines*; Abbé de Mably, *Observations sur les Grecs* and *Entrétiens de Phocion*; Helvétius, *De l'Esprit*.

72. ["On a dit que 'la pitié était la meilleure des aumônes.' Comment la pitié sincère et discrète peut-elle soulager les malheureux qui en sont l'objet?"] *Revue Universitaire* (1902:1), 540.

73. ["Montrez, avec exemples à l'appui, les nuances de sens qui existent entre la pitié, l'indulgence, la bienveillance. Montrez aussi que ce sont les qualités souhaitables par excellence chez la femme, mais les plus dangereuses à exercer pour soi et pour autrui si l'on ne les soumet au frein de la raison."] *Revue Universitaire* (1910:2), 459.

74. ["Evolution historique du sentiment de la pitié. Montrez comment il tend à se substituer, de nos jours, au sentiment du devoir dont il est un élément essentiel,

nécessaire, non suffisant."] *Revue Universitaire* (1909:2), 86.

75. ["'Un siècle de pitié n'est fécond, a-t-on dit, que s'il est aussi un siècle d'énergie.' Les deux qualités ne vous paraissent-elles pas également nécessaires pour fonder une société juste et noble?"] *Revue Universitaire* (1910:1), 276.

76. ["La douleur et la tristesse. Montrer leurs rapports et leurs différences; leur valeur morale et leur danger. Explications générales: la douleur nous révèle à nous-mêmes; elle nous révèle aussi les autres: la pitié et la solidarité naissent de la souffrance, c'est pourquoi elles sont plus habituelles chez les humbles."] *Revue Universitaire* (1906:1), 459.

77. ["Comment peut-on développer les sentiments de la pitié dans l'âme de l'enfant?"] *Revue Universitaire* (1913:1), 214.

78. See J. Vaillant, "Pour le maintien du cours de morale sociale," (*Revue Universitaire* [1912:1], 291), who argued for the leading role of literature in moral instruction; and also Georges Fonsegrive, *L'Enseignement féminine* (Paris: Librairie Victor Lecoffre, 1898).

79. On the development of a scholastic canon in French pedagogy, see Daniel Milo, "Les Classiques scolaires," in *Les Lieux de mémoire*, vol. 2: *Nation III* (Paris: Gallimard, 1986).

80. ["La Fontaine a dit en parlant des enfants: 'cet âge est sans pitié.' Réfléchissez sur votre cruauté enfantine, puisque vous êtes à l'âge où l'on sort de l'enfance."] *Revue Universitaire* (1913:1), 274.

81. ["Recherche des causes: 1. Etourdérie, inexpérience, incapacité à se mettre à la place d'autrui; 2. égoisme et vanité; 3. révolte contre l'autorité."] *Revue Universitaire* (1913:1), 275.

82. ["Un philosophe allemand contemporain prétend que le vrai grand homme, l'homme sans pair, le 'surhomme,' doit être aussi dur que le diamant, indifférent aux souffrances des autres et dégagé de tout pitié. Vous recherchez d'abord s'il serait désirable, à supposer la chose possible, de renoncer à la pitié. Ensuite, vous montrerez que les types de 'surhomme' que nous trouvons chez Corneille,—et notamment don Diègue, le vieil Horace, Auguste—ne sont ni inéxorables, ni insensibles."] *Revue Universitaire* (1919:2).

83. ["Boileau a reproché à Corneille d'avoir introduit dans la tragédie un nouveau ressort: l'admiration. Faut-il en blâmer Corneille, et la mesure dans laquelle il a eu recours à l'admiration lui a-t-elle fait vraiment négliger les deux grandes passions tragiques: la terreur et la pitié?"] *Revue Universitaire* (1913:2), 366.

84. ["Le sens de la 'pitié' dans les *Pensées* de Pascal. Montrez comment elle imprègne ce livre si écrasant pour la faiblesse humaine."] *Revue Universitaire* (1910:1), 383.

85. ["Commentez cette pensée d'Anatole France: 'La souffrance, quelle divine méconnue! Nous lui devons tout ce qu'il y a de bon en nous, tout ce qui donne du prix à la vie; nous lui devons la pitié, nous lui devons le courage, nous lui devons toutes les vertus.'"] *Revue Universitaire* (1919:1), 320.

Part III: The Patrimony of Literary Pity in Fin-de-Siècle Fiction

The poet's, the writer's, duty is to help man endure by lifting his heart, by reminding him of the courage and honor and hope and pride and compassion and pity and sacrifice which have been the glory of his past.

William Faulkner, Accepting Nobel Prize in Literature

Many representative French writers of the *fin-de-siècle* inherited the belief that the qualities on Faulkner's list should be fundamental to their work. Pity was especially germane to their patrimony, not only because of its pressing connections to wider philosophical and social debates but because many novelists were conscious of pity as a narrative strategy and, not incidentally, because in a period of vehement position-taking in literary politics, pity's ancestry as a *locus classicus* in French literary tradition made of it a conceptual critical arbiter. Literature of *fin-de-siècle* France was always more than literary, absorbing and inflecting politics, social dissensions, even philosophical awareness, and pity provided many writers of fiction, *littérateurs*, and philosophers with an expedient point of critical entry. Moreover, the positive valuation of pity in *fin-de-siècle* French literary discussion transcended ideological and religious divisions, thus emphasizing for us the status of pity as a vaunted key word in—and potential pacifier of—*fin-de-siècle* culture.

Literary debates in the *fin-de-siècle* were always about more than literature: philosophers adverted to literary works, and literary types ranged themselves around social and philosophical positions, metaphysical or "scientific." In this part, I first outline the dimensions of writers' and critics' acknowledgment of pity as a thematic and then schematize the most important assessments and orientations toward literary pity, especially the nationalistic anxiety over the supposed neglect and squandering of the French pro-pity legacy. The position-taking on pity's patrimony and its centrality to literature will then set the stage for our analysis in the following chapters of how pity was used as a narrative strategy, with varying degrees of self-consciousness, by representatives of dominant literary genres.

Chapter 7: Debating at the Goncourts' *Grenier*

In his *Journal* entry for January 13, 1895, Edmond de Goncourt registered this impression of Léon Daudet, Alphonse's melodramatic son and soon-to-be right-wing gadfly:

Léon Daudet who, in order to wrestle with all the sadness in his life at the moment, immerses himself even more in his work and spent the entire day writing in his brother's room, asks us after dinner to read the beginning of an article on "Pity and Sorrow" which makes me cry out: "It's odd, no? It is Catholicism that brought about pity for the wretched, and it has taken eighteen centuries so that this pity could finally make a start in literature, a development that began with Dickens"… "and carries on with you!" it is shouted out.[1]

Goncourt's self-congratulatory *aperçu*—placing himself at the center of attention, his chronic chronicler's gambit—was consistent with his other claims to be the pioneer of the literary representation of pity, as attested by another journal entry dated June 23 of the same year: "He entertained me this morning, Bauër, with his piece on Pity in Literature, whose discovery he attributes absolutely to the Russians, forgetting however that there is not a little pity in *Germinie Lacerteux*."[2]

What is going on here, over and above Edmond de Goncourt's ritual protestation of literary preeminence and precedence (he even charged Zola with plagiarizing him!)? Is it mere coincidence that, at such brief intervals, regulars of Goncourt's *grenier* at 67, Boulevard de Montmorency in Auteuil, took up the theme of pity in literature, and that Goncourt would hitch his own ego to this venture? The subject of pity attracted the attention of literary chroniclers who felt compelled to classify and analyze it. This sizing up had much to do with squabbles in literary politics, especially over "Naturalism;" much also had to do with a battle over literary "cosmopolitanism" and the chauvinism of literary genius. But it was also a portent of an emerging phenomenon: a rising doctrinaire pity, a literary virtue of a stable and supposedly unanimous nature.

The article auditioned by Daudet to a bemused Goncourt was intended for his series "Quinzaine Littéraire" that appeared bimonthly in the journal that Daudet coedited, *La Nouvelle revue*. Daudet's critical musings for the early part of 1895 centered on how to judge literature by the standards of passionate needs. The first article, "L'Objet de la littérature," laid out the argument that the common denominator of all "great works" is "sentimental communion."[3] The "concern of art is to move," Daudet proclaimed, and since we all lead lives of inescapable sorrow, pity is our most transmissible sentiment: "Honor to the apostles of pity! The names of Dickens and Dostoyevsky will never disappear as long as there are social wolves, the humble, the hurt; children, workers, or the feeble who are tortured."[4] Daudet concluded that the reading public would sanction authors who ignore or disdain pity: "Humanity loves those who love or have loved it. It makes its choice with an infallible tact, since it comes from the heart and not the head."[5]

The next issue of *La Nouvelle revue* contained a thorough assessment of "Sorrow and Pity Communicated by Literature," two characteristics that Daudet glossed as "those two sentiments, so useful to social life, which set up human solidarity."[6] The pretext for this latter discussion was a review of a recent French translation of Daniel Defoe's *Moll Flanders*, but Daudet's true focus was on the paramount "apostles of pity"—Dickens, Dostoyevsky, and Tolstoy. They were the writers who, together with Hugo, discerned that the pathetic is the aesthetic: "Whoever has suffered will understand another's suffering. Every wound is an opening through which truth infiltrates body and soul.... To bend over this abyss of misery...make oneself the interpreter of so many undeserved abuses, inexpressible tortures, what more noble task."[7] Literature's goal as well as its representational mode is cataleptic suffering.

Daudet's pathetic credo inspired a chronological march past pro-pity literature. Daudet diminished the "lyric" poets as "egotistical children," and Pascal, "as a good Jansenist, restrains his pity."[8] The secular advocates of pity have done more for humane sentiment than many a Christian authority who turned Jesus' original misericordious message into fixed metaphysical dogmas: "But I imagine that the compassionate hand has done more than the punishing hand and that the greatest number of conversions were won beside the gentle little glimmer of pity."[9] Alighting on the contemporary period, Daudet sees an advance in pity: "If sorrow and pity are eternal, we must admit that modern times have granted them a larger place than they have ever received."[10] Why? Daudet's response reprises the teleological litany of pro-pity reasoning, alighting on all the traditional names:

During the 18th century, Diderot, whose vision was truly encyclopedic, realized that in a social system it was necessary to take into account the lower strata, and did not ignore those who were sickly; but his interest remained scientific in the celebrated *Lettre sur les aveugles*. This interest was singularly humanized by Rousseau.... Jean-Jacques did more than point out injustices; he created a sentimental and quivering state of mind whose waves have washed over us and which is the source of modern pity. It is his greatest title to glory.[11]

Diderot and Rousseau were the *loci classicus* of humanitarian pity. The nineteenth century, the Rousseauian century, was both the beneficiary of the enlightenment of the tender passions and reinforced it. The vector of progress was literature, thus making writers and novelists, more so than philosophers, the heirs to the Enlightenment project of human self-knowledge: "In this century, other than the *Misérables*, we have the majestic effusions of Michelet.... As for George Sand, she is the successor of Rousseau."[12]

Pity was a key arbiter in adjudicating the contest between literature and philosophy for pride of place in forging a rhetoric of French humanitarianism. So Daudet concluded his survey by urging that pity be taken out of philosophers' hands and placed in those of imaginative writers: "A profound sense of sorrow is rare. Philosophically, it leads to pessimism. Humanely, it leads to sympathy. The domain of literary revelation is the most comforting of all. It has neither walls nor frontiers. It is open to all."[13] Daudet carves up a doctrinaire pity, slicing away the choice morsel of literature from the ranker portions of philosophical pessimism.

Daudet advanced his thesis with beatific generality, leaving the polemics to Henry Bauër, whose article for *L'Echo de Paris* of June 24, 1895 occasioned Goncourt's other instance of co-optive narcissism. Titled "La Lumière du Nord," Bauër supported the claims of "Northern" European literature to pity's patrimony, so as to shame French "bourgeois literature" for squandering what is rightfully its own legacy. Wagner is his innovating figure in crafting an anti-naturalist art around pity, followed by "the great Russians, Tolstoy and Dostoyevsky, who imparted pity, the criticism of brute force and the hazards of war, the study of individualities hidden in bleakness, about which French literature no longer cares."[14] Yet another key figure is Ibsen—he shared this estimation with the "naturalists," including Zola, who began championing Ibsen in 1888. Unlike Daudet, who added writers within the French tradition to his advocacy of Dickens, Dostoyevsky, and Tolstoy, Bauër ignored French writers, the better to exaggerate the enormity of the appropriation by non-French literature of thematic pity.

Indeed, Bauër assaulted contemporary French literature, specifically drama: "they rebelled against the Slavic pity allotted to the unfortunate, they for whom sufficed a bourgeois sensibility offered up to petty adulteries and to motherless little boys."[15] Bauër then disingenuously disavowed any intention of charging the idea of patrimony with anxiety, since literature is universal and cosmopolitan: "We have no intellectual homeland; we simply consider the superior individual; it little matters whether the accident of birth placed him in Saint Petersburg, Berlin, London, Christiana, or Paris. A good book brings us together wherever it appears; it becomes the real homeland and establishes a moral companionship with its author."[16] Bauër's conclusion was not so much a paean to pity as a derisive jeer at the Parisian literary scene:

The men from the North arrived in their light, powerful and shining wooden boats, one waving in front the blue banner of *Pity*, the other hoisting on its great mast the supreme flag of the *Individual*, and sounding the fanfare of freedom, that antisocial trumpet, before the cities of hypocrisy, lies, and legal inequalities. While the old boat anchored to the muddy bottom of the Seine, inundated, dismasted by the stream of ideas, has fallen apart.[17]

Bauër assumed knowledge that his targets were the dramatists of the Boulevard, whom he designated as the "bourgeois" writers in his reviews. His less polemical assertion was that "new ideas" in literature were predicated on the valorization of pity and individuality—the truly humane agenda.

Bauër's screed highlights the value of pity as a normative term. This value is truly beyond analysis—it is a doctrinaire pity that, for both Daudet and Bauër, evokes emotive qualities cherished by advanced world literatures, whether that of eighteenth-century France or contemporary Northern Europeans. Pity as a doctrine was a prophet's article of faith, possessing a sociophilosophical dimension of practical acuity: pity sounds out a human soul, brings it attention, and so combats alienation, anonymity, and socioeconomic conflict.

This dimension had personal resonance for Bauër. Life experience had led him to an emotive investment in pity that surpassed his brief against contemporary drama. He had affectively compassed what he preached, and so his idea of pity was an amalgam both doctrinaire and lived. A year after publishing the article on "Northern Light," Bauër wrote a midlife biography that placed his experiences immediately after the Commune of 1871 under pity's tutelary star. Bauër envisions two metaphorical divinities, Disappointment and Pity, come to offer him contrasting allegorical options:

DISAPPOINTMENT points out to me the city laid out beneath our feet, the city of royalty, palaces and domains, statues, disturbances, revolutions, and poverty, today shrouded by boredom worse than death. She broke out in laughter, a strident laughter that ended in tears. *PITY* kissed my face, and suddenly a bright autumnal sun illuminated her intelligent face with divine beams, and in the visage of this friend, just as between the golden trees of that nature as calm as the depths of that soul, I glimpsed the continuous change of things, stirrings in the near future, the world's renewal through love, hope and faith.[18]

Pity, disappointment's better half, enables recollection in tranquillity and in hope. Elevated to allegory, it possesses the same representational powers as classical myth and Christian virtues—it is to consciousness what Ariadne is to time and Charity to social bonds, a thread of continuity. In Bauër's hands, pity is personified as guide and goal in a secularized Morality-play that preserves the fervor of faith.

Bauër, Daudet, and Goncourt were not an exceptional triad in their preoccupation with pity. For that matter, they did not agree among themselves about the authors that best exemplified pity.[19] Bauër, for instance, was a fan of the Théâtre Libre but wished it to be dogmatically committed to work of the Tolstoy-Ibsen-Zola school, which he saw as a cluster. "Pity in literature" was a catchy rubric for internecine literary battles, as well as a doctrinaire analytic in *fin-de-siècle* debates. That three particularly vehement bickerers in the overheated world of literary journalism deployed pity as criterion and cause shows the extent to which the concept gained ascendancy in critical discourse.

A heightened perception of pity had a reciprocal relationship to major literary developments of the period, for example, the reception of Tolstoy, the battles over "naturalism" and Zola's stature, and debates on the relationship of the novel to society. Perhaps not incongruously, both the doctrinaire promoters of pity and their opponents helped propagate a totalizing criticism of systematic ethical and aesthetic standards that gave the *fin-de-siècle* community of literary practitioners a discursive unity.

Fouillée and Bouillier exemplify this unity. In discussing fiction, Fouillée yoked together a sentimental communicability similar to Daudet's tenet and Aristotle's pity-centered theory of tragedy:

Why are novels understood by everybody and have such an influence on the masses? It is because they awaken and stimulate in each person a whole set of sentiments that, in everyday life, do not have the chance to manifest themselves.... And if a large portion of the French public can follow the novels even of the great masters, is it not proof that, in the majority of readers, all the sentiments slumber, vengeance or pardon, pity, generosity, zeal, etc., which "only await the opportunity to appear in the light of day of conscience?"[20]

For Fouillée, good works overcome hierarchies by their universal appeal to, and catharsis of, sentiments. They are a civilizing and moralizing force for modernity. So the aesthetic element of literature is, and must be, ethical, psychological, and social—an emotive aesthetics.

Françisque Bouillier combined an analogous aesthetic with Christian faith in a synoptic portrait of French nineteenth-century literature: "Alone against egoism, Christianity provides the power to love others and give to charity...these two presiding spirits (Christianity and egoism) are in constant battle in the literature of the nineteenth century. How many loathsome works born of the evil spirit; but how many other admirable ones on pity toward the unfortunate, on love, on the sentiment of nature, and on honor, has not the good spirit inspired!"[21]

Lucien Arréat tackled a topic comparable to that of the visitors to the Goncourt's *grenier*. For him, literature reflects moral progress, and pity especially is a hallmark of contemporary improvement:

"Pity," la Rochefoucauld had already written, "is often a feeling of our own woes in those of another, and a clever foretaste of the misfortunes that may befall us." Vauvenargues, on the contrary, held that pity does not need a self-conscious dimension in order to be stimulated, as is often believed...."Is our soul incapable of disinterested sentiment?" Certainly, I would reply, the sight of a wound causes a distressing sensation, but it is one of disgust, and our first instinct is to turn away our eyes; the same with blood dried on the skin, which is so disagreeable to us that our hands seek to clean themselves from such a stain. It is not until then but an emotion of our sensibility, and in order to become pity, it must pass through a superior sphere of thoughts and sentiments.[22]

The progression of ideas on pity inherent in the trajectory from la Rochefoucauld to Vauvenargues to contemporary society allows Arréat to confirm Fouillée and Bouillier's earlier contentions on the civilizing imperative behind a literature of pity:

The feelings of pity and sympathy assume a role only slightly less important in the lives of the primitives. What touching expressions and tender and generous sentiments we admire in Homeric verses! The epics of Northern races are less rich than these, but the sweet note in them is so exact, so sincere, that it makes up for the absence of the old Greek charms. The uncouth valor of the Norse hero does not preclude pity or softness.[23]

Animadversions on literary pity, whether flowing from the pens of philosophers, literary theorists, or *littérateurs*, always twined advocacy and diagnosis. This was a distinctively *fin-de-siècle* doctrinaire pity: for if pity found one theoretical support in Aristotle,[24] this was of a descriptive, classificatory nature, rather than that of sentimental prescription. The supporters of "Northern light," as these French commentators labeled the European current of pro-pity literature in the *fin-de-siècle*, went beyond Aristotle in championing virtues and attitudes that they believed literature must declaim. They entrusted the author with a sacred hegemony over sentiments, which would always hit its mark—pity intended is, *ipso facto*, pity communicated; authorial pity results in unmediated reader's pity; thus, fictional emotion expands the readers' moral universe and offers social solace. Analysis followed advocacy, as was especially the case with Tolstoy's novels, whose contents helped authorize the criteria of doctrinaire pity.

NOTES

1. ["Léon Daudet qui, dans ce moment, pour combattre les tristesses de sa vie, se plonge plus avant dans le travail et a écrit toute la journée dans la chambre de son frère, nous demande à nous lire après dîner un commencement d'article sur la Pitié et la Douleur, qui me fait m'écrier: 'C'est curieux, n'est-ce pas? C'est le catholicisme qui a apporté dans le monde la pitié pour les miséreux et il a fallu dix-huit siècles pour que cette pitié eût son développement en littérature, développement qui commence à Dickens'...-'et continue avec vous!' me crie-t-on."] Edmond de Goncourt, *Journal*, vol. 4 (Paris: Flammarion, 1959), 718.
2. ["Il m'amusait, ce matin, Bauër, avec son morceau sur la Pitié en littérature, dont il attribue absolumment la découverte aux Russes, oubliant qu'il y a pas mal de pitié cependant dans *Germinie Lacerteux*."] Goncourt, 808.
3. Léon Daudet, "L'Objet de la littérature," *La Nouvelle revue* 92 (January 15, 1895), 407.
4. ["Honneur aux apôtres de la pitié! Les noms de Dickens et de Dostoievsky ne passeront pas tant qu'il y aura des loups sociaux, des humiliés, des offensés, des enfants ou des ouvriers ou des idiots que l'on torture."] Daudet, 409.
5. ["L'humanité aime celui qui l'aime ou qui l'a aimée. Elle fait son tri avec un tact infallible, parcequ'il vient du coeur, non du cerveau."] Daudet, 410.
6. ["ces deux sentiments, si utiles à la vie sociale et qui établissent la solidarité entre les hommes."] *La Nouvelle revue* 92 (February 1, 1895), 620. Daudet even preached pity to his wife. Goncourt records this entry for March 13, 1895: "Dîner chez Hébrard avec le ménage Daudet. Daudet reproche à sa femme, gentiment et d'une manière philosophique, de ne pas connaître la pitié pour le malheur" (*Journal* 2, 1175). ["Dinner at Hébrard's with the Daudet household. Daudet accuses his wife, gently and in a philosophical way, of not knowing pity for misfortune."]
7. ["Quiconque a souffert comprendra la souffrance d'autrui. Toute plaie est une

ouverture par où la vérité pénètre l'âme et le corps....Se courber sur cet abîme de misères...se faire l'interprète de tant d'injures imméritées, de tortures inexprimables, quelle plus noble tâche."] Daudet, *La Nouvelle revue* (February 1, 1895), 621.

8. ["en bon janséniste, il maintient et contient sa pitié."] Daudet, 622.

9. ["Mais j'imagine que la main compatissante a plus fait que la main châtiante et que les plus nombreuses conversions se sont accomplies à la petite lueur si douce de la pitié."] Daudet, 622.

10. ["si la douleur et la pitié sont éternelles, il faut avouer que les temps modernes leur ont accordé une place plus grande qu'elles n'avaient jamais obtenue."] Daudet, 622.

11. ["Au XVIIIème siècle, Diderot, dont le regard était vraiment encyclopédique, comprit bien que, sur la coupe sociale, il faudrait tenir compte des couches inférieures et ne négligea pas les infirmes; mais son intérêt demeure scientifique dans la fameuse *Lettre sur les aveugles*. Cet intérêt s'humanise singulièrement avec Rousseau....Jean-Jacques fit mieux que d'indiquer les injustices; il créa un état d'esprit sentimental et vibrant dont les ondes se sont propagées jusqu'à nous et il est la source de la pitié moderne. C'est son plus beau titre de gloire."] Daudet, 623.

12. ["En ce siècle, outre les *Misérables*, nous avons la majestueuse expansion de Michelet....Quant à George Sand, elle est la continuatrice de Rousseau."] Daudet, 624.

13. ["le sens profond de la douleur est rare. Philosophiquement, il porte au pessimisme. Humainement, il porte à compatir. Ce domaine de la révélation littéraire est de tous la plus réconfortante. Il n'a ni murs ni barrières. Il est ouvert à tous."] Daudet, 624.

14. ["les grands russes, Tolstoï et Dostoiewsky, lesquels apportèrent la pitié, la critique des forces brutes et du hasard de la guerre, l'étude des individualités effacées en grisaille, dont la littérature française ne se souciait pas."] Henry Bauër, "La Lumière du Nord," *L'Echo de Paris*, Monday June 24, 1895, 1. Bauër (1851–1915) was the illegitimate son of Alexandre Dumas and the latter's married lover, Anna Bauër. A radical Republican student during the Second Empire, he fought for the Commune and was arrested and sentenced to deportation on September 25, 1871. He lived in deportation in New Caledonia from 1872 to 1879. As the theater critic for *L'Echo de Paris* throughout most of the 1890s, he championed realist theater and Zola—and sided openly with Zola during the Dreyfus affair—but (inconsistently?) denigrated "bourgeois" fiction, which he allied with realism. For biographical information, see Lucien Scheler, "Louise Michel et Henry Bauër: correspondants de Paul Meurice," *Europe* 48 (1971), 253–64; the short biography by Marcel Cerf, *Le Mousquetaire de la plume: la vie d'un grand critique dramatique, Henry Bauër, fils naturel d'Alexandre Dumas, 1851–1915* (Paris: Académie d'histoire, 1975). On Bauër's notoriety as a duelist, see Nye, *Masculinity and Male Codes of Honor in Modern France*, 123, 189, 192. (Bauër often engaged in journalistic outrages—hence Cerf's title of "mousquetaire de la plume").

15. ["ils s'insurgèrent contre la pitié slave répandue sur tous les misérables, eux à qui suffisait une sensibilité bourgeoise offerte aux petits adultères et aux garçonnets sans mamans."] Bauër, 1.

16. ["Nous n'avons pas de patrie intellectuelle; nous considérons seulement l'individu supérieur; peu nous importe que le hasard de la naissance l'ait placé à Saint-Petersbourg, à Berlin, à Londres, à Christiana ou à Paris. Un beau livre nous rassemble où qu'il paraisse; il devient la vraie patrie et détermine notre compagnonage moral avec son auteur."] Bauër, 2.

17. ["Les hommes du Nord sont venus sur leurs nefs de bois légères, puissantes et lumineuses, l'un portant à l'avant l'étendard d'azur de la *Pitié*, l'autre arborant à son grand mât le pavillon souverain de *l'Individu*, et sonnant la fanfare de liberté, la trompette antisociale devant les cités d'hypocrisie, de mensonges, d'iniquités légales. Alors le vieux bateau ancré au fond boueux du port de la Seine, submergé, démâtibulé par le flot des idées,

s'est disjoint."] Bauër, 2.

18. ["La *DÉCEPTION* me désigna du doigt la ville étalée à nos pieds, la ville des royautés, des palais, des parcs, des statues, des agitations, des révolutions et des misères, aujourd'hui entourée d'un ennui pire que la mort. Elle éclata de rire, d'un rire strident qui finit en sanglot. La *PITIÉ* me baisa au front, et soudain un clair soleil automnal illumina de divines lueurs son visage d'intelligence et sur le front de l'amie comme entre les arbres dorés, en cette nature assoupie comme au fond des âmes, je lus le mouvement continu des choses, les réveils prochains, le renouveau du monde par l'amour, l'espérance et la foi."] *De la vie et du rêve* (Paris: H. Simonis Empis, 1896), 154–55.

19. To the examples from Goncourt's *Journal* already cited may be added a dispute between Goncourt and Bauër over the merits of Tolstoy's "The Power of Darkness" and Strindberg's "Miss Julie." See *Paris and the Arts, 1851–1896: From the Goncourt Journal*, George J. Becker and Edith Philips, eds. and trans. (Ithaca, NY: Cornell UP, 1971), 301–2. Tolstoy's play was put on by André Antoine's subscription-based company, the Théâtre Libre, at the Théâtre Montparnasse in November 1887. This company also helped introduce Ibsen to theatergoing Parisians.

20. ["Pourquoi des romans sont-ils compris de tout le monde et ont-ils une telle influence sur les masses? C'est qu'ils éveillent et exercent en chacun tout un groupe de sentiments qui, dans la vie ordinaire, n'ont pas l'occasion de s'exercer....Et si de très larges portions du public français peuvent suivre les romans mêmes des grands maîtres, n'est-ce point la preuve que, chez la majorité des lecteurs, tous les sentiments dorment, vengeance ou pardon, pitié, générosité, enthousiasme, etc, qui 'n'attendent que l'occasion de paraître au grand jour de la conscience?'"] Alfred Fouillée, *La France au point de vue morale*, 364.

21. ["Seul, à l'encontre de l'égoisme, le christianisme donne la force d'aimer les autres et de pratiquer la charité...ces deux génies [sont] aux prises dans la littérature du XIXème siècle. Que d'oeuvres détestables enfantées par le mauvais génie, mais que d'autres admirables sur la pitié envers les misérables, sur l'amour, sur le sentiment de la nature, sur l'honneur, le bon génie n'a-t-il pas inspirées!"] Bouillier, "Rapport verbaux: *De la vertu morale et sociale du Christianisme*, par M. le comte Guy de Brémont d'Ars," in *Séances de l'Académie des sciences morales et politiques* 134 (1890) [Paris: Alphonse Picard, 1890], 483.

22. ["'La pitié,' avait écrit déjà la Rochefoucauld, 'est souvent un sentiment de nos propres maux dans les maux d'autrui, et une habile prévoyance des malheurs où nous pouvons tomber.' Vauvenargues disait, au contraire, que la pitié n'a pas besoin d'être excitée par un retour sur nous-mêmes, comme on le croît....'Notre âme est elle incapable d'un sentiment désintéressé?' Assurément, répliquerais-je, la vue d'une plaie nous cause une sensation pénible, mais elle est de dégoût, et notre premier mouvement est d'en détourner les yeux; de même le sang gluant sur la peau nous est si désagréable, que nos mains cherchent à se nettoyer de cette souillure. Ce n'est jusque-là qu'une émotion de notre sensibilité, et il faut, pour qu'elle devienne pitié, qu'elle traverse un milieu supérieur de réflexions et de sentiments."] Lucien Arréat, *La Morale dans le drame: l'épopée et le roman* (Paris: Félix Alcan, 1889), 6–7.

23. ["Les sentiments de pitié, de sympathie, ont un rôle à peine moins important dans la morale des peuples primitifs. Que d'expressions touchantes des sentiments tendres et généreux nous admirons dans les chants homériques! L'épopée des races du Nord en est moins riche; mais la note douce y est si juste, si sincère, que l'absence de l'ancienne grâce grècque en est rachetée. La valeur si rude du héros norse n'excluait pas la pitié, ni la douceur."] Arréat, 179.

24. Aristotle's views on pity and tragedy are found in two extant works—the *Rhetoric*, II.8, and the *Poetics*, VI, 1449b. His analysis of pity and tragedy, more structural and

descriptive than normative, are not readily transposable to the modern novel. But he did stress literature's intersubjective value—which he valorized over that of history—and among his *fin-de-siècle* French acolytes, this was not a negligible point.

Chapter 8: Cosmopolitanism or *Francité*?

Leo Tolstoy facilitated the task of making doctrinaire pity into a programmatic mode of criticism. "Tolstoy's pity" was as much a truism in the *fin-de-siècle* as "Zola's naturalism." One of Tolstoy's earliest French translators and patrons was Eugène-Melchior, Vicomte de Vogüé (1848–1910), member of the ASMP and promulgator of a doctrine of literary pity.[1] Vogüé's epochal *Roman russe*[2] of 1886 promoted Tolstoy and Tolstoyan pity.

Vogüé favorably contrasted Tolstoy's sense of pity to that of his French peers: "Stendhal and Balzac—I speak only of those who are dead—made themselves into the judges of their fellow men; they present every creature to me as deserving their pity. On behalf of what higher principle?"[3] Tolstoy's pity, Vogüé then claimed, is the real thing, since it is not condescending or manipulative but is based on a "higher principle:" an explicatory religion of love and charity. For him, pity has legitimate narrative value—a doctrinaire literary pity—when it comprises a global aesthetic of moral and theological communication, not when it emanates from a solipsistic pen that draws attention to the author rather than the ethic.

Vogüé is especially edifying for us on the difference between pity as analytic and pity as doctrine, for in an interval of two years he alternately adopted both modes in two different assessments of the great Russian novelists. In an article for the *Revue des deux mondes* he first approached Dostoyevsky's and Tolstoy's achievements by means of an analytic pity that was far from lionizing. Exploiting a commonplace, he linked both writers to Schopenhauer's notional Buddhism: "Under the combined influence of the masses' old Aryan spirit and Schopenhauer's lessons among the cultivated classes, we are witnessing an indisputable resurrection of Buddhism…. This Buddhist mentality, in its desperate efforts to enlarge ever more an Evangelical charity, has infused into the national literature a frantic affection for nature, for the humblest creatures, for the suffering and dispossessed."[4] Tolstoy was the best exemplar of this development: "Tolstoy has been one of the originators of this movement; after having written for his peers, for the literate classes, he turns his attention, with dread and pity, to the people.... Tolstoy, in a sense, is the first apostle of pity; but because of his origins and beginnings, he is one of those who stoop from on high into the abyss."[5] For Vogüé, this is not an unadulterated blessing, since it has a negative undercurrent—the revolutionary implications of Rousseau's sentimentalism: "Unfortunately, I am reminded and I reflect on the fact that we too had our century of sensitivity and pro-peasantry: twenty years before 1793.... The almost mathematical law of historical fluctuations has it that these outpourings are followed by terrible reactions, that pity sours and that sensitivity turns into fury."[6] Vogüé reprised the post-Revolutionary response to sensibility and sentimentalism that had informed the early nineteenth century's emotional climate. The comparison between Tolstoy and Rousseau was ready-made, as condignly patented as it was contentious—a comparison countenanced by Tolstoy himself, who claimed Rousseau as a model, especially in his pedagogical treatises and autobiographical writings on childhood and youth. Part of Tolstoy's fascination for the literary scene, then, was the possibilities he offered to revisit some of the most passionate sites of past literary controversy.

Vogüé's unease concerned the political consequences of literary pity. So his critical perspective in *Le Roman russe* focused mostly on apolitical, literary pity rather than on Rousseauian pity. His arguments, especially those in a chapter on "le réalisme en Angleterre et en Russie," prefigured Daudet's and Bauër's arguments by a decade, particularly his classificatory distinction between "Nord" and "France."[7] Vogüé, following Taine and like Daudet and Bauër, discerned direct filiations running from Dickens through Tolstoy: "Mr. Taine says of Stendhal and Balzac, in comparing them to Dickens: 'They love art more than humans...they do not write out of sympathy for the unfortunate, but out of love for beauty.'—That is all true, and that difference becomes more obvious the more one tracks it between our present-day realists and the successors of Dickens or the Russian realists."[8] For Vogüé, the essence of literature is the ethical message it offers and not craft like concerns or a word-picture of the world as it may be thought to exist; a really consequential realism weds our concerns to our ideals, as the "Russians" and the "English" have correctly fathomed: "But other writers, the Russians, extricated realism from these excesses and, like the English, imparted to it a superior beauty attributable to the same moral inspiration: compassion, from which has been filtered all impure elements, and has been sublimated by the evangelical spirit."[9] This compassionate ideal is the motive force of story-telling, aesthetic delight, and enlightenment. Vogüé saw this compassionate ideal at work everywhere in the literature from the "North"—especially in Tolstoy, more so than in Dostoyevsky, whose pity, according to Vogüé, was attached to unhealthy principles and psychological needs: "Dostoyevsky has revealed a completely opposite genius, uneducated and subtle, warmed by pity, tortured by tragic and atypical visions."[10] In Vogüé's words, Tolstoy becomes the measure by which doctrinaire pity would assess contemporary literature.

Tolstoy's French critics quickly comprehended the social and philosophical message underpinning his stories. Bauër, for example, discussed the Russian's work in terms similar to Vogüé's: "In the sweetness of love, fine pity, and overflowing humanity of Tolstoy's works, the myths of wars and lonely heroes are swept along…. *War and Peace* is one of the three or four if not the book of the nineteenth century."[11] Alphonse Darlu cited Tolstoy as the literary equivalent of Schopenhauer's pity-ethics: "That excellent thought could be Tolstoy's…. In order to know the secret of life, it suffices to look at it with the eyes of a dying man"[12]—the latter a reference both to *War and Peace* and to "The Death of Ivan Illych."

Darlu discloses why Tolstoy was crucial to the proselytism of pity: his ready comparability to Rousseau, Schopenhauer, and Nietzsche and his status as a lightning rod for contemporary French fiction. Tolstoy had a profound impact in France because he was easily grouped with these three philosophers. For example, Vogüé had stretched the parallels between Tolstoy and the first two, writing in reference to Rousseau that "Tolstoy…expands upon Rousseau's ideas: the thinking being is not only a depraved animal, but an ugly plant."[13] The philosopher G. Dwelshauvers compared Tolstoy's and Rousseau's supposedly pity-based misology and primitivism: "Tolstoy undoubtedly found in Rousseau a model for the condemnation that he directed at the state of society…in contrast to Hobbes's view of man, it is pity which is man's primary sentiment; his manners are soft; avoiding the complicated sentiments that, among the civilized, cause disorder and lust."[14] Frédéric Paulhan, commenting on the ambient sentimentalism he labeled "le nouveau mysticism" ("the new mysticism"), attributed this mood to the success of Tolstoy and the "Russian novel:" "Literature, more than philosophy, doubtlessly allows us to see precisely a group of desires and ideas that are beginning to liberate themselves…. The first or one of the first was the triumph of the Russian novel."[15]

Literary debates in the *fin-de-siècle* were philosophic in the sense that narrative styles were credited with the ability to disclose ultimate ethical and social concerns. Literary alignments on pity perforce equaled philosophical alignments. The goal of doctrinaire pity was to simplify this concordance by insisting on the consistent equivalence of philosophical and literary positions. This approach to pity was never philosophical in an Aristotelian vein: it attended to literature for the sake of advocacy, not of the technics of purgation. Rousseau, not Aristotle, was its guiding and warning light; Tolstoy its contemporary champion.

Some voices were raised to question the aesthetic aptness of doctrinaire pity. How does pity achieve its narrative ends? Is it part of a larger emotive strategy? When does it become lugubrious or sadistic? Is a spectator's pity really a kind of moral or aesthetic knowledge?[16] Most *fin-de-siècle* critics did not allow themselves to be thrown off-stride by such reservations. Even the few who did so rendered a sort of inverse homage to doctrinaire pity by premising its very terms and values. (Nietzsche's Zarathustra, we should recall, must overcome, not simply condemn, pity.)

Jules Lemaître (1853–1914) of the Académie Française was one literary figure that accepted pity as an analytic while opposing its sponsorship. A *littérateur* and critic—together with Émile Faguet and Brunetière, he was part of the triumvirate of politically and literarily conservative figures dominating *fin-de-siècle* criticism—whose discernments ranged from Virgil and St. Thomas à Kempis to Anatole France, he espoused an unsystematic critical method that he labeled, after artistic fashion, "impressionism" (in all his reviews he used the term *peintures* for narrative depictions).[17] This undoctrinaire doctrine required a rejection of "objectivity," which he defined as the attempt to bring a "whole system of aesthetics and a whole system of ethics" to bear on literature and an insistence instead on the reader's personal response to the inner qualities of a particular writing's structure and voice. Lemaître repugned pity, appraising it as an "objective" quality sustaining an entire aesthetic and ethical "system."

Lemaître wanted to subvert the supposed divide between the "North" (which he always called "septentrionale") and French. In an article on "l'influence récente des littératures du Nord," he argued against Vogüé that French authors such as George Sand, Théophile Gautier, Alexandre Dumas, Victor Hugo, and Gustave Flaubert superseded George Eliot, Dickens, and Tolstoy in their sympathetic commitments.[18] He began, appropriately enough, with Tolstoy and Dostoyevsky: "Let us first consider Russian pity and goodness.... Nothing surprises me more than the astonishment of those who claim to have discovered in those pages (of *War and Peace* and *Crime and Punishment*) charity, pity, respect for goodness and for moral beauty insulted by humble and sordid appearances. Do I need to remark that Victor Hugo and the Romantics did not at all wait for Dostoyevsky and Tolstoy?"[19] Moreover, Hugo and the Romantics, unlike Dostoyevsky and Tolstoy, were impregnated by a nonreligious and justice-based humanitarianism; and for Lemaître, the more humane faith in a secular justice is preferable to the Russians' religion-premised pity, which was precisely what had made them preeminent for Vogüé.

Lemaître's plaint was also similar to Goncourt's. Indeed, he partly accepted Zola and Goncourt as Tolstoy's equals in pity but favored Flaubert over them all: "Is not Flaubert's soul, in regards to the herdswoman Elisabeth Leroux, essentially in the same moral position as Tolstoy's soul vis-à-vis the Mudjik Platon Karatief?"[20] There is more than one aesthetic approach to pity; indeed, there is also a concealed pity that an "impressionist" approach may be best able to discern: "Ah, there can be a huge pity, by all that it leaves implicit, in refusing to represent specific pities!"[21] If there is pity in literature, Lemaître holds, this can never be communicated in narrative innocence.[22] Lemaître is not inclined to dismiss pity itself in pejorative terms; rather, he endorses Flaubert's pity over Tolstoy's. "Generalized pity is too simplistic," he writes,[23] and what he is after is a pity that is neither exclusively patrimonial nor dogmatically lisible.

In an essay critical of Brunetière (Lemaître's criticism was never simply an anti-"Naturalist" polemic), Lemaître once again cited Flaubert in accepting pity as an analytic while severing its external moral and philosophical links to altruism:

Brunetière...believes in the necessity of a certain optimism, or at least in a "sympathy for the miseries and sufferings of humanity." But, first of all, that sympathy may be articulated in many different ways: there is a contempt of humanity that does not at all exclude a sort of pity and that, moreover, implies precisely a lofty ideal of generosity, disinterestedness, and goodness. And I believe that, despite everything, this was the case for poor Flaubert, who was such an excellent man but unbending in his feelings, like a child.[24]

Lemaître comes close here to a Nietzschean-Stoic outlook on pity and hardness, which combines disappointment at humanity's weakness and a refusal to compound it through tender assent. Indeed, Lemaître argued about the apostles of pity that "they can well show us the world as infinitely sad and pitiable: they hesitate to show it as simply revolting, which it is also."[25] According to this school of thought, a realistic portrayal of suffering can lead to enlarged aesthetic and ethical awareness, but doctrinaire pity tries to attain this latter awareness without the hard work of the former. The gap between doctrinaire pity and a truly pitying social order struck Lemaître, and so he decried doctrinaire pity. Like the painting after which he named his approach, Lemaître was searching to disfranchise literature's easily identifiable attributes so as to concentrate instead on its formal properties. But since he was not a systematic critic, Lemaître repudiated doctrinaire pity without extracting all of its conclusions.

Yet Lemaître, not unlike Zarathustra harried by his acolytes, could not get rid of pity. After alternately minimizing it or inverting the supposed North-French scission, he welcomed signs that French pity was redressing the imbalance: "But already you can see that this inferiority is on the way to being put right.... The same seriousness and same pity of Russian novelists, the gift they possess of making us feel for the most commonplace human dramas, the shadows of the unknown, all that gives much value to the exceptionally sincere books of Mr. Paul Margueritte."[26] What to make of this? It is clear that situating literary movements and their social dimensions on the map of *fin-de-siècle* French culture invariably involved summoning pity. The Frenchness of French literature was indissociable from pity, and vice versa; anxieties about the patrimony of pity were a response to thinking about literature's social function and about the schools that would best comply with it. Pity offered a metaphysics of national comfort, and even those critics who did not valorize it could not avoid it in judging contemporary literature.

Lemaître was not alone—André Hallays, for example, also championed Flaubert as a worthy alternative to the Russians: "finally, pity, tenderness for the poor, worries about the universal mystery, all which seemed new and original in Russian novelists can be found in the French romantics and realists, even in Flaubert."[27] But Hallays went further than Lemaître in uncoupling an analytical from an ethical pity, in a way that curiously resembles Rousseau's argument in "Lettre à d'Alembert" as well as discussion today: "To admire a work of art is not always a sure indication that one will be influenced by it. I can find Tolstoy's novels quite beautiful without my beliefs changing, without my life being disturbed. I know of men who, by temperament, are the least lyrical and the least mystical on earth, but who cannot hear *Parsifal* without being moved to tears."[28] Pitying fictions does not always educate us to pity our fellows; pitying our fellows does not perforce guarantee that we will "pity" with imaginary tales.

The critic Joseph Texte (1865–1900) proposed a related argument. In a book on Rousseau's relation to English literature, Texte practiced a clever inversion of the "Northern light" debate, proposing a corrective to the unsubtle extremes subtending the disagreement. The dialectic he proposed in its stead is this: that French writers of the eighteenth century, especially Voltaire and Rousseau, were in the grip of an "Anglomania" that manifested itself in their borrowing the "sentiment de la nature" ("feelings for nature") of Thomas, Gray, Young, and "Ossian" (when still believed to be an authentic author) as well as the "sentimental novel" of Sterne and Richardson; with the Revolution, French classicism expropriated this literary terrain, forcing the retreat of Rousseau and Anglo-German literature; but the return of the repressed was inevitable in the form of Rousseau's reemergence in the works of the Romantics—German, English, and Russian. So Texte reverses the patrimonial trajectory feared by others: "I have tried to show that literary cosmopolitanism has, for the past century and a half, consisted in the spreading of the French mentality, in the wake of Rousseau, to Northern Europe."[29] Texte hoped to demonstrate that "cosmopolitanism" is an accretion of French tradition, even by way of such a divisive and hybrid figure as Rousseau, who both imposed the French on foreigners and then foreigners on the French: "In two or three centuries, or even earlier, Jean-Jacques Rousseau will appear as the Dante of modern times, he who opened for us, not the gates of the ancient world, but those of a Germanic and Northern Europe, whose prestige for the French character will have been so great in this century."[30] Texte cherished foreign literature precisely for its Frenchness. What he located and revered in both is a Romantic sensibility of emotional and sentimental ripeness—and for him, as for others, the term "cosmopolitanism" was a code for pity. In fact, it was employed in this sense by figures as diverse as Vogüé and André Hallays—as the virtue recognized by a polyglot readership and sanctioning cross-cultural influence and anxiety, hence "cosmopolitan." This is not a fortuitous connection, since pity was theorized as negotiating the relationship between social proximity and alienation in much the same way as cosmopolitanism did between chauvinism and universalism: Gabriel Tarde used the terms "cosmopolitanism" and "pity" as corrival in much the same way. Rousseau was the pivotal figure in forging a piteous cosmopolitanism.

If the differences over pity's true homeland permitted a wide range of appreciations on influence and precedence, and if literary-philosophical valorizations of doctrinaire pity could be challenged, pity as a moral property emerges clearly as a critical tool for the literary field. Literary chauvinism presupposed a pro-pity anxiety about, and support of, the challenge of "Northern Light" to French literary superiority. How did works of fiction—as distinguished from criticism—reflect this?

NOTES

1. In his *Regards historiques et littéraires* (Paris: Armand Colin, 1892), Vogüé declared by way of advice "to those who are twenty years old:" "Art must have in view a social goal: it is not a matter of composing a sermon; but instead of falling back on itself, it should broaden out, convey all of modern life, bring together the crowds that escape it, reach them through simplicity and sympathy" (9). ["à ceux qui ont vingt ans:" "L'art doit se proposer

une fin sociale: il ne s'agit pas d'en faire un prêche; mais au lieu de se replier sur lui-même, il doit s'élargir, exprimer toute la vie moderne, ramasser les foules qui lui échappent, atteindre ce peuple par la simplicité et la sympathie"]. This is precisely the canonical and systematic approach to literature that brought pity within its purview and that, in turn, occluded formal and craft concerns.

2. Vogüé, *Le Roman russe* (Paris: 1886). Vogüé rested on his Russian laurels; for the remainder of his life, he would be known as the man who fanned the flames of fortune for Tolstoy in France. See for example *L'Illustration*, which published a profile of him on June 8, 1889—the date at which his work in publicizing Russian literature had earned him a chair in the Académie Française—comparing him with Mme. de Staël and her promotion of German culture. For a biographical and cultural study of Vogüé's importance, see Michel Cadot, *Eugène-Melchior de Vogüé, le héraut du roman russe* (Paris: Institut d'études slaves, 1989). See also Christophe Charle's analysis in *Paris, fin de siècle*, 179.

3. ["Stendhal et Balzac—je ne parle que des morts—se sont institués juges de leurs semblables; ils me donnent toutes les créatures pour dignes de leur pitié. Au nom de quel principe supérieur?"] Vogüé, *Le Roman russe*, 323–24. On Vogüé's sponsorship of Tolstoy as a form of conservative politics of the literary field, see Victor Giraud, *Les Maîtres de l'heure: Essais d'histoire moral contemporaine* (Paris: Hachette, 1912), 214–15; Maxime du Camp, "Les Académiciens de mon temps," in Bibliothèque de l'Institut, MS 3748; Christophe Charle, *Paris, fin-de-siècle*, 181.

4. ["Sous l'influence combinée du viel esprit aryen dans le peuple, des leçons de Schopenhauer dans les classes cultivées, nous assistons en Russie à un véritable résurrection du Bouddhisme....Cet esprit du bouddhisme, dans ses efforts désespérés pour élargir encore la charité évangélique, a pénétré la littérature nationale d'une tendresse éperdue pour la nature, pour les plus humbles créatures, pour les souffrans et les déshérités."] Vogüé, "Les Ecrivains russes contemporains," *Revue des deux mondes* (July 15, 1884), 300.

5. ["Tolstoï aura été un des initiateurs de ce mouvement; après avoir écrit pour ses pairs, pour les lettrés, il se penche avec effroi et pitié sur le peuple....Tolstoï est en un sens le premier apôtre de la pitié; mais, par ses origines et ses débuts, il est encore de ceux qui en descendent de haut dans le gouffre."] Vogüé, 300.

6. ["Malheureusement, je me souviens et je réflechis; je me souviens que nous eûmes, nous aussi, nôtre siècle de sensibilité et de paysannérie: vingt ans avant 93....La loi presque mathématique des oscillations historiques veut que ces effusions soient suivies de réactions terribles, que la pitié s'aigrisse et que la sensibilité se tourne en fureur."] Vogüé, 300–301.

7. For recent discussions of the debate pitting "Nord" and "France," see Christophe Charle's chapter, "Champ littéraire français et importations étrangères: la naissance du nationalisme littéraire," in *Paris: fin du siècle*; and Christophe Prochasson, *Les années électriques (1880–1910)*, 60, 63–64.

8. ["M. Taine dit de Stendhal et de Balzac, en les comparant à Dickens: 'Ils aiment l'art plus que les hommes...ils n'écrivent pas par sympathie pour les misérables, mais par amour du beau.'—Tout est là, et cette distinction devient plus évidente, à mesure qu'on la poursuit entre nos réalistes actuels et les continuateurs de Dickens ou les réalistes russes."] Vogüé, *Le Roman russe*, 181.

9. ["Mais d'autres écrivains, Russes, dégageaient le réalisme de ces excès, et, comme les Anglais, ils lui communiquaient une beauté supérieur, due à la même inspiration morale: la compassion, filtrée de tout élément impur et sublimée par l'esprit évangélique."] Vogüé, 181. In "Les Ecrivains russes contemporains," Vogüé wrote: "les idées générales qui transforment l'Europe et nôtre propre pays ne sortent plus de l'âme française" ["the broad ideas that transform Europe and our own country no longer emanate from the French soul"] (277).

10. ["Dostoïevsky nous a montré un génie tout contraire, inculte et subtil, échauffé par la pitié, torturé par les visions tragiques peu communs."] Vogüé, *Le Roman russe*, 279.

11. ["Dans la douceur de l'amour, dans la belle pitié et l'humanité débordant de l'oeuvre de Tolstoï, est emportée la légende des guerres et des héros accidentels....*Guerre et Paix* est l'un des trois ou quatre livres sinon le livre du 19ème siècle."] Henry Bauër, *Idée et réalité*, 268, 270.

12. ["Cette belle pensée pourrait être de Tolstoï....Pour connaître le secret de la vie, il suffirait de la regarder avec les yeux de l'homme qui va mourir."] Darlu, *Morale Sociale. Leçons professées au Collège libre des sciences sociales*, 31.

13. ["Tolstoï...c'est le mot de Rousseau élargi: l'homme qui pense n'est pas seulement un animal dépravé, il est une plante enlaidie."] Vogüé, "La Renaissance latine," *Revue des deux mondes* (1895:1), 187.

14. ["Tolstoï a trouvé, incontestablement, chez Rousseau un modèle pour les critiques qu'il a adressés à l'état social...à l'opposé de l'homme selon Hobbes, c'est la pitié qui est leur sentiment originaire; leurs moeurs sont douces; elles échappent aux sentiments compliqués qui, chez les civilisés, causent le désordre et la luxure."] G. Dwelshauvers, "Rousseau et Tolstoi," *Revue de métaphysique et de morale* 20:2 (March 1912), 474. For similar examples, see Ossip-Lourié (Ossip Davidovitch Lourié), *La Philosophie de Tolstoï* (Paris: Félix Alcan, 1899), and *La Philosophie de Tolstoï: opinions diverses* (Paris: V. Giard et E. Brière, 1900). For a contemporary account that revises the equation of sentiment with realism, see Michael Bell, "Tolstoy: Truth of Feeling and the 'Sentiment of Reality,'" in *The Sentiment of Reality: Truth of Feeling in the European Novel* (London: George Allen and Unwin, 1983).

15. ["La littérature, plus encore que la philosophie, permet sans doute de voir avec précision un ensemble de désirs et d'idées qui commence à se dégager....Le premier ou l'un des premiers a été le succèss du roman russe."] Frédéric Paulhan, *Le Nouveau mysticisme*, 187.

16. For recent works that grapple with these questions, in addition to those cited later in this chapter, see Margo Jefferson, "What Is Wrong with Sentimentality?" *Mind* 1983 (92), 368; Karl Frederick Morrison, *I am You: the Hermeneutics of Empathy in Western Literature, Theology and Art* (Princeton: Princeton UP, 1988); David L. Norton, *Imagination, Understanding, and the Virtue of Liberality* (Lanham, MD: Rowman and Littlefield, 1996); Martha Nussbaum, "Fictions of the Soul," in *Love's Knowledge: Essays on Philosophy and Literature* (New York: Oxford UP, 1990); Walter J. Slatoff, *The Look of Distance: Reflections on Suffering and Sympathy in Modern Literature—Auden to Agee, Whitman to Woolf* (Columbus: Ohio State UP, 1985). Douglas Walton, in *Appeal to Pity: "Argumentum ad misericordiam"* (SUNY Series in Logic and Language [Albany, NY: SUNY Press, 1997]), argues that *argumentum ad misericordiam* do not always involve a logical fallacy: "This book reveals the underlying structure of how appeals to pity, compassion, sympathy, and mercy can correctly be used as species of practical reasoning in a type of argument from need for help" (xiv–xv).

17. An early Parnassian, Lemaître abandoned a university career for professional writing—and succeeded spectacularly, both financially and popularly. He was a poet, storyteller, critic, and playwright, composing at least a dozen productions for the stage. Elected to the Académie in 1895, Lemaître also opted for political combat: he headed the *Ligue de la Patrie française* at the turn of the century and then, when this disbanded, was a member of the *Action Française*. For an analysis of Léon Blum as cutting his literary teeth in opposition to Lemaître, see Charle, *Paris, fin de siècle*.

18. It is perhaps not incidental to note that more recent observers continued to perpetuate a "North"-French divide. Erich Auerbach, for example, wrote: "When the great

Russians, especially Dostoevsky, became known in Central and Western Europe, the immense spiritual potential and the directness of expression which their amazed readers encountered in their works seemed like a revelation of how the mixture of realism and tragedy might at last attain its true fulfillment" (*Mimesis: The Representation of Reality in Western Literature*, Willard R. Trask, trans. [Princeton: Princeton UP, 1953], 523).

19. ["Voyons d'abord la pitié, la bonté russes....Rien ne m'étonne plus que l'étonnement de ceux qui ont cru découvrir dans ces pages [*War and Peace, Crime and Punishment*], la charité, la pitié, le respect de la bonté et de la beauté morale offusquées par d'humbles et de sordides apparences. Ai-je besoin de faire remarquer que Victor Hugo et les romantiques n'avaient point attendu Dostoyevsky et Tolstoï?"] Jules Lemaître, "L'Influence récente des littératures du nord," *Revue des deux mondes* (126:6) (December 15, 1894), 856–57. Also reprinted in *Les Contemporaines: études et portraits littéraires* 6 (Paris: Nouvelle bibliothèque littéraire, 1896), 243.

20. ["L'âme de Flaubert n'est elle point, à l'égard de la bouvière Elisabeth Leroux, sensiblement dans la même position morale que l'âme de Tolstoï vis-à-vis du moujick Platon Karatief?"] Lemaître, *Les Contemporaines: études et portraits littéraires* 6, 247.

21. ["Ah! la grande pitié qu'il peut y avoir, par tout ce qu'il sous-entend, dans le renoncement à l'expression des pitiés particulières!"] Lemaître, 248.

22. Wayne C. Booth's ideas of "implied author" and "coduction" can be related to Lemaître's position: "*Coduction* will be what we do whenever we say to the world (or prepare ourselves to say): 'Of the works of this general kind that I have experienced, *comparing my experience with other more or less qualified observers*, this one seems to me among the better (or weaker) ones, or the best (or worst)" (*The Company We Keep: An Ethics of Fiction* [Berkeley: U of California P, 1988], 72). Martha Nussbaum defines the former idea this way: "Booth is famous for a distinction that we need to bear in mind: between the narrator or characters and the 'implied author,' that is, the sense of life embodied in the text taken as a whole. A work that contains few or no sympathetic, admirable characters may still promote sympathy and respect in the reader through the sort of interaction the work as a whole constructs" ("Fictions of the Soul," 101).

23. Lemaître, *Revue des deux mondes*, 870.

24. ["Brunetière...croit à la nécessité d'un certain optimisme, ou du moins de la 'sympathie pour les misères et les souffrances de l'humanité'. Mais d'abord cette sympathie peut s'exprimer de bien des façons: il y a un mépris de l'humanité qui n'est point exclusif d'une sorte de pitié et qui, d'autre part, implique justement un idéal très élevé de générosité, de désintéressement, de bonté. Et je crois que, malgré tout, c'était bien le cas pour ce pauvre Flaubert, qui était un si excellent homme, mais entier dans tous ses sentiments, comme un enfant."] Lemaître, *Les Contemporaines: études et portraits littéraires*, 232.

25. ["ils peuvent bien nous montrer le monde infiniment triste et pitoyable: ils hésitent à le montrer simplement dégoûtant, ce qu'il est pourtant aussi."] Lemaître, *Revue des deux mondes*, 868.

26. ["Mais déjà, voyez vous, cette infériorité est en bon train d'être réparée....Et la même gravité et la pitié des romanciers russes, et le don qu'ils ont de nous faire sentir, autour des médiocres drames humaines, les ténèbres et l'inconnu, tout cela donne un très grand prix aux livres singulièrement sincères de M. Paul Margueritte."] Lemaître, 869.

27. ["enfin, la pitié, la tendresse pour les humbles, l'inquiétude du mystère universel, tout ce qui nous a paru neuf et original chez les romanciers russes, peut se retrouver chez les romantiques ou les réalistes français, même chez Flaubert."] Lemaître, 869.

28. ["Admirer une oeuvre d'art n'est pas toujours l'indice qu'on doit en subir l'influence. Je puis trouver fort beaux les romans de Tolstoï sans que mes convictions en soient modifiées, sans que ma vie en soit troublée. Je sais des hommes qui, par

tempérament, sont les gens les moins lyriques et les moins mystiques du monde, et qui ne sauraient écouter *Parsifal* sans être bouleversés jusqu'aux larmes."] Lemaître, 879.

29. ["J'ai essayé de montrer que le cosmopolitisme littéraire a été, depuis un siècle et demi, l'expansion de l'esprit français, à la suite de Rousseau, vers l'Europe du Nord."] Joseph Texte, *Jean-Jacques Rousseau et les origines du cosmopolitanisme littéraire* (Génève: Slatkine Reprints, 1970), xxii–xxiii. The book was originally published in 1895 and dedicated to Brunetière. For Paul Janet's favorable review—"À tout prendre, un ouvrage de cette valeur fait honneur à la science et à la sagacité de la critique littéraire universitaire"—see *Journal des savants* (April 1896), 205–18.

30. ["Dans deux ou trois siècles, ou peut-être avant, Jean-Jacques Rousseau apparaîtra comme le Dante des temps modernes, celui qui nous a ouvert, non pas les portes du monde antique, mais celles de cette Europe germanique et septentrionale, dont le prestige aura été si grand, en notre siècle, sur le génie français."] Texte, 455.

Chapter 9: From *Germinie* to *Germinal*: Effects of Pity, Effective Pity

INTERLUDE: ILLOCUTIONARY AND PERLOCUTIONARY PITY

Consensual or unconscious of their polemical ground, French critics mostly welcomed or rejected the pitying messages in works such as Tolstoy's *Anna Karenina* that today have been problematized into the issue of how pity can be put into words at all. If our *fin-de-siècle* French reviewers asked, "are there French equivalents of *Anna Karenina*," today's interrogation is, "how can anyone 'pity' 'Anna Karenina'"?[1]

The literalness of responses to pity was often matched by the eagerness with which authors deployed it in their fiction. It is time to turn to an analysis of how pity figured in some important and representative novels of the *fin-de-siècle*. This discussion will help us see the relationship between theory and practice, thus disclosing the confluences and contradictions between what critics could read in contemporary invention and what they valorized.

As a preamble we should note that an apparently monolithic pity in these narratives might be divided into two logics of appeal. This divergence can be usefully equated to that between an illocutionary and a perlocutionary pity: in the former, pity functions as an emotive term of vocabulary, as both noun and adjective putatively evoking a semasiologically pure response; the latter, an oblique pity that, through a complex interplay of semantics and thematic structure, intentionally elicits the sentiment. This distinction is similar to that drawn by Friedrich Schiller in his classic *On the Naïve and Sentimental in Literature*, where he argues for an "artful idealism" in these terms: "This kind of expression, where the term completely vanishes in what is being referred to and where speech leaves the thought which it expresses as it were naked, while the other type can never represent it without at the same time concealing it; this is what in style one calls above all inspired and the work of genius."[2] This is the distinction between a rhetoric of pity and a poetics of pity; the former is assimilable to the didactic, doctrinaire pity championed by critics, the latter is harder to wrestle into critical debate. If for our contemporary minds and hearts the latter is more effective and ennobling to the reader, for the *fin-de-siècle* the former was worth advocating.

We will flesh out this synopsis in a discussion of characteristic works from a range of male novelists who related to traditional *fin-de-siècle* thinking on pity in important ways: the Goncourt brothers, Émile Zola, Paul Bourget, Octave Mirbeau, Léon Bloy, Marcel Proust, and Pierre Loti. These writers are representative on the grounds of prominence and range—they epitomize different positions in the literary field. Yet they all shared a concern with the "democratization of inner life," in Simmel's phrase,[3] in which pity was either depicted or proposed as a subjective response to increasing propinquity, as either buffer against or conduit to social, psychological, or metaphysical suffering. It is not incidental, moreover, that these authors summoned, apostrophized, or challenged pity as a specifically gendered virtue, as a feminine quality.

"LES FRÈRES DE GONCOURT: OR THE TWO AJAXES IN BATTLE WITH HOMER—MUSIC BY OFFENBACH."

Nietzsche[4]

It is only fitting that we heed Edmond de Goncourt's earlier claim that "there is not a little pity in *Germinie Lacerteux*." Since we have been taking critics at their word, we should now look more closely at their referents, at the works they took to be illustrative of literary pity. In this section, however, the principle of interpretive charity has its limits; namely, the paraphrasing of authorially overt *argumentum ad misericordiam* will give way to the detection of strategies for pity that may have escaped the authors' dominion or that point to inconsistencies. This approach implies neither the existence of an idealized fictional pity nor the superiority of current definitions or criticism. It simply means that we try to verify the positivist claim that there *is* "pity" in a literary work and try to understand what features can possibly justify such a claim.[5] This tactic has the advantage of combining analyses and issues common to both intellectual and literary history by focusing on the rhetoric of appeal swathed around a word, "pity," heralding both intellectual tradition and narrative communion.

The Goncourts, known today for their precious aestheticism, informative diaries, and eponymous annual prize, were in their own day more esteemed or maligned for a Zolaesque naturalism that combined morbidity with sentimentalism. Nietzsche criticized "the religion of the heart" in the *Twilight of the Idols* by singling out the brothers: "The worst in this respect is accomplished by the Goncourts; they do not put three sentences together without really hurting the eye, the psychologist's eye."[6] Victor Hugo, on the other hand, had complimented their romantic humanitarianism in 1865: "Now the sentiment of progress, of pity for the weak, love for the suffering, shine more and more in your eloquent pages."[7] Erich Auerbach, in a chapter from *Mimesis* on "Germinie

Lacerteux," analyzed the synthetic and faulty realism that guided the Goncourts' vision while acknowledging its sentimental dimension: "The conclusion of the preface, it is true, introduces a less modern position, a turn toward ethics, charity, and humanitarianism. A number of motifs of very different origin enter into this. The reference to the *heureux de Paris* and the *gens du monde* who ought to think of their fellow-men belongs to the mid-century socialism of sentiment...and finally there is the religion of humanity of the Age of Enlightenment."[8] Nietzsche, Hugo, and Auerbach are all correct in that *Germinie Lacerteux* (1864) was envisaged as an *argumentum ad misericordiam*.

The Goncourts laid claim to pity three decades before Edmond's defensive journal entry of 1895, as Auerbach noted, in the "Preface" to *Germinie Lacerteux*: "We were curious to know whether Tragedy, that conventional form of a forgotten literature and a vanished society, was really dead; whether, in a land without caste or legal aristocracy, the miseries of the humble and poor would mean as much to interest, to emotion, to pity as those of the great and rich; whether, in a word, the tears shed below could touch as deeply as those shed above."[9] The brothers clearly thought and hoped so, for not only did they premise their story on it, but also more generally, they maintained that the purpose of literature was to broaden compassionate horizons. As if good Aristotelians, the Goncourts believed that the aim of tragedy was to awaken pity, claiming that their innovation consisted in arousing the "superior" class's pity for the poor and working classes. In so doing they claimed to be forging a Tragic character for the modern novel. This was the outsized contention on behalf of their aesthetic practice; yet the scope of their emotive achievement was far more modest.

The story of *Germinie* is a simple one.[10] The first character introduced, Sempronie de Varandeuil, is the daughter of a petty aristocrat and place-holder under the ancien régime; she survived the Revolution by hiding in Paris, during which time she received an education in hardship, selflessness, and survival. History and destiny are the two forces that, counteracting her parents' and her class's selfishness as well as the ambient villainy of the Revolution, combine to shape a pity-character, which the Goncourts trace as follows: "She was, so to speak, impersonal through her greatness of heart, a woman who did not belong to herself: God seemed to have made her solely to give to others."[11]

This piteous character is twined to her sororal class-opposite, Germinie Lacerteux, an impoverished orphan led to Paris from the provinces by her cruel sisters, who are Grimm Brothers archetypes. In order to earn a living, Germinie is first employed at a café, where she is brutalized and then raped, and finally as a *bonne* at Mlle de Varandeuil's, in whose building one of her sisters already worked as a *portière*. Germinie and Sempronie share a symbiotic relationship based on caring and a mutual need to forget childhood hurts. Indeed, Sempronie's small, tidy apartment, where Germinie spends her days, is a cloistral bulwark of compassion.

The novel narrates the debauch to which Germinie sinks by a conspiracy of uncaring forces and from which she returns to Sempronie's apartment as if by a moral homing instinct. Sempronie's ignorance of Germinie's dissolute hidden life (posited and judged as such by authorial requirements) and the latter's fear of exposure are the source of the dramatic tension invented by the Goncourts for their macabre morality tale.

That the protagonists are female is crucial to the story's dramatic intent, for the Goncourts drew on the maternal *pietà* current in the pity tradition to reinforce their audience's emotive associations. Doctrinaire pity was a feminine pity; literary pity was even more so. The Goncourts reinforce this feminizing aspect by giving the women different ages and classes, for these are then factored out as the crucial source for Plot, as the social differences that propel the dramatic tension forward, leaving behind a harmony of sentiments in which Woman is the major chord. The feminization of the Goncourts' pity gains from the fact that no male character—except for the inconsequential example of the former actor who employs Germinie as his domestic just before his death—ever evinces a trace of it.

Female, maternal, procreative sensuality is at the heart of the Goncourts' pity as it was to be for Zola and Paul Bourget. For them, social-sexual contagion is a form of both sentimental and physical promiscuity. Germinie's openness to others involves both; receptive to their hurts, she searches out their bodies. In one scene, she battles her body's reactions to Jupillon *fils*—for whose love she will bring herself to perdition, after the death of the baby they conceive out of wedlock and the financial ruination his upkeep entails—in the same terms she wrestles with her emotions. On the other hand, Sempronie's pity is that of a chaste *pietà*—hence, Germinie's horror lest her mistress discover her debts, drinking, profligate liaisons, nocturnal escapades, and hygienic lapses.

Edmond de Goncourt was strictly correct that "there is not a little pity in *Germinie Lacerteux*." The novel flaunted its pity for women and the weak; there is in it a traditional, demotic pity comprehensible to all who were steeped in traditional thinking on pity. But in the more complicated sense of an effective literary pity—the sense to which Edmond was, in part, laying claim—does the novel substantiate his boast?

Among its many shortcomings, the novel is a just-so story, with little dialogue; and much of that is created for the exoticism of transcribing contemporary argot—of some sociolinguistic value, to be sure, but narratively condescending and, more importantly, casting doubt on the attribution to the novel of the appellation of "sentimental novel."[12] More troubling is the Goncourts' declamatory procedure of pity-by-adjective: a demotic pity declared but never narrated. The readers are cued to pity, rather than educated by or for it. There are many examples of this: "What sadness, what bitterness, what loneliness for her in this existence with a morose, embittered old man, always grumbling and muttering round the house, reserving his charm for the outer world and leaving her alone every evening."[13] In this sentence, the thesaurus of pitiable adjectives preempts the narrative expansion of the terms invoked. Germinie is more pitied against than pitiable, at least from what the Goncourts supply for our inference. When Jupillon *fils* abandons Germinie: "and he hastened to get away from her, with no charity, no pity;"[14] or when Mlle de Varandeuil gathers a dying Germinie into her bed: "Mademoiselle took pity on her and forced her to lie on her own bed."[15] Even "Germinie" ventriloquizes the Goncourts' evaluative standpoint on her fictitious character in this outburst at the selfish, inebriate housepainter, Gautruche: "Have you ever given up one glass of wine for me? Did you even have any pity for me when I dragged about in the mud and snow at the risk of kicking the bucket?"[16]

The Goncourts issued adjectives that were designed to bear the sentimentally communicative brunt of narrative. Moreover, their conception of the poor and oppressed, which are the intended beneficiaries of a romantic-humanitarian pity, was also problematic. For there is a lack of coherence between the Goncourts' dispensing pity for a traditional underdog, on the one hand, and their goal of updating it as an excuse for a lubricious anecdotal account of contemporary Paris, on the other. The Goncourts, in assuming a bourgeois readership for their fiction, were convinced that a recitation of the seamy underside of their city would arouse both interest and pity. Thus, they set about cataloging the quotidian curiosities of life among *le peuple*;[17] thus, they apostrophized the city itself as a locus and dispenser of pity: "O Paris, heart of the world, great human city of charity and fraternity! You possess the luxuries of the mind, age-old kindliness of manners, sights that prompt people to give alms!"[18] This formula displaces dramatic intensity from character to characteristic, from persons to personification, from specificity to abstraction.

The novel's sense of time is both problematic and an instructive example of how pity was worked into narrative. Throughout the story, there are forced transitions and improbable chronologies; the brothers are saved from developing a sense of elapsed time by *deus ex machina*, usually in the form of implausible deaths ("Then one day, by sheer chance, she found out that her niece had died a few weeks after her sister")[19]—which perfectly fits their pity-by-adjective strategy. Still, both the sense of pastness and the reliance on death are intrinsically linked to pity, whether illocutionary or perlocutionary. The Goncourts' demotic pity is closely related to ideas of death and pardon, in a manner dictated by traditional philosophical pity and literary form.

Pardon, for example, is inextricably allied to pity in the novel's plot. Germinie fears discovery and retribution from Sempronie, and indeed the Goncourts first make the latter's character refractory to pardon: "Wonderfully good, there was yet something lacking in her goodness: forgiveness. Never had she succeeded in bending and adapting her character to that extent. Any hurt, any behavior, any little thing that cut her to the heart, wounded her forever. She never forgot. Time, nor death itself, did not disarm her memory."[20] Yet Germinie's death does change Mlle de Varandeuil, allowing her to feel, after a first furious umbrage at the discovery of her *bonne*'s past, a dolorous acceptance of a piteous fate. Death, pity, and pardon are the transforming triad in Sempronie's move from remonstrance to tender remembrance. The Goncourts, in delineating the ambivalence of Sempronie's efforts to absorb Germinie's destiny whole, for once provide an example of a narrative method appropriate to their subject: "and yet gradually, slowly, from these stirred-up memories, these evocations intended to bring bitterness, this far-off sweetness of past days, there rose within her a first tender feeling of mercy."[21] Sempronie finally acquiesces in the pardon that pity—the physiognomy of pity—facilitates: "As the expression on the face continued to soften, Mademoiselle finally saw there an imploring supplication, a supplication that finally captured her pity...life, circumstances, the misfortunes of her body and destiny had made her into the creature she had been, a creature of love and pain."[22]

The ability to pardon finally completes Sempronie's character of piteous vocation. Hers is the character that, in the classic tragic pattern, moves to full recognition through pity and fear. Whereas Germinie fulfills a destiny dictated by the Goncourts' lurid didacticism—stalked implacably by Paris, "circumstances," her "body"—Sempronie becomes the stand-in for our own enlarged awareness. If we have beat her to the punch in learning of Germinie's debauches and have been prompted to receive these with a tolerant pity, Sempronie retrospectively ties these together in a literary mode that is all the more effective for being sited in the most apposite of settings: Germinie's unmarked grave.

The Goncourts' demotic pity of death, unlike Proust's or Loti's later versions, is not an embracing valedictory; it is too facilely morbid. If death is connected to pardon and hence to a fuller conception of individual fate and of life's dolent cruelties and plangent absurdities, the Goncourts are content to dispense melancholy adjectives about it. By creating a narrative wherein pity's referent is so clear and so prodded, they gave themselves no room for experimenting with the novel's (the "*Roman,*" as they self-consciously had it) possibilities for evoking and transforming emotive responses.

Germinie Lacerteux is an *argumentum ad misericordiam* that articulated a pity of unchanging characteristics: feminine, maternal, traditional ("old-Christian," as Auerbach put it), and directed at the poor and weak. What had changed throughout the nineteenth century were the conditions for actuating pity—the social circumstances and psychological appreciations—and the Goncourts believed that by giving a simplistic and prurient account of these psychosocial transformations, they had revived fictional pity. But they could not democratize the fiction of inner life, because of the shortcomings we have identified. Zola, from a related but altogether different starting point, did better.

Zola is the last great representative of nineteenth-century romantic humanitarianism. I wish to argue here a point that parallels Naomi Schorr's arguments about George Sand—that what was adjudged her literature of "realism" was really a form of sentimental and romantic idealism.[23] Whereas Schorr attributes Sand's fall from the canon to the subsequent depreciation of this (feminine) dimension to her writing, I wish to persuade that Zola has maintained his dominant position precisely because of the hidden resources of romantic idealism in his novels.[24]

For all of Zola's ambivalence about Hugo, he was the latter's most consequential heir. As it was for Hugo, pity was a cardinal point of Zola's romantic imagination, central to both the architecture of his fiction and the social message he wished it to articulate. That this was not discerned by Vogüé, Brunetière, or the other naysayers of naturalism confirms yet again our suspicion that a discourse of pity was so pervasive that this sentimental quality could be altogether overlooked or ignored if its setting was disagreeable—as was supposedly the case with Zola's "naturalism."

Zola's claims for the place of pity in his fiction were as forthright as the Goncourts'. Expressing himself on the genesis and goal of *Germinal*, for example, he declared, "At the risk of being labeled a socialist, I must tell you that when I saw how miners lived, pity overwhelmed me. My book is a work of pity, nothing else, and if readers experience this feeling, I shall be happy, I shall have achieved the goal I set for myself."[25] Indeed, pity is the communicative strategy and emotional leitmotif of much of Zola's fiction, and he was more faithful to, and successful with, it than the Goncourts. If it was not one of his "Evangelic" virtues—the titles of his last, incomplete tetralogy, *Les Évangiles*, were "work," "fecundity," "truth," and "justice"—it was only because pity comprised at least three, if not all four, of these. An examination of three very different novels, *Germinal*, *La Joie de vivre*, and *Lourdes*, will confirm Zola's insistent dedication to a perlocutionary pity and emphasize some reasons for its effectiveness. Yet almost any of Zola's novels would serve the same representative purpose, for the emotive strategy of his oeuvre is virtually uniform.

Zola's fiction, especially the Rougon-Macquart series, is notable for the constancy of its preoccupations and characterizations and its appeals to pity. This pity is likewise coherent and in harmony with traditional romantic-humanitarian pity—sensitivity to the weal and woe of others. In Zola's conception of his often-bewildered protagonists, pity typifies the author's standpoint to his material, to the empirical world of actual suffering that this material is supposed to dramatize (Zola's so-called realism or naturalism) and rouses our reactions to the fictional characters' plight. It is the latter dimension—the pathos with which the protagonists come to grasp the situation in which the author has placed "them"— that is designed to trigger the reader's response of pity.

There are three notable elements in Zola's sentimental strategy: first, a piteous narrative presenting conditions that, having provoked the author's pity, are meant to elicit the same emotion in the reader, in an Aristotelian and perlocutionary manner; next, a declamatory pity whereby both author and his characters apostrophize the word in order to telegraph the narrative's dramatic import (similar to the Goncourts' strategy); lastly, pity as the emotion needed or withheld from the situation narrated and therefore providing an ethical flash point for the drama. At all levels, Zola imbues pity with the positive, romantic valuation of an other-regarding, morally salient, hence emotionally meaningful social virtue.

The second level, the declamatory property, most clearly reveals the degree to which pity suffuses Zola's imagination and vocabulary. Yet in *Germinal* (1885), perhaps Zola's most successful fictional evocation of pity, it is the first level—an enveloping narrative of human moral impoverishment that incites Aristotelian pity—that is most vitally present and makes this novel largely successful. In *Germinal*, characters are offered, and thus offer us, moments of moral awareness through their capacity for pity, moments that are clearly indicated to the reader through adjectives. There is a certain naïveté in rendering characters corrival with the emotion they are meant to embody, but Zola's narrative is that of a moralist.

The steps in the moral bafflement and edification of *Germinal*'s main character, Étienne Lantier, are indicated by his growing pity for those about whom he is most befuddled. Étienne's conscience is racked by the conflicts among his "hereditary" alcoholism, atavistic violence, the social misery that he sees around him but that he is impotent to ameliorate, and the need for acceptance. He ultimately reproves the violent strike that he had fomented, because he had convinced himself it was the only means of promoting workers' equity, but that he now views through the pity induced by such a cataclysmic struggle.

At first, the strike at the Voreux colliery is an inertial standoff that further immiserates miners, especially those in the Maheu family, with whom Étienne lodges and who form the centerpiece of Zola's doleful portrait of miners' misery. Étienne slowly exchanges an initial anger for pity: "What wretchedness! And odors! And the bodies in a heap! And a terrible pity caught him by the throat,"[26] is Zola's description of Étienne's return to the Maheu residence while their infirm eight-year-old daughter, Alzire, lies dying during the strike. The Maheu's eldest daughter, Catherine, for whom Étienne feels a disturbing mixture of lust, fraternal solicitude, and resentment, becomes the particular beneficiary of Étienne's pity; this emotion reconciles him to her after she has gone off with another man, the abusive Chaval, and permits him to feel a less ambivalent love for her. "'My poor dear,' said Étienne softly, overcome with pity" for Catherine; and then "but he remained near her; he had put his arms around her waist in a caress of grief and pity."[27] Their reconciliation and final scenes together at the apocalyptic flooding of the coal pit, where Catherine will perish after nine days of entombment within the collapsed veins, are all the more pathetic because of Étienne's piteous rapprochement to her.

Zola's voice seems to want to persuade us, through his characters, that pity is most useful as an antidote to anger and retribution—to violence and cruelty. Throughout the novel, savagery is the counterpoint to social harmony and moral sensitivity; indeed, the overarching message of *Germinal* could be interpreted as declaring that a world without both pity and justice is a world of obdurate brutality—one where justice remains incapacitated unless buttressed by pity. Étienne rethinks the dangerous social catastrophe he has helped precipitate after its violence overwhelms his best intentions, and this reassessment triggers pity even more so than regret or remorse.

This is especially true of the murder of a young Breton conscript, Jules, who is called in by the government to secure the mine and whose throat, Jeanlin--the guilelessly savage son of the Maheus—then slits. The scene is made all the more pathetic in that it has been foreshadowed through a previous narration in which Zola has Étienne encounter Jules, in the hopes of converting him to the strikers' cause, and is instead moved by the young man's homesickness for his widowed mother and only sister. Étienne reacts with a powerful and regretful pity when he next encounters Jules, a corpse in the snow: "and deep pity came over him in front of this fair gentle face, marked with freckles."[28]

Germinal's denouement is an unhappy one; the declamatory pity that has operated as a goad to moral refinement in the reader has not brought felicitous results within the timeframe or terms of the novel; rather, the Götterdamerung-like ending makes for a morality-tale warning the reader of what comes of a pitiless world. Those whom pity could have saved—especially the Maheus (the father, Alzire, and Catherine); but also the charitable Cécile from the prosperous local family, the Grégoires—are dead before pity has become operative in society. The selfishly insensate bourgeoisie, represented by the Grégoires, are finally sensitized to pity, but only after disaster has struck: "Their excursion was to be completed by a visit of charity. Zacharie's death had filled them with pity for this tragic Maheu family, about whom the whole country was talking."[29] With her husband dead and her young children in need of material support, Mme Maheu, 40 years old, is forced to return to work in the pits. Her coworkers, when interrogated on her whereabouts by Étienne, who is on the brink of leaving the area for good, react: "They made no reply. One made a sign that she was coming. Others raised their arms, trembling with pity. Ah, poor woman! What wretchedness!"[30] The characters themselves have been educated to pity, realizing the double lesson that emotionally they must feel pity, and socially their conditions warrant it.

Therein lies Zola's "realistic," yet ultimately idealistic, use of pity—he does not wish to have the characters' pity do the work of the readers'. The pity in *Germinal* overflows its narrative bounds, coursing from Zola's intentions to the audience's workable responses toward elements in their milieu similar to those encountered in the fictional account. For these readers, literary pity has not done the work of the real-life pity Zola would like them to achieve.

The overall tone of the novel retains a tenebrous sense of pain and injustice that may lead an individual to perform social actions out of pity. The relationship between pity and activism is thus much more complicated and vexed in Zola than in the Goncourt brothers. What sets apart Zola is his view of pity as an individual and sentimental communion prior to justice, outrage, and violence. The workings of social reform do not interest Zola as much as the moral predispositions to it— for social activism without pity would still be a failure of moral imagination. This hortatory intent informs a pity that is less declarative and more narrative. That is, Zola indulges a piteous plot in *Germinal* wherein the emotional component of concern for misery is the object, rather than simply the language, of pity. It is to this that Zola spoke when he commented that "and if readers experience [pity], I shall be happy."

They "experience" it partly because Zola creates narratives of unrelieved and undeserved socioeconomic suffering. This represents one of Zola's "realistic" contributions to romantic humanitarian literature: he located the sphere of pity's possible operation not only in the unavoidable heartbreaks of human passion but in the social forces that make pity as thorny as it is indispensable. If classical tragedy elicited pity through accounts of love, exile, compulsion, early death, and other trajectories of an aleatory fate, Zola also firmly grounded it in hunger and physical necessity. Hard hearts are confronted by aching bellies in Zola's narrative. Étienne's first stirrings of revolt, which will lead him to strike, had been aroused by this misery:

Outside, night was already coming on, a frosty night; and with lowered head Étienne walked along, sunk in dark melancholy. It was no longer anger against the man, or pity for the poor ill-treated girl. The brutal scene was effaced and lost, and he was thrown back on to the sufferings of all, the abominations of wretchedness. He thought of the settlement without bread, these women and little ones who would not eat that evening, all this struggling race with empty bellies.[31]

Étienne first responds by a revolt premised on justice, not pity. Indeed, a defining moment in Zola's development of Étienne's character is the latter's temporary but hugely consequential spurning of pity: "That was a confession on his part. He jested over his illusions of a novice, his religious dream of a pity in which justice would soon reign among men who had become brothers."[32] Étienne attempts to personify the vengeful justice preached by the Russian exile anarchist Souvarine, until pity later reclaims its precedence after tragic events continue. The seesaw dynamic between a just vengeance and pity thus creates the story's central moral tension and propaedeutic lesson. *Germinal* is a long perlocutionary appeal to social melioration through subjective emotional awareness and engagement, both premised on pity.

La Joie de vivre (1884), by contrast, works at a more ideological level—the novel is Zola's attempt to rescue a romantic-humanitarian pity from the clutches of Schopenhauer's pessimism.[33] He did so by reinforcing the maternalist aspects of traditional thinking on pity, updating them for the *fin-de-siècle* gender arena. In this, *La Joie de vivre* approaches the work of those whose sense of pity was most gendered and elementary—the Goncourts and Léon Bloy, especially. In its pedagogical foundations, moreover, Zola's story conforms to the ambient maternalism of the Republican milieu and its educational precepts.

In this novel of intellectual psychology, the orphaned Pauline is sent from Paris to the Channel coast to live with relatives, a self-absorbed bourgeois couple that will subsequently cannibalize her inheritance, forcing upon her an education in diffidence. Their son, her cousin Lazare, is the focus of her preoccupations and disappointments; a ne'er-do-well who aspires to many careers, first as a doctor and then as an engineer on a quixotic quest to erect barrages against coastal flooding in his village. He is seized by constant existential panics, triggered by the thought of death and concomitant doubts on the value of engaging life. Pauline battles against his *idée-fixe* with a joyous solicitude while keenly observing and responding to the pain and suffering around her. This contrast in temperament is the focus of the rather limited plot and its thin veneer of philosophy: the reliance on pity as a distinguishing trait between the narrative protagonists is what makes the novel an important source for Zola's views on pity.

Zola wanted to argue in *La Joie de vivre* (a facilely ironic title) that if pain, suffering, and death are inevitable, both religious consolation and nihilism are still inadequate responses; rather, an empathic innocence of vitality is the best adaptation. In contrast to both Schopenhauer and Nietzsche, Zola argued through his characters that pain and suffering can strengthen the self's attachments to life, if confronted by a robust pity.

Pauline incarnates this contention. For her, pity is an agent of knowledge and action: "Her heart ached with pity, she renewed her old dream of knowing everything in order to heal everything"[34]—much as it was for the novelist himself. In Pauline he fuses both a suffering-based awareness of others—"Pauline...alone remained calm, in her pity for so much pain"[35]—and the most exalted capacities for devoted action: "Everything was submerged in the depth of an immense pity, she wished she could love even more, devote herself, give herself, abide injustice and insults, in order to better assuage others."[36]

Zola insists—for this is a moralist's tale—throughout *La Joie de vivre* that the pain of suffering is not defeatist; it primes his characters to vigorous opposition against affliction, personal and social, and to a renewed commitment to life. This is the substance of Zola's dispute with Schopenhauer: "Pessimism made its appearance there, a badly digested pessimism, of which the only elements that remained were the ingenious glibness and dark poetry of Schopenhauer."[37] Pauline picks up the German philosopher's name and ideas from Lazare's discussions of his readings, and Zola has her retain only Schopenhauer's popularized preaching on asceticism and renunciation, not his pity-ethics: "Oh, didn't I tell you? Last night I dreamed that your Schopenhauer learned of our marriage from the other world and that he came in the night to drag us off!"[38] That Zola sunders the two elements central to Schopenhauer's legacy—pessimism and pity—may reveal that he wanted to battle the former without implicating the latter.

Pauline's pity is a willful attempt at ablating her selfishness and, paradoxically, her self-consciousness. Self-forgetfulness is just what Lazare lacks and what she tries to instill in him by her example: "finally, she was happy to connect Lazare to her charities, hoping to distract him and to lead him to self-forgetfulness through pity."[39]

Elsewhere in Zola's oeuvre, pity is a means of expanding moral self-awareness, operating from self to others and then back to a heightened conscience. Zola's characterization of Pauline suggests that she had started out with this heightened conscience, from which a socially valuable pity emanated, and that Lazare's problem was that his pity was disabled by solipsistic obtuseness. In Lazare's experience, pity is an untrustworthy and patronizing quality that he particularly associates with and laments in religious consolations: "He suffered before that charitable lie of all religions, wherein pity hides the terrible truth from the weak. No, everything ends in and at death, none of our affections would be reborn, it was goodbye for always."[40] Understanding religious pity as a shield against accepting mortality, Lazare reacts with muffled anger. His attitude comes closest here to joining Pauline's, since it seems to invite a noncondescending relation to suffering—only, in his case, this suffering takes the form of his own death-bound cognition, while in hers it seems to be directed to others' weal and woe.

The static psychological drama pitting *mal de vivre* against *joie de vivre* gains some narrative momentum when Louise, another female possessed of a vital and visceral attachment to life, enters the household and competes for Lazare's affection. Her relation to others is more sensual (the third character trait, with pessimism and pity, contesting for Zola's own allegiance, no less masked than the second by being given feminine personification) and less sorrowful, and she attracts Lazare through her coquettish innocence. Pauline's reaction to her rival is a jealousy ultimately vanquished by her pitying sensibility.

Given the battle between affirmation and negation that Zola wished to see waged at the pith of his tale, Louise becomes an expendable character after testing the central pair's strongly held convictions. Louise becomes pregnant soon after marrying Lazare and just as quickly dies at childbirth (a *deus ex machina* worthy of the Goncourts). The couple's tragedy, coming on the heels of Pauline's uncle's slow death and her discovery of the financial chicanery perpetrated against her by the aunt, tests her acceptance of the random suffering meted out by life. Her capacious pity allows her to decide in favor of affirmation as she takes the deceased Louise's newborn to her lap: "In self-forgetfulness, she placed him in her lap, shedding some more tears in which were merged a lament for her own wasted motherhood and her pity for the woes of all living beings."[41] Lazare, who is less shaken by the death of loved ones than by the prospect of his own end, is finally won over to Pauline's perspective when he sees fructifying compassion conjugated by the presence of his baby boy and his cousin's care: "'Yes, you alone were wise. Life becomes so easy when the household is in such good humor and when one lives for others.... If the world should burst with woes, let it burst at least with some jolly in taking pity on itself.'"[42] Lazare's endorsement of pity—he summons the world's reflexive pity for itself, which is a hardy and mocking pity—shows Zola's consistent refusal to allow this character an easy psychological and emotional relation to that sentiment. Lazare has not really learned pity, only acquiesced in its comforts as blandished by others.

Zola's poetics of pity failed most acutely, not surprisingly, when he tackled Schopenhauer head-on in *La Joie de vivre*. The problem with Zola's attempt to unhitch pity from pessimism is that his pity becomes character-driven instead of inhering in the narrative, as it had done in *Germinal*. He merely tests pity in his characters, and pity comes through, predictably. Here, Zola's use of pity demonstrated neither an illocutionary strategy nor a perlocutionary appeal; it is a static variable objectified for a story's sake.

In contradistinction to *Germinal*, moreover, there is no wide social dimension to this character-driven pity. Zola shifted wholly to a domestic ideal of pity, to a fully feminized, maternalist version of doctrinaire pity, which seems both inadequate to the task of rebutting Schopenhauer (given the latter's misogyny) and to call for action. By eliding creature comforts into metaphysical succor, Zola collapsed the social into the personal without binding them with any view to action, or relating them in an illocutionary appeal to the readers' own moral or social awareness. This approach to pity was inscribed in the Republican maternalist consensus of the period. Let us recall Buisson's idealized feminine pity:

Whatever the case may be, women appear to us today, more than at other times, governed by the Heart, sensibility, imagination, by all that sort of affective and intuitive qualities in which we earlier perceived its intimate powers and irresistible charm.... The treasures of sensibility and imagination that overflow your Heart, do you know where they must unfold? Around yourselves, in the humble and sweet circle of your family. You dream of being an angel: be an angel of the household.[43]

We cannot expect even Zola to escape the sentimentalist tropes and ideological blinders of his day.

Lourdes (1894) is no less obsessive a *roman à thèse* than *La Joie de vivre* and yet succeeds in its didactic goal of contrasting a romantic-humanitarian to a religious pity. The tag line of *fin-de-siècle* humanitarianism, "the religion of suffering humanity"—a label often wielded against it by the critics of the literature of pity—conveyed a secular, anti-clerical concern for the human predicament. *Lourdes* is Zola's attempt to understand the pitying impulses underlying religious belief while proposing to his readers a this-worldly channeling of such compulsions; and to battle religion inside its own suffering-based cosmology so as to argue the superiority of secular compassion. *Lourdes* indeed is the rather ghastly hymn Zola composed for the secular "religion of suffering humanity."

The novel was part of the *Trois villes* trilogy, whose two other place-titles, *Paris* and *Rome*, as well as the symbolism of an experimental series in the form of a trinity (trilogy), betray Zola's fascination with the religious urges and the clerical habitus of a fallen world. Like some prototypes from the earlier Rougon-Macquart series, *Lourdes* unites a young girl with a doubting priest: in this case, Marie, a paralytic young girl, and Pierre, whom she had known earlier in life and who, now a priest, travels on the train transporting the lame and ill from Paris on a pilgrimage to Lourdes. The Boschian portrait that Zola paints of crippling physical pain and deformity is a more effective foil for the sympathetic, and perhaps condescending, impulses of his vision than the domestic world of Pauline and Lazare. Zola is convinced that religion functions as a rationalization and palliative for such overwhelming affliction, and he wants to test the premise that a nonreligious, humane pity can serve as a substitute without risking misanthropic lassitude or chimerical denials. As in most of his works, Zola's aesthetic pedagogy is premised on *pathei mathos*, that pathos educates, and his ethical stance is that pity encourages social action and redeems the individual. In addition, the grotesque descriptions and bizarre but topical setting of *Lourdes* give panache to Zola's inspiration.

Pierre is one of those sensitive souls for whom suffering acts as a social and ethical stimulus, and through it he will triumph over his calling and come to love Marie fully. Pity is the suffering-based virtue he will harness toward these ends: "And immense pity overflowed from Pierre's heart, human compassion for all the suffering and all the tears that consumed weak and naked man. He was sad unto death and ardent charity burnt within him, the inextinguishable flame as it were of his fraternal feelings towards all things and beings."[44] As was the case with *La Joie de vivre* and contrary to *Germinal*, Zola sketches this moral panorama for us through characterization, not narrative poetics, which tips us to the fact that Zola is ventriloquizing Pierre. Zola extends his authorial sympathy to almost all characters that, if capable of pity, then appeal to it when self-conscious of their own predicament.

Marie reacts to the dolent stories of her fellow pilgrims with piteous solicitude: "and Marie, listening to her, felt great pity for her."[45] Soeur Hyacinthe, a nun who had nursed Pierre back to health many years before, when they were both young, and who is also now a pilgrim, is given only motives from maternalist pity: "And she was a mother also, a mother who helped him to rise, and who put him to bed as though he were her child, without aught springing up between them save supreme pity, the divine, gentle compassion of charity."[46]

Zola has Pierre fervently wish to possess the simple religious faith of Marie and Hyacinthe; indeed, he undertakes the pilgrimage in the hope of fortifying his always-shaky faith. Instead, he ends up reinforced in his conviction that religious belief is misinterpreted pity, a misericordious self-delusion about suffering. Pierre/Zola, the only Voltairean in the cast, is the omniscient arbiter who alone can adjudicate among pity's supernatural and humane claims. A converted atheist called Sabathier, who had lost his wife and daughter and now undertakes an annual voyage to the grotto out of religious duty as well as gratitude for his religious epiphany, is introduced by Zola as a counterpoint to Pierre: "'And then, after long living without a thought of religion, I was led back to God by the idea that I was too wretched, and that Our Lady of Lourdes could not do otherwise than take pity on me.' 'Is it not so, Monsieur l'abbé? Is not suffering the best awakener of souls?'"[47] Pierre holds fast to both his skepticism and his pity, and this allows him to see through religious faith and gives him a tender resignation in the face of others' belief, especially Marie's. Zola cuts short Pierre's account to Marie of his spiritual torments with the following remark: "Why should he discourage her with his doubts, since he wanted her to heal? So he held on to her little wet, sickly hand with an infinite tenderness, overcome by fraternal suffering and wanting to believe in the pity of all things, in a higher goodness that spares pain for the hopeless."[48]

Zola has Pierre share the pathetic sensibility both see at work in religion, and this accentuates the priest's crisis of faith and Zola's drama about the ineluctable but regrettable role of religion in human life. Confronting the physical and mental torments along his journey, Pierre reacts with a pity that touches on religious exaltation: "and his pitiful feelings at the sight of so much suffering were so intense that he regained some little of his faith. It was long indeed since he had prayed like this, devoutly wishing that there might be a God in Heaven, whose omnipotence could assuage the wretchedness of humanity."[49] A megalomaniac element inheres in this drama and in the author's position, for Zola equates his view of religion as an appeal to supernatural pity with Pierre's capacity for lucid pitying; thus, author and character's pity make of both secular deities.

Zola evidenced a more condescending version of pity in his narrative treatment of the historical figure of Bernadette Soubirou, interpreting her visions as good-faith efforts to alleviate human suffering and vouchsafe a noble view of the world. Pity is the keyword in Zola's rendition of both Pierre's and Dr. Chassaigne's view of her, as well as of Mgr. Laurence's decision to issue a decree accepting the miracles associated with her grotto. Of Pierre he writes: "Pierre, who knew Bernadette so well, and who felt a fraternal pity for her memory, the fervent compassion with which one regards a human saint, a simple, upright, charming creature tortured by her faith, allowed his emotion to appear in his moist eyes and trembling voice."[50] Zola deploys his emotive language in order to liken Pierre's temperament to Bernadette's naïveté, thereby furthering his attempt to relegate religious belief to a pitying impulse. Dr. Chassaigne similarly parrots Zola's perspective: "'Yes,' remarked Doctor Chassaigne in his turn, 'it is the wretched lodging, the chance refuge, where new religions are born of suffering and pity.'"[51] This is also the case with Zola's telepathic fictional rendering of Mgr. Laurence's motives: "He did not believe in the apparitions; he had a loftier, more intellectual idea of the manifestations of the Divinity. Only, would he not be showing true pity and mercy in silencing the scruples of his reason, the noble prejudices of his faith, in presence of the necessity of granting that bread of falsehood which poor humanity requires in order to be happy?"[52] Pierre/Zola's rhetorical interrogation is at a great remove from the Enlightenment mockery of religious convictions; the pathetic credo shared by both romantic humanitarianism and religion prohibits Zola any ridicule. Zola's rhetoric of pity and his psychology of religion were guided by a hybrid of perennial atheism: religion is a metahistorical symptom of the need for a "consoling illusion;" counteracting and perhaps displacing old-fashioned religion is a newfangled emotivism with its immanent deity of "pity and hope" anchoring a "new religion."

The rhetorical weight of the novel shifts inexorably toward the latter, which Zola recuperates on behalf of a compassionate humanism. *Lourdes* is, in this sense, an emotive brief for secularism, battling religious belief not on the narrow grounds of rationalism but on the fertile soil of pathos. The pilgrims descended upon Lourdes are described, for example, as nothing less than physical embodiments of an apostrophized pity: "and pity came to the heart, a pity full of anguish, at the sight of this flock of wretched beings lying there in heaps in loathsome rags, whilst their poor spotless souls no doubt were far away in the blue realm of some mystical dream."[53] In the presence of this pitiful humanity, Pierre responds to its spiritual hunger with a sympathetic indulgence that deigns to comprehend faith: "In the midst of all his sadness Pierre felt deep pity penetrate his heart. He was upset by the thought that mankind should be so wretched, reduced to such a state of woe, so bare, so weak, so utterly forsaken, that it renounced its own reason to place the sole possibility of happiness in the hallucinatory intoxication of dreams."[54] As the story moves to its unsurprising climax—Pierre will leave the priesthood; his love for Marie remains chaste while becoming sentimentally richer—Zola again employs the phrase "the religion of suffering humanity" as a cue that Pierre has effected the very absorption of dogmatic religion into a secular pathetic credo intended by the author:

And of his journey there already only remained to Pierre an immense feeling of pity…it would never do to drive the wretched to despair. Lourdes must be tolerated, in the same way that you tolerate a falsehood which makes life possible. And, as he had already said in Bernadette's chamber, she remained the martyr, she it was who revealed to him the only religion which still filled his heart, the religion of human suffering.[55]

Zola's work of apostasy imposes: Bernadette, like Pierre, is taken from the Catholic Church and delivered over to the secular "religion of suffering humanity."

Zola's story sets out to convince us—this is the overarching perlocutionary appeal centered on pity—through Pierre's example, that the "religion of suffering humanity" can fulfill the psychological and emotional demands, which Zola sums up as "tears and love," theretofore the exclusive province of dogmatic religion. Zola's narrative in *Lourdes* was an insistent threnody on suffering and its emotive meaning and ethical purport, and since he wants a wide-eyed endorsement of the pathetic to supplant religion's otherworldly bromides, he must certify the value of suffering.

Zola was acutely aware of the pessimistic possibilities in his narrative stance in *Lourdes*, of not offering a more healthy-minded alternative to the religious belief he assimilated to the "religion of suffering humanity." Indeed, Pierre, in a last-second revolt against his own temperament near the end of the novel, is tempted by a rational eudamonism that contradicts his pathetic impulses:

No, no, even human suffering, the hallowed suffering of the poor, ought not to prove an obstacle, enjoining the necessity of ignorance and folly. Reason before all; in her alone lay salvation. If at Lourdes, whilst bathed in tears, softened by the sight of so much affliction, he had said it was sufficient to weep and love, he had made a dangerous mistake. Pity was but a convenient expedient. One must live, one must act; reason must combat suffering, unless it be desired that the latter should last forever.[56]

Pity conceived of as a convenient expedient, suffering as self-perpetuating fatalism—these were the tenets of Zola's rationalist superego, and his recognition of such counterhypotheses curiously marks his distance from us, since these may be more consonant with our own estimations. But Zola will not undermine his melodrama with such far-seeing quibbles; he will stick to his hope for a new religion:

A new religion; a new religion. Doubtless it must be a religion nearer to life, giving a larger place to the things of the world, and taking the acquired truths into due account. And, above all, it must be a religion which was not an appetite for death—Bernadette living solely in order that she might die, Doctor Chassaigne aspiring to the tomb as to the only happiness— for all that spiritualistic abandonment was so much continuous disorganization of the will to live....Could a new religion ever place that garden of eternal happiness on earth?[57]

The "new religion," the "religion of suffering humanity," would profess a suffering that does not negate life, a suffering that leads to more vital connections with others, with nature, with the hard realities of our terrestrial condition. No less so than *La Joie de vivre*, *Lourdes* is Zola's attempt to convince us—and himself— that Schopenhauer was wrong about the relation of suffering to life, but right about the role of pity as the principle behind both pathos and ethos.

Zola's novels may be too melodramatic for some tastes; they are often read today as guides to the socioeconomic "realities" of late-century France—a purpose, moreover, that perhaps would have satisfied his wishes for posterity. But even as they are consulted for their lessons on French *fin-de-siècle* social history, they should also be mined for their valuable insights into the consensus on sentimentalism. Zola's oeuvre is never merely analytical or graphic, as both he and his vituperators often agreed it was; it was very much a sentimental portrait of human suffering, an *argumentum ad misericordiam*. It was romantic, humanitarian, and idealist, in its precedents and narrative scope. He was most successful when he crafted a poetics of pity that weaved together sociological details and an emotive narrative, covertly communicating his own or his character's overt appeals to the reader's pity—as in *Germinal*. But so close was Zola to his own apostolate of pity that he often brought the terms of his pathetic appeal to the very surface of his tales, as he did in both *La Joie de vivre* and *Lourdes*. If these are less effective literary creations as a result—if their characterizations are more schematic, their narrative architecture more transparent, manipulations more rhetorical—they highlight the place of pity in a fiction that meant to be indivisibly moral and social—the way philosophers and critics thought it should be.

NOTES

1. Current reflections updating Aristotelian poetics, as well as Rousseau's argument in "Lettre à d'Alembert"—an often unacknowledged precursor—include the following works: Colin Radford's "How Can We Be Moved by the Fate of Anna Karenina?" which bases itself on the "paradox of belief;" that is, what is the reality of an emotion elicited by a fiction? Radford detects an incommensurability between the epistemology of fictional representation and emotional responses: "What seems unintelligible is how we could have a similar reaction to the fate of Anna Karenina, the plight of Madame Bovary or the death of Mercutio. Yet we do. We weep, we pity" (*Proceedings of the Aristotelian Society*, Supp. vol. 49 [1975], 69). Radford concludes that this incommensurability involves, at the level of brute fact, illogic. In his "Response" to Radford's article in the same issue, Michael Weston argues that affective responses are directed to aesthetic experience, not veridical events. A whole collegium of respondents has subsequently anatomized this topic. Susan L. Feagin, distinguishing between "empathetic emotions" and "emotions with which I empathize," sides with and expands upon Weston's position ("Imagining Emotions and Appreciating Fictions," *Canadian Journal of Philosophy* 18:3 [September 1988], 496, 500). Don Mannison partly agrees with both Radford and Weston by introducing Stanley Cavell's distinction between the actual "true" and the potential "truthful:" "although it is not Anna Karenina whom we pity, perhaps it is Anna's 'fate' which moves us....So, what in Tolstoy moves me? Radford was half right. We are moved by the fate of Anna Karenina; but, I have argued, not by her" ("On Being Moved by Fiction," *Philosophy* 60 [1985], 82, 87). Robert J. Yanal also splits the differences between Radford and Weston: "Such examples suggest that it is the thought that counts, that is, the mere entertaining of thoughts is often sufficient to induce emotion. When we read a novel or view a film we are inspired to thoughts not believed true—for example, the thought that Anna Karenina is suicidal—and such thoughts even in the absence of belief can inspire pity" (*Paradoxes of Emotion and Fiction* [University Park, PA: Penn State UP, 1999], 159–60). Kendall Walton comes close to a full endorsement of the "suspension of disbelief" model: "Representative works of art generate make-believe truths....Rather than somehow fooling ourselves into thinking fictions are real, we become fictional. So we end up 'on the same level' with fictions" ("Fearing Fictions," *The Journal of Philosophy* 75 [1978], 12, 24.) See also idem., *Mimesis and Make-Believe: On the Foundations of the Representational Arts* (Cambridge, MA: Harvard UP, 1990). Peter Lamarque argues that literary descriptions become thoughts, but thoughts that are states of consciousness and not formal representations: "Our feelings of pity can have real and intentional objects. The real object of our pity, what we are moved *by*, is what arouses our emotions....We do not pity thoughts; but thoughts can be pitiful and can fill us with pity" ("How Can We Fear and Pity Fictions?" *British Journal of Aesthetics* 21 [1981], 293–94). William Charlton argues for the mediating impact of fictional emotions; that is, they instill a desire for comforting action in the real world: "The analysis of 'we feel for Anna' which I am proposing here is not that we categorically pity hypothetical persons; it is that we hypothetically desire to benefit real persons....If any of my friends had a husband like Karenin or a lover like Vronsky, would that I might help her to do what is best" ("Feeling for the Fictitious," *British Journal of Aesthetics* 24 [1984], 211–12.) R. T. Allen replies: "we respond to the events and characters and scenes themselves, and not because we are always breaking off to think about what we would wish for people we know in real

life....This brings me to my main objection: viz, that I do not find myself making wishes about what I might do with regard to real people and that to do so would be always to cease attending to the story and to think about something else" ("The Reality of Responses to Fiction," *British Journal of Aesthetics* 26 [1986], 65). Allen concludes by articulating what a nineteenth-century reader might have dumbfoundedly responded had they been pressed to defend their literary sensations: "What I then propose is that 'we feel for Anna' needs no analysis at all: it says exactly what we mean, no more and no less. The emotional response to fiction is not a 'problem' but a daily fact. We *feel* (not wish nor anything else) and we feel *for Anna* (not a real person nor Anna taken wrongly to be a real person). All that we need to do is to recognize the phenomenon for what it is" (66). More recently, Glenn A. Hartz has responded by relying on advances in cognitive neurophysiology—on "empirical and phenomenological facts about us;" "I very much suspect that the *real* answer to Radford lies, not in the esoterica of aesthetic theory, but in the brutally technical details of cognitive neuroscience" ("How We Can Be Moved by Anna Karenina, Green Slime, and a Red Pony," *Philosophy* 74:290 [October 1999], 578). His explanation for our responses to a fictional Anna Karenina is: "So, to return to *Anna*: the pity that erupts during reading, though caused by thoughts about the story, is often as automatic, passive, involuntary, and forceful as the one-year old's barely cogitated fellow-feeling directed towards her friend. By ignoring the fact that adult emotions retain vestiges of primitive responses, philosophers have found paradox where there is none" (567). See also Jennifer Wilkinson, "The Paradox(es) of Pitying and Fearing Fictions," *South African Journal of Philosophy* 19:1 (March 2000), 8–25; Alex Neill, "Fiction and the Emotions," *American Philosophical Quarterly* 30:1 (1993), 1–13.

2. Schiller, *On the Naïve and Sentimental in Literature*, Helen Watanabe-O'Kelly, trans. and intro. (Manchester, UK: Carcanet New Press, 1981), 30.

3. See Georg Simmel, *Nietzsche and Schopenhauer*, Helmut Loiskandl, Deena Weinstein, and Michael Weinstein, trans. (Amherst: U of Massachusetts P, 1986).

4. Nietzsche, "Skirmishes of an Untimely Man," *Twilight of the Idols*, 513.

5. Nor is this to be understood as implying a claim on behalf of the ethical status of literary pity. The analysis that follows is concerned with an author's attempts to use pity as both subject and trope. There is a good contemporary discussion on the question of the ethical and philosophical status of fiction. See, for example, Wayne C. Booth, *The Company We Keep: An Ethics of Fiction*; Richard Eldridge, *On Moral Personhood: Philosophy, Literature, Criticism, and Self-Understanding* (Chicago: U of Chicago P, 1989); S. L. Goldberg, *Agents and Lives: Moral Thinking in Literature* (Cambridge: Cambridge UP, 1993); J. Hillis Miller, *The Ethics of Reading* (New York: Columbia UP, 1987); Martha Nussbaum, *Love's Knowledge: Essays on Philosophy and Literature*; David Parker, *Ethics, Theory and the Novel* (Cambridge: Cambridge UP, 1994); Alexander Nehamas, "What Should We Expect from Reading (There Are Only Aesthetic Values)," *Salmagundi* 111 (Summer 1996), 27–58. If I agree with Hillary Putnam that "commentary on literature can be philosophy while the literature cannot"—hence the ever-growing citation of fiction by contemporary philosophers—some works of literature are more purposive in either trying to generate such commentary or forestall it. Nehamas argues that "but in order to assume that the text and its paraphrase concern the same situation we must in turn presuppose that the literary work describes something actually independent of itself, something we can vaguely call reality itself. Without such an independent object and without access to it, we will not be able to determine that text and paraphrase are concerned with it and that some of its features are repeatable while others are not" (37). I would argue, however, that if the reality described and appealed to are emotions, which themselves should be reinforced by the reader's (commentator's) awareness, then this subjective response will serve as one way of

verifying, qualifying, or rejecting the possibility that the manipulation of such an emotion has indeed come close to making it appear an "independent object." However, I would not go so far as Justin Oakley's argument in *Morality and the Emotions* (New York: Routledge, 1992), 52.

6. Nietzsche, "Skirmishes of an Untimely Man," 517.

7. ["Déjà le sentiment du progrès, la pitié pour le faible, l'amour pour le souffrant éclatent de plus en plus dans vos éloquents pages."] Cited in Jules et Edmond de Goncourt, *Germinie Lacerteux*, Philippe Desan, ed. and intro. (Paris: Librairie Générale Française, 1990), xlix.

8. Erich Auerbach, *Mimesis*, 496–97.

9. ["Il nous est venu la curiosité de savoir si cette forme conventionelle d'une littérature oubliée et d'une société disparue, la Tragédie, était définitivement morte; si, dans un pays sans caste et sans aristocratie légale, les misères des petits et des pauvres parleraient à l'intérêt, à l'émotion, à la pitié, aussi haut que les misères des grands et des riches; si, en un mot, les larmes qu'on pleure en bas pourraient faire pleurer comme celles qu'on pleure en haut."] *Germinie Lacerteux*, 4; *Germinie Lacerteux*, Leonard Tancock, trans. and intro. (New York: Penguin, 1984), 15. Where there are two sources for a citation, the first is for the French-language edition, the second for its published English-language edition (in parentheses).

10. And born of a simplistic biographical reflex: the Goncourts' discovery at her death in 1862 that their maid, Rose, had led a duplicitous life.

11. ["C'était une femme impersonelle pour ainsi dire à force de coeur, une femme qui ne s'appartenait point: Dieu ne semblait l'avoir faite que pour la donner aux autres."] Goncourt, 33 (32).

12. See Nancy K. Miller, *French Dressing: Women, Men, and Ancien Régime Fiction* (New York: Routledge, 1995): "What is a *roman sentimental*? Henri Coulet, in his classic study, *Le roman jusqu'à la révolution*, puts the matter this way: 'Under this heading are included, somewhat arbitrarily, novels that have different subjects and forms, but whose purpose is to depict and analyze feelings rather than to describe manners.'" (69). According to this view, the Goncourts' emphasis on manners, despite their own pronouncements, makes it difficult to consider *Germinie* a sentimental novel. But see also the claim made by Suzanne Clark in *Sentimental Modernism: Women Writers and the Revolution of the Word* (Bloomington: Indiana UP, 1991), that sentimentalism involved female abjection and abnegation—which is consistent with the Goncourts' depiction.

13. ["Que de tristesses, que d'amertumes, que de solitude pour elle, dans cette vie avec ce vieillard morose, aigri, toujours grondant et bougonnant au logis, n'ayant d'amabilité que pour le monde et qui la laissait tous les soirs."] Goncourt, 20 (25).

14. ["Et il ne tarda pas à s'en écarter, sans charité, sans pitié."] Goncourt, 8 (65).

15. ["Mademoiselle en avait pitié: elle la forçait à se jeter sur son propre lit."] Goncourt, 215 (154–55).

16. ["M'as-tu jamais sacrifié un verre de vin? As-tu eu seulement pitié de moi, quand je trimais dans la boue, dans la neige, au risque de crever?"] Goncourt, 196 (141).

17. For a similar point see Auerbach, *Mimesis*, 505.

18. ["O Paris! tu es le coeur du monde, tu es la grande ville humaine, la grande ville charitable et fraternelle! Tu as des douceurs d'esprit, de vieilles miséricordes de moeurs, des spectacles qui font l'aumône."] Goncourt, 236 (169).

19. ["puis un beau jour, par un hasard, elle apprit que sa nièce était morte quelques semaines après sa soeur."] Goncourt, 58 (50).

20. ["Excellemment bonne, quelque chose pourtant manquait à sa bonté: le pardon. Jamais elle n'avait pu fléchir ni plier son caractère jusque-là. Un froissement, un mauvais

procédé, un rien qui atteignait son coeur, la blessait pour toujours. Elle n'oubliait pas. Le temps, la mort même ne désarmait pas sa mémoire."] Goncourt, 34 (33–34).

21. ["...peu à peu, lentement, de ces souvenirs remués, de ces évocations dont elle cherchait l'amertume, de la lointaine douceur des jours passés, il se levait en elle un premier attendrissement de miséricorde."] Goncourt, 231 (166).

22. ["Et l'expression de cette tête s'adoucissant toujours, mademoiselle finissait par y voir une supplication qui l'implorait, une supplication qui, à la longue, enveloppait sa pitié...si, la vie, les circomstances, le malheur de son corps et de sa destinée, n'avaient pas fait d'elle la créature qu'elle avait été, un être d'amour et de douleur."] Goncourt, 233 (167).

23. Schorr, *George Sand and Idealism* (New York: Columbia UP, 1993): "My thesis then is this: Sand's spectacular aesthetic devaluation cannot be ascribed in any simple terms to her gender; it is not because Sand was a woman but rather because (like so many other women authors) she is associated with a discredited and discarded representational mode that she is no longer ranked among the canonical authors" (32); "demeaning association with the feminine, i.e., sentimentalism, sensationalism, and idealism" (43); "I have argued throughout what precedes that, for all its embryonic naturalist elements, French social romanticism—at least as it was exemplified by Sand—relied heavily on techniques of idealization that strained against the particularization we (and she) associate with realism" (165–66). For more on George Sand's sentimentalism, especially concerning her first novel, *Indiana*, see William Reddy, *The Navigation of Feeling*, 249–53.

24. In "Before the Castle: Women, Commodities, and Modernity in *Au Bonheur des Dames*," Schorr has interpreted this novel of Zola as a "gothic" novel—as a stereotypical female *bildungsroman* and a sentimental novel. See *Bad Objects: Essays Popular and Unpopular* (Durham, NC: Duke UP, 1995), 149–55.

25. Cited by Frederick Brown, *Zola: A Life* (Baltimore: Johns Hopkins UP, 1996), 544. This is the same remark that Zola made about his endeavors on behalf of Captain Dreyfus.

26. ["Quelle misère, et l'odeur, et les corps en tas, et la pitié affreuse qui le serrait à la gorge."] Émile Zola, *Germinal* (Paris: Fasquelle, 1983), 375. (Zola, *Germinal*, Havelock Ellis, trans. [London: Nonesuch Press, 1942], 276).

27. ["'Ma pauvre petite!' dit tout bas Étienne, saisi d'une grande pitié;" "mais il demeurait près d'elle, il l'avait prise à la taille, dans une caresse de chagrin et de pitié."] Zola, 391 (324).

28. ["Et une grande pitié le saisit, en face de cette douce figure blonde, criblée de taches de rousseur."] Zola, 395 (290).

29. ["C'était une pensée charitable, qui devait compléter l'excursion. La mort de Zacharie les avait emplis de pitié pour cette tragique famille des Maheu, dont tout le pays causait."] Zola, 466 (345).

30. ["Ils ne répondirent point. Un fit signe qu'elle allait venir. D'autres levèrent leurs bras, tremblants de pitié: ah! la pauvre femme! quelle misère!"] Zola, 494 (368).

31. ["Dehors, la nuit tombait déjà, une nuit glaciale, et la tête basse, Étienne marchait, pris d'une tristesse noire. Ce n'était plus de la colère contre l'homme, de la pitié pour la pauvre fille maltraitée. La scène brutale s'effaçait, se noyait, le rejetait à la souffrance de tous, aux abominations de la misère. Il revoyait le coron sans pain, ces femmes, ces petits qui ne mangeraient pas le soir, tout ce peuple luttant, le ventre vide."] Zola, 224 (162).

32. ["C'était, de son côté, une confession. Il se raillait de ses illusions de néophyte, de son rêve religieux d'une pitié où la justice allait régner bientôt, entre les hommes devenus frères."] Zola, 230 (167).

33. On Zola and Schopenhauer, see especially René-Pierre Colin, *Schopenhauer en France: Un mythe naturaliste*, 120–21, 170.

34. ["Son coeur se brisait de pitié, elle reprenait son ancien rêve de tout connaître, afin

de tout guérir."] Zola, *La Joie de vivre* (Paris: Fasquelle, 1985), 68. The translations from this novel are all mine.

35. ["seule restait calme, dans sa pitié pour tant de douleur."] Zola, 179.

36. ["Tout se noyait au fond d'une pitié immense, elle aurait voulu pouvoir aimer davantage, se dévouer, se donner, supporter l'injustice et l'injure, pour mieux soulager les autres."] Zola, 210.

37. ["Le pessimisme avait passé par là, un pessimisme mal digéré, dont il ne restait que les boutades de génie, la grande poésie noire de Schopenhauer."] Zola, 103.

38. ["'Ah, je ne t'ai pas dit? J'ai rêvé que ton Schopenhauer apprenait nôtre mariage dans l'autre monde, et qu'il revenait la nuit nous tirer par les pieds.'"] Zola, 104, 108.

39. ["enfin, elle avait eu la joie d'associer Lazare à ses charités, espérant le distraire, l'amener par la pitié à un oubli de lui-même."] Zola, 251.

40. ["Il agonisait devant ce mensonge charitable des religions, dont la pitié cache aux faibles la vérité terrible. Non, tout finissait à la mort, rien ne renaissait de nos affections, l'adieu à jamais."] Zola, 237.

41. ["Et, dans l'oubli d'elle-même, elle le prit sur ses genoux, pleurant encore des larmes, où se mêlaient le regret de sa maternité et sa pitié pour la misère de tous les vivants."] Zola, 374.

42. ["'Oui, toi seule étais sage. L'existence devient si facile, lorsque la maison est en belle humeur et qu'on y vit les uns pour les autres!...Si le monde crève de misère, qu'il crève au moins gaiement, en se prenant lui-même en pitié."] Zola, 376.

43. ["Quoi qu'il en soit, la femme nous semble aujourd'hui, plus encore qu'autrefois, dominée par le Coeur, par la sensibilité, par l'imagination, par tout cet ordre de qualités affectives et intuitives dont nous devinions tout à l'heure, dans une si fine et si sobre analyse, la puissance intime et l'irrésistible charme....Ces trésors de sensibilité et d'imagination dont votre Coeur déborde, savez-vous où il faut les répandre? C'est autour de vous, dans l'humble et doux cercle de la famille."] Fernand Buisson, *La Foi laïque*, 28–29. See Chapter 6.

44. ["Et une immense pitié déborda du coeur de Pierre, la religion humaine de tant de maux, de tant de larmes dévorant l'homme faible et nu. Il était triste à mourir, et une ardente charité brûlait en lui, comme le feu inextinguible de sa fraternité pour toutes les choses et pour tous les êtres."] Zola, *Lourdes* (Paris: Gallimard, 1995), 50 (Émile Zola, *Lourdes*, Ernest Alfred Vizetelly, trans. [Dover, NH: Alan Sutton, 1993], 18).

45. ["Et Marie, écoutant, était prise d'une grande pitié."] Zola, 39 (8).

46. ["Elle était une mère aussi, le levait, le couchait comme son enfant, sans que rien autre chose grandît entre eux qu'une pitié suprême, le divin attendrissement de la charité."] Zola, 73–74 (40).

47. ["'Alors, moi qui avais vécu sans religion, j'ai été ramené à Dieu par cette idée que j'étais trop misérable et que Nôtre-Dame de Lourdes ne pourrait pas faire autrement que d'avoir pitié de moi. N'est-ce pas, monsieur l'abbé, la souffrance est le meilleur réveil des âmes?'"] Zola, 40 (9).

48. ["Pourquoi donc l'aurait-il découragée par son doute, puisqu'il souhaitait sa guérison? Aussi gardait-il avec une tendresse infinie, cette petite main moite de malade, bouleversé de fraternité souffrante, voulant croire à la pitié des choses, à une bonté supérieur qui ménageait la douleur aux désespérés."] Zola, 74.

49. ["sa pitié devant tant de souffrance était si grande, qu'il retrouvait un peu de sa foi: depuis bien longtemps, il n'avait pas prié ainsi, souhaitant qu'il y eût au Ciel un Dieu, dont la toute-puissance pût soulager l'humanité misérable."] Zola, 193–94 (152).

50. ["Pierre, qui connaissait bien Bernadette, et qui gardait à sa mémoire une pitié fraternelle, la ferveur qu'on a pour une sainte humaine, une créature simple, droite et charmante dans le supplice de sa foi, laissa voir son émotion, les yeux humides, la voix

tremblante."] Zola, 230–31 (186–87).

51. ["'Oui, dit le docteur Chassaigne à son tour, c'est le logis misérable, l'asile de rencontre, où naissent les religions nouvelles de la souffrance et de la pitié."] Zola, 438 (371).

52. ["Il ne croyait pas aux apparitions, il avait des manifestations de la divinité une idée plus haute, plus intellectuelle. Seulement, n'était-ce pas pitié et miséricorde que de faire taire les scrupules de son intelligence, les noblesses de son culte, devant la nécessité de ce pain du mensonge, dont la pauvre humanité a besoin pour vivre heureuse?"] Zola, 238 (193–94).

53. ["Et une grande pitié, une sourde pitié d'angoisse montait de ce troupeau de misérables, écroulés en tas, dans le dégoût de leurs guénilles, tandis que, sans doute, leurs petites âmes blanches voyageaient ailleurs, au pays bleu de leur rêve mystique."] Zola, 319 (266).

54. ["Mais, au milieu de cette tristesse sans bornes, Pierre sentit une pitié profonde le gagner. Ah! cette humanité misérable, elle le bouleversait, réduite à cet excès de malheur, si nue, si faible, si abandonnée, qu'elle renonçait à sa raison, pour ne plus mettre le bonheur possible que dans l'ivresse hallucinée du rêve."] Zola, 430 (363).

55. ["Et, de son voyage, il ne restait déjà plus à Pierre qu'une immense pitié...il ne fallait désespérer personne, il fallait tolérer Lourdes, ainsi qu'on tolère le mensonge qui aide à vivre. Et, comme il l'avait dit dans la chambre de Bernadette, elle restait la martyre, elle lui révélait la seule religion dont son coeur fût encore plein, la religion de la souffrance humaine."] Zola, 570–71 (483–84).

56. ["Non, non! la souffrance humaine elle-même, la souffrance sacrée des pauvres ne devait pas être un obstacle, une nécessité d'ignorance et de folie. La raison avant tout, il n'y avait de salut que dans la raison. Si, baigné de larmes, amolli par tant de maux, il avait dit à Lourdes qu'il suffisait de pleurer et d'aimer, il s'était trompé dangereusement. La pitié n'était qu'un expédient commode. Il fallait vivre, il fallait agir, il fallait que la raison combattît la souffrance, à moins qu'on ne voulût l'éterniser."] Zola, 573 (486).

57. ["Une religion nouvelle! Une religion nouvelle! Il la faudrait sans doute plus près de la vie, faisant à la terre une part plus large, s'accommodant des vérités conquises. Et surtout une religion qui ne fût pas un appétit de la mort. Bernadette ne vivant que pour mourir, le docteur Chassaigne aspirant à la tombe comme à l'unique bonheur, tout cet abandon spiritualiste était une désorganisation continue de la volonté de vivre....Une religion nouvelle pourrait-elle jamais mettre sur la terre ce jardin de l'éternel bonheur?"] Zola, 575–76 (488).

Chapter 10: A Rhetoric of the Feminine: Paul Bourget, Octave Mirbeau, and Léon Bloy

Paul Bourget's *Le Disciple* is a breathtakingly guileless testament to the ideological use of traditional pity in fiction. It is a novel that uses pity as a clue to an intellectual mystery, yet the dimensions and quality of this pity hold no mystery for the author and retain none for the reader: so doctrinaire that it can be treated as a stock figure. This very fact betrays the presumptive consensus about pity on which Bourget drew his inspiration.

Bourget (1852–1935), a *littérateur* remembered as much for the multivolume thumbnail sketches of his contemporaries, gathered as *Essais de psychologie contemporaine*, as for his novels, specialized in the "drama of ideas," which in more creative guises he crafted into cunning psychological fictions.[1] Abhorring naturalism and all forms of materialist reductionism (a trend he espied everywhere), Bourget set about cataloguing the anti-idealist vices of his day as a "spiritualist psychologist"—for example, his novel *L'Étape* was an attack on the Solidarity movement. *Le Disciple* (1889) is yet another product of this monomania. It is a straightforward tale, dressed up as a first-person epistolary novel, in the service of a simple proposition: that ideas have consequences.[2]

The ideas in the occurrence are those of a philosopher, Adrien Sixte, who is the "Spencer français," modeled mostly on Ribot and Taine—the titles of the three works that Bourget has "Sixte" write are a pastiche of titles from these two: *Anatomie de la volonté*, *Théorie des passions*, and *Psychologie de Dieu* (*The Anatomy of Will*, *A Theory of the Passions*, and *The Psychology of God*).[3] Sixte is the misanthropic mouthpiece for the materialist doctrine that Bourget reduces to (for he combats reductionism through a reductive narrative mode) the following cliché: "'If we could know correctly the relative position of all the phenomena which constitute the actual universe, we could, from the present, calculate with a certainty equal to that of the astronomers the day, the hour, the minute when

England, for example, will evacuate India, or Europe will have burned her last piece of coal, or such a criminal, still unborn, will assassinate his father, or such a poem, not yet conceived, will be written."[4]

Unbeknownst to Bourget's Sixte, the young Robert Greslou has become an avid disciple and, worse, been implicated in the death of Charlotte, daughter of the Marquis de Jussat and sister of the young man entrusted to Greslou's tutelage. She had committed suicide after being seduced by Greslou, who had plotted it as one would a move in a chess match or a meteorological experiment.[5]

The point of Bourget's novel-cum-manifesto is that Sixte's teachings are responsible for Greslou's behavior.[6] Both the Marquis and Greslou summon Sixte from Paris to the judicial proceedings in Riom, and this order prompts Sixte into reexamining his relations with Greslou and the moral scope of his ideas.

Among the nugatory precepts that Sixte supposedly instilled in Greslou was a hostility to pity: "On this point he agreed with Spinoza who has written in the fourth book of the *Ethics*: 'Pity, for a wise man who lives according to reason, is bad and useless.' This Saint Lais, as he might have been called as justly as the venerable Émile Littré, hated in Christianity the excessive fondness for humanity."[7] Sixte's Spinozian animus against pity would be inconsequential if a corrosive additive that changes Greslou's behavior had not accompanied it. For Bourget, the loss of an innocent relation to "pity" leads to amoral, criminal behavior. Robert confesses by letter to Sixte that the denigration of the moral sentiment of pity and his manipulation of it in those holding naively to it were his keys to success as confidence-man and seducer:

I had copied the passage on pity which is found in your "Theory of the Passions;" you remember it, my dear master, it begins: "There is in the phenomenon of pity a physical element, and which, especially in women, is confined to the sexual emotion." It was through pity then, that I proposed to act first upon Charlotte. I would profit by the first falsehood by which I had already moved her, combining with it a succession of others, and thus make her love me by making her pity me. There was, in this use of the most respected of human sentiments for the profit of my curious fancy, something particularly contrary to the general prejudice, which flattered my pride most exquisitely.[8]

This bifurcated avowal, with its opposition between a feminine pity, linked to female sexuality, and an acknowledgment of it as a universal virtue, the "most respected of human sentiments," reflects both contemporary positions on pity and Bourget's wish to see the matter taken on faith rather than narrative exploration.

Given the thematic distribution of the story, pity is portrayed as both universal and yet more innocently embodied in the Feminine. That Bourget need not have elaborated or defended this view but rather caricatured others' attempts to theorize it testifies to his confidence in pity's lisibility as doctrine and sentiment. Bourget's is the same demotic pity to which the Goncourts knew they could appeal a quarter century earlier. For these authors, their readership, incarnating the "préjugés généraux," would unself-consciously summon up the pity tradition, from Christian *pieta* to romantic humanitarianism, and sneer at the irreverent, blasphemous travesty served up in the name of "science."[9] Bourget also saw himself, however, as the defender of a virile will and would have detected in the Goncourt's pity a "maladie de la volonté," an atonic and dysthemic sentimentalism instead of a truly "Christian" pity. In an essay on the brothers' writing, Bourget castigated the errors of mistaking will-lessness for a truly tender perspicacity: "This weakening of the will, which is the Goncourts' habitual object of study, is truly this century's malady...there is something stricken about our epoch's moral energy, the presence among many of us of a morbid element and a want of a healing element.... The more that modern man suffers from an underdeveloped will, the more he feels the intensification of indulgence for errors and for weakness."[10] Bourget argued against the Goncourts that a "mediocre will" is a fertile ground for the wrong sort of pity.

Bourget's disagreement with the Goncourts and the disarming directness of the belief in doctrinaire pity in Le Disciple both point to his deeper didactic objective: endorsement of religious modes of feeling and sociability over those explored and promoted by liberalism. Bourget fought against the disenchantment of pity, which he regarded as consonant with decadence and whose consequences he equated with moral disorder. Such disenchantment is the goal of scientism, understood caricaturally, and of the detached yet controlling dissection of the passions and extraction of pity as practiced by Greslou:

In order to draw from this pity which had been surprised rather than provoked, all the result demanded, it must first be prolonged.... I had succeeded in touching the chord of pity, I wished to touch that of sentimental emulation and that of self-love.... The germ of pity, of jealousy, and of dangerous example planted by my ruse in the soul of Charlotte must develop its action, but only after days and days, and this action would be the more irresistible as she believed me to be in love with another and that in consequence she would not think to defend herself against me.[11]

That Greslou's ruse—and subtending it, Sixte's ideas—revolves around a psychosexual view of feminine pity helps explain why Bourget wrote of Charlotte's emotional intelligence as if it would be powerless against this ploy; as the hierophant of Christian dualism, Bourget believed in the relative weakness of the spirit in its struggle against the flesh. The materialists' gravest sin in desacralizing pity consisted in their seeing it as the province of the latter, which they would then exploit rather than mitigate. The inversion and manipulation of pity's locus are Bourget's metonym for the topsy-turvy reevaluations with which liberalism and materialism (and, not incidentally, feminism) would proceed if given free rein—or if given enough "master-disciple" pairings as Sixte-Greslou.

Bourget's contrivance of pity is not naive—the polemic drives the plot—but his view of it is. Put another way, if Aristotle discerned the mechanics of pity and had a presumed psychology for it, Bourget began with the presumed psychology, precisely because it was a traditionally consecrated supposition, and then mechanically worked it into his plot.

This corresponded to Brunetière's critical method, so it is not surprising that he devoted a laudatory review to Le Disciple that trumpeted its plain message. In fact, there is no heuristic distance between fiction and its response in Brunetière's rhetorical doubling of the practical effects of "Sixte"'s supposed teachings:

In teaching him, along with Spinoza, that "pity, for a wise man who lives according to reason, is bad and useless," he simply taught him that in exempting himself from humanity, he could use others as instruments or victims of his passions. And in ridding him of remorse as "the silliest of human illusions"—Spinoza, in his *Ethics*, said something along those lines—he disposed him to all the criminal desires that can be produced by the sap of youth in a twenty year-old.[12]

Brunetière perceived no distance between philosophical teachings and fictional representations of those teachings; between pity-as-premise and pity-in-literature; between, finally, an argument and a plot.

Bourget had touched the proper didactic chord when Brunetière read *Le Disciple*'s use of pity as yet another opportunity to take up cudgels against "naturalist" literature. Brunetière's blows are obviously delivered against Zola: "It is obvious that between two beasts battling over their prey, it is brutality that will be determinant, not justice, even less so pity; but that's precisely not human."[13] By forcing a reprise of these themes, Bourget's work rigidly upheld Brunetière's doctrinaire discourse of pity:

Life is interesting because it is full of a bottomless pity.... While our realistic novels convey only the foul humor to which our novelistic fiction has reduced an informed reader, Russian observers have an opinion of Man and that belief is that we are, above all, worthy of misericord.... Sympathy, necessary to society, is not any less so to art: it becomes more so every day. Among the signs that allow us to hope that we are beginning to appreciate its value, the "Preface" of *The Disciple* and M. Paul Bourget's novel itself are not the least.[14]

Pity so permeated the literary field that a fictional use of it could be overtly rhetorical and simplistically perlocutionary. Even a critical response diametrically opposed to Brunetière's accepted the literalness of *Le Disciple*'s ideas. Fouillée, for example, took the novelist to task for misrepresenting mainstream philosophy's consensus on pity, with the Schopenhauer-Nietzsche split as his criterion: "But the philosophy of the 'disciple' and the 'master' appear to us equally belated by more than a century.... Contemporary philosophy, instead of seeing in pity, like Nietzsche, an 'illusion,' sees in it, with Schopenhauer, the primary and surest way of stripping away the illusion of a solitary and autonomous self."[15] *Le Disciple* thus succeeded in its basic narrative goal, which was no different from those of Vogüé's *Le Roman russe*, Bauër and Daudet's articles, or Bouillier's essay—to vouchsafe a pity that is didactic and doctrinaire. His pity was exceptional only in adding an extra dollop of condescension to its gendered version—an attempt at what has been labeled the "identificatory reading" expressly cognizant of a growing female readership.[16] *Le Disciple* and responses to it were also suggestive of the turf wars between philosophy and literature for the right to the *mise-en-scène* of sentiments and fundamental human values.

Octave Mirbeau's *Journal d'une femme de chambre* is marked by an animus toward Paul Bourget: not only toward Bourget's fiction, but his person and ideas, an animus that Mirbeau renders in the voice of his fictional alterego and exercise in *déclassement*, Célestine the chamber maid. Bourget is an idol of the household in which she had been employed as maid:

Monsieur Paul Bourget, the famous novelist, was the intimate friend and spiritual guide of Countess Fardin, where, last year, I was employed as a housemaid. I was always hearing it said that he was the only man who really understood women's complex nature to its very depths.... It is generally accepted that our minds are influenced by those of our employers, and that what is said in the drawing room will be repeated in the servants' hall. The only trouble was that, in the servants' hall there was no Paul Bourget capable of elucidating and resolving the feminine problems that we used to discuss there.[17]

Given the class-consciousness with which Mirbeau imbues Célestine, the idolatry of Bourget is merely a setup:

One day, however, my mistress sent me with an urgent letter for the illustrious master, and he himself brought me the reply. This emboldened me to lay before him the problem that was tormenting me; though, of course, I attributed the scabrous story to one of my friends. Monsieur Bourget asked me, "And what kind of a woman is your friend? A woman of the people? One of the poorer classes?" "A maid like myself, sir." Monsieur Bourget assumed a most superior and disdainful expression. Heavens! He certainly doesn't like poor people! "I'm not really concerned with such people," he said...."They are too small-minded, completely lacking in soul.... They do not fall within the scope of my psychology." I realized at once that, in the circles in which he moved, no one with an income of less than 100,000 francs a year was expected to have a soul.[18]

This emphasis on the gap between rhetoric and reality, between literary pity and social understanding, was the gist of both Mirbeau's broad and more pettily *ad hominem* attack on Bourget's practice. Mirbeau prefers the demotic virtue of pity to its philosophic and religious equivalents—denigrating Bourget's pretensions and social milieu as inauthentic.

Mirbeau's contestatory convocation of Bourget is issued on the grounds of class and femininity; the battle between the two men is over who can best speak for women and best plumb their pitying souls through literature. Like the Goncourt brothers' "Germinie," Mirbeau's "Célestine" is a ventriloquized version of the authors' ideal of feminine virtue and forbearance, all the more effective in that, since both are domestics, they afford the imagined connections and distancing of playing across class lines. Mirbeau, however, goes further than the Goncourts could dare to in chastising the very class basis of feminine pity: bourgeois rapacity and hypocrisy are what rouse pity in Mirbeau's *Journal*. His message is that if it were not for the Bourgets and other "masters" of the social order, pity would not be as essential a corrective as it has theretofore been. The melodrama of indignation propels the *Journal*, which then searches its equipoise in pity; indeed, part of the narrative high-wire act performed by Mirbeau, balancing his novel between bathos and acute social perception, is the delineation of a tensile dynamic between righteousness and pity.

Célestine's working and living conditions are depicted in a narrative that beckons a reader's pity. The novel, dressed down as a domestic's journal, is a scathing portrait of the cupidity, villainy, and scabrous corruption of the bourgeoisie. Put in the words of Célestine, who is portrayed as endearingly indulgent toward her "masters'" faults, Mirbeau's indictment carries the full force of sentimental and moral wrath:

Those who only see humanity from the outside, and allow themselves to be dazzled by appearances, can have no idea of how filthy and corrupt the great world, "high society," really is. It is no exaggeration to say that the main aim of its existence is to enjoy the filthiest kinds of amusement. I have had plenty of experience of the middle class, and of the nobility, and only very rarely have I seen love that was accompanied by any noble feeling or real tenderness, the kind of self-sacrifice and pity that alone make it something great and holy.[19]

Mirbeau's bilious yet tenderhearted gambit is to present Célestine as the embodiment of all the latter qualities and the social classes to which she is subservient as their antitheses. Mirbeau creates a Célestine who desires to be pitied and to pity others. He does this without making her a self-abasing or self-abnegating figure like the Goncourts' "Germinie." Like the Goncourts, Mirbeau aspires to enter the gendered transitive world of a feminine domestic so as to discover what he always expected he would find there: a piteous soul. Unlike the Goncourts, however, Mirbeau does not indulge the need for sacrificial tragedy— Mirbeau grants Célestine an abandonment of her journal at a point in her fictional life that is both fulfilled and hopeful.

Célestine's social world is neither caricaturally bleak, like Germinie's or that of Zola's novels, nor as intellectually depraved as that of Sixte's and Greslou's in Bourget. There are no obscure or self-destructive forces at work in her universe except for crass class exploitation:

No one has any idea of all the worries that servants have to put up with, nor of the monstrous way in which they are continually exploited.... Everybody lives, grows fat, and amuses himself at the expense of someone more miserable and hard-up than himself.... When all's said and done, the truth is that a girl like me is defeated even before she starts, wherever she may go and whatever she may do...poor human dung, nourishing the harvest of life and happiness for the rich to gather and use against us.[20]

But Mirbeau gives us a Célestine who is not in fact defeated in advance, for he provides her the use of pity as a sentimental tool with which she can both connect to and separate from others' weight.

Pity is Célestine's hope for escape from fatality. Without being self-pitying, she beckons others' pity: "Among so many mouths that have spoken to me, so many eyes that have tried to peer into my soul, perhaps—who can tell?—I shall one day find a friendly mouth and pitying eyes."[21] The piteous gaze of the Other would provide comfort, friendship, and affirmation. When Célestine is on the verge of destitution, pity does come to her rescue: "With all this, I don't know what would have become of me in this hellish existence at Audierne, if the Little Sisters of Poncroix, finding me intelligent and pretty, had not taken charge of me out of pity."[22]

Célestine wants to show pity for others, as a way both to connect with them and to maintain a pathos of distance. This is her reaction to her first mistress, who had a penchant for afternoon trysts and erotic self-abuse, as well as to Père Pantois, an old man who performed odd jobs for this same household. Both the downtrodden and the foppishly stupid stir her pity. When the cuckolded and cuckolding husband of the household is ambivalent about seducing Célestine, she responds: "And off I went to the linen-room, having made up my mind never to allow him the pleasure of what, without the least feeling of desire on my part, I had sometimes dreamt of giving him out of pity."[23] Here pity is an amatory proxy, substituting emotional for carnal connection. The gardener who is hired at the provincial estate from which Célestine will finally escape the world of domestic service inspires her pity in these terms: "What follows is an impersonal account of the simple, human drama, which he described to me one day, when, feeling very upset by all his misfortunes, I had been more than usually interested and pitying."[24] "Interest" and "pity:" we take an interest in pitying; we take an interest in others by pitying them; and we pity others by taking an interest in them. Moreover, the gardener's pathetic story is conveyed to us within an iterative narrative of story-within-a-journal-within-a-story; his tale is appropriated by the sympathetic imagination of Célestine, who then fulfills the same function for Mirbeau and hence for the reader.

Mirbeau's pity is not the doctrinaire pity of Bourget; rather, it is a metonym for the choices presented by social propinquity and promiscuity. The pity he gives Célestine is a finely calibrated social tool for both affective affinity and moral disdain; it is a variable and varying social quantum that allows her to meet her changing circumstances with a changing disposition. Pity is Célestine's way of both adapting and changing while protecting herself from being "defeated in advance"—depending on others' obtuseness to social and personal needs.

Most instances of pity in the *Journal* occur as an emotion of recognition in female-to-female relationships. Indeed, Célestine judges other women by their quickness to and worthiness of pity. Those who rouse pity are usually fellow domestics, and they become piteous at the hands of their employers, also female. Célestine responds to Marianne, her pathetic colleague at her last household in the provinces, with piteous sentiments: "I felt genuinely sorry for this poor woman, with her dull brain, stuffed with hazy ideas. Pathetic, unhappy creature!"[25] This declamatory and exclamatory pity turns into a more ethical trait when Célestine learns of Marianne's sexual abuse by their (male) employer: "Never again should I laugh at her, and the pity I feel for her becomes more and more a real and painful tenderness."[26] The last phrase affords us a fictional equivalent of the cognitive definition of pity as a moral and psychological good, alerting us to others' weal and woe.

The narrative dynamics and psychological permutations of Mirbeau's pity are most evident in Célestine's interaction with Louise Randon, a sad and repulsive domestic whom she meets at Mme Paulhat-Durand's, the placement agency in Paris that both exploits and furthers their livelihood. Pity is tested by Louise's unsightliness in their first encounter: "She was ugly, with that special kind of ugliness that excludes all idea of pity and arouses people to savagery, because they see in it an offense against themselves."[27] Mirbeau's pity is true to the paradoxical sense of cruelty that weakness and ugliness at first inspire and that then become the grounds for a sympathetic overcoming. For Célestine's pity both acknowledges and is transmuted by Louise's weakness and hideousness:

Though sometimes just to be like the others I joined in this savage by-play, I could not help feeling a kind of pity for her. I realized that she was one of those beings predestined to suffer, a creature who, whatever she did, wherever she went, would always find herself rejected by man and beast...for there is a certain degree of ugliness, a certain kind of physical deformity, that even animals will not tolerate.[28]

Mirbeau's pity validates its quality as an intuition that facilitates both distance and intersubjectivity. He complexifies pity's entwinement of egoism and disinterestedness—for example, when Louise, truly "defeated in advance," is rejected at a job-placement interview, Célestine comforts her with this blend of intentions: "The thought that here, at least, was someone worse off than myself!...that egoistical thought revived in my heart pity for her."[29] Recognition of Louise's plight and her ugliness, of others' cruel reactions to her, of the impossibility of finding employment and the interest this recognition takes on, involves Célestine in Louise's fate, which can be softened, if not undone, by pity.

But not all women are susceptible to pity. Louise is the victim of this dichotomizing by class of a gendered attribute, when a prospective employer sadistically humiliates her. After mercilessly dissecting Louise's appearance, the bourgeoise begins to haggle over remuneration in these terms: "'Thirty francs,' she screamed. 'But have you never looked at yourself in the glass? You must be insane! Why, nobody will employ you.... If I take you on, it will simply be out of the goodness of my heart, because I pity you. And you ask for thirty francs!'"[30] Pity manipulated for class exploitation creates a rhetorical distance that is used by the character so as to preserve the very cruelty that it supposedly overcomes, as it had done for Célestine. Later in this encounter, when the employer becomes aware of the malodorous miasma emanating from Louise's body (Mirbeau does load the dice against her), the exchange becomes an even more cruel exercise in the distortion of pity on behalf of exploitation: "'Why, you'll poison the whole house.... I couldn't bear you near me.... You ought to be only too grateful that I'm prepared to pay you ten francs.... I offer them because I pity you.... Don't you understand that it's an act of charity, that I may well be sorry for later on.'"[31] The abuse of pity makes plain its consecration in common speech; here it avows the unavowable. Mirbeau does not empty out the content of pity through this malevolent misuse; he exposes, on the contrary, the class misuse of an inherently tender sentiment. Célestine and the prospective employer represent the two poles of pity around which the fixed, pathetic point of Louise orients the reader. One is intricate and more humane; the other false and meretricious. The former is spoken of confessionally; the latter is spoken to manipulatively.

Mirbeau cannot escape the gendered attributions of pity that held sway in his culture. Nor does he fully escape the same doctrinaire use of declamatory pity for denoting his characters' sentimental qualities. Yet Mirbeau escapes the confines of the Goncourts and Bourget by conjoining pity to the limits of class and gender maltreatment—his view of the latter informed by anarchist rather than socialist leanings, which perhaps helps explain Céléstine's final escape from her milieu as well as Mirbeau's preference for subjective, autonomous values.[32] Paradoxically, Mirbeau vivifies pity by placing it in a world of simple and desiccated exploitation. He means to show up the confusion of sentiment with inhumanity that afflicts bourgeois society, and pity is a key to this enterprise—and to a parting shot at Bourget:

It was there that I met Monsieur Paul Bourget, at the height of his fame—need I say more?...He is precisely the kind of philosophizing, poeticizing, moralizing writer that suits the pretentious nullity, the intellectual snobbery, the fundamental untruth of that social stratum for whom everything is artificial: elegance, love, cooking, religious feeling, patriotism, art, charity...yes, even vice itself, which, on the pretext of literature and good manners, decks itself out in tawdry mysticism and hides behind a mask of sanctity....A world in which there is but one genuine desire...the ruthless desire for money, a desire that adds an odious and savage quality to the absurdity of these puppets.[33]

Nowhere is Mirbeau so vituperative on the facticity of sentiment and its literary pretensions than in this *ad hominem* attack on Bourget, on the very grounds of feminine *argumentum ad misericordiam* over which they contested.

Léon Bloy's entire oeuvre is a peculiar mixture of vituperation and piteous sentimentalism. His fiction is a fascinating juxtaposition of misanthropic objurgations and Catholic mysticism. He does not fight a single straw man, as does Mirbeau with Bourget; his vitriol extends to the entire unspecified range of worldly authors. Bloy's *La Femme pauvre* is similar to these two novelists' works in that it feigns to speak of a quintessentially feminine pity, and it, too, is a lachrymose tale of social hardness; yet it differs from both in lacking demotic and humanitarian elements, plainly summoning an old-Christian pity that few other novelists, even Bourget, petitioned. It is useful to study Bloy's singular novel in order to observe the secular-religious schism around the valorization of pity. Bloy's novel is, in this limited sense, the converse of Zola's *Lourdes*.

The entirety of Bloy's socioreligious repertory is disclosed by his title: *La femme*, the locus of a feminine pity with roots in Christian *pieta*; *pauvre*, the material and spiritual poverty of his *fin-de-siècle* milieu. They go together as the indispensable crucible of pity—as is indeed the point of his novel, for *La Femme pauvre* has a purpose, is no less didactic than those of his sentimentalist contemporaries, except that the didacticism here is a catechism. The catechism censures the bourgeoisie as much as it preaches old-Christian values.

To the bourgeois pity that could be implied by the expression "pauvre femme!" Bloy retorts with the sternly anti-bourgeois *La Femme pauvre*. Pity in this work partakes of the same paradox at the heart of all of Bloy's work: the piteous feel pity despite others, they pity precisely because others are pitiless. The bourgeois, since they are not poor, perforce lack pity. Bloy rejects the demotic and humanitarian pity we have seen everywhere at work at this time, for his is a metaphysical pity that overhangs the social order, rather than erupting from humanity. For him, there are social and spiritual conditions that make it impossible for some people—the well-off, diffident, and obtuse—to feel others' weal and woe. Bloy's pity is a throwback to a medieval *pieta*-pity, wholly Christian in tenor—it invokes and enacts Jesus Christ's passion.

If this-worldly engagements subtract from the capacity for pity, it is nonetheless the case that socioeconomic privation is the ground propitious to pity.

For Bloy, if only the poor and meek inherit the Kingdom of God, they also are alone in both feeling pity for others and deserving it from fellow-sufferers, from the author who fictionalizes their plight, and, it is to be hoped, a few like-minded readers. Bloy's anger at the social preconditions of pity is real—he is not a fatalist, nor does he counsel resignation. Foolish, fallen mortals have rejected Heaven on earth and are therefore berated (thus accounting for the authorial vituperation and crass vocabulary omnipresent in Bloy's fiction); the few who have not rejected and are therefore exempt from excoriation can pretend to a measure of dignity and pity—a coupling of qualities that Bloy promulgates as his distinctive version of pity: the dignified and pitying are theologically blessed and socially exceptional.

Bloy's pity-narrative is, at first sight, remarkably like that of the Goncourts and Mirbeau: Clotilde, the protagonist, is the victim of exploitative petit-bourgeois, first and foremost in the person of her mother, Mme Maréchal, of whom Clotilde lives in perpetual fear. Seconding this harpy is her common-law husband, Isidore Chapuis—"by temperament and training he belonged to that world of perfect squalid vice that is to be found nowhere but in Paris, unparalleled by the vulgar dissipation of any other nation under the sun."[34] Chapuis, a leftist former Communard, conspires with Mme Maréchal to force Clotilde as a model upon the painter Gacougnol, in order to exploit her earnings.

Like the other female victims/heroines deserving of ethical and narrative pity, Clotilde is self-effacing and tenderhearted, a character made expressly for the author's pity but, consistent with Bloy's law of inverse narrative and social proportions, not for that of her peers: "She mused, as she stared into the blackness, that it was peculiarly cruel, above all, not to have the right to weep in a wretched corner. For, even if the horror of fouling her tears had not inhibited her from shedding them now and then in the reeking filth of that pigsty, such a dismal indulgence would have been condemned out of hand as evidence of selfishness and criminal cowardice."[35] What is distinctive from the very beginning of Bloy's conception of Clotilde is that he does not assume readers' pity for her. *La Femme pauvre* is, in this sense, a hermetic novel: Bloy wants to *show* us how an author can conceive a pity-character and how certain noble religious types can pity each other. But he wants to boast this from a privileged and catechistic perspective, rather than educate the reader unto *feeling* it. Not for Bloy the intersubjective tenderness of pity.

The narrative strategy of masculine ventriloquy is central to Bloy's aesthetic of socioreligious pity. If the Goncourts, Mirbeau, and others also appropriated the supposed feminine subjectives of pity for their rhetoric, Bloy did so with a difference: he surrounds Clotilde with a coterie of males who serve to activate, absorb, and reflect her pity. Pélopidas Gacougnol, the writer Marchenoir, the poet Bohémond de L'Isle-de-France, the painters Folantin and Lazare Druide, and especially the enamel-painter Léopold are the real foci of Bloy's pity-narrative— the Josephs and apostles to Clotilde's Mary in this narrative of *pieta*.

Bloy's novel *uses* "la femme pauvre," Clotilde, in order to preach a pity of and for Christian males at a time when Catholicism was becoming increasingly feminized. A summary of the dual narrative of vitriol and dolorous compassion will bear out this interpretation of Bloy's contriving to proselytize feminine pity for and in the company of men.

Clotilde meditates her prospective fate as Gacougnol's prostitute-model with a mixture of horror and resignation and recalls the memory of a mysterious missionary who had consoled her in an earlier period of despair: "'Alas!' ran her thought. 'He would be so sorry for his child, he would save me, he *would*! But is he still alive, even?'"[36] Clotilde's only hope, as well as her only revolt against fate, is to call upon the Christian pity of past and future intercessors, not only this missionary but Jesus Christ:

She remembered a picture she had once admired in the gilder's shop, and would have loved to possess...the gentle Christ of Galilee, surrounded by His glory, as He had appeared to the Magdalene in the garden of the Resurrection, standing immobile in the light, His sorrowful countenance expressing a Divine pity, and His hands outstretched, filled with pardon, toward one of the women, quite a young girl, who had drawn away from the rest of the group, and was crawling on her knees toward Him with an imploring fervor.[37]

Mary-Magdalene, the fallen woman, prepares the Christic pity that will forever twine sexuality and pardon, feminine exploitation and pity.

At Gacougnol's studio, Clotilde cannot bring herself to disrobe; stricken and crying, she receives the same response from him as she had from the missionary in her earlier fortuitous encounter: "Gacougnol, surprised and touched, suddenly conceived the thought that his burst of laughter just now had been an accompaniment to those extraordinary tears, and, bending over the weeping girl with some emotion, said: —'My child, why are you crying?'"[38] Clotilde's hope to be released from what she perceives to be her humiliating quandary and achieve her unarticulated desire for comprehension by another sensitive being is granted through Gacougnol's capacity for pity, which surprises her and is meant to surprise the reader: "All the same, just at that moment it was uncalculating admiration and disinterested pity that were working in him."[39] Gacougnol is the first and most consequential male character to activate and reflect Clotilde's pity-character: "She was so vividly aware of the pity in this good man, blaming himself for the sake of reassuring her!"[40]

Gacougnol introduces her to like-minded male friends, who respond to her guilelessness, nobility of character, and poverty with instructive theological disquisitions on subjects such as post-Edenic nature and pity. Marchenoir, especially, is Bloy's chosen disserter on Bloian Catholicism. Having been introduced as Bloy's misericordious but vehement alter ego in the earlier *Le désespéré*, Marchenoir here has a more pedagogical, less incriminatory role. Clotilde is already a "good Christian;" but to remain a good person and to avoid society's pitfalls, she must learn of arch-Catholic ideals—and especially theological pity—from others. Bloy has her reveal this in her nightly prayers to Eve (rather than the Virgin Mary)—"cette Mère des Vivants:" "'If there is some dangerous little reptile round about me, be pitiful and warn me. Place upon its head a crown of burning coals, so that I may recognize it by the way I shall be afraid of it.'"[41] Those others who have taken pity on her are the exemplary Catholic males that Bloy recommends to our attention.

These men are artists and inspired outcasts who inescapably recall Bloy himself, especially Druide. Take, for example, Marchenoir's judgment on L'Isle-de-France: "'He is one of the innocents of Bethlehem, not properly slain by Herod's murderers,' he would tell himself; and he always found a boundless pity welling up in him afresh for that aged infant's unparalleled unhappiness."[42] This inescapably self-referential quality to *La femme pauvre* contributes to the feeling in Bloy's narrative of a hermetic quality and of preaching to the already-angry converts.

Now that Clotilde's self-effacing and tenderhearted character has received validation from her new male acquaintances—Gacougnol employs her as a live-in factotum and protégé but not as a nude model—she can afford to take pity on her erstwhile exploiters: "But for her dread of meeting her mother's horrible 'protector,' Clotilde would have been tempted to see her again, for the delightful peace that had swallowed up the memory of past tribulations inclined her to a sort of pity for her wretched mother."[43] Yet her painful journey, in which she must inspire and absorb others' pity, has only begun; indeed, the sentimental narrative takes force only after Clotilde has benefited from others' pity. Gacougnol, trying to keep Chapuis and Mme Maréchal from blackmailing him and Clotilde, is killed by Chapuis. Feeling culpabilized and alone in the world, Clotilde prays: "'Lord Jesus, have pity on me! It is written in your Book, that in your Agony you were afraid, when your soul was sick unto death, and you were afraid even to the sweating of blood.'"[44] It is Bloy's position that human and Divine pity grow from the same theological roots; those who acknowledge the latter will instantiate the former.

The paramount embodiment of Christian misericord (Bloy never employs that Latinate term—everywhere he uses the French *pitié* to denote both theological and sentimental values) is Léopold, who replaces Gacougnol's paternalistic pity with a romantic love premised on pity. Their first encounter after Gacougnol's death reveals the tenor of their subsequent marriage: "'Unhappily, I had only to look at you. And I was overwhelmed with pity, at once, and wanted to take you into my heart.'"[45] Bloy, fearing lest the reader has not grasped the Christic parallel in Clotilde's salvation by Christian male pity, drives home the point: "There was only one point, one vital, essential point, that was common to the two adventures. A man, in both cases, had taken pity on her distress."[46]

For Bloy, pity begets pity, especially in a postlapsarian world of social hardness. So it is that Léopold and Clotilde's child must die an infant, to underscore Bloy's socioreligious message. For the eleven-month-old baby boy dies from poverty, and in a larger sense, from the Fall for which poverty is a litote: "Every affliction of the body or the soul is one of the pains of Exile, and the heart-rending pity, the devastating compassion, that bend above tiny little coffins is, surely, the most powerful of all the reminders we have of that famous Banishing for which humanity without innocence has never been able to find any consolation."[47] Mortality is no less a sign of poverty by contrast to salvation than economic poverty is a sign of social cruelty in an unredeemed world. Bloy again offer us his pity-inducing socioreligious catechism in the thoughts of Clotilde: "If she roused in Him who watches the revolution of the worlds enough pity for a flood of tears to be sent to aid her, and assuage her torment, it left her dazed, stupefied, hallucinated...and the memory of that life extinguished at eleven months was so inextricably blended in her mind with the *lustral* conception of Poverty, that she would see him about her, again, *five years* old—the soul's capacity for suffering is something of which we know nothing."[48] Presumably, Bloy does, and so do those inspired by a Catholic pity.

Does Bloy therefore forswear a non-Catholic readership? Interestingly enough, given Bloy's abhorrence of Zola[49] and Zola's agnosticism, they were similar in buttressing their distinctive narrative versions of pity with a larger social and metaphysical ideology for which exploitation and bad faith, death and consolation were the central concerns. If in *La joie de vivre* and *Lourdes* Zola fought the suffering- and death-based hold of religion over pity and in *Germinal* made the reader feel the poverty in which his characters were mired, Bloy took an analogous path in order to arrive at an opposite ideological point.

After the death of their child, the cross that Léopold and Clotilde must bear is the persecution of their wicked neighbors, who try to debase them with constant rumors and harass them with the goal of driving them away. Their landlord, for example, makes ever more absurd demands of them. Bloy once again develops this narrative line as a pretext for a theological point—he includes verbatim the Gospel passage on the "Two Debtors:" "'Shouldest thou not also have had pity on thy fellow-servant, even as I had pity on thee?'"[50] The Gospel serves as a preamble to a larger socioreligious paragraph, Bloy's own catechism:

The irreligious think themselves heroes to put up a fight against the Almighty. They are proud men, some of them not inaccessible to pity, but they would weep with shame could they but see the feebleness, the poverty, the infinite desolation and destitution of Him Whom they defy and insult. For God made Himself Poor when He made Himself Man, and, in a certain sense, He is forever being crucified, forever being abandoned, and forever expiring in torments. But what are we to think of these people, here, who are incapable of pity, of shedding a tear, and who do *not* consider themselves irreligious?[51]

Human qualities are authentic only insofar as they are based on their Divine models, are patterned after the example of Jesus Christ. Here the contrast to Zola's and to the other romantic humanitarian models of the "religion of suffering humanity" is most complete. The salient quality in Bloy's anathemas and excommunications is pity—the blasphemous are not logically refractory to it and indeed could perhaps be made believers were they to extend their pity to the suffering Christ, he claims; even worse than the pridefully irreverent are the supposed believers who are nonetheless incapable of pity, which by its status in this logic becomes the cardinal theological virtue.

Bloy's pity-based theology venerates the importance of universal suffering and death, which the crucified Christ exactingly embodies. The death of their child is the trial of Léopold's and Clotilde's pity, and they pass it as true Bloian Catholics, with a wider awareness of the metaphysical and socioeconomic fatalities that does not simply single out their offspring: "Léopold and Clotilde had a great pity for those forgotten ones, but what pierced them to the heart with loving pity was the crowd of tiny graves. One must visit the great necropolises around Paris to realize how great is the slaughter of children in the shambles of poverty."[52] Just as *La femme pauvre* connotes in its title the twofold theme of femininity and poverty, "misery" for Bloy denotes both Fallen humanity and socioeconomic deprivation. An active pity is the good-faith response to both.

The sense of Bloy's title and its link to "misery" are united in the novel's conclusion. It is significant that by then he has peeled away most of the cast of supporting males; the fictional and universal *deus ex machina* of death has spared only Clotilde and Druide by the narrative's finale. Death and poverty have fired her character into that of a saintly martyr, Bloy's ideal of feminine pity: "By dint of suffering, this woman, a living and strong, courageous Christian, has learned that there is only one way of making contact with God, and that this way, for a woman especially, is Poverty. Not that facile, interesting, *accommodating* poverty, that gives alms to the hypocrisy of this world, but the difficult, revolting, scandalous poverty that must be helped with no hope of glory and that has nothing to give in return."[53] Poverty is Divine in so far as it is the means by which suffering is accepted and mastered in good faith. And "especially for woman"— poverty and suffering in a male-dominated world need a Mary, both Virgin and Magdalene, for the bearing of witness—as reflection of suffering and pity. Bloy does not solicit or condemn charity, either the charity of Evangelic virtue or the pecuniary charity that was such a hotly contested political topic in his time. Poverty is about more than the sharing of bread, which is only an external manifestation of the spiritual sharing that is vaster, more encompassing—"la pauvreté difficile." It is to this latter notion that pity, rather than charity, is correlative and a corrective.

Men spur Clotilde's actualization as noble witness of suffering and pity; but *La femme pauvre* begins and ends in her subjectivity, for it is she who must transcend the world of men and their activities (painting, writing, music, craftsmanship) for the sake of Salvation. In Bloy's narrative, there can be no pity without a commitment to the ideas of Christian theodicy; but there can be no human attentiveness to this theodicy without feminine pity.

NOTES

1. Armand E. Singer's *Paul Bourget* (Boston: Twayne, 1976) is an adequate biography and discussion of Bourget's work.

2. Following Bourget, a question for the *Agrégation de l'enseignement secondaire des jeunes filles* in 1902 asked: "Existe-t-il une responsabilité intellectuelle? Dans quelle mesure le maître est-il responsable de son disciple?" (*Revue Universitaire* [1902], 356). ["Is there such a thing as intellectual responsibility? Is a teacher liable for his disciple?"]

3. For Taine's sharp response to Bourget's appropriation of him, see *Vie et correspondance*, vol. 4 (Paris: Hachette, 1907), 287–93.

4. ["Si nous connaissions vraiment la position relative de tous les phénomènes qui constituent l'univers actuel,—nous pourrions, dès à présent, calculer avec une certitude égale à celle des astronomes le jour, l'heure, la minute où...tel criminel, encore à naître, assassinera son père, où tel poème, encore à concevoir, sera composé."] Bourget, *Le Disciple* (Paris: Editions de la Table Rond, 1994), 21–22. (Bourget, *The Disciple* [London:

T. Fisher Unwin, 1901], 32–33).

5. Bourget's novel was inspired by a real-life case in the city of Constantine (France), where in 1888 a young man by the name of Henri Chambige supposedly killed his mistress, Mlle Grille, and then harmed himself in what he claimed was a double-suicide attempt but in which he was charged with murder and with staging his own suicide attempt as an alibi. He was condemned to seven years' imprisonment and, after release, became a contributor to *La Revue blanche*.

6. Jean-Louis Fabiani places Bourget's caricature of Sixte within the context of *fin-de-siècle littérateurs'* battle against professional philosophy. See *Les philosophes de la République*, 112–13. But a contemporary actor in this debate offers a different perspective—Paul Janet, in "De la responsabilité philosophique, à propos du *Disciple*, de M. Paul Bourget," part of his lessons at the Sorbonne, lectured his students: "Philosophy is then, concerning humans, a type of abstract literature, and literature a sort of vivacious, sensitive, dynamic philosophy" (*Principes de Métaphysique et de Psychologie*, 289).

7. ["Il pensait sur ce point comme Spinoza qui a écrit dans le livre quatrième de l'*Éthique*: 'La pitié, chez un sage qui vit d'après la raison, est mauvaise et inutile.' Ce Saint Laïque, comme on l'eût appelé aussi justement que le vénérable Émile Littré, haïssait dans le Christianisme une maladie de l'humanité."] Bourget, 18 (28–29).

8. ["J'avais recopié le passage sur la pitié qui se trouve dans votre *Théorie des passions*, vous vous souvenez, mon cher maître, c'est celui qui commence: 'Il y a dans ce phénomène de la pitié un élément physique, et qui, chez les femmes particulièrement, confine à l'émotion sexuelle'....C'est par la pitié aussi que je me proposais d'agir d'abord sur Charlotte. Je voulais profiter du premier mensonge par lequel je l'avais déjà remuée, l'enlacer par une suite d'autres, et achever de me faire aimer en me faisant plaindre. Il y avait, dans cette exploitation du plus respecté des sentiments humains au profit de ma fantaisie curieuse, quelque chose de particulièrement contraire aux préjugés généraux qui flattait mon orgueil jusqu'au délice."] Bourget, 188 (187–88).

9. See Gérard Peylet, "À la limite du roman sentimentale: *Un crime d'amour* de Paul Bourget ou comment un romancier bourgeois exploite la veine du roman d'analyse," in *Le roman sentimental: actes du colloque de 14–15–16 mars 1989 à la faculté des lettres de Limoges* (Limoges: TRAMES, 1989), 143–52.

10. ["Cet affaiblissement de la volonté, habituel objet de l'étude des frères de Goncourt, c'est vraiment la maladie du siècle...il y a quelque chose d'atteint dans l'énergie morale de notre âge, la présence chez beaucoup d'entre nous d'un élément morbide et l'absence d'un élément réparateur....À mesure que l'homme moderne devient d'une volonté plus chétive, il sent croître son indulgence pour les erreurs et les fautes de la faiblesse."] Bourget, *Études et portraits*, vol. 3: *Sociologie et littérature* (Paris: Plon-Nourrit, 1906), 156, 158.

11. ["Pour tirer de cet effet de pitié, surpris plutôt que provoqué, tout le résultat demandé, il s'agissait d'abord de le prolonger....J'avais réussi à toucher en elle la corde de pitié, je voulais toucher d'un coup celle de l'émulation sentimentale et celle de l'amour-propre....Le germe de pitié, de jalousie et de dangereux exemple déposé par ma ruse dans l'âme de Charlotte devait y développer son action, mais après des jours et des jours, et cette action serait d'autant plus irrésistible que la jeune fille me croyait épris d'une autre et que par suite elle ne songeait pas à se défendre contre moi."] Bourget, *Le Disciple*, 189, 194, 200 (188, 193, 199).

12. ["En lui répétant avec Spinoza que 'la pitié chez un sage qui vit d'après la raison est mauvaise et inutile,' il lui a tout simplement appris, en s'exceptant lui-même de l'humanité, à ne se servir de ses semblables que comme des instruments ou de victimes de ses passions. Et en le débarassant enfin du remords 'comme de la plus niaise des illusions humaines,'— Spinoza, dans son *Éthique*, a dit encore quelque chose de cela,—il l'a rendu prêt à tout ce

que peuvent soulever de criminels désirs dans un jeune homme de vingt ans la fougue de l'âge."] Ferdinand Brunetière, "À Propos du *Disciple*, de M. Paul Bourget," *Revue des deux mondes* (July 1, 1889), 223. A contrasting evaluation was provided by Paul Janet in "De la responsabilité philosophique," 313–14.

13. ["Il est naturel qu'entre deux brutes acharnées sur la même proie, ce soit la brutalité qui décide, et non pas la justice, encore moins la pitié; mais précisément, cela n'est pas humain."] Brunetière, "A Propos du *Disciple*," 221.

14. ["La vie est intéressant, parce qu'elle est remplie d'une pitié sans fond....Tandis que nos romans réalistes n'expriment, en somme, que la mauvaise humeur où nos fades romans romanesques ont mis un lecteur sensé, les observateurs russes ont une opinion sur les hommes et cette opinion, c'est que nous sommes, avant tout, dignes de miséricorde....La sympathie, nécessaire à la société, ne l'est pas moins à l'art: elle le devient même chaque jour davantage. Entre autres symptômes qui donnent lieu d'espérer que l'on commence d'en sentir le prix, la *préface* du *Disciple* et le roman lui-même de M. Paul Bourget ne sont pas l'un des moindres."] Brunetière, 225–26.

15. ["Mais la philosophie du 'disciple' et celle du 'maître' nous semblent également en retard de plus d'un siècle....La philosophie actuelle...au lieu de voir dans la pitié, avec Nietzsche, une 'illusion,' la philosophie actuelle y voit, avec Schopenhauer, le premier et le plus sûr moyen de dépouiller l'illusion du moi isolé et se suffisant à lui-même."] Alfred Fouillée, *Morale des idées-forces*, 306–7.

16. See Lise Queilfelu, "Héroïne et martyre: La figure de la femme dans le roman sentimental de la fin du XIXème siècle:" "Terreur et pitié (les composantes du sublime, donc) sont les sentiments requis du lecteur dans une lecture identificatoire, de même qu'ils sont les sentiments essentiels éprouvés par les personages" (253); "Plus encore qu'à l'accroissement du lectorat féminin en cette fin-de-siècle, qui voit l'alphabétisation féminine rattraper à peu l'alphabétisation masculine, le roman sentimental de cette époque est une réponse ambiguë donnée au défi lancé par la montée, dans la société, du sujet féminin" (261).

17. ["M. Paul Bourget était l'intime ami et le guide spirituel de la comtesse Fardin, chez qui, l'année dernière, je servais comme femme de chambre. J'entendais dire toujours que lui seul connaissait, jusque dans le tréfonds, l'âme si compliqué des femmes....C'est un fait reconnu que notre esprit se modèle sur celui de nos maîtres, et ce qui se dit au salon se dit également à l'office. Le malheur était que nous n'eussions pas à l'office un Paul Bourget, capable d'élucider et de résoudre les cas de féminisme que nous y discutions."] Octave Mirbeau, *Journal d'une femme de chambre* (Paris: Bookking International, 1993), 110. (*The Diary of a Chambermaid*, Douglas Jarman, trans. [Cambridge, UK: Dedalus, 1991], 79).

18. ["Un jour, ma maîtresse m'envoya porter une lettre 'urgente,' à l'illustre maître. Ce fut lui qui me remit la réponse. Alors, je m'enhardis à lui poser la question qui me tourmentait, en mettant, toutefois, sur le compte d'une amie, cette histoire scabreuse et obscure histoire....M. Paul Bourget me demanda: 'Qu'est-ce que c'est que votre amie? Une femme du peuple? Une pauvresse, sans doute?' —'Une femme de chambre, comme moi, illustre maître.' M. Bourget eût une grimace supérieure, une moue de dédain. Ah sapristi! il n'aime pas les pauvres. —'Je ne m'occupe pas de ces âmes-là, dit-il....Ce sont de trop petits âmes....Ce ne sont même pas des âmes....Elles ne sont pas du ressort de ma psychologie'....Je compris que, dans ce milieu, on ne commence à être une âme qu'à partir de cent mille francs de rentes."] Mirbeau, 111 (79).

19. ["Ah! ceux qui ne perçoivent, des êtres humains, que l'apparence et que, seules, les formes extérieures éblouissent, ne peuvent pas se douter de ce que le beau monde, de ce que 'la haute société' est sale et pourrie....On peut dire d'elle, sans la calomnier, qu'elle ne vit que pour la basse rigolade et pour l'ordure....J'ai traversé bien des milieux bourgeois et

nobles, et il ne m'a été donné que très rarement de voir que l'amour s'y accompagnât d'un sentiment élevé, d'une tendresse profonde, d'un idéal de souffrance, de sacrifice ou de pitié, qui en font une chose grande et sainte."] Mirbeau, 131 (94).

20. ["On ne se doute pas de tous les embêtements dont sont poursuivis les domestiques, ni de l'exploitation acharnée, éternelle qui pèse sur eux….Chacun vit, s'engraisse, s'amuse de la misère d'un plus pauvre que soi….pour une fille comme je suis, le résultat est qu'elle soit vaincue d'avance, où qu'elle aille et quoi qu'elle fasse. Les pauvres sont l'engrais humain où poussent les moissons de vie, les moissons de joie que récoltent les riches, et dont ils mésusent si cruellement, contre nous."] Mirbeau, 282 (211).

21. ["Parmi tant de bouches qui m'ont parlé, parmi tant de regards qui m'ont fouillée l'âme, je trouverai, peut-être, un jour—est-ce qu'on sait?—la bouche amie et le regard pitoyable."] Mirbeau, 26 (18).

22. ["Avec tout cela, je ne sais ce que je serais devenue dans cet enfer d'Audierne, si les Petites Soeurs de Pont-Croix, me trouvant intelligente et gentille, ne m'avaient recueillie par pitié."] Mirbeau, 112 (80).

23. ["Et je me retirai, dans la lingerie, bien résolue à ne plus lui accorder jamais rien du bonheur que ma pitié, à défaut de mon désir, avait parfois rêvé de lui donner."] Mirbeau, 119 (85).

24. ["Je mets sous forme de récit impersonnel le drame si simple, si poignant qu'il me conta, un jour que, très émue par son infortune, je lui avais marqué plus d'intérêt et plus de pitié."] Mirbeau, 348 (263).

25. ["J'éprouve une vraie pitié pour cette pauvre femme dont le cerveau est si noir, dont les idées sont si obscures. Ah! Qu'elle est mélancolique et lamentable!"] Mirbeau, 306 (229).

26. ["Maintenant, je ne ris plus, je ne veux plus jamais rire de Marianne, et la pitié que j'ai d'elle devient un véritable et presque douloureux attendrissement."] Mirbeau, 307 (230).

27. ["Elle était laide de cette laideur définitive qui exclut toute idée de pitié et rend les gens féroces, parce que, véritablement, elle est une offense envers eux."] Mirbeau, 329 (248).

28. ["Bien que je me mêlasse, quelquefois, pour faire comme les autres, à ces jeux féroces, je ne pouvais me défendre, envers la petite Bretonne, d'une espèce de pitié. J'avais compris que c'était là un être prédestiné au malheur, un de ces êtres qui, quoi qu'ils fassent, où qu'ils aillent, seront éternellement repoussés des hommes, et aussi des bêtes, car il y a une certaine somme de laideur, une certaine forme d'infirmités que les bêtes elles-mêmes ne tolèrent pas."] Mirbeau, 331 (249).

29. ["Il y en avait donc de plus malheureuses que moi! Cette pensée égoïste ramena dans mon coeur la pitié évanouie."] Mirbeau, 334 (252).

30. ["'Trente francs! Mais vous ne vous êtes donc jamais regardée? C'est insensé! Comment? personne ne veut de vous...personne jamais ne voudra de vous—si je vous prends, moi, c'est parce que je suis bonne, c'est parce que, dans le fond, j'ai pitié de vous!—et vous me demandez trente francs!'"] Mirbeau, 338 (255).

31. ["'Mais vous allez empester toute ma maison, vous ne pourrez pas rester près de moi….Et ces dix francs, vous devriez m'en remercier. C'est par pitié, par charité que je vous les offre. Comment ne comprenez-vous pas que c'est une bonne oeuvre, dont je me repentirai, sans doute, comme des autres.'"] Mirbeau, 341(257).

32. See R. Carr, *Anarchism in France: The Case of Octave Mirbeau* (Manchester, UK: Manchester UP, 1977).

33. ["Là, j'ai connu M. Paul Bourget en sa gloire, c'est tout dire….Ah! c'est bien le philosophe, le poète, le moraliste qui convient à la nullité prétentieuse, au toc intellectuel, au

mensonge de cette catégorie mondaine, où tout est factice: l'élégance, l'amour, la cuisine, le sentiment religieux, le patriotisme, l'art, la charité, le vice lui-même qui, sous prétexte de politesse et de littérature, s'affuble d'oripeaux mystiques et se couvre de masques sacrés...où l'on ne trouve qu'un désir sincère: l'âpre désir de l'argent, qui ajoute au ridicule de ces fantoches quelque chose de plus odieux et de plus farouche."] Mirbeau, 391 (298).

34. ["par tempérament et par culture, il appartenait à l'élite de cette superfine crapule qui n'est observable qu'à Paris et que ne peut égaler la fripouillerie d'aucun autre peuple sublunaire."] Léon Bloy, *La Femme pauvre*, 32nd ed. (Paris: Mercure de France, 1937), 9. (*The Woman Who Was Poor*, I. J. Collins, trans. [London: Sheed and Ward, 1947], 3).

35. ["Elle songeait, en regardant les ténèbres, que c'était pourtant bien cruel de n'avoir pas même le droit de pleurer dans un misérable coin. Car, en supposant que l'horreur de salir ses larmes ne l'eût pas empêchée de les répandre quelquefois sur le fumier de cette étable à cochons, une effusion si mélancolique eût été blamée à l'instant comme une preuve d'égoisme et de lâcheté criminelle."] Bloy, 30 (29).

36. ["'Hélas!' pensait-elle, 'il aurait grande pitié de son enfant, il me sauverait, sans doute! Mais vit-il encore, seulement?'"] Bloy, 39 (40).

37. ["Elle se souvint d'une image qu'elle avait admiré autrefois....Le doux Christ galiléen environné de sa gloire, tel qu'il apparut à Madeleine au jardin de la Résurrection, se tenait immobile dans la clarté, sa Face douloureuse exprimant une pitié divine, et tendait ses mains pleines de pardon à l'une des femmes, une toute jeune fille qui s'était détachée du groupe et se traînait sur ses genoux, en l'implorant avec ferveur."] Bloy, 42 (40–41).

38. ["Gacougnol, surpris et apitoyé, fut aussitôt saisi de cette pensée que son rire de tout à l'heure avait été l'accompagnement de ces larmes extraordinaires et se penchant avec émotion sur la douloureuse: 'Mon enfant,' dit-il, 'pourquoi pleurez-vous?'"] Bloy, 49 (51).

39. ["Toutefois, en cet instant, l'admiration sans calcul et la pitié seules agissaient immédiatement sur lui."] Bloy, 50 (53).

40. ["Elle sentait si bien la pitié de ce brave homme qui s'accusait lui-même pour la rassurer."] Bloy, 51 (54).

41. ["'S'il y a quelque reptile dangereux dans mon voisinage, avertissez-moi par pitié. Mettez-lui sur la tête une couronne de charbon ardents pour que je le reconnaisse à force d'en avoir peur....M'abandonnerez-vous aujourd'hui, parce que d'autres ont eu pitié de Votre enfant?'"] Bloy, 127–28 (146).

42. ["'C'est un Innocent de Bethléem, disait-il, que les assassins d'Hérode ont mal égorgé.' Et une pitié sans bornes renaissait en lui, chaque fois, pour l'incomparable misère de ce vieil enfant."] Bloy, 162–63 (190).

43. ["Sans la crainte de rencontrer l'horrible voyou, Clotilde aurait déjà tenté de la revoir, car la paix charmante où s'engourdissait le souvenir des tribulations d'autrefois l'inclinait à une sorte de pitié pour sa misérable mère."] Bloy, 178–79 (211).

44. ["'Seigneur Jésus, ayez pitié de moi! Il est écrit dans votre Livre que vous avez eu *peur* en votre Agonie, lorsque votre âme était triste jusqu'à la mort, et que vous avez eu peur jusqu'à suer le sang.'"] Bloy, 189 (225).

45. ["'Hélas! il m'a suffi de vous regarder. Aussitôt je me suis sentie fondre de pitié et j'aurais voulu vous faire entrer dans mon coeur.'"] Bloy, 196 (233).

46. ["Un seul point, très essentiel, il est vrai, reliait les deux aventures. Dans l'une et l'autre, un homme avait eu pitié de sa détresse."] Bloy, 197 (235).

47. ["Toute affliction du corps ou de l'âme est un mal d'exil, et la pitié déchirante, la compassion dévastatrice inclinée sur les tout petits cercueils est, sans doute, ce qui rappelle avec le plus d'énergie le Bannissement célèbre dont l'humanité sans innocence n'a jamais pu se consoler."] Bloy, 225 (264).

48. ["Si elle faisait assez de pitié à Celui qui regarde tourner les mondes pour qu'un flot

de larmes vint la secourir et que le supplice diminuât, elle en demeurait étourdie, somnolente, halucinée...et le souvenir de cet être mort à onze mois se confondait tellement dans son esprit avec l'idée *lustrale* de la Pauvrété, qu'elle le revoyait auprès d'elle, âgé de *cinq* ans. On ne sait pas ce que les âmes peuvent souffrir."] Bloy, 235 (277).

49. Bloy was notoriously anti-Dreyfusard and wrote the anti-Zola screed *Je m'accuse: Pages irrespectueuses pour Émile Zola* (Paris: Editions de la Maison d'art, 1900).

50. ["'Ne te falloit-il pas aussi avoir pitié de ton compagnon en service, ainsi que j'avoye pitié de toy?'"] Bloy, 281 (333).

51. ["Les impies se croient héroïques de résister à un Tout-Puissant. Ces superbes, dont quelques-uns ne sont pas inaccessibles à la pitié, pleureraient de honte, s'ils pouvaient voir la faiblesse, la misère, la désolation infinies de Celui qu'ils bravent et qu'ils outragent. Car Dieu, qui s'est fait pauvre en se faisant homme, est, en un sens, toujours crucifié, toujours abandonné, toujours expirant dans les tortures. Mais que penser de ceux-ci qui ne connurent jamais la pitié, qui sont incapables de verser des larmes, et qui ne se croient pas impies?"] Bloy, 283–84 (336).

52. ["Léopold et Clotilde ont grande pitié de ces oubliés, mais ce qui les navre de charité, c'est la foule des petites tombes. Il faut visiter les vastes nécropoles de la banlieue de Paris pour savoir ce qu'on tue d'enfants dans les abattoirs de la misère."] Bloy, 287–88 (341).

53. ["À force de souffrir, cette chrétienne vivante et forte a deviné qu'il n'y a, surtout pour la femme, qu'un moyen d'être en contact avec Dieu et que ce moyen, tout à fait unique, c'est la Pauvreté. Non pas cette pauvreté facile, intéressante et *complice*, qui fait l'aumône à l'hypocrisie du monde, mais la pauvreté difficile, révoltante et scandaleuse, qu'il faut secourir sans aucun espoir de gloire et qui n'a rien à donner en échange."] Bloy, 298–99 (355).

Chapter 11: Moving the Past: Marcel Proust and Pierre Loti

Marcel Proust's maxim in *Le temps retrouvé*, "a work in which there are theories is like an object which still has the ticket that shows its price,"[1] would have been fittingly addressed to some of the works we have analyzed and helps define the difference between illocutionary and perlocutionary logics of appeal. Proust's milieu and literary culture overlapped with those of our other authors, yet much had changed in the three decades separating the Goncourts, Bourget, and Zola from *À la recherche du temps perdu*. Proust's magnum opus fundamentally engages questions of pity in literature as in life and does so both in response to, and as a reworking of, traditional ideas on pity. Proust succeeded in crafting a complex poetics of pity that conserved some of its traditional ethical content within an innovatory fictional setting.

One manner of understanding Proust's affiliation with pity is a grossly analogous one: he is Wagner's Parsifal to Nietzsche's Zarathustra.[2] Proust's relationship to Nietzsche and Wagner, both of whose work he knew, is a problematical one, and his novel is obviously not an embellishment of themes or ideas borrowed from either German.[3] But it may be useful to imagine Proust as committed to repositioning Nietzsche's critique of pity and its link to the aesthetic impulse in such a way as to draw nearer to Wagner. Viewed in this light, Proust would invert Zarathustra's concluding epiphany: "My suffering and my pity for suffering—what does it matter? Am I concerned with happiness? I am concerned with my work!"[4] For Proust's own epiphany is that his work is built on the pursuit of happiness and its corollaries, suffering and pity, as these are reshaped by mnemonic refluxes. Work, "mon oeuvre, cette idée du Temps," which the narrator beckons as the creative mission that will fulfill his life and draw a circle around time, is a reworking and redescription of suffering. This takes Proust down aesthetic and ethical paths that crisscross Nietzsche's and Wagner's.

Another way of appreciating Proust's contribution to the *mise-en-scène* of pity using Nietzschean terms is to understand how his masterpiece is an elaboration of, and corrective to, what Nietzsche diagnosed as one of "the Four Great Errors:"

Most of our general feelings—every kind of inhibition, pressure, tension, and explosion in the play and counterplay of our organs, and particularly the state of the *nervus sympathicus*—excite our causal instinct: we want to have a reason for feeling this way or that—for feeling bad or for feeling good. We are never satisfied merely to state the fact that we feel this way or that: we admit this fact only—become conscious of it only—when we have furnished some kind of motivation. Memory, which swings into action in such cases, unknown to us, brings up earlier states of the same kind, together with the causal interpretations associated with them—not their real causes.[5]

The motions of the Proustian consciousness move away from such causal simplifications and from memory's reductive capabilities and toward an emancipation of past and present from the tyranny of their contemporaneous meanings, by substituting an archaeological for a causal reasoning.[6] "The intermittences of the heart are related to troubles of memory," Proust wrote in the famous section that begins: "Upheaval of all my being."[7] This disturbance results from the narrator's fresh awareness of his grandmother's death, earlier, and affects "Marcel's" perception of time and others, a change of outlook to which death, suffering, and pity are inextricably linked. "Time is elastic, the passions we feel expand it, those we inspire contract it," Proust aphorized elsewhere,[8] and pity is one of the sentiments that he portrays as exercising a singular hold on time.

For Proust then, *contra* Nietzsche, a literary awareness of the work of memory and suffering can be a moral accomplishment, and reciprocally the moral awareness of pity and pathos can help readers expand their connection to the imaginary aesthetic. Proust's illocutionary poetics of pity is thus as far removed from that of the Goncourts, Bourget, and Zola as from Nietzsche's.

Pity is intrinsic to Proust's hybrid accomplishment as aesthetician and moralist. Malcolm Bowie has placed it at the heart of *À la Recherche*'s "moral architecture."[9] Bowie correctly argues, it seems to me, that:

Proust's book, in its culminating vision of the moral life, crosses the threshold that the narrator establishes for himself in his account of art and dares to re-create a sense of community and communicativeness between those who write and read and the innumerable company of those who do neither. The emotion that comes into play here is pity, and the virtue accompanying it is an unconditional and improbably versatile charity. Pity of an active and inclusive kind, and a charity that is extended disinterestedly to the living, the dead, and the unborn.[10]

One of the crucial sources Bowie cites as an inspiration for Proust is Hugo's romantic humanitarian vision of pity: "'J'avais une pitié infinie même d'êtres moins chers, mêmes d'indifférents, et de tants de destinées dont ma pensée en essayant de les comprendre avait, en somme, utilisé la souffrance, ou même seulement les ridicules'....Proust has a source here...a still abundantly flowing one in the French culture of Proust's maturity, tells us something important about the scale and the tone of these closing pages. I am referring to the Victor Hugo of *Les*

Contemplations."[11]   Proust embraced, as Bowie argues, romantic French thinking on pity and concluded *Le temps retrouvé* with a citation and explication of Hugo:

Victor Hugo says: "Il faut que l'herbe pousse et que les enfants meurent." To me it seems more correct to say that the cruel law of art is that people die and we ourselves die after exhausting every form of suffering, so that over our heads may grow the grass not of oblivion but of eternal life, the vigorous and luxuriant growth of a true work of art, and so that thither, gaily and without a thought for those who are sleeping beneath them, future generations may come to enjoy their "déjeuner sur l'herbe."[12]

Proust here marshals Hugo's support in offering another sort of response to Nietzsche's postulate of the eternal recurrence and reworks the Nietzschean image of grass as the cud of iterative bovine experience into the ground of monumental art.

But Proust's achievement does not lie in having fallen back on Hugo's sentimentalism or in rejecting some of Nietzsche's severity. For Proust, too, is a poet of hardness, an anatomist of egoism who proposes pity as a curative to the savagery of selfishness, much as manners, art, and beauty were seen as civilizing the savage breast. The "fecund" of "oeuvres fécondes" in the preceding passage is also the adjective Proust utilizes elsewhere to qualify egoism: "Every fecund altruism in nature develops along an egotistic line." It is this aspect of Proust's altruistic aesthetic—the narrative and mnemonic shifts between egoism, even a cruel egoism, and a piteous altruism ("the role of disinterested sentiment in the life of humans is greater than is believed"[13])—that partly innovates the narrative signification of pity.

This is the aspect of Proust's work of art that I wish to propose as a supplement to Bowie's insights. Proust places the self's complicated and refractory relation to time, alterity, suffering, and regret at the center of sentimental modalities, dispensing with both the selfless naïveté and temporal stasis of psychological and literary narratives of pity. "Indeed, the whole art of living is to make use of the individuals through whom we suffer as but a step enabling us to draw nearer to the divine form which they reflect and thus joyously to people our life with divinities,"[14] Proust writes, and the transmutation of suffering into idealized forms is one way of changing otherness into pity. By confronting egoism and selfless altruism in a dialectic in which temporality is the key variable, Proust gives us both the form and content of an effective literary pity.

There is no recognition in Proust of an instantaneous pity, no possibility of an undifferentiated, immediate cognition that would correspond to the contagious and irruptive feeling that philosophers and psychologists of the sentimentalist consensus took to be the essence of sentiment or emotion. Pity can present itself only as a moral cognition in two adjacent frames: one contemporaneous yet carrying with it an accumulated personal history of countervailing motives and assumptions; the other, retrospective. Since it is the task of a work of art to show the bifocal way in which these frames interact and expand our vision of fate, we understand pity necessarily as literary pity, as both retrieval and dispensation.

Proust comes close to casting this vision into literary dogma in the following passages, one relating to the act of authorship, the other to reading:

Unfortunately, I should have to struggle against that habit of putting oneself in another person's place, which, if it favors the conception of a work of art, is an obstacle to its execution.[15]

Even if this goodness, paralyzed by self-interest, is not exercised, it nonetheless exists, and any time that an egoistic motive does not keep it from doing so, for example when reading a novel or a newspaper, it expands, turns toward the weak, the righteous, the persecuted, even in the heart of one who, an assassin during the day, remains kindhearted when reading serial dramas.[16]

Throughout *À la Recherche*, he helps the reader corroborate subliminally these perceptions, rather than constantly declaiming them.

Proust presents pity as a sentiment whose full flowering requires time in both a character's life and a reader's attention; it is an instrument and reward of our emotional education, not a spur or consequence of acts. This is best exemplified by the narrator's love for his grandmother and his gratitude for her understanding of his more egotistical suffering. Throughout the work, she is the person who incarnates the highest virtues and most tender affects. Her love for him—the very selfless adoration that will be cruelly counterbalanced by love as "Swann" and "Odette," "Marcel" and "Albertine" will come to know it—creates the greatest opening up of self to another that the novel will disclose. This he learns retrospectively, realizing it through the love and pity he feels because of her: "I knew, when I was with my grandmother, that, however great the misery that there was in me, it would be received by her with a pity still more vast; that everything that was mine, my cares, my wishes, would be, in my grandmother, supported upon a desire to save and prolong my life stronger than was my own; and my thoughts were continued in her without having to undergo any deflection, since they passed from my mind into hers without change of atmosphere or of personality."[17] Pity is the indispensable faculty for surpassing solipsism. Recognizing how powerful for the narrator's sensibility is the suspicion of an irreducible subjectivity—"from ourselves comes only that which we drag forth from the obscurity which lies within us, that which to others is unknown"[18]—we can understand the importance Proust confers on pity as a counterweight in his sentimental education.

The narrator's relationship to his grandmother begets the impression that pity is the greater part of love, an impression that is reinforced by the narrator's observation on his sadomasochistic love for Albertine:

It was because I placed myself at a standpoint that was purely human, external to both of us, from which my jealous love had evaporated, that I felt for Albertine that profound pity, which would have been less profound if I had not loved her. However, in that rhythmical oscillation which leads from a declaration to a quarrel (the surest, the most effectively perilous way of forming by opposite and successive movements a knot which will not be loosened and which attaches us firmly to a person), in the midst of the movement of withdrawal which constitutes one of the two elements of the rhythm, of what use is it to analyze further the refluences of human pity, which, the opposite of love, though springing perhaps unconsciously from the same cause, in any case produce the same effect?[19]

The un-eudemonistic premise of Proust's morality is that love is always refractory to our possibilities of escape from the self, teaches us onto subjectivity, whereas pity attaches us less passionately but more effectively to others.

Proustian pity is anchored firmly to subjective feelings of pain. The education in caring that the narrator receives from his grandmother is possible because it is prompted by physical sufferings: "Sometimes I went too far; and that dear face, which was no longer able always to control its emotion as in the past, would allow an expression of pity to appear, a painful contraction...my body had wished to secure exactly the amount of pity that it deserved, and, provided that someone knew that it 'had a pain' in its right side."[20] This is generalized into a blanket assertion on the superior strength of pity and pain compared to pleasure: "For the issue is no longer of a specific pleasure—become through use, and maybe even through the mediocrity of its object, almost nil—against other, more tempting and delightful, pleasures; but between the latter and something much stronger than they, pity for suffering."[21]

The message that pain and suffering are educative, that *pathei mathos*, would not constitute an advance in literary pity if this were the gist of Proustian morality. But it is the particular education about time and others imparted by pathos that serves as the basis of Proust's ethics of pity. It is the intersubjective play of individual sufferings that creates the space for pity, which in turn facilitates the affective distances and proximities of attachment:

My thoughts kept constantly turning to the last days of my grandmother's illness, to her sufferings which I relived, intensifying them with that element, still harder to bear than even the sufferings of others, which is added to them by our pity; when we believe we are merely re-creating the grief and pain of a beloved person, our pity exaggerates them; but perhaps it is our pity that speaks true, more than the sufferers' own consciousness of their pain, they being blind to that tragedy of their existence which pity sees and deplores.[22]

This is another sort of response to Nietzsche, who judged pity as contagiously debilitating. Proust, on the contrary, sees in it an apperceptive faculty that the pitier exercises independently of the pitied. This lesson becomes axiomatic, repeated again in another tome in almost the same terms: "And yet, our pity for misfortune is perhaps not very exact, since in our imagination we recreate a whole world of grief by which the unfortunate who has to struggle against it has no time to think of being moved to self-pity."[23] The operative word in both passages is "recreate," which removes the simultaneity from pity and aligns it with the narrative mode appropriate to Proustian fiction. Pity is the pastness of the suffering that the sufferer cannot see, as grasped by the empathic mind.

The sentimental strategy of Proustian fiction is, first, to disclose the sufferings and disappointments of characters whose vanity and narcissism cannot register these as anything but momentary frustrations of their *amour-propre*; then to confront these individual mortifications so as to distill their essence from social dross; finally, to summon the sweet pathos that saves them from the comedy of social errors, which can be accomplished only in the shadows of retrospective time.

This is the sense of one of Proust's most clever and aphoristic credos on pity, in *La Prisonnière*. Guiltily acknowledging his often-preemptory treatment of the housekeeper Françoise, the narrator reflects:

With this a feeling of melancholy invaded me. We have thus in our sleep a number of Pities, like the "Pietà" of the Renaissance, but not, like them, wrought in marble, being, rather, unsubstantial. They have their purpose, however, which is to make us remember a certain outlook upon things, more tender, more human, which we are too apt to forget in the common sense, frigid, sometimes full of hostility, of the waking state. Thus I was reminded of the vow that I had made at Balbec that I would always treat Françoise with compassion.[24]

Proust's analogy reveals the linguistic link between pity and piety still preserved in the French lexicon and also discloses the hiatus between them in this temporal mode. As a motive for action, pity is inconstant, a pious wish no more effective than a *riposte d'escalier*. Both the narrator and Françoise are ensnared in a web of social plenitude whose vitality calls for hardness and error; there can be no room for evaluating hurts. Pity is not propaedeutic; rather, it is a restorative recollection.

The retrospective element in pity is nowhere more palpable than in its link to death. In the scene where Swann discloses his imminent death to Oriane, Proust takes note of the conflict between an unguarded pity and the social straitjacket that helps deny death:

Placed for the first time in her life between two duties as incompatible as getting into her carriage to go out to dinner and showing pity for a man who was about to die, she could find nothing in the code of conventions that indicated the right line to follow, and, not knowing which to choose, felt it better to make a show of not believing that the latter alternative need be seriously considered, so as to follow the first, which demanded of her at the moment less effort, and thought that the best way of settling the conflict would be to deny that any existed.[25]

The narrator, in contrast to Oriane, comes to his own sense of misericord and clement *amor fati* through the recognition of his mortality. The nearly Schopenhauerian vision of the final volume and its anxious equation of dwindling time and creativity is the setting for the affective reevaluation of the past, of which pity is one keynote.

Throughout this final volume, the narrator extends to other characters the tragic affirmation that binds pity and time. Indeed, if pity is a sentiment of retrospective cognition, impotent in the hurly-burly of worldly passions and social imperatives, it nonetheless holds sway under the sign of Death. For Proust, pity like art presents a key to the door of our life when its objects and secrets have already been gathered together in near-darkness. The will is finally able to accommodate pity by projecting itself backward across time. Not only is this a different sense of the relationship between will and pity than shared by such dissimilar figures as Bourget, Schopenhauer, Nietzsche, and Ribot, but it also offers a contrast to Nietzsche's version of a tragic affirmation: whereas Nietzsche says to death, "Was that life? Well then again!" thus inviting an eternal recurrence, Proust writes: "And once one understands that suffering is the best thing that one can hope to encounter in life, one thinks without terror, and almost as of a deliverance, of death."[26] Suffering's lessons are once and for all time, late and retrospective, redemptive and misericordious.

Proust's pity is a successful literary pity, in two senses: retrospective, it cannot be a ground of prospective action; it is the "once upon a time" of suffering. It can be connected to our moral lives only in the same way we read fiction: as a provisional unfolding in time of an achieved whole.[27] The affective content of Proust's pity is fundamentally traditional—it would confirm a contemporary's sense of it as a tender feeling of compassionate concern with others' weal and woe. But the role he assigns to pity in moral cognition goes against the grain of the practitioners of a demotic and doctrinaire pity, with their rhetorical investment in a literary pity whose emotive propaganda offered moral suasion and instruction to its readers.

It is perhaps apposite to point out here that in his youth Proust's favorite authors were Anatole France and Pierre Loti (Julien Viaud). He recognized in both a dedication to themes of nostalgic longing and remembrance, a marmoreal stance on social passions, and a high-minded moralism. Loti's dual fascination with death and pity shares much with Proust's vision in *À la recherché*. Indeed, when Proust's real-life grandmother died, he recommended to his mother that she read Loti's *Roman d'un enfant*. We will look at how Loti set out to enact a thanoptic pity in his fiction, especially in *Le livre de la pitié et de la mort*, that preserved the acknowledged affective dimensions of pity while positioning it astride an asocial subjectivity unknown to doctrinaire pity.

We should also recall that Alphonse Darlu had related Loti's work to Schopenhauerian pity: "Schopenhauer's morality of pity...we must surely acknowledge the powerful action that it has brought to bear on European thought in the last half-century.... I am not sure that our own Loti, whose most beautiful books have a taste of ash, is not indebted to him."[28] Whether Loti owed much to, or read any of, Schopenhauer is not really the question for us; rather, the link between pity and the "taste of ash" is what inscribes his fiction in *fin-de-siècle* sentimentalism and makes it relevant here.

Loti's *Le livre de la pitié et de la mort*, like Bloy's *La femme pauvre*, reveals its range by its very title: pity and death are the two covers of one book, compelling literary expression. For Loti, pity is the human response to the fact that people, animals, and places are transitory; we concede this through reason and anticipate it emotionally, and the only way we can palliate the attendant pain is through pity—self-pity and other-directed pity. Just as Proust assimilated all behavior to "habitude" and "oublie" ("habit and forgetfulness"), for Loti experience is hostage to the *oublie* anticipated in all *habitude*, including, especially, the "habitude" of cherishing loved ones: "Perhaps, mon Dieu, it is the last time the sorrow for Aunt Claire will come to me with this intensity and in the special form that brings tears. For everything in this world grows less acute; everything becomes customary and is forgotten. For a veil of mist, ashes, I know not what, is thrown as though in haste and suddenly, across our memory of beings that have returned into eternal nothingness."[29]

Death, which prompts remembrance of things past and melancholic anticipation of the annihilation of things to come, haunts Loti's imagination: "The past—all the accumulation of what has gone before us—possesses my imagination almost unceasingly…. Already there rose up in my pathway the revolting mystery of the brutal annihilation of human beings, the blind continuation of families and races."[30] In fact, Loti avows this is his governing motive as a writer: "This craving to struggle against death, besides—next to the desire of doing something of which one believes oneself capable—is the sole spiritual reason one has for writing at all."[31] This is the "taste of ash" to which Darlu referred.

This taste was part of the palate of contemporary thought, but for Loti this was not a social fact: each person had to savor it individually and privately. Loti's paradigmatic pity-sequence involves an individual (usually his alter ego) facing an animal whose suffering triggers the claustral idea of nothingness. "Une bête galeuse" is the simple anecdotal account of a cat confronting euthanasia. The narrator wants to be present at the animal's final moments, for he craves contact with the horrible mystery of Death: "The annihilation of a thinking animal, even though it be not a human being, has in it something to dumbfound us. When one thinks of it, it is always the same revolting mystery, and death besides carries with it so much majesty, that from the instant its shadow appears it has the power of giving sublimity in an unexpected, exaggerated form to the most infinitesimal scene."[32] The narrator, embarrassed by his prurient interest in the cat's death and fearing that his attempts to put it out of its misery have been motivated by an erroneous pity, confesses: "In fact, I was afraid that I had done something wrong. In this world in which we know nothing of anything, men are not allowed to even pity intelligently."[33]

The "intelligence" of pity consists in the cognition prior to feeling, an awareness based on the very self-consciousness of death particular to humans. Just as it is in Proust's work, the interstitial opening between individuals' knowledge of their situations and the sympathetic observer's position is the anoetic setting for pity. In Loti this gap is provided distinctively by the assumed difference between animal and human self-consciousness. In "Vie de deux chattes," Loti writes: "and I have perhaps felt a deeper pity for the souls of animals than for those of my brothers, because they are without speech and incapable of coming forth from their semi-night, especially when they belong to the humblest and most despised of their kind."[34] About yet another cat that has caught his fancy aboard a ship cruising in the distant waters of Asia: "And the happiness of young animals is complete, perhaps, because they have no sense of the inexorable future…. She had arrived at the port, remote and tranquil, at the last halting place in her life, and she rested herself, unconscious of the coming end."[35]

It was a characteristic trope of *fin-de-siècle* fiction to point to animals as a reminder of the distance that separates animate beings as well as the self-consciousness of time. But Loti's zoophilic pity is far from Bloy's, for example, who wrote: "When we see a beast suffering, the pity that we feel is only so keen because it impinges in us on our prescience of Redemption…since it has no hope beyond this present life, and that thus it is a terrible injustice."[36] By contrast, for

Loti the confrontation between homo sapiens sapiens and other animals, between life and death, offers no religious consolation, no theodicic revelation. The Tragedy inherent in a cat's death is a tragedy of nature, of time, played to nothing but empty space: "that cry which no longer hopes for anything, which is addressed to nobody—which is like the last grand remonstrance to Nature herself, an appeal to some unconscious spirits of pity in the air! The plants, the things, seemed to sing cruelly the triumph of their perpetual renewal, without pity for the fragile beings who heard them, already saddened by the anticipation of their inevitable end."[37] Lest Loti leave the impression that a pet's domestic nature is what brings it close to cozily anthropomorphic pity, he discloses similar feelings about a cow led to slaughter: "The cry of that ox was one of the saddest sounds that ever made me groan, and at the same time was one of the most mysterious things that I had ever heard... 'and my turn will come soon, and not another being in the world will have pity on me any more than on him!' Ah yes, I did have pity on him; I experienced a sense of pity, indeed, that was almost quixotic, and an impulse came upon me to go and take hold of his head."[38] It is the revolt against cruelty, not only of beings toward other animals but of the mercilessness of time toward Being, that inspires Loti's pity—a pantheistic pity similar to that mentioned by Mélinand in his article for the *Grande Encyclopédie,* which he considered a merit distinguishing it from other moral criteria.

Loti's pity for animals is divulged within a narrative that makes it the effect of a source both authorial and impersonal—Loti's tone of loss and sentimental rupture is not the mark of a unique persona nor specific to his alter ego; it is proposed as that of Consciousness and Conscience themselves, of sentience groping its way, with words, through loss and time—hence, the existential magnitude of language, of poesy, and of literature in making the poignant intersubjective, and hence Loti's literary mission, similar in this to the Japanese sensibility of *mono no aware,* which essayed the description of "the poignancy of things." If, for his portrayal of poignant things, Loti must still employ the word "pity," with its semasiological overload, traditional lisibility, and demotic overtones, this is not because he lacks an imaginative lexicon—it is because "pity," *la pitié* as noun and concept, is the term in the lexicon most capable of carrying this poignant charge.

The tale of poignancy that anchors *Le livre de la pitié et de la mort* is "Tante Claire nous quitte," relating the death of Loti's beloved Aunt Claire. Pity and death are here adjoined to the figure of an adored person, in keeping with traditional ideas that presupposed that people closest to one inspire the most pity. So Loti records his Aunt's last moments: "And I hear her whisper quite low, with an accent of sweet and sublime pity, 'How long! How long!' This thing, which she does not name and which we all know, is the last agony."[39] Loti crafts his account so that death speaks to us and through us in the accents of pity. The authorial reporting and the specific persona of his Aunt are synonymous with the sympathetic solidarity all beings should share in the face of oblivion.

Loti's narrative technique, with the amalgamation it brings about between a language of poignancy and a sensitive persona, operates by constituting the observant mind and language as piteous instruments communicating mortality, since these means can extend a farewell embrace to finite beings. But this technique does not create a fictional setting that is ultimately as appropriate to conveying pity as Proust's. In Loti, it is the narrative voice rather than the fictional account that helps conserve the literal innocence of traditional pity. One of Loti's contemporary critics wrote favorably of him: "it disposes him to a profound and moving pity for all who suffer from life, for all the humble souls with whom he comes into contact and which he has put into his books.... And he deserved to have written that work of poetry, of anguished tenderness, of dolorous pity and poignant sadness that is titled *An Iceland Fisherman*."[40] Yet Loti's authorially overt sensitivity short-circuits an education unto pity. Zola and Mirbeau, for example, worked by letting us imagine ourselves into characters and situations that evoked social specificity and then allow us to oscillate between anger or incomprehension and "feeling for"—since the reader begins with an affectivity that should be confirmed and indulged throughout the account. This is why, in a work titled *Le livre de la pitié et de la mort*, Loti need not have constantly made a perlocutionary appeal to those two terms—the poignancy of each narrative allows the terms to transpire.

Loti seemed to admit as much in his most autobiographical writings, *Le roman d'un enfant* and *Prime jeunesse*, where he depicted a childhood marked by nostalgic sadness, but often confesses in them that: "But I would exhaust myself in vain trying to find the words to express all that, whose vague depths escape me."[41] It was, of course, Proust's goal and great achievement to have successfully pulled off this type of endeavor. A further concrete example of this contrast would be Loti's description of the "citron-aurore," a butterfly that he first sees during a childhood summer stay in the Limoise and that will be a specimen of pride in the "museum" that he amasses of his childhood. We sense that this is for him what the "madeleine" was for Proust. Yet in describing this importance he avows: "and I well see that with all my lengthy descriptions in these dead pages, I have not been able to convey any of that."[42] If poignancy, nostalgia, and nothingness are subjects which triumph over their *mise-en-scène*, they can rarely disclose a narratively enlightening pity.

There is no social drama in Loti's illocutionary pity because pity, like death, renders all equal, and social fiction, whether that of the Goncourts, Zola, Mirbeau, or Bloy, must premise human difference. Yet Loti still achieves something of a successful literary pity, because his version of sensibility helps his readers acknowledge their own finitude and neediness and thus come to know these in others, if only as "generalized" fellow-mortals. Like Proust, Loti highlights the pastness of pity—the prospect of mortality makes of all phenomena a transitive becoming backward that casts everything into the shadows of weal and woe. In this Loti agrees with the psychosociologically affective nature of pity as depicted in Mélinand's article for the *Grande Encyclopédie*, with which we began.

Postscript: Anatole France

The other of Proust's early favorites was Anatole France (part of the composite figure of the fictional "Bergotte" in *À la Recherche*). France was that rare author, a "classic" in his own day, much as Voltaire and Hugo had been in theirs. It is significant that he, too, fastened himself to traditional pro-pity philosophy in a manner that is instructive for us, as it was for his contemporaries.

France practiced the poetics of pity in many works. But for this brief "Postscript" we concentrate on *Le Jardin d'Épicure*, a composition that draws on two literary traditions central to the *mise-en-scène* of pity: aphorisms and the morality tale. Pity had been especially pertinent to old-Christian morality tales and passion plays. This background informed how Bauër personified pity in his biographical fable of the conflict between "Pity" and "Disappointment." Anatole France similarly animated "Pity" and "Irony." This is an instructive pairing in that France approves of the one as much as the other: and so, to those who might hypothesize that the declining fortunes of pity in our century are partly due to the increase in value of the ironic sensibility, the author would not have credited this possibility in his own ethical and literary concerns. And whereas Bauër dramatizes the confrontation between Pity and Disappointment so as to emphasize what hangs in the balance of their antagonism, France dramatizes the partnership of Pity and Irony in their combat against all of life's "Disappointments:" "The more I think over human life the more I am persuaded we ought to choose Irony and Pity for its assessors and judges, as the Egyptians called upon the goddess Isis and the goddess Nephtys on behalf of their dead. Irony and Pity are both of good counsel; the first with her smiles makes life agreeable; the other sanctifies it to us with her tears."[43] Of the two vital metaphors implored as palliatives for the living, it is Pity that renders life sacred, since tears and sadness are the most elevated responses to the human mystery. More than just a panacea, pity is also a "witness" and "judge" of this mystery—it underwrites the dolent finitude of existences.

France, similarly to Proust, calls upon pity as a bulwark against time: "Time, as it flies, wounds or kills our most ardent and tenderest sentiments. It tones down admiration, robbing it of its two staple aliments—surprise and wonder; it destroys love and love's pretty follies, it shakes the foundations of faith and hope, it strips bare of blossom and leaf every growth of simple innocence. At any rate, may it leave us pity, that we be not imprisoned in old age as in a charnel-house."[44] This plea for a timeless and time-defying pity recalls Bouillier and other apostles of an apostrophized pity. France reprises the terms of these earlier deliberations and turns them into aphorisms. He accepts foremost the fundamentally pain-centered view of human consciousness and sociability. Indeed, France calls on pity as a cosmic spectator to the terrestrial drama of suffering:

No, no! Be the earth great or small, what matter is that to mankind? It is always great enough, provided it gives us a stage for suffering and for love. To suffer and to love, these are the twin sources of its inexhaustible beauty. Suffering, pain—how divine, how misunderstood! To it we owe all that is good in us, all that makes life worth living; to it we owe pity, and courage, and all the virtues. The earth is but a grain of sand in the barren infinity of worlds. Yet, if it is only on the earth creatures suffer, it is greater than all the rest of the universe put together.[45]

Anthropomorphized suffering and apostrophized pity meet in fully abundant humaneness:

It is through pity we remain truly men. Let us not change into stone like the defiers of the gods in the old myths. Let us commiserate the weak because they suffer persecution, and the fortunate of this world, because it is written: "Woe unto you that laugh." Let us choose the good part, which is to suffer with them that suffer, and let us say with lips and heart to the victims of calamity, like the good Christian to Mary, "Fac me tecum plangere,"—Make me to lament with thee![46]

France takes up again and aphoristically reenacts all the themes valued by the pro-pity tradition: the lofty moral value ("la bonne part") of cognitively feeling for the weal and woe of others; the congruence within pity of old-Christian and secular virtues; the omnipresence of suffering and the obligation to alleviate it.

France so pertinently phrased his pro-pity themes within a tradition that had become so steeped in them that the words we cited earlier became part of the education of contemporary students. For example, in 1906 students in *l'enseignement secondaire des garçons* were expected to answer the following essay question: "What thoughts are inspired in you by these words of a contemporary author: 'The more I think over human life the more I am persuaded we ought to choose Irony and Pity for its assessors and judges.... Irony and Pity are both of good counsel; the first with her smiles makes life agreeable; the other sanctifies it to us with her tears' (Anatole France, *Le Jardin d' Épicure*)."[47] In 1919, female students in the class of the "4ème année, Morale" were asked: "Comment on this thought of Anatole France: 'Suffering, pain, —how divine, how misunderstood! To it we owe all that is good in us, all that makes life worth living; to it we owe pity, and courage, and all the virtues.'"[48]

Anatole France's words thus retrace for us the typical trajectory in *fin-de-siècle* discourse from a sentimentalist pro-pity thematic, to literary narrative, aphorism and criticism, to a pedagogical pity susceptible of catechistic treatment. What changed, if anything, after 1919?

NOTES

1. ["une oeuvre où il y a des théories est comme un objet sur lequel on laisse la marque du prix."] Marcel Proust, *Le temps retrouvé* (Paris: Gallimard, 1989), 189. (Proust, *Time Regained*, Andreas Mayor, trans. [London: Chatto and Windus, 1970], 244).

2. See Jean-Jacques Nattiez, "*Parsifal* comme modèle rédempteur de l'oeuvre rédemptive," in *Proust musicien* (Paris: 1984); Margaret Mein, "Proust and Wagner," *Journal of European Studies* 19 (1989), 205–22.

3. See Paul de Man, *Allegories of Reading: Figural Language in Rousseau, Nietzsche, Rilke, and Proust* (New Haven, CT: Yale UP, 1979), who wrote: "I was struck to find many more traces of Nietzsche in Proust than assumed" (103); Edward Andrew, *The Genealogy of Values: The Aesthetic Economy of Nietzsche and Proust* (Lanham, MD: Rowman and Littlefield, 1995); Émile Bedriomo, *Proust, Wagner et la coïncidence des arts* (Paris: J.-M. Place, 1984); Duncan Large, "Proust on Nietzsche: The Question of Friendship," *Modern Language Review* 88 (July 1996), 612–25. Anne Henry has argued for the essentially Germano-romantic inspiration behind Proust's aesthetic—by way of Lachelier and Séailles, especially since in the latter's class on "Étude de la sensibilité" Proust supposedly came to his fictional vision through the influence of Schelling and Schopenhauer (See *Marcel*

Proust: Théories pour une esthétique [Paris: Klincksieck, 1983], 81).

4. Nietzsche, "Thus Spoke Zarathustra," in *The Portable Nietzsche*, 377.

5. Nietzsche, *Twilight of the Idols*, 496.

6. Proust's gloss, at the end of the novel, on the meaning of his famous episode of the madeleine is a quintessential example of this: "This explained why it was that my anxiety on the subject of my death had ceased at the moment when I had unconsciously recognized the taste of the little Madeleine, since the being which at that moment I had been was an extra-temporal being and therefore unalarmed by the vicissitudes of the future. This being had only come to me, only manifested itself outside of activity and immediate enjoyment, on those rare occasions when the miracle of an analogy had made me escape from the present. And only this being had the power to perform that task which had always defeated the efforts of my memory and my intellect, the power to make me rediscover days that were long past, the Time that was Lost" (*Time Regained*, 229).

7. ["Car aux troubles de la mémoire sont liées les intermittences du coeur"..."Bouleversement de toute ma personne."] *Sodome et Gomorrhe* (Paris: Gallimard, 1988), 152–53. On this passage and its relation to pity, see also Michel Guérin, *La Pitié*: "En ce sens, la Figure des 'intermittences du Coeur,' pourvu qu'on l'affranchisse des dîmes qu'elle paie à une psychologie datée, touche juste....Et c'est bien la géniale intuition de Proust, de manière générale, que d'avoir, non seulement exhibé le lien fatale entre les deux propositions: l'amour est en moi et du moi; il est fugitif ou jaloux—mais d'en avoir fait le ressort d'une écriture indéfinie" (*La Pitié: apologie athée de la religion chrétienne* [Arles: Actes Sud, 2000], 620).

8. Proust, *Swann's Way*, C. K. Scott Moncrieff, trans. (London: Chatto and Windus, 1925), 159.

9. Malcolm Bowie, *The Morality of Proust: An Inaugural Lecture delivered before the University of Oxford on 25 November 1993* (Oxford: Clarendon Press, 1994), 3. Bowie's premise is that "the book as a whole has an overarching moral drama as well as an elaborate and cogent plot. The book is concerned, among many other things, with the discovery and the assumption by the narrator of a morality that was not available to him at the start of the tale" (11).

10. Bowie, 20.

11. Bowie, 21.

12. ["Victor Hugo dit: 'Il faut que l'herbe pousse et que les enfants meurent.' Moi je dis que la loi cruelle de l'art est que les êtres meurent et que nous-mêmes mourions en épuisant toutes les souffrances, pour que pousse l'herbe non de l'oubli mais de la vie éternelle, l'herbe drue des oeuvres fécondes, sur laquelle les générations viendront faire gaiement, sans souci de ceux qui dorment en dessous, leur 'déjeuner sur l'herbe.'"] Proust, *Le temps retrouvé*, 343. (*Time Regained*, 459–60).

13. ["car la part des sentiments désintéressés est plus grande qu'on ne croit dans la vie des hommes."] Proust, *À l'ombre des jeunes filles en fleur*, 366.

14. ["Tout l'art de vivre, c'est de ne nous servir des personnes qui nous font souffrir que comme d'un degré permettant d'accéder à leur forme divine et de peupler ainsi joyeusement nôtre vie de divinités."] Proust, *Le temps retrouvé*, 205 (*Time Regained*, 267).

15. Proust, *Time Regained*, 387–88.

16. ["Même si cette bonté paralysée par l'intérêt, ne s'exerce pas, elle existe pourtant, et chaque fois qu'aucun mobile égoïste ne l'empêche de le faire, par exemple pendant la lecture d'un roman ou d'un journal, elle s'épanouit, se tourne, même dans le coeur de celui qui, assassin dans la vie, reste tendre comme amateur de feuilletons, vers le faible, vers le juste et le persécuté."] Proust, 290.

17. ["je savais, quand j'étais avec ma grand-mère, si grand chagrin qu'il y eût en moi,

qu'il serait reçu dans une pitié plus vaste encore; que tout ce qui était mien, mes soucis, mon vouloir, serait, en ma grand-mère, étayé sur un désir de conservation et d'accroissement de ma propre vie autrement fort que celui que j'avais moi-même; et mes pensées se prolongeaient en elle sans subir de déviation parce qu'elles passaient de mon esprit dans le sien sans changer de milieu, de personne."] Proust, *À l'ombre des jeunes filles en fleur*, 224. (Proust, *Within a Budding Grove*, C. K. Scott Moncrieff, trans. [London: Chatto and Windus, 1924], 344).

18. ["ne vient de nous-mêmes que ce que nous tirons de l'obscurité qui est en nous et que ne connaissent pas les autres."] Proust, *Le temps retrouvé*, 187 (*Time Regained*, 241).

19. Proust, *Sodom and Gomorrha*, vol. 4 (London: Chatto and Windus), 266.

20. ["Parfois j'allais trop loin; et le visage aimé qui n'était plus toujours aussi maître de ses émotions qu'autrefois, laissant paraître une expression de pitié, une contraction douloureuse...mon corps avait voulu obtenir exactement ce qu'il méritait de pitié et pourvu qu'on sût qu'il avait une douleur en son côté droit."] Proust, *À l'ombre des jeunes filles en fleur*, 69. (*Within a Budding Grove*, 96–97).

21. ["Car la question ne se pose plus entre un certain plaisir—devenu par l'usage, et peut-être par la médiocrité de l'objet, presque nul—et d'autres plaisirs, ceux-là tentants, ravissants, mais entre ces plaisirs-là et quelque chose de bien plus fort qu'eux, la pitié pour la douleur."] Proust, *La Disparue*, 60.

22. Proust, *Sodom and Gomorrha*, 201–2.

23. ["Et pourtant, de même que la pitié pour le malheur n'est peut-être pas très exacte, car par l'imagination nous recréons toute une douleur sur laquelle le malheureux, obligé de lutter contre elle, ne songe pas à s'attendrir."] Proust, *Le côté des Guermantes*, 178. (*The Guermantes Way*, C. K. Scott Moncrieff, trans. [London: Chatto and Windus, 1925], 234).

24. Proust, *La Prisonnière* (Paris: Gallimard, 1984), 220. (*The Captive*, 163).

25. ["Placée pour la première fois de sa vie entre deux devoirs aussi différents que monter dans sa voiture pour aller dîner en ville, et témoigner de la pitié à un homme qui va mourir, elle ne voyait rien dans le code des convenances qui lui indiquât la jurisprudence à suivre et ne sachant auquel donner la préférence, elle crut devoir faire semblant de ne pas croire que la seconde alternative eût à se poser, de façon à obéir à la première qui demandait en ce moment moins d'efforts, et pensa que la meilleure manière de résoudre le conflit était de le nier."] Proust, *Le côté des Guermantes*, 601. (*The Guermantes Way*, vol. 2, 392).

26. ["Et comme on comprend que la souffrance est la meilleure chose que l'on puisse rencontrer dans la vie, on pense sans effroi, presque comme à une délivrance, à la mort."] Proust, *Le temps retrouvé*, 216. (*Time Regained*, 281). On the relationship between Proust and Ribot—less obvious than Bergson's—see D. W. Alden, "Proust and Ribot," *Modern Language Notes* 58 (November 1943), 501–7.

27. See the thesis of Michael Bell in *Sentimentalism, Ethics, and the Culture of Feeling* (Hampshire, UK: Palgrave, 2000): "that fiction provides an intuitive appreciation of the ontology of feeling" (5); and "Fiction, however, has both an especially self-conscious focus on the sphere of feeling and a genetic appropriateness in presenting it. The examined life of feeling is more like a lived fiction in that its object is always mediated by imagination, conditioned by context, and modified by time" (206).

28. ["la morale de la pitié de Schopenhauer...il faut bien reconnaître l'action puissante qu'il a exercée sur la pensée européenne dans ce dernier demi-siècle....Je ne sais pas si notre Loti, dont les plus beaux livres ont un goût de cendre, ne lui doit pas quelque chose."] Alphonse Darlu, "Classification des idées morales du temps présent," 31. See also Alain Buisine, *Tombeau de Loti* (Paris: Aux amateurs de livres, 1988).

29. ["Peut-être, mon Dieu, est-ce la dernière fois que le regret de tante Claire se produira en moi avec cette intensité et sous cette forme spéciale qui amène les larmes,

puisque tout s'apaise, puisque tout devient coutume, s'oublie, et qu'il y a un voile, une brume, une cendre, je ne sais quoi, de jeté comme en hâte et tout de suite sur le souvenir des êtres qui s'en sont retournés dans l'éternel rien."] Pierre Loti, "Tante Claire nous quitte," *Le livre de la pitié et de la mort* (Joué-les-Tours: Christian Pirot, 1991), 146. (*The Book of Pity and of Death*, T. P. O'Connor, trans. [London: Cassell and Co., 1892], 233).

30. ["Le temps passé, tout l'antérieur amoncélé des durées, obsède mon imagination d'une manière presque constante....Déjà se dressait devant ma route le sombre et révoltant mystère de l'anéantissement brutal des personnalités, de la continuation aveugle des familles et des races."] Loti, "Dans le passé mort," *Le livre de la pitié et de la mort*, 98, 100. (143, 146).

31. ["Ce besoin de lutter contre la mort est d'ailleurs—après le désir de faire quelque bien si l'on s'en croit capable—la seule raison immatérielle que l'on ait d'écrire."] Loti, "Préface," 23. (8).

32. ["L'anéantissement d'une bête pensante, tout autant que celui d'un homme, a de quoi nous confondre; quand on y songe, c'est toujours le même révoltant mystère. Et la mort d'ailleurs porte en elle tant de majesté qu'elle est capable d'agrandir un instant, d'une façon inattendue, démesurée, les plus infimes petites scènes, dès que son ombre est près d'y apparaître."] Loti, 41. (36–7).

33. ["En vérité, j'avais peur de m'être égaré; dans ce monde où nous ne savons rien de rien, il ne nous est même pas permis d'avoir pitié d'une façon intelligente."] Loti, 42. (38).

34. ["Et j'ai peut-être eu plus de pitié encore pour ces âmes des bêtes que pour celles de mes frères, parce qu'elles sont sans parole et incapables de sortir de leur demi-nuit, surtout parce qu'elles sont plus humbles et plus dédaignées."] Loti, "Vie de deux chattes," 46. (51).

35. ["Et le bonheur des bêtes jeunes est complet peut-être, parce qu'elles n'ont pas comme nous l'appréhension de l'inéxorable avenir....Elle était arrivée au port lointain et tranquille, à l'étape dernière de sa vie,—et s'y reposait sans avoir conscience de la fin."] Loti, "Madame Moumoutte Chinoise," 67. (85).

36. ["Quand nous voyons une bête souffrir, la pitié que nous éprouvons n'est vive que parce qu'elle atteint en nous le pressentiment de la Délivrance...puisqu'elle ne peut espérer d'autre bien que la vie présente et qu'alors c'est une effroyable injustice."] Bloy, *La femme pauvre*, 71. (*The Woman Who Was Poor*, 79).

37. ["ce cri qui n'espère plus rien, qui ne s'adresse plus à personne, qui est comme une protestation suprême jetée à la nature elle-même, un appel à je ne sais quelles pitiés inconscientes épandues dans l'air....Les plantes, les choses, semblaient cruellement chanter le triomphe de leur recommencement perpétuel, sans pitié pour les êtres fragiles qui les écoutaient, déjà angoissés par le présage de leur irrémédiable fin."] Loti, "La Moumoutte chinoise," 85–86. (115, 117).

38. ["Oh! le cri de ce boeuf, c'est un des sons les plus lugubres qui m'aient jamais fait frémir, en même temps que c'est une des choses les plus mystérieuses que j'aie jamais entendues...'Et mon tour sera bientôt, et pas un être au monde n'aura pitié, pas plus de moi que de lui'...Oh! si, j'avais pitié! J'avais même une pitié folle en ce moment."] Loti, "Viande de boucherie," 149. (240–41).

39. ["Et je l'entends dire tout bas, avec un accent de douce et sublime pitié: 'Comme c'est long!'—Cette chose qu'elle ne nomme pas et que nous connaîtrons tous, c'est l'agonie."] Loti, "Tante Claire nous quitte," 119. (185).

40. ["elle l'incline à une profonde et touchante pitié pour tous ceux qui souffrent de la vie, pour tous ces humbles qu'il coudoie et qu'il a mis dans ses livres....Et il a mérité d'écrire ce chef-d'oeuvre de poésie, de tendresse inquiète, de douleureuse pitié et de poignante tristesse qui s'appelle *Pêcheur d'Islande*."] Victor Giraud, *Les Maîtres de l'heure: Essais d'histoire morale contemporaine*, 16.

41. ["Mais je vais m'épuiser en vain à chercher des mots pour dire tout cela, dont l'indécise profondeur m'échappe."] Loti, *Roman d'un enfant suivi par Prime jeunesse* (Paris: Gallimard, 1999), 46.

42. ["et je vois bien alors qu'avec mes longues descriptions, dans ces pages mortes, je n'ai rien su mettre de tout cela."] Loti, 182.

43. ["Plus je songe à la vie humaine, plus je crois qu'il faut lui donner pour témoins et pour juges *l'Ironie* et la *Pitié*, comme les Égyptiens appelaient sur leurs morts la déesse Iris et la déesse Nephtys. L'Ironie et la Pitié sont deux bonnes conseillères; l'une, en souriant, nous rend la vie aimable; l'autre, qui pleure, nous la rend sacrée."] Anatole France, *Le Jardin d'Épicure* 162nd ed. (Paris: Calmann-Lévy, 1926), 94-95. This volume was originally published in 1894 and included extraits from some popular articles published in journals. (*The Garden of Epicurus*, Alfred Allinson, trans. [London: John Lane, the Bodley Head: 1908], 106).

44. ["Le temps, dans sa fuite, blesse ou tue nos sentiments les plus ardents et les plus tendres. Il affaiblit l'admiration en lui ôtant ses aliments naturels: la surprise et l'étonnement; il anéantit l'amour et ses belles folies, il ébranle la foi et l'espérance, il défleurit, il effeuille toutes les innocences. Du moins, qu'il nous laisse la pitié, afin que nous ne soyons pas enfermés dans la vieillesse comme dans un sépulcre."] France, 98–99. (112).

45. ["Non! Non! Que la terre soit grande ou petite, il n'importe à l'homme. Elle est assez grande pourvu qu'on y souffre, pourvu qu'on y aime. La souffrance et l'amour, voilà les deux sources jumelles de son inépuisable beauté. La souffrance! quelle divine méconnue ! Nous lui devons tout ce qu'il y a de bon en nous, tout ce qui donne du prix à la vie; nous lui devons la pitié, nous lui devons le courage, nous lui devons toutes les vertus. La terre n'est qu'un grain de sable dans le désert infini des mondes. Mais, si l'on ne souffre que sur la terre, elle est plus grande que tout le reste du monde.'"] France, 43 (50).

46. ["C'est par la pitié qu'on demeure vraiment homme. Ne nous changeons pas en pierre comme les grandes impies des vieux mythes. Ayons pitié des faibles parce qu'ils souffrent la persécution et des heureux de ce monde parce qu'il est écrit: 'Malheur à vous qui riez!' Prenons la bonne part, qui est de souffrir avec ceux qui souffrent, et disons des lèvres et du cœur, au malheureux, comme le chrétien à Marie: 'Fac me tecum plangere.'"] France, 100. (112).

47. ["Quelles réflexions vous inspire cette pensée d'un auteur contemporain: 'Plus je songe à la vie humaine, plus je crois qu'il faut lui donner pour témoins et pour juges l'Ironie et la Pitié. L'Ironie et la Pitié sont deux bonnes conseillères: l'une, en souriant, nous rend la vie aimable; l'autre, qui pleure, nous la rend sacrée.'"] *Revue Universitaire* (1906:1), 179.

48. ["Commentez cette pensée d'Anatole France: 'La souffrance, quelle divine méconnue! Nous lui devons tout ce qu'il y a de bon en nous, tout ce qui donne du prix à la vie; nous lui devons la *pitié*, nous lui devons le courage, nous lui devons toutes les vertus.'"] *Revue Universitaire* (1919:1), 320.

Conclusion

This book first surveyed the philosophy of sentimentalism in the eighteenth and early nineteenth centuries and then analyzed and argued for its rehabilitation during the end of the nineteenth century, especially as this was connected with the probing and promotion of pity as a sentiment of a cognitive origin and moral destination. In order to bring to a fuller conclusion this examination, we would need to learn about the aftermath of a renascent sentimentalism and its pro-pity rhetoric: whither pity in the twentieth century and this *fin-de-siècle*? We would also have to cast a comparative glance at other national traditions and schools of thought in order to determine how much of the story we told was a synchronic expression of cross-cultural discursive consensus and how much was due to a specific *francité*. Moreover, we would need to give an incisive look at other sentiments and emotives—love, mercy, anger, vengeance, honor, shame, guilt, and gratitude, for example—to ascertain whether we could detect for any of them a prominence similar to that of pity within the frameworks of the sentiment-reason divide, literary strategies and debates, and social pacification. Any of these three inquiries would require at least a self-standing tome, as well as a methodology and command of materials that are beyond my resources here. But I can point to a few topics and sources briefly, in the hope of contributing to these larger projects.

It is apparent, for example, that pity as a rhetorical *enjeu* did not completely collapse with the political and military catastrophes of the twentieth century. For example, in the midst of World War I the sentiment was invoked as an ideal response to soldiers' hardship, if a lesson in 1916 for the *classes de l'enseignement secondaire des jeunes filles* is any indication: "You will have attended a military review for the distribution of decorations to various heroes of the war, among whom there are several gravely wounded and disfigured. Express the sentiments of admiration, pity, and appreciation that you would take away with you from this ceremony."[1] We would need to know how much the century's subsequently bigger and more ideological disfigurations affected the valuation of pity; and how much the dispersion of pedagogical sites of certified rhetoric, the mandated literary and philosophical syllabi, may have hidden or help expose the evidence of such an outcome. Moreover, we would have to confront the promoters of pity to ideological movements in the *fin-de-siècle* fixated on the supposed threats of decadence, deracination, and de-natality.

The lexicographical evidence substantiates some continuity. The pejorative sense of "pity" is not as widespread in French as it is in English. Georges Matoré's *Dictionnaire du vocabulaire essentiel (les 5,000 mots fondamentaux)* lists *pitié* as one of the 5,000 "essential" words of French vocabulary and defines it as "a sentiment that arouses us to become interested in the weal and woe of others."[2] Yvette Yannick Mathieu's *Les verbes de sentiment: de l'analyse linguistique au traitement automatique* also lists "pity" as a "nom de sentiment" that subsumes: "to soften; commiserate; touch; relent; penetrate; bend."[3]

In contemporary French philosophical thought, pity has attracted attention mostly in reference to its *loci classicus*—especially Rousseau. One example is Jacques Derrida's sensitive deconstruction of Rousseau's explanation of pity's representative capacities, which is an intriguing rendezvous with the pity tradition.[4] Another is Claude Lévi-Strauss' valedictory to Rousseau as the "founder of the sciences of Man"[5] as well as his discussion of the structural implications of Rousseauian pity in "Totemism from Within," which places pity at the interior of the totemic relationship.[6] In these examples, exceptional and iconoclastic, pity has become a historical artifact, a concept deposited within a precise epoch alongside its unique protagonist. If the rendezvous with Rousseau attests to a sense of continuity, it also is evidence of a certain mustiness in the pity tradition.

A recent exception that proves the rule is Michel Guérin's *La Pitié: apologie athée de la religion chrétienne*. It, too, is highly indebted to the *loci classicus* to which *fin-de-siècle* theorists also referred: Descartes,[7] Pascal, Rousseau,[8] Tocqueville,[9] Nietzsche, and Schopenhauer.[10] Guérin does interject Pierre Janet and Freud into his discussion, as those of the *fin-de-siècle* did not or could not do. He also explicitly argues against making pity synonymous with compassion or other altruistic sentiments: "And if compassion (one would say today 'humanitarianism') stands for pity, it is doubtlessly as its shadow, as marker more of absence than of presence…. For the scandal of pity is that it has nothing to do with what is called altruism: this sensibility, as we have seen, verticalizes itself—its abyss is not a knowledge—whereas sentiments horizontalize themselves (addressing themselves to, representing themselves as, exchanging)."[11]

As an example of a postphenomenological philosophy Guérin, following Michel de Certeau's *L'Écriture de l'histoire*,[12] calls "Figurologie"—"as a first intuition, we would say that pity is that which is *Without-Fear*. This book seeks to conjure up this Figure"[13]—his work endeavors to reinvigorate thinking on pity, even if *La Pitié* lacks sociological and historical context and often engages in clever wordplay in lieu of explication. But unlike writings of the earlier pity tradition, Guérin's book undertakes to bring together Christian (*apologia*) and secular ("atheist") conceptions of pity: "If pity is not just a form of altruism, but a generous invention of human sensibility, we must deduce that it is the other form of love. So how not to credit Christianity with the comprehension of this *agapè* or this *caritas*?"[14] Guérin's book especially represents a different approach by embracing a cognitive theory of sentiment that conspicuously excludes pity as the one exceptional sentiment. Indeed, for Guérin the singularity of the Figure of Pity consists in that it is not founded on cognition: "Pity is decidedly a singular sentiment: unique in its genre, in the world, it is the *Without-Fear*.... pity is unique because it alone does not play the game of substitution, has no place in the commonplaces (the treatises) of the passions, places itself right away *beyond belief*."[15] This entails, according to Guérin and *contra* the pity tradition, that it is not a pro-social virtue: "Let us keep in mind these two chief intuitions: a. pity belongs to a body; b. it is not a form of exchange: I would want said of it that it is 'ethical,' even 'political,' but never 'social.'"[16]

The definition of *Pitié* that Guérin offers is phenomenological and yet still partial to the traditions of Rousseau and Schopenhauer: "Pity undifferentiates the self.... Pity is not a sentiment for another; it is sensibility without an 'Other.' The Without-Fear. Or rather: pity is a sentiment that cannot be a sentiment.... Pity has no space, because it is itself a space. Pity must first know (inopportune) woes before actually seeing actual suffering."[17] Guérin's alignment with Schopenhauer and Rousseau is frankly declared:

We assert with Schopenhauer: all love is pity. Let us rather ask: how does the "demon" of pity differ from the "demon" of love.... Thus our hypothesis, shored by our reading of Rousseau: whereas the sentiments of the various Treatises are representational evolutions of emotion, or rather, of Love-Fear, pity "revolutionizes" feeling, turns it around completely, translates/overturns unrefined emotion (by which a living person becomes "hypermetrically" consonant with his being) into sensibility.... The paradox of pity, signaled by Rousseau and Schopenhauer, is that the most comparative (and thus most reflexive) of affects turns into the routing of all representation (or mediation).[18]

Guérin repeats this theme in a conclusion that also returns to the distinctiveness of pity as opposed to compassion:

Pity, despite ill-considered assimilations, is not synonymous with compassion (mitfühlen) nor with empathy (sich einfühlen), both of which are attitudes that remain "sentimental" and, all things considered, imaginary...."Feeling with" even appears to be, under a certain point of view, the opposite of compassion, if the latter views itself as identically reconstituting in a person the passion (suffering) experienced by another. Compassion, which implies sociability and belief, belongs to the domain of sentiments; pity merges into the pure sensibility of "feeling with," free of all fear.... Pity does not know any individuality and chooses silence...because the proximus is not the person I come up against, nor that whom I address, but rather the being that "a-stounds" me for as long as I can recall.[19]

Guérin's book thus prolongs the enthrallment of pity in philosophical thinking that has been scrutinized in this book, as well as the hold of Rousseau and Schopenhauer over this engagement, at the same time that it outstrips this thought by insisting on the radical uniqueness of pity. The question remains, of course, as to the representativity of Guérin or *La Pitié* of a wider movement in the contemporary French philosophy of emotions and in ethics. Not very, I believe.[20]

Literary expressions of pity in the course of the twentieth century similarly seemed to be marked by continuity and change. The tension between an illocutionary and perlocutionary rhetoric of appeal has persisted. Given the transformation of literary genres and tastes at the same time as a literary *francité* has perdured,[21] reiterations of the debates and narratives of the *fin-de-siècle* in different forms could probably be identified.[22] Two examples of this continuity within change that may be representative of the larger literary field are Jean Giono's *Solitude de la Pitié* and Camus' *La Peste*.

Giono's collection of stories is an exemplar of nondoctrinaire literary pity of the twentieth century. In these tales, pity is solitary, not social; a quality in need of solitude for its flowering and expression, not—*contra* most *fin-de-siècle* narratives—the social turmoil of inequality and propinquity. Guérin glossed Giono's sense of pity: "Giono shows us two poles of human solitude: sedentary egoism, 'normal' and rendered stupid by custom; the almost irrationally incessant solicitude of the hobo who, by himself, is nothing and has nothing, but continues on his way while lugging behind him the sickly man.... Not only has [pity] no need of words, but also it secretly knows that its wave breaks against its reefs. Pity is alone because it is aphasic."[23]

Guérin's line of reasoning here may apply only to the first, eponymous story in the collection, in which two nameless characters—*le gros* and *le maigre* (the big and skinny ones) —in search of handiwork in order to survive, arrive at a parish. The priest, a supercilious and solitary man, offers them the chance to clean out the well, a job he knows is at best useless, at worst lethal. The *gros*, against odds and with great difficulty, succeeds in reattaching a rope to the source and is remunerated meagerly, a sum he must share with the unhelpful and helpless *maigre*: "A cold and tenacious rain continued to fall. Under the lamplight, the man opened his hand. There were ten *sous*. The others' blue eyes glanced at the small coin and the hand completely muckled by scratches and mud—'You'll tire yourself out,' he says, 'I am a fetters to you, I who am sick. You'll get too tired, just leave me behind.'—'No, said the big one, come.'"[24] This is a *mise-en-scène* evocative of fellow feeling in its characters, despite the absence of any altruistic vocabulary in the entire narrative—or precisely because of the word "pity" in the title.

Yet Giono's pity "has no need of words" not because it is "aphasic," but because, like Loti's, it appears as a subjective and pantheistic quality, transcending humans and society, turned equally toward animals and nature. For example, in "Prélude de Pan," "Pan," the pagan personification of nature, responds to human cruelty to animals through a stern pity. In a visit to a pub, "Pan" encounters a dove whose pitiless owner has broken its wing to subdue it and to which he responds with pity: "He cast looks that were rivers of pity and pain."[25] Angrily, "Pan" commands the owner:

"Let go of that creature." The dove was also moved by that voice. And that voice must have been a ray of hope for it....."I'll keep her," said the man (Pan). "She is mine. By what right have you taken her, have you broken her? By what right have you, the strong, the solid one, have you crushed that gray creature? Tell me! It has blood, just like you; it has blood of the same color and it has the same right to the sun, the wind, as you do. You have no more rights than the creature."[26]

"Pan" captures the dove, and everyone is forced into dancing a bacchanalic Panic, as punishment and release.

But in "La Grande Barrière," Giono lamented the "barrier" of fellow-feeling separating humans and animals. In this lovely tale of nature's cruelties and little mercies, a rook attacks a doe hare and her newborns, consuming the baby rabbits and ripping at the mother. The author's persona responds to her suffering: "On my knees next to her, I softly caressed her thick fur, burning with fever, and especially there, at the nape of her neck, where caresses are sweeter. The only thing I could give was pity; that was the only thing to do: pity, a Heart full of pity, to soften, ease, to say to the animal: 'No, you see, someone suffers by your suffering, you are not alone. I cannot heal you, but I can stay by your side.'"[27] But Giono/the narrator realizes, in the fissure between feeling and reflection, that the doe hare, in contrast to the dove, cannot acknowledge his fellow-feeling: "But it was not comfort I had brought there, next to that death-struggle, but terror, a terror so great that it was henceforth useless to moan or to call for help. The only thing to do was to die. As a human I had killed all hope. The creature was dying out of fear for my uncomprehending pity; my caressing hand was crueler than the rook's beak. A great barrier separated us."[28] Pity thus becomes the quality that best invokes the regret over nature's refusal of a sentimentally pellucid pantheism: "I who am just as much an animal among them all, by the great weight of those hills, those juniper trees, thyme, wild air, herbs, sky, wind, rain, that is in me; I, who have more pity for those animals than for humans, if there is anyone for whom this great barrier should fall.... But no, it is there. It has taken centuries of accumulated wickedness to render it as solid as it now is."[29] Giono's mix of perlocutionary and illocutionary uses of pity in order to dramatize the human presence and perplex in nature is thus similar in many respects to that of Loti.

Camus' work is more representative of a strictly illocutionary and social appeal to pity as fellow feeling. In some suggestive respects, Camus is the heir to the Durkheimian mentality, with its implied ideal of a sustaining collective moral community from which to draw upon and justify the meaning of our acts and the resulting alienation or *anomie* when this is no longer possible. *La Peste*, the fablelike story of Dr. Rieux's battle against a mysterious plague in Oran, Algeria, is paradigmatic of Camus' understated and illocutionary insistence on the need for moral recognition of others' weal and woe. Camus is aware of the limits of perlocutionary pity: "Once the epidemic was diagnosed, the patient had to be evacuated forthwith. Then indeed began 'abstraction' and a tussle with the family who knew they would not see the sick man again until he was dead or cured. 'Have some pity, doctor!' It was Mme. Loret, mother of the chambermaid at Tarrou's hotel, who made the appeal. An unnecessary appeal; of course he had pity. But what purpose could it serve? He *had* to telephone, and soon the ambulance could be heard clanging down the street."[30] But the moral universe of Camus's fiction cannot dispense with a comprehensive sense of fellow-feeling, even, at times, an apostrophized pity: "Oh! It is all too true that humans cannot do without each other, that he was as needy as all the unfortunate, and that he warranted the same quiver of pity that he allowed to expand in him whenever he left one of them."[31] By the end of this harrowing tale of the limits of human endurance in the face of the unknown and the inhuman, Camus presents us with a Dr. Rieux and the soon-to-die Tarrou having learned the particular lesson of sympathetic solidarity with the deprived and the suffering: "'That's why I decide to take, in every predicament, the victim's side—so as to reduce the damage done. Amongst them I can at least try to discover how one attains to the third category; in other words, to peace.' Tarrou was swinging his leg, tapping the terrace lightly with his heel, as he concluded. After a short silence the doctor raised himself a little in his chair and asked if Tarrou had an idea of the path to follow for attaining peace. 'Yes,' he replied. 'The path of sympathy.'"[32]

So pity has not vanished, whether as a moral sentiment studied and disputed by philosophers and other thinkers or as a guiding narrative trope. But this continuity should not occlude from us a capital dissimilarity from the tradition I have portrayed: the earlier writers organized themselves self-consciously around a project of promoting a pro-social virtue, marveling at, capitalizing on, or striving against the renewed attention to sentiments. What they may share is a sort of rhetorical futility: how much were the theorizing and fictional *mise-en-scène* of pity able to persuade social actors to a greater concern with others' weal and woe? This book has established the rhetorical *desiderata*; a causal link to actuality, to effective reality, remains to be determined. Since renewed attention to pity has been the province of English-language philosophy, psychology, and cultural studies for the past few decades, while the lexicon remains obstinately ambiguous on the value of pity, perhaps we can keep a closer eye on the socio-emotional community comprising our present ambit.

NOTES

1. ["Vous avez pu assister à une prise d'armes pour la remise de décorations à divers héros de la guerre dont plusieurs grièvement blessés et mutilés. Dites les sentiments d'admiration, de pitié, et de reconnaissance que vous emportez de cette cérémonie."] *Revue Universitaire* (1916:1), 159.

2. ["sentiment qui pousse à s'intéresser aux malheurs des autres."] Georges Matoré, *Dictionnaire du vocabulaire essentiel (les 5,000 mots fondamentaux)* (Paris: Librairie Larousse, 1963), 240.

3. ["amadouer; apitoyer; attendrir; désarmer; entamer; fléchir."] Yvette Yannick Mathieus, *Les verbes de sentiment: de l'analyse linguistique au traitement* (Paris: CNRS Editions, 2000), 152, 179.

4. Jacques Derrida, *Of Grammatology*, Gayatri Chakravorty-Spivak, trans. (Baltimore and London: Johns Hopkins UP, 1976). In a chapter on the relationship between Rousseau's *Second Discourse* and *Essay on the Origin on Language* entitled "The Present Debate: The Economy of Pity," Derrida writes: "Pity is a voice. As opposed to writing,

which is *without pity*, the voice is always, in its essence, the passage of virtue and good passion....One might then say that the natural law, the gentle voice of pity, is not only uttered by a maternal solicitude, it is inscribed in our hearts by God. It concerns the natural writing, the writing of the heart, which Rousseau opposes to the writing of reason. Only the latter is without pity, it alone transgresses the interdict that, under the name of natural affection, links the child to the mother and protects life from death. To transgress the law and the voice of pity is to replace natural affection by perverse passion" (173–74). Derrida also analyzes how Rousseau relates pity to death as a representative capacity: "For him, pity never stops being a natural sentiment or an inner virtue that only imagination has the power to awaken or reveal. Let us note in passing that Rousseau's entire theory of the theater also establishes a connection, within representation, between the power of identification—pity—and the faculty of the imagination. If now it is remembered that Rousseau gives the name terror to the fear of death (*Discourse*), one perceives together the entire system which organizes the concepts of terror and pity on the one hand, and of the tragic scene, representation, the imagination, and death, on the other" (184–85).

5. Claude Lévi-Strauss, *Structural Anthropology*, vol. 2, Monique Layton, trans. (New York: Basic Books, 1976). In the chapter on "Jean-Jacques Rousseau, Founder of the Sciences of Man," Lévi-Strauss situated Rousseauian pity at the junction of social-science epistemology: "But its discovery [respect for others] forces him to see an equal in any being exposed to suffering and, by the same token, indefeasibly entitled to pity. The only hope, for each of us not to be treated as an animal by his fellow men, is that all his fellow men (and himself first) feel themselves immediately as suffering beings. Thus they cultivate inwardly this aptitude for pity which, in nature, takes the place of 'laws, customs, and virtue,' and without whose exercise we realize that there can be neither laws, customs, nor virtues" (41).

6. In *Totemism* (Rodney Needham, trans. [Boston: Beacon Press, 1963]), Lévi-Strauss located pity at the interior of the totemic relationship: "Rousseau's answer consists in defining the natural condition of man, while still retaining the distinctions, by the only psychic state of which the content is indissociably both affective and intellectual, and which the act of consciousness suffices to transfer from one level to the other, viz., pity, or, as Rousseau also writes, identification with one another, the duality of terms corresponding, up to a certain point, to the above duality of aspect. It is because man originally felt himself identical to all those like him (among which, as Rousseau explicitly says, we must include animals) that he came to acquire the capacity to distinguish himself as he distinguishes *them*, i.e., to use the diversity of species as conceptual support for social differentiation."

7. ["De m'être recommandé de Descartes ne m'empêchera pas de lui fausser compagnie pour essayer un autre dénombrement des passions primitives. Il se trouve qu'elles sont encore six: l'amour, la peur, la joie, la tristesse, la mélancholie, la pitié."] ("Having referred to Descartes does not prevent me from parting ways with him in order to attempt a different enumeration of the basic passions. In this one, there are still six: love, fear, joy, sadness, melancholy, pity.") Guérin, *La Pitié: apologie athée de la religion chrétienne*, 65.

8. ["Telle est, pour Rousseau, l'expérience de la pitié; elle suppose une spiritualité dégagée de toute intellectualité....Ainsi s'éclairit la définition que Rousseau propose de la pitié: 'se sentir dans ses semblables.' La pitié est une double trans-position du 'composé' humain: transport de notre sensibilité, transport 'hors de nous,' autrement dit identification avec 'l'animal souffrant'....*La pitié, qui se place au degré le plus élevé de la sensibilité, soit la bonté ou l'humanité, se fonde radicalement dans l'amour de soi ani-*

mal, en tant qu'il enveloppe le couple indéfectible du plaisir et de la douleur....savoir que l'amour de soi est toujours *en acte*, tandis que la pitié, faute que soient réunies les circonstances qui favorisent son éveil, demeure lettre morte, étouffée dans l'oeuf; de là l'importance qu'elle revêt pour l'*éducation*, dont le propos est de guider 'naturellement' le jeune homme en lui faisant, pour ainsi parler, escalader les reliefs de la condition humaine: du *nécessaire* à l'*utile* et puis au *bon*. Or, le seuil de la *pitié* est la pierre de touche et la fin de l'éducation."] Guérin, 182, 183, 186, 189 ("Such is, for Rousseau, the experience of pity, which supposes a spirituality removed from all intellectuality....Thus is clarified Rousseau's definition of pity: 'to feel oneself in our fellow humans.' Pity is a double trans-position of the human 'composite': transfer of our sensibility, transfer 'outside of ourselves,' or put another way, with 'the suffering animal'....*Pity, which places itself at the highest degree of sensibility, meaning goodness or humanity, dissolves itself radically in creaturely self-love in as much as it wraps together the indestructible couple, pleasure and pain*....knowing that self-love is always at work whereas pity, lacking the circumstances favoring its arousal, remains a dead letter, still-born; thus arises the importance of education, whose purpose is to lead the young man 'according to nature,' by making him, so to speak, climb the outcroppings of the human condition: from the *necessary* to the *useful* and then to the *good*. The threshold of pity is the touchstone and goal of education.")

9. ["Tocqueville, à la différence de Rousseau, réduit pour ainsi dire à rien l'écart entre la nature du sentiment et sa condition d'exercice....Or, si nous ne nous trompons pas, 'l'*éthos*' démocratique comme *éthique du semblable* est, dans les textes tocquevilliens, polarisé par deux sentiments: l'ambition et la pitié. À première vue, la pitié obéit à une motivation inverse, qui tend à résorber la différence entre moi et mes semblables, entre un peuple et les gens....J'ai extrapolé d'un Tocqueville constatatif à une Hannah Arendt polémique pour mobiliser, l'une contre l'autre, deux figures sociales de la pitié: la première, modeste, s'économise en se politisant; la seconde prétend changer radicalement la politique."] Guérin, 163, 164, 167. ("Tocqueville, as opposed to Rousseau, reduces to almost nothing, so to speak, the gap between the nature of sentiment and the conditions of its performance....But if we are not mistaken, the democratic '*ethos*' like the *morality of the other* is, in Tocquevillian texts, split into two sentiments: ambition and pity. Pity seems to obey a contrary impulse, which tends to reduce the difference between me and others, between peoples and nations....I have extrapolated from a Tocqueville who establishes facts to an Arendt who polemicizes in order to put into play against each other two social Figures of pity: the first, modest, conserves itself in becoming political; the second claims to radically alter politics.")

10. ["'En Italien, remarque Schopenhauer, la pitié et la tendresse pure ont le même nom, pieta.' Alors que l'homme infecté de remords continue de haïr l'autre *dans sa propre personne*, le véritable amour—*agapè, caritas*, pitié—est libéré du joug du vouloir: il est touché par toute souffrance parce qu'il n'est pas attaché à la sienne."] ("'In Italian,' comments Schopenhauer, 'pity and pure tenderness share the same name, pieta.' Whereas the man infected by guilt continues to hate the Other *in his own person*, real love—*agapè, caritas*, pitié—is freed from the yoke of Will: it is moved by all suffering because it is not fixed on its own.") Guérin, 281.

11. ["Et si la compassion (on dirait aujourd'hui 'l'humanitaire') figure la pitié, c'est sans doute d'en être l'ombre, de porter absence plus que présence....Car le scandale de la pitié, c'est qu'elle n'a rien à voir avec ce qu'on appelle l'altruisme: la sensibilité, on l'a déjà dit, se verticalise—son abîme n'étant savoir—au lieu que les sentiments s'horizontalisent (s'adressant, se représentant, s'échangeant."] Guérin, 9, 226.

12. See Michel de Certeau, *The Writing of History*, trans. Tom Conley (New York:

Columbia UP, 1988).

13. ["En première intuition, la pitié, c'est le *Sans-peur*. Ce livre cherche à en forger la Figure."] Guérin, 13.

14. ["Si la pitié n'est pas un altruisme, mais l'invention généreuse de la sensibilité, force est d'en conclure qu'elle est l'autre forme de l'amour. Et comment ne pas porter au crédit du christianisme l'intelligence de cette *agapè* ou de cette *caritas*?"] Guérin, 229.

15. ["La pitié est décidément un sentiment *singulier*: seul dans son genre, seul au monde, c'est *le Sans-peur*....La pitié est seule parce qu'elle ne joue pas le jeu des échanges, n'a pas de place dans la topique (le traité) des passions, se met d'emblée *hors croyance*."] Guérin, 158, 160.

16. ["Gardons présentes à notre esprit ces deux intuitions majeures: a. la pitié fait masse avec un corps; b. elle ne s'échange pas: je veux bien qu'on la puisse dire 'éthique,' voire 'politique,' mais non pas 'sociale.'"] Guérin, 171.

17. ["La pitié indifférencie le moi....La pitié n'est pas un sentiment pour l'autre, c'est une sensibilité sans Autre. Le Sans-peur. Ou plutôt: la pitié est un sentiment qui ne peut pas être un sentiment....La pitié n'a pas d'espace, parce qu'elle est espace....La pitié...il faut qu'elle sache la misère (intempestive) avant de voir la souffrance actuelle."] Guérin, 201, 205, 206, 209.

18. ["Nous affirmons avec Schopenhauer: tout amour est pitié. Demandons plutôt: en quoi le démon de la pitié diffère-t-il du démon de l'amour?....De là notre hypothèse, étayée par la lecture de Rousseau: alors que les sentiments du Traité sont des développements représentationnels de l'émotion, autrement dit de l'amour-peur, la pitié 'révolutionne' le sentir, le retourne complètement, elle qui traduit/renverse l'émoi brut (par quoi un vivant d'abord coincide 'hypermétriquement' avec son être) en sensibilité....Le paradoxe de la pitié, que Rousseau et Schopenhauer ont décliné, c'est que le plus comparatif (et donc le plus réflexif) des affects tourne à la déroute de la représentation (ou de la médiation)."] Guérin, 220, 226, 338.

19. ["La pitié, malgré les assimilations hâtives, n'est pas synonyme de compassion (*mit-fuhlen*) ni d'empathie (*sich einfühlen*), toutes attitudes qui demeurent 'sentimentales' et, en fin de compte, imaginaires....Le 'consentir' apparaît même, sous un certain angle, comme l'opposé de la compassion, si du moins celle-ci se figure qu'elle reconstitue à l'identique dans le sujet la passion (la souffrance) vécue par un autre. La compassion, qui implique la sociabilité et la croyance, ressortit au domaine des sentiments; la pitié se confond avec la pure sensibilité du 'consentir,' libre de toute peur....La pitié ne connaît pas de sujets et elle choisit le silence...parce que le *proximus* n'est pas l'homme que je rencontre ni celui à qui je m'adresse, mais bien l'être qui 'métonne' d'aussi loin que je me souvienne."] Guérin, 341.

20. But see A. T. Nuyen, who argues that Emmanuel Levinas's ethics are impregnated by pity: "I have tried to show that it is the feeling of pity that fully accomplishes Levinas's metaphysics of morals. In a passage that comes closest to what I have argued here, Levinas claims that it is 'through the condition of being hostage that there can be in the world pity, compassion, pardon, and proximity.' My claim is that it is in fact through the condition of being hostage to pity that there can be in the world morality as we know it" ("Levinas and the Ethics of Pity," *International Philosophical Quarterly* 160:40 [December 2000], 421). We have also cited Vladimir Jankélévitch's *Les Vertus et l'Amour*, vol. 2: *Traité des vertus*.

21. See Priscilla Parkhurst Ferguson, *Literary France: The Making of a Culture* (Berkeley: U of California P, 1987).

22. Examples of further continuity not analyzed in this Conclusion are the perlocutionary works of Maurice Leblanc, "La Pitié," a boulevard play first performed in 1906 to

some acclaim and popularity, as well as Mathilde Osso's *La Pitié plus forte que l'amour, roman sentimental* (Paris: J. Ferenczi, 1929).

23. ["Giono montre deux pôles de la solitude humaine: l'égoisme sédentaire, 'normal,' abruti d'habitudes; la sollicitude, déraisonnablement continuée, du trimardeur qui, par soi, n'est rien et n'a rien, va son chemin en tirant le malade derrière lui....Non seulement elle n'a pas besoin des mots, mais elle sait sourdement que sa vague se brise sur leurs récifs. La pitié est seule parce qu'elle est aphasique."] Guérin, 156–57.

24. ["Il tombait une pluie tenace et froide. Sous le réverbère, l'homme ouvrit sa main. C'était dix sous. Les yeux bleus regardaient la petite pièce et la main toute mâchurée d'égratignures et de boue.— 'Tu te fatigueras, dit-il, je te suis une chaîne, moi, malade. Tu te fatigueras, laisse-moi'. –'Non, dit le gros. Viens.'"] Jean Giono, *Solitude de la pitié* (Paris: Gallimard, 1932), 19.

25. ["Il en coulait des regards qui étaient des ruisseaux de pitié et de douleur."] Giono, 40.

26. ["'Laisse cette bête.'...Et la colombe avait été touchée par cette voix, aussi. Et cette voix, ça avait dû être un peu d'espoir pour elle....'Je la garde, disait l'homme. Elle est à moi. De quel droit, toi, tu l'as prise, et tu l'as tordue? De quel droit, toi, le fort, le solide, tu as écrasé la bête grise? Dis-moi! Ça a du sang, ça, comme toi; ça a le sang de la même couleur et ça a le droit au soleil et au vent, comme toi. Tu n'as pas plus de droit que la bête.'"] Giono, 34.

27. ["A genoux à côté d'elle, je caressais doucement l'épais pelage brûlant de fièvre et surtout là, sur l'épine du cou où la caresse est plus douce. Il n'y avait qu'à donner de la pitié, c'était la seule chose à faire: de la pitié, tout un plein Coeur de pitié, pour adoucir, pour dire à la bête: 'Non, tu vois, quelqu'un souffre de ta souffrance, tu n'es pas seule. Je ne peux pas te guérir, mais je peux encore te garder.'"] Giono, 159.

28. ["Ce n'était pas apaisement ce que j'avais porté là, près de cette agonie, mais terreur, terreur si grande qu'il était désormais inutile de se plaindre, inutile d'appeler à l'aide. Il n'y avait plus qu'à mourir. J'étais l'homme et j'avais tué tout espoir. La bête mourait de peur sous ma pitié incomprise; ma main qui caressait était plus cruelle que le bec du freux. Une grande barrière nous séparait."] Giono, 159.

29. ["moi qui suis une bête d'entre elles toutes par ce grand poids de collines, de genvriers, de thym, d'air sauvage, d'herbes, de ciel, de vent, de pluie que j'ai en moi; moi qui ai plus de pitié pour elles que pour les hommes, s'il en est un pour qui la grande barrière devait tomber...Non, elle est là. Il en a fallu de nos méchancetés entassées pendant des siècles pour la rendre aussi solide."] Giono, 160.

30. ["Alors commençaient l'abstraction et la difficulté en effet, car la famille du malade savait qu'elle ne verrait plus ce dernier que guéri ou mort. 'Pitié, docteur!' disait Mme. Loret, la mère de la femme de chambre qui travaillait à l'hôtel de Tarrou. Que signifiait cela? Bien entendu, il avait pitié. Mais cela ne faisait avancer personne. Il fallait téléphoner."] Albert Camus, *La Peste* (Paris: Gallimard, 1947), 86. Camus, *The Plague*, in *The Collected Fiction of Albert Camus*, Stuart Gilbert, trans. (London: Hamish Hamilton, 1960), 121.

31. ["Ah! Il était bien vrai que les hommes ne pouvaient se passer des hommes, qu'il était aussi démuni que ces malheureux et qu'il méritait ce même tremblement de pitié qu'il laissait grandir en lui lorsqu'il les avait quittés."] Camus, 176. (164).

32. ["'C'est pourquoi j'ai décidé de me mettre du côté des victimes, en toute occasion, pour limiter les dégâts. Au milieu d'elles, je peux du moins chercher comment on arrive à la troisième catégorie, c'est-a-dire à la paix.' En terminant, Tarrou balançait sa jambe et frappait doucement du pied contre la terrasse. Après un silence, le docteur se souleva un

peu et demanda si Tarrou avait une idée du chemin qu'il fallait prendre pour arriver à la paix. —'Oui, la sympathie.'"] Camus, 229 (219).

Bibliography

MANUSCRIPT SOURCES

Archives Nationales (AN)
Series AJ, 16/985, 1000, 1025, 1028, 1076, 1153, 1434, 5885, 6066
Series F17, 3612, 12964, 20340, 20343, 20993, 21253, 21577, 21879, 22028, 22331, 22983, 24348

Bibliothèque de l'Institut de France
MS 18742, 18174, 18742: Papiers Théodule Ribot

Bibliothèque Nationale de France (BNF)
Salle des Manuscrits (MS): N. A. Fr. 18183–18184: Lettres de Th. Ribot; N. A. Fr. 25170: Papiers Lavisse, vol. 5
N. A. Fr. 15995: Papiers Poincaré, vol. 4; N. A. Fr., 18340

BOOKS AND ARTICLES

Philosophy and Psychology of the Emotions

Arnold, Magda B. *Emotion and Personality.* Vol. 2: *Neurological and Physiological Approaches.* New York: Columbia UP, 1960.
Badiou-Monferran, C., Anne Coudreuse, and Bruno Delignon. "La promotion esthétique du pathétique dans la seconde moitié du XVIIème siècle: Passions, émotions, pathos." *La Licorne* 43 (1997): 75–94.
Blesius, Rita. "The Concept of Empathy." *Psychology* 26:4 (1989): 10–15.
Brandt, Richard B. "The Psychology of Benevolence and Its Implications for Philosophy." *The Journal of Philosophy* 73:14 (12 August 1976): 429–53.
Damasio, Antonio. *Descartes' Error: Emotions, Reason, and the Human Brain.* New

York: G. P. Putnam, 1994.

—. *Looking for Spinoza: Joy, Sorrow, and the Feeling Brain*. Orlando: Harcourt, 2003.

Davis, Mark. *Empathy: A Social Psychological Approach*. Boulder, CO: Westview Press, 1996.

Davitz, Joel R. *The Language of Emotion*. New York and London: Academic Press, 1969.

De Sousa, Ronald. *The Rationality of Emotions*. Cambridge: MIT Press, 1987.

Dooley, Pamela A. "Perceptions of the Onset Controllability of AIDS and Helping Judgements: An Attributional Analysis." *Journal of Applied Social Psychology* 25:10 (May 1995): 858–69.

Eisenberg, Nancy, and Janet Strayer. *Empathy and Its Development*. Cambridge: Cambridge UP, 1987.

Febvre, Lucien. "Sensibility and History: How to Reconstitute the Emotional Life of the Past." *A New Kind of History: From the Writings of Febvre*. Peter Burke, ed. K. Folca, trans. London: Routledge & Kegan Paul, 1973.

Goldie, Peter. *The Emotions: A Philosophical Exploration*. Oxford: Clarendon Press, 2000.

Gordon, Robert M. *The Structure of Emotions*. Cambridge: Cambridge UP, 1987.

Graham, Sandra, Catherine Doubleday, and Patricia A. Guarino. "The Development of Relations between Perceived Controllability and the Emotions of Pity, Anger, and Guilt." *Child Development* 55:2 (April 1984): 561–65.

Hacking, Ian. *Rewriting the Soul: Multiple Personality and the Sciences of Memory*. Princeton: Princeton UP, 1995.

Hardie, C. D. "The History of the Emotive Theory of Ethics." *Mind* 1966 (75): 492.

Harré, Rom, ed. *The Social Construction of the Emotions*. Oxford: Blackwell, 1986.

Hatfield, Elaine, John Cacioppo, and Richard Rapson, Eds. *Emotional Contagion*. Cambridge: Cambridge UP, 1994.

Hecht, Anthony. "The Pathetic Fallacy." *The Yale Review* 74:4 (Summer 1985): 481–99.

Heidsieck, Arnold. "Adam Smith's Influence on Lessing's View of Man and Society." *Lessing Yearbook* 15 (1983): 125–43.

Hobbes, Thomas. *Elements of Law*. Tönnies, Ed. London: 1889.

Hochschild, Arlie Russell. *The Managed Heart: Commercialization of Human Feeling*. Berkeley: U of California P, 1983.

Lutz, Catherine A., and Lila Abu-Lughod, Eds. *Language and the Politics of Emotion*. Cambridge: Cambridge UP, 1990.

Monroe, Kristen Renwick. *The Heart of Altruism: Perspectives of a Common Humanity*. Princeton: Princeton UP, 1996.

Morrow, G. R. "The Significance of the Doctrine of Sympathy in Hume and Adam Smith." *The Philosophical Review* 32 (1923): 60–78.

Morse, Janice M., Gwen Anderson, et al. "Exploring Empathy: A Conceptual Fit for Nursing Practice?" *Image: The Journal of Nursing Scholarship* 24:4 (Winter 1992): 273–80.

Murphy, Jeffrie G., and Jean Hampton. *Forgiveness and Mercy*. Cambridge: Cambridge UP, 1988.

Nussbaum, Martha. "Compassion: The Basic Social Emotion." *Social Philosophy and Policy* 13:1 (1996): 1–40.

—. "Emotion in the Language of Judging." *St. John's Law Review* 70 (Winter 1996): 23–30.

—. "Fictions of the Soul." *Love's Knowledge: Essays on Philosophy and Literature*. New York: Oxford UP, 1990.

—. *The Fragility of Goodness: Luck and Ethics in Greek Tragedy and Philosophy.* Cambridge: Cambridge UP, 1986.

—. *The Therapy of Desire: Theory and Practice in Hellenistic Ethics.* Princeton: Princeton UP, 1994.

—. *Upheavals of Thought: The Intelligence of Emotions.* Cambridge: Cambridge UP, 2001.

Oakley, Justin. *Morality and the Emotions.* New York: Routledge, 1992.

Richendoller, Nadine R., and James B. Weaver III. "Exploring the Links between Personality and Empathic Response Style." *Personality and Individual Differences* 17:3 (September 1994): 303–11.

Rorty, Amélie, ed. *Explaining Emotions.* Cambridge: Cambridge UP, 1980.

—. "From Passions to Emotions and Sentiments." *Philosophy* 57 (1982): 159–72.

—. "The Historicity of Psychological Attitudes." *Studies in the Philosophy of Mind (Midwest Studies in Philosophy 10).* Minneapolis: U of Minnesota P, 1986.

Rosenwein, Barbara H. "Worrying about Emotions in History." *American Historical Review* 107:3 (June 2002): 821–45.

Shelton, Mary Lou, and Ronald W. Rogers. "Fear-Arousing and Empathy-Arousing Appeals to Help: The Pathos of Persuasion." *Journal of Applied Social Psychology* 11:4 (1981): 366–78.

Sherman, Nancy. *The Fabric of Character: Aristotle's Theory of Virtue.* Oxford: Oxford UP, 1989.

Snow, Nancy. "Compassion." *American Philosophical Quarterly* 28 (1991): 195–205.

Solomon, Robert C. *A Passion for Justice: Emotions and the Origins of the Social Contract.* Reading, MA: Addison-Wesley, 1990.

—. *The Passions.* New York: Anchor Books, 1977.

Stearns, Carol Z., and Peter N. Stearns, eds. *Emotion and Social Change: Toward a New Psychohistory.* New York: Holmes and Meier, 1988.

Stearns, Peter N., with Carol Z. Stearns. "Emotionology: Clarifying the History of Emotions and Emotional Standards." *American Historical Review* 90 (1985): 813–36.

Stocker, Michael. "Affectivity and Self-Concern: The Assumed Psychology in Aristotle's Ethics." *Pacific Philosophical Quarterly* 64:3 (1983): 210–29.

—. "Emotional Thoughts." *American Philosophical Quarterly* 24 (1987): 59–69.

—. and Elizabeth Hegeman. *Valuing Emotions.* Cambridge: Cambridge UP, 1996.

Tarada, Rei. *Feeling in Theory: Emotion after the "Death of the Subject."* Cambridge, MA: Harvard UP, 2001.

Toi, Miho, and C. Daniel Batson. "More Evidence That Empathy Is a Source of Altruistic Motivation." *Journal of Personality and Social Psychology* 43:2 (August 1982): 281–92.

Williams, Bernard. "Morality and the Emotions." *Problems of the Self: Philosophical Papers, 1956–72.* Cambridge: Cambridge UP, 1973.

Wilmer, Harry A. "The Doctor–Patient Relationship and the Issues of Pity, Sympathy, and Empathy." *Encounters between Patients and Doctors: An Anthology.* John D. Stoeckle, ed. Cambridge: MIT Press, 1987, 403–11.

Wispé, Lauren. *The Psychology of Sympathy.* Perspectives in Social Psychology. New York: Plenum Press, 1991.

Pity

Ackerman, Felicia. "Pity as a Moral Concept/The Morality of Pity." *Midwest Studies in*

Philosophy. Vol. 20. Notre Dame, IN: U of Notre Dame P, 1996: 59–66.

Alford, C. Fred. "Greek Tragedy and Civilization: The Cultivation of Pity." *Political Research Quarterly* 46 (June 1993): 259–80.

Arendt, Hannah. *On Revolution*. New York: Penguin, 1977.

Aristotle. *Rhetoric and the Poetics*. New York: Modern Library, 1954.

Bécamier. *Pitié pour les pauvres*. Lons-le-Saunier: J. Mayet, 1887.

Bergson, Henri. *Essai sur les données immédiates de la conscience. Oeuvres complètes.* André Robinet, Ed. Henri Gouhier, Intro. Paris: Presses universitaires français, 1970.

Bock, J.-N. Étienne de. *Recherches philosophiques sur l'origine de la pitié et divers autres sujets de morale*. London: 1787.

Brueckner's French Contextuary. John H. Brueckner, ed. Englewood Cliffs, NJ: Prentice-Hall, 1975.

Brunot, Ferdinand. *Histoire de la langue française: des origines à 1900*. Vol. 6: *Le XVIIIème siècle. Deuxième partie: la langue postclassique*. Paris: Armand Colin, 1932.

Callan, Eamonn. "The Moral Status of Pity." *Canadian Journal of Philosophy* 18:1 (March 1988): 1–12.

Cameron, Frank. "Beyond Pity and Cruelty: Nietzsche's Stoicism." *De Philosophia* 13:2 (1997): 191–206.

Carpentier, J.M.L. *Le Gradus français*. Paris: A. Johanneau, 1822.

Carr, Brian. "Pity and Compassion as Social Virtues." *Philosophy* 74:289 (July 1999): 411–29.

Cartwright, David E. "Compassion." *Zeit der Ernte: Studien zum Stand der Schopenhauer. Forschung. Festschrift für Arthur Hübscher*. Wolfgang Schirmacher, ed. Stuttgart: Frommann-Holzboog, 1982: 60–69.

Chamfort, Sébastien-Roch-Nicholas. *Maximes et anecdotes*. Monaco: Incidences, 1944.

Chazaud, Henri Bertaud de. *Le Robert, Dictionnaire des synonymes*. Paris: Dictionnaires le Robert, 1983.

Connolly, Oliver. "Pity, Tragedy, and the Pathos of Distance (Aristotle, Nietzsche)." *European Journal of Philosophy* 6:3 (December 1998): 277–96.

Delille, J. *Œuvres complètes*. Amar Du Riviere, ed. Paris: J.G. Michaud, 1824.

Descartes, Rene. *Passions of the Soul. The Philosophical Works of Descartes*. Vol. 1. Elizabeth S. Haldane and G. R. T. Ross, eds. and trans. Cambridge: Cambridge UP, 1973.

Dictionnaire historique de la langue française. vol. 2. Paris: Dictionnaires le Robert, 1992.

Dumonceaux, Pierre. *Langue et sensibilité au XVIIème siècle: l'évolution du vocabulaire affectif*. Publications Romanes et Françaises 131. Génève: Librairie Droz, 1975.

Encyclopédie, ou Dictionnaire raisonné des sciences, des arts et des métiers. Diderot and d'Alembert, eds. Paris: Briasson [etc.], 1757.

Encyclopédie philosophique universelle: II. Les Notions philosophiques, dictionnaire. vol 2: *Philosophie occidentale, M-Z*. Sylvain Auroux, ed. Paris: Presses Universitaires de France, 1990.

Etia, Abel Moumé. *La Pitié, sermon*. Cahors: A. Coueslant, 1948.

Feraud, Abbé. *Dictionnaire critique de la langue française*. Marseilles: J. Mossy père et fils, 1787.

Giessler, Willy. *Das Mitleid in der Neueren Ethik*. Halle: C. A. Kaemmerer, 1904.

Godefroy, Frédéric. *Dictionnaire de l'ancienne langue française et de tous ses dialectes, du IXème au XVème siècles*. Paris: F. Vieweg, 1889. Repr. New York: Kraus Reprint Corp, 1961.

—. *Léxique de l'ancien français*. J. Bonnard and A. Salmon, eds. Paris: Librairie Honoré Champion, 1964.

Gougenheim, Georges. *Les Mots français dans l'histoire et dans la vie*. vol. 1. 2nd ed. Paris: A & J. Picard, 1966.

Guérin, Michel. *La Terreur et la Pitié*. vol. 1: *La terreur*. Arles: Actes sud, 1990.

—. *La Pitié: apologie athée de la religion chrétienne*. Arles: Actes sud, 2000.

Guyot, Abbé Pierre François. *Racine vengé, ou examen des remarques grammaticales de M. l'Abbé d'Olivet sur les verses de Racine*. Avignon: 1739.

Habib, Claude. "Le Sadisme et la pitié." *La Revue des lettres modernes. Séries Victor Hugo*. Vol. 3: *Femmes* (1991): 111–24.

Hastings. *Encyclopedia of Religion*. Vol. 10: *Pity*: 48–50.

d'Holbach, Baron. *La Morale universelle, ou les devoirs de l'homme fondés sur sa nature*. Amsterdam: Marc-Michel Rey, 1776.

Huguet, Edmond. *Dictionnaire de la langue française du seizième siècle*. Vol. 6. Paris: Didier, 1965.

Kemp, John. "Hobbes on Pity and Charity." *Thomas Hobbes: His View of Man. Elementa: Schriften zur Philosophie und ihrer Problemgeschichte*. Vol. 21. Amsterdam: Rodopi, 1982: 57–62.

Kimball, Robert H. "Moral and Logical Perspectives on Appealing to Pity." *Argumentation* 15:3 (August 2001): 331–46.

Konstan, David. *Pity Transformed*. London: Duckworth, 2001.

Laquièze, Armand. *La pitié, étude analytique*. Lyon: E. Vitte, 1943.

Le Brun, Charles. *Conférence de M. Le Brun sur l'expression générale et particulière*. Los Angeles: U of California P, 1980.

Littré, Paul-Émile. *Dictionnaire de la langue française*. Vol. 5. Chicago: Encyclopedaeia Britannica, 1994.

Mathieu, Yvette Yannick. *Les verbes de sentiment: de l'analyse linguistique au traitement automatique*. Paris: CNRS Editions, 2000.

Matoré, Georges. *Dictionnaire du vocabulaire essentiel: les 5,000 mots fondamentaux*. Paris: Librairie Larousse, 1963.

—. *La Méthode en léxicologie*. Paris: M. Didier, 1953.

Meillet, A. "Comment les mots changent des sens." *L'année sociologique* 9 (1906): 1–39.

Michaud, M. *Le Printemps d'un proscrit, suivi de plusieurs lettres à M. Delille sur la pitié*. Paris: Chez Giguet et Michaud, 1803.

Michelet, Jules. *Bible de l'humanité*. Paris: Ernest Flammarion, s.d.

—. *Oeuvres complètes XXI (1872–74)*. Paul Viallaneix, ed. Paris: Flammarion, 1982.

Montesquieu, Charles-Louis de Secondat, baron de. *Lettres Persanes*. Paris: Bookking Intl., 1993.

Moulard, Abbé Jacques. *La Pitié dans Virgile*. Lyon: E. Vitte, 1905.

Nicot, Jean. *Thrésor de la langue français*. Paris: A. et Je. Picard, 1960.

Nuyen, A. T. "Lévinas and the Ethics of Pity." *International Philosophical Quarterly* 160:40 (December 2000): 411–21.

—. "Pity." *The Southern Journal of Philosophy* 37:1 (1999): 77–87.

Olivet Girard, abbé d'. *Synonymes françois, leurs différentes significations, et le choix qu'il en faut faire*. Amsterdam: Chez J. Wetstein & G. Smith, 1737.

Philippe, J. "Revue : 'La Pitié.'" *Revue Philosophique de la France et de l'étranger* 52 (July–December 1901): 703–11.

Ridgeway, R. S. *Voltaire and Sensibility*. Montreal: McGill's-Queen's UP, 1973.

Robert, Guy. *Mots et dictionnaires (1798–1878) [Annales littéraires de l'université de Besançon]*. Paris: Les Belles Lettres, 1971.

Rochefoucauld, Francois, Duc de La. *The Maxims of La Rochefoucauld*. Louis Kronenberger, trans. New York: Vintage Books, 1959.

Rousseau, Jean-Jacques. *The "Discourses" and Other Early Political Writings*. Victor Gourevitch, ed. and trans. Cambridge: Cambridge UP, 1997.

—. *Politics and the Arts: Letter to M. d'Alembert On the Theatre*. Allan Bloom, ed. and trans. Glencoe, IL: Free Press, 1960.

Saunders, F. H., and G. Stanley Hall. "Pity." *American Journal of Psychology* 11:1–4 (October 1899-July 1900): 534–91.

Scheler, Max. *The Nature of Sympathy*. Peter Heath, trans. Hamden, CT: P. Books, 1970.

Schultz, Èmile. *La Miséricorde: conciliation des notions d'amour et de justice*. Strasbourg: E. Hubert, 1894.

Spink, John. "Diderot et la réhabilitation de la pitié." *Colloque International Diderot (1713–84)*. Anne-Marie Chouillet, ed. Paris: Aux Amateurs de Livres, 1985: 51–60.

Spinrad, Phoebe S. "Dramatic 'Pity' and the Death of Lear." *Renascence* 43 (Summer 1991): 231–40.

Sprigge, T.L.S. "Is Pity the Basis of Ethics? Nietzsche versus Schopenhauer." *The Bases of Ethics*. William Sweet, ed. Milwaukee, WI: Marquette UP, 2000.

Thesaurus Larousse: des mots aux idées, des idées aux mots. Daniel Pechoin, ed. Paris: Larousse, 1991.

Trésor de la langue française: Dictionnaire de la langue du XIXème et du Xxème siècle (1789–1960): Vol. 13. Paris: Editions du Centre national de recherche scientifique (Gallimard): 1988.

Thompson, Homer A. "The Altar of Pity in the Athenian Agora." *Hesperia* 21 (1952): 47–82.

Travlos, John. *Pictorial Dictionary of Ancient Athens*. New York: Praeger, 1971.

Vauvenargues, Luc de Clapiers, Marquis de. *Réflexions et maximes*. Paris: Editions Gallimard, 1971.

Walton, Douglas N. *Appeal to Pity: "Argumentum ad misericordiam."* SUNY Series in Logic and Language. Albany: State U of New York P, 1997.

Williams, Raymond. *Key Words*. New York: Oxford UP, 1976.

Literature, Philosophy, and Sentiments

Abdulla, Adnan K. *Catharsis in Literature*. Bloomington: Indiana UP, 1985.

Allen, R. T. "The Reality of Responses to Fiction." *British Journal of Aesthetics* 26 (1986): 64–68.

Auerbach, Erich. *Mimesis: The Representation of Reality in Western Literature*. Willard R. Trask, trans. Princeton: Princeton UP, 1953.

Ballanche, P. S. *Du sentiment considéré dans ses rapports avec la literature*. Lyon: Ballanche et Barret, 1801.

Barine, Arvède. "Hors de France: Des influences étrangères en littérature." *Journal des débats politiques et littéraires* 107 (8 January 1895): 2–5.

Bayne, Sheila Page. *Tears and Weeping: An Aspect of Emotional Climate Reflected in Seventeenth-Century French Literature*. Études littéraires française: 16. Tübingen: Gunter Narr Verlag, 1981.

Bedrioni, Émile. *Proust, Wagner et les coïncidences des arts*. Paris: J.-M. Place, 1984.

Bell, Michael. *Sentimentalism, Ethics and the Culture of Feeling*. Hampshire, UK: Palgrave, 2000.

—. "Tolstoy: Truth of Feeling and the 'Sentiment of Reality.'" *The Sentiment of Reality: Truth of Feeling in the European Novel*. London: George Allen and Unwin, 1983.

Bénichou, Paul. *The Consecration of the Writer, 1750–1830* (*Le sacre de l'écrivain*). Mark J. Jensen, trans. Lincoln: U of Nebraska P, 1999.

—. *Man and Ethics: Studies in French Classicism.* Elizabeth Hughes, trans. Garden City, NY: Anchor Books, 1971.

—. *Le Temps des prophètes: Doctrines de l'âge romantique.* Paris: Gallimard, 1977.

Bernardin de Saint-Pierre, J. H. *Études de la nature de la morale.* Paris: Firmin Didot Frères, 1853.

Bersani, Leo. "'The Culture of Redemption': Marcel Proust and Melanie Klein." *Critical Inquiry* 12 (Winter 1985–1986): 399–421.

Booth, Wayne C. *The Company We Keep: An Ethics of Fiction.* Berkeley: U of California P, 1988.

Bowie, Malcolm. *The Morality of Proust: An Inaugural Lecture Delivered before the University of Oxford on 25 November 1993.* Oxford: Clarendon Press, 1994.

Burke, Kenneth. *A Rhetoric of Motives.* Berkeley: U of California P, 1969.

Charlton, William. "Feeling for the Fictitious." *British Journal of Aesthetics* 24 (1984): 206–16.

Chernovitz, M. E. "Bergson's Influence on Marcel Proust." *Romanic Review* 27:1 (January-March 1936): 45–50.

Daudet, Léon. "L'Objet de la littérature." *La Nouvelle revue* 92 (January 15, 1895): 407– (February 1, 1895): 620.

de Man, Paul. *Allegories of Reading: Figural Language in Rousseau, Nietzsche, Rilke, Proust.* New Haven, CT: Yale UP, 1979.

Denby, David. *Sentimental Narrative and the Social Order in France, 1760–1820.* Cambridge: Cambridge UP, 1994.

Derrida, Jacques. *Of Grammatologie.* Gayarti Chakravorty-Spivak, trans. Baltimore and London: Johns Hopkins UP, 1976.

Eldridge, Richard. *On Moral Personhood: Philosophy, Literature, Criticism and Self-Understanding.* Chicago: U of Chicago P, 1989.

Feagin, Susan L. "Imagining Emotions and Appreciating Fiction." *Canadian Journal of Philosophy* 18:3 (September 1988): 485–500.

Goldberg, S. L. *Agents and Lives: Moral Thinking in Literature.* Cambridge: Cambridge UP, 1993.

Hartman, Elwood. *French Literary Wagnerism.* New York: Garland, 1988.

Hartz, Glenn A. "How We Can Be Moved by Anna Karenina, Green Slime, and a Red Pony." *Philosophy* 74:290 (October 1999): 557–78.

Jefferson, M. "What Is Wrong with Sentimentality?" *Mind* 92 (1983): 368.

Kocay, Victor. *L'Expression du sentiment dans l'oeuvre de Benjamin Constant.* Studies in French Literature 48. Lewiston, NY: The Edwin Mellen P, 2001.

Lamarque, Peter. "How Can We Fear and Pity Fictions?" *British Journal of Aesthetics* 21 (1981): 291–304.

Mannison, Don. "On Being Moved by Fiction." *Philosophy* 60 (1985): 71–87.

Miller, J. Hillis. *The Ethics of Reading.* New York: Cambridge UP, 1987.

Morrison, Karl Frederick. *I Am You: The Hermeneutics of Empathy in Western Literature, Theology and Art.* Princeton: Princeton UP, 1988.

Mullan, John. *Sentiment and Sociability: The Language of Feeling in the Eighteenth Century.* Oxford: Clarendon Press, 1988.

Nehamas, Alexander. "What Should We Expect from Reading? (There Are Only Aesthetic Values)." *Salmagundi* 111 (Summer 1996): 27–58.

Neill, Alex. "Fiction and the Emotions". *American Philosophical Quarterly* 30:1 (1993): 1–13.

Norton, David L. *Imagination, Understanding, and the Virtue of Liberality*. Lanham, MD: Rowman and Littlefield, 1996.

Parker, David. *Ethics, Theory and the Novel*. Cambridge: Cambridge UP, 1994.

Radford, Colin, and Michael Weston. "How Can We Be Moved by the Fate of Anna Karenina?" *Proceedings of the Aristotelian Society*. Supp. Vol. 49 (1975): 67–93.

Le Roman sentimental: actes du colloque des 14–15–16 mars 1989 à la faculté des lettres de Limoges. Limoges: TRAMES, 1989.

Schiller, Friedrich. *On the Naïve and Sentimental in Literature*. Helen Watanabe-O'Kelly, trans. Manchester, UK: Carcanet New Press, 1981.

Slatoff, Walter J. *The Look of Distance: Reflections on Suffering and Sympathy in Modern Literature—Auden to Agee, Whitman to Woolf*. Columbus: Ohio State UP, 1985.

Todd, Janet. *Sensibility: An Introduction*. London: Methuen, 1986.

Walton, Kendall. "Fearing Fictions." *The Journal of Philosophy* 75 (1978): 5–27.

—. *Mimesis and Make-Believe: On the Foundations of the Representational Arts*. Cambridge, MA: Harvard UP, 1990.

Wilkinson, Jennifer. "The Paradox(es) of Pitying and Fearing Fictions." *South African Journal of Philosophy* 19:1 (March 2000): 8–25.

Yanal, Robert J. *Paradoxes of Emotion and Fiction*. University Park: Penn State UP, 1999.

Nietzsche and Schopenhauer (see also **Pity**)

Albert, Henri. *Nietzsche*. Paris: Bibliothèque internationale d'édition, 1903.

Andrew, Edward. *The Genealogy of Values: The Aesthetic Economy of Nietzsche and Proust*. Lanham, MD: Rowman and Littlefield, 1995.

Ansell-Pearson, Keith. *Nietzsche Contra Rousseau: A Study of Nietzsche's Moral and Political Thought*. Cambridge: Cambridge UP, 1991.

Baillot, Alexandre. *L'influence de Schopenhauer en France (1860–1900)*. Paris: Librairie Philosophique J. Vrin, 1927.

Bernardini, L. "Les Idées de Frédéric Nietzsche." *La Revue de Paris* 2:1 (January-February 1895): 197–224.

Bianquis, Geneviève. *Nietzsche en France*. Paris: Félix Alcan, 1929.

Birot, Abbé. "Recherches sur la philosophie de F. Nietzsche." *Annales de philosophie chrétienne* 43 (1900–1901): 38–52.

Bridel, Ph. "Pessimisme." *Encyclopédie des sciences religieuses*. Vol. 10. F. Lichtenberger, ed. Paris: Librairie Sandoz et Fischbacher, 1881.

Brunetière, Ferdinand. "'Le Pessimisme au dix-neuvième siècle:' Revue." *Revue des deux mondes* (January 15, 1879): 478–80.

—. "La Philosophie de Schopenhauer et les conséquences du pessimisme." *Revue des deux mondes* (October 1, 1886): 694–706; (November 1, 1890): 210–21.

Caro, Elme. "La Maladie du pessimisme au dix-neuvième siècle." *Revue des deux mondes* (November 15, 1877): 241–68; (December 1, 1877): 481–514.

—. *Le Pessimisme au XIXème siècle*. Paris: Hachette, 1878.

—. "Schopenhauer." *Dictionnaire des sciences philosophiques, par une société de professeurs et de savants*. Adolphe Franck, ed. 2nd ed. Paris: Hachette, 1875.

Cartwright, David E. "Kant, Schopenhauer, and Nietzsche on the Morality of Pity." *Journal of the History of Ideas* (January 1984): 83–98.

—. "The Last Temptation of Zarathustra." *Journal of the History of Philosophy* 31 (1993): 49–68.

—. "Schopenhauer's Compassion and Nietzsche's Pity." *Schopenhauer-Jarbuch* 69 (1988): 57–69.

Challemel-Lacour, Paul-Armand. *Études et réflexions d'un pessimiste. Un Bouddhiste contemporaine en Allemagne: Arthur Schopenhauer* (Corpus des oeuvres de philosophie en langue français). Paris: Fayard, 1993.

Charbonnel, J. Roger. "Les deux pôles de la morale contemporaine: la solidarité et l'individualisme de Nietzsche." *Annales de philosophie chrétienne* 3 (1904): 360–85.

Colin, René-Pierre. *Schopenhauer en France: Un mythe naturaliste.* Lyon: Presses Universitaires de Lyon, 1979.

Dauer, Dorothea W. *Schopenhauer as Transmitter of Buddhist Ideas.* Berne: Herbert Land, 1969.

Deudon, Eric Hollingsworth. *Nietzsche en France: L'antichristianisme et la critique, 1891–1915.* Washington, DC: UP of America, 1982.

—. "'Requiescat in Inferno:' La Maladie de Nietzsche et les psychiatres français." *Revue de littérature comparée* 54:3 (July-September 1980): 360–65.

Donnellan, Brendan. *Nietzsche and the French Moralists.* Bonn: Bouvier, 1982.

Doumic, Rene. "Deux Moralistes 'fin de siècle:' Chamfort et Rivarol." *Revue des deux mondes* (February 15, 1896): 277–78.

Droit, Roger-Pol. "Schopenhauer et le Bouddhism: une 'admirable concordance'?" *Schopenhauer: New Essays in Honor of His 200th Birthday.* Eric von der Luft, ed. Lewiston, NY: Edwin Mellen Press, 1988: 123–28.

Droz, Théophile. "La Revanche de l'individu: Nietzsche." *La Semaine littéraire* (November 3, 1894): 518.

Ducros, Louis. *Schopenhauer: les origines de sa métaphysique.* Paris: Germer Baillière, 1883.

Forth, Christopher E. "Nietzsche, Decadence, and Regeneration in France, 1891–95." *Journal of the History of Ideas* 54 (1993): 97–118.

Foster, John Burt. *Heirs to Dionysus: a Nietzschean Current in Literary Modernism.* Princeton: Princeton UP, 1981.

Fouillée, Alfred. *Nietzsche et l'immoralisme.* Paris: Félix Alcan, 1902.

—. "La religion de Nietzsche." *Revue des deux mondes* (January-February 1901): 563–94.

Gaultier, Jules de. *De Kant à Nietzsche.* Paris: Editions Mercure de France, 1900.

—. *Nietzsche et la reforme philosophique.* Paris: Editions Mercure de France, 1904.

Green, Michael S. "Nietzsche on Pity and 'Ressentiment.'" *International Studies in Philosophy* 24:2 (1992): 63–76.

Haaz, Ignace. *Les Conceptions du corps chez Ribot et Nietzsche.* Paris: L'Harmattan, 2002.

Hamburger, Kate. "Zum Problem der Mitleids-Ethik—Rousseau und Schopenhauer." *Philosophisches Jahrbuch* 92:1 (1985): 68–78.

Hollinrake, Roger. *Nietzsche, Wagner, and the Philosophy of Pessimism.* London: George Allen and Unwin, ltd., 1982.

Janet, Paul. "Un Philosophe misanthrope: Schopenhauer." *Revue des deux mondes* (May 15, 1877): 269–87.

—. "Schopenhauer et la physiologie française: Bichat et Cabanis." *Revue des deux mondes* (May 15, 1880): 35–59.

Lampl, Hans Eric. "Flair du Livre: Friedrich Nietzsche und Théodule Ribot." *Nietzsche-Studien* 18 (1989): 573–86.

Large, Duncan. "Proust and Nietzsche: The Question of Friendship." *Modern Language*

Review 88 (July 1996): 612–25.

Lasserre, Pierre. *La morale de Nietzsche*. Paris: Editions de la Mercure, 1902.

Lichtenberger, Henri. *La Philosophie de Nietzsche*. Paris: Félix Alcan, 1894.

Luft, Eric von der, ed. *Schopenhauer: New Essays in Honor of His 200th Birthday*. Lewiston, NY: Edwin Mellen P, 1988.

Maehle, Andreas-Holger. "The Ethical Discourse on Animal Experimentation, 1650–1900." *Clio Medica* 24 (1991): 203–51.

Meštrovic, Stjepan. "Moral Theory Based on the 'Heart' versus the 'Mind:' Schopenhauer's and Durkheim's Critiques of Kantian Ethics." *Sociological Review* 37:3 (August 1989): 431–57.

Molner, D. "The Influence of Montaigne on Nietzsche: A Raison d'Etre in the Sun." *Nietzsche-Studien* 22 (1993): 80–93.

Nietzsche, Friedrich. *On the Genealogy of Morals*. New York: Vintage, 1986.

— .*The Viking Portable Nietzsche*. Walter Kaufmann, ed. New York: Peguin, 1968.

—. *Twilight of the Idols*. New York: Penguin, 1968.

Parkes, Graham. "The Orientation of the Nietzschean Text." Parkes, ed. *Nietzsche and Asian Thought*. Chicago: U of Chicago P, 1991: 3–19.

Pécaud, Dominique. "'Ce Brave Guyau.'" *Nietzsche-Studien* 25 (1996): 239–54.

Pinto, Louis. *Les neveux de Zarathoustra: la réception de Nietzsche en France*. Paris: Editions du Seuil, 1995.

Renouvier, Charles. "Kant et Schopenhauer." *La Critique philosophique* 9:1 (February 1880): 23-30.

—. "Schopenhauer et la Métaphysique du pessimisme." *L'année philosophique* 3 (1892): 1–61.

Ribot, Théodule. *La Philosophie de Schopenhauer*. Paris: Germer Baillière, 1874.

Rod, Edouard. "Le père du pessimisme: Schopenhauer." *Revue des jeunes filles* (January 20, February 5, 1896). Reprinted in *Nouvelles études sur le XIXème siècle*. Paris: Perrin, 1899.

Safranski, Rudiger. *Schopenhauer and the Wild Years of Philosophy*. Ewald Osers, trans. Cambridge: Cambridge UP, 1989.

Schacht, Richard. *Nietzsche*. London: Routledge and Kegan Paul, 1983.

— , ed. *Nietzsche: Morality and Genealogy*. Princeton: Princeton UP, 1994.

Schopenhauer, Arthur. *On the Basis of Morality*. E.F.J. Payne, trans. David Cartwright, Introd. Providence, RI: Berghahn Books, 1995.

Sellière, Ernest. *Arthur Schopenhauer*. Paris: Blond et cie, 1911.

—. "Taine et Nietzsche." *Revue des deux mondes* 71 (1909): 538–56.

Simmel, Georg. *Schopenhauer and Nietzsche*. Amherst: U of Massachusetts P, 1986 [1907].

Smith, Douglas. *Transvaluations: Nietzsche in France, 1872–1972*. Oxford Modern Languages and Literature Monographs. Oxford: Clarendon Press, 1996.

Stambaugh, Joan. "Thoughts on the Innocence of Becoming." *Nietzsche-Studien* 14 (1985): 164–79.

—. "Thoughts on Pity and Revenge." *Nietzsche-Studien* 1 (1971): 27–35.

Taylor, Charles S. "Nietzsche's Schopenhauerianism." *Nietzsche-Studien* 17 (1989): 45–73.

Varner, G. E. "The Schopenhauerian Challenge in Environmental Ethics." *Environmental Ethics* 7 (1985): 209–29.

Vyvyan, John. *In Pity and in Anger: A Study of the Use of Animals in Science*. Marblehead, MA: Micah, 1988.

West, Thomas. "Schopenhauer, Huysmans and French Naturalism." *Journal of European*

Studies 1 (1971): 313–24.

Williams, W(illiam) D(avid). *Nietzsche and the French*. Oxford: Blackwell, 1952.

French *Fin-de-Siècle* Philosophy, Psychology, and Social Sciences

Académie des sciences morales et politiques. *La solidarité sociale, ses nouvelles formules* (Eugène d'Eichthal); *La solidarité sociale comme principe des lois* (Charles Brunot); *Observations* (Frédéric Passy), et al. Paris: A. Poncet, 1903.

——. *Notices biographiques et bibliographiques, membres titulaires et libres, associés étrangers* (31 décembre 1918). Paris: Imprimérie nationale, 1918.

Angot des Rotours, J. "La Morale en France, de 1888–1898." *Congrès Bibliographique international tenu à Paris du 13 au 16 avril 1898*: 130–36.

Annuaire du Collège de France. Paris: Ernest Leroux, 1901–s.d.

Arreat, Lucien. *Dix ans de philosophie*. Paris: Félix Alcan, 1901.

——. *La morale dans le drame: l'épopée et le roman*. Paris: Félix Alcan, 1889.

Bayet, Albert. *La morale scientifique: essai sur les applications morales des sciences sociologiques*. Paris: Félix Alcan, 1905.

Beaussire, Émile. "La Crise actuelle de la morale." *Revue des deux mondes* 4 (August 1, 1884): 551–574.

——. *La morale laïque, examen de la morale évolutionniste de M. Herbert Spencer*. Paris: A. Picard, 1881.

——. *Les principes de la morale*. Paris: Félix Alcan, 1885.

Benrubi, Isaac. *Contemporary Thought of France*. Ernest B. Dicker, trans. New York: Alfred A. Knopf, 1926.

Bérenger, Henry. *La Conscience nationale*. Paris: Armand Colin, 1898.

Berthélot, André, ed. *La Grande Encyclopédie: Inventaire raisonné des sciences, des lettres, et des arts*. Vol. 26. Paris: Société anonyme de la Grande Encyclopédie, 1885–1902.

Blanc, Abbé Elie. *Dictionnaire de philosophie ancienne, moderne, et contemporaine* (1906). Rep: New York: Burt Franklin, 1972.

Boirac, Émile. *Cours élémentaire de philosophie*. 7th ed. Paris: Félix Alcan, 1894.

——. *La Dissertation philosophique*. Paris: Félix Alcan, 1890.

Bonnet, H. *Alphonse Darlu (1849–1921): Le Maître de philosophie de Marcel Proust*. Paris: A. G. Nizet, 1961.

Bouglé, Célestin. *Vie spirituelle et action sociale*. Paris: Edouard Cornély, 1902.

Bouillier, Françisque. *De la conscience en psychologie et en morale*. Paris: Germer Baillière, 1872.

——. *De la querelle des anciens et des modernes en morale*. Paris: Académie des sciences morales et politiques, 1869.

——. *Morale et progrès*. Paris: Didier, 1875.

——. *Nouvelles études familières de psychologie et de morale*. Paris: Hachette, 1887.

——. *Questions de morale pratique*. Paris: Hachette, 1889.

Bourdeau, Jean. "Le Bonheur dans le pessimisme: Schopenhauer d'après sa correspondance." *Revue des deux mondes* (August 15, 1884): 916–34.

——. *L'évolution du socialisme*. Paris: Félix Alcan, 1901.

——. *Les maîtres de la pensée contemporaine*. Paris: Félix Alcan, 1904.

——. "Le néo-cynisme aristocratique—Nietzsche." *Journal des débats politiques et littéraires* (April 20, 1893): 1–2.

——. *La Philosophie affective: nouveaux courants et nouveaux problèmes dans la philosophie contemporaine*. Paris: Félix Alcan, 1912.

—. *La Rochefoucauld*. Paris: Hachette, 1895.

Bourdon, B. *L'expression des émotions et des tendances dans le langage*. Paris: Félix Alcan, 1892.

Bourgeois, Léon. *Essai d'une philosophie de la solidarité*. Paris: Félix Alcan, 1902.

—. *Solidarité*. Paris: Armand Colin, 1912.

Boutmy, Émile. *Académie des sciences morales et politiques: Funérailles de M. Beaussire*. Paris: Firmin Didot, 1889.

—. *Académie des sciences morales et politiques: Notice sur la vie et les travaux de M. Bardoux*. Paris: Firmin Didot, 1902.

—. *La Solidarité humaine*. Paris: s.d.

—. *Taine, Scherer, Laboulaye*. Paris: Armand Colin, 1901.

Boutroux, Émile. *The Beyond That Is Within and Other Addresses*. Jonathan Nield, trans. London: Duckworth, 1912.

—. "Les idées philosophiques et religieuses de Rousseau." *Revue métaphysique et morale* (May 1912): 265–74.

—. "Morale et Religion." *Revue des deux mondes* (September 1, 1910): 5–37.

—. *Morale sociale*. Paris: Félix Alcan, 1895.

—. "Observations sur la solidarité sociale." *Académie des sciences morales et politiques* 160 (1903): 399–408.

—. "La Philosophie en France depuis 1867." *Nouvelles études d'histoire de la philosophie*. Paris: F. Alcan, 1927.

—. *Questions de morale et d'éducation*. Paris: Charles Delagrave, 1895.

—. *Science et religion dans la philosophie contemporaine*. Paris: Flammarion, 1908.

Boutry, Camille. *De la solidarité humaine*. Paris: A. Chaix, 1877.

—. *La loi morale et le sens commun*. Paris: A. Chaix, 1875.

Brémont d'Ars, Comte Guy de. "Rapports verbaux: Bouillier, *De la vertu morale et sociale du Christianisme*." *Séances de l'Académie des sciences morales et politiques*. Vol. 134. Paris: Alphonse Picard, 1890.

Brunetière, Ferdinand. "L'idée de la solidarité." *Journal des débats* (December 17, 1900): 7–8.

—. *La Moralité de la doctrine évolutive*. Paris: Firmin Didot, 1896.

—. *La Science et la religion*. Paris: Firmin Didot, 1895.

Brunot, V. "Solidarité et charité." *Revue politique et parlémentaire* 28 (June 10, 1901): 543.

Buisson, Ferdinand Edouard, ed. *Dictionnaire de pédagogie et d'instruction primaire*. 4 vols. Paris: Hachette, 1887.

—. *La foi laïque: extraits de discours et d'écrits (1878–1911)*. Paris: Hachette, 1912.

—. *Leçons de morale à l'usage de l'enseignement primaire*. Paris: Hachette, 1927.

Cadot, Michel. *Eugène-Melchior de Vogüé, le héraut du roman russe*. Paris: Institut d'études slaves, 1989.

Cahen, Léon. "Les idées charitables à Paris au XVIIème et au XVIIIème siècles, d'après des compagnies paroissales." *Revue d'histoire moderne et contemporaine* 2 (1900): 5–22.

Canivez, André. *Jules Lagneau: Essai sur la condition du professeur de philosophie jusqu'à la fin du XIXème siècle*. Strasbourg: Association des publications de la Faculté des Lettres de Strasbourg, 1965.

Caro, Elme. *Étude morale sur le temps présent*. Paris: Hachette, 1875.

—. *Philosophie et philosophes*. Paris: Hachette, 1888.

—. *Problèmes de morale sociale*. Paris: Hachette, 1887.

—. "La Solidarité morale." *Revue politique et littéraire* 3:1 (January 1881): 11.

Carrau, Ludovic. *La conscience psychologique et morale dans l'individu et dans l'histoire*. Paris: Perrin, 1887.

—. "L'Evolution de la morale: la moralité chez les sauvages." *Revue politique et littéraire* 2:1 (July 10, 1880): 27–33.

Catalogue des thèses et écrits académiques. Paris: Librairie Ernest Leroux, 1908.

Centenaire de Théodule Ribot: Jubilé de la psychologie scientifique française. 1839–1889–1939. Agen: Imprimérie Moderne, 1939.

Clemenceau, Georges. *La Honte*. Paris: P.-V. Stock, 1903.

—. *L'Iniquité*. Paris: P.-V. Stock, 1899.

—. *Vers la réparation*. Paris: P.-V. Stock, 1899.

Constant, Benjamin. *De la Religion considérée dans sa source, ses formes et ses développements*. Paris: Bossange père, 1824–1831.

Curinier, C.-E., ed. *Dictionnaire national des contemporains*. 5 vols. Paris: B. Brunel, s.d.

Dareste, Rodolphe. *Études d'histoire du droit*. Paris: L. Larose et Forcel, 1889.

Darlu, Alphonse. "Classification des idées morales du temps présent." *Morale sociale: Léçons professées au Collège libre des sciences sociales*. Émile Boutroux, pref. Paris: Félix Alcan, 1899.

—. "La Morale chrétienne et la conscience contemporaine." *Revue métaphysique et morale* 8 (1900): 257–73.

Dessaignes, J.-P. *Études de l'homme moral*. 3 vols. Paris: 1881.

Dictionnaire des philosophes. 2 vols. Denis Huisman, Dir. Paris: Presses Universitaires de France, 1993.

Donaudy, Joseph. *Les questions sentimentales en sociologie*. Paris: V. Giard et E. Brière, 1905.

Dubost, Paul. "L'idée de justice sociale et sa transformation depuis 100 ans." *La Reforme sociale* (August 1, 1896): 299–317.

Dumas, Georges. *Les Etats intellectuels dans la mélancolie*. Paris: Félix Alcan, 1895.

Dumont, Léon. *Théorie scientifique de la sensibilité*. 3rd ed. Paris: Germer Baillière, 1881.

Durkheim, Émile. *On Morality and Society: Selected Writings*. Chicago: U of Chicago P, 1977.

Dwelshauvers, G. "Rousseau et Tolstoï." *Revue de métaphysique et de morale* 20:2 (March 1912): 461–82.

Ehrhardt, Eugène. *La notion du droit et le christianisme: introduction historique. La Crise actuelle de la philosophie du droit*. Paris: Fischbacher, 1908.

Espinas, Victor-Alfred. "Le Système de J.-J. Rousseau." *Revue de l'enseignement* (1895).

—. *Études sur l'histoire de la philosophie de l'action: Descartes et la morale*. Vol. 1. Paris: Editions Bossard Pais, 1925.

Études sur la philosophie morale au 19ème siècle, léçons professées à l'Ecole des hautes études sociales. Paris: Félix Alcan, 1904.

Faure, Sébastien. *La douleur universelle: Philosophie libertaire*. Paris: Albert Savine, 1895.

Favre, Pierre. "Les professeurs de l'Ecole libre des sciences politiques et la constitution d'une science du politique en France." *Le Personnel de l'enseignement supérieure en France aux 19ème et 20ème siècles*. Charle, Christophe, and Régine Ferré, eds. Paris: Editions du CNRS, 1985.

Fonsegrive, Georges. *'Kultur' et civilisation*. Paris: Bloud et Gay, 1914–1916.

—. *Léon Ollé-Laprune*. Paris: Victor Lecoffre, 1898.

—. *Morale et société*. Paris: Librairie Bloud et Cie, 1907.

—. *Regards en arrière*. Paris: Librairie Bloud et Cie, 1908.

—. *Solidarité, pitié, charité: Examen de la nouvelle morale*. Paris: 1912.

Fouillée, Alfred. *Critique des systèmes de morale contemporains*. Paris: Germer Ballière, 1883.

—. *L'Evolutionnisme des idées-forces*. Paris: Félix Alcan, 1890.

—. *La France au point de vue morale*. Paris: Félix Alcan, 1911.

—. *Morale des idées-forces*. Paris: Félix Alcan, 1908.

—. *La Morale, l'art et la religion d'après Guyau*. Paris: Félix Alcan, 1889.

—. "La morale socialiste." *Revue des deux mondes* (July 15, 1901): 390–91.

—. *Le Moralisme de Kant et l'immoralisme contemporain*. Paris: Félix Alcan, 1905.

—. *Le Mouvement idéaliste et la réaction contre la science positive*. Paris: Félix Alcan, 1896.

—. *Le Mouvement positiviste et la conception sociologique du monde*. Paris: Félix Alcan, 1896.

—. *La Psychologie des idées-forces*. 2 vols. Paris: Félix Alcan, 1893.

—. "La Psychologie des sexes et son fondement physiologique." *Revue des deux mondes* 119 (1893): 400.

—. "La Question morale, est-elle une question sociale?" *Revue des deux mondes* (August 1, 1900): 481–512.

—. "La solidarité humain et les droits de l'individu." *Revue des deux mondes* (August 15, 1883): 803–34.

Franck, Adolphe. ed. *Dictionnaire des sciences philosophiques*. 3rd ed. Paris: Hachette, 1885.

Garnier, Adolphe, ed. *Traité des facultés de l'âme*. 2nd ed. Paris: Hachette, 1865.

Giraud, Victor. *Les Maîtres de l'heure: Essais d'histoire morale contemporaine*. Paris: Hachette, 1912.

Godfernaux, André. *Le sentiment et la pensée, et leurs principaux aspects physiologiques: Essai de psychologie expérimentale et comparée*. Paris: Félix Alcan, 1894.

Guyau, Jean-Marie. *Esquisse d'une morale sans obligation ni sanction*. Paris: Félix Alcan, 1885.

—. *Solidarisme et christianisme*. Reims: 1906.

Haussonville, Othénon-Bernard-Gabriel de Cléron. *Misères et remèdes*. Paris: Calmann-Lévy, 1892.

—. "Socialisme d'état et socialisme chrétien." *Revue des deux mondes* (June 15, 1890): 839–68.

—. *Socialisme et charité*. Paris: Calmann-Lévy, 1895.

Hayward, J.E.S. "Solidarity: The Social History of an Idea in Nineteenth Century France." *International Review of Social History* 4 (1959): 261–84.

Hémon, Camille. "Conflit des sentiments égoistes et des sentiments sociaux." *Revue des cours et conférences* 9:2 (June 20, 1901): 705–14.

Izoulet, Jean. *La Saint-cité ou l'anti-Marxisme*. Paris: Albin Michel, 1895.

Jacquard, Charles. "L'éducation morale à l'école." *Le Volume* 20:1 (1907–1908): 35.

Janet, Paul. *Cours de morale à l'usage des écoles normales primaires*. Paris: Charles Delagrave, 1881.

—. *Cours de psychologie et de morale: 2ème année—morale théorique et morale pratique*. Paris: Charles Delagrave, 1891.

—. *La Crise philosophique*. Paris: Germer Ballière, 1865.

—. *Eléments de morale*. Paris: Charles Delagrave, 1870.

—. *Eléments de morale pratique*. Paris: Charles Delagrave, 1889.

Bibliography 291

—. *Eléments de morale pratique et scientifique*. Paris: Charles Delagrave, 1890.

—. *Histoire de la science politique dans ses rapports avec la morale*. Paris: Ladrange, 1872.

—. and Gabriel Séailles. *History of the Problems of Philosophy*. 2 vols. Henry Jones, ed. Ada Monahan, trans. London and New York: Macmillan, 1902.

—. *Lectures variées de littérature et de morale*. Paris: Charles Delagrave, 1890.

—. *Les Maîtres de la pensée moderne*. Paris: Calmann-Lévy, 1883.

—. *La Morale*. Paris: Charles Delagrave, 1874.

—. *La Philosophie française contemporaine*. Paris: Calmann-Lévy, 1879.

—. *Principes de métaphysique et de psychologie: Leçons professées à la faculté des lettres de Paris (1888–1894)*. Vol. 3. Paris: Delagrave, 1897.

—. *Les Problèmes du XIXème siècle*. Paris: Michel Lévy Frères, 1873.

—. *The Theory of Morals*. Mary Chapman, trans. New York: Charles Scribner's Sons, 1883.

—. *Traité élémentaire de philosophie*. 6ème éd. Paris: Librairie Charles Delagrave: 1889.

Janet, Pierre. *Manuel du baccalauréat de l'enseignement secondaire: Philosophie*. Paris: Librairie Nony, 1896.

Joly, Henri. *Eléments de morale*. Paris: Delalain, 1880.

—. *Le socialisme chrétien*. Paris: Hachette, 1892.

Jourdain, Charles. *Notions de philosophie*. 8th ed. Paris: Hachette, 1863.

LaCapra, Dominick. *Émile Durkheim: Sociologist and Philosopher*. Ithaca, NY: Cornell UP, 1972.

Lachelier, Jules. *The Philosophy of Jules Lachelier*. Edward G. Ballard, trans. and ed. The Hague: Nijhoff, 1960.

Lalande, Andre. *La Dissolution opposée à l'évolution dans les sciences physiques et morales*. Paris: Félix Alcan, 1899.

—. *Vocabulaire technique et critique de la philosophie*. Paris: Félix Alcan, 1932.

Laloi, Pierre. *La Première année d'instruction morale et civique*. Paris: Armand Colin, 1899.

Lapie, Paul. *La Justice par l'état: étude de morale sociale*. Paris: Félix Alcan, 1899.

Laplaigne, H. *La morale en maximes*. Paris: V. Girard, 1903.

Laserre, Pierre. *Le Romantisme français: essai sur la révolution dans les sentiments et dans les idées au XIXème siècle*. 4th ed. Paris: Mercure de France, 1907.

LeBon, Gustave. *The Crowd: A Study of the Popular Mind*. New York: Viking Press, 1960.

—. *Gustave Le Bon: The Man and His Works*. Alice Widener, ed. Indianapolis: Liberty Press, 1979.

—. *The Psychology of Socialism*. New York: Macmillan, 1899; Wells, VT: Fraser, 1965.

Lemaître, Jules. *Les Contemporains: études et portraits littéraires*. Paris: H. Lecène et H. Oudin, 1886.

Létourneau, Charles Jean Marie. *L'Evolution de la morale: leçons proféssées l'hiver de 1885–86*. Paris: L. Battaille et cie., 1894.

Levy-Bruhl, Lucien. *La Morale et la science des moeurs*. Paris: Félix Alcan, 1903.

Maillet, Eugène. *De l'essence des passions: étude psychologique et morale*. Paris: Hachette, 1872.

Maneuvrier, Edouard. "Une thèse individualiste sur l'idée de l'état." *Revue universitaire* (February 15, 1896): 333–350.

Mantegazza, Paolo. *La Physionomie et l'expression des sentiments*. Paris: Félix Alcan, 1889.

Marion, Henri. *De la Solidarité morale: essai de psychologie appliquée*. Paris: Germer

Ballière, 1880.

—. *Leçons de morale*. 9th ed. Paris: A. Colin, 1898.

—. *Pages et pensées morales: Extraits des auteurs français du XVIIème, XVIIIème, et XIXème siècles*. 4th ed. Paris: H. Dereux, 1925.

Mélinand, Camille. *Cours de philosophie morale*. Paris: Ecole universelle par correspondence, s.d.

—. *Notions de psychologie appliquées à l'éducation: 1ère année des écoles normales (programmes du 20 août 1920)*. Paris: F. Nathan, 1923.

Mézières, Alfred-Jean-François. *Éducation morale et instruction civique à l'usage des écoles primaires*. Paris: Charles Delagrave, 1883.

Mignard, M. "Emotion, Sentiment, Tendance." *Revue des idées* 84 (December 1910): 418–25.

Milsand, Joseph. "Les Sentiments et les idées." *La critique philosophique* (9:1): 109.

Ministère de l'instruction publique. *L'inspection de l'enseignement primaire*. Paris: Imprimérie nationale, 1900.

Montier, Edward. *Éducation du sentiment*. Paris: Boivin, 1921.

Morales et religions: leçons professées à l'Ecole des hautes études sociales. Paris: Félix Alcan, 1909.

Nourrison, Jean-Félix. *Spinoza et le naturalisme contemporain*. Paris: Didier et cie., 1866.

Nye, Mary Jo. "The Boutroux Circle and Poincaré's Conventionalism." *Journal of the History of Ideas* 40 (1979): 107–20.

Ollé-Laprune, Léon. *De la certitude morale*. Paris: Belin Frères, 1880.

—. *De la responsabilité de chacun devant le mal social*. Paris: Comité de défense et de progrès social, 1895.

—. *Essai sur la morale d'Aristote*. Paris: Belin Frères, 1881.

Paulhan, Frederic. *The Laws of Feeling*. C. K. Ogden, trans. New York: Harcourt, Brace, 1930.

—. *Le Nouveau mysticisme*. Paris: Félix Alcan, 1891.

—. *La Physiologie de l'esprit*. Paris: Germer Baillière, s.d.

—. *Les Phénomènes affectifs et les lois de leur apparition*. Paris: Félix Alcan, 1887.

Payot, Jules. *Cours de morale*. Paris: Armand Colin, 1904.

—. *La Morale à l'école*. Paris: Armand Colin, 1907.

Picot, Georges. *L'Institut de France*. Paris: Librairie Renouard, 1907.

Pioger, Julien. *La vie sociale, la morale et le progrès*. Paris: Félix Alcan, 1894.

—. "Origines et conditions sociales de la moralité." *Revue philosophique de la France et de l'étranger* 37 (January-June 1894): 634–56.

Ponthière, Charles de. *Charité, Justice, Propriété*. Paris: X. Rondélet et Cie., 1899.

Prat, Louis, ed. *Charles Rénouvier: derniers entrétiens*. Paris: A. Colin, 1904.

Pressensé, M. E. de. "La morale de l'intérêt et l'obligation morale." *Revue politique et littéraire* 3:2 (November 11, 1882): 619–21.

Proal, Louis Joseph. *Passion and Criminality: A Legal and Literary Study*. Paris: C. Carrington, 1901.

Rabier, Elie. *Leçons de philosophie*. 5th ed. Paris: Hachette, 1896.

Rauh, Frédéric. *Études de morale*. Paris: Félix Alcan, 1911.

—. *De la Méthode dans la psychologie des sentiments*. Paris: Félix Alcan, 1899.

Ravaisson-Mollien, Félix. *Essai sur le stoïcism*. Paris: Imprimérie impériale, 1856.

—. *La philosophie en France au XIXème siècle*. Paris: Imprimérie impériale, 1868.

Rée, Paul. *De l'origine des sentiments moraux*. Michel-François Demet, trans. Paris: Presses Universitaires de France, 1892.

Renan, Ernest. *Correspondance*. Vol. 2: 1872–1892. Paris: Calmann-Lévy, 1928.

—. *La réforme morale et intellectuelle*. Paris: Lévy Frères, 1871.

Renouvier, Charles. *Philosophie analytique de l'histoire: les idées, les religions, les systèmes*. Vol. 4. Paris: Ernest Leroux, 1897.

—. "Revue: Henri Marion, *De la solidarité morale*." *La Critique philosophique* 9:1 (October 1880): 148-160.

—. *Science de la morale*. 2 vols. Paris: Librairie Philosophique de Ladrange, 1869.

Revue universitaire. Paris: Armand Colin, s.d.

Ribot, Théodule. *Diseases of Memory; Diseases of Personality; Diseases of the Will*. In *Significant Contributions to the History of Psychology, 1750–1920*. Daniel N. Robinson, ed. Washington, DC: University Publications of America, 1977.

—. *Essai sur les passions*. Paris: Félix Alcan, 1906.

—. *La Logique des sentiments*. Paris: Félix Alcan, 1904.

—. *La Psychologie allemande contemporaine*. Paris: Germer Baillière, 1879.

—. *La Psychologie des sentiments*. Paris: Félix Alcan, 1896.

Richard, Gaston. *La Question sociale et le mouvement philosophique au XIXème siècle*. Paris: Armand Colin, 1914.

—. *Manuel de morale*. Paris: Charles Delagrave, 1903.

Ritti, Jean Marie Paul. *De la méthode sentimentale*. Paris: P. Ritti, 1904.

—. *Quelques vues théoriques sur la sympathie*. Paris: P. Ritti, 1899.

Les sentiments desintéressées: étude psychologique, dialogue. Vannes: Librarie Lafoyle, 1900.

Shand, Alexander F. *The Foundations of Character: Being a Study of the Tendencies of the Emotions and Sentiments*. London: Macmillan and Co., 1914.

—. "Mr. Ribot's Theory of the Passions." *Mind* 16 (1907): 477–505.

Sollier, Paul. "Recherches sur les rapports de la sensibilité et d'émotion." *Revue philosophique de la France et de l'étranger* 37 (January-June 1894): 241–66.

Strowski, F. "Le Romantisme humanitaire et philosophique." *Revue des cours et conférences* 21:1 (1913): 209– ; 21: 2 (1913): 34– ; 22:1 (1913): 105.

Sully-Prudhomme. *Oeuvres de Sully Prudhomme: Prose. L'expression dans les beaux-arts*. Paris: Alphonse Lemerre, 1893.

Taine, Hippolyte. *Philosophie de l'art*. 18th ed. Paris: Hachette, 1921.

—. *Vie et correspondance*. Vol. 4: *L'historien*. Paris: Hachette, 1907.

Tarde, Gabriel. *Études de psychologie sociale*. Paris: 1898.

—. "La logique sociale des sentiments." *Revue philosophique de la France et de l'étranger* 36 (July-December 1893): 561–94.

—. *On Communication and Social Influence: Selected Papers*. Terry N. Clark, ed. Chicago: U of Chicago P, 1969.

Tersen, Émile. *Histoire des idées sociales et religieuses de 1815–1914*. Paris: Centre de documentation universitaire, 1961.

Thamin, Raymond. *Cours de psychologie et de morale, 1ère année*. Paris: Charles Delagrave, 1891.

—. *Extraits des moralistes*. Paris: Hachette, 1897.

Thomas, P.-Félix. *L'Éducation des sentiments*. Paris: Félix Alcan, 1899.

—. *Morale et éducation*. Paris: Félix Alcan, 1899.

Vaillant, J. "Pour le maintien du cours de morale sociale." *Revue Universitaire* (1912): 1.

Vincent, K. Steven. "Benjamin Constant, the French Revolution, and the Origins of French Romantic Liberalism." *French Historical Studies* 23:4 (Fall 2000): 607–37.

Worms, Frédéric. "Au-delà de l'histoire et du caractère: l'idée de philosophie française, la Première Guerre mondiale et le 'moment 1900.'" *Revue de Métaphysique et de*

Morale (July-September 2001): 63–81.

France and the Study of Gender

Accampo, Elinor A., Rachel Fuchs, and Mary Lynn Stewart. *Gender and the Politics of Social Reform in France, 1870–1914*. Baltimore: Johns Hopkins UP, 1995.

Ancel, J., and Léon Dugas. *Leçons de morale théorique et notions historiques. Enseignement secondaire des jeunes filles: Ecoles normales*. 3rd ed. Paris: Fernand Nathan, 1918.

Boiraud, H. "Sur la création par l'état d'un enseignement secondaire féminin en France." *Paedagogica Historica* 21 (1977): 21–36.

Clark, Linda L. "A Battle of the Sexes in a Professional Setting: The Introduction of *Inspectrices Primaires*, 1889–1914." *French Historical Studies* 16:2 (Spring 1989): 96–125.

—. *Schooling the Daughters of Marianne: Textbooks and the Socialization of Girls in Modern French Primary Schools*. Albany: SUNY Press, 1984.

Clark, Suzanne. *Sentimental Modernism: Women Writers and the Revolution of the Word*. Bloomington: Indiana UP, 1991.

Dubreuil, Léon. "Paul Bert et l'enseignement secondaire féminin." *Revue d'histoire économique et sociale* 18 (1930): 205–40.

Fonsegrive, Georges. *L'Enseignement féminin*. Paris: Victor Lecoffre, 1898.

Gemie, Shariff. "Docility, Zeal, and Rebellion: Culture and Sub-Cultures in French Women's Teacher Training Colleges, c.1860–1910." *European History Quarterly* 24 (1994): 213–44.

Gréard, Octave. *L'Enseignement secondaire des filles: Mémoire présenté au conseil académique dans la séance du 27 juin 1882*. Paris: Delalain, 1882.

Gullickon, Gay L. *Unruly Women of Paris: Images of the Commune*. Ithaca, NY: Cornell UP, 1996.

Janet, Paul. "L'éducation des femmes." *Revue des deux mondes* (September 1, 1883): 48–85.

Juranville, Clarisse. *Manuel d'éducation morale et d'instruction civique à l'usage des jeunes filles*. Paris: Vve. P. Larousse, 1889.

Koven, Seth, and Sonya Michel. "Womanly Duties: Maternalist Politics and the Origins of Welfare States in France, Germany, Great Britain, and the United States, 1880–1920." *American Historical Review* 95 (October 1990): 1076–1108.

Lamy, Étienne. *La Femme de demain*. Paris: Perrin, 1914.

—. "La Femme et l'enseignement de l'état." *Revue des deux mondes* (April 1, 1901): 601–29.

Lapie, Paul. *La Femme dans la famille*. Paris: Octave Doin, 1908.

Marion, Henri. *Étude de psychologie feminine: l'éducation des jeunes filles*. Paris: Armand Colin, 1902.

Maugue, Annelise. *L'identité masculine en crise au tournant du siècle, 1871–1914*. Paris: Editions Rivages, 1987.

Mayeur, Françoise. *L'Éducation des filles en France au XIXème siècle*. Paris: Hachette, 1979.

—. *L'Enseignement secondaire des jeunes filles sous la Troisième République*. Paris: Presses de la fondation nationale des sciences politiques, 1977.

Michelet, Jules. *Les Femmes de la Révolution*. Paris: A. Delahays, 1854.

Offen, Karen. "Ernest Legouvé and the Doctrine of 'Equality in Difference' for Women: A Case Study of Male Feminism in Nineteenth-Century French Thought." *Journal of Modern History* 58:2 (1986): 479–81.

— "The Second Sex and the Baccalauréat in Republican France, 1880–1924." *French Historical Studies* 13 (1983): 252–86.

Queilfelu, Lisa. "Héroine et martyre: La figure de la femme dans le roman sentimental de la fin du XIXème siècle." *Le roman sentimental: actes du colloque des 14–15–16 mars 1989 à la faculté des lettres de Limoges.* Limoges: TRAMES, 1989: 253–81.

Reval, Gabrielle. *Les Sèvriennes.* Paris: Ollendorff, 1900.

Rousselet, Paul. *La Pédagogie féminine.* Paris: Charles Delagrave, 1881.

Sée, Camille. *Lycées et collèges de jeunes filles: documents, rapports et discours à la chambre des Députés et au Sénat; décrets, arrêtés, circulaires, etc.* Paris: 1896.

Teutscher, F. "Sur Quelques insuffisances de l'enseignement féminine." *Revue Universitaire* 1911 (1): 33–37.

Villemot, Antoine. *Étude sur l'organisation, le fonctionnement et les progrès de l'enseignement secondaire des jeunes filles en France, de 1789 à 1887.* Paris: Paul Dupont, 187.

— .ed. *Enseignement secondaire. Documents, publications et ouvrages récents relatifs à l'éducation des femmes et à l'éducation secondaire des jeunes fille.* Paris: Paul Dupont, 1889.

Waelti-Walters, Jennifer. "'New Women' in the Novels of *Belle Epoque* France." *History of European Ideas* 8:4/5 (1987): 537–48.

French *Fin-de-Siècle* Literature

Alden, Douglas W. "Proust and Ribot." *Modern Language Notes* 58:7 (November 1943): 501–7.

Barrès, Maurice. *Journal de ma vie extérieure.* François Broche et Eric Roussel, eds. Paris: Editions Julliard, 1994.

—. *Mes Cahiers: 1896–1923.* Guy Dupré, ed. Paris: Plon, 1994.

Bauër, Henry. *De la vie et du rêve.* Paris: H. Simonis Empis, 1896.

—. *Idée et réalité.* Paris: H. Simonis Empis, 1899.

—. "La Lumière du nord." *L'Echos de Paris* (June 24, 1895): 1–3.

—. *Mémoires d'un jeune homme.* Paris: Charpentier, 1895.

Bloy, Léon. *La Femme pauvre.* 32nd ed. Paris: Mercure de France, 1937.

Bourget, Paul. *Le Disciple.* Paris: Editions de la Table Ronde, 1994.

—. *Essais de psychologie contemporaine.* 9th ed. Paris: A. Lemerre, 1893.

—. *Études et portraits.* Vol. 3: *Sociologie et littérature.* Paris: Plon-Nourrit, 1906.

Brown, Frederick. *Zola: A Life.* Baltimore: Johns Hopkins UP, 1996.

Brunetière, Ferdinand. "A Propos du *Disciple* de M. Paul Bourget." *Revue des deux mondes* (July 1, 1889): 223.

—. *Essais sur la littérature contemporaine.* 3rd ed. Paris: Calmann-Lévy, 1892.

—. *Le Roman naturaliste.* Paris: Calmann-Lévy, 1883.

Buisine, Alain. *Tombeau de Loti.* Paris: Aux amateurs de livres: 1988.

Cerf, Marcel. *Le Mousquetaire de la plume: la vie d'un grand critique dramatique, Henry Bauër, fils naturel d'Alexandre Dumas, 1851–1915.* Paris: Académie d'histoire, 1975.

Faguet, Émile. *Dix-neuvième siècle: Études littéraires.* Paris: Société Française d'imprimérie et de librairie, 1900.

France, Anatole. "Conte pour commencer gaiement l'année." *Opinions Sociales.* Paris: G. Ballais, 1902.

—. *Le Jardin d'Epicure.* 132nd ed. Paris: Calmann-Lévy, 1926.

Giono, Jean. *Solitude de la pitié*. Paris: Gallimard, 1932.

Goncourt, Edmond, et Jules de. *Germinie Lacerteux*. Paris: Librairie Générale Française, 1990.

—. *Journal des Goncourt*. 4 vols. Paris: Flammarion, 1959.

—. *Paris and the Arts, 1851–1896: From the Goncourt Journal*. George J. Becker and Edith Philips, eds. and trans. Ithaca, NY: Cornell UP, 1971.

Hallays, André. "De l'influence des littératures étrangères." *Revue de Paris* (February 15, 1895): 884.

Hemmings, F.W.J. *The Russian Novel in France, 1884–1914*. Oxford: Clarendon Press, 1950.

Henry, Anne. *Marcel Proust: Théories pour une esthétique*. Paris: Klincksieck, 1983.

Hugo, Victor. "La Pitié suprême." *Oeuvres Complètes*. Vol. 10. Jean Massin, ed. Paris: Club Français du Livre, 1967.

Janet, Paul. "J.-J. Rousseau et les origines du cosmopolitisme littéraire." *Journal des savants* (January, April 1896): 5–14; 205–18.

Lemaître, Jules. "De l'influence récente des littératures du Nord." *Revue des deux mondes* (December 15, 1894): 847–73.

—. "Le Mouvement poétique en France." *Revue politique et littéraire* 2ème série: 6 (August 9, 1879): 121.

Lévinas, Emmanuel. "L'Autre dans Proust." *Deucalion* 2 (1947): 117–23.

Loti, Pierre. *Le Livre de la pitié et de la mort*. Joué-lès-Tours: Christian Pirot, 1991.

—. *Le roman d'un enfant, suivi de Prime jeunesse*. Paris: Gallimard, 1999.

Mauclair, Camille. "Le Sentimentalisme littéraire et son influence sur le siècle." *La Grande revue* 5:1 (May 1900): 371–404.

Mein, Margaret. "Proust and Wagner." *Journal of European Studies* 19 (1989): 205–22.

Michiels, Alfred. *Histoire des idées littéraires en France au XIXème siècle, et de leurs origines dans les siècles antérieurs*. Paris: 1863. Génève: Slatkin Reprints, 1969–1970.

Mirbeau, Octave. *Journal d'une femme de chambre*. Paris: Bookking International, 1993.

Nathan, Jacques. *La morale de Proust*. Paris: Nizet, 1953.

Nattiez, Jean-Jacques. "*Parsifal* comme modèle rédempteur de l'oeuvre rédemptive." *Proust musicien*. Paris: 1984.

Newman-Gordon, Pauline. *Répertoire des thèmes de Marcel Proust. Cahiers Marcel Proust: 7*. Paris: Gallimard, 1935.

O'Brien, Justin. *Contemporary French Literature: Essays*. New Brunswick, NJ: Rutgers UP, 1971.

Ossip-Lourié. *La Philosophie de Tolstoï*. Paris: Félix Alcan, 1899.

Ouvrard, Pierre. *Zola et le prêtre*. Paris: Beauchesne, 1986.

Peylet, Gérard. "À la limite du roman sentimentale: *Un crime d'amour* de Paul Bourget ou comment un romancier bourgeois exploite la veine du roman d'analyse." *Le roman sentimental: actes du colloque des 14–15–16 mars 1989 à la faculté des letters de Limoges*. Limoges: TRAMES, 1989: 143–52.

Proust, Marcel. *À l'Ombre de jeunes filles en fleur*. Paris: Gallimard, 1989.

—. *Albertine Disparue*. Paris: Gallimard, 1990.

—. *The Captive*. C. K. Scott Moncrieff, trans. London: Chatto and Windus, 1925.

—. *Le Côté des Guermantes*. Paris: Gallimard, 1988.

—. *The Guermantes Way*. C. K. Scott Moncrieff, trans. London: Chatto and Windus, 1925.

—. *La Prisonnière*. Paris: Gallimard, 1984.

—. *Sodome et Gomorrhe*. Paris: Gallimard, 1988.

—. *Sodom and Gomorra*. C. K. Scott Moncrieff, trans. London: Chatto and Windus, 1951.

—. *Swann's Way*. C. K. Scott Moncrieff, trans. London: Chatto and Windus, 1924.

—. *Le Temps retrouvé*. Paris: Gallimard, 1989.

—. *Time Regained*. Andreas Mayor, trans. London: Chatto and Windus, 1970.

—. *Within a Budding Grove*. C. K. Scott Moncrieff, trans. London: Chatto and Windus, 1924.

Saint-Marc Girardin. *Lectures on Dramatic Literature, or, The Employment of the Passions in the Drama*. Robert Gibbes Barnwell, trans. New York: Appleton & Co., 1849.

Schalk, David L. "Tying up the Loose Ends of an Epoch: Zola's *Docteur Pascal*." *French Historical Studies* 16 (Spring 1989): 202–16.

Scheler, Lucien. "Louise Michel et Henry Bauër: correspondants de Paul Meurice." *Europe* 48 (1971): 253–64.

Schor, Naomi. *Bad Objects: Essays Popular and Unpopular*. Durham, NC: Duke UP, 1995.

—. *George Sand and Idealism*. New York: Columbia UP, 1993.

Shattuck, Roger. *Marcel Proust*. New York: 1974.

Singer, Armand E. *Paul Bourget*. Boston: Twayne, 1976.

Texte, Joseph. *Jean-Jacques Rousseau et les origines du cosmopolitisme littéraire*. Génève: Slatkine Reprints, 1970.

—. "La Philosophie d'Elizabeth Browning." *Revue des deux mondes* (August 15, 1892): 847.

Vogüé, Eugène Melchior, Comte de. "Le Débacle." *Revue des deux mondes* (July 15, 1892): 443–59.

—. "Les Ecrivains russes contemporains." *Revue des deux mondes* (July 15, 1884): 300.

—. *Pages choisies*. Paris: Plon-Nourrit, 1912.

—. *Regards historiques et littéraires*. Paris: Armand Colin, 1892.

—. "La renaissance Latine." *Revue des deux mondes* (January-February 1895): 187–207.

—. *Le Roman russe*. Paris: Plon-Nourrit, 1886.

Zola, Émile. *Germinal*. Paris: Fasquelle, 1983.

— *My Hatreds/Mes Haines*. Palomba Paves-Yashinsky and Jack Yashinsky, trans. *Studies in French Literature* 12. Lewiston, NY: Edwin Mellen Press, 1991.

—. *La Joie de Vivre*. Paris: Fasquelle, 1985.

General Works on History, Philosophy, and Education

Barrows, Susanna. *Distorting Mirrors: Visions of the Crowd in Late Nineteenth-Century France*. New Haven, CT: Yale UP, 1981.

Barthes, Roland. *Michelet*. Paris: Editions de Seuil, 1995.

Baustert, Raymond. "L'Honnêteté en France et à l'étranger: étude comparative de quelques aspects." *Horizons Européens de la littérature française au XVIIème siècle*. Wolfgang Leiner, ed. Tubingen: 1988.

Bell, David A. "The Unbearable Lightness of Being French: Law, Republicanism and National Identity at the End of the Old Regime." *The American Historical Review* 106:4 (October 2001): 1215–235.

Borchard, Edwin M., and George Wilfred. *Guide to the Law and Legal Literature of France*. Washington, DC: Library of Congress, 1931.

Brédin, Jean-Denis. *The Affair: The Case of Alfred Dreyfus*. New York: George Brazilier, 1986.

Brooks, John I. III. *The Eclectic Legacy: Academic Philosophy and the Human Sciences in Nineteenth Century France*. Newark: U of Delaware P, 1998.
—. "Philosophy and Psychology at the Sorbonne, 1885–1913." *Journal of the History of the Behavioral Sciences* 29 (April 1993): 123–45.
Brown, Richard Harvey. *Social Science as Civic Discourse: Essays on the Invention, Legitimation, and Uses of Social Theory*. Chicago: U of Chicago P, 1989.
Carr, R. *Anarchism in France: The Case of Octave Mirbeau*. Manchester: Manchester UP, 1977.
Carroll, John. *Break-Out from the Crystal Palace: The Anarcho-Psychological Critique, Stirner, Nietzsche, and Dostoyevsky*. Boston: Routledge and Kegan Paul, 1974.
Carroy, J., and R. Plas. "The Origins of French Experimental Psychology: Experiment and Experimentalism." *History of the Human Sciences* 9 (1996): 73–84.
Certeau, Michel de. *The Writing of History*. Tom Conley, trans. New York: Columbia UP, 1988.
Charle, Christophe. *Paris, fin de siècle: culture et politique*. Paris: Editions du Seuil, 1998.
—. *Les Professeurs de la faculté des lettres à Paris: Dictionnaire biographique*. Paris: Editions du CNRS, 1985.
—. and Régine Ferré, eds. *Le Personnel de l'enseignement supérieur en France aux 19éme et 20éme siècles*. Paris: Editions du CNRS, 1985.
Charmasson, Thérèse, ed. *L'Histoire de l'enseignement, XIXème-XXème siècles: guide du chercheur*. Paris: Institut national de recherche pédagogique, 1986.
Clark, Terry N. *Prophets and Patrons: The French University and the Emergence of the Social Sciences*. Cambridge, MA: Harvard UP, 1973.
Dejean, Joan. *Ancients against Moderns: Culture Wars and the Making of a Fin-de-Siècle*. Chicago: Chicago UP, 1997.
Digeon, Claude. *La Crise allemande de la pensée française*. Paris: Presses Universitaires de France, 1959.
Dunn, Susan. *The Deaths of Louis XVI: Regicide and the French Political Imagination*. Princeton: Princeton UP, 1994.
—. "Michelet and Lamartine: Regicide, Passion, and Compassion." *History and Theory* 28:3 (November 1989): 275–95.
Elias, Norbert. *The Civilizing Process: The History of Manners and State Formation and Civilization*. Edmund Jephcot, trans. Oxford: Blackwell, 1994.
Ellenberger, Henry. *The Discovery of the Unconscious*. New York: Basic Books, 1970.
Fabiani, Jean-Louis. *Les Philosophes de la République*. Paris: Editions de Minuit, 1988.
Ferguson, Priscilla Parkhurst. *Literary France: The Making of a Culture*. Berkeley: U of California P, 1987.
Hazard, Paul. *The European Mind: The Critical Years, 1680–1715*. New York: Fordham UP, 1990.
L'Histoire de l'enseignement, XIXème-XXème siècle: guide du chercheur. Thérèse Charmasson, dir. Paris: Institut National de recherche pédagogique, 1986.
Jankélévitch, Vladimir. *Les Vertus et l'Amour*. Vol. 2: *Traité des vertus*. Paris: Flammarion, 1986.
LaCapra, Dominick. *History and Reading: Tocqueville, Foucault, French Studies*. Toronto: U of Toronto Press, 2000.
Laval, Rose. "The Newest Academy of the Institut-de-France (A Portrait of the Académie des sciences morales et politiques)." *Historia* 579 (March 1995): 94–96.
Leiner, Wolfgang. *Horizons européens de la littérature française au XVIIème siècle: l'Europe, lieu d'échanges culturels? La circulation des oeuvres et des jugements au*

XVIIème siècle. Études littéraires françaises 41. Tubingen: G. Narr, 1988.

Le Senné, René. *Traité de morale générale*. Paris: Presses Universitaires de France, 1967.

Levi, Anthony. *French Moralists: The Theory of the Passions, 1585 to 1649*. Oxford: Clarendon Press, 1964.

Levi-Strauss, Claude. *Structural Anthropology*. Vol. 2. Monique Layton, trans. New York: Basic Books, 1976.

—. *Totemism*. Rodney Needham, trans. Boston: Beacon Press, 1963.

Logue, William. *Charles Renouvier: Philosopher of Liberty*. Baton Rouge, LA: LSU Press, 1993.

—. *From Philosophy to Sociology: The Evolution of French Liberalism, 1870–1914*. DeKalb: Northern Illinois UP, 1983.

Maisonneuve, Jean. *Les Sentiments (Que sais-je?)*. Paris: Presses Universitaires de France, 1973.

—. *Recherches diachroniques sur une représentation sociale: Persistance et changement dans la caractérization de 'l'homme sympathique.'* Paris: Editions du CNRS, 1978.

Maza, Sarah. *Private Lives and Public Affairs: The "Causes Célèbres" of Prerevolutionary France*. Berkeley: U of California P, 1993.

Mestrovic, Stjepan. *The Coming Fin-de-Siècle: An Application of Durkheim's Sociology to Modernity and Postmodernism*. London and New York: Routledge, 1991.

—. *Durkheim and Postmodern Culture*. New York: Aldine de Gruyter, 1992.

Miller, Nancy K. *French Dressing: Women, Men, and Ancien Régime Fiction*. New York: Routledge, 1995.

Milo, Daniel. "Les Classiques scolaires." *Les Lieux de mémoire*. Vol. 2: *Nation 3*. Pierre Nora, ed. Paris: Gallimard, 1986.

Montagu, Jennifer. *The Expression of the Passions: The Origin and Influence of Charles le Brun's "Conférence sur l'expression générale et particulière."* New Haven, CT: Yale UP, 1994.

Nora, Pierre. "Le *Dictionnaire de pédagogie* de Ferdinand Buisson: Cathédrale de l'école primaire." In *Les Lieux de mémoire*. I: *La République*. Paris: Gallimard, 1984.

Nye, Robert A. *Masculinity and Male Codes of Honor in Modern France*. Berkeley: U of California P, 1998.

—. *The Origins of Crowd Psychology: Gustave LeBon and the Crisis of Mass Democracy in the Third Republic*. Beverly Hills, CA: Sage, 1975.

Ozouf, Mona. *L'Ecole, l'Eglise et la République*. Paris: Seuil, 1982.

Paléologue, Maurice. *My Secret Diary of the Dreyfus Case, 1894–99*. Eric Mosbacher, trans. London: Secker & Warburg, 1957.

Paterson, Ronald. *The Nihilist Egoist: Max Stirner*. London: Oxford UP, 1971.

Prochasson, Christophe. *Les Années électriques (1880–1910)*. Paris: Editions de la Découverte, 1991.

— , and Anne Rasmussen. *Au nom de la Patrie: les intellectuels et la première guerre mondiale (1910–1919)*. Paris: Editions de la Découverte, 1996.

Reddy, William. *The Invisible Code: Honor and Sentiment in Postrevolutionary France, 1814–1848*. Berkeley: U of California P, 1997.

—. *The Navigation of Feeling: A Framework for the History of Emotion*. Cambridge: Cambridge UP, 2001.

—. "Sentimentalism and Its Erasure: The Role of Emotions in the Era of the French Revolution." *The Journal of Modern History* 72:1 (March 2000): 109–52.

Ringer, Fritz. *Fields of Knowledge: French Academic Culture in Comparative Perspective, 1890–1920*. New York: Cambridge UP, 1992.

Rorty, Richard. *Contingency, Irony, and Solidarity.* Cambridge: Cambridge UP, 1989.
— , J.B. Schneewind, and Quentin Skinner, eds. *Philosophy in History: Essays on the Historiography of Philosophy.* Cambridge: Cambridge UP, 1984.
Rosanvallon, Pierre. *Le Moment Guizot.* Paris: Gallimard, 1985.
Roth, Michael S. "Remembering Forgetting: *Maladies de la Mémoire* in Nineteenth-Century France." *Representations* 26 (Spring 1989): 49–68.
Smith, W. M. "The 'Two Cultures' in Nineteenth-Century France: Victor Cousin and Auguste Comte." *Journal of the History of Ideas* (1965): 45–58.
Vincent-Buffault, Anne. *Histoire des larmes, XVIIIème-XIXème siècles.* Paris: Rivages, 1986

Other Works

Apollodorus. *The Library.* Michael Simpson, trans. Amherst, MA: U of Massachusetts P, 1989.
Augustine. *The City of God.* New York: Penguin, 1984.
Boileau Despreaux, Nicolas. *Satires, Epitres, Art poétique.* Paris: Gallimard, 1985.
Diodorus of Sicily. *Complete Works.* Vol. 5. C.H. Oldfather, trans. Cambridge, MA: Harvard UP, 1950.
Du Bos, Abbé. *Réflexions critiques sur la poésie et sur la peinture.* Paris: Pissot, 1770.
Gengler, Olivier. "Les traductions françaises de Pausanias." *Les Études classiques* 67:1 (1999): 63–70.
Guizot, François. *De la peine de mort.* Bruxelles: Hauman, 1838.
Jay, Martin. "Two Cheers for Paraphrase: The Confessions of a Synoptic Intellectual Historian." *Fin-de-Siècle Socialism and Other Essays.* New York: Routledge, 1988: 52–63.
Knight, Roy C. *Racine et la Grèce.* 2nd ed. Paris: Librairie A.-G. Nizet, 1974.
Letters of Alciphron, Aelian, and Philostratus. Allen Rogers Benner and Francis H. Fobes, trans. Cambridge: Harvard UP, 1949.
Myers, Robert L. "Racine's *La Thébaïde*: Politics, Morals, and Aesthetic Dimensions." *Rice University Studies* 67:2 (Spring 1981): 1–51.
Pausanius. *Description of Greece.* Wilt S. Jones, trans. Cambridge: Harvard UP, 1959.
Senault, Jean-François. *De l'usage des passions. The Use of the Passions.* Henry, Earl of Monmouth, trans. London: John Sims, 1671.
—. *Natural History of the Passions.* London: Printed by T.N. for James Magnes, 1674.
Statius. *Thebaïs.* H. J. Mosely, trans. Cambridge: Harvard UP, 1959.
Tritle, Lawrence A. *Phocion the Good.* London: Croom Helm, 1988.
Venesoen, Constant. "La *Thébaïde* et les dieux de Racine." *Revue d'histoire littéraire de la France* 79 (1979): 755–71.
Weber, Max. *From Max Weber: Essays in Sociology.* H. H. Gerth and C. Wright Mills, ed., trans., and introd. New York: Oxford UP, 1958.
Ziolkowski, Théodore. *Virgil and the Moderns.* Princeton: Princeton UP, 1993.

Index

centennial of, 110; cruelty and, 112; crying and, 115; Dareste on, 116; Ehrhardt on, 150; *fin-de-siècle* France, reception of, 3, 109, 110–11, 118, 129 n.3; Fonsegrive on, 117–18, 149; Fouillée on, 114, 124–25, 232; *francité* of, 107, 110, 113, 119; French moralists' tradition and, 111, 119; French philosopher-psychologists and, 45; Guérin on, 266–67; Paul Janet on, 93, 110, 114, 127; Jourdain on, 93; Kant and, 53, 110, 113–115; Loti and, Darlu on, 255; Mélinand on, 26–28; Nietzsche and, 107, 109, 111, 113, 114, 118, 119–123, 124, 135–136 n.73; Nourrisson on, 114; pessimism and, 111–19 passim., 128; — , in Zola's *La Joie de vivre*, 216–18; Pioger on, 75; pity and: — , definition of, 111–13; — , politics and, 109, 111, 129–30 nn.5, 6; — , revival of, 3; Proust and, 254, 260–61 n.3; Renouvier on, 114–16, 171; Ribot on, 83–84, 110, 118; la Rochefoucauld and, 110, 113, 116; Tolstoy and, 122, 197, 199; Vogüé on, 197–98; will and, 110, 111, 112, 115, 116, 118; Zola and, 216–18, 222, 226 n.33. Works: *Aphorisms*, 110, 118; *On the Basis of Morality*, 111–13, 131 n.21; *The World as Will and Representation*, 110, 111, 113

Schorr, Naomi, 38 n.95, 212, 226 nn.23, 24

Séailles, Gabriel, 57, 66 n.39, 260–61 n.3

secularism. *See* justice and pity, religious-secular split over

Sée, Camille, 161, 163, 175 n.4

Sée, Ida-R., 163

Senault, Jean-François, 30 n.14

Seneca, 43

sensibility: Bernardin de Saint-Pierre and, 19–20; Boirac on, 94; in Compayre's *Dictionnaire de pédagogie*, 94; gender and, 161–63, 169; Jourdain on, 93; literature and, 198; Loti and, 257 (*see also mono no aware*); moral value of, 95; Paulhan on, 88; pity and, 16–17, 18, 19, 21,

125, 145–46, 266, 267; *"sensiblérie"* and, 56; Thomas on, 92. *See also* sentimentalism

sentimental idealism, Sand and Zola on, 212

sentimental novel, 210, 225 n.12, 237

Sentimentalism: "affective philosophy" and, 2, 50–61 passim.; Bouillier and, 72–73; Bourdeau on, 53, 83; Bourget and, 230; Boutroux and, 41, 98; Carrau and, 76; Christianity and, 143, 144; cognitive dimensions of, 86; Benjamin Constant and, 23; defined, 20, 25, 26; David Denby on, 21–22; Eclecticism and, 26; eclipse of, 20, 26; emotional contagion and, 73; Enlightenment and, 17, 20, 44, 61, 122; ethics and, 51, 95; — , crisis of, 49; Fouillée and, 59; gendered pity and, 56, 108, 163, 167–70, 173; Helvétius and, 57; impact of, 151; Paul Janet and, 56, 93; Kantianism as, 53; Loti and, 255; Paulhan and, 57; — , defined as "new mysticism," 199; pedagogy of pity and, Boirac on 94; — , official philosophy textbooks and, 93; — , *Revue universitaire* and, 95–96; philosophy, *fin-de-siècle* revival of, 2, 26, 43, 44–45, 58, 265; post-revolutionary, 21, 146, 198, 306; as pro-pity, Bernardin de Saint-Pierre and, 19, 20; — , Bouillier and, 72; — , Darlu's contrast of individualism and socialization, 146; — , Fonsegrive and, 149; — , Anatole France and, 260; — , LeBon and, 150; — , Mélinand and, 27; — , Nietzsche, Schopenhauer and, 121; — , Tarde and 77; Proust and Hugo on, 251; reason-sentiment divide and, 52–53, 85; William Reddy on, 20–21; Renouvier and, 53, 55–56, 116; Ribot and, 85–86; rise of, 20; romanticism and, 43; Schopenhauer, pity and, 110–11, 113–15, 116; Solidarity and, 145; in twentieth century, 265; Waddington on, 55; Zola's fiction and, 213

sentiments: "affective philosophy" and, 77, 83; altruistic, 52, 54, 55, 58, 87, 109, 123 (*see also* altruism); as

About the Author

GONZALO J. SÁNCHEZ JR. is Professor of Liberal Arts at the Juilliard School. Educated at Columbia, he has published extensively in 19th-century European cultural history. His previous teaching assignments include both Columbia and Boston Universities, and he received fellowships from the French Government (Chateaubriand), the American Philosophical Society, and Columbia University. He was also a Visiting Scholar at the Centre national de recherche scientifique, Paris.